Kremelin.

Porte du Sauv

5th edition **An Introduction**

D. VAN NOSTRAND COMPANY, INC.

to Russian History and Culture

IVAR SPECTOR

University of Washington

PRINCETON, NEW JERSEY · TORONTO · LONDON · MELBOURNE

Van Nostrand Regional Offices: *New York, Chicago, San Francisco*

D. Van Nostrand Company, Ltd., *London*

D. Van Nostrand Company (Canada), Ltd., *Toronto*

D. Van Nostrand Australia Pty. Ltd., *Melbourne*

Published simultaneously in Canada by
D. Van Nostrand Company (Canada), Ltd.

Library of Congress Catalog Card No. 69–11742

PRINTED IN THE UNITED STATES OF AMERICA

To my father

VLADIMIR LVOVITCH

Preface

This book is a product of more than thirty years of teaching undergraduates in the field of Russian history and civilization, in the Far Eastern and Slavic Department and Far Eastern and Russian Institute of the University of Washington. In its present form, it represents a thorough revision and an appreciable expansion of previous editions.

Since World War II, new emphasis has been placed not only on formal history, but on cultural backgrounds. The author, therefore, has devoted considerable space to Russian and Soviet culture. This is particularly important because, as explained in this text, current events and culture in Russia are so closely interwoven.

In the United States, where a constitutional system of government has always prevailed, where Party platforms and Congressional debates have reflected the thinking and needs of the people at large, and where daily events have been chronicled by a free press, it is possible to teach formal history and still provide a key to understanding the American people. In the case of Russia, however, where there has never existed a strictly civilian government, where policies both domestic and foreign reflected not the will of the people so much as the will of the ruler, we must turn to the novels, dramas, poems, music, and art—in other words, to Russian culture—for an understanding of the history of the people and their achievements. That is why no study of Russian history can be complete without a parallel study of Russian culture. Moreover, since the launching of the first sputnik in 1957, Soviet scientific progress has attracted more and more attention in the Western World. I have, therefore, included material on the achievements of leading Tsarist and Soviet scientists.

This revision brings the history of the Soviet period up to date. In recent years, even in the United States, foreign policy has taken priority over domestic affairs. There have been substantial additions, therefore, to the material on Soviet foreign policy, especially as it pertains to Asia. As a result of three trips to the Middle East, 1958, 1963, and 1967, and a trip to the Soviet Union in the summer of 1963, I have been able to add new material pertaining to domestic conditions in the USSR and to Soviet relations with Asia.

I wish to express my thanks to all those professors and instructors who have used this book and taken the trouble to offer suggestions for its improvement.

I.S.

University of Washington

Contents

PART I. RUSSIA FROM 862 TO 1682

ix

PART III. IMPERIAL RUSSIA, 1894–1917

PART IV. SOVIET RUSSIA, 1917–1941

PART V. THE SOVIET UNION, 1941–1968

List of Maps

Part One

Russia from 862 to 1682

I

Kievan Russia

and the Mongol Invasion

ORIGINS OF KIEVAN RUSSIA

The Chronicle. The traditional interpretation of the origin of the Kievan Russian state is largely based on the *Chronicle of Ancient Years,* sometimes called the *Primary Chronicle,* ascribed to the monk Nestor (1056–1114) of the Pechersky Monastery at Kiev. Today, this work is believed to be a product of the twelfth century. According to the *Chronicle,* the Russian state was established about A.D. 862 when the Slavonic tribes invited the *Rūs* Varangians, a people of Scandinavian origin living in the north, to end the prevalent state of confusion and anarchy by sending a prince to rule over their domains. The invitation, as recorded in the *Chronicle,* was extended in these words: "Our land is great and rich, but there is no order in it; come and rule and govern us." In response to this message, three brothers established themselves in the land of the Slavs: Rurik, the eldest, in Novgorod; Sineus, the second, on Lake Byelo-ozero; and Truvor, the youngest, in Izborsk, not far from Pskov. After their deaths, Igor, son of Rurik, fell heir to their joint domains.

"Normanist Theory." The *Chronicle* thus records a Norman conquest of Russia not long after the Danish incursions against England began (787) and approximately two centuries prior to the Danish (1017) and Norman (1066) conquests of England. This "Normanist theory" of the origin of the Russian state, based on the *Chronicle,* distinguishes the *Rūs,* as Scandinavians, from the Slavs. The same distinction is to be found in some early Byzantine and Arab sources, including the writings of the Byzantine Emperor Constantine Porphyrogenitus and those of the tenth century Arab traveller Ibrahim Ibn-Yakub. This theory is still accepted by most Western scholars.

Soviet Theories. Because the USSR emerged from World War II with an attitude of superiority toward Western Europe, Soviet historians have intensified their efforts to repudiate the traditional Normanist theory. They have attributed it mainly to "reactionary German historians" living in Russia in the eighteenth century, especially to G. Z. Bayer, G. F. Mueller, and A. L. Schloezer, who sought by this means to justify their preeminence in Russian

3

historical scholarship. Soviet historians point out that this German theory was challenged by the distinguished Russian scholar and educator M. V. Lomonosov as early as 1749, when he denounced Mueller's address, "The Origin of the People and the Name Russia," at the Russian Academy. In the USSR the Normanist theory has also been rejected as "politically harmful," because it was used by "bourgeois historians" to distort the Russian past and to disparage the Russian people by denying their ability to form an independent state.

As further proof that the Russian state was established in the south prior to the coming of the Norsemen, Soviet historians claim that as late as the tenth and twelfth centuries the grand princes of Kievan Russia bore the title *kagan,* adopted from the Khazars, a Turkish tribe which established a state along the lower Volga. By using the title of the Khazar rulers, the Kievan princes declared themselves independent from the Khazar empire. In the Cathedral of St. Sophia in Kiev there are granite inscriptions dating back to the eleventh and twelfth centuries, which state: "Save, O Lord, our Kagan" (*Spasi, gospodi, kagana nashego*). One concession has been made by Soviet scholars to the Normanist theory. They have admitted that one of the warring Slavic tribes may have called upon the "semi-legendary Rurik" who ruled over Ladoga, for military aid, but that Rurik seized power in Novgorod in 862, an event which led to the uprising of Vadim the Courageous two years later.

Soviet scholars have likewise contended that Byzantine influence on Kievan Russia has been greatly exaggerated by Western historians. In rewriting Russian history, the Soviet trend has been to consider developments in Kievan Russia as a natural outgrowth of Russian conditions and of the native genius.

Soviet scholarship has increasingly tended to identify the *Rūs* with the Slavs and to deny their Scandinavian origin. B. A. Rybakov, one of the foremost anti-Normanists, maintains that the name *Rūs* was established in South Russia for several centuries prior to the coming of the Varangians, or Norsemen. His studies, and Soviet archeological investigations, have led him to conclude that the Slavs were the autochthonic, or native, population of this region. According to him, the *Rūs* represented a confederation of Slavonic tribes that later developed into a Russian state, although not all the Slavs belonged to this confederation. It is Rybakov's contention that the Novgorod chroniclers of the eleventh and twelfth centuries, who interpreted *Rūs* as the name applied to the state founded by the Varangians, were pro-Varangians seeking to elevate the rulers under whom they served.

The majority of Russia's pre-Soviet historians accepted the premise that the state of Kievan *Rūs* was exclusively, or chiefly, created by outsiders no earlier than the ninth or tenth century. Even one of Russia's foremost early twentieth-century historians, V. O. Kliuchevsky, however, and some others, admitted the possibility that a sixth-century "political union" known as Volynia might have existed in the western Ukraine, while other Soviet historians, led by B. D. Grekov, have transformed this hypothesis into an indisputable fact. On the basis of what is at best fragmentary and inconclusive evidence derived from historical sources and archeological artifacts that neither prove definitively nor disprove the existence of Volynia, they have reached dogmatic conclusions in conformity with Marxist doctrine. All this has made it possible for the Soviets to claim that Russia did not lag behind Western Europe in the creation of a state, and that Russia was the first of the Slavic peoples to establish a state.

Russian Language. Linguistically, the Slavs belong to the broad family of Indo-European peoples inhabiting Europe and part of Asia, including India. The Indo-European languages are related, and form several linguistic branches: Slavic, Germanic, Celtic, Italic, Iranian, Indic, and others. In all these languages, there are analogous words, some believed to date back to primitive times.

The four centers of Eastern Slavic concentration in the ninth century, as described by Arab geographers, were located in the vicinity of Lake Ilmen, on the Oka River near Ryazan, at Kiev on the Dnieper, and in Galicia. The *Chronicle,* written in the twelfth century, but with reference to past conditions, lists the tribes on Russian soil as the Croats, Polyane, Volhynians, Dulebians, Buzhane, Dregovichians, Polotians, Novgorod Slavs, Severians, Krivichians, Radimichians, Vyatichians, Ulichians, and Tivercians.

According to their speech, these tribes fell into three categories, reflecting the three basic Russian dialects of today. Those in the north, the Slovenes of Novgorod and Krivichians, spoke what was the basis of the Great Russian dialect, or standard Russian literary language. Of those in the center—Dregovichians, Radimichians, Vyatichians, and Severians—the eastern section eventually combined with the Great Russian element; the western tribes, the Dregovichians and Radimichians, came to form the second category, the White Russians centering around Minsk. The Polyane, Derevlians, Volhynians, Ulichians, Tivercians, and Croats, located in the south, became the Ukrainian, or Little Russian (*Malo Rossiya*), element, the latter term having been used since the fourteenth century.

Pre-Rurik Society. Pre-Rurik sources indicate that the ancestors of the Russians were organized as tribes. In some areas, there was a loose confederation of tribes. Politically, it was an anarchic society. This term is not used in a derogatory sense to denote chaos; it simply means a society in which there was no organized political regime in the Western sense. Byzantine writers visiting the Slavs in the sixth century reported that they found *ataxia* and *anarchia,* that is, the absence of a political order and a government. The Russian historian S. F. Platonov found substantiation of this interpretation in old Russian manuscripts, some of which used the terms *ustroistvo, naryad,* and *naryadnik,* which signify the absence of a political structure rather than confusion or chaos.

In pre-Rurik times, the basic economy was agrarian, although in the towns there were many craftsmen. In matters of religion, the Slavs of this period may be designated as polytheists. Their major deities were Dazhbog, god of the sun; Veles, god of the earth and livestock; Svarog, god of fire; and Perun, god of the storm, the Russian version of Mars.

Islam and the Khazars. The rise and growth of Islam in the seventh and eighth centuries had a profound impact upon the Mediterranean world and the emerging states of Eastern Europe. The expanding Muslims rimmed the southeastern periphery of Europe, engulfing Persia, Armenia, Daghestan, Transcaucasia, and Transoxiana. They raided Anatolia annually and on several occasions even attacked Constantinople, capital of the Byzantine Empire.

Two factors protected the early Slavonic tribes from Islamic expansion: the Byzantine Empire to the south and southwest and the Turco-Slavic Khazar Khanate to the east, both of which put up a valiant struggle against the Muslim invaders. Continuous and powerful Khazar attacks on the Arabs in the eighth century exhausted the Arab invaders, diverted their armies to the Caucasus, and prevented their further advance on Byzantium and Eastern Europe. The Khazars were overwhelmed by the Arabs *c.* 737 and their ruler was temporarily forced to accept Islam. In general, however, the allied Khazar and Byzantine states, their relations strengthened by dynastic inter-marriage, collaborated effectively in their struggle against the expansion of Islam.

Although the Byzantine role in stemming the tide of Islam is well known, comparatively little attention has been paid to the Khazars, even in the *Chronicle.* The center of the Khazar state in the ninth and tenth centuries was the town of Atil, situated on both banks of the Volga. On the same site the "Golden Horde" later established its first capital under the name of Saray-i-Butu (see page 18). In the ninth century the Khazar ruling class and some of its subjects became converts to Judaism; this development, rather unique for the Middle Ages, enabled the Khazars to maintain a neutral position between Arabs and Byzantines. For over three hundred years, from the seventh to the eleventh century, the Khazars formed a bulwark on the steppes of eastern Europe and from the Urals to the Crimea against invaders from the east and south. In the eighth century, they fought their greatest battles against Muhammad Marwan II (*r.* 744–750), the last of the fourteen Umayyad caliphs of Damascus. Their struggle gave the Slavonic tribes a breathing spell and enabled them to lay the foundations of the Kievan state. The seizure of the Khazar capital, Sarkil (Biela Viezha), in 966 by the Russian Prince Svyatoslav, was the prelude to their downfall and eventual obliteration.

By the ninth century, the Russian Slavonic tribes, through their trade contacts with the declining Khazars and Byzantium, must have become more conscious of the Islamic threat and of the need for collective security. Unorganized and weak states in Asia had fallen, one after another, before the onslaught of the Muslim hordes. Though reluctant to abandon their "anarchic" mode of life, in all probability the external threat was a significant factor in forcing the tribes to resort to political organization for reasons of security. In other words, the Russian state would seem to have been established in response to an emergency. Thus began the Rurik dynasty and the state of Kievan Russia. Khazaria was the first state with which Kievan Russia came into contact. According to A. I. Artamonov, this is an historical fact which cannot be denied and which is indispensable to a correct understanding of the historical development, not only of Kievan Russia, but of all Eastern Europe.

THE RURIK DYNASTY

The rulers of the Rurik dynasty, canonized or uncanonized, were recognized as saints. Under pressure from internal strife and the external threat of Muslim expansion, the Slavonic tribes of the pre-Rurik "anarchic" society were constrained to establish a regime of law and order. Thus, anyone who assumed the responsibility of ruling—and according to the *Chronicle,* the people resorted to a foreigner, Rurik—became, *ipso facto,* a martyr and therefore a saint. The fact that the people made the supreme sacrifice of surrendering their authority to a ruler, according to later interpretation, made them a holy people. Thus, the land made holy by the ruler and people became "Holy Russia" (*Svyataya Rus*).[1]

Two of the most vital developments of the Rurik period were the adoption of Christianity from Byzantium and the invasion of the Mongols from Asia. The chief weakness of the regime lay in its failure to establish a strong, centralized authority, capable of dealing effectively with rival claimants to the throne and with endless dissension among semi-feudal principalities.

Oleg (r. 879–912). Rurik (*r.* 862–879), from his headquarters in Novgorod, established order among the Slavonic tribes of the surrounding area through a network of forts, and made statesmanlike arrangements for the succession. After his death, his kinsman Oleg served as regent for Rurik's minor heir, Igor. Oleg seized Kiev, the chief trading center of the lower Dnieper valley, made it his capital, and laid the foundations for the Kievan state of south Russia. According to the Russian chroniclers of the eleventh and twelfth centuries, a legendary hero named Kii was the real founder of the city and principality of Kiev, as Romulus was the founder of Rome; they record that Kii travelled to Byzantium where he was royally treated by the emperor.

After Oleg had seized the city of Kiev and the surrounding area, he pursued his objective of expansion to the south and east, at the expense of the Khazars and the Magyars, to open a route to the Black Sea and reach Byzantium. The

---

1. See Michael Cherniavsky, *Tsar and People: Studies in Russian Myths* (New Haven: Yale University Press, 1952). Although this work contains a few discrepancies and inaccuracies in translation, it breaks new ground in this field.

Chronicle appears to have embellished his military prowess. In 907 his forces are said to have attacked the suburbs of Byzantium by land and sea; the Greeks were forced to pay tribute and to conclude a commercial treaty granting Russian merchants special privileges in the city. Thus, Oleg successfully opened a route from Kiev to the Black Sea and the Dardanelles, and cleared the way for the lucrative Russo-Byzantine trade described by Emperor Constantine Porphyrogenitus in his *De Administrando Imperio.*

Turning his attention to Asia, two years before his death Oleg dispatched an exploratory expedition (909–910) to the southern shores of the Caspian Sea. For his achievements, the Russian chroniclers named him *Vieshchi,* the seer, the sage, the holy. His successor, Igor (*r.* 913–945) was responsible for two more plundering expeditions, recorded in Arab writings, to the Caspian and to Muslim Azerbaijan in the Trans-Caucasus. In 945, Igor, following a costly campaign to the Danube, negotiated a more definitive commercial treaty with Byzantium, one of his more important achievements.

Olga (r. 945–962). Upon Igor's death his widow, Princess Olga, assumed power on behalf of her infant son Svyatoslav. A clever, rich, and resourceful woman, Olga revealed her sound judgment by administrative reforms, which included the substitution of taxes for tribute. The first Russian ruler to accept Christianity, she journeyed to Byzantium in 957 for baptism at the Byzantine court, an episode described by Constantine Porphyrogenitus in his *Book of Byzantine Ceremonies.* Her failure to secure autonomy for a Russian church, opposed by her pagan son, Svyatoslav, postponed the adoption of Christianity by the Kievan state for three decades.

Svyatoslav (r. 962–972). Within the brief span of a decade, Svyatoslav vastly extended the bounds of the Kievan state to Bulgar, capital of the Volga Bulgars (about 965); to the Balkans, where he established his headquarters at Pereyaslavets (967) commanding the Danube delta; and to the Khazar stone fortress at Sarkil on the Don (968–969). Svyatoslav's overthrow of the Khazar Khanate left his realm vulnerable to attack by the Pecheniegs (Patzinaks), a Slavic-Turkic tribe from Asia. They temporarily occupied Kiev during his reign and eventually killed him in action.

Vladimir (r. 980–1015) and Christianity. After prolonged struggle over the succession, one of Svyatoslav's sons, Vladimir, a shrewd and ruthless warrior, emerged triumphant with the aid of Varangian mercenaries. Vladimir's reign was memorable for the adoption of Christianity as the official religion of the Kievan state (988–989). Already the country was surrounded by peoples who had abandoned paganism for Christianity, Judaism, or Islam. About 865 the Khazars became converts to Judaism. In 922 the Volga Bulgars chose Islam. From 966 to 985 the Polish, Danish, Norwegian, and Hungarian rulers accepted Roman Catholicism. Since the reign of Igor, there appears to have been a growing Christian minority in Kievan *Rūs.* Vladimir, according to the *Chronicle,* investigated Islam and Judaism, as well as Greek and Latin Christianity, before he decided in favor of the Greek Orthodox faith. He took the Byzantine princess Anna as his bride, and by 990 imposed

This fourteenth-century miniature shows the army of Svyatoslav in its campaign against the Bulgars on the Danube. The artist dressed the soldiers and horses in the armor of his own era.

a general baptism upon the population of his domains. By the end of the tenth century, Orthodox Christianity was firmly established in Kievan *Rūs*. As late as the twelfth century, however, according to Boris Rybakov, two centuries after the introduction of Christianity, pagan survivals were still in evidence. Russian women continued to wear bracelets depicting pagan dances known as *Rusalii*.

The adoption of Christianity was undoubtedly a great landmark in the history of Russia. Henceforth, the country was linked, spiritually as well as commercially, with the advanced civilization and culture of the Byzantine Empire, thereby enhancing its prestige throughout Europe. Some historians have even suggested that Slavic civilization (Kievan and Bulgar) showed signs of emerging in the tenth century as "a third cultural power, competing with the Latin and Greek."[2] Christianity led to the introduction by the Greek bishops, Kirill and Methodius, of a Slavonic alphabet, which contributed to the development of a written language. Vladimir's decision, however, resulted in the permanent religious division of the Slavs, some of whom, like the Croatians, Czechs, Slovaks, and Poles, accepted Roman Catholicism. To a very considerable degree the antagonism between Poles and Russians appears to have stemmed from religious differences.

Yaroslav the Wise (r. 1036–1054). Following another bitter struggle for the succession among the sons of Vladimir, Yaroslav, prince of Novgorod, known as Yaroslav the Wise, established his authority in Kiev. It was during his reign that the Kievan state reached the peak of its greatness. About 1039, on the basis of an agreement with Byzantine authorities, the first metropolitan[3] of Kiev, Theotemptus, arrived from Byzantium, signifying that Kiev had become the ecclesiastical, as well as the political, capital of the state. With Byzantium as a model, Yaroslav proceeded along lines already laid down by Vladimir to make Kiev equally renowned as an artistic and cultural center. Several churches, including the Cathedral of St. Sophia, equipped with five apses and thirteen cupolas and elaborately decorated with Byzantine frescoes and mosaics, were constructed with the aid of Greek artisans, sculptors, architects, and ikon painters who flocked to the city following the adoption of Christianity. The so-called Golden Gate of Kiev and the renowned Pechersky Monastery date from his reign. A devotee of learning, Yaroslav employed many scribes to translate Greek works into Slavic and to collect a library, thereby transforming the cathedral into what M. Hrushevsky, Ukrainian historian, has called Russia's first learned academy. Schools were established for the education of the clergy and the ruling class. One of his most significant contributions was the promulgation in Novgorod and later in Kiev of the first Russian code of laws, the *Russkaya Pravda,* based on Norse and Slavic precedents. As pointed out by historian George Vernadsky, it affords many parallels with Frankish (Salic) law and with Anglo-Saxon law as represented by the Wessex Code of Alfred the Great (848–899).

In order to free himself from too great a dependence on Byzantium, Yaroslav made important international contacts in Europe through a series of dynastic alliances. He himself married a Swedish princess. His sister Maria was wed to King Kazimir I of Poland; his daughters married the kings of France, Norway, and Hungary. Three of his sons took German princesses as brides, and a fourth married a relative of Constantine Monomachus, the

2. As, for instance, George Florovsky. See *Slavic Review,* Vol. XI (No. 1, March, 1962), 1–15.

3. The bishop who presides over the other bishops of a province.

Byzantine emperor. In another demonstration of his independence from Byzantium, he assembled the Russian bishops for the election of Hilarion as the first Russian metropolitan of Kiev. The great prestige of the Kievan state, however, depended largely on Yaroslav's own ability and intellect. His arrangements for the succession, involving the partition of the realm among his sons in order of seniority, led to prolonged dissension during which much of the progress he had made was lost.

Vladimir Monomakh (r. 1113–1125). The internecine conflict and confusion that followed Yaroslav's death marked the beginning of the decline of the Kievan state. The reign of Vladimir Monomakh, grandson of Yaroslav, temporarily stemmed the tide. A deeply religious man with a social conscience and his grandfather's love of learning, he was the author of several epistles, among them his "Testament," a very human and revealing document for the instruction of his sons. The *Chronicle,* which is often regarded as a product of his time, hailed him as a popular hero for his military prowess against the Polovtsy (Cumani), a nomadic Turkic tribe from the steppes, and for his success as a peacemaker. His death brought a renewal of disorder, from which the Kievan state failed to recover. The turmoil was marked by the decline of commerce and agriculture due to the inroads of warlike tribes, such as the Polovtsy. The final disruption of Kievan trade with Byzantium followed the sacking of that city by the Venetians in 1204 during the fourth Crusade.

ORGANIZATION OF THE KIEVAN STATE

Political Structure. The Kievan state was in reality a loose federation of city-states, on which the grand prince of Kiev imposed his authority through his lieutenants, usually his sons or an occasional boyar.[4] In this fashion, his sway extended from Kiev to Novgorod, Vladimir-Suzdal, Smolensk, Chernigov, Rostov, Pereiaslav, and many lesser cities. Although this semblance of unity was strengthened by the church after the adoption of Christianity, it remained tenuous. Rivalry for the possession of Kiev, which according to a mode of succession based on genealogical seniority went to the "senior prince," too often proved the signal for a general redistribution of thrones, which was accompanied by conflict. Following the death of Yaroslav, instead of one strong center at Kiev in the south, there were other secondary principalities in Galicia (west), Novgorod (north), and Vladimir-Suzdal (northeast).

The government of the Kievan city-states, patterned after that of Kiev, was a mixture of three elements: the monarchic, represented by the ruling prince; the aristocratic, the prince's Boyar Council comprised of the leaders of his *druzhina* (private army); and the democratic, a popular gathering of the adult

---

4. A member of the Russian aristocracy next in rank below the ruling princes.

males known as the *vieche*. All three elements were present in the Kievan city-states, but in varying degrees. In the twelfth century, the monarchic element prevailed in Suzdalia, the aristocratic in Galicia, and the democratic in Novgorod. After the death of Vladimir Monomakh in 1125, Novgorod took advantage of the absence of any strong central authority and secured the right to elect its own prince.

Social Structure. The social structure of Kievan Russia was composed basically of three groups: freemen, semifreemen, and slaves. Actually, this is an oversimplification of a complex society in which there existed no such rigid class barriers as prevailed in feudal Europe during the same period. The freemen included both upper and middle classes. Those of the upper class comprised a heterogeneous assortment of boyars: descendants of the tribal aristocracy; members of the *druzhina* of Norse, Slavic, Magyar, Turkish, or other origin; churchmen; and wealthy landowners. Together they belonged to boyardom. The middle-class freemen included merchants, craftsmen, and tradesmen in the towns, and peasant landowners or farmers in rural areas. Although serfdom, as such, did not exist in the Kievan state, the *zakupy,* or semifreemen, included debtors (merchants, artisans, hired laborers, etc.) forced to settle their obligations by their labor if they were unable to meet payment. This group also included persons in distress, who temporarily "gave themselves" to a lord in return for succor in the form of money or grain. The third class, the slaves, originally consisted of captives taken in war; in the course of time it also included those who sold themselves into slavery, married slaves, or entered into service without specific guarantees of their personal freedom. In Kievan Russia, in contrast to the later Muscovite period, women enjoyed a large measure of freedom and independence, legally and socially; they could own property and be entrusted with the management of a deceased husband's estate.

Under the Soviet regime, much attention has been paid by Soviet scholars, such as B. D. Grekov, to the controversial issue of the extent of feudalism in Kievan Russia, a subject largely ignored by tsarist historians. Approaching feudalism from the Marxist standpoint, the Soviets have stressed the existence of economic feudalism—the increasing exploitation of the peasants by the lords of the manor during the Kievan period. Their conclusion has been, with some reservations, that Kievan society was feudal rather than slaveowning.

In contrast to the Soviet position, George Vernadsky, historian and specialist on ancient and medieval Russia, contends that large numbers of small farms existed alongside the large landed estates, not all of which were of the manorial type; that Russian boyars and princes depended not only on the land, but on trade, especially foreign trade, which involved the growth of a money economy as opposed to barter and services characteristic of feudalism; that serfdom, as a legal institution, did not exist in Kievan Russia and that Soviet writers have underestimated the extent of slavery; and that property in Kievan Russia could be disposed of without restriction. Although Vernadsky concedes a measure of political feudalism, as revealed by the relations between suzerains and vassals by the middle of the twelfth century, this was more characteristic of areas, such as Lithuania, which were adjacent to other European countries. In Kievan society he finds more resemblance to the Byzantine Empire than to Western Europe.

Religious Structure. The Russian Holy Catholic and Apostolic Orthodox Church, as it was officially called, played an important role in the spiritual, political, and economic life of Kievan Russia. Although it was the state religion, it enjoyed a large measure of autonomy, for all practical purposes existing as a state within a state. Officially a diocese of the Patriarchate of Byzantium after 1037, it nevertheless sought to establish and maintain its own identity as a Kievan institution, a position in which it frequently secured support from the state. It conducted its services in Church Slavonic (Slavonic Bulgarian) and adapted and simplified Byzantine ritual to correspond with local conditions. With but two exceptions, however, the appointments of Hilarion (1051) and Kliment (1147), the metropolitans of Kiev were Greeks appointed by the Greek patriarch.

Sovfoto

Ikons such as this Virgin and Child played an important role in Orthodox devotions. They were not regarded as pictures, but as symbolic objects of worship and veneration.

In many other respects, the Russian church followed the pattern set by Byzantium. It encouraged the spread of Byzantine law, established monasteries in accordance with Byzantine models, translated Greek liturgies and prayers, and in its church art and architecture followed and adapted Byzantine models. Influenced by Byzantine reaction to the iconoclastic dispute that rocked the Christian church in the eighth century, the Kievan church made important use of the ikon (pictures of Mary or members of the Holy Family) in its services, but excluded sculptured figures. Byzantine church festivals, especially those connected with the Easter season, likewise became an integral part of the Russian ritual.

The Russian clergy was divided into two groups: the "black clergy," or monks; and the "white clergy," the priests and deacons. With the support of church and state, fifty-eight monasteries and twelve convents were established in Kievan Russia, most of them of the communal type. It was in the Monastery of the Caves in Kiev that the first Kievan *Chronicle* was written. Russian bishops were ordinarily chosen from the monks, who led a celibate life. In contrast to the practice of Roman Catholicism, Russian priests were required to marry. Because the family was regarded as the foundation of society, and priests were consulted on all family matters, lay and spiritual, the church believed that its priests should have more than a bookish knowledge of family life.

Although the Russian Orthodox and Roman Catholic churches recognize the same seven sacraments, they differ fundamentally on certain aspects of dogma. The Dogma of the Immaculate Conception, insofar as it involves the concept of original sin for all mankind except the Holy Virgin, was rejected by the Russians. They have likewise rejected the doctrine of papal infallibility, affirming that Jesus Christ is the sole head of the church and has no vicar on earth. According to their belief, Christ still lives, not in visible form as during his life on earth, but transfigured in spirit, and therefore no one can take his place. In general, it may be said that in matters of ritual the Russian church remains in close affinity with the Roman Catholics, but in matters of dogma it approaches Protestantism, especially Episcopalianism.

The Rurik dynasty of Kievan Russia in the pre-Mongol period, was distinguished by a high level of spiritual activity and notable political and social progress. The stage was set for great cultural development, which might have had a far-reaching and beneficent influence not only upon Russia but upon the entire Western world. Outside foes, aided by internal discord, interrupted and retarded its development for many years to come.

THE MONGOL PERIOD: ASIAN COLONIALISM, 1240–1480

"Mongol" and "Tatar." The Mongol forces which invaded Russia in the thirteenth century were comprised mainly of Tatars from central Asia. For this reason, the Russians have employed the terms "Mongol" and "Tatar"

interchangeably. When these Tatar hordes were converted to Islam in the fourteenth century (1341), Russians likewise began to identify Islam with their Asian oppressors, just as many Asians and Africans in the twentieth century regarded Christianity and colonialism as synonymous. In other words, the Mongol period made Russians conscious of Islam and Muslims as mortal enemies of Russia and Christendom. No sooner did they cast off the Mongol "yoke" than they entered into a crusade against the Muslims, which lasted for nearly four hundred years. Western historians usually interpret this crusade simply as Russian territorial expansion.

Impact of Islam. From the seventh to the eleventh centuries the tide of Muslim expansion in Eastern Europe was contained mainly by the Byzantine Empire and the Khazar Khanate. The respite thus provided made possible the establishment of the Kievan state and its high level of political, economic, and cultural achievement. It also turned the scales in favor of a Christian rather than a Muslim Kievan state. The Western crusades against Islam, which lasted nearly two hundred years (1097–1291) once again saved Kievan Russia, and provided time for its consolidation and for the transition from the principality concept to a national consciousness which survived the Mongol period. Kievan Russia as a state took no part in the crusades of Western Christendom against Islam. There is no evidence of Russian hatred for Muslims until the Mongol period.

The rapid rise and spread of Islam in Asia and the Mediterranean world was possible because no political power following the decline of Rome was strong enough to prevent it. The two powers that might have contained Islam in the early stages, the Byzantine and Persian empires, exhausted themselves in a series of hot and cold wars, thus creating a vacuum which the Muslims penetrated. At the end of the Western crusades a somewhat comparable situation existed; the Western powers had exhausted themselves in two centuries of struggle against Islam. The vacuum thus created was filled by the Mongols, whose invasions began as the crusades petered out. Before they were converted to Islam, the Tatar hordes literally wiped out the Abassid Caliphate at Baghdad, which had flourished from 750 to 1258, as well as other parts of Asia and Russia, destroying civilizations much in advance of those in the West at that time. The Mongol objective was Western Europe. This time it was the Russian turn to reciprocate what the West had inadvertently done for Kievan Russia by stemming the Mongol tide in the eastern Mediterranean. The Kievan state faced the Mongols alone on the eastern front, bearing the full brunt of the Tatar hordes. By so doing, it saved Western Europe from depredation.

Chingis Khan. It was in 1206 that the general assembly of Mongol clans proclaimed one of its leaders, Temuchin, supreme emperor (Chingis Khan), and the era of Mongol expansion began. Turning first toward China, the Mongols seized Peking in 1215. Chingis Khan then looked to the west, to Khorezm in central Asia. At the beginning of the thirteenth century, Khorezm was the capital of a rich and powerful empire ruled by Muhammad Shah (*r.* 1200–1220), whose authority extended throughout most of Turkestan, northern Persia, and Azerbaijan. When the shah summarily rejected the Mongol offer of an alliance, Chingis Khan's forces invaded Turkestan and the Khorezmian Empire collapsed before them.

Our knowledge of the career of Chingis Khan (1155?–1227), the leader of the Mongol invasion of 1223, is extremely limited. Even the real meaning of his title *Chingis* (or *Jenghis*) is unknown, although many scholars and historians have suggested translations and interpretations. The following scanty facts may be regarded, however, as more or less authentic.

He was born of a Mongol father and a Turkish mother at Delium-Boldak on the Onon River and died in August 1227, while engaged in a campaign against the Tanguts. He was buried on Mount Burkan-Kaldun. Like the majority of his countrymen, he practiced polygamy extensively, having four senior wives, a great number of junior wives, and in addition numerous concubines and maid servants. As a military organizer he had unusual ability, but his genius alone would have been insufficient to institute and inspire the great Mongol invasion. He was the able warrior, but the driving and controlling spirit of the movement was supplied by another man, Ye-liu Chu-tsai, whom Chingis Khan met in Peking in 1215.

Ye-liu Chu-tsai was a statesman of great renown, possessed of a sound liberal education. Learning of Chingis Khan's plans for conquest of western territory, he became deeply interested; his motive was ethical from his standpoint—the domination of the territory in question by a higher and more ancient culture. It was through the inspiration of this Chinese statesman and philosopher that the Mongol invasion and devastation of the world assumed in the eyes of the invaders the aspect of a Mongol "mission," and their conquests, from their point of view, assumed the form of crusades.

The prologue to the Mongol invasion of Kievan Russia occurred in 1223, when Tatar forces led by two of Chingis Khan's foremost generals, Djebe and Subutai, attacked the Polovtsy (Cuman) Horde, a pastoral people, who had controlled the south Russian steppe since the eleventh century. The Polovtsy lands lay athwart the overland caravan route from Khorezm to Kievan Russia and the Black Sea, and they collected duties on the transit trade. For years their constant raids on Kievan borders in search of booty and captives to be sold as slaves had antagonized the Kievan princes and drained the resources of the people. By the thirteenth century, however, relations had improved, and the Polovtsy even joined the Kievan forces as allies against the Poles and Hungarians.

When the Mongols struck, Kotyan Khan, leader of the Polovtsy, did not hesitate to appeal in person for Russian aid. "Today the Tatars have seized our land," he warned. "Tomorrow they will take yours." Unfortunately, only a few principalities responded, and they lacked a unified command. In pursuit of the retreating Mongol vanguard, the Kievan forces and their allies suddenly confronted the main ranks of the enemy on the River Kalka, near the Sea of

Azov, in May, 1224. After a memorable three-day battle the Russians, including the princes of Kiev and Chernigov, were wiped out. On this occasion the Tatars, who were merely reconnoitering the "western lands," failed to follow up their victory beyond the Dnieper and retreated as quickly as they had come. Of them the chronicler wrote: "Only God knows whence they came and whither they went." It was not until 1237 that the Mongols reappeared on Russian soil, this time fully prepared to assume the offensive in earnest.

Fall of Kiev, 1240. The Kievan state meanwhile failed to heed the warning of the Battle of the Kalka. Reports of a successful attack by the Volga Bulgars on the retreating Mongols may have engendered over-optimism. Although their chief bulwark, the empires of the Khazars and Khorezm had vanished, the Russians apparently overestimated the strength of the Muslim Bulgars and the Polovtsy as a shield against invasion from Asia. In the winter of 1237–1238, the Mongol forces of Ugedey Khan, under command of Chingis Khan's grandson, Batu, overwhelmed the Volga Bulgars near Kazan, crossed the river, and sacked the city of Ryazan. Ravaging the country far and wide, they also burned the city of Vladimir. This time the Mongols remained in Russia, setting up their quarters near the mouth of the River Don. On December 12, 1240, according to the *Chronicle,* they overran Kiev, sacked the Cathedral of St. Sophia and the nearby monasteries, and "all the people from small to large, they slew by the sword." Only about two hundred houses remained intact in Kiev and thousands of people were enslaved. After witnessing the downfall of one principality after another, Novgorod in 1259 voluntarily submitted to the "Tatar yoke," thereby avoiding the destruction that had befallen Kiev.

So extensive was the slave traffic during this period of East-West invasion of Russian territory that in al-Zahra the Umayyad caliph of Cordova surrounded himself with a bodyguard of 3750 Slavs. The term *Slav* seems to have been used at first to denote slaves and prisoners captured by the Germans and others from the Slavonic tribes and subsequently sold to the Arabs; it was later applied to all purchased foreigners, Franks, Galicians, Lombards, etc., who as a rule were acquired young and raised as Muslims. "With the aid of these 'Janissaries' or 'Mamluks' of Spain," says Philip K. Hitti, "the Caliph not only kept treason and brigandage in check but reduced the influence of the old Arab aristocracy."

Thus the conquest of Russia by the Mongols was accomplished from 1237 to 1240. The loss of Kiev created panic in Western Europe. Writing to the English king Henry III (*r.* 1216–1272), Frederick II of the Holy Roman Empire (*r.* 1212–1250) announced the fall of "noble Russia." The Tatars justified European fears by pressing west to defeat the Poles at Liegnitz, overwhelm the Hungarians, and appear before the gates of Vienna. Three strenuous years of conflict had nevertheless exhausted the invaders, who sustained heavy losses in men and equipment. Following the sudden death of the great khan, Ugedey, the Mongols withdrew from Central Europe. Batu established his capital at Sarai (Saray-i-Batu) on the Volga below the present city of Volgograd (Stalingrad). From this center the Tatars controlled Russia for two centuries.

Alexander Nevsky. Irrespective of Frederick II's tribute to "noble Russia," the Mongol conquest encouraged Europeans, especially the Lithuanians, Swedes, and Germans, to invade from the west. Ostensibly, they sought strategic positions from which to repulse any new Mongol penetration of the West. The Lithuanians professed paganism until the end of the fourteenth century, but the Swedes and Germans proclaimed their intention of saving Russia for Christianity, which at the time meant Roman Catholicism. Whatever their motives, Russia's distress proved to be Europe's opportunity. The Swedes were the first to attack in force, their goal being the seizure of the Neva, Ladoga, and even Novgorod. They were defeated outright in 1240 by the rising military leader, Prince Alexander Nevsky (1219–1263), who was well versed in Western strategy. It was this victory on the Neva which won him the appellation "Nevsky." No sooner had he disposed of the Swedish threat, however, than he confronted the crusading Teutonic Knights, who captured Izborsk and Pskov. The people of Novgorod, alarmed by this new invasion, called on Alexander Nevsky to assume command of their hastily assembled forces. In the famous "Battle of the Ice" at Lake Peipus in 1242, he outmaneuvered the Teutonic Knights and destroyed their forces.

To secure this victory, Alexander Nevsky broke with tradition and adopted a strategic maneuver that remained characteristic of Russian military tactics for many years to come. Aware that the Germans would attack in force at the center, he greatly strengthened the flanks of his army. When the Germans penetrated the weakly held center and regarded the victory as won, the Russians encircled them from both flanks and destroyed them. The Soviet film *Alexander Nevsky,* produced by Sergei Eisenstein on the eve of World War II, presents a graphic demonstration of this strategy.

Alexander Nevsky, who regarded the West as a greater threat to Russia than the Tatars, accepted Tatar aid to repel the European encroachment. Confronted by the pincer movement from East and West, he is reputed to have said: "The Mongol can wait." In comparable circumstances, these tactics have been pursued by Russians under the tsars and under the Soviets. The Orthodox church appears to have shared the views of Alexander Nevsky, perhaps because the Tatars refrained from interference with Russian religious beliefs, whereas the Western invaders crusaded to substitute Roman Catholicism for Orthodoxy. For saving Russia from Roman Catholicism, Alexander Nevsky was later canonized as a saint.

Results of Mongol Rule. The Mongols did not colonize Russia as the Soviets have colonized the Muslim areas of Soviet Central Asia. Nor did they interfere with the Russian Orthodox church. Instead, they taxed the conquered people and, taught by experience, they employed Russian princes as tax collectors. The princes of Moscow competed successfully with their rivals for this privilege and the benefits it entailed. In 1328 the Tatars conferred the title of grand prince on the wily Muscovite Ivan I, "Kalita" (bag, i.e., moneybag), whose success as a collector of tribute had won him great favor, including the hand of a Tatar princess. Thus the Tatars themselves contributed to the rise of the Moscow state, which soon fought to cast off the Tatar yoke.

The Tatar domination of Russia (1240–1480) made the Russians Islam-conscious. The Russian struggle against Asian colonialism, begun under Ivan Grozny (1530–1584) assumed religious overtones. Islam, represented by the Turks, became for the Russians a legitimate target. There were no fewer than twelve Russo-Turkish wars from 1672 to 1914. Even when the Cossacks and other Russians invaded Siberia in the sixteenth century, their zeal for conquest and their mistreatment of the natives were due in part to the fact that they regarded them as Tatars. The Mongol period colored Russian foreign policy vis-à-vis Asia, especially Muslim Asia, for nearly four centuries. As Count Vladimir N. Lamsdorff, tsarist minister of foreign affairs (1900–1906), once stated, "the entire foreign policy of Tsarist Russia was, first of all, an Asiatic policy."

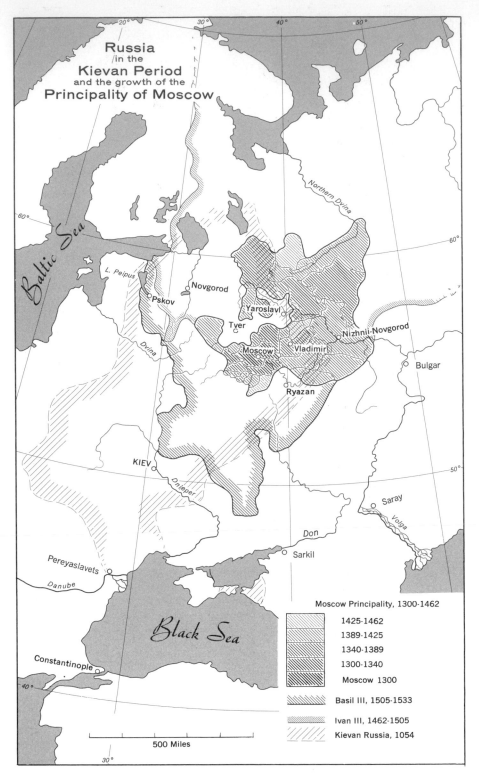

Russia
in the
Kievan Period
and the growth of the
Principality of Moscow

Northern Dvina

Baltic Sea

L. Peipus

Pskov

Novgorod

Yaroslavl

Tver

Moscow Vladimir

Nizhnii-Novgorod

Bulgar

Ryazan

Dvina

KIEV

Dnieper

Saray

Volga

Don

Sarkil

Pereyaslavets

Danube

Black Sea

Constantinople

500 Miles

Moscow Principality, 1300-1462

1425-1462
1389-1425
1340-1389
1300-1340
Moscow 1300

Basil III, 1505-1533

Ivan III, 1462-1505

Kievan Russia, 1054

2

The Rise and Expansion

of the Moscow State

Origins of the Moscow State

Moscow, which was first mentioned in the chronicles in 1147, was a relative newcomer among the Russian principalities. It was destroyed by the Mongols in 1238, but suffered less than many other Russian cities from subsequent Mongol raids. Its location, at the hub of Russia's great network of water communications, was of strategic and economic significance. Not only did it become the residence of the grand duke, but the metropolitan of the Orthodox church, Peter, selected it in preference to Vladimir as his ecclesiastical capital, and was buried there in 1342. The princes of Moscow proved to be good business managers, who carefully husbanded the resources of the principality.

Dimitri Donskoi. Whereas Alexander Nevsky represented the princely camp that accorded priority to the European threat to Russia as opposed to that of the Mongols, Dimitri Donskoi (1350–1389), grand duke of Moscow, voiced the sentiment of those whose main concern was the overthrow of the "Mongol yoke." The expulsion of the Mongols from China in 1368 convinced Dimitri and his followers that the Mongol Empire was far from invincible and could be overthrown in Russia.

Before he could emulate the Chinese example, Dimitri had to fulfill two prerequisites. He needed recognition by rival princes of his supreme authority as grand prince of Moscow and fortification of his new capital by the construction of a kremlin (walled fortress). Dimitri began construction of a stone kremlin in 1368. Among his main assets in the contest for power were the support of the church and the financial backing of the city of Novgorod. Opposition to the political ascendancy of Moscow centered in the rival principalities of Suzdal-Nizhegorod, Tver, and Ryazan.

The watchful Tatars, warned by the Chinese debacle and operating in Russia on the principle of "divide and rule," proceeded to check Dimitri's ambitions by extending support to his chief rival, the prince of Tver. The adjacent European powers, especially Lithuania, likewise viewed with apprehension any demonstration of centralized authority in Moscow. Like the

Mongols, they regarded the construction of the Kremlin as a forerunner of a policy of aggrandizement. The Mongols responded by conferring on Prince Mikhail Alexandrovitch of Tver the title (*yarlyk*) sought by Dimitri, that of grand prince.

Under the leadership of Grand Duke Oligerd, the Lithuanians invaded Russia; their main objective was Moscow. They made three attempts to capture the city, the first in the winter of 1368, the second in November, 1370, and the third in the summer of 1372. During this last invasion, the Russians seized the initiative and inflicted on them an overwhelming defeat.

Dimitri's triumph led him to abandon his defensive tactics and to assume the offensive against Tver. In this he was aided by other princes and by popular revolt against the "foreign" Mongol aid provided his opponent. In 1375 the prince of Tver was forced to abandon his pretensions to the title of grand prince and to become the vassal of Moscow in matters of foreign policy. With the exception of Ryazan, Dimitri was now the recognized suzerain of all east Russia.

Confronted with this demonstration of the growing power of Moscow, the khans of the Golden Horde under Mamai suspended their bickering and

Renowned chiefly as a military leader, Dimitri Donskoi made a further contribution to the consolidation of Muscovy. He abandoned the practice of dividing the country among a ruler's heirs and introduced in its place the system of primogeniture.

united for military action against Dimitri. For this purpose they hired Genoese infantry and concluded alliances with Grand Duke Yagailo Ol'gerdovitch of Lithuania and Prince Oleg of Ryazan. Once the Mongols assumed the offensive, Dimitri secured the full backing of the church, under the leadership of Metropolitan Cyprian. On September 8, 1380, with an army probably not in excess of thirty thousand men, he confronted and defeated the forces of Mamai Khan in the bloody battle of Kulikovo Pole (Meadow) on the River Don, thereby earning for himself the title Dimitri Donskoi ("of the Don"). According to the chronicler, "The black earth under the horses' hoofs was sown with Tatar bones and watered with their blood." The khan's allies, still en route to join Mamai, beat a hasty retreat. In commemoration of this hard-won victory, the Russian church appointed the Saturday preceding October 26 as a memorial day, to be observed "as long as Russia exists." The Mongols, chafing at this debacle, reorganized. Under Mamai's successor, Tokhtamysh, vassal of the great Timur (Tamerlane), they retaliated by the ruthless sack of Moscow in 1382 and reimposed Tatar suzerainty over the Russian princes. Dimitri's struggle appeared to have been in vain.

In the long run, the psychological effect of the Kulikovo victory on the Russian people was enormous. In the first place, it afforded proof that through unity the Russians could evict the Tatars, as the Chinese had done before them. Timur himself was a vassal of the Ming dynasty of China. Second, it marked the beginning of the disintegration of the Golden Horde on Russian soil. Dimitri's son and successor, Vasily I (*r*. 1389–1425), played off one foe against another, as the Chinese had done, and won a large measure of independence for Moscow at the expense of the Tatars. Another century was to pass, however, before the last Tatar remnants were driven from Russian territory by Ivan III.

Effects of Mongol Occupation. In many respects, the Mongol invasion proved highly detrimental to Kievan Russia's economy, especially during the first century of occupation. The death or enslavement of at least 10 per cent of the population in itself produced economic concussion. As might be expected, the cities suffered more than the agricultural areas. The cities of Kiev, Chernigov, Pereiaslav, Ryazan, Suzdal, and Vladimir-in-Suzdalia were utterly destroyed. Others in the west and north, like Smolensk, Novgorod, and Pskov, lay beyond the circumference of the devastated area and their recovery occurred earlier. The Mongol practice of requisitioning jewelers, goldsmiths, armorers, sadlers, potters, carpenters, cobblers, and other craftsmen and artisans seriously depleted the ranks of Russia's skilled manpower and affected all types of construction and industrial production. Most of east Russia, according to Vernadsky, who has made a special study of the impact of the Mongol invasion on Russia, was subjected to a century-long industrial depression.

On the other hand, there were some positive economic results. Agriculture expanded in the south to provide food for the great khan's armies. As the population shifted to the central and northern areas, around Moscow and Tver and beyond the Volga, which were less subject to Mongol encroachment, new agricultural regions were opened up. The Mongols had a vested interest in the major trade routes, not only between Asia and Russia, but between Russia and the West. They encouraged the trade of Novgorod and of the Italian colonies in the Crimean and Azov areas. After the first century of Mongol domination and the breakdown of the Mongol trade monopoly, Russian merchants assumed an increasingly active role in commerce.

Ivan III, the Great

Withdrawal of the Golden Horde. In 1480 Ivan III, known as Ivan the Great (*r.* 1462–1505), repudiated the overlordship of the Golden Horde and refused to pay tribute any longer. Akhmat Khan, like Mamai Khan in the time of Dimitri Donskoi, promptly invaded the Moscow principality to enforce his suzerainty. Before the panic had subsided, he unexpectedly withdrew his forces without engaging in battle for Moscow, and the Golden Horde never again threatened the heart of Russia. The fragments of the disintegrating Horde, the Khanates of Kazan, the Crimea, and Astrakhan proved much less formidable, although marauding bands of Tatars continued to threaten peace and order along the periphery of the Russian state.

Unification and Expansion. The second contribution of Ivan III was the successful unification into one state of the majority of Russian lands. In general, all his changes tended toward the centralization of power in Moscow. In 1478 even the free republic of Great Novgorod became an integral part of Russia. In 1485 the former rival principality of Tver followed suit. Viatka was added in 1489. Moscow also strengthened its influence over Pskov, finally annexed by Ivan's son and successor, Vasily III, in 1510. Even Ryazan, although not formally incorporated until 1517, became the ward of Moscow. Officially, Ivan became "Ioann, by the Grace of God, *Gosudar* (Sovereign) of all *Rūs,* and grand prince of Vladimir and Moscow and Novgorod and Pskov and Tver and Yugria and Viatka and Perm and Bolgary and others."

Not content merely to establish his preeminence at home, Ivan reached out to acquire all former Russian lands lost to European powers, such as Lithuania, Sweden, and Livonia (Esthonia, Courland, the Island of Oesel, and other islands). In 1495–1496 he waged war against Sweden for the return of possessions formerly held by Novgorod. From 1500 to 1503 he fought the Livonian Order (remnants of the Teutonic Knights) to repossess former Russian territory. Attracted by his success, many aspiring Lithuanian landholders, with or without their estates, attached themselves to the new Russia. The westward expansion of the Russian state had begun.

Once he had rounded out his domains, Ivan established formal diplomatic relations with European sovereigns, including the pope, the Holy Roman emperor, the kings of Hungary and Denmark, the sultan of Turkey, and the shah of Persia. In this respect, he was helped by his wife, Sophia Palaeologa, a niece of the last of the Byzantine emperors, who took refuge in Naples after Byzantium fell to the Turks in 1453. Upon her insistence, he assumed the Byzantine coat of arms, the double-headed eagle used by the Roman legions, and began to refer to himself as "tsar" and successor to the Byzantine emperors. His primary concern, however, was the reconstruction of Russia, and he refused to lead a crusade to drive the Turks from Europe and restore the Byzantine Empire.

Internal Developments. Inside Russia, the shrewd and competent Ivan resorted to various means of consolidating his authority. A much more complex administrative apparatus was developed. By means of an elaborate system of post roads and mail service, which aroused the admiration of European travellers, he was able to keep the various parts of the state under constant surveillance. The confiscation and redistribution of large areas of land acquired in the process of expansion and consolidation of his hegemony greatly increased the number of *pomeshchiki* (landholders), who received their grants in return for services, including military service, rendered to him. Another step toward centralization was afforded by the compilation of the *Sudebnik,* the first unified code of laws for the expanded Russian state, comprising sixty-eight articles based largely on *Russkaya Pravda* and *Pskovskaya Sudnaya Gramota* (1497). Ivan's contributions to the codification of Russian law likewise elicited admiration from Europeans, including the English.

To convert Moscow into a capital befitting his new dignity, Ivan lost no time in inviting foreign specialists and architects, principally Italians, to Russia to assist with the reconstruction. The Kremlin was enlarged and the walls and chapels constructed in his reign survive today. Among the outstanding architectural achievements of his period are the Uspenskii Sobor (Cathedral of the Assumption), constructed between 1475 and 1479 by Russian master craftsmen under the direction of the Italian architect Aristotle Fioravanti, which became the coronation church of the tsars; the Blagoveshchenskii Sobor (Cathedral of the Annunciation), which served as the royal chapel; and the Granovitaya Palace, built from 1487 to 1491, where the ruler received foreign ambassadors and celebrated Russian victories.

"Third Rome" Concept. By the time Ivan III died in 1505, the Moscow state, with its mixture of native Russians and assimilated Tatars, had become in every respect but name a centralized military monarchy. Under his successor, Vasily III (Basil III, *r.* 1505–1533), the authority and prestige of the ruler was further enhanced by the enunciation of the thesis that Moscow had become the Third Rome. By the deposition of the Metropolitan Isidore in 1441, the Russian church and state had already repudiated the reunion of the Byzantine and Roman Catholic churches (Eastern and Western Catholicism) effected at the Council of Florence in 1439. Beginning in 1448, Russian

metropolitans were appointed by a synod of Russian bishops without reference to Byzantium. The fall of Byzantium to the Muslim Turks in 1453, although a blow to Orthodoxy, was regarded by many Muscovites as the judgment of God for the church's heresy. When in 1472 Ivan III married Sophia Palaeologa, his claim to inherit the Byzantine throne was established. After Ivan's death, the monk Philotheus impressed upon Vasily III the thesis that Moscow was the heir of Byzantium, the defender of the faith, the new and legitimate center of Orthodox Christendom:

> The first Rome collapsed owing to its heresies, the second Rome fell victim to the Turks, but a new and Third Rome has sprung up in the north, illuminating the whole universe like a sun. . . . The first and second Rome have fallen, but the third will stand till the end of history, for it is the last Rome. Moscow has no successor; a fourth Rome is inconceivable.

Henceforth, the self-imposed mission of Russian Orthodoxy was the liberation of Constantinople from the Musslim yoke.

IVAN GROZNY—THE FIRST TSAR

The Russians emerged from over two centuries of Mongol domination with a Tatar complex. This situation has its parallels even in modern times. The Soviets emerged from World War II with a German complex, the Americans with a Pearl Harbor complex, and the peoples of Asia and Africa with a complex about colonialism. The primary concern of victims of aggression and foreign occupation, irrespective of time and place, may be summed up in one word—security. They emerge with a determination that this will never happen to them again. Thus at the close of the Mongol period Russia was ready for an autocratic ruler capable of preserving the internal and external security of the state at all costs. Such a ruler was Ivan IV, or Ivan Grozny,[1] grandson of Ivan III.

When Vasily III died in 1533, his son and heir, Grand Prince Ivan, was but three years of age. Only the sound foundations laid by Ivan III and the power of the church forestalled a period of utter chaos during the prolonged period of his minority. Although Ivan assumed the title "Tsar and Grand Prince of all Russia" in 1544, upon the initiative of Metropolitan Macarius (1542–1564) he remained under the tutelage of the church until 1553.

---

1. The customary English translation of *grozny* as "terrible" or "dreadful" is an incorrect rendition of the Russian term, which in reality means "awe-inspiring," "great," "wonderful," or "dreadful" in a reverential sense. It is entirely possible that Ivan Grozny's title was appropriated from Sultan Selim the Grim (r. 1512–1520) of the Ottoman Empire. "Grim" is a better rendition than "Terrible." Muslim and Byzantine patterns of autocratic monarchy were studied by scholars in the reign of Ivan IV, the better to justify the new Russian autocratic ideology.

Boyar Struggle. Convinced that Russian security was contingent upon Russian unity, Ivan IV strove to complete the work of his grandfather by the consolidation of the various principalities into a single unified state under an autocratic ruler. Not all the boyars shared this point of view, and a struggle inevitably resulted. Impressed during the period of his tutelage by the fact that the boyars often subordinated the interests and security of the state to their own personal aggrandizement, Ivan Grozny ruthlessly suppressed all opposition. The church, although it opposed his senseless atrocities, believed that the welfare of Orthodoxy required an autocratic monarchy. Metropolitan Macarius had impressed on his young charge the concept of a Third Rome. Ivan's challenge to boyar ascendancy was likewise aided by Ivan Semyonovitch Peresvietov, a man of Lithuanian-Russian extraction; before he entered the service of Moscow, he had carved out a colorful career for himself in Poland, Hungary, Bohemia, and Lithuania. In his "Legend of Sultan Mahomet," Peresvietov presented a political program for Ivan's guidance, urging him to rule "in terror and wisdom." To his enemies, according to Peresvietov, the tsar must always be formidable, for "Tsardom without terror is like the Tsar's horse without a bridle." Ivan executed some of the boyars, the lands of others were confiscated, and many escaped to become refugees in the Tatar Khanates of Kazan and the Crimea, where they continued to plot the overthrow of the tsar.

The Conquest of Kazan. Ivan Grozny decided to assume the offensive against the Kazan Khanate, which was supported by Crimea and the Turks, and which constituted a threat to the security of the Russian state. He selected Kazan because it was the strongest remnant of the Golden Horde, and because a "holy war" against the Muslim enemy—a legitimate target to which no one could object—would promote internal unity. Also, as Peresvietov pointed out, it afforded an opportunity to open up new lands for the tsar's supporters. Even Western Europe was sure to applaud such a crusade.

In preparation for this struggle, the tsar began the organization of a regular army, fully equipped with firearms (*pishchali*). In 1550, he formed six regiments of infantry from the untaxed elements (*netyaglye*) of the population, which came to be known as the *streltsy*. In fact, on a limited scale, he introduced compulsory military service. His military preparations included the erection not far from Kazan of the "prefabricated" fortress of Svieyazhsk, numbered sections of which had been floated down the Volga.

On October 2, 1552, with an army of around 150,000 men, and as reported by Prince Kurbsky, 150 large cannon, Ivan Grozny seized the stronghold of Kazan. According to Russian historians, this marked the first time that explosives were used to undermine the walls of a fortress. The fall of Kazan sealed the fate of Astrakhan at the mouth of the Volga, which was incorporated into the Russian state in 1556. Russian forces even advanced to the Caucasus and constructed a fort on the River Terek. For a time it appeared that the next Russian military objective was the Khanate of the

Crimea. Ivan was soon diverted from this task by his campaigns in the west against Livonia.

Kazan, which had been a prosperous city and an important Muslim cultural center, was destroyed, its population decimated by massacres, and the remnants expelled, or if they entered Russian service, restricted to a special Tatar district (*sloboda*). In the early stages, the alternatives open to the conquered population were often conversion or annihilation. The best lands of the former Khanate were confiscated and the area subjected to systematic colonization by Russians, the loyal followers of Ivan Grozny, who were protected by a ring of fortresses from incursions by the nomads of the steppes. Vis-à-vis their former oppressors the Russians in many respects appeared to be following the ruthless tactics pursued by the Mongol invaders of Kievan Russia.

The seizure of Kazan inaugurated the Russian crusade against the Muslim world, which has continued for more than four centuries to the present day. When Ivan Grozny returned to Moscow the metropolitan Macarius ascribed to him the combined virtues of Alexander Nevsky, Dimitri Donskoi, Saint Vladimir, and Constantine the Great. In the *History of the Empire of Kazan,* written to celebrate Ivan Grozny's victory, which appeared in 1564–1566, is to be found the moral of Kazan's downfall and a tribute to the victor: "The bulwark of any empire is a wise tsar, not its protecting walls; armies with mighty generals can stand firm without a wall."[2] To commemorate the victory

The capture of Kazan opened the Volga to Russian trade and settlement. This seventeenth-century print shows the city fifty years after it was destroyed by Ivan IV.

2. N. K. Gudzy, *History of Early Russian Literature* (New York: Macmillan, 1949), p. 349.

over the Kazan Khanate, the fantastic Russian cathedral, known since 1588 as St. Basil's Cathedral, was constructed (1555–1561) in Red Square just outside the Kremlin walls by the Russian master craftsmen Barma and Poyetnik.

Although Ivan's primary concern was Russian security, he inadvertently opened a gateway for Russian expansion across Siberia to the Pacific. This expansion was to a large extent the work of individual landowners, adventurers, outlaws, prospectors, fur traders, etc. The crusade against the Muslims, however, was initiated and organized by the government, and enthusiastically supported by the majority of the Slavic population. In one sense, Kazan symbolized a reversal of the trend of history. The intermittent invasion of Europe by Asians now gave way to the Western invasion of Asia, which continued until by the nineteenth century most of that continent was subject to European occupation or control.

Livonian Wars. Once Ivan Grozny had accomplished his purposes in Kazan he turned to the West, with the objective of seizing Livonia, home of the German Baltic barons, which in 1557 became a vassal of Poland. Through the possession of Livonia, he hoped to secure an outlet to the Baltic Sea and to appropriate the profitable trade of the Hanseatic League.

The Livonian Wars (1558–1583) proved to be a lengthy and ultimately an inglorious struggle, which strained the economic resources of the country to the limit. Nor was this conflict against the Christian West popular at home as was the struggle with the Muslim East. It was opposed by the boyars; one of their leaders, Prince Kurbsky, even deserted to the enemy camp in 1564. The initial Russian successes, which included the capture of Narva, Dorpat, Marienburg, and Polotsk, aroused apprehension in Europe, especially among the Lithuanians, Poles, and Germans. The Poles under Sigismund II (1520–1572) instigated the Crimean Tatars to attack Russia. Between 1556 and 1576 they undertook five major raids and numerous small incursions. In 1571 Devlet Girei, the Crimean khan, conducted a raid deep into the heart of Russia, which culminated in the sack and burning of Moscow, and in the death and capture of thousands of Russians. The next year, when he tried to repeat this maneuver, he was driven back, but at great cost. Ivan was soon involved in conflict with Stephen Bathory (1533–1586), his successful Magyar rival for the Polish throne in 1575, over the possession of Livonia. Bathory, who had once served the sultan of Turkey, promptly entered into an alliance with the Crimean Tatars. The Russians were driven east to Pskov. In 1582, unable to raise the soldiers and taxes essential to continue a conflict which had lasted over twenty years, Ivan was forced to abandon his pretensions to Livonia, as well as his Lithuanian acquisitions, and make peace. In 1583 he relinquished Esthonia to the Swedes.

Establishment of Autocracy. The Livonian Wars from the beginning greatly intensified Ivan's domestic problems. To quell the opposition of the boyars and assert his own authority, Ivan Grozny resorted to a dramatic course of

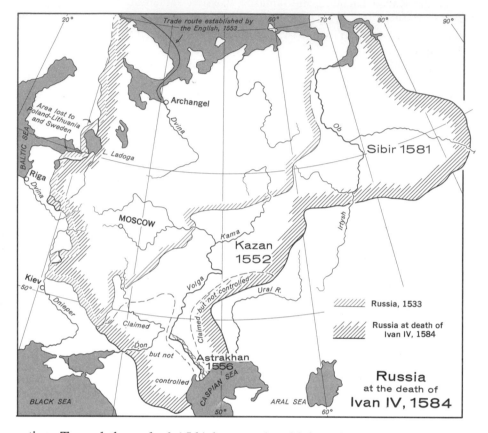

Russia
at the death of
Ivan IV, 1584

action. Toward the end of 1564 he secretly withdrew from Moscow, established himself in the village of Alexandrovskaya Sloboda, near Trinity Monastery, and backed by his bodyguard, announced his abdication. What happened thereafter bore all the earmarks of a prearranged plan. Since his early victories had made him popular with the masses and to some extent with the church, and since he was strongly reinforced, it was not difficult for his agents to organize a group of boyars, churchmen, and common people, who trekked to the monastery to beg Ivan to reconsider. This he agreed to do, provided he was given a mandate from the people to deal with the boyars, the main stumbling block in the implementation of his policies.

Ivan's first step was the creation of an organization known as the *oprichnina* (1565–1572), his own private guard. Its members, who represented a cross section of the population, irrespective of rank or station, were carefully selected and screened, and their sole purpose was to serve the tsar. Hence the name *oprichniki* (detached). To insure their unquestioned loyalty, they were from the beginning separated from family, the people, and property. Later they were ranked as monks (*dukhovnoe bratstvo*) and equipped with special black uniforms. All members of this organization were required to take the following oath of allegiance:

> I swear to be loyal to the sovereign and Grand Duke and his state, to the young princes, and Grand Princess, and not to remain silent about the evil that I know, have heard, or will hear, which is being plotted against the Tsar and Grand Duke and his state, the young princes, and the Tsarina. . . . In witness thereof, I kiss the cross. . . .

According to the historian Nicholas M. Karamzin, the *oprichnyi* court was a product of the extravagant and unfounded fears of Ivan Grozny for his own personal safety. The entire territory assigned to it was enclosed by a strong wall. Here the tsar used to stay when he came from Aleksandrovskaya Sloboda. At one time the *oprichniki* included Nikita Romanov, Ivan's brother-in-law; Boris Godunov, who subsequently occupied the Russian throne; and the Stroganov brothers, Moscow merchants and colonizers of the Trans-Urals. It was this organization, which eventually numbered six thousand, that ruthlessly carried out Ivan's purge of the boyars, who were literally disfranchised and deprived of all protection of life and property. The lands confiscated from the boyars were set aside for the tsar as a kind of Russian version of crown lands, and also came to be known as the *oprichnina*. Many members of the tsar's special guard eventually replaced the boyars on the *oprichnyi* lands. We must differentiate between the *oprichniki,* the bodyguard organized by Ivan Grozny to combat disaffection and treason, and the *oprichniki* settled by the tsar on the *oprichnyi* lands.

In brief, Ivan Grozny reinforced his authority by a reign of terror, comparable in some respects to that instituted by Stalin through the OGPU (secret service) and by Hitler through the Gestapo. Although he was a prejudiced witness, Prince A. M. Kurbsky's correspondence with Ivan and his *History of the Great Prince of Moscow,* written in Lithuania, bitterly condemned this "persecution" of the boyars. The new aristocracy that replaced the boyars became known as the *dvoryanie.* It was this new class of land-owners (*pomeshchiki*) rather than the boyars that spread the institution of serfdom. When the *oprichnina* failed to save Moscow from the Crimean Tatars in 1571, the tsar's confidence in it was shaken, its members were purged, and many of the former property owners were reinstated.

Ivan Grozny's defense of autocracy and his divine right to rule, challenged by the boyars and churchmen of his time, is best illustrated in his correspondence (1564–1579) with Prince Kurbsky:

> But as for the Russian autocracy, from the beginning the rulers themselves, and not the boyars and not the notables, have governed their entire realms. And according to your understanding, would it be dishonest to refuse to subordinate the power given us by God to govern by ourselves and

not be subject to the authority of a certain priest or to your nefarious schemes? . . .

Or do you call this "light," for a priest and arrogant, cunning servants to rule and the tsar to be respected only by virtue of his chairmanship, with power no greater than that of a servant? And do you call this "darkness," for the tsar to rule and govern his kingdom, and for his servants submissively to obey his orders? How can one be called an autocrat if he himself does not build? . . . But we, by the grace of Christ, have reached the age of maturity set by our father, and it is not fitting that we should remain under governors and tutors. . . .[3]

In order to win support for the continuation of the Livonian Wars, Ivan Grozny in 1566 summoned the first "genuine" Zemsky Sobor, an assembly composed of representatives of the clergy, the boyars, the government bureaucracy, and the merchants and traders. This was the first occasion when merchants and traders had been included in such an assembly. This astute move recalls the comparable action in England by Simon de Montfort in 1265 and Edward I in 1295. Temporarily, at least, it appeared to place the country solidly behind Ivan's war policy.

Rise of Serfdom. It was in the reign of Ivan Grozny that the foundations of Russian serfdom were laid. These years brought great changes in the relations between landlords and peasants. Several factors contributed to this: the greater demands on the landlords due to the rise of autocracy; the decline of the former aristocracy and rise of the *pomeshchiki;* the growth of trade and demand for money; and the exhausting Livonian Wars which sapped the country's resources, and which, together with the terrorism instituted under the *oprichnina,* led to severe labor shortages.

The growth of serfdom was by no means a simple process. In the years following the Mongol period, the growth of the lord's demesne increased the demand for labor services from the peasants, sometimes from one to three days a week, or more. According to Soviet historians, serfdom began with the *barshchina,* or forced labor, which, they contend, was a sixteenth-century version of conditions prevalent in the Kievan era. Generally speaking, this is refuted by Western scholars, who regard the payment of the *obrok,* a tax in cash and kind, as of greater significance.

In any event, the peasants in the time of Ivan IV were burdened by increased money dues and other taxes, and by a general reduction in the size of their holdings, without any improvement in agricultural techniques. Many became indebted to their landlords and were forbidden to leave the land. Although they were not slaves, they were transferred with the land in case of sale. The position of the *kholopy,* or house servants, who belonged to their owners, was one of virtual slavery.

3. See Spector, Ivar, and Marion Spector, eds., *Readings in Russian History and Culture* (Boston: Allyn and Bacon, 1965), pp. 45–47.

It was the restriction on the peasant's right of movement, which in its turn was promoted by the terror and by competition among landlords for their labor, that accelerated the rise of serfdom. Already in 1497, because of labor shortages, Ivan III had restricted the peasant's freedom of movement to a two-weeks' period coinciding with St. George's Day (November 25), and heavy fees were exacted for his departure. During the prolonged Livonian Wars even the restricted migration permitted by this ruling proved disadvantageous to the *pomeshchiki*. In 1581 they secured legislation which forbade the peasant to leave the estate during certain years. Ultimately, of course, all years were prohibited and the peasant became permanently "attached" to the land. By such means, serfdom was well established by the close of the reign of Ivan Grozny.

Cossacks. In Russian history the Cossacks are first mentioned in the Mongol period (1240–1480), during which time they were organized into light cavalry regiments. The term *Kazak,* which should not be confused with the Kazakh people of Central Asia, was used by both Turks and Tatars. *Kazak* is the Turkish word for "free man" or "free adventurer." In the Tatar language, it denotes "a light-armed warrior."

When Ivan Grozny abolished the appanages,[4] the Cossacks were scattered throughout Russia, in the interior as well as on the borderlands. In protest against Ivan's reign of terror and the spread of serfdom, many of his subjects fled to the "wild south," where they were able to live as "free Cossacks." In the middle of the fifteenth century, refugees from the Ukraine (borderland), chafing under Lithuanian control, took refuge in the lower reaches of the Dnieper River. Cossacks appeared on the Don in the sixteenth century. This area became a center for fugitives, nonconformists, adventurers, and vagabonds, most of whom were Russians and Ukrainians of lowly origin and of strong Orthodox persuasion, but whose ranks included Poles, Tatars, Armenians, Turks, and others.

In the beginning, Cossack life on the steppes appears to have resembled an anarchic society or primitive collectivism. In a sparsely populated region, the Cossacks roamed at will, hunting, fishing, robbing, and plundering, sharing what they had and enjoying a high degree of freedom from outside control. Just as the camel is always associated with the desert, the horse is connected with the steppes. The Cossack and his horse became inseparable.

In time the Cossacks settled down, cultivated the land which they owned in common, and established two unique republics: the Host of the Don in the southeast and the Zaporog Host in the southwest. Literally, the term "zaporog" means "beyond the cataracts," the reference being to those of the Dnieper, near which the Soviet government has constructed the Dnieprostroy, the largest hydroelectric plant in Europe. Indicative of the democratic spirit that prevailed among them, the ataman, or hetman, at the head of the

---

4. Appanages were estates or territories assigned by a ruler to his younger sons for their maintenance.

Cossack state was elected by universal suffrage and his military authority was
strictly limited. Judicial authority rested in the "Circle," or popular council.
Compulsory military service began at the age of eighteen, when the Cossack
youth became a member of the *stanitsa* (Cossack village), and continued for
seventeen years, of which twelve were devoted to active service.

Fighting now on one side and now on the other, the Cossacks of Ivan
Grozny's reign and for some time thereafter, acknowledged no allegiance to
Russia. Prior to 1676 they frequently served the Moscow state as mercenaries. In that year, Fyodor Alexeyevitch, father of Peter the Great, forced
them to take the oath of allegiance. After 1725 they became an integral part
of the regular Russian army.

In spite of their revolt against Russian authority, the Cossacks were largely
instrumental in adding vast stretches of the Khanate of Sibir (Siberia), a
loose federation of vassal states headed by Kuchum Khan, to the expanding
empire of Ivan Grozny. By 1555 following the victory at Kazan, Siberians
had begun to recognize the supremacy of Moscow and agreed to pay an
annual tribute in furs. Kuchum Khan's defiance of this arrangement led Ivan
in 1574 to bestow upon the powerful family of the Stroganovs, wealthy
Novgorod boyars, a huge territory east of the Urals on the Tobol and Irtysh
rivers, within the khan's domains. With the assistance of a band of Cossacks
under Ataman Yermak, hero of Cossack folklore, who in 1581 entered

USSR Information Bulletin

Ilya Repin worked from 1878 to 1891 on "The Zaporozhian Cossacks Write
a Letter to the Turkish Sultan." Muhammed IV (1641–1691) had proposed
that the Cossacks become his subjects, and this famous painting depicts their
exuberant negative response.

Siberia, the Stroganovs established their claim to the region. Using firearms against the khan's bows and arrows, Yermak captured Iskar, the Siberian capital, on the Irtysh River. In 1584 Siberia was annexed to Russia. Thus Cossack refugees from Ivan's absolutism helped to make his kingdom one of the largest in the world at that time. They performed an important service to Christian civilization by serving as buffers against Muslim Tatar and Turkish encroachment.

By 1914 the Cossacks numbered about 3,000,000, divided into eleven hosts or corps, of whom 300,000 were available for active military service. The Cossack hosts were the Don, Kuban, Terek, Astrakhan, Orenburg, Ural, Siberian, Semiryetchensk, Transbaikal, Amur, and Ussuri. Russian literature has been enriched by many colorful tales of the Cossacks. These include *Taras Bulba,* a short historical novel of the Zaporog Cossacks, by Nikolai Gogol; *The Cossacks* and *Hadji Murad,* fictional accounts by Leo Tolstoy; and *The Silent Don,* an epic of Cossack life in the era of World War I, the Russian Revolution and Civil War, by Mikhail Sholokhov, recipient of the Nobel prize for literature in 1965.

Trade with the West. Russian trade in the reign of Ivan IV was controlled by government edict and determined by the interests of the state, especially by the needs of the treasury. Russian merchants were not organized into corporations, guilds, or companies. They remained the servants of the state. Foreigners visiting Russia expressed surprise at the lack of independent enterprise. Ivan Grozny nevertheless displayed a keen interest in the development of foreign trade and in Western technical progress.

One of the principal trade routes to the West opened up during this period was the Dvina, White Sea, Arctic route. The other was through the conquered port of Narva and the Baltic Sea. In 1553 Richard Chancellor, a survivor of the ill-starred expedition of Sir Hugh Willoughby in search of an Arctic passage to the Orient, reached the mouth of the Dvina River and made his way to Moscow. There he successfully arranged for the shipment of English cloth and military supplies to Russia via the Dvina. The Muscovy Company, charted by Queen Mary of England in 1554, which was a forerunner of the English and Dutch East India Companies, shortly thereafter secured a monopoly of English trade with Russia. As this trade developed, a chain of towns from the new port of Archangel soon lined the route from the mouth of the Dvina to Moscow. After 1558 the English were permitted free access to Narva on the Gulf of Finland. English warehouses were constructed in the larger Russian towns.

The English were particularly interested in trade via Russia with the Orient. With the Volga route in Russian hands, they were able to secure from Ivan Grozny exclusive rights to trade with the newly won Muslim centers of Kazan and Astrakhan, together with free transit via the Volga to Persia and Central Asia. Anthony Jenkinson, an agent for the Muscovy Company (1555–1669), in 1558 penetrated as far east as Khiva and Bukhara. Ivan IV even permitted an English company to prospect for iron on the Vychegda River and to erect a smelter, to mint money at Russian mints, to use Russian post horses, and to hire Russian labor. Little wonder that he was sometimes referred to as the "English Tsar." The Muscovy Company actually sponsored and covered the expenses of English embassies in Moscow for almost a century. After the execution of Charles I of England in 1649, however, all its trading privileges in Russia were cancelled by Tsar Alexis I. With the restoration of the Stuarts, the English government reestablished the embassy at its own expense in 1663, but the tsar refused to renew the trading privileges so long enjoyed by the Muscovy Company, which terminated in 1669.

The German merchants of Lübeck (an old Hanse center) viewed the development of Russian trade with great apprehension, and strongly recommended that European technicians and strategic goods be barred from Russia. Ivan Grozny's interest in English trade, as in trade with Denmark, stemmed in part from the determination of the three powers to strike a final blow at the Hanseatic League, which had lost its privileged position in Russia in 1494 as a result of Ivan III's subjugation of Novgorod. It was also due to English readiness to furnish Russia with war materials and military men. In the national interest, however, he steadfastly rejected English efforts to secure a monopoly of all Russian commerce.

Printing. The Western impact on Russia included plans for the development of printing. The first printing shop was established in Moscow in 1553 (1563?) by Ivan Fedorov and Peter Mstislavets. Their first book, *The Apostle,* said to be beautifully illustrated, was published in 1564. It soon became evident that the time was not propitious for the success of this venture. Accused of heresies by high government and church officials, the two printers abandoned Russia for Lithuania, where a second edition of *The Apostle* appeared in 1574. According to the testimony of the Jesuit Antonio Possevino (1534–1611) who visited Moscow in 1581, Ivan Grozny maintained his own printing office for government business at Alexandrovskaya Sloboda.

Evaluation of Ivan IV. Ivan's private life bore some resemblance to that of Henry VIII of England (1491–1547). Married seven times, he killed his eldest son in 1580 in a fit of insane fury, and left behind him at his death only two young boys. His wives, five of whom were crowned, included Anastasia Romanov, Maria Temriukovna (Circassian), Martha, Anna, Anna Vasiltchikuf, and Maria Nagaya, who outlived him. As trade relations developed with England, he is said to have proposed marriage to Queen Elizabeth, and perhaps anticipating her refusal, to Lady Mary Hastings.

Ivan Grozny's excessive cruelty, although characteristic of the time, has long beclouded his reputation at home and abroad. One of his tangible achievements was the welding together of Russian principalities into a unified state with Moscow as its center. This step in the development of a Russian national state had its parallels in the concentration of power in national monarchies in Western Europe during the same period. As a result of the Mongol invasion, Muscovite Russia succeeded Kievan *Rūs*. Whereas the political structure of the latter was decentralized, a blending of monarchical, aristocratic, and democratic elements, Muscovite Russia emerged strongly centralized and autocratic. A glimpse of what Russia might have become, had Ivan IV not ruthlessly crushed the power of the boyars, can be seen in the relations between monarch and nobility in seventeenth- and eighteenth-century Poland. Another outstanding event of Ivan's reign was the seizure of Kazan in 1552, which inaugurated the Russian crusade against the Muslim world and precipitated an era of Russian expansion which, from 1552 to 1905, averaged about fifty square miles per day. World War II produced a reevaluation of Ivan Grozny in the Soviet Union. His Soviet biographer, R. Wipper, has described him as "one of the great political and military leaders of Europe of the sixteenth century."

Current Soviet interest in Ivan Grozny's contribution to the national unification of Russia led in the summer of 1963 to the disinterment of his remains and those of his two sons, Ivan and Fyodor, from their graves in Archangel Cathedral in the Kremlin and their transfer to the Institute of Ethnography of the USSR Academy of Sciences. In April 1964 a leading Soviet anthropologist, Mikhail M. Gerasimov, already noted for his reconstruction of the likeness of the prehistoric Java man and the Peking man, displayed a bust of Ivan IV constructed from the skull of the former Russian ruler.

Historians have long emphasized the "great divide" between Kievan and Muscovite Russia, geographically, politically, and culturally. A Soviet scholar of distinction, D. S. Likhachev, member of the USSR Academy of Sciences, has taken issue with this interpretation, contending that, geographically speaking, Kievan *Rūs* included both Novgorod and Vladimir-Suzdal, the land in which the rise of Moscow occurred; that throughout Kievan *Rūs* one culture prevailed; and that following the emergence of the Moscow state there was a great revival of interest in Kievan and Byzantine culture, religion, and art. Today this view is shared by some scholars outside the Soviet Union.

END OF THE RURIK DYNASTY

Boris Godunov. Ivan Grozny, whose objective was stability under autocracy, left a legacy of discontent, disunity, and confusion. His son, Fyodor I (*r.* 1584–1598), lacked all the qualities necessary for the preservation of the autocracy on which the stability of the country rested. Russia, according to Giles Fletcher (1549?–1611), an English traveller, was "so full of grudge and mortall hatred" that civil conflict appeared inevitable. Power was vested in a Council of Regents, set up by Ivan IV during his lifetime. It was soon superseded by the regency of Boris Godunov, a boyar of remote Tatar origin, whose position was greatly strengthened by his own marriage to the daughter of Maliuta Skuratov, a notorious member of the *oprichniki* and favorite of Ivan Grozny, and by his sister Irina's marriage to Ivan's son, Fyodor. Boris Godunov became the real ruler of the Moscow state during the decade 1588–1597.

Although he discontinued the terror, Boris carried on Ivan Grozny's domestic and foreign policies. He removed from office the members of the prominent Shuisky and Romanov families. Like Ivan, he sought to win the middle classes—the lesser nobility and gentry—by grants of land, money, and increased authority over the peasantry. He enhanced the prestige of church and state by forcing the Greek patriarch, during a visit to Moscow in 1589, to consecrate the metropolitan Job as patriarch of Russia, thereby recognizing an autocephalous, or self-governing, Russian church. In foreign policy, his main objectives were to reverse the losses of the Livonian Wars and to restore the prestige of the Russian state. By 1595 he had recovered from Sweden (Peace of Tyavzin) the former possessions of Novgorod on the Gulf of Finland and Karelian Isthmus, with the exception of the port of Narva. On the whole, his administration earned him a reputation, even among his enemies, for efficiency and enlightenment.

The death of Fyodor's younger brother, Dimitry, in 1591, in unexplained circumstances, beclouded the remaining years of Boris Godunov's reign. The official explanation was that Dimitry accidentally stabbed himself during a fit of epilepsy while playing a game of soldiers. Rumors were circulated, however, that Dimitry was removed by Boris Godunov's agents, in order to eliminate the latter's chief rival for the throne. Russian historians have long disagreed as to his guilt or innocence. N. M. Karamzin and V. O. Kliuchevsky have expounded his guilt, which has been perpetuated in Pushkin's drama, *Boris Godunov,* and in Count A. K. Tolstoy's trilogy: *Ivan the Terrible, Tsar Fyodor Ivanovitch,* and *Boris Godunov.* Other leading Russian historians, including S. F. Platonov, D. S. Mirsky, and Godunov's biographer, Stephen Graham, have discounted or denied it.

"Time of Troubles." When Tsar Fyodor died in 1598 and the Rurik dynasty came to an end, the Patriarch Job summoned the Zemsky Sobor, which elected Boris Godunov (r. 1598–1605) as tsar. It was "the cutting off of the old dynasty," according to Kliuchevsky, which precipitated Russia's "Time of Troubles" (1598–1613), marked by political and social upheaval, and accompanied by the "interposition of Cossack and Polish offscourings of the Muscovite and Lithuanian Empires."

The reign of Boris Godunov was beset by economic crises, in part the aftermath of Ivan Grozny's domestic and foreign policies. Due to prolonged warfare, serfdom, and colonization of newly won territory, large areas in the northwest and center of the Moscow state were depopulated. Giles Fletcher in 1588 testified to the great number of deserted villages en route to Moscow, in an area that had formerly been reported to be thickly populated. The districts around Moscow, Novgorod, and Pskov were the most seriously affected. The country's economic recovery received a severe setback in 1601–1604 from a series of crop failures, which brought in their wake plague, famine, and social unrest. Although Boris Godunov sought to relieve the distress, he was only partially successful.

The tsar's prestige suffered another blow in 1604, with the appearance on Russian soil, abetted by Sigismund III of Poland, of the First False Dimitry. In reality a runaway monk, he claimed to have escaped Boris Godunov's murderous designs in 1591 by taking refuge in Poland. Renewed warfare, resulting in further devastation and depopulation of the countryside, agravated Russian economic problems. Peasants and Cossacks of the Ukraine flocked to the banners of Dimitry. Disgruntled boyars exploited the situation by declaring Boris Godunov's election by the Zemsky Sobor null and void.

Upon Boris Godunov's sudden death on April 13, 1605, the armed forces and leading boyars deserted his sixteen-year-old son and heir for the pretender Dimitry, who was crowned in Moscow. This artificial recreation of the old dynasty failed to end the dissension. Dimitry's large retinue of Poles and Jesuits, his disregard of the boyars, and deliberate insult to the Crimean khan which precipitated further hostilities, soon disillusioned his supporters. Within eleven months he was murdered by the boyars and his body dragged through the streets of Moscow. In a popular revolt against the Poles, the Moscow city mob, in search of a "good tsar," elected Prince Vasily Shuisky (r. 1606–1610).

The boyars' choice was promptly repudiated by the restless peasants and Cossacks of the Ukrainian borderlands. This, the first of a long series of peasant revolts in Russia, was led by Ivan Bolotnikov, a much-travelled fugitive slave, who reached the gates of Moscow in 1606. Associated with the peasants and once again abetted by the Poles, was the Second False Dimitry, known as the thief of Tushino, where he established his rival court and ravaged the country far and wide. The intervention of Sweden soon led the Poles to abandon the hapless Dimitry. In 1610, with the Moscow state facing complete disruption, seven leading boyars invited Sigismund III of Poland to permit his son Vladislav to accept the vacant throne, under conditions guaranteeing the rights of the boyars. The Poles, having seized Smolensk, once again entrenched themselves in the burned city of Moscow.

Resistance to the Polish "take-over" began almost immediately, encouraged by the Patriarch Hermogen, who denounced the boyars as traitors. Some dissident elements supported another pretender, called Sidorka, whose forces seized Pskov in 1611. The Swedes took advantage of the situation to occupy Novgorod. The complete disruption of the Volga trade resulting from this chaos led Kuzma Minin, a cattle-dealer from Nizhny-Novgorod, to raise funds for the support of a "peoples' army," which was placed under the leadership of the *dvorianin,* Prince Dimitry Pozharsky. This "peoples' army," joined by several troops of Cossacks enveloping Moscow, starved the Poles into submission, and liberated the city on October 26, 1612. Even today, the statues of Minin and Pozharsky occupy a place of honor in the Red Square in Moscow. In November, the liberators of Moscow issued a summons for a Zemsky Sobor, to elect a new tsar. This Zemsky Sobor, which convened in Moscow in 1613, was the largest yet held and the most representative of the various strata of society, including boyars, dvorianie, clergy, a cross section of the urban population, streltsy, peasants, and Cossacks. After long and painful deliberation, they discarded the foreign Polish and Swedish candidates, and elected a "born tsar," sixteen-year-old Michael Romanov (r. 1613–1645), nephew of Tsar Fyodor, who became the founder of the Romanov dynasty. Following his release from Polish capitivity in 1619, Michael's father, Philaret Romanov, as patriarch and co-sovereign, was the real ruler of the country until 1633.

ESTABLISHMENT OF THE ROMANOV DYNASTY

With the election of Michael Romanov, the "Time of Troubles" officially came to an end. The aftermath of internal confusion, foreign intervention, and poverty, which had characterized the period, continued to plague Michael, his son Alexis, and his grandson Fyodor, all of whom began their reigns as minors and who were far from being strong and competent rulers.

The external enemies of the new regime, the Swedes and the Poles, continued to occupy Russian territory. Under the circumstances, Michael was in no position to pursue an aggressive foreign policy. By the peace treaty with Sweden at Stolbovo in 1617, the Russians retrieved Novgorod, but the Swedes continued to occupy the vitally important Baltic coast. Under the fifteen-year truce with Poland at Deulino near the Troitse-Sergiev Monastery, in December, 1618, the Poles retained possession of Smolensk, Chernigov, and Novgorod-Seversk. It was not until 1634 that "permanent" peace with Poland was achieved, whereby Vladislav, now King Ladislas IV, renounced his claim to the Russian throne in return for Smolensk and payment of an idemnity. The Russian international situation remained sufficiently precarious that when the Don Cossacks offered Azov as a gift to the tsar in 1637, Michael was constrained to reject it for fear of conflict with the Turks, from whom the Cossacks had seized it.

Russian Expansion. Under Alexis I (r. 1645–1676) Russian expansion was resumed, this time in support of the struggle of the Zaporozhian Cossacks against Poland. In 1649, under the leadership of Bogdan Khmelnitsky, the Cossacks and Ukrainian peasants successfully challenged Polish authority. To secure their position, they offered to place the Zaporozhian Host under Russian protection, and in 1654 took an oath of allegiance to the tsar. In the inevitable conflict with Poland which followed, the reorganized forces of Alexis succeeded in recovering Smolensk. War with Poland and Sweden continued intermittently. Finally, by the Peace of Andrusovo in 1667, the

Ukraine was divided between Poland and Russia, the Russians securing the entire left bank of the Dnieper, together with Kiev on the right bank. What was intended to be a temporary solution became permanent.

In contrast to the military holding action and slow gains in the West, in the seventeenth century Russian expansion across Siberia proceeded apace, with little or no resistance from the native population, until in 1639 the Russians reached the Sea of Okhotsk on the Pacific. The only substantial resistance encountered was from the Buddhist Buryats around Lake Baikal. Much of Siberia could be traversed by the Yenisei and Lena river systems, a type of travel with which Russians had long been familiar. The trade in furs, especially in sables, provided a constant incentive. Russian arms were vastly superior to those of the native population. The Russian government, partly because of the importance of the fur trade, backed up the traders by establishing a rudimentary form of government and a defense system consisting mainly of armed stockades along the river routes.

When, under Alexis, the Russians pushed south to the Amur River, and encountered the Chinese Empire under the Manchu Ch'ing dynasty, conditions changed. After a quarter of a century of intermittent hostilities, the Russians represented by Count F. A. Golovin and the Chinese by a Jesuit missionary concluded peace at Nertchinsk on August 26, 1689. In this, the first treaty China concluded with a Western power, the Chinese retained the Amur River and blocked Russian expansion in the Far East until the middle of the nineteenth century. The treaty included a provision for the establishment of a Russian mission in Peking and permitted state-organized merchant caravans to enter China.

Further Development of Serfdom. In the seventeenth century, the gradual transformation of the Russian peasants into serfs continued. In 1607, during the Time of Troubles, Tsar Vasily Shuisky once again extended the period of recovery of fugitive peasants from five to fifteen years. In this chaotic period, many peasants found it possible to evade these restrictions on their freedom of movement. Under Bolotnikov, however, they had failed to recover their freedom. During the restoration of law and order under the early Romanovs, there was increasing pressure from the *dvoryanie* for further restrictions on peasant movement. Prince N. I. Odoyevsky, appointed by Tsar Alexis to restore order, undertook a codification of the laws, which, after its approval by the Zemsky Sobor of 1649, was known as the *Sobornoe Ulozhenie,* or Assembly Code. This code, which prevailed until the Speransky reforms of the nineteenth century (see page 110), formalized the existing relations between lords and peasants and the transformation of the latter into serfs. The key feature in this code was the complete abolition of the time limit for the recovery of fugitive peasants, their families, crops, and personal possessions. Although the code was designed to protect the landlord from the loss of his labor force, it failed to define the rights of the laborers, and the position of the vast majority continued to deteriorate.

In spite of the code, the chief form of peasant protest continued to be flight. They succeeded in running away, even from the estates of Tsar Alexis. Their alternative to flight was sporadic fighting and violence which ordinarily constituted no serious threat to the regime. In 1670, however, a mass uprising of peasants on the Volga, led by the filibustering Don Cossack Stepan (Stenka) Razin, led to widespread destruction. The rebels seized the lower and middle reaches of the Volga, including Astrakhan and Tsaritsyn (Volgograd), a city founded by Boris Godunov. In their northward progress, however, they proved to be no match for the regular armed forces of the tsar. Razin himself was turned over to the government by Cossack "elders," who opposed the revolt, taken to Moscow in a cage, and beheaded in Red Square.

Patriarch Nikon and the Raskol. In the middle of the seventeenth century, the Russian Orthodox church, which over the centuries had been relatively free from doctrinal disputes, was rocked by the *Raskol,* or Schism. Isolated from foreign, even from Byzantine, influences throughout the Mongol period and almost untouched by the Protestant Reformation in Europe, the Russian church had clung tenaciously to the ritual and customs of the Kievan era. As

Seventeenth-century Moscow is the scene of this Easter celebration. The tsar and his subjects join in procession outside the Kremlin wall.

contacts between the Moscow state and Kievan and Greek scholars were resumed, there came to light numerous discrepancies between the Greek and Russian services in matters of ritual. There was some recognition of the need to raise the standards of the Russian clergy, to improve their education, and to return to the Greek ritual. Patriarch Nikon (1605–1681), an ambitious and redoubtable leader of humble birth, assumed office in 1652 with a determination to revise the Service Books and reform the ritual. His pastoral Letter of 1653 directed the clergy to join three fingers when making the sign of the cross, denoting the trinity, instead of the customary two fingers, symbolizing the dual nature of Christ. These and other "reforms" were bitterly resented by large numbers of the clergy and laity, who regarded Moscow as the Third Rome, the Russian church as the purest form of Christianity, and the Greek church as corrupted under Turkish rule.

Nikon relentlessly forced through his reforms against all opposition. They were recognized by Church Councils in 1654, 1655, and 1656. Those who joined the ranks of the opposition called themselves Old Believers (*Raskolniki*). Under the leadership of Archpriest Avvakum, they preferred martyrdom to conformity. In the schism that rent the church, thousands like Avvakum died at the stake or were buried alive. Others were exiled to the far Arctic, to Siberia, or to the Caucasus, where they established new settlements, and inadvertently became effective agents of Russian expansion. Still others fled abroad.

Although he was successful in enforcing "reform," Nikon met defeat when, as head of the church, he challenged the authority of the state. He insisted upon the superiority of the spiritual power over the temporal, as so many European churchmen had done in the Middle Ages, and his action produced the first serious clash between church and state in Russia. The church and Nikon emerged the losers. Nikon was deposed and banished to a distant monastery by an Ecumenical Council meeting in Moscow in 1666–1667, the very council which approved his reforms in ritual. The *Ulozhenie* of 1649, which drastically reduced the power and jurisdiction of the Russian church and its monasteries, and the fall of Nikon were but preludes to the final victory of secular authority over the church in the time of Peter the Great.

Trade and Industry. Under the early Romanovs, contacts with Western Europe which had developed so propitiously in the reign of Ivan Grozny, once again improved. Michael sought loans from the Dutch and English to help stabilize his position and pay for the reorganization of the armed forces. After 1649 neither the English nor the French were successful in their efforts to negotiate trade monopolies such as the Muscovy Company had previously enjoyed. Attempts by the Dutch, who were interested in the grain trade, to secure an export monopoly and to engage in grain cultivation in Russia came to nought. The Romanovs found it more profitable to maintain their own monopolies of divers commodities. Foreign control of trade inside Russia was no longer considered commensurate with Russian national interests. Russian

merchants, to their own profit, managed to prevent foreigners from engaging in retail trade with the Russian population. The state, operating in accordance with the principles of mercantilism, was primarily interested in making Russia economically independent and militarily strong. In pursuit of this objective, foreign technicians and organizers were encouraged to enter the country, in order to stimulate the growth of Russian industry. In 1632, for example, Andrew Vinnius, a Dutchman, established three foundries, operated by water power, near Tula, which became the chief center for iron production.

With few exceptions, industrial development in seventeenth-century Russia was on a small scale. Those industries which were of value to the armed forces prospered. Altogether, during this period there were only about thirty factories in the country, some of which operated temporarily. The principal industries, aside from iron, salt, and potash, included woolen cloth, silk, and other textiles and consumer goods. By the end of the century the Solkamskaya Salt Works were producing seven million poods (one pood equals thirty-six pounds of salt) per annum. Moscow, Pskov, Tikhvin, and later Smolensk became centers for flax and hemp, an appreciable amount of which was exported via Archangel.

Much of the trade and industry of Russia during this period was concentrated in a handful of wealthy families. Among the chief capitalists were the Stroganovs, who controlled vast salt works, operated iron mines, shipped large quantities of grain and fish, sold sables and other furs abroad, and maintained their own agents in Holland and Flanders. They also collected the *yasak* (fur tribute) for the tsar and undertook numerous lucrative government contracts.

In the towns and cities, there were no guilds in the Western sense. During the seventeenth century, however, there developed three groups of privileged traders: the *gosti* (guests), royal commercial counselors and factors of the tsar, of whom in 1649 there were thirteen including the Stroganovs; the *gostinaya sotnya* (guest hundred), who numbered one hundred fifty-eight; and the *sukonnaya sotnya* (cloth hundred), numbering one hundred sixteen. The *gosti* comprised an exclusive group of wealthy capitalists, many of whom grew rich on "pork barrel" army contracts, and who managed all sorts of state enterprises, supervised the collection of customs dues, engaged in the fur trade, the salt and fish industries, etc. Nikitinov, the most outstanding among the *gosti* and a competitor of the Stroganovs, traded in wool cloth, salt, and fish, and owned a fleet of ships plying to Astrakhan. Merchant capitalists in the other two categories operated, for the most part, independently of the government. The most "substantial" member of the *gostinaya sotnya*, Y. A. Graditsyn, owned over forty villages, fisheries, salt works, and other stores. Voronin, a Moscow merchant, had thirty stores for the sale of woolen cloth, a large ironworks, and was at the same time a grain industrialist, shipowner, lease operator, and army contractor. According to Giles Fletcher, some of the *gosti* were worth up to three million rubles.

Among the principal reasons for the weakness of Russian economic and industrial development at this time, as compared with Western Europe, were the lack of adequate communications and the absence of a public credit system. Although some wealthy merchants, like the Morozovs, advanced credit, the monasteries remained the chief moneylenders.

Growth of Cities. Under the early Romanovs, there was a marked growth in the urban population of Russia. Soviet economic studies have indicated that in the sixteenth century the country boasted only about 180 cities. By the middle of the seventeenth century this number had increased to 226, exclusive of cities and towns in Siberia and those on the left bank of the Dnieper in the Ukraine. Moscow's population at this time was about 200,000. Although the early Romanovs actively encouraged the settlement of tradesmen and craftsmen in the towns, by no means every town included a *posad,* or business settlement. Most Russian towns, many of which were founded as armed outposts for protection against foreign or internal marauders, were primarily administrative and military centers. Even Moscow in 1638 included only 2,367 craftsmen (except for the "white," or tax-exempt, categories). Those towns with the largest business districts were located mainly in the central and northern parts of the Moscow state. Moscow, with its Kitaigorod and German settlement, led all the rest. Other towns of outstanding economic significance included Kazan; Nizhny-Novgorod on the Volga, center of the great fair of St. Macarius; Archangel, the chief port as long as Russia was cut off from the Baltic; Yaroslavl; and Novgorod. The old cities of Kiev and Novgorod were no longer, as in the medieval period, on the main trade routes.

Siberia. In the seventeenth century, Siberia made rapid strides in economic development. Every year, by various routes, hundreds of businessmen or their agents, trekked east in search of sables, beaver, Arctic foxes, and other furs. The fur trade provided a substantial amount of the income of the government. Products in great demand in Siberia, for which furs were often exchanged, were textiles, footwear, haberdashery, hides, manufactured wares of iron, copper, and zinc, and other consumer goods. As previously indicated, the government protected the trade routes by construction of many towns, or armed outposts which became towns. The number of government employees in the region by the end of the century exceeded 10,000. Towns such as Tobolsk, Tomsk, and Yeniseisk, included appreciable urban settlements, with many settlers dividing their time among trade, business, and agriculture. By the close of the century, it is estimated that more than 2,500 urban families were engaged in business in Siberia. To feed the growing population, the government encouraged the migration of peasants from European Russia, with the result that by 1700 at least 17,000 peasant families, half the Russian population of the area, had settled in Siberia, and most of them were engaged in agriculture.

Part Two

Imperial Russia, 1682-1894

3

Peter I, the Great:

The Reformer, 1682-1725

WHEREAS THE TATARS *trans*formed Russia, it was Peter I's purpose to *re*form the country in accordance with Western ideas and customs. In current terminology, he sought to create a modern state from an underdeveloped country. A man of such volcanic energy, diverse interests, and ruthless determination could not fail to evoke controversy. Inside Russia, Peter and his policies were, for decades, the subject of bitter controversy, especially by Slavophiles opposed to Russia's Western orientation. Russian history, as the Russian historian Kliuchevsky has pointed out, was divided into pre-Petrine and post-Petrine periods, with Peter's reforms used as the focus for study of the past and clarification of the future. Leo Tolstoy (1828–1910), repelled by the alleged immorality and vulgarity of the monarch and his court, abandoned all plans for a biography of Peter. In Soviet times Alexei N. Tolstoy (1882–1945) produced a novel, filmed by Sergei Eisenstein, which unabashedly depicted the debauchery of Peter's court; also, by implication, the book drew laudatory comparisons between Peter's policies and those of Stalin.

In recent years, a new image of Peter I has emerged, which describes him, not as a "dynamic barbarian," but as a humble and selfless man dedicated to Russia and the Russian people.[1] He has been portrayed as the antithesis of Louis XIV of France; as "an autocrat uncorrupted by power," whose cruelty and barbarities reflected the age in which he lived; and as one of the "very great princes of history." This new image extends to the emperor's moral behavior. Allegations of Peter's gross immorality, it is claimed, have stemmed largely from disgruntled foreign hirelings, who disparaged his reputation abroad. The new image includes Peter's "only love," his second wife, Catherine I, who bore Peter twelve children. Even those who accept this rehabilitation of Peter will recognize British biographer Ian Grey's judgment of his long reign as "a hard reign for the whole nation. . . ."

1. Ian Grey, *Peter the Great, Emperor of All Russia* (Philadelphia and New York: Lippincott, 1960).

THE REGENCY

The inauspicious events connected with ten-year-old Peter I's accession to the tsardom made a lasting impression on the young monarch. Upon Tsar Fyodor's death in 1682 the boyars bypassed the sickly Ivan and selected instead his gifted half-brother Peter as tsar. The bloody palace revolution which followed made Ivan co-sovereign with Peter (until 1696) under the regency of the latter's older half-sister, Sophia.

Fearing an attempt on his life by the ambitious Sophia, Peter and his disappointed mother, who had been the second wife of Tsar Alexis and wished her son to succeed to the throne, moved to Preobrazhensk; this village was not far from the German Suburb of Moscow in which Tsar Alexis had in 1652 ordered all foreigners to reside. The foreign district was founded by English adventurers and German soldiers from the army of General Albrecht von Wallenstein, who acquired fame during the Thirty Years' War (1618–1648). Several thousand Scottish refugees joined the community, following the imprisonment of Charles I of England. Since few of these foreigners spoke Russian, the Russians applied to one and all the name *nemetz* (German), derived from *nemoi,* meaning speechless. B. H. Sumner, the English historian, appropriately termed the colony "a little fragment of industrious, ingenious, Protestant Europe."[2]

The youthful Peter, left largely to his own devices after his formal education was interrupted by Fyodor's death, made numerous friends in the German Suburb. Under the Dutch merchant Timmerman, he zealously studied arithmetic, geometry, ballistics, the art of fortification, and other military subjects. From this foreign settlement, Peter drew most of the colonels, majors, and captains, for mock regiments (*poteshnye*), which formed the nucleus of the later Preobrazhensky and Semyonovsky regiments, and the cell from which the regular Russian army developed. Instead of studying politics and statesmanship, Peter spent his time on live military maneuvers with his make-believe regiments, which were equipped with real cannon and other weapons and included many young boys from Russian aristocratic families.

One event which appears to have made a lasting impression on Peter's thought and action was his visit with Timmerman to a storehouse some five miles from Moscow on the estate of a forebear of the Romanovs, where he saw his first English boat. Rightly or wrongly, he later referred to this ship as the "grandfather of the Russian Navy." Henceforth, Peter's determination to make Russia a sea power became an obsession. The impression is given that Peter's subsequent decisions on domestic and foreign policy were subordinated to this objective. It likewise conditioned his attitude toward England. "The English island," he remarked, "is the best, most beautiful, and happiest that there is in the whole world."

2. *A Short History of Russia* (New York: Reynal and Hitchcock, 1943), p. 319.

The Early Years of Peter's Reign

In 1689 Peter received word that Sophia was instigating an attempt on his life. His subsequent suppression of the triumvirate and relegation of Regent Sophia to a nunnery made little change in his way of life. He continued his military maneuvers on a larger scale, in association with such friends in the German Suburb as General Patrick Gordon, who taught him valuable lessons in military tactics; Franz Lefort, the Genevese who encouraged him in riotous living and urged him to travel abroad; and others like them. Here it was he learned European crafts and languages, became imbued with Western ideas, and resolved to Europeanize Russia at any cost.

First European Tour. After successfully seizing Azov from the Turks in 1696 Peter, determined to unite Western Christendom in a holy alliance against the "infidel" Turk, dispatched a "grand embassy" of 250 persons to Western Europe in March, 1697. Ignoring tradition and the opposition of the church, the tsar joined the embassy incognito as Peter Mikhailovitch. His tour included many leading European cities—Riga, then under Swedish control, Königsberg, Amsterdam, London, Leipzig, Dresden, Prague, and Vienna. Peter spent eighteen months abroad, four in Holland working in shipyards and inspecting factories, and three in England, studying the theory of naval architecture, visiting the Royal Society, Parliament, and other English institutions. A revolt of the *streltsy* cut short his tour, and he returned to Russia more determined than ever to change the customs, ideas, and character of his people. Although much ado has been made of Peter's subsequent regulations requiring his subjects to adopt European dress, the men to shave their flowing beards, and the women to abandon Oriental seclusion, these were but the outward and visible symbols of his goal—the modernization of Russian institutions.

Peter's tour of the principal countries of Western Europe left an indelible impression upon many of the young men who accompanied him abroad. No sooner did Peter die than they called for a constitutional government in Russia. These young "ambassadors" may, in fact, be regarded as the progenitors of the Decembrist revolutionaries of 1825 and of subsequent political leaders who fought against Russian autocracy. Any study of political development, especially of political parties, in Russia should begin with this trip. Russian society was never the same after the return of these young persons selected with the greatest care by Peter himself. The controversy over the Europeanization of Russia that stemmed from this tour eventually became crystallized in the Slavophile and Westernizer movements of the nineteenth century. This "window to Europe" created in Russia an effervescent political climate that lasted for over two hundred years.

Church Reforms. Peter soon turned to the church, the guardian of tradition in Russia, which opposed change, especially Westernization. To raise the iron

Peter I returned from his European travels determined to Westernize Russia. The European style he imposed upon his own court is evident in this painting.

curtain between Orthodox Christianity and European Christendom, he encouraged the erection of Lutheran and Roman Catholic churches in Moscow and elsewhere. Due to his tolerance, foreigners in Russia ceased to regard the Russians as "baptized bears," and Russians, in turn, stopped labelling Protestants and Roman Catholics as "damned and unbaptized." His action convinced many that in Russia there was no head-on clash between church and state, as in the West. Peter was not forcing a revolution in doctrine and ideas, but one in customs and institutions. In many documents, he is represented as a deeply religious man, well versed in theology, although far removed from the bigotry of many of his subjects. For some years, even the Old Believers, some of whom were reputed to be valuable workers in the iron industry, enjoyed a modicum of freedom of worship. In 1716, because he disapproved of their tenacious adherence to beliefs and customs of the past, and because he needed more revenue, Peter ordered a census of these nonconformists. They were then subjected to double taxation, declared ineligible for government service, and forced to wear a special dress.

Peter's attitude toward the church suggests that he was opposed to the Orthodox hierarchy which stubbornly resisted progress rather than to Russian Orthodoxy. On the death of the patriarch Adrian in 1700, he simply neglected to appoint a successor. In 1701 the Monastery Bureau was reestablished, and an exacting census was undertaken to determine the real-estate and peasant holdings of the 557 monasteries and nunneries in Russia. This census resulted in rigid restrictions on the numbers permitted, strict assignment of occupations, as well as in the secularization of schools (other than those for training priests), printing, and almshouses. In 1721, after a prolonged ecclesiastical vacuum, Peter substituted for the Patriarch an ecclesiastical college, which came to be known as the Holy Governing Synod, to handle the spiritual and temporal affairs of the church, subject, of course, to his direction. Church schools were established to elevate the quality of the priesthood. In effect, Peter emerged as the real head of the Russian church. His removal of the capital to the new city of St. Petersburg on the Baltic, founded in 1703, undermined the theory of Moscow as the Third Rome.

Moves Against Boyardom. After asserting his undisputed power over the church, Peter dealt with the boyars, whose influence he regarded as reactionary and detrimental to his plans for modernization. Irrespective of their motives, the boyars acted as a curb on the absolute power of the monarch. Peter did not seek to liquidate them, as did Ivan Grozny. Instead, he effectively deprived them of political and social power. In 1711, on the eve of his military campaign on the Pruth, he established the Administrative Senate, a body of nine officials. In practice, the Senate superseded the Boyar's Duma and soon began to exercise supervision over government finance, the judiciary, and provincial governors. In reality, it was an executive, rather than a legislative, body. Quarrels among its members and between them and the provincial governors seriously interfered with its successful functioning. To supervise the activities of the Senate, Peter in 1722 created the office of procurator-general (attorney general), to which he appointed Yaguzhinsky, one of his favorites.

Perhaps prompted, as Kliuchevsky suggests, by Prince Jacob Dolgoruky's criticism in 1717 that nothing had been done to improve the country's internal administrative machinery, Peter devoted the closing years of his reign to this matter. In 1718, using Sweden as a model, he further reorganized the Muscovite bureaucracy, reducing some forty *prikazy* (government departments), which had accumulated in haphazard fashion, to eight *collegia* (colleges), each headed by a board, on the ground that collective rule might prove more effective and less corrupt than the old system. Two new colleges were added, one for commerce and another for mines and manufactures. This reorganization relieved the hard-pressed Senate of much routine administration. The collective principle did not work out as well in Russia as in Sweden, however, and many of the colleges, as adapted to Russian practice, came to resemble the old *prikazy*. In the search for trained personnel to establish the new colleges, Peter had to import foreigners, and friction developed between Russians and foreigners employed in the colleges.

One of the most effective blows against boyardom was the well-known "Table of Ranks," published in January, 1722, which gave legal recognition to the concept of an aristocracy based on service to the government. The new *dvorianstvo* superseded the old aristocracy of birth. Military, civil, and court services were organized in an ascending series of ranks (*chiny*): fourteen for military and naval service, and another fourteen for civilian service. The upper eight ranks came to be identified with the nobility. Peter thus opened the door for advancement to persons with talent, irrespective of birth and social origin. Several of his top administrators, including his long-time favorite, Alexander D. Menshikov (1670–1729), were of humble origin. The Table of Ranks lasted until the Russian Revolution, when it was abolished by the Soviet regime on December 10, 1917.

Urban and National Reforms. Peter likewise had elaborate plans for the reorganization of local urban administration. As early as 1699 a measure of self-government was granted to Moscow by permitting that city to elect *burmisters* (mayors), according to the German practice. These elected offices were suppressed in 1708. In 1718 Peter decided in favor of urban town councils, modelled after those in Riga and Reval. Urban reform, however, proved to be a slow process. In 1720 Prince Trubetskoy was directed to establish a magistracy on the collegial pattern in St. Petersburg, to serve as a model elsewhere. To Peter's great disappointment, his urban reforms failed to develop the strong middle class he had so admired in Holland and England.

In a move toward decentralization, Peter in 1708–1709 divided the country into eight (later twelve) *guberniyas,* which were in turn subdivided into *provintsii* in 1712. Ultimately, what local autonomy these units were intended to have was lost, and the "provinces" were closely tied to the central government. In general, Peter's new institutions, in many instances borrowed from other countries where conditions and customs were different, failed to take root in Russia. His legislative façade concealed much disorder, corruption, and brigandage throughout the country. The Zemsky Sobor, which might have developed into a parliament, was abandoned during his reign.

FROM TSAR TO EMPEROR

In 1721, at the successful conclusion of the Swedish Wars, Peter abandoned also the title of "tsar," with its Oriental and ecclesiastical implications, for the Western title of "imperator" (emperor). The "Grand States of the Russian Tsardom" became the "Empire of All the Russias." Academically speaking, the title of "tsar" is used to designate Russian monarchs from Ivan Grozny to Peter I. The title of "emperor," beginning with Peter the Great was used until the downfall of the Romanov dynasty. In popular terminology, however, the people continued to call their rulers "tsars."

Industrial Development. By Europeanization, Peter had in mind the industrialization of Russia. Like his immediate predecessors, it was his objective to develop Russian industry to make the country economically independent of foreigners. Peter did not initiate Russian mercantilism, but he extended and strengthened it; many of his projects were launched with both financial and military considerations in view: to increase income and to provide the armed forces with uniforms, weapons, training, and transportation, etc. Historians, prone to criticize Peter's paternalism and the forced introduction of new methods and new industries, underestimate the difficulties he confronted. As Peter himself frequently averred, if an enterprise was new "our people will not do it without compulsion." In the process of industrialization, he was handicapped by the absence of a middle class, willing and capable of building up the mining and manufacturing industries essential to provide the nation with iron, munitions, and textiles.

Peter established the College of Mining and Manufactures to supervise and encourage factory development, and state control of industry was greatly extended during his reign. Among the state enterprises launched by Peter were new armament and metallurgical plants, a sail plant in Moscow, saltpeter plants in Kazan and the south, numerous glass factories (including one still in operation in Leningrad), and textile and tobacco plants. Bad management and lack of skilled workers caused the failure of some enterprises, and others were eventually transferred to private hands.

Because of the wastefulness of government-owned industry, Peter was forced to induce private capital to develop certain industries by attaching villages of serfs to their factories to provide the necessary labor, thereby instituting factory serfdom. He resorted to a policy of generous state subsidies for private industries, advanced loans, granted tax exemptions and freedom from military service. As a result of his efforts, around two hundred factories and mills were established in Russia, most of them during his reign, including important new ironworks and textile mills in the Urals. Only Sweden and England led Russia in the production of iron in Europe.

Soviet scholars assert that many establishments listed as "factories" and "foundries" during Peter's reign were in reality little more than centralized workshops run by artisans and craftsmen. Many were operated largely by serf labor, using hand-operated machines or none at all. The St. Petersburg market was not large enough to supply consumer goods for the city's population. This was done by the many small tradesmen and craftsmen in the capital. St. Petersburg, however, boasted many shipyards and munitions plants. The capital also teemed with foreigners who were instrumental in establishing close relations with Western Europe.

In 1721–1722 Peter sought to organize urban workers along Western lines into two major guilds: one for large merchants, doctors, apothecaries, goldsmiths, and painters; the other for petty traders and small artisans. As in Western Europe, the master workmen of each guild were entitled to employ and train journeymen and apprentices. The attempt to graft this European system on Russian crafts proved largely ineffective. The prevailing form of industry in Russia remained the petty household or *kustar* industry, whereby small artisans worked in their homes and disposed of their wares through jobbers in the markets. Much of the linen exported from Russia appears to have been produced in this fashion.

Lack of transportation facilities handicapped the development of trade and industry. Peter developed plans for the improvement of land and water communications, most of which were not completed in his lifetime. A five-hundred mile highway connecting St. Petersburg and Moscow was constructed. Of the six canals Peter envisaged, one was completed, linking Moscow with the new capital. The basic soundness of his program is indicated by the fact that the great Volga-Don Canal has become a reality under the Soviet regime and the White Sea-Baltic Canal is under construction.

Education. Peter I's educational policy emphasized the training of good officers and technical specialists. Thus the curriculum dealt mostly with the sciences and foreign languages. The group of young noblemen dispatched by Peter to Holland to learn seamanship and navigation in 1697 were the first of a long line of young Russians sent abroad to study Western armies, navies, new trades, and the sciences. Peter's hopes of introducing compulsory ele-

Embassy USSR

Envisioned by Peter I, it was not until 1952 that the Volga-Don Canal was constructed near Volgograd. At this point the two rivers are only sixty-three miles apart.

mentary education for children of landowners and the middle class proved premature. In 1701 an Artillery School and a School for Navigation were established in Moscow, with an enrollment of three hundred in the latter. In 1707 foundations were laid for a Medical School. In St. Petersburg in 1715 a Naval Academy, the second in Europe, was established. Many schools for engineers were opened.

Peter's adoption of the Julian Calendar on January 1, 1700, was meant to bring Russia into line with the majority of countries in Western Europe. Many of these countries, however, had abandoned the Julian for the Gregorian Calendar (1582–1583), and the time lag (eleven days in the eighteenth century, twelve in the nineteenth, and thirteen in the twentieth) prevailed in Russia until February 14, 1918. The Imperial Academy of Sciences, patterned after a similar institution in Paris and the Royal Society in London, was founded in 1725 at the close of Peter's reign. It was intended as an organization for scientific research and special assignments, as well as for supervision of the country's institutions of higher learning and secondary schools. Since Russia lacked scholars to staff the new academy, they were imported from the West, especially from the German states.

To assist the work of the technical schools, Peter had Western books on technical and scientific subjects translated into Russian. In 1703 L. F. Magnitsky wrote the first Russian text on arithmetic published in Moscow; this work, a kind of encyclopedia of mathematics, surveying, astronomy, and navigation, was the earliest Russian book to use Arabic figures instead of letters. In 1703 the first public newspaper, *Vedomosti* ("News"), made its appearance. Peter I was likewise responsible for the simplification of the old Church Slavonic script in order to facilitate the production of secular literature. Interested himself in Russian history, Peter ordered historical manuscripts, books, and papers to be collected and preserved. He commissioned a history of Russia, which, however, he found unsatisfactory. In the years from 1699 to 1725 about six hundred books and other publications were issued in Russia. To facilitate their sale and distribution, book stores were opened in Moscow and St. Petersburg.

Serfdom. Many of the reforms which Peter forced upon his people, and which Stalin in 1928 termed "a peculiar attempt to jump out of the framework of backwardness," contributed in general to their welfare and progress. Unfortunately the institution of serfdom became more firmly established during this period. Peter's vast building program required much forced labor by serfs. By the capitation census of 1718 he sought to increase the country's revenues by making the entire population subject to taxation ("idling" and "free," "royal" and "serfs"), so that "none shall remain without being included in the tax." The new poll tax, intended for the maintenance of the army, was first levied in 1724 with very satisfactory results as far as revenue was concerned. Peter's passport system, which made it illegal for peasants to move from a locality without the proper credentials further bound them to the soil. The only mitigation in the lot of the serfs was his decree to the Senate in 1721, asking that the retail sale of individual serfs be ended, and that henceforth, "the family should be disposed of as a unit."

Toward the close of his reign, Peter was urged to abolish serfdom as a means of promoting the industry and commerce of Russia through free labor. Such a policy appears to have been advocated by the publicist Ivan Pososhkov, who objected, in particular, to the "soul-killing" per capita tax which precipitated a new epidemic of flights from the land. Although Peter was apparently conscious of the negative aspects of serfdom, his military campaigns and construction projects required more and more taxation and heavy requisitioning of labor, horses, and supplies. The construction of St. Petersburg alone led to the drafting of tens of thousands of peasants from all parts of Russia.

Widespread peasant discontent throughout Peter's reign led to renewed uprisings, provoked by heavy taxation and serfdom. The most serious occurred at Astrakhan (1705) and among the Don Cossacks (1707) led by Hetman Bulavin. The Bulavin uprising engulfed the area between the lower Don and Volga and the middle Volga, affecting some non-Russian minorities such as the Bashkirs, Tatars, and Cheremis. As in previous revolts, the poorly organized peasant forces proved no match for the regular army.

Foreign Policy. By the time of Peter the Great, Russia already embraced the greater part of what has come to be recognized as Russian territory proper, and Russian boundaries extended far to the east in Siberia. It was Peter's objective to secure outlets on the Black and Baltic Seas, as well as the coast of the Caspian Sea. In the beginning, his foreign policy was coexistence in Europe and expansion in Asia. As leader of "the Great Ambassadors of the Tsar" to Western Europe (1697–1698), he labored for eighteen months to unite European Christendom in a "holy alliance" against the "infidel" Turk. The time was not propitious: first, Europe was torn by the conflicts of the Hapsburgs and the Bourbons; and second, the great European powers had no faith in Russian leadership. Convinced that Sweden was responsible for his failure to form this Western coalition, Peter abandoned his crusade against Islam in order to conduct the Great Northern War against Charles XII, a conflict that dragged on for twenty-one years.

While Peter was touring Western Europe, the Swedes had managed to conclude alliances with England, Holland, and France, which provided security against the attack from the West in the event of war with Russia. Immediately following this first European tour, Peter hastily began preparations for a preventive war against Sweden. These preparations included alliances with Augustus II of Poland and King Christian of Denmark. After protracted and trying negotiations with the sultan, word was received in Moscow on August 8, 1700, from E. I. Ukraintsev, Russian ambassador in Constantinople, of the conclusion of a thirty-year truce with Turkey. Although the Turks had rejected Russian demands for free navigation in the Black Sea, they finally accepted the Russian seizure of Azov (1696), and terminated Russian obligation to pay tribute to the Crimean khan. On the very next day, following the receipt of this good news, Russia declared war on Sweden. Thus began the Great Northern War (1700–1721), which spanned most of Peter's reign.

Great Northern War. In his initial efforts Peter, who had apparently over-estimated the strength of his new allies and underestimated that of Sweden under the young military genius, Charles XII, met with a series of reverses. Augustus II, who in February, 1700, besieged Riga with a force of twelve thousand Saxons, abandoned the siege in September and retreated. After the bombardment of Copenhagen by combined Anglo-Dutch-Swedish naval action, Denmark on August 8, 1700, the very eve of Russian entry into the war, concluded peace with Sweden.

It was against this unfavorable background that the Russian army, under the command of Field Marshal Fyodr Golovin, undertook the siege of Narva, which ended in inglorious defeat and consequent loss of Russian prestige in Europe. It was to take four years of stubborn fighting for the Russians to acquire Ingria, which provided Peter with the site for his new capital of St. Petersburg and his long-desired "window to Europe." Meanwhile Charles XII, due to this initial Russian defeat, underestimated Peter's determination and ability. Instead of heading for Moscow, he turned south in pursuit of the Saxon troops of Augustus II, thereby providing Peter with a breathing spell for the reorganization of his forces.

Reorganization of Armed Forces. From his early youth, Peter was absorbed in military affairs. The military organization he inherited, based on ill-equipped feudal levies of nobles with their retinues of serfs, who served for a campaign and then disbanded, no longer met the requirements of an absolutist state. Peter knew that they were no match for Western armies. The Crimean campaign also demonstrated, in its early stages, the need for better organized forces—for a professional army. The haste with which Russia launched the Swedish War had not provided time for adequate reform of the Russian military system. Peter took advantage of the breathing spell to achieve much-needed modernization.

To build a professional army, conscription was introduced. Men were recruited from all classes of society, not for short-term service, but for life. In 1705 Peter introduced a system of annual general levies, based on the ratio of one recruit from every twenty households on landed estates and in villages. This resulted in a great expansion of the armed forces and the availability of substantial reserves. By 1725 Peter had a regular army of around 200,000 men, together with 100,000 Cossacks (cavalry) and other units. His emphasis on the production of armaments in Russia paid off in better equipped forces. It is estimated that in Moscow alone, from 1700 to 1708, about 1,000 cannon were cast—a number which increased to 10,000 by the end of Peter's reign. The output of Russian rifles reached approximately 10,000 per year. Equally determined to make Russia a sea power, Peter devoted much time and expense to this task. Between 1703 and 1725 he accumulated forty-eight ships-of-the-line. The Russian navy, however, proved to be of less strategic significance than his reorganized army.

Russo-Turkish War. The resounding victory of the Russians at Poltava in the Ukraine in 1709, which climaxed the duel between Peter I and Charles XII, followed in the wake of the reorganization of the Russian army. Russian forces seized Riga, Reval, and other Baltic ports in the summer of 1710. With Swedish power broken, the Swedish army assumed the defensive. Charles XII himself, having escaped to Turkey, successfully instigated the Turks to declare war on Russia on November 20, 1710, depriving the Russians of a much-needed respite.

In the struggle which followed, although Peter posed as a crusader against Islam, he suffered a series of humiliating defeats. His troops were greatly outnumbered, his supply lines overextended, and the Orthodox Christians, on whose support he had counted, failed to rise in force against the "infidel" Turk. The situation became so hopeless that Peter was prepared to sue for peace on almost any terms. The Turks, however, were apparently unaware of their advantages and made overtures for the cessation of hostilities. By the Treaty of Pruth in 1711, Russia lost Azov, the prized outlet to the Black Sea, and other territory acquired in the campaign of 1696. The interpretation and implementation of the Treaty of Pruth led to continued intermittent hostilities with the Turks until the Treaty of Adrianople in 1713. Peter then accepted more definitive Turkish terms, which freed him for renewed conflict in the Baltic.

End of Great Northern War. Despite the blow to Russian prestige resulting from the Turkish War, Peter continued his efforts to acquire additional territory from Sweden. The war-weary Russians were forced to endure several more years of conflict before the objective was achieved. In 1714 the Russians defeated the Swedish navy in the Battle of Hango, a victory which Peter, always determined to make Russia a sea power, rated on a par with Poltava. In 1716–1717, to secure more effective aid from the West, Peter undertook a second journey to London, Paris, and other capitals. He was encouraged by the fact that George I of Hanover, now king of England, was known to be opposed to the Swedes. Unable to secure help from the West to bring the Northern War to a close, Peter entered into direct negotiations with Charles XII. That monarch's death in December, 1718, altered the Swedish position in Europe, although it postponed a peaceful settlement with Russia.

Peace finally came in September, 1721, by the Treaty of Nystadt. By this agreement, Sweden ceded to Russia the entire Baltic coast, including Livonia, Esthonia, Ingria, and part of Karelia, from the strategic port of Viborg (Viipuri) to Riga, thus crowning for Russia several centuries of conflict to secure an outlet to the sea. Finland remained in Swedish possession until 1809. Peter's acquisitions enabled him to divert European trade gradually from Archangel to St. Petersburg. A grateful Senate bestowed upon Peter the titles "Father of his Country," "Emperor," and "The Great" (*Pater Patriae, Imperator Maximum*).

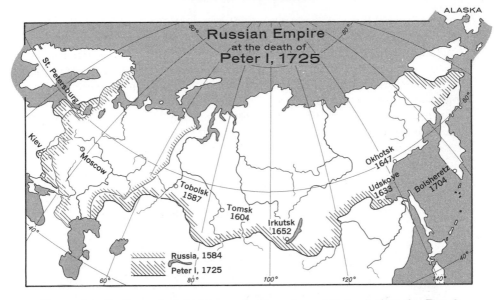

Expansion in Central Asia. It was in the reign of Peter I that the Russian offensive against the South Siberian steppes and Central Asia was launched. Hitherto the eastward expansion of Russia had followed the forest belt to the north, where fur-bearing animals could be found in abundance. The steppes to the south were peopled by nomadic tribes of Mongol origin, remnants of the Golden Horde, who still engaged in periodic attacks on Russia's south-eastern frontiers. Rumors of gold to the south, however, led Peter to dispatch several military expeditions, one under Buchholz, 1714–1716, and another by Likhachev in 1719, across the Irtysh and along the Erketi-Yarkend. According to the usual procedure, armed outposts were erected at Omsk, Semipalatinsk, and Ust-Kamenogorsk to hold the area and pave the way for further expansion. In 1716 Peter dispatched a third expedition, under Prince Cherkassy-Bekovitch, to Khiva and Bukhara in Central Asia, via the Caspian Sea and the Amu-Darya River. Peter's objective was to secure the Khivan khan's cooperation in the search for gold and for the dispatch of an expedition to India. In view of recent Soviet projects on the Amu-Darya, it is of interest to note that Peter ordered a study of the course of that river, with the intent of restoring it to its old bed leading into the Caspian. Unfortunately for Peter's project, the expedition ended in disaster when the khan summarily executed all its members.

With the "window" on the Baltic secure, Peter in 1722 once more turned to the Caspian. In the course of the following year, he was able to win an important cession of territory, including Baku, from the shah of Persia.

The territorial expansion of Russia in Asia was a determining factor in the development of Russo-Chinese relations. In spite of the Treaty of Nertchinsk in 1689, Russian merchants importing furs and other wares into Manchuria were, according to Russian sources, frequently mistreated. In an effort to secure a rapprochement with China, Peter in 1720 sent Captain L. V. Izmailov on a diplomatic and trade mission to Peking. This proved to be a complete failure. Another effort, shortly after Peter's death, by the Russian ambassador S. L. Raguzinsky, resulted in the Kyakhta Treaty of 1727, which regulated Russian trade with China and provided for permanent Russian diplomatic representation in Peking.

Explorations. Between 1700 and 1715 Peter was instrumental in bringing about the discovery and exploration of Kamtchatka and the Kurile Islands. These expeditions aroused the interest and respect of the European scientific world. When Peter made his second European tour, Oxford University conferred upon him an honorary doctor's degree, and the Paris Academy made him one of its members. Before his death in 1725 Peter drafted orders for additional explorations, paving the way for the Bering expeditions, 1725–

East-West trade was carried on via the overland route long before the construction of the Trans-Siberian Railway. This print shows Russian and Chinese caravans meeting at Kyakhta in the Russian Far East.

1730 and 1733–1742. "When Bering's second expedition came to an end in 1749," according to F. A. Golder, "Bering Strait had been discovered, the Arctic coast of Asia from the White Sea to the Kolyma River had been charted, and the North Pacific coast of America from Cape Addington to Bering Island had been placed on the map. This was Russia's share in the work of discovery and exploration, and a very important contribution to geographical knowledge it was."

A "DARK ERA": PETER'S IMMEDIATE SUCCESSORS

The death of Peter the Great in 1725 left a political vacuum which was difficult to fill. Peter's failure to provide for the succession and the absence of any candidate with his ability and driving personality enabled the new nobility to acquire power and privilege. Peter's immediate successors were in a very real sense creatures of the guards' regiments and the *dvorianstvo*. With the exception of the brief interludes provided by the boy monarch Peter II (1727–1730) the babe-in-arms, Ivan VI (r. 1740), and the incompetent Peter III (r. 1762), the Russian throne was occupied by four women: Peter the Great's second wife, Catherine I (r. 1725–1727); the daughter of Peter's stepbrother Ivan V, and widow of the Duke of Courland, Anna Ivanovna (r. 1730–1740); Peter's daughter, Elizabeth (r. 1741–1762); and Catherine II, the Great (r. 1762–1796).

Empress Anna. The absence of Peter's strong hand and dominant personality soon resulted in what he himself had feared—a challenge to the principle of autocracy and to his program of Europeanization. Following the death of Catherine I, when the Supreme Secret Council invited Anna of Courland to become empress, it required her to accept conditions ("points") which would have established a limited monarchy, comparable in some respects to that achieved by the "glorious" English Revolution of 1688. This movement stemmed partly from the impact of Western ideas upon the members of Peter's grand embassy to Western Europe, and partly from the reassertion of its former power by the old Russian nobility, as represented by the Dolgoruky and Golitsyn families. The eighteenth-century Russian historian Vasily Tatishchev at this time submitted a plan for the replacement of the Supreme Secret Council by a bicameral legislature, consisting of a senate of twenty-one members and a lower house of one hundred, representing the gentry. All plans to limit Russian autocracy failed, however, due to strong opposition among the service nobility created by Peter I and the guards' regiments. On the ground that the movement for a constitutional monarchy lacked widespread support, Anna publicly tore up the "scrap of paper" she had signed in Courland.

German Favorites. Some concessions were made to the nobility; instead of a modicum of constitutional government, however, Russia under Anna was subjected to a "German yoke," beside which the autocracy of Peter the Great paled into insignificance. According to many historians, this decade proved to be a "Dark Era" in the history of Russian autocracy. Due to her lack of education and limited intelligence, Anna played a minor role in the administration of the country and the formulation of its policies. She surrounded herself with Balts and Germans, whose haughty and domineering attitude aroused Russian national pride and whose efficiency in the forcible collection of back taxes evoked resentment and discontent. Some of these foreigners, feeling no particular concern for the welfare of the Russian state and its people, pursued a goal of self-enrichment.

The country appeared to be run by Germans, headed by the notorious favorite Baron Ernst Johann Biron (Bühren, 1690–1772), who earned the unenviable reputation of being the most unpopular German in Russian history, at least prior to Hitler. Biron was accused of taking advantage of his position to rob the treasury, engage in speculation, resort to bribery, and practise terrorism. It is claimed that in 1734 English merchants of the Russia Company[3] bribed him by payment of 100,000 rubles to sign a trade treaty granting British merchants privileges and immunities that were not enjoyed by Russians. One of Anna's cabinet ministers, A. P. Volynsky, authored a "General Project" to remove all Germans from the Russian government and to increase the role of the gentry at all levels. Until his arrest, he participated with others in a "circle" of opponents of the regime established in St. Petersburg. More recent evaluations of Anna's regime have modified the prevalent opinion of misgovernment by Germans, while giving full recognition to Russian resentment of foreigners in high places.

Foreign policy under Anna was conducted by another German, Vice-Chancellor Andreas I. Ostermann (1686–1747), who had entered Russian service under Peter the Great and who pursued a pro-Austrian course. In 1732 Russia was forced to relinquish to Persia certain cities on the Caspian Sea acquired by Peter I. The Austrian alliance led, in the War of the Polish Succession (1733–1735), to Russia's first major intervention in Polish internal affairs, by which the pro-Swedish candidate, Stanislas Lesczinsky, was ousted in favor of pro-Austrian Augustus III (r. 1734–1763) of Saxony. In this engagement, Russian troops first reached the Rhine. The Austrian alliance also involved Russia in an expensive and prolonged conflict with Turkey, 1735–1739. Russian forces under General Burkhard Christoph Münnich (1683–1767) seized Azov, but due to Austrian reverses failed to secure access by the Treaty of Belgrade (1739) to the Black Sea and Sea of Azov for Russian ships and fortifications. Continuing her pro-Austrian orientation, Russia approved and guaranteed the "pragmatic sanction," by which Emperor Charles VI provided for the succession of his daughter Maria Theresa. Active participation in the War of the Austrian Succession (1740–

3. By the eighteenth century the Muscovy Company had been replaced by the Russia Company.

1748) which followed was forestalled only by Anna's death in 1740 and Russian involvement in a war with Sweden (see page 67). Prior to her death Anna named as her successor her three-months-old grand nephew, Ivan VI, with Biron as regent. By this time, however, the country, including many of the Germans, had had more than enough of "Bironism" (*Bironovshchina*). As a result of two palace revolutions, Biron was overthrown by Münnich, imprisoned and sentenced to death, although the sentence was later commuted to exile. Shortly thereafter, in the words of the Russian historian Karamzin, with shouts of "Death to foreigners! Honor to Russians!," a French doctor and some drunken guardsmen raised Elizabeth, youngest daughter of Peter the Great, born before his second marriage was legalized, to the Russian throne.

THE REIGN OF ELIZABETH

Elizabeth (*r.* 1741–1761) was hailed by church and state—in bishops' sermons and in the poems of Lomonosov—as Russia's liberator from the "German yoke." Russians who had denounced Peter as the "Anti-Christ" now welcomed a return to his policies of reform and modernization and made him a national hero. "Foreigners," were blamed for undoing what Peter had achieved and for keeping Russia "backward." Such was the change wrought by Bironism only fifteen years after Peter's death.

Favored Aristocracy. Elizabeth utilized this wave of anti-foreignism to establish her position as a truly Russian empress, and replaced many German ministers and officers with talented and energetic members of the Russian *dvorianstvo*. Instead of German "favorites," however, key positions were occupied by such Russian "favorites" as the wealthy Count P. I. Shuvalov, in charge of domestic affairs; Chancellor A. P. Bestuzhev-Ryumin and Vice-Chancellor M. I. Vorontsov, handling foreign affairs. Count Kyrill Razumovsky, another favorite, in 1746 became Russian president of the Academy of Sciences at the age of eighteen. In a dramatic demonstration of her return to Peter's policies, Elizabeth in 1741 abolished Anna's Cabinet of Ministers and restored the Senate as the highest organ of internal administration, as well as some other government institutions created by her father.

Although Peter had undertaken to curb the power of the boyars, the women who succeeded him, including Anna and Elizabeth, showered favors upon the *dvorianstvo,* to whom they were largely indebted for their crowns. They were in effect empresses of the nobility rather than of the people at large. Thus Anna in 1731 established a Military Academy for children of the nobility, which enabled them upon graduation to enter the army as officers instead of rising through the ranks. In 1736 she reduced the term of service of the nobility from life to twenty-five years and exempted from military service one son from each family to manage the family estates.

Under Elizabeth, the Shuvalovs and Vorontsovs were given rich metallurgical foundries in the Urals. By a decree of December 4, 1747, she authorized landowners to sell their serfs. One businessman, I. B. Tverdyshchev, subsequently acquired 15,000 serfs for his factories in the South Urals. Various measures were taken to rescue the nobility from bankruptcy. In 1752, setting a precedent followed by her successors, Elizabeth wiped out all arrears in taxes, amounting then to 5,000,000 rubles. Two years later she established the Noble Bank, with a capital of 750,000 rubles, from which loans were available on easy terms. A decree of December 13, 1760, permitted landowners to banish their serfs to Siberia for major offenses, with replacements guaranteed.

French Influence. Reverting to Peter the Great's policy of Europeanization and no doubt reacting against the "German yoke," Elizabeth encouraged French influence at court. French fashions, books, manners, and language came to the fore. Whereas Peter had sent young Russians abroad to learn mathematics, navigation, and Western technology, during Elizabeth's reign they returned from Western Europe with French clothes, hair styles, language, and dance steps—a cultural veneer which, in Kliuchevsky's terms, made them "foreigners at home," or rootless cosmopolitans. Francomania reached its peak in Russia from 1755 to 1775. Even earlier, these "Parisian Russians" were satirized in the plays of Prince Antiokh Dmitryevitch Kantemir (1709–1744). In a comedy written in 1750 Alexander Sumarokov (1718–1777), known as the Russian Racine, castigated Russian "foreigners" who neglected their obligations to their own society. In one of his plays, a Russian dandy even challenged his rival to a duel because he was called a Russian.

In spite of satires against French manners, however, French influence was not hated in Russia as Bironism had been during Anna's reign. Even during the Napoleonic Wars, the Russian aristocracy continued to speak and read French, sometimes to the consternation of Russian peasants. One reason for the difference may have been that in France Russians discovered the liberal arts (humanities), whereas from Germans they acquired science, technology, and military techniques. In the nineteenth century, when Russians became better informed about German philosophy, literature, and music, their attitude toward things German changed. This transformation found its best expression in the works of Turgenev.

Social and Cultural Development. Although subject like her father to furious outbursts, Elizabeth was in the main kindly and courteous. Her horror of violence led her to commute sentences of capital punishment to banishment or flogging, and to weep over military casualties. During her reign Freemasonry was tolerated, and several lodges in St. Petersburg and Moscow included Russians whose names became household words under Catherine the Great. For a time, Elizabeth also pursued a policy of tolerance toward religious minorities. Pressure from the Orthodox clergy, however, led to the closure of Roman Catholic churches and Muslim mosques and to the exile of many Jews.

However indolent and lax Elizabeth may have been in matters of business, she was addicted to pomp and ceremony, and to extravagance in clothing and entertainment, setting an example in these respects to the members of her court. The English merchant Jonas Hanway, an agent of the Russia Company, in commenting on Grand Duke Peter's wedding to Catherine of Anhalt-Zerbst (later Catherine the Great), wrote that a man might spend a lifetime travelling throughout the world without encountering anything comparable to this display.

Two outstanding Russian cultural institutions were established during Elizabeth's reign: Moscow University in January, 1755, and the Russian Theatre in August, 1756. The theater was founded for educational purposes rather than for entertainment. One of the foremost scholars at the new university was Mikhail V. Lomonosov (1711–1765), son of a peasant fisherman and member of the Academy of Sciences, who because of his encyclopedic knowledge, is often compared with Leonardo da Vinci. Moscow University, which today bears his name, was set up in accordance with his plans. As distinguished from other universities of his time, it became a purely secular institution, with faculties of law, medicine, and philosophy, but with no theological school. According to Soviet historians, Lomonosov laid the foundations for Russian materialistic philosophy. As the author of the first Russian grammar and other textbooks, he made significant contributions to the development of a Russian national language and belles lettres. He worked hard to create a Russian scientific terminology. Russian patriot that he was, he insisted on lecturing in Russian rather than in Latin which was in vogue. This patriotic fervor, as indicated earlier, he carried over into historical studies, when he opposed the Normanist theory of the origin of the Russian state advanced by German scholars in the Academy of Sciences (see page 3). Perhaps his greatest achievement was in the field of physical chemistry. It was upon his initiative that the first chemical laboratory was established in Russia. In recognition of his accomplishments, he was made a member of the Swedish Academy of Science and an honorary member of the Bologna Academy in Italy.

Like Peter the Great, Elizabeth demonstrated a zeal for the construction of fine buildings. In no other reign, it is claimed, were so many churches built. The eminent Italian architect, Rastrelli the Younger, was brought to Russia to embellish the capital; he constructed the Winter Palace, a fine example of Russian baroque style, and the summer residence, Tsarskoe Selo. During his visit to Russia in the mid-seventeenth century Jonas Hanway was able to report that St. Petersburg had become an "elegant and superb city." In 1758 the Academy of Arts was separated from the Academy of Sciences and staffed with French artists from the Académie Française, who trained a new generation of Russian architects, among them, Starov, Bazhenov, Kazakov, Veronikhin, and Zakharov.

Foreign Policy. In 1741 Sweden, hoping to profit from the unsettled state of the Russian monarchy, declared war. Thus Elizabeth inherited the problem which had supposedly beeen settled by the Treaty of Nystadt in 1721 (see page 60). The war was concluded in Russia's favor in 1743, with the acquisition of additional Finnish territory. Reverting to Anna's pro-Austrian policy, Elizabeth lined up with the Hapsburgs and Bourbons in the "diplomatic revolution of 1756" against the Hohenzollerns and the Hanoverian dynasty of Great Britain. In the Seven Years' War (1756–1763) which followed, General Peter S. Saltykov, in spite of heavy losses in Russian manpower, inflicted a resounding defeat on the armies of Frederick the Great at Künersdorff in 1759; Russian troops occupied Berlin in 1760. This war against Prussia was the occasion of much dissension, intrigue, and confusion inside Russia. The empress was unqualifiedly opposed to Frederick the Great, but her heir apparent, Grand Duke Peter, Duke of Holstein, was a fanatical supporter of the Prussian king. When Frederick's forces were on the verge of collapse, the death of Elizabeth (December 25, 1761, O.S.[4]), followed by the accession of Peter III, led to a military about-face; Russia withdrew from the conflict and concluded an alliance with her erstwhile enemy. Prussia was freed from a war on two fronts which otherwise might have proved disastrous. Russia emerged from the Seven Years' War without territorial acquisitions, although the arduous Russian military campaigns may have forestalled Prussian territorial gains in the east at the expense of Poland and Russia.

---

4. The Julian Calendar (Old Style, or O.S.) prevailed from January 1, 1700, until the Revolution, at which time (February 14, 1918) it was replaced by the Gregorian calendar (New Style, or N.S.). The necessary corrections involved a difference of thirteen days in the twentieth century, twelve in the nineteenth century, and eleven in the eighteenth century. Thus the Bolshevik Revolution, popularly called the "October" Revolution (October 25, 1917, O.S.) is celebrated in the USSR on November 7 (N.S.). For purposes of clarification, both dates are sometimes used: October 25/November 7, 1917.

4

Catherine II, the Great: Empress

of the Nobility, 1762-1796

CATHERINE II, who regarded herself as a feminine counterpart of Peter the Great, cast a spell over her contemporaries in Russia and Western Europe. Viewed in perspective, however, one gleans the impression that she was a great personality rather than a great empress, a first-rate opportunist rather than an idealist, and a borrower of ideas from Peter the Great, the French philosophers, and the Empress Elizabeth, rather than a monarch whose contribution was distinctively original and creative. She emerges from the pages of history as a consummate actress, and as an eighteenth-century publicity expert who threw up a façade— a glorified Potemkin village[1]—and surrounded herself thereby with an aura of success.

Catherine II, according to Paul Miliukov, was a representative of enlightened absolutism in its "truer and finer" form. Her father was a member of the German petty nobility, who served as a general in the Prussian army. Princess Sophia (her maiden name) of Anhalt-Zerbst arrived in Russia in 1744 at the age of fifteen, where she accepted the Orthodox faith and was baptized Catherine. Empress Elizabeth had selected her as the wife of her nephew and heir, Karl Peter Ulrich, duke of Holstein. He, too, received Orthodox baptism as Grand Duke Peter Fyodorovitch, later known as Peter III.

ACCESSION OF A GERMAN PRINCESS

In order to become empress, Catherine was prepared to make any sacrifice. German in origin, she consciously became more Russian than the Russians. Born a Lutheran, she nevertheless paraded her devotion to her adopted Russian Orthodox church. For eighteen years she endured public insults inflicted upon her by her retarded and wholly incompetent husband. During these years, her "greatness" was largely due to the studied contrast between her own behavior and that of the juvenile pro-German grand duke.

1. The expression originated from Catherine's tour of New Russia (part of southern Russia seized from the Turks) in 1787. Her "favorite" Potemkin erected fake villages along the banks of the Volga in order to impress the empress.

Coup d'État. During the reign of Elizabeth, Catherine gained valuable experience in court intrigue and the struggle for power. She profited from this knowledge in the palace revolution that brought her to the throne. She also capitalized on the unpopularity of her husband, Peter III, who was accused of restoring Bironism in Russia. One week after the coup d'état that removed him from the throne he was allegedly choked to death by one or more of Catherine's favorites. Another attempt by the officer Mirovitch to place Ivan VI, who had been imprisoned in Schluessenburg fortress during Elizabeth's reign, on the throne in Catherine's stead ended with the death of Ivan during a prison break and the capture and execution of the plotter. Rumors as to the selection of Catherine's young son, Paul, to replace Peter III were completely silenced when Catherine rapidly entrenched herself in the position of empress.

Having once acquired the throne, Catherine's primary objective was to keep it. Her emphasis on Russian culture, native Russian virtues, Russian folk music, the greatness of the Russian language, and her pose as the defender of Orthodoxy, won for her the appelation "Mother of the Fatherland." She was ever conscious of the strength of Russian nationalism, which as a doctrine is said to date from her reign. Because Catherine was German whereas Elizabeth was the daughter of Peter the Great, she was indebted to the nobility, army, and Orthodox church to an even greater degree than her predecessor. Catherine in reality became empress of the nobility, and watered down or abandoned her vast programs for constitutional, legal, social, and economic reform. In this the golden age of the Russian nobility, the privileges of the aristocracy were extended and confirmed at the expense of the masses of Russian peasants. Catherine virtually ignored the evils of serfdom, the real challenge of her time, with the result that reform without revolution became practically impossible.

The Peasantry. During his brief reign as emperor, Peter III issued the manifesto of March 2, 1762, to appease the nobles who opposed his pro-Prussian foreign policy. This document freed the entire nobility from compulsory service to the state. The Russian peasants, who regarded the manifesto as the prelude to their own liberation from compulsory service, were soon disillusioned. In August, 1762, Catherine decreed that in the future serfs could not be bought for industrial labor apart from the land, that their services must be voluntary and recompensed by mutual agreement. This initial step raised hopes so high that all serfs in Kazan and Perm districts went on strike. Thereafter, Catherine not only reaffirmed the freedom of the gentry, but following the precedent set by Elizabeth, she increased the power of the nobles over the serfs and greatly extended serfdom. By a decree of 1765 she gave landowners the right to sentence their serfs to exile with hard labor or to send them to the army. Another decree in 1767 provided that peasants complaining of ill-treatment from their landowners were to be condemned to exile and hard labor for life.

Catherine's Free Economic Society, founded in 1765 in St. Petersburg to improve the conditions of agriculture and rural life, did discuss the peasant question. The empress, by expressing interest in emancipation, again raised hopes unduly. At the time, she did forbid the further reduction of freemen to a state of serfdom, and created a new category of state ("economic") peasants from those taken over from church lands, most of which were confiscated during her reign and that of her husband. When the Crimea was annexed in 1783, however, Catherine herself bestowed hundreds of thousands of acres of land on her current favorites on the ground that the Crimean Tatars, not being members of the nobility, had no right to hold land. It is estimated that during her reign, Catherine granted 800,000 peasants to her courtiers.

Catherine granted favors to the nobility, not only because of her dependence upon them, but because of her unfamiliarity with other strata of Russian society. Her Russian experience had taught her that the nobility performed the most important tasks in the internal and military affairs of the state, that they made and unmade emperors and empresses. The masses were the creatures of the nobility. She had no reason to anticipate that they would rise in a rebellion which would constitute a threat to the nobility and the throne. As a result, she largely ignored them.

The Pugachev Rebellion. Catherine's decrees pertaining to the peasantry literally reduced them to chattels, with no protection from arbitrary abuse of power by the landowners. Thus the peasantry—the bulk of the population—abandoning hope of any amelioration of their plight, had nothing to lose by revolt. Their predicament resulted in a number of sporadic disturbances, including the plague revolt of 1771. These uprisings were suppressed without difficulty. A leader was needed who was capable of organizing and uniting the discontented peasants with other dissatisfied elements in Russian society. Such a leader was Yemelyan Ivanovitch Pugachev (1726–1775), an army deserter and runaway Don Cossack from Kazan jail. Pugachev had appeared in 1772 among the Yaik Cossacks of the Urals, most of whom were Old Believers, bitterly opposed to government exactions and the Orthodox church.

With a motley army of peasants, Cossacks, Bashkirs, Kalmyks, Kirghiz, and Volga peoples such as the Udmurti, Mariitsi, Mordva, and Chuvashi, over-worked industrial serfs, and other malcontents, in May, 1773, Pugachev invaded the Orenburg region, although he failed to take the city of Orenburg (Chkalov). As the rebellion spread rapidly throughout east and southeast Russia, it assumed the character of a social revolution of peasants versus landlords. Posing as Peter III,[2] the rightful monarch whom Catherine had prevented from liberating the serfs, this pretender established a court in imitation of hers. He issued *ukazy,* outlining his plans to kill the landowners, distribute land to the peasants, and relegate Catherine II to a nunnery. "We shall behead every noble in the land," proclaimed Pugachev. "We shall make the true faith prevail and take over the land for ourselves."

---

2. There was enough mystery surrounding Peter's death to give rise to rumors that he was still alive. Pugachev was one of a number of impostors.

By the close of 1773 Pugachev was reputed to have 30,000 rebels under his command and eighty-six cannon at his disposal. Shortly thereafter, he had seized ninety-two factories, or three-quarters of the industrial enterprises of the Urals. With Russian armed forces engaged in the First Turkish War (1768–1774), Catherine was seriously handicapped in dealing with the rebels, whose atrocities spread panic among large numbers of refugee nobles in Moscow and other towns, where defenses were regarded as inadequate.

Pugachev's early successes stemmed in part from the fact that his appeal electrified the masses. It offered them a ray of hope for liberation from eternal slavery. It stands to reason that not all the rebels believed Pugachev to be Peter III, Emperor of All the Russias. Even if they suspected him of being an impostor he was their only hope. They could see no other alternative. His supporters, too, were not only peasants, but representatives of minority groups. This was not only a peasant revolution, but a colonial revolt of discontented minorities, especially of the Muslim elements against subjugation by Russians.

The Pugachev revolt came to an end when its unfortunate leader was brought in chains to Moscow and executed. Catherine thereupon ordered that the Yaik River be renamed the Ural, and the Yaik Cossacks, the Ural Cossacks.

As long as Pugachev's successes mounted, his followers remained loyal. In 1774, however, the Treaty of Kuchuk-Kainardji brought to a favorable close the war between the Russians and Turks. Like Stenka Razin and other rebel leaders before him, Pugachev met reverses once he was called upon to resist the regular armed forces. Moreover, the non-Russian minorities who had flocked to his standard were an asset to Pugachev as long as the fighting continued on or near their territories. They became a liability as they approached the heart of Russia proper. Great Russians united in fierce resistance to domination by the minorities represented in his army. War brought famine to the Volga. Pugachev's army, confronted in defeat by dissension and desertion, never reached Moscow. He was betrayed by his followers, sent to Moscow in a cage, and publicly executed in Red Square in January, 1775.

Unfortunately, the lesson of the terrible Pugachev upheaval went unheeded by most of the Russian nobility. Fifteen years later, Alexander N. Radishchev published *A Journey from St. Petersburg to Moscow* (see also page 75) the first Russian book to denounce the institution of serfdom. "Tremble, hard-hearted landlord," wrote Radishchev, "for on the brow of each of your peasants I read your condemnation." In general, however, the nobility called for the ruthless suppression of revolt rather than for reform. Catherine, although she was thoroughly shaken by the revolt, proceeded to extend serfdom throughout the Ukraine and the conquered Crimea. The Cossacks were divided into Hosts, their local autonomy dependent upon military service in special Cossack brigades.

EMPRESS OF THE ENLIGHTENMENT

Determined to serve as a model of European enlightenment, Catherine in early life immersed herself in the works of the leading French philosophers. Although she carried on an extensive correspondence with Voltaire for fourteen years and became a patron of the financially embarrassed Diderot, Catherine looked to Montesquieu as her political mentor. In his assumption that autocracy was the only form of government feasible for Russia with its vast empire, Catherine found justification for her own predilections. For a time she paid lip service to the proposals of Count Panin, tutor of her son Paul, for a limitation of autocratic power along the lines developed in Sweden and England. In actuality, she effectively deprived the Senate of legislative power, without substituting for it the Imperial Council recommended by Panin.

The Nakaz. Under the influence of the *philosophes* and to impress Europe that a new era had dawned in Russia, Catherine drafted the *Nakaz,* or Instruction (1765–1767), a vast project for the codification of Russian laws. This Instruction was not based on Russian experience, but on Montesquieu's *Esprit des Lois* and Beccaria's *Of Punishment and Crimes,* the latter published in 1764, from which she copied large sections verbatim. The cautious

Catherine subjected it to the censorship of her foremost lay and spiritual advisers. The *Nakaz* proclaimed Russia to be a "European nation" and its sovereign an absolute ruler. Other sections encouraged greater freedom for internal and foreign commerce, opposition to any unnecessary expansion of serfdom and at the same time to any general program of emancipation. In spite of the reassertion of absolutism, the Instruction gave the impression, in tune with Western trends, that the best government was the one which shackled freedom the least. Voltaire, whose ideas were well represented, called the Instruction, which was quickly translated into other European languages, the finest monument of the eighteenth century.

Once the *Nakaz* was ready, Catherine summoned by imperial manifesto in December, 1766, a Legislative Commission of 658 deputies (565 attended) from all parts of Russia and from virtually all classes and creeds, with the exception of the landowners' serfs, the largest part of the population. After two years of ineffective struggle to cope with a variety of seemingly insoluble problems, the commission was shelved by Catherine, apparently without regret. She had demonstrated her liberal propensities, basked in the acclaim of Voltaire, Frederick the Great, and the civilized world, and strengthened her absolute control.

Education. As early as 1762 Catherine II embodied her views on education in a statute calling for the education of boys and girls from five to eighteen years of age in state schools. Among the concerns of the Legislative Commission was the drafting of a Russian public school system to include elementary, secondary, and higher schools; this task was assigned to a special Commission on Education. Unlike Peter I, Catherine placed cultural education ahead of vocational training. That she envisaged a veritable revolution in the education of Russian children, most of whom were schooled at home by private tutors, is clear from her intention to eliminate class distinction and to make education compulsory. Like her other grandiose schemes, however, Catherine's plans for general education foundered when her energies were diverted by the First Turkish War, the partition of Poland, and the Pugachev Rebellion. The two schools dating from the early years of her reign were the Smolnyi Institute for daughters of the nobility, modelled after one set up by Madame de Maintenon at St. Cyr, and the Novodyevichy Institute for daughters of townsmen, both in St. Petersburg.

In 1782 under the influence of another "enlightened" despot, Joseph II of Austria, Catherine returned to her plans for public schools in Russia, which then included a gymnasium in every provincial capital. Once again she was diverted from the task by wars and the French Revolution. By 1800, shortly after her death, however, there were 315 public schools in Russia, with an estimated 19,915 students in attendance. Although many *pensions* and private schools were opened during Catherine's reign, these were all placed under government supervision in 1784. Since the majority of the teachers in all Russian schools were non-Russians, usually French or German, the education of Russian youth remained European rather than Russian in spirit.

In 1782 Catherine breathed new life into the disorganized Academy of Sciences by her appointment of the inimitable Princess Catherine Dashkov (1743–1810), a member of the Vorontsov family, as director. At Dashkova's suggestion the Russian Academy, an institution for the study and development of the Russian language, was established in 1783. In her capacity as president, the Princess commissioned and helped to prepare the first Russian etymological dictionary. She appears to have shared Catherine's belief that Russian "would one day become the universal language."

Printing. As part of the intellectual ferment characteristic of the age, there was an upsurge in printing and publishing during Catherine's reign, under the aegis of both private and state institutions. The versatile Catherine herself produced numerous essays and plays of mediocre caliber. As late as 1771 there was in Russia only one press in private hands, that for the printing of foreign books, and even this was subject to supervision by the Academy of Sciences and the police. Nikolai Ivanovitch Novikov (1744–1818), a member of the lesser gentry, with encouragement from the empress published a series of satirical magazines from 1769 to 1774. A few years later, he undertook the publication of *Moskovskie Vedomosti,* the official journal of the University of Moscow. In 1768 Catherine had established a Translator's Commission, with which Novikov and the Princess Dashkov were actively concerned, and which was responsible for the publication during the next twelve years of 154 books, among them *Pilgrim's Progress* and *Paradise Lost.*

In 1783 under the influence of Emperor Joseph II, Catherine removed all restrictions on the establishment of private printing in Russia. The question of how much freedom of thought and expression is compatible with autocracy is one which all absolute rulers have confronted. Catherine's auspicious beginning was short-lived. The Masonic movement, with which Novikov was associated and which spread rapidly in the 1770's among Russian landowners and bureaucrats, took advantage of the newly acquired freedom to publish. The historian Vernadsky has estimated that from one-sixth to one-third of all men in government service joined the Masons, with the result that their impact was profound. The movement, with its secret rituals and secret publications, soon aroused suspicion and distrust. The French Revolution, especially the execution of Louis XVI and the trek of French Royalist refugees to Russia, evoked sharp political reaction. Russians were soon forbidden to travel to France and to receive French publications. The Russian press was brought under close surveillance and unwelcome books were banned and destroyed.

Alexander N. Radishchev, a Russian nobleman who had imbibed the ideas of the Enlightenment while studying abroad at the University of Leipzig, was condemned to death for his daring attack on the institutions of serfdom and autocracy in *A Journey from St. Petersburg to Moscow,* printed by his own private press. The sentence was commuted to exile in eastern Siberia, where Radishchev remained during Catherine's lifetime and where he devoted some time to the study of Russo-Chinese trade. Following the appearance of his highly unfavorable history of the Jesuit order, Novikov himself was arrested and imprisoned. Even the Princess Dashkov, who, as head of the Russian Academy, arranged for the publication of Yakov Knyazhnin's (1742–1791) tragedy, *Vadim Novgorodsky,* ran the gamut of Catherine's displeasure when the book, due to its republican sentiments, was confiscated and burned in 1793. Toward the end of her reign, Catherine closed all private presses and maintained a rigid censorship in the major cities and ports. No amount of censorship and persecution of writers, however, could blot out the ferment of ideas which Catherine herself had unleashed but could not control. Among other things, it contributed much to the development of the Russian theater in the decades from 1770 to 1790.

Architecture. Like other enlightened despots of her age, Catherine indulged in a passion for building. In this respect, she was ably assisted by a galaxy of outstanding Russian and foreign architects. With characteristic energy, she devoted herself to the construction of numerous palaces, public buildings, villas, and private residences. The Russian architect Ivan Starov (1743–1808), a graduate of Elizabeth's Academy of Fine Arts, abandoned the baroque and rococo styles of the past for Roman classicism. He constructed for Catherine the Alexander Nevsky Cathedral and the magnificent Tauride Palace, famous throughout Europe, which Catherine bestowed upon her favorite, Prince Grigory Potemkin. In the twentieth century it housed the Russian Duma. Vallin de la Mothe, a French architect, built the Hermitage, an addition to Elizabeth's Winter Palace, and Yuri Velten, a pupil of Rastrelli, added to it the famous art gallery which housed Catherine's unique and growing collection of paintings and art objects. Other noted structures of her time included Antonio Rinaldi's Cathedral of St. Isaac, Quarenghi's Theater of the Hermitage, the Scottish architect Charles Cameron's addition to Tsarskoe Selo, and his restoration of the fifteenth-century Palace of the Khans in the Crimea. Throughout Russia the new architectural style was widely emulated on a smaller scale on the estates of members of the Russian nobility. Catherine's reign is regarded as a "golden age of architecture in Russia."

FOREIGN POLICY

Russian foreign policy under Catherine the Great focused on Europe and the Near East. Russia's position as a leading European power was insured by brilliant victories of the armed forces on land and sea under the leadership of Generals P. A. Rumyantsev (1725–1796) and A. V. Suvorov (1730–1800), and Admirals G. A. Spiridov (1713–1790) and F. F. Ushakov (1743–1818). Some of the goals of Russian foreign policy conceived in the seventeenth century—in particular, the extension of Russian territory on the Black Sea and the stabilization of Russian borders on the Baltic—the attainment of the so-called natural frontiers, were achieved during the reign of Catherine II.

By the partition of Poland, perhaps the phase of Catherine's European policy most bitterly assailed abroad, Russia acquired the "Western Lands" which had formed part of the state of Kievan *Rūs*. In the second half of the eighteenth century, Russian prestige in Europe reached a new zenith.

Upon her accession to the throne in 1762 Catherine, under the guidance of Count Nikita Panin, skillfully avoided further entanglement in the Seven Years' War through a Declaration of Neutrality. Panin's main objective in Europe was the restoration of the balance of power by means of a "Northern Accord," in which the combined power of France and Austria would be offset by an alliance of Russia, Prussia, Poland, Sweden, Denmark, and England. European politics proved too unstable for the permanence of any such objective.

Partitions of Poland. Polish membership in the "Northern Accord" failed to prevent Catherine's maneuvers to secure coveted Polish territory. The first crisis she faced concerned the Polish succession. In 1763 she successfully intrigued to place on the Polish throne her former lover, Stanislas Poniatovski, whose candidacy was supported by the pro-Russian Czartoryski family. It was Poland's misfortune that the country lacked strong leadership in the eighteenth century. Belated Polish efforts to rectify the weakness of Poland's political organization by constitutional reform resulted in opposition and intervention by her neighbors, Austria, Russia, and Prussia, none of whom viewed with equanimity a strong Poland. Dissident factions inside Poland, including members of the nobility and priesthood, as well as the Jewish population of the Polish Ukraine persecuted by the Ukrainian Cossacks, or "Haidamaki," welcomed foreign intervention. On the pretext of Polish persecution of religious minorities, Catherine II joined hands with Frederick the Great and the tearful Maria Theresa of Austria to effect the first partition of Poland in 1773. By this agreement, Russia acquired mainly White Russian territory formerly annexed by the grand duchy of Lithuania, including the strategic commercial cities of Vitebsk and Mogilev.

The new Polish Constitution of 1791, which substituted an hereditary for an elective monarchy, abolished the outmoded *liberum veto,* and provided for a bicameral legislature, produced renewed internal dissension which afforded a pretext for further intervention. Taking advantage of the preoccupation of Austria and Prussia with revolutionary France, Catherine's troops invaded Poland in 1793, ostensibly to curb "Jacobinism" in Warsaw. By a subsequent Russo-Prussian bargain in the same year, the second partition of Poland brought Russia western White Russia and most of the right bank of the Dnieper.

Polish refusal to accept this humiliation led to a national uprising under the leadership of the Polish hero Tadeusz Kosciuszko (1746–1817), who served with the Colonial army in the American Revolution, but who went down to defeat before the armies of General Suvorov. The third partition effected by Austria, Prussia, and Russia in 1795 removed Poland from the map of

Although the outspoken General Suvorov frequently incurred royal displeasure, both Catherine and Paul recognized the value of his military skill.
Paul exiled Suvorov to his country estate, but was forced to recall him to
lead the Russo-Austrian armies against France in 1799. The Italian and
Swiss campaigns were his last, and he died in Moscow the following year.

Europe as an independent state until 1918. The new Russian frontier, except
for eastern Galicia, which had gone to Austria in 1773, was comparable to
that arranged by the USSR and Hitlerite Germany in 1939, following the
outbreak of World War II. Only in the third partition did Russia acquire any
substantial number of Poles.

By the Polish partitions Russia acquired approximately one million Jews, thereby encountering for the first time a major Jewish problem and anti-Semitism. As late as 1762 Catherine had excluded Jews from an edict permitting foreigners to settle in Russia. The "Pale of Settlement" of 1791[3] restricted Jewish settlement in Russia to the provinces seized from Poland and Turkey, where they were subjected to double taxation.

Expansion in the East. A significant passage in the memoirs of Catherine the Great indicates that in the middle of the eighteenth century the Russians let slip an opportunity to purchase from the Turks the right to free navigation of the Black Sea, over which so much blood was spilled in later years: "In 1757 or 1758 a favourite of the Sultan Osman offered M. Obreskov, the Russian envoy in Constantinople, free navigation for the Russian Empire in the Black Sea on condition Russia paid about 30,000 ducats. The Russians replied that owing to excessive expenditure on the war against the king of Prussia, this further expenditure could not be met."

As regards Russian expansion in the Near East, Catherine the Great began where Peter left off. In 1768 the Turks, incited by the French to take advantage of Catherine's preoccupation with the Poles, declared war on Russia. Catherine had no difficulty in arousing the support of the Russian population against the Muslim aggressor. Under Count Rumyantsev the Russian forces defeated the Turkish army, overran the Crimea, seized Turkish outposts on the Dniester and Danube, and occupied Moldavia and Wallachia. The Russian Baltic fleet, which under Count Alexei Orlov proceeded to the Mediterranean, annihilated the Turkish navy at Chesme. During Russia's naval campaign in the eastern Mediterranean, Russian forces occupied Beirut in 1772 and 1773 at the invitation of insurgent Arab leaders. From "October 1773 to February 1774, Beirut was effectively under Russian control. During this time the Muscovite flag flew over Beirut, the portrait of the Empress [Catherine] was raised over the principal gate, before which passers-by were obliged to do reverence . . . For five months the Russian flag flew over an Arab population."[4] As a wartime expedient, the Russian expedition supported the pretensions of Ali Bey, who in 1768 declared Egyptian independence of the Ottoman Empire, and his ally, Dahir al-'Umar of Syria.

Because of war fatigue on the part of both belligerents, and the Pugachev Rebellion (1773–1775) which shook the Russian throne to its foundations, the Russo-Turkish War was concluded in 1774 by the Peace of Kuchuk-Kainardji. By this treaty, a landmark in Russian relations with the Near East, Russia obtained control of the northern shores of the Black Sea from the Bug to the Dnieper and the right to free navigation of its waters. By exacting a pledge from Turkey to permit freedom of religion in Moldavia and Wallachia, Russia emerged as the champion of Orthodoxy in the Balkans. The treaty of

3. The "Pale" was extended in 1794, after the second partition of Poland, to include all of the Ukraine.
4. W. Person, "The Russian Occupation of Beirut, 1772–1774," *Royal Central Asian Journal*, XLII (July–October 1955), p. 283.

1774 set the pattern for future international settlements pertaining to the Black Sea and the Dardanelles, as well as the protection of Orthodox Christians in the Ottoman Empire. The stage was set for the "Eastern Question" and for the role of Turkey as the "sick man of Europe" in the nineteenth century.

Meanwhile, neither side recognized the Treaty of Kuchuk-Kainardji as definitive. In preparation for the next phase of the struggle, Catherine, following the suggestion of Voltaire, developed the "Greek Project" (1782). This plan envisaged the partition between Austria and Russia of the European possessions of the Ottoman Empire. Russia was to secure a protectorate over the Turkish provinces of Wallachia, Moldavia, and Bessarabia. The Byzantine Empire (Greek), comprising Constantinople and the provinces of Thrace and Macedonia, was to be restored. Austria's share was to be Serbia, Bosnia, and Herzegovina. It was no accident that Catherine's grandson, born in 1779, was named Constantine.

When the conflict was renewed by the Turks in 1787, the Russian forces under General Suvorov once again defeated them. In 1790 he captured Izmail, one of the strongest fortresses in Europe, a victory lauded by the Russian poet G. R. Derzhavin (1743–1816). By the peace concluded at Yassy in January, 1792, Russia retained the Crimea (first annexed in 1783) and expanded Russian territory along the shores of the Azov and Black Seas to include the fortress of Otchakov. The Russian government at once proceeded to establish Cossack settlements along the Kuban River to spearhead an advance into the Caucasus. Already in 1785, following the annexation of the Crimea, Catherine had guaranteed her Muslim subjects freedom of religion. By 1796 she was pursuing her objective to acquire Persia and the Middle East as far as Tibet. When her death intervened and brought that conflict to a close, Russian forces had captured Derbent and Baku.

Catherine left the Russian advance in the Far East largely to private initiative. In 1777 the merchant Grigory Shelekhov dispatched the first Russian ship to the Kurile Islands. From its base in Kodiak, the merchant company he founded laid plans for the exploration of Alaska.

American Revolution. Although the French Revolution had a more powerful impact on Russia, the American Revolution, 1775–1782, did not pass unnoticed. In 1780 Catherine rejected an English bid for a Russian alliance in her struggle against the American colonies, in return for the island of Minorca. Russia, on the contrary, proclaimed the "Act of Armed Neutrality" to uphold the right of neutral ships to trade with belligerents in all commodities save war supplies. From the British standpoint, this was an unfriendly move, likely to obstruct English efforts to subdue the American "rebels." It was not to be expected, however, that Catherine, with the Pugachev revolt in mind, would look with favor on American revolutionaries. Francis Dana, dispatched by the Continental Congress in 1781 to St. Petersburg, completely failed to secure Russian recognition of the new republic. Not until 1809—

thirty-three years after the American Declaration of Independence—did Imperial Russia finally recognize the United States.

THE REIGN OF PAUL, 1796–1801

The frustrated and unbalanced Paul, who had been deprived of the throne of Russia by his mother since 1762, hated everything that Catherine II stood for. In the "reign of terror" that followed his accession, he swept her appointees from office, including the military hero General Suvorov. According to Princess Dashkov, herself a logical victim because of her participation in the coup d'état that brought Catherine to the throne, every family among the nobility had at least one member exiled to Siberia or imprisoned. On the other hand, Paul released many of Catherine's victims, including Radishchev, Novikov, and large numbers of Polish prisoners in St. Petersburg. One of them, Kosciuszko, was granted 60,000 rubles and permitted to leave for the United States.

Censorship. Paul displayed an unequivocal hatred of the French Revolution. In this respect, he outdid the censorship instituted by Catherine II in her closing years. Convinced, as Catherine never was, that ideas could be combatted and suppressed by force, he reestablished the political police, suspended all reforms, closed all private schools, prohibited the importation of foreign books and music, and recalled Russian students studying abroad. He even forbade the wearing of French hats or clothing, and the use of the terms "citizen," "Fatherland," and "society," which were reminiscent of French revolutionary practice. The iron curtain erected by Paul, which was intended to preserve Russians from the slightest taint of French influence, produced intellectual stagnation.

Prussian Influence. A fanatic admirer of Frederick the Great of Prussia, Paul enthusiastically adopted Prussian military tactics and discipline. While he was still the heir-apparent, isolated in Gatchina, he organized and trained a small army in the Prussian style. As emperor, he introduced corporal punishment in the army. The constant drilling, parades, and requirement of blind obedience on the part of members of the armed forces reflected a type of martinetism which in the past had not been characteristic of Russian military technique. The introduction of Prussian uniforms, including powdered wigs, buckled shoes, and other unsuitable paraphernalia, is said to have elicited the following comment from General Suvorov: "Wig powder is not gun powder; curls are not cannons; a pigtail is not a sabre; I am not a Prussian, but a Russian."

Reassertion of Autocracy. During his brief reign, Paul challenged the position of the nobility by the reassertion of his own personal authority as autocratic ruler. To prevent a recurrence of what had happened to him, he introduced the principle of primogeniture in Russia with the issuance of the

"Law of Succession to the Throne" on April 5, 1797. Paul's subjects were required to pay him the most servile homage, falling upon their knees in token of submission as he passed through the streets. The first to give precise expression to the doctrine that "The Tsar is head of the Church," Paul made the Orthodox church the ally of autocracy and directed its efforts toward the suppression of ideological subversion and the maintenance of law and order among the lower classes. This alliance of the church with the government, which was continued by Nicholas I, permanently alienated the aristocracy and the intelligentsia, who henceforth associated the church with reaction. One mitigating factor in Paul's pursuit of reaction was his toleration of non-Orthodox minorities, Christian and non-Christian, including Roman Catholics and Old Believers.

The Peasantry. With respect to the Russian peasantry, Paul's reign marks a departure from the policies of his immediate predecessors. He was the first ruler for many generations to enact legislation in their favor. From the reign of Ivan Grozny to Catherine II the bondage of the peasants had been progressively intensified, until they became chattels at the mercy of their landlords. Paul did nothing to revolutionize the position of the serfs. He did, however, seek to limit their obligations by an edict of 1797 prohibiting the exaction of forced labor (*barshchina*) on Sundays and by recommending that three days per week should be sufficient for the upkeep of the landowners' estates. Although this edict was not strictly enforced, it set an important precedent for future concessions. Paul also banned the sale of peasants without land in the Ukraine. To offset the deplorable effects of recurring famine in rural areas, he ordered the storage of food for emergencies in village bins.

On the other hand, Paul reaffirmed the right of the landowners to banish peasants to Siberia, in 1796 extended serfdom to the "New Lands" of the southern Ukraine and Caucasus, and forbade southern landowners to appropriate runaway serfs. In his short reign, he distributed more than 500,000 state peasants among private landowners, a ratio much higher than that of Catherine II. Prone to respond to the whim of the moment, Paul is said to have given 2,000 souls to one who dedicated a poem in his honor. During his reign, it is estimated that there were 278 peasant disturbances in thirty-two different provinces.

Foreign Policy. In foreign affairs, it was logical that Paul should pursue an anti-French course, which he appears to have hoped would lead to a Christian crusade against the French revolutionaries. When the Knights of St. John on the Island of Malta, deprived of French aid by the Revolution, appealed to him for support in negotiating their property rights in Poland, Paul concluded a treaty with the order on January 15, 1797, and provided financial assistance. Tentative arrangements for a Russian protectorate over Malta were forestalled by French occupation in 1798, following which Europe was treated to the curious situation of an Orthodox Russian emperor becoming grand master of a Roman Catholic religious order!

French expansion into Holland, Malta, Italy, and Egypt under Napoleon led to Russian participation in the Second Coalition, 1798–1800, with Austria, Turkey, England, and the kingdom of Naples. The Turks and Russians were alarmed by the rise of French power in the Mediterranean; on January 3, 1799, they formed for the first time in history an alliance for joint naval action against a common foe. A secret clause in this alliance formally recognized the freedom of passage of Russian ships through the Straits of the Bosporus and the Dardanelles to the Mediterranean, and the closure of this strategic passage to the warships of other foreign powers. A squadron of thirteen Russian naval vessels under Admiral Ushakov thereupon passed through the Dardanelles and joined forces with the Turkish navy. After Russia declared war on France in July, 1799, Ushakov proceeded, with the support of the Greek population and the patriarch of Constantinople, to liberate the Ionian Islands; there, curiously enough, a republic was established with Russian blessing under the nominal protection of Turkey. The Russian fleet then proceeded to patrol the Italian coast, drove the French from Naples, and entered Rome in 1799. In the same year, the prince-bishop of Montenegro, whose country had maintained relations with Russia since the time of Peter the Great, sought an alliance with Paul. Temporarily, at least, Russia had secured bases in the Mediterranean from which to conduct further operations against the French.

Under Austrian pressure, Paul finally agreed to dispatch a Russian expeditionary force of 52,000 men under General Suvorov to Austria to lead the allied campaign for the liberation of northern Italy. The indefatigable Suvorov reorganized the sluggish Austrian forces and taught them how to achieve complete destruction of the enemy by "on-the-spot decisions, speed, and charges." Together with the well-equipped and experienced Russian army, they entered Italy as liberators of the country from French "imperialism"; they rapidly occupied Milan and Turin, drove the hitherto undefeated French national army from Lombardy, and cleared the way to Genoa. An avalanche of Suvorov medals, hats, portraits, and feathers demonstrated the popularity of the Russian military genius. When the Austrians prevailed upon Suvorov to evict the French from Switzerland, he accomplished the virtually impossible feat of leading his forces across the Alps by way of St. Gothard Pass late in the season, only to find that the Austrians had withdrawn, leaving him to face greatly superior French armies and encounter heavy losses. In spite of this so-called "Austrian treachery," Suvorov escaped.

The expeditionary force of 12,000 men, which Paul had dispatched via the Baltic to join the English in effecting a landing in Holland, likewise confronted disaster, allegedly due to the incompetence of the English commander, the "famous" duke of York. Paul, incensed at what he regarded as betrayal by his allies, abruptly withdrew from the war in 1800. The rise of Napoleon to first consul convinced the emperor that the French Revolution was over, and he entered into peace negotiations with the "Little Corporal."

The English occupation of Malta, and their failure to return the island to the Knights of St. John, led to a new orientation of Russian policy. Paul, in this instance emulating Catherine II, proceeded to revive the League of Neutrals: Denmark, Sweden, Prussia, and Russia.

Paul wreaked his wrath upon England by placing an embargo on English merchant vessels, by altering the customs tariff, and finally, by cutting off all

Mens turpe, corpore turpi.

The Magnanimous Ally. — Painted at Petersburg

Tsar Paul, believing he had been betrayed by the Austrians and the English, began peace negotiations with Napoleon in 1800. The Allies considered that Paul was betraying them, and this British cartoon is indicative of their reaction.

exports and imports to and from England. With more venom than wisdom, he hastily dispatched a Don Cossack expedition of forty regiments (22,000 men) overland via Orenburg and Bukhara to seize England's prize possession, India, and destroy British colonial supremacy. The British effectively retaliated by sending the British fleet under Admiral Nelson to the Baltic. Unfortunately for Paul, his hostile measures against England had upset the entire Russian foreign trade and aroused widespread opposition at home. Paul's general unpopularity led to a well-laid plot to remove him from the throne. The British ambassador was implicated, and even Paul's son Alexander was cognizant of the conspiracy. Paul was murdered in his bedchamber on March 23, 1801, thereby terminating the quixotic course of Russian foreign policy during his reign.

5

Alexander I: The Enigmatic Tsar,

1801-1825

ALEXANDER I, the eldest son of Paul I, ascended the throne March 24, 1801. Great things were expected of Alexander, who had been tutored by the Swiss liberal republican, Frederick Caesar de La Harpe (1754–1836), "in accordance with the laws of reason and the principles of virtue." His grandmother, Catherine II, had encouraged in Alexander liberal and humanitarian views; she herself read and explained to him the French Declaration of Rights. Although she looked forward to his becoming an "ideal" tsar, she neglected to provide the practical training essential to the position. Alexander's pleasing personality was an asset in diplomacy, but his background under Catherine and Paul made him inclined toward compromise, evasion, and hypocrisy rather than toward vigorous and forthright leadership. By some of his contemporaries, he was characterized as being "as sharp as a pin, as fine as a razor, and as false as seafoam." One of his biographers, G. M. Paléologue, has called him the "enigmatic Tsar."

DOMESTIC POLICY

Advisory Committee. Alexander, therefore, came to the throne as a liberal, ready to undo the reactionary measures of his unpopular father. Although he restored some of Catherine's appointees to office, he was distrustful of the plotters who had murdered his father, and found opportunities to remove them from the capital. In their place, he soon surrounded himself with a group of young friends of liberal persuasion, including Victor P. Kochubey, Nicholas N. Novosiltsev, Count Paul A. Stroganov, and Prince Adam Czartoryski. These men comprised a privileged Advisory Committee (*Neglasnyi Komitet,* sometimes translated as Secret Committee), that met with Alexander informally to draft a program of reform for Russia. According to Czartoryski's *Memoirs,* every useful reform initiated in Alexander's reign originated with this group.

The Advisory Committee devoted a great deal of effort to the question of administrative reform of the higher branches of the government, in accordance with the spirit of the times. Anglophiles in their political thinking, their model was the English system of constitutional monarchy. The consensus was, however, that the introduction of this system into Russia was premature. They, therefore, recommended no constitutional limitations on the autocratic power of the emperor, but sought rather to make the autocracy "legitimate." For the collegiate system which Catherine II had abolished and which Paul had restored under individual directors, Alexander in 1802 substituted the ministerial system. At the outset, the Senate exercised a modicum of control over the activities of the ministers; later the Senate's functions were restricted to judicial matters. The advantages of the new system over the old lay in the direct relationship between the emperor and his ministers, who were both appointees of the crown and heads of departments. The Committee of Ministers, a new institution presided over by the tsar himself, met to discuss matters of common concern. Although it lacked the authority to make decisions which characterizes a modern cabinet, during Alexander's prolonged absence from Russia in the conflict with Napoleon, 1805–1807, it performed the functions of the ruler.

Speransky was no more successful with his program for the reorganization Speransky (1772–1839), sometimes regarded as the greatest man of Alexander's epoch, the transformation of Russian political and legal institutions; the ultimate goal was the establishment of a constitutional monarchy. Impressed by the French system that had evolved during the revolutionary and Napoleonic periods, Speransky envisaged a centralized, rather than a federal, form of government, with emphasis on the separation of the executive, judicial, and legislative powers. His elaborate blueprint for reform provided for an enlarged State Council as the supreme administrative institution, a Governing Senate to supervise the ministries vested with executive power, a Judicial Senate, and a representative Duma. Only two parts of this project—the Imperial Council (1810) and the eleven ministries (1811)—were achieved. Nicholas Karamzin, who secured access to Speransky's draft proposals (made public only in 1905), unqualifiedly denounced the program in his memorandum to Alexander in 1812, entitled *Ancient and Modern Russia.* He called for the *status quo* in the form of a strong monarchy free from constitutional trappings.

Speransky was no more successful with his program for the reorganization of Russian law, based on the Napoleonic Code. His financial reforms, badly needed to offset inflation and bankruptcy resulting from the war with Napoleon, fared better. His recommendations, which were implemented, included higher taxes to stabilize the Russian currency; increased duties on imported luxury goods; and revival of Russia's European trade by relaxation of the observance of the Continental Blockade imposed by Napoleon under the Treaty of Tilsit (1807). In spite of his contributions, Speransky, who had labeled serf owners "a handful of parasites," had many enemies. In 1812 they secured his removal from office and banishment from St. Petersburg.

Federalism. Following the Napoleonic Wars, in 1815 Alexander once again turned his attention to political reform. Nicholas Novosiltsev (1761–1836) drafted a charter providing for a federal system of government, modelled after that of the United States. Alexander for a time even corresponded with President Jefferson in regard to the American system. In spite of the emperor's life-long contention that he was at heart "a republican," this correspondence did not result in a practical program for Russia. Novosiltsev's project, completed in 1820, was shelved during the extreme reaction that followed in the wake of the mutiny of the Semyonovsky Regiment[1] of the Guards.

Education. Since Alexander's Advisory Committee and Michael Speransky regarded education as of paramount importance, in fact as a prerequisite to constitutional reform, much attention was devoted to this area during the first five years of the emperor's reign. One of the new ministries established was the Ministry of Public Instruction, an innovation in Russia and one acclaimed even by the conservative historian Karamzin. There was great need, following the reign of Paul, for the reorganization of the educational system. The University of Moscow had no more than one hundred students. The Academy of Sciences had practically ceased to exert any influence on the intellectual life of the nation. In the National Schools set up by Catherine II, the quality of teaching had greatly deteriorated. The new ministry spent more money on education. Catherine's peak allocation had been 780,000 rubles a year; in 1804 Alexander assigned 2,800,000 rubles. The existing universities— Moscow, Vilna, and Dorpat—received substantial endowments, and three new ones were founded: the Institute of Pedagogy in St. Petersburg (renamed the University of St. Petersburg in 1819), Kharkov, and Kazan. Under the reorganization of the educational system, each of the six universities supervised and inspected the schools in its own district.

Alexander's hopes of providing an apportunity for every Russian child to secure an education and thereby to improve his status failed to materialize. There was a drastic shortage of teachers, schools, and funds. After 1805 the funds that might otherwise have been devoted to educational purposes were diverted to the needs of the armed forces in the war against Napoleon. After 1815 when peace was finally restored, Alexander's submersion in mysticism and reaction, and the supremacy of Arakcheyevism (see page 90), proved highly detrimental to the schools of higher learning. Many professors were accused of disseminating un-Russian ideas, lectures were censored, and text-books revised. Under the influence of the Bible Society imported from England, Prince A. N. Golitsyn, super-procurator of the Holy Synod and minister of education, sought to combine education and spiritual matters. Biblical themes were introduced even in mathematical and scientific studies. One by one the universities, beginning with Kazan, were completely transformed. In other words, much of what had been achieved in the early years of

---

1. One of the guards regiments organized by Peter the Great, which had enjoyed special privileges. Many of its officers were known to have been connected with the secret societies. In 1820 a coarse and brutal German, Colonel Schwartz, was appointed as their commander. His inhuman disciplinary measures led to the mutiny.

Alexander's reign in the field of education was cancelled. By this time, however, Russia had 6 universities, 48 gymnasia (secondary schools), 3 lyceums, including the Imperial Alexander Lyceum founded in 1811, and 367 grade schools.

Serfdom. The other major problem considered by the Advisory Committee was serfdom. Alexander and his associates wanted to do something about the agrarian situation, not only on humanitarian grounds, but to forestall any serious disturbances at home in view of the critical international situation. Even his liberal advisers were forced to admit, however, the danger of antagonizing the *dvorianstvo* and merchants who profited by the institution of serfdom. Although they concluded that emancipation, like constitutional government, was premature, they did recommend measures designed to ameliorate some of the worst abuses of serfdom.

In 1801 the right to buy uninhabited land was extended from the *dvorianstvo* to merchants, the urban population, and state peasants. The following year the right of the landlords to exile their serfs to hard labor was abolished. In February, 1803, the Law of Free Agriculturists, attributed to Count N. P. Rumyantsev, gave landlords the right to free their serfs individually or by entire villages, with land allotments. Such agreements, arrived at by mutual consent of the landlord and those to be liberated, were presented to the emperor for sanction. Peasants freed under this law belonged to a special category of free agriculturists, who were subject to certain assessments and service to the state. During the reign of Alexander I, 47,153 male souls were freed in this fashion—less than 0.5 per cent of the entire serf population of the Empire. In addition, Alexander set aside one million rubles per annum to redeem land from private owners. By this ruse, 50,000 serfs attached to the land were redeemed and brought directly under state control.

In 1804 the Advisory Committee, in collaboration with representatives of the Baltic nobility, instituted a number of reforms in the status of the Baltic peasants. In 1808 the public sale of serfs in the market place was banned. Under French occupation, Polish serfs in the duchy of Warsaw were liberated in 1807. Following the Napoleonic Wars, the peasants of the Baltic Province were emancipated (Esthonia, 1816; Courland, 1817; and Livonia, 1819), although failure to provide them with land led to their exploitation by the landowners and to serious unrest.

Arakcheyev: Emperor's Deputy. As Alexander's position became more secure, his meetings with the Advisory Committee tapered off, and ceased entirely by the close of 1803. Its place was ultimately taken by the honest, upright, but wholly reactionary Alexei Arakcheyev (1769–1834), former commandant of St. Petersburg, known for his dogged loyalty to the emperor Paul. Alexander made Arakcheyev his "deputy," the sole representative of the Council of Ministers reporting directly to him.

Military Colonies. Although the idea did not originate with him, Arakcheyev is best known for his efforts to transform Russia into a military barracks by the establishment of military settlements across the country from the Baltic to the Black Sea. The settlement of military regiments on state-owned land had two purposes: the availability of trained soldiers for defense in case of need, without the expense attached to their maintenance in the regular army; and the preservation of law and order by means of colonies maintained by rigid military discipline. Even children at the age of seven were dressed in uniforms, drilled, and severely punished for infractions of discipline. The first of these military colonies was founded in 1810 in the province of Mogilev. The project was interrupted by the Napoleonic invasion of Russia in 1812, but was resumed in earnest after the conflict was over. Strangely enough, these settlements, which eventually made Arakcheyev the most hated man in Russia, were approved by men as far removed from one another in their political outlook as the ultra-conservative Karamzin and the liberal Speransky.

Reactions Against Despotism. A wave of protests and uprisings, ruthlessly suppressed by Arakcheyev, followed the expansion of the program of military settlements after 1815. A large-scale uprising occurred in January, 1818, following the establishment of military colonies in the Ukraine, where existing settlers were impressed into the settlements instead of being transferred elsewhere. The most serious uprising took place in Chuguyev in the summer of 1818; before it was subdued, it required four regiments of infantry and eighteen squadrons of cavalry and artillery. Far from abandoning this pet project in the face of opposition, Alexander is reputed to have said that he would maintain the military settlements, even at the cost of strewing the entire road from St. Petersburg to Moscow with corpses. By the close of his reign, these settlements comprised 300,000 male souls.

The reaction, which reached its peak under Arakcheyev and Golitsyn following the Napoleonic Wars, produced what is known as the Decembrist Movement, which culminated in a revolt upon the accession of Nicholas I in 1825. The conflict with Napoleon had greatly increased Russian contacts with the rest of Europe—a situation which, historically speaking, has always led to the growth of liberalism and of demands for reform in Russia. Large numbers of Russian officers saw active service in Germany, Holland, and France, where they read books and newspapers and had ample opportunity to compare conditions with those in Russia. As war veterans, many of these members of the aristocracy and gentry hoped that under postwar conditions Alexander would revive his earlier projects for political reform. Their hopes had risen when the tsar in 1815 granted a constitution to Poland and internal autonomy to Finland; he had also been instrumental in forcing the restored Bourbons in France to operate under a constitution. In 1818 Alexander, speaking at the opening of the Warsaw Diet, expressed his hope of extending "liberal institutions to all the lands under his scepter." His Warsaw speeches, as Karamzin noted, made a strong impact upon young Russians, who, sleeping and waking, dreamed of a constitution. When the Novosiltsev plan for a federal government died aborning and the revolt of the Semyonovsky Regiment in 1820 turned Alexander's mind from reform to stark reaction, their disillusionment was profound. Alexander, the liberator abroad, remained the despot at home.

Secret Societies. Many veterans of the European wars, having come into contact with Masonry in the West, returned to join Masonic societies in Russia. This paved the way for other secret organizations, modelled in some respects after those of the German Tugendbund and Italian Carbonari. The first such Russian underground organization, the Union of Salvation, was formed in 1816 to abolish serfdom and autocracy. The Union of Welfare, organized two years later, included an inner core determined to infiltrate the armed forces and civil administration to secure at some opportune time in the future a constitutional regime, the abolition of serfdom, a reduction in the term of military service, the abandonment of military settlements, and civil rights. As reform receded into the background, some members of the Union of Welfare championed republicanism rather than constitutional monarchy.

After the Semyonovsky mutiny in 1820, the danger of membership in secret organizations involving officers led to the disbanding of circles of the Union in St. Petersburg and Moscow. The organization revived, however, after a division into a Northern Society and a Southern Society, the latter including more extremists. The leaders of the Northern Society were Nikita and Alexander Muraviev, heirs to vast estates and thousands of serfs; the poet Kondratii Ryleyev (1795–1826), an employee of the Russian-American Company and an admirer of the American constitution; and the Princes Sergei Trubetskoy and Yevgeny Obolensky, officers of the guard. Nikita Muraviev, their leading spokesman in the early stages, favored a federal constitution of thirteen Russian states, obviously based on American precedent; a hereditary monarch with limited powers; a bicameral National Assembly, chosen by an electorate with high property qualifications; the introduction of trial by jury; and guarantees of civil liberties. Muraviev favored the emancipation of the serfs, but without land.

The Southern Society, farther from the capital, survived the Semyonovsky outbreak without disbanding. Its leader was Colonel Paul Pestel, son of the German governor-general of Siberia, and a veteran of the Battle of Borodino (1812). More radical than the leaders of the Northern Society, and Machiavellian in tactics, he was known as a "Jacobin republican." Pestel's "republic" resembled a centralized, totalitarian police state. He preached Russification, or assimilation, of all minorities, with the exception of the Poles, and proposed to banish the Jews, if they refused to assimilate, to Asia Minor to establish their own state.

It is significant that all members of these societies were aristocrats, many of them wealthy serf owners. Their ranks included no "bourgeois" merchants, regarded by Ryleyev as "ignoramuses." Neither faction supported a popular uprising, which they appeared to fear as much as they feared the existing

Colonel Pestel drew up the Southern Society's plan for the Russian constitution. He was a ringleader of the Decembrist Revolt, and was executed for
his role in the uprising.

autocracy. Although their plans for action remained vague and uncertain, they
seem to have envisaged the kind of military coup which had already unseated
several Russian rulers, rather than a Russian version of the French Revolution. Many believed, as Pestel did, that the assassination of Alexander was
inevitable. The two societies maintained close communications, although
Pestel's efforts to fuse them were unsuccessful.

Decembrist Revolt. While these plotters were still debating their course of
action, Alexander I died suddenly on November 19, 1825, in Taganrog in
southern Russia. Uncertainty over the succession provided the long-awaited
opportunity for revolt. Alexander was childless, and according to Paul's Law

of Succession, his brother Constantine was the legitimate heir to the throne. Because of Constantine's extreme reluctance to assume this responsibility and his morganatic marriage to a Polish commoner, Alexander in 1823 appointed his other brother, Nicholas, next in line, as his heir. Alexander's manifesto providing for the succession was kept secret. In the confusion that followed Alexander's death, Constantine, who was in Poland, swore allegiance to Nicholas, who, due to ignorance or pressure resulting from his unpopularity, swore allegiance to Constantine. It was not until December 12 that the situation was clarified and Nicholas accepted the throne. The fact that Nicholas was known to be a reactionary with Prussian leanings, whereas his brother was erroneously believed to be more liberal, precipitated action by the plotters. The revolt was set for December 26, 1825 (hence the name Decembrists), to coincide with the oath of allegiance by the guards to Nicholas I.

The Decembrists were too few in numbers, too poorly organized, and they lacked resolute leadership. The three thousand mutineers who lined up in military formation in the Senate Square in St. Petersburg failed to take effective action. There were cheers for Constantine and the constitution. Allegedly, some of the ignorant soldiers involved were under the impression that "constitution" was Constantine's wife. Nicholas, alerted to the uprising in advance, was soon in a position to confront the rebels with vastly superior forces. He had no trouble suppressing the revolt in the capital and a subsequent rising in the south. After a Commission of Inquiry had spent six months investigating the uprising, five of the ringleaders were hanged, more than one hundred were exiled to Siberia, and the remainder received a conditional pardon.

The defeat of the Decembrists amounted to a serious setback for the Russian constitutional movement. It proved that political and social reform could not be achieved by a palace revolution. In the long run, it was the example of the Decembrists that counted. Unlike Razin and Pugachev, the Decembrist leaders represented the flower of the Russian nobility and their numbers included the scions of some of the most powerful families in Russia. It was not long before they were acclaimed by the poet Pushkin and the writer Alexander Herzen as martyrs to the constitutional cause. Subsequent revolutionaries, including even Vladimir Lenin, traced their lineage to the Decembrists, who, in the words of Avrahm Yarmolinsky, fought "the opening skirmish in Russia's battle for democracy."

FOREIGN POLICY

Russia's outstanding international position under Alexander I during and after the Napoleonic Wars is comparable to that of the USSR during and following World War II. As a result, there has been a revival of interest in the reign of Alexander I and a reinterpretation of his policies.

Russia was the leading continental opponent of French expansion, a guarantor of the Holy Roman Empire under the Peace of Teschen (1779), and a prime mover in the Third, Fourth, and Fifth European Coalitions against Napoleon. Alexander, the creator of the Russian Ministry of Foreign Affairs, had a strong flair for diplomacy. His messianic complex convinced him that he had a special role to play, first as the liberator of Europe and later as preserver of international peace and order on the European continent. In matters of foreign policy, his reign can be divided into two periods: the first from 1801 to 1815, in which Russian policy focused on the struggle with Napoleon; and the second from 1815 to 1825, when, under the aegis of the Holy Alliance, Alexander sought to preserve the European *status quo* against the resurgent forces of revolution.

Upon his accession to the throne in 1801, Alexander quickly mended his international fences. He placated England by recalling Paul's India expedition and rejecting the grand mastership of the Knights of St. John. He then resumed diplomatic relations with Austria. Third, he established a *modus vivendi* with Napoleon, by means of the peace convention of October 8, 1801. Finally, through Alexander's personal visit to Memel in 1802, he established friendly and intimate relations with Friedrich Wilhelm III and Queen Louise of Prussia.

War of the Third Coalition, 1805–1807. The interests of Russia and France, however, continued to clash in Central Europe, and relations between the two powers steadily deteriorated, as Napoleon annexed, in succession, the kingdom of Sardinia in Italy and Hanover in Germany. The kidnapping of the Bourbon Duke d'Enghien from Baden on March 15, 1804, and his subsequent murder, together with the assumption by Napoleon of the title of emperor of France on May 18, 1804, led the indignant Alexander to break off diplomatic relations with France in September. Alexander's repeated challenge of Napoleon's actions in Europe resulted from the stabilization of his own position on the Russian throne. In posing more as a European than as a Russian leader, he was acting, in part at least, under pressure from foreign advisers at his court. These included the English, who in 1803 reentered the war against Napoleon, and his own minister of foreign affairs, Prince Adam Czartoryski, who hoped by Russian intervention in Europe to secure the restoration of his native kingdom of Poland. The wisdom of dragging Russia into another conflict with France was questionable, from the standpoint of Russian interests. Nevertheless, upon Alexander's initiative, the Third Coalition (England, Austria, Russia, Sweden, 1805; Prussia, 1806) clearly indicated that the emperor already envisaged the creation of a new European order for the preservation of peace in which Russia would play a leading role.

The war went badly for the allies. The Austrians were soundly defeated at the Battle of Ulm (1805). Alexander, after flouting the advice of his commanding general, Michael Kutuzov, a pupil of Suvorov, was overwhelmed at the Battle of Austerlitz (1805). The entry of Friedrich Wilhelm into the conflict, without waiting for Russian reinforcements, was followed by the collapse of Prussia in the Battle of Jena (1806). Alexander was humiliated by the defeat at Austerlitz, a severe blow to Russian prestige—following, as it did, the great victories of Suvorov in his father's time. He nevertheless determined to continue the struggle against Napoleon, on the ground that Russian strategic interests in Poland and the eastern Mediterranean were seriously threatened by French victories in Germany and Italy. For the campaign against Napoleon, he had raised an army of 150,000 men and a militia of 612,000. This was done at great cost and by sacrificing internal reforms. The Russian army managed to hold the French at bay in the Battle of Eylau (1807), where both sides lost 50,000 men, but it was badly beaten a few months later at Friedland (1807), with Russian losses reaching 15,000 men. The collapse of allied support, the impossibility of securing additional Russian reinforcements, and the outbreak of war with Turkey made the continuation of the conflict untenable.

Treaty of Tilsit. Alexander, following the pattern of Paul's *volte–face* toward Napoleon in 1800 (see page 83), negotiated peace with the French emperor at Tilsit on a raft on the Niemen River on June 25, 1807. The deal between Napoleon and Alexander, with the division of their spheres of interest, is strongly reminiscent of the Hitler-Stalin Pact of August 23, 1939. Alexander had little alternative but to recognize the French conquests. The three major problems confronted by the two contestants were the fate of Prussia, Russian relations with England, and the Near East. Alexander saved Prussia from complete annihilation, although not from heavy loss of territory and an exorbitant indemnity. He agreed to act as mediator between Napoleon and England, and barring a successful conclusion of the conflict, to join forces with Napoleon against his erstwhile ally. Alexander also capitulated to Napoleonic pressure by consenting to join his Continental System, a blockade to throttle English trade. In return, Napoleon agreed to intervene with the sultan of Turkey on behalf of Russia. When the vital issue of the partition of the Ottoman Empire was raised, Napoleon clearly indicated that he had no intention of permitting Constantinople to fall to the Russians. Alexander, however, was given a free hand against Sweden, including the right to annex Finland and thereby provide greater security for the Russian capital of St. Petersburg.

Other Wars. Alexander's deal with Napoleon was highly unpopular among the Russian nobility, French émigrés in Russia, and English representatives, all of whom looked for opportunities to overthrow it. The new Russian foreign minister, Count Nicholas Rumyantsev (1754–1826), a staunch supporter of the Franco-Russian alliance, regarded the Treaty of Tilsit as an opportunity for the fulfillment of Russia's historic mission in the Near East against the Ottoman Empire. The rupture of diplomatic relations with England on November 7 was followed by war, which, although it involved no major engagements, lasted until 1812. There is reason to believe that from the beginning Alexander regarded the Treaty of Tilsit as a temporary truce rather than as a permanent settlement of Franco-Russian problems. He took advantage of the breathing spell thus afforded to seize Finland (1808–1809) in a war against Sweden, the ally of England; to acquire Bessarabia in the protracted conflict with Turkey (1806–1812); and to reorganize the Russian forces in preparation for a renewal of the conflict with Napoleon. Although Alexander proved to be "as stubborn as a mule" in his dealings with Napoleon on European issues, the fact that Russia was already involved in three wars made him most reluctant to engage in a fourth with France.

Napoleon's Continental System. The Continental System, which completely upset Russian foreign trade oriented toward England, proved to be the greatest cause of friction between France and Russia. Both sides violated the Treaty of Tilsit: Napoleon by the annexation in 1811 of the duchy of Oldenburg, whose reigning duke was an uncle of the tsar; and the Russians by flouting the strict observance of the Continental System to engage in trade with England. Speransky's prohibitive tariffs on French luxury goods in 1810, designed to prevent the drain of Russian currency from the country, also aroused the ire of Napoleon. Quarrels over the anti-English blockade are generally regarded as the primary reason for the collapse of the Franco-Russian alliance and the outbreak of war in 1812.

Napoleonic Invasion. For the invasion of Russia, Napoleon raised a Grand Army of 600,000 men, with a nucleus of French soldiers, but with large levies of troops from the French-occupied states of Naples, Switzerland, Poland, Portugal, Spain, Croatia, Belgium, and Holland. Formidable as it was, this polyglot force lacked the cohesion of an army fighting for national survival. With Austerlitz in mind, Napoleon fully expected, by using *blitzkrieg* tactics, to destroy in one climactic battle the much smaller active Russian forces, numbering 210,000. He thus disregarded the timely warning of General Armand de Caulaincourt (1772–1827), French ambassador in St. Petersburg, to the effect that on Russian soil the French army would encounter united and prolonged resistance from the entire Russian nation. Just one month prior to Napoleon's invasion of Russia, the Turks by the Treaty of Bucharest, May 16, 1812, ended the Russo-Turkish conflict (1806–1812). The French were thereby deprived of a valuable ally, and the Russians relieved of fighting a major war on two fronts.

In June, 1812, Napoleon's Grand Army crossed the River Niemen near Kovno. In a heavy engagement around Smolensk, both contestants lost around 20,000 men, but the Russian army under Barclay de Tolly escaped Napoleon's grasp by a tactical retreat. Thus began the Russian tactics of "defense in depth," which were adopted by Kutuzov, who was recalled by popular demand after the loss of Smolensk. Napoleon, who had expected to destroy the Russian army in this first engagement, instead pursued it to Moscow. Only a country with vast territorial expanses could afford to avoid major engagements with the advancing enemy, the object being to draw him far into the interior and there destroy him. Like most agrarian peoples, the Russians rose en masse to the defense of the Fatherland against the presence of foreigners on Russian soil. Kutuzov risked one major battle at the village of Borodino, seventy-five miles west of Moscow, where both sides suffered extreme losses. Based upon recent Soviet estimates, the French lost 58,000 men and the Russians, on the defensive, 38,500. The Russian army, still intact, resisted in rear-guard actions every inch of the route to Moscow, but avoided decisive encounters with the French. Time was gained for the evacuation of the historic capital, justified by Kutuzov in the following terms:

> As long as there exists an army and it is in a condition to oppose the enemy, so long will I be able to preserve the hope of ultimate victory. But when the army is destroyed, both Moscow and Russia will perish. I order the retreat.

Napoleon entered "that celebrated city," only to find that it was practically deserted. He assumed that the war was finished. In Europe the fall of a capital ordinarily heralded the collapse of resistance in a country. Although Moscow was no longer the official capital, Russia in reality had two capitals, and Moscow was the traditional center of the Moscow state. No sooner had Napoleon taken up residence in the Kremlin, however, than fires, spread by high winds, within a few days reduced three-quarters of the city to rubble.

The burning of Moscow proved to be the turning point of the war. The French blamed the Russians, and they in turn blamed the French. Recent Soviet accounts emphasize that the conflagration was deliberately carried out by the French forces. Actually, it seems to have been a joint responsibility. The retreating Russians destroyed military, but not civilian supplies. Some individual Russian patriots set fire to their residences and possessions rather than see them fall to Napoleon's troops. Drunken French soldiers in search of loot and booty played their part in the destruction. Irrespective of who was to blame, the burning of Moscow destroyed all possibility that Napoleon might win over the infuriated Russian population. He also lost essential food supplies and winter quarters for his troops. Moreover, he lost valuable time, with winter approaching, while he tried to negotiate a dictated peace to Alexander.

French Retreat. Meanwhile, the Russian army, encamped on the road to Riazan, rested, was reequipped, and reinforced up to 110,000 men. Brigadier-General Sir Robert Thomas Wilson, dispatched by the English government to Russia at the outset of the Napoleonic invasion, had high praise for the morale of the Moscow refugees and Russian armed forces, to whom he brought word that Alexander would continue the war as long as a single Frenchman remained on Russian soil. He wrote of the reinforcement and provisioning of the Russian army as "one of the most extraordinary efforts of national zeal ever made."[2] The whole nation responded to the effort, providing whatever could be of service. When Napoleon, unable to advance toward

2. Peter Putnam, ed., *Seven Britons in Imperial Russia, 1698–1812* (Princeton, N.J.: Princeton University Press, 1952), p. 389.

St. Petersburg or to the south with his demoralized forces, on October 20 began his disastrous retreat over the same route by which he had come, Prince Kutuzov allowed the French no rest. Partisan regiments formed spontaneously, and together with the Cossack cavalry, harried the enemy's rear. Once again, the cautious Kutuzov avoided a general engagement with Napoleon's army. Before Napoleon reached Smolensk early in November, the first snows of winter began to fall, adding to the hardships of the retreating army. A Russian pincer movement failed to capture Napoleon and his army at the Berezina River. When the remnants of Napoleon's Grand Army re-crossed the Niemen into Prussia, there remained no more than 20,000 or, at most, 30,000 men. It was a "phantom" army, which had abandoned its baggage and had to forage for its food supplies.

Various reasons have been assigned for this cataclysmic Napoleonic disaster: the weather, the vast open spaces, the polyglot composition of the French forces, Kutuzov's tactics of defense in depth, the over-extension of the French lines of communication, and the furious resistance of the Russians in their war for national survival. Lobanov-Rostovsky, a historian of this conflict, after attributing the French defeat to a number of factors—military, national, and geographical—denies the traditional concept that Napoleon was de-stroyed by "General Winter":

> No war has been more generally misinterpreted in history than Napoleon's campaign in Russia. Too readily it has been dismissed with the statement that Napoleon was driven out by the cold. In saying this, historians forget that they thereby merely endorse Napoleon's "war propaganda"—the official explanation which Napoleon gave Europe to account for his defeat and make it appear an "act of God" for which he could not be responsible. Thus accepted, the legend of the defeat of the Grand Army by the cold in Russia has crept into history, and this superficial view has been repeated glibly ever since.[3]

The contemporary Soviet historian, Eugene Tarle, interpreted the War of 1812 as "a people's war" against an enemy invader:

> Not the cold and not Russia's vast expanses conquered Napoleon, but the resistance of the Russian people.
>
> The Russian people asserted their right to an independent national exist-ence; they asserted it with an indomitable will to victory, with the true hero-ism that despises all phrases, with a surge of spirit unequalled by any other nation save the Spanish.
>
> The Russians revealed greater physical strength and material potentialities than Spain. Within six months Napoleon's hordes were dispersed and de-stroyed in Russia, while the Spaniards, despite their equally indisputable

3. Andrei A. Lobanov-Rostovsky, *Russia and Europe, 1789–1825* (Durham, N.C.: Duke University Press, 1947), p. 212.

heroism, took five years, even with the immense help given them by England, to get rid of Napoleon—and ultimately succeeded in 1813 in direct consequence of Napoleon's defeat in Russia.[4]

Conflicting Interpretations. Although Russian interpretation of the 1812 war with Napoleon has varied greatly, in general pre-Soviet historians have treated it as a "Patriotic War," in which Russian military leaders emerged as "heroes." Soviet interpretation, which has fluctuated with changes in the party line, is best represented by the writings of Mikhail Nikolayevitch Pokrovsky and Eugene (Evgeny Viktorovitch) Tarle, two outstanding historical scholars.

Pokrovsky, the leading Soviet historian of the 1920's and early 1930's, unqualifiedly debunked the 1812 campaign. In line with Marxist concepts, he emphasized economic factors, especially the continental blockade, as the basic cause and justification of the Napoleonic invasion. Contending that Napoleon was defeated, not by a popular uprising but by poor organization and by his own tactical errors, Pokrovsky denied the existence of any "planned retreat" on the part of Russia's generals, who simply withdrew because of necessity, and further revealed their ineffectiveness during Napoleon's retreat from Moscow.

Tarle was a non-Marxist before the Revolution of 1917, and was exiled to Alma Ata during the early years of the Stalin regime. Perhaps of necessity he followed the main lines of the Pokrovsky thesis in his 1936 biography of Napoleon. Within two years, however, as revealed in his *Napoleon's Invasion of Russia: 1812* (1938), he had completely reversed his position to one corresponding with the new emphasis in Soviet historiography on the positive achievements of tsarist Russia in foreign policy. As indicated in the passage quoted above, he now glorified the "heroic" Russian people and, for the most part, its military leadership. Tarle still criticized some aspects of Russian military organization, including the supply services, and recognized the weakness and indecision of Kutuzov, in spite of his military genius.

World War II led to even greater emphasis by Soviet historians on the traditional patriotic approach to 1812, with inevitable comparisons between Hitler's invasion of Russia and that of Napoleon. With Khrushchev's de-Stalinization campaign, however, the so-called planned retreats of 1812 and 1941, as well as the "victories" at Borodino and Stalingrad have all been subjected to historical criticism.

Wars of Liberation. The Russian war for national survival had a tremendous impact on Europe, most of which was still under French occupation. The French retreat eventually proved to be the signal for an uprising of the conquered peoples in their own wars of liberation. Inside Russia, there were two schools of thought as to whether or not the war should be carried beyond the Russian-Polish frontiers to support the liberation of other suppressed

4. Eugene Tarle, *Napoleon's Invasion of Russia—1812* (New York: Oxford University Press, 1942), pp. 408–409.

peoples. Prince Kutuzov, already ailing, contended that France no longer constituted a danger to Russia, and that any further pursuit of the French armies could only redound to the advantage of England, the probable successor to France as the world's major power. This isolationist point of view was opposed by many of the foreign advisers surrounding Alexander I, including Baron Stein of Prussia. The emperor, himself, who relished the role of liberator of Europe, leaned toward the interventionists, who reasoned that only by the overthrow of Napoleon could Russian and European problems be solved. He therefore decided to continue the conflict until Napoleon's downfall had been accomplished. This involved another two years of hard fighting. Casualties were heavy, and Russian losses were greater than those of any other allied power.

Following the Treaty of Kalish on February 28, 1813, which restored peace between Russia and Prussia and reestablished their alliance, Kutuzov's forces entered Prussia, as liberators, on their westward march to Paris. By April the Russian army had cleared eastern Germany of the French forces. In succession, Berlin, Hamburg, and Dresden were taken and Russian troops reached the River Elbe. The Fourth Coalition, including Russia, Prussia, Austria, England, and Sweden, was formed to carry on the war. It was the great Battle of Leipzig, September 16–19, 1813, often called the Battle of the Nations, that sealed Napoleon's downfall and forced him to withdraw beyond the Rhine.

First Treaty of Paris. The disposition of Emperor Francis of Austria and his foreign minister, Prince Metternich, to make peace at the Rhine was strongly resisted by Alexander I and his Prussian ally. Early in 1814, the allied armies crossed the Rhine into France. The four great powers signed the Treaty of Chaumont, a twenty-year alliance by which they pledged themselves to continue the war until victory was achieved. Alexander and the allied troops marched through the streets of Paris in triumph on March 31. Napoleon's abdication followed shortly thereafter, and the Bourbons were restored under Louis XVIII as constitutional monarch. By the First Treaty of Paris, May 30, 1814, France emerged from the war with the frontiers of 1792 and no indemnities.

The intense friction and distrust among the allies, which had already been manifested before they crossed the Rhine, now increased with the removal of Napoleon to the Island of Elba. Metternich resented the lenient terms Alexander had won for the defeated French. The English, represented by Viscount Castlereagh, were seriously concerned about the future of Poland. Both feared that the unaccustomed presence of Russian armed forces in Western Europe was a prelude to further Russian expansion. The new colossus, Alexander the Liberator and savior of Europe, appeared to the English and Austrians as a threat second only to Napoleon.

Congress of Vienna. The rift reached its climax at the Congress of Vienna, which opened in October, 1814, to redraft the map of Europe. Alexander's plan for the reconstitution of a united Poland under the Russian crown, with compensation elsewhere to Austria and Prussia for their former Polish holdings, split the Congress wide open. For Russia, this was the major issue, and Alexander faced the combined opposition of his former allies. So bitter was the dispute that Castlereagh secretly offered Austria and France a military alliance against Prussia and Russia. The deadlock was broken by news of the escape of Napoleon from Elba and the need to use Russian troops against him. A compromise was reached whereby the greater part of Poland was established as a constitutional monarchy under Alexander, and Prussia was compensated by receiving two-fifths of Saxony. The final act of the Congress of Vienna was signed on June 9, a few days before the Battle of Waterloo.

By this European settlement, Russia acquired some 2,100 square miles of territory, as compared to 2,300 square miles for Austria, and 2,217 for Prussia. Alexander had compromised at the conference table and his allies had fared well. The settlement at Vienna, without any "cooling-off period," lasted for a century. France, by the Second Treaty of Paris, November 20, 1815, was forced to accept the frontiers of 1790, a minor territorial adjustment, to pay a substantial indemnity, and to submit to an allied army of occupation for five years. Under this agreement, Russia left 27,000 men in France.

Holy Alliance. Before Alexander left Paris, he proclaimed the much-publicized Holy Alliance of the European powers, pledged to conduct their relations according to the "precepts of justice, Christianity, charity, and peace." Its Covenant provided that "the supreme truths dictated by the eternal law of God the Saviour" would serve as the basis for the operation of the league. International problems were, henceforth, to be decided "by no other rules but the commandments of this sacred faith, the commandments of love, truth, and peace." The pact further stipulated, in a provision that achieved added significance in subsequent years, that members of the Holy Alliance were to govern their peoples as "fathers of their families," and each was pledged to go to the help of the other as need arose.

Alexander was too powerful for his personal "League of Nations" to be ignored. Metternich regarded the agreement as a harmless, empty chimera, but Austria accepted it, as did Prussia. The English prince regent, although in sympathy with the principles expressed, was unable to commit his country without Parliamentary consent. Castlereagh, his foreign minister, labelled the whole thing "a piece of sublime mysticism and nonsense." In the end, all Europe—except England, the Papacy, and the Ottoman Empire—paid lip service to the Holy Alliance. Since the precepts enunciated by Alexander appeared too mystical and pietistic to be practical, Austria, Prussia, Russia, and England believed it necessary to insure the implementation of the Holy Alliance. By the Second Treaty of Paris in 1815 the four great powers renewed their twenty-year Chaumont agreement, forming the Quadruple Alliance which provided the machinery for maintaining peace and order in

A remarkable international outlook, combined with mysticism, led Alexander I to initiate the Holy Alliance. Russian nationalists were critical of this tsar who they believed subordinated the interests of his own nation to those of Europe as a whole.

Europe. This attempt at international cooperation, often called the Concert of Europe, was to be effected through frequent congresses.

Actually, the project for a league of European powers to maintain the peace had been conceived by Alexander as early as 1803, but under the impact of the pietist movement which had become fashionable in Europe as a result of the Napoleonic holocaust, it was expressed in Christian terms. After what Russia had suffered during and after the years of invasion, there is no reason to doubt that Alexander was wholly sincere in his program for world peace.

Concert of Europe. In the first years that followed the European settlement of 1815, Russian prestige remained high. Alexander continued to exert a direct and powerful influence on major and even on minor European affairs. At the Congress of Aix-la-Chapelle in 1818, he used that influence to secure the withdrawal from France of the allied occupation army, and French admission on a basis of equality to the Concert of Europe. Thus was France liberated from "the foreign yoke." Much to the consternation of Metternich, in 1816–1817 Alexander supported liberal constitutional movements in the German states of Saxe-Weimar, Württemburg, and Baden.

But the resurgence of violence and revolutionary agitation in Germany, as marked by the murder of the German writer Kotzebue, who had spent many years in Russian service, alarmed Alexander. At the Congresses of Troppau (1820) and Verona (1822), summoned to deal with revolutions in Naples and Spain respectively, Metternich no longer had reason to rant against the liberalism of the Russian emperor. Revolution abroad, combined with the revolt of the Semyonovsky Regiment at home in 1820, had transformed the tsar's outlook; henceforth, the two leaders entered into a personal "entente-cordiale" to stem the tide of revolution and preserve the *status quo* in Europe. After the death of Alexander in 1825, his brother Nicholas I became an even more dependable ally of Metternich in the preservation of conservatism and autocracy in Europe. In 1821, when the Greek Christians, under Alexander Ypsilanti, rose in rebellion against Ottoman despotism, they received no assistance at first, on the ground that they had disobeyed their legitimate ruler. Alexander, having no desire to cope with revolution in the Balkans, subordinated Russia's Eastern policy to the strengthening of the Holy Alliance.

Even the United States soon feared the alliance would intervene in the New World, Spanish efforts to recover former Latin American their freedom by revolution. The United States proclamation of the Monroe Doctrine, December 2, 1823, warned Russia and the other involved powers against intervention in the American hemisphere. Fortunately, the rift already developing among the great powers over intervention in the internal affairs of European countries placed England on the side of the United States.

Territorial Expansion. The reign of Alexander I brought significant territorial acquisitions to the already vast Russian Empire. Hitherto, most additions to the Russian state had involved large areas occupied mainly by Slavic peoples: Russian settlers in the south; White Russians; Little Russians or Ukrainians; and Poles, occupying land much of which had belonged to Kievan *Rūs*. In the East, the Russian state had expanded to the Pacific, mainly across the northern section of Siberia, sparsely populated by native tribes. The non-Slavic peoples, like the Tatars, Buryat Mongols, and Baltic nationalities had remained small minorities in a Slavic sea.

The territories acquired under Alexander I, on the contrary, located along the fringes of the Empire, emphasized its growing multinational character. They were obtained, as were earlier acquisitions, for reasons of security or trade, and because their possession by other foreign powers would have constituted a threat to Russia. Although Russia was reaching out for overseas possessions, such as Sakhalin and Alaska, the territory actually annexed was adjacent. Basically Russia was pursuing a policy of continental rather than overseas expansion.

In 1809, as a result of the conflict with Sweden, sanctioned by Napoleon, Russia acquired Finland and the Aaland Islands, further consolidating her position on the Baltic. The grand duchy of Finland was granted internal autonomy under the tsar as grand duke. The Treaty of Bucharest, May 16, 1812, terminated the protracted Russo-Turkish War (1806–1812); Bessarabia (Moldavia), between the Dniester and Pruth rivers, and a two-hundred-kilometer stretch of the Black Sea coast were ceded to Alexander by the sultan. The Ottoman Empire also was forced to grant autonomy to Serbia. The peace with the Turks made it possible for the Russians to concentrate substantial forces against Persia and to terminate the prolonged Russo-Persian conflict. In 1801 Georgia, which had earlier sought Russian protection against the Turks and Persians, was annexed by Russia. Although this step provoked a new war with Persia, in 1813 the shah formally ceded to Russia not only Georgia but also the adjacent Muslim areas of Baku, northern Azerbaijan, and Daghestan in the Transcaucasus. Thus, Russia

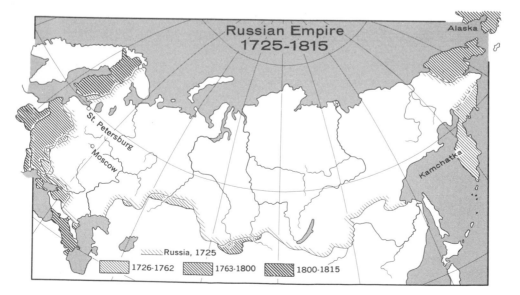

acquired a solid block of territory stretching from the Black to the Caspian Seas.

Soviet scholars interpret these manifestations of Russian imperialism, with the exception of Finland, more as a progressive step which brought these peoples freedom from "backward" countries, such as Turkey and Iran, than as the imposition of a "colonial yoke" on the new minorities. What amounts to Soviet justification of Russian territorial expansion at the expense of the Ottoman Empire and Persia is strongly suggestive of a Soviet "white man's burden."

6

Nicholas I: The Containment
of Democracy, 1825-1855

NICHOLAS I'S GRANDMOTHER CATHERINE II and his brother Alexander I ascended the throne by palace revolutions. Whereas the palace revolutions had been launched in their favor, Nicholas was confronted by a revolt organized by the Russian nobility in opposition to his accession. Nicholas realized, moreover, that this was not the conventional palace revolution, out to substitute one ruler for another. The Decembrist movement was opposed not only to him as a person but also to the institution of autocracy. The aim of the Decembrists was political revolution, to be followed by drastic social changes.

DOMESTIC POLICY

Third Division. The immediate concern of Nicholas I, therefore, was to crush the revolt and to establish an agency to insure that this would never occur again. As already indicated, the Decembrist movement was suppressed and its ringleaders sentenced to death or to Siberian exile.

To prevent a recurrence of the revolt, one of the emperor's first moves was the reorganization of the police. Following the example of Ivan Grozny, in 1826 he organized his own version of an *oprichnina,* which became known as the Third Division, or *Gendarmerie.* As its chief, he selected one of his favorites, Count A. Benckendorff (1783–1844), a Baltic German and a supporter of Arakcheyevism. The entire nation was divided into seven *Gendarmerie* districts. It was the function of the Officers of the Third Division to submit to the proper authorities confidential reports of conditions in their districts and of individuals under surveillance. Although for reasons of prestige many of these officers came from the best families, they were chosen for their lack of scruples and brutality, with the result that police standards deteriorated. Frequently uneducated themselves, they had no compunction about the suppression of freedom of speech and the press. No section of the population was immune from their high-handed tactics.

Even conservative writers, such as Yuri Samarin (1819–1876) and Fyodor Dostoyevsky (1821–1881), fell victims to the Third Division. Alexander

Herzen (1812–1870) was arrested; Vissarion Belinsky (1811–1848) was expelled from the University of Moscow; Alexander Pushkin (1799–1837) was killed in a "duel," the contemporary equivalent of a purge; Mikhail Lermontov (1814–1841) was exiled to the Caucasus, the warm Siberia; and Peter Chaadayev (1793–1856), for offensive statements against the Orthodox church in his *Philosophical Letters,* was declared insane. Professors and students alike were carefully screened and their conduct reported to the authorities. Two popular periodicals which reflected the thinking of the intellectuals, *Moscow Telegraph* and *Telescope,* were banned from publication.

The "police state" thus established drove liberals and radicals underground. Writers took refuge in fiction as the only available medium for the expression of social and political ideas. In 1848, the year of revolutions in Europe, Nicholas even sought to delete the word "progress" from official reports. The historian and journalist Mikhail Pogodin (1800–1875) compared Russia to a "graveyard."

Unpopular as it was, the *Gendarmerie* continued to function until 1917. The Third Division was only one of twelve agencies which exercised censorship in the reign of Nicholas I. In their zeal they often carried matters to ridiculous extremes. It seems likely that the Third Division provided the pattern for the *Cheka* (secret police) and subsequent variations of it under the Soviets.

German Officials. To Nicholas, most intellectuals were tainted with the poison of free thinking. He therefore either drew mainly upon mediocrity or risked conferring responsibility upon former victims of the autocracy, such as Speransky, whose unhappy experiences served as a guarantee against their departure from the straight and narrow path laid down by Nicholas. For many key positions in the government, army, police, and bureaucracy, Nicholas favored the appointment of Germans, mainly of Baltic extraction, rather than Russians. Their main asset was their "blind obedience" to the will of the monarch. Since most prominent Russian families were linked directly or indirectly with the Decembrists, and were therefore subject to guilt by association, and others lacked the qualifications necessary for government service, Nicholas relied greatly on the German element. In the Ministry of Foreign Affairs, for example, five out of six of Count Nesselrode's immediate subordinates in the period from 1830 to 1850 were Baltic Germans.

Nicholas' predilection for Germans can be partly attributed to his own background and training. He was born on July 6, 1796, the year in which Catherine the Great died. His father, Paul I, was descended from the ruling German houses of Holstein and Anhalt-Zerbst. His mother, the Grand Duchess Marie, was a German princess. Nicholas was surrounded by numerous relatives of German extraction. Although he had a Scottish nurse for the first seven years of his life, much of his early training and education was in the hands of Baltic Germans, such as Countess Lieven and General Mathew Lamsdorff. The German influence was greatly accentuated by his marriage to the Princess Alexandra, daughter of Frederick William III of Prussia. This background also helps to explain the emperor's devotion to militarism, specifically to Prussian militarism. No doubt the Napoleonic Wars, 1812–1815, also increased his preoccupation with military affairs. In 1814 at the age of eighteen he was permitted to join the Russian army but excluded from active service. Napoleon's escape from Elba enabled Nicholas to join the active army in 1815, although he did not take part in combat.

Reaffirmation of Autocracy. The thirty-year reign of Nicholas I was the high watermark of Russian autocracy. Unlike his brother Alexander, Nicholas was "the most consistent of autocrats" both at home and abroad. At no time did he lend support to the concept of constitutional monarchy for Russia. As he informed the Marquis de Custine, a trenchant critic of Russian conditions, in 1839:

> I can understand the republic—it is an open and sincere government, or at least it can be; I can understand the absolute monarchy, since I am the head of such a government; but I cannot comprehend the representative monarchy—it is a government of lies, of fraud and corruption, and I would withdraw as far as China rather than ever adopt it.[1]

Nicholas successfully bypassed the existing machinery of the Russian government—the Committee of Ministers, the Senate, and State Council—by setting up "His Majesty's Own Chancery," the chief vehicle for the implementation of his personal rule. The Third Department of his Chancery provided his own "political police." Nicholas also displayed a penchant for dealing with major problems by means of secret *ad hoc* committees, and by the appointment of special emissaries to undertake foreign missions. Probably no one worked harder than Nicholas at being an autocrat. He travelled incessantly throughout his Empire on tours of inspection, handed out awards and punishments arbitrarily, and even intervened in the trivial concerns of school discipline, the details of army life, and breaches of morality. His energy approached that of Peter the Great, although it was directed toward disciplinary matters and the maintenance of the *status quo* rather than toward change and modernization.

Landowners and Serfs. After the Decembrist revolt Nicholas I, fearful of another uprising of landowners, took steps to control and to appease them. To protect them from the taint of Western liberalism he greatly restricted their study and travel abroad. On the other hand, he made extensive use of them in the bureaucracy, aided them financially, and provided educational facilities for their children. On the vital issue of serfdom, Nicholas in the spring of 1826 took pains to reassure the landowners by stating that "all talk about freeing the crown peasants from payment of assessments and the landlords'

---

1. P. P. Kohler, ed. and trans., *Journey for Our Time: The Journals of the Marquis de Custine* (New York: Pellegrini & Cudahy, 1951). Many parallels have been drawn between the Russia of Nicholas I as Custine found it and the Russia of Stalin.

peasants and serfs from obeying their masters is baseless rumors." Those responsible for spreading such rumors were threatened with severe punishment. This declaration was read in churches and bazaars throughout Russia. Nicholas' whole attitude toward serfdom was conditioned by his dependence on the gentry to maintain the existing order. The landlords served as his special police agents in rural areas.

In 1839 Count A. Benckendorff, head of the *Gendarmerie,* warned Nicholas that something should be done to forestall a social upheaval of the peasant masses:

> The institution of serfdom is a powder keg beneath the state. I recommend the adoption of measures to ease the sharp controversy between landowners and peasants. One has to begin sometime, and somehow. It is better to start gradually, with caution, than to wait until it comes from below, from the people.

Nicholas I was aware that serfdom was an "evil, palpable and evident to everyone." Revolution, either by the landowners or the serfs, was equally abhorrent to him and he lived in fear of both. However, he had actually confronted the Decembrist revolt from above. Although there were from 556 to 700 peasant uprisings during his reign, 41 before 1830, the Pugachev type of revolt was what he feared most. For Nicholas, change in the existing regime, with all its unknown and incalculable repercussions, spelled greater danger than the existing evil, which he could see and understand. Moreover, he associated concessions to the peasants at the expense of the landowners with demands from the latter for a constitutional regime. Those two conditions had been inseparable issues in the Decembrists' program.

Although from 1826 to 1854 ten separate secret committees assiduously studied the problem of serfdom in one or more of its aspects, the results were far from commensurate with the effort expended. In the interval of peace following the overthrow of Napoleon, the serf population of Russia substantially increased from 9,800,000 males (1816) to 10,872,000 (1835). Their numbers were becoming a source of embarrassment to the landowners, who often could not provide them with land or work. Some landlords, their property already heavily mortgaged to maintain their improved standard of living, favored the emancipation of the serfs without land as the most feasible solution to their own problem. For others, especially for those on the poorer lands of north Russia, the serfs were their only capital. Heinrich Storch, one of Nicholas' tutors in political economy and a disciple of Adam Smith, regarded serfdom as incompatible with Russia's national economic development. Opinion as to the correct solution was sharply divided.

Partial Emancipation. Like his predecessor, Nicholas cautiously left the liberation of the serfs to the discretion of the landowners; he contented himself with the correction of specific abuses, such as the sale of a serf's family to more than one buyer. He lectured the landowners on their mistreatment of the serfs, and also warned of the danger of educating them beyond their station in life. In 1826 serfdom was officially banned in Siberia. In the following year a law forbade the purchase of peasants unless they could be provided with sufficient land to eke out a living. In 1842, following the publication of Gogol's social satire *Dead Souls,* provision was made for the emancipation of serfs by landlords, although they remained "bound" by the terms imposed. Only three landowners, it is said, took advantage of this opportunity, and it remained a dead letter. Serf labor in factories having become unprofitable, in 1840 a law was passed permitting factory owners to liberate their peasants. The peasants of the west Russian provinces in juxtaposition to Poland fared best, probably because Nicholas, who favored a policy of national integration, was less circumspect in dealing with their Polish and Lithuanian landlords. The Baltic Germans were sufficiently powerful in all areas during the reign of Nicholas to prevent any serious inroads on their authority.

General P. D. Kiselev (1788–1872), head of the emperor's new Fifth Department for the management of peasant affairs (1837), worked for eighteen years to improve conditions among peasants on crown lands, and thereby set an example to private landlords. An early advocate of emancipation, his goal was the creation of a well-to-do class of landed, free peasants. The crown peasants during this period numbered over one-third of the agrarian population, or more than 16,000,000 (7,649,000 male souls). Their condition was appreciably improved. Nicholas appeared to be consciously, although over-cautiously, paving the way for eventual emancipation.

All the committees and legislation dealing with serfdom in the reign of Nicholas I failed to produce any radical change in their condition. After 1848 Nicholas practically abandoned even the pretense of social reform. Speransky's codification of Russian law did at least clarify and generalize the various limitations on the landowners' power over their serfs.

Speransky: Digest of Laws. In 1826 Michael Speransky, released from exile by Nicholas, was appointed head of the Commission of Laws which became the Second Department of the emperor's Chancery. Speransky, whom Nicholas termed "the most loyal, reliable, and zealous servant," had "done penance" for past mistakes, and the emperor entrusted to him the reexamination of the Russian legal code, with the object of bringing order out of chaos. Speransky abandoned his earlier project of constructing a new Russian legal system based on the alien Napoleonic Code for the more practical plan of collecting and codifying existing Russian laws from the time of the *Ulozhenie* of Tsar Alexis (1649). This tremendous and vitally important task was accomplished by 1833. The energetic, hard-working Speransky first collected some 30,000 laws and arranged them in chronological order in forty-five bulky volumes. To these were added six separate volumes on the laws issued since 1826 by Nicholas I. On the basis of these findings, a *Digest of the Laws of the Russian Empire* was prepared and issued in 1833 in fifteen volumes, replacing the *Ulozhenie* of Alexis. This code remained in force until 1917. Speransky's extraordinary contribution consisted not so much in reforming the law as in making available and clarifying the existing laws. What Peter the Great, Catherine the Great, and Alexander I had tried in vain to achieve was accomplished in the reign of Nicholas I. This in itself was an important step in the so-called "modernization" of Russia.

Russification of Minorities. The centralized autocracy of Nicholas I was not compatible with freedom for religious and national minorities. Nicholas and his cohorts, who were not race conscious, under the banner of "Orthodoxy and Nationality" purposefully pursued a policy of integration—the assimilation of Poles, Ukrainians, Jews, Caucasians, and others into Russian life. In other words, from a heterogeneous Empire they sought to create one homogeneous nation.

The Jewish population of Russia, confined to the Pale of Settlement by Catherine II in 1791, had remained largely isolated from Russian life, education, and customs. This situation Nicholas sought to change. During his reign some six hundred laws were promulgated concerning the Jews, the object of which was their integration into the national life. In 1827 Jews became subject to active military service, with no further provision for buying exemption through substitutes. Nicholas believed that twenty-five years of compulsory military service, far from home, family, and religious observances, would solve the Jewish problem. The Jewish soldiers would forget their early training and religion and become members of the Orthodox faith. To encourage religious integration, baptized Jews were offered all the rights and privileges of Christians, including a life beyond the Pale. Other measures designed to promote integration included the opening of Russian schools to Jews and permission for them to engage in agricultural pursuits. Some Jewish colonies were established in the provinces of Ekaterinoslav (now Dnepropetrovsk) and Kherson, but the Jews in general did not take kindly to agriculture. Those who did were less subject to discrimination and pogroms in subsequent years.

Other dissenters, such as the Dukhobor and Molokane sects, because of their anti-state proclivities, were viewed by Nicholas as rebels against Orthodoxy. Beginning in 1839 the Dukhobor and Molokane settlements were liquidated. Many sectarians were dispatched to the Transcaucasus and others were sent to Siberia to serve in the armed forces. Nicholas, as was his custom, established a special committee, on which Yuri Samarin and Ivan Aksakov served, to investigate the schismatics and the ever-increasing number of sects. The government continued to carry on a relentless persecution against them, which does not appear to have reduced their numbers, although it increased their hostility to the administration. From 1847 to 1852 the number brought to trial was 26,456.

Education. Unlike Alexander I, Nicholas was never interested in a program of universal education for Russia. He foresaw that an educated public would

The Dukhobors, or spirit wrestlers, the sect to which these women belong, believed that the individual must battle earthly things while he sought the world of the spirit. Because they denied the authority of the civil government and refused military service, they were considered a menace to the state.

resist the regimentation and militarization of the country, which were an essential part of his twenty-five-year plan. Count Benckendorff, chief of the *Gendarmerie,* regarded learning as a poisonous drug, which should be dispensed only by government prescription. Thus education, especially higher education, was consciously restricted to the upper classes, mainly to the nobility, although some members of the *raznotchintsy* (plebeians)—children of rich merchants and lesser bureaucrats—managed to take advantage of the limited facilities available. Children of peasants were not expected to rise above the primary grades of the parish schools, those of the merchants beyond the gymnasia.

Count S. S. Uvarov (1786–1855) served as minister of education from 1833 to 1849. Formerly an advocate of freedom and education, he had adapted himself completely to the new climate of official opinion in Russia by prescribing the erection of "mental dikes" against the spread of subversive ideas among Russian youths. Uvarov devised the triple formula "Orthodoxy, Autocracy, and Nationality," signifying "One Faith, One Ruler, and One Nation," as the basic principles underlying the Russian system of education. In 1835 the primary and secondary schools were removed from the jurisdiction of the universities and placed under the supervision of district curators, a change which did not promote the quality of education. Although the uni-

versities enjoyed some autonomy and academic freedom during the early
years of the reign of Nicholas, they lost it subsequently, especially after 1848.
With the new emphasis on "Nationality," more attention was paid to Russian
language, history, and literature. Michael Pogodin (1800–1875), historian
and journalist, in 1835 became the first professor of Russian history at the
University of Moscow. Uvarov introduced a classical curriculum into the
gymnasia, whose number increased from forty-eight in 1826 to seventy-four in
the 1850's.

Technical education, less dangerous from the ideological standpoint, received special emphasis during this period, with the establishment in St.
Petersburg of a technological institute (1828), a school of law (1835), and a
school of architecture (1842). Agricultural and veterinary schools and
teachers' colleges were founded in various parts of the Empire.

In the final years of unremitting reaction after 1848, when Uvarov himself
became too liberal for the regime, the curriculum was narrowed by the
banning of philosophy and constitutional law. Study abroad for students and
teachers was prohibited. All students were subjected to rigid military training
and discipline. The number of non-scholarship students in each university was
restricted to three hundred. This type of education was intended to graduate
standardized conformists, who could be relied on not to do too much thinking
or to foment radicalism.

The Russian Intelligentsia. Nevertheless, in spite of militarism, censorship,
and stifling intellectual conformity, the Russian intelligentsia, or intellectual
class, dates from this reign. Before Nicholas I, intellectuals were confined to
the nobility, who, because of their background and training, tended on the
whole to remain conservative, content with the established order. The Decembrists, all members of the aristocracy who rejected collaboration with those of
lesser status, were the great exception to the general rule. The opportunities
afforded at first by Nicholas for the education of the *raznotchintsy,* limited as
they were, were promptly grasped. As a result, the intelligentsia was soon
extended to an entirely new class with a totally different background which
made them welcome new and radical ideas. In the 1830's the University of
Moscow included such students as Vissarion Belinsky, later a prominent
critic, Michael Bakunin, the future anarchist, and Alexander Herzen. In the
next decade, many students were stimulated by professors who had been
educated abroad before foreign travel was banned. In subsequent years, the
new intelligentsia manifested more and more revolutionary tendencies.

Slavophiles and Westernizers. During this period, intellectual stimulus was
also found in two opposing theories as to how Russia could best fulfill her
destiny—those of the Slavophiles and Westernizers, each of whom developed
a well-defined ideology, but drafted no political platform. The Slavophiles, vis-
à-vis Europe, were isolationists. Immersed in German romanticism, they
came to believe that Russia possessed its own distinctive national culture and
personality, superior to that of the West. This culture, based on the Orthodox

faith and on tsardom, would eventually supersede European civilization, the offspring of materialism and rationalism. The Slavophiles were traditionalists who deplored the efforts of Peter the Great to modernize and Westernize Russia. The salvation of the country lay, in their estimation, not in imitation of the West but in a return to the old beliefs, ideals, and customs of the pre-Petrine era.

According to A. S. Khomyakov (1804–1860), a leading Slavophile during the reign of Nicholas I, the chief factor in the Russian historical process was not the state as in the West, but the people. In contrast to the West, where absolutism was imposed upon the people, he claimed that in Russia the people created the autocracy and thereby achieved spiritual emancipation from politics. The Russian autocracy, in other words, was an expression of the political asceticism and anarchistic spirit of the Russian people, whose aim was to free themselves from all the obligations of government. Khomyakov believed that the Russian people delegated to the tsar not only their political power but also their authority in ecclesiastical matters. Such a people, he concluded, was messianic in character—a chosen people–whose mission was to found not an empire but a Holy Russia.

Some Slavophiles, including the poet and translator V. A. Zhukovskii (1783–1852), justified the autocracy on the ground that the tsar ruled by the grace of God, by divine right, whereas European rulers governed by the will of the people. The Reformation, in Zhukovskii's opinion, had undermined both divine and human authority. Its legacy was rationalism, pantheism, and atheism. The rationalists rejected the divinity of Christ. The sequel was pantheism, which destroyed the personality of God and resulted in atheism, which denied the existence of God. The revolt against autocracy, according to Zhukovskii, could only lead to democracy, which in its turn spawned socialism and communism. The outcome was the destruction of the family, the very foundation of society. The real source of evil, as Zhukovskii understood it, was not the autocracy of the tsar, but the autocracy of the human mind and the autocracy of the people. It was essential that Russians should ward off these evils through the holy authority of the Orthodox church and divine autocracy, the powers established by God Himself and the only ones befitting a Christian state. It was his conclusion that autocracy supported by God's truth was superior to all paper constitutions.

Although they were closer to "official Nationality" than the Westernizers, not all the Slavophiles were outright reactionaries. Many, especially during the early stages of the movement, stood for civil liberties, freedom of conscience, and the emancipation of the serfs. They idealized the collectivist elements in peasant life rather than the individualism of the West. Other leading Slavophiles of the period were the Kireyevsky brothers, Yuri Samarin, and the Aksakov brothers.

The Westernizers, on the other hand, claimed to be disciples of progress and modernization, the elements which they understood to comprise Europeanization. They favored institutional reform, liberalism, and even socialism. They had nothing good to say about the Russian "dark ages" prior to Peter the Great, and they welcomed change. Lacking the messianic outlook of the Slavophiles, the Westernizers regarded the Orthodox church as a reactionary influence, toadying to despotism.

One of the best rebuttals by a Westernizer of the Slavophile point of view is to be found in the well-known letter of the literary critic Vissarion Belinsky to N. V. Gogol, famous novelist and dramatist, denouncing the latter's *Correspondence with Friends* (1847), which reflected the Slavophile views of Zhukovskii on serfdom, autocracy, and Orthodoxy:

. . . Therefore you have now observed that Russia sees her salvation lies not in mysticism, not in asceticism, not in pietism, but in the achievements of civilization, of education and humanity. Russia does not stand in need of sermons—she has heard plenty of them—but of an awakening among the people of a sense of human dignity, which was for so many centuries trampled in the mire and the dung—and of rights and laws, conforming not to the teaching of the Church, but to common sense and righteousness, and as far as possible strict fulfillment of them. But instead of that Russia presents the horrible spectacle of a country where men traffic in men, without having even that justification which American plantation owners so hypocritically resort to, by asserting that a Negro is not a human being; the spectacle of a country where people do not refer to themselves by their real names but by nicknames: Vankas, Vasskas, Stepkas, Palashkas; the spectacle of a land where there is a complete absence of any guarantees whatsoever of the rights of the individual, his honor or his property, where even the police do not maintain order, but where there exist only huge corporations of sundry bureaucratic thieves and robbers!

The most burning contemporary national issues in Russia now are: the abolition of serfdom, the relaxation of corporal punishment, and the strict execution of at least those laws which already exist. That this is realized even by the Government itself (which is well aware how the landowners mistreat their peasants, and how many of the former die at the hands of the latter every year), is substantiated by its timid and fruitless half measures in favor of our white Negroes and by the comic substitution of a knout with one tail instead of one with three tails. These are the issues with which Russia is so uneasily preoccupied in her apathetic slumber! And at this very time a great writer, who with his marvellously artistic, profoundly realistic creations, was so greatly instrumental in making Russia conscious of herself, making it possible for her to see herself as in a mirror—this writer brings out a book wherein, in the name of Christ and Church, he encourages the barbaric landowner to extract more money from his peasants, cursing their unwashed snouts. . . . And that was not supposed to arouse my indignation? . . .

If you were discovered making an attempt to assassinate me, I would not hate you more than I do because of these shameful lines. And after that you expect people to believe in the sincerity of the purpose of your book! No. If you were actually filled to overflowing with the truth of Christ, and not with the teaching of the Devil, you would have written something altogether different to your agent the landowner. You would have written him that since his peasants are his brothers in Christ, and since a brother cannot be the slave of his brother, the landowner is in duty bound either to give his peasants their freedom, or at least to use their labor as much for their own benefit as possible, realizing that he is in a false position in relation to them. . . .

I am not going to dwell at length on your panegyric about the bonds between the Russian people and their masters. I will say without circumlocution that this panegyric did not meet with sympathy from anyone and has lowered your prestige in the eyes of those who were otherwise your staunch followers. As far as I am concerned, I leave it to your conscience to bask in the contemplation of the divine beauty of autocracy (it is ever so peaceful and profitable for you); only continue to contemplate it prudently from your beautiful, far-off place; for near at hand it is neither beautiful nor safe.

Other leading Westernizers of the time included T. N. Granovsky, A. I. Herzen, and I. S. Turgenev. Although it was the ideas of Westernizers that caught the imagination of the young, both groups were suspect in the reign of Nicholas I and suffered from the rigid censorship.

Economic Expansion. In spite of the desire of the emperor to stop the clock of progress, the forces of change were also at work in the Russian economy during his reign. Russian credit was vastly improved by the sound financial and tariff policies and by the currency reforms of Count Y. F. Kankrin, minister of finance from 1823 to 1844. Russian exports and imports increased substantially during the reign of Nicholas—exports from 75,000,-000 rubles to 230,000,000 (silver), and imports from 52,000,000 to 200,-000,000 rubles (silver). The bulk of Russian exports consisted of grain, especially wheat, and sundry agricultural products, cattle, hides, lumber, and other raw materials. Exports of lumber from 1815 to 1850 advanced more than 100 per cent. Russian importation of machinery increased rapidly during the same period, as did that of woolen textiles.

Inside Russia, silk, cotton, and linen factories increased to meet the demands of the domestic market; by 1850 there were 492 cloth factories. In the first half of the nineteenth century, the *kustarny* (household) industry greatly expanded. Some workers, like Savva Morozov, who began as a serf, prospered sufficiently to purchase their freedom. Even as early as 1825, 54 per cent of Russian laborers in industry were "free." An edict of 1840 enabled owners of "possessional" factories (those operating with serf labor) to emancipate their workers, on the ground that the growth of industrial capitalism and serfdom were not compatible. Sugar was an important new industry in Russia in the first half of the century. The first sugar foundry had been established in 1802. By 1845 there were already 206 foundries, with a capacity production of 484,000 *puds* (1 pud = 38 pounds). These had increased by 1848 to about 340 foundries, producing 900,000,000 *puds.*

In the fields of transportation and communications, the signs of change were already apparent. The first Russian railroad, a sixteen-mile private venture, was completed from St. Petersburg to Tsarskoe Selo in 1838. A state-financed railroad, from St. Petersburg to Moscow, was begun in 1842 and completed by slave labor in 1850 at a cost of 100,000,000 rubles. In 1851 telegraph communication was established between the two capitals. Permission was given in 1843 for the operation of steamships on all Russian rivers. In general, however, Russian transportation and communications, as compared with Western Europe, remained backward. The lack of good roads, railroads, and steamship lines proved to be an important factor in the defeat of Russia in the Crimean War.

Autocrat or Liberal? There are two schools of thought in regard to the domestic policies of Nicholas I. One holds that he shared the liberal views of his brother Alexander I and wished to continue the reforms already inaugurated, especially those on behalf of the serfs. He was prevented from so doing, however, by circumstances. The other school contends that Nicholas was a confirmed autocrat, opposed to any change on the ground that it would upset the *status quo* in Russian society. Those changes that he did authorize were introduced under pressure, because revolution might occur unless some steps were taken from above to avert it. Unlike Peter the Great, Nicholas thought that Russia had a glorious past. Nor did he make any apologies for the Russian present. With the preservation of "Orthodoxy, Autocracy, and Nationality," he foresaw a magnificent Russian future. The point of view of Nicholas and those who followed his lead was perhaps best summed up by Count Benckendorff, chief of his *Gendarmerie:*

> Le passé de la Russie a été admirable; son présent est plus que magnifique; quant à son avenir il est au delà de tout ce que l'imagination la plus hardie se peut figurer.

FOREIGN POLICY

In the field of foreign policy, Nicholas I had at least two main objectives: (1) a firm determination to contain liberalism and democracy in Europe; (2) acquisition of the Dardanelles and Constantinople.

To achieve the first objective, Nicholas worked through the Holy Alliance, for which his extensive army provided the "teeth." He considered essential the preservation intact of the European settlement established in 1815 under the guidance of his brother Alexander I. In Europe Nicholas was careful not to infringe on that settlement by extending Russian boundaries to the West. In his stand for the *status quo,* he was as consistent as in his pursuit of reaction at home. What he expected to achieve by autocracy inside Russia, he hoped to realize through support of legitimism abroad. The long tenure of K. V. Nesselrode as foreign minister helped to provide continuity in Russian foreign policy during his reign. In reality, however, Nicholas I was his own foreign minister.

As the ally of legitimism, Nicholas was seriously disturbed by the rising tide of liberalism and nationalism in Western Europe. The Revolution of 1830 in France overthrew the regime of Louis XVIII, established after the fall of Napoleon. Another revolution resulted in the independence of Belgium from Holland. Nicholas was prepared to intervene by the dispatch of Russian armed forces. He probably would have done so, but Louis Philippe of France and the new Belgian regime received prompt recognition in the West, and Prussia and Austria refused to collaborate with him. He had also been diverted by the Polish Revolution nearer home.

Convention of Berlin. After this manifestation of disunity in the Concert of Europe, Nicholas aligned Russia more closely with Austria and Prussia to checkmate the designs of France and England, both out of step with the Holy Alliance. By the Convention of Berlin in 1833 the three monarchs agreed to come to one another's aid when confronted by internal trouble or external threat. The Hapsburgs and the Hohenzollerns still regarded the Romanovs as the guarantor of the existing European system and of their way of life. One factor, of course, which helped to perpetuate the alliance of the three East European monarchies was their common interest in the preservation of what amounted to a fourth Polish partition at the Congress of Vienna in 1814.[2] In 1836 Nicholas actually reached an agreement with the Hapsburgs for the incorporation of the free Polish city of Cracow into Austria, an agreement implemented in 1846.

"Gendarme of Europe." The climax of the Russian policy of intervention came in 1848, when virtually all Europe, except England and Russia, was beset by revolution. When Louis Philippe of France was overthrown, Nicholas assembled from 300,000 to 400,000 troops with the intent of marching to the Rhine. In July, 1848, he did intervene in Moldavia and Wallachia on behalf of the Turks to crush the Rumanian national movement. He provided diplomatic and financial aid to the beleaguered Hapsburgs through a loan of six million rubles to bring about the restoration of Austrian power in Italy. In 1849, following the revolt in Hungary led by Louis Kossuth, which received some support from dissident Poles, Nicholas sent a Russian force of about 200,000 men under General Paskevitch to suppress the uprising. This costly episode, which calls to mind Soviet intervention in Hungary in 1956, was extremely unpopular not only in Europe but even in Russia. Nicholas was

---

2. In this partition, Prussia kept Poznan and Danzig, Austria held Galicia, and Cracow was made a free city. The rest of Poland became a kingdom in Russian hands.

seriously disturbed by the surrender of the Prussian king, Frederick William
IV, to the revolutionaries, and by his acceptance of a constitution, albeit a
highly conservative one. In 1850 he stepped in to prevent Prussia from seizing
Schleswig-Holstein from Austria, thereby postponing a major upset of the
Vienna settlement, which would have been caused by the reorganization of
Germany.

In 1848 Nicholas earned his reputation as "the gendarme of Europe." In
general, Russian intervention proved to be an important, if temporary factor,
in the restoration of the *status quo*. With the collapse of the revolutions of
1848–1849, the position of Russia appeared on the surface to be impregnable. Nicholas was satisfied not only because Russia had avoided revolution,
but also because liberal groups and nationalist aspirations had been crushed
in Central Europe. In 1850 on the twenty-fifth anniversary of his accession to
the throne, Nesselrode assured the emperor that the position of Russia was
better than it had been since 1814. The dikes erected against liberalism and
nationalism during more than thirty years of reaction, however, produced in
1848 the Communist Manifesto of Karl Marx.

War with Persia, 1825–1828. Wars in the Near and Middle East broke out
shortly after the accession of Nicholas I. The first of these was with Persia,
where English officers had entered the service of the shah, and the mullahs

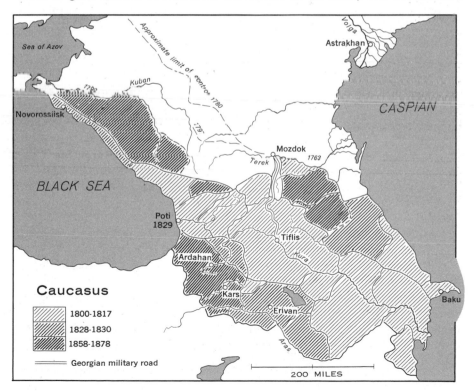

preached a holy war against Russia. This war was a sequel to that conducted by Alexander I from 1804 to 1813. The Persian forces, which initiated the conflict, retreated before the army of General Paskevitch, who seized the important stronghold of Yerevan, crossed the Araxes, and proceeded to march on Teheran, the capital. Alarmed by the Persian debacle, the shah, who had failed to receive the expected aid from England, in 1828 hastened to conclude the Treaty of Turkmantchay; the Russians acquired the left bank of the Araxes and a large part of Armenia, including Yerevan. In addition Persia paid a huge indemnity of thirty-six million rubles, abandoned her claim to the Caucasus, and conceded to Russia the exclusive right to maintain a navy in the Caspian Sea. Nicholas, true to his respect for legitimacy, refused to support a Persian plot for the overthrow of the Kajar dynasty.

Shamyl and the Muridist Revolution, 1829–1859. Almost immediately the Muridist revolution, a religious movement, broke out among the Muslim mountaineers in the Caucasus. Under the leadership of able imams and sheiks, the best known of whom were Kazi-Mullah, who was killed in 1831, and Shamyl (1797–1871), who was ultimately captured by the Russians in 1859, the revolutionaries maintained a long and stubborn resistance and were not finally subdued until the reign of Alexander II.

Shamyl, the dedicated Avar prophet and warrior, reached the zenith of his power and prestige in the Caucasus between 1845 and 1850. He was the last of the Caucasian "Mohicans." Indeed, the hopeless struggle between the Caucasian tribes and religious sects, on the one hand, and the Russians on the other, had much in common with the resistance of the North American Indians to the westward migration of the white man. Based on Sufism[3] and non-warlike in its origins, Muridism recognized three aspects of Islam; the Shariat (the law), Tarikat (the Path) and Hakikat (the Truth). Shamyl, the austere Muridist leader who revived and imposed the Shariat on the entire Caucasus, regarded himself as Allah's Second Prophet and as Allah's chosen mouthpiece on earth. Convinced of his divine mission, he transformed Muridism into a Holy War (Ghazavat) under the slogan, "Death to the Giaour [Russians, or any infidels]!" Paradise was the prize for all followers killed in battle. For him, the Russians were like poisonous snakes crawling across the Moughan steppe.

During the Crimean War (1853–1856), the Russian defeat at Sevastopol, which prevented the realization of Russian dreams of the acquisition of Constantinople from the Turks, diverted the full fury of the Russian crusade toward the Islamic peoples of the Caucasus and Central Asia. For Nicholas I, however, and his immediate successors, Constantinople was the stepping stone to the erection of the cross over the crescent at Jerusalem. In the Caucasus, the Russian crusade confronted a counter-crusade to establish the supremacy of the crescent over the cross. Strictly speaking, Shamyl's Murid

---

3. The Sufists were an order of Muslim pantheistic mystics that emerged after the Mongol overthrow of the Baghdad Caliphate in 1258.

Wars were but the final climax of Russian efforts to conquer the Caucasus, which persisted for 137 years, from 1722 to 1859, the year of Shamyl's dramatic surrender.

Russo-Turkish War, 1828–1829. Scarcely had peace been concluded with Persia in 1828 than Russia was again involved in war, this time with the Ottoman Empire. This conflict grew out of the Greek struggle (1821–1829) for independence from Turkey. Nicholas I, who stood for the *status quo* in Western Europe, by no means applied the same principle to Turkey and the Balkans. The ruthless campaign of the Sultan's vassal, Ibrahim Pasha of Egypt, against the Greeks had aroused popular opinion throughout Europe. This led to joint intervention on the part of England, France, and Russia to enforce a diplomatic settlement, and when that failed, their combined fleets destroyed a Turko-Egyptian squadron in the Battle of Navarino in 1827. The same year, the sultan aroused the righteous wrath of Nicholas I by proclaiming the Russian government "an irreconcilable foe of the Ottoman Empire." Encouraged by the success of the joint action at Navarino, Nicholas appears to have concluded that England and France would give him a free hand against the Turks. Acting unilaterally in 1828, he declared war on Turkey, and the Russian army, supported by the Serbs, almost reached Constantinople.

In view of the Turkish debacle, Nicholas in 1829 appointed a special committee, headed by Count V. Kochubey and including Foreign Minister Nesselrode, to consider what action should be taken. It was this committee's considered opinion, in which Nicholas concurred, that the advantages of the preservation of a weak Ottoman Empire in Europe, subject to Russian influence, outweighed the advantages of dismemberment. Moreover, such a policy would prevent open conflict with England. On this basis, the victorious Russians settled for what was then generally considered a moderate peace.

Treaty of Adrianople. The Treaty of Adrianople, which brought the war to a close in September, 1829, was highly favorable to Russia and marked an important stage in the weakening of the Ottoman Empire. By its terms Russia gained possession of the mouth of the Danube and the coast of the Black Sea to Poti. Turkey also acceded to Russia's demand for a protectorate over Orthodox peoples living in Turkish territories and granted commercial privileges to Russian subjects in the same regions. In addition to her other concessions to Russia, Turkey agreed to recognize the independence of the Greeks (1830) and to open the Bosphorus and Dardanelles to Russian merchant ships. Certain dependencies of Turkey, namely, Moldavia, Wallachia, Serbia, and the principalities of the Danube, were granted autonomy under Turkish suzerainty.

Intervention in the Near East, 1833. Nicholas might have exacted far more by the Treaty of Adrianople, but he preferred to moderate his demands and pursue a policy of expansion by peaceful penetration, in conformity with the tactics of Catherine II in the Middle and Far East and those of Paul in the

Near East. Thus, when Mehemet Ali, the pasha of Egypt, began hostilities against the sultan, Nicholas managed to secure from the reluctant Porte an invitation to send 10,000 Russian troops to Asia Minor to protect Constantinople and the Straits. In Mehemet Ali's war to establish an Arabic Empire comprised of Egypt, Abyssinia, Turkey, and Syria, Nicholas saw an unwelcome manifestation of the revolutionary spirit against a legitimate ruler. The Egyptian pasha was ordered to render homage to his sovereign, the sultan.

Treaty of Unkiar Skelessi. The unusual example of a Russian expeditionary force at the Bosphorus, ostensibly to support the sultan in line with the precedent set by the Emperor Paul in 1799, startled all Europe. There is reason to believe that Nicholas expected to establish a Russian base on the Bosphorus.[4] Instead, by the Treaty of Unkiar Skelessi (Iskelesi), signed July 8, 1833, the sultan agreed to an eight-year mutual aid pact with Russia. A secret clause released the Turks from going to the assistance of Russia in exchange for a commitment to close the Straits to the warships of all foreign powers. Although this provision, in regard to the closure of the Straits, has been interpreted in a variety of ways, the Soviet *Diplomatic Dictionary* still contends that it was applicable "upon the demand of Russia." A literal interpretation of the mutual-aid terms seemed to indicate that although the Russians avoided any guarantee of the territorial integrity of Turkey, in the event of an international crisis Turkey was obligated to turn first to Russia for assistance. In any event, the emperor's foreign minister, Nesselrode, assumed that Russia had obtained for the future a prior right of intervention at the Straits, which would enable her armed forces to be on hand first, and in the greatest strength, either to preserve the Ottoman Empire or to preside over its dissolution. Although the advantages of this treaty to Russia were perhaps more potential than actual, the implementation of its terms would have made a Russian satellite of the Ottoman Empire, with Russia in control of the Straits.

European Reactions. The unilateral policy of Nicholas in regard to Turkey in 1828 and 1833 aroused the fear of Austria and the antagonism of England and France. In spite of the Holy Alliance, Austria found herself increasingly at odds with Russia over the Christian principalities in the Balkans as a result of the Treaty of Adrianople. Since the reign of Catherine II, England had watched, with increasing concern, the expansion of Russia at the expense of Turkey, Persia, and Afghanistan along the vital route to India. With the appointment of Viscount Palmerston as foreign secretary in 1830, Anglo-Russian relations began to deteriorate rapidly. France, as the ally of Mehemet Ali, had her own reasons for discomfiture in regard to Russian policy toward Turkey. The groundwork was being laid for the formation of an anti-Russian bloc, which was soon to challenge Russia in the Crimean War.

---

4. Philip E. Mosely, *Russian Diplomacy and the Opening of the Eastern Question in 1838 and 1839* (Cambridge, Mass.: Harvard University Press, 1934), pp. 22–23.

In order to preserve a united front of the conservative powers—Austria, Prussia, and Russia—against France and England, and thereby prevent the formation of an anti-Russian bloc, at Münchengrätz on September 18, 1833, and by the subsequent Berlin Convention of October 15, Nicholas sought and reached an understanding with Austria in regard to the preservation of the Ottoman Empire in the Near East. Having voluntarily limited their freedom of action in the Balkans, the Russians turned their attention to Persia and Afghanistan. In 1837 they established Russian diplomatic relations with Kabul for the first time. The following year they engineered a Persian-Afghan alliance to strengthen their strategic and economic position in the Middle East against England, and thereby paved the way for the first Anglo-Afghan War (1838–1842). The revival in 1838 of Mehemet Ali's pretensions against the sultan soon engaged the attention of all the major powers of Europe.

London Convention and Treaty of London. In 1839 Nicholas, envisaging an opportunity to collaborate with England in the solution of the Turkish problem, agreed to let the objectionable Treaty of Unkiar Skelessi lapse. In 1840, in what was ostensibly a move to isolate France, the four great powers—Russia, Prussia, England, and Austria—signed the London Convention, which defined the position of Mehemet Ali in the Ottoman Empire and closed the Straits of the Bosphorus and Dardanelles to warships of all foreign powers in time of peace. These terms were confirmed by the Treaty of London in 1841, in which France participated. Thus, an international guarantee of the Ottoman Empire by the five great powers replaced the unilateral guarantee by Nicholas in 1833. In spite of his loss of unilateral freedom of action in regard to the Straits and Turkey, Nicholas appeared satisfied with the results, possibly because they insured the *status quo* against France and Mehemet Ali, and a workable arrangement with the British in the eastern Mediterranean.

Still seeking an understanding with England on the Near East, Nicholas visited London in person in 1844. His discussions with Lord Aberdeen on the future of Turkey, which Nicholas labelled "the sick man of Europe," were summed up by Nesselrode in an official memorandum, certified by the British to be accurate. This discussion emphasized the desirability of preserving the Ottoman Empire as long as possible, but implied an understanding between England and Russia if it should become necessary to proceed with dismemberment of Turkey. No doubt unaccustomed to British affirmations of "agreement in principle" as a matter of courtesy, Nicholas left London with the conviction that he had reached a firm understanding with England on a matter which the British regarded as a mere exchange of views. The complete suppression of the revolutions of 1848 in Europe apparently increased the self-assurance of the emperor and made him more arrogant. Certain that he would encounter no resistance from Austria and Prussia because of the Münchengrätz discussions, or from England as a result of his visit to London, Nicholas soon had occasion to intervene once again in the affairs of the Ottoman Empire—intervention which led to the Crimean War.

Crimean War, 1853–1856. The immediate cause of the Crimean War grew out of the efforts of Napoleon III of France to strengthen French influence and prestige in the Near East, particularly in the Holy Land. He demanded and obtained from Turkey concessions for Roman Catholics living in the Holy Land. He also obtained for them possession of the keys of the Church of Bethlehem, which by the Treaty of Kuchuk-Kainardji (1774) had been assigned to the keeping of the Orthodox church. Nicholas reacted promptly and energetically. In February, 1853, Prince Menshikov, his ambassador extraordinary, arrived in Constantinople and in high-handed fashion demanded the removal of the Turkish minister of foreign affairs because of his action in regard to the Holy Places. To his successor, Menshikov presented a series of Russian secret demands which would have made of Turkey another Danubian principality.

The Russians demanded a reaffirmation and clarification of the terms of the treaties of 1774 and 1829, which established the Russian right of protection of Orthodox Christians in the Ottoman Empire. This was now interpreted, however, as giving the emperor control of the Orthodox church in Turkey and making nine million Orthodox Christians there subjects of the tsar of Russia. Had the sultan demanded the right to protect the Kazan Tatars inside Russia, the Russians would have given an unequivocal denial. The sultan, however, agreed to issue a *firman,* solemnly reaffirming all the rights and privileges of the Orthodox church in Turkey, provided his Orthodox subjects remained under his jurisdiction. Since neither side would compromise on this point, Menshikov broke off diplomatic relations and Russia thereupon occupied the Danubian principalities.

When it became apparent that, contrary to expectations, Russian policy was vigorously opposed by England and even by Austria, Nicholas made a valiant effort to avert war by withdrawing from the Danubian principalities. The sultan, however, encouraged by Lord Stratford de Redcliffe (Stratford Canning), the English ambassador in Constantinople, to believe that English and French aid would be forthcoming, declared war on Russia on October 1, 1853.

Russia's first move was to dispatch Russian warships to Sinope, where a Turkish squadron was destroyed. Anglo-French naval forces entered the Black Sea, and after a futile effort to achieve a diplomatic settlement at Vienna, England and France declared war on Russia on March 27, 1854. They were later joined by the ambitious king of Sardinia. Austria and Prussia, from whom Nicholas expected a display of friendship, preserved a hostile neutrality. Russia was thus left alone to face an enemy alignment of the chief powers of Western Europe. In September, 1854, the allied forces landed in the Crimea near Eupatoria and laid siege to Sevastopol. After a historic siege, which lasted almost a year, the city surrendered. Nicholas I did not live to witness its downfall, for he died on March 2, 1855. Rumors spread that he committed suicide because he was unable to face the collapse of Russian military power and the downfall of his system at home and abroad. Peace was concluded in 1856 by his son Alexander II, under the terms of the Treaty of Paris.

The Crimean War provided a startling revelation of the backwardness of Russian military and naval equipment and the lack of adequate transportation and communication facilities. Even good maps of the Crimean peninsula were unavailable. The Russian fleet, still predominantly a sailing fleet, confronted the ironclad British and French warships run by steam, whose guns had a range double that of the Russian shore batteries. Unlike the British and French, however, the Russians not only fought in the Crimea, but had to maintain other fronts in the Caucasus against the Muridists, and on the Baltic, while substantial forces were immobilized throughout the war on the Austrian frontier. In the Pacific, units of the Anglo-French fleets attacked the Russian port of Petropavlovsk on the Kamchatka Peninsula in 1854. In spite of this "encirclement," Russian forces won a notable victory against the Turks at Kars in Asia, following the fall of Sevastopol. In the final analysis, the Crimean War afforded a demonstration of the ineffectiveness of naval power without the backing of huge armies, when pitted against a great land power. Anglo-French military forces never penetrated more than a few miles beyond the Crimean coast. Leo Tolstoy, in his *Sevastopol* sketches, has provided an interesting and revealing first-hand account of the Crimean engagement.

All the belligerents suffered heavily in the Crimean War, although the Russian loss of 250,000 men was the greatest. French losses amounted to 80,000 and the English to 22,000. The name of Florence Nightingale is ordinarily associated with the care of the wounded in the Crimea. Less well known is the record of the famous Russian surgeon, Nicholas Pirogov (1810–1881), who did much to develop antiseptic surgery in the field, to establish first-aid stations behind the Russian lines, and to organize an order of nursing sisters to tend the wounded. Darya Sevastopolskaya, one of these nurses, became as famous in Russian annals as Florence Nightingale in England.

Treaty of Paris. The Treaty of Paris (1856) destroyed the results of two hundred years of tsarist effort in the Near East. Russia retained Sevastopol, but lost control of the Black Sea. She was likewise forced to surrender her exclusive protectorate over Orthodox Christians in the Ottoman Empire, and to accept multilateral responsibility on the part of the great powers for the welfare of Christians in Turkish lands. The loss of southern Bessarabia also excluded Russia from the mouth of the Danube. In addition the Bosphorus and the Dardanelles were closed to the armed fleets of all nations. Thus, the military prestige which Russia had built up through the victories of Suvorov and Kutuzov, and the influence she had exerted throughout Europe in the first half of the nineteenth century, were sacrificed in the Crimea. The Treaty of

Paris marked the beginning of the end of tsarist expansion in Europe. More important still, Russia was isolated from the Concert of Europe during the years following 1856, when the balance of power in the West was completely upset by the rise of the German and Italian national states at Hapsburg expense.

Aftermath of Crimean War. Although the Crimean War marked the end of an era in Russian foreign policy, it by no means put an end to Russian territorial expansion. Holding more than one thousand miles of Black Sea coastline, it was hardly to be expected that Russia would permanently accept the unrealistic provision of the Treaty of Paris that banned her fleet from that sea and forbade the fortification of the shoreline. Russians likewise considered intolerable their exclusion from the mouth of the Danube. Alexander II merely awaited a favorable opportunity to dispose of these "two nightmares."

Evidence that Russia had not abandoned her long-term goals in the Near East as a result of the Crimean War was furnished by an ambitious scheme emanating from the Grand Duke Constantine Nikolayevitch, younger brother of Alexander II, for the development of a Russian merchant marine in the Black Sea and Mediterranean, and for the revival of the Russian pilgrim trek to Palestine.[5] Having attributed Russia's defeat, in part, to Allied naval superiority and to the efficiency of Anglo-French supply services, the navy-minded grand duke clearly hoped to remedy Russia's backwardness in this respect and, at the same time, to obviate the restrictions imposed upon the country by the Crimean settlement. The Russian Steam Navigation Company founded in 1856, comprised of vessels easily convertible to military purposes, was never in a position to compete seriously with Austrian and French lines in the Mediterranean, but it did serve a useful purpose in the Black Sea. In the Russo-Turkish War of 1879, its ships were used to transport Russian troops to the Ottoman Empire. This step in the direction of Russian sea power and the fairly elaborate provisions made for the care of Russian pilgrims in Palestine, including hostels, a hospital, and churches, amounted to economic and cultural penetration of the Turkish Empire which was designed to pave the way for eventual political intervention.

In the final analysis, however, Anglo-French success in blocking Russian expansion in the Mediterranean in 1856 merely deflected the tsarist program of expansion to the Middle and Far East, with the result that England, in particular, soon had even greater reason to fear Russian designs on India. Within the next twenty years Russia carved out a new Asian Empire, which from the strategic point of view constituted a roundabout route to Constantinople.

5. W. E. Mosse, "Russia and the Levant, 1856–1862: Grand Duke Constantine Nicolaevich and the Russian Steam Navigation Company," *Journal of Modern History,* XXVI (No. 1, March 1954), pp. 39–48.

7

Alexander II: Liberator and Reformer, 1855-1881

ALTHOUGH NICHOLAS I was a confirmed autocrat, he trained his son Alexander in the event of emergency to adopt new methods essential to the preservation of the existing regime. Alexander II, who was thirty-seven years of age when he came to the throne, was prepared, first and foremost, to be a military disciplinarian. This narrow regimentation was leavened somewhat, however, by his tutor, the poet Zhukovsky, who warned that Alexander as emperor would not only command armies but make laws to uplift his people, and for this purpose a broader and more enlightened education was required. The climate of opinion under Nicholas I militated against a liberal education. However, Alexander did receive some instruction from Speransky on the laws of the Russian Empire and from Kankrin on its finances. It stands to reason that he must have learned from these able ministers that changes were indispensable to avert the rising tide of revolution from below. Nevertheless, to all intents and purposes, Alexander, as heir apparent, remained the friend of the landowners and the champion of their rights and privileges. To alienate them might have imperilled his chances of accession to the throne.

Before his death, Nicholas I was aware that his twenty-five year program for the preservation of the autocratic regime and the empire had failed. As demonstrated by the Crimean War, the results of all his regimentation, reaction, and militarization were far from commensurate with the sacrifices entailed. In the words of Samarin, a prominent Slavophile, the Russians had collapsed "not before the forces of the Western Alliance, but as a result of our own internal weakness." The emperor's legacy to Alexander is strongly reminiscent of Boris Godunov's legacy to his son, as presented in Alexander Pushkin's famous drama, censored in person by Nicholas I. Although the Russian poet put the words in the mouth of Boris Godunov, he was no doubt speaking in reality to Nicholas, coaching him how to train his son:

> Of late I have been driven to restore
> Bans, executions—These thou canst rescind;
> And they will bless thee, as they blessed thy uncle
> When he succeeded to the Terrible.

Emancipation of the Serfs

Thus Alexander II, seeking to relieve the internal tensions which accompanied a costly war and military defeat, even before peace was declared made minor concessions which aroused Russian hopes that a new day was dawning. The surviving Decembrists of 1825, some Petrashevists, and Polish revolutionaries of the 1830's were amnestied. Limitations on the number of university students and the ban on foreign travel were lifted. In an open letter to the emperor, published in his new review, *The Polar Star,* which was circulated surreptitiously in Russia, Alexander Herzen called for freedom of the press, abolition of corporal punishment, and emancipation of the serfs.

Serfdom. As yet, however, Alexander showed no intent of abolishing serfdom. The first circular issued by his minister of the interior, Count Sergei Lanskoy (1787–1862) on August 28 (O.S.), 1855, appeared to confirm in full the rights of the *dvorianstvo.* In his Manifesto of March 19, 1856, announcing the end of the Crimean War, Alexander minimized the military losses, implying that they would be outweighed by the blessings of peace, which would bring substantial benefits to the people, including equal justice and protection for all. This message, although it made no explicit reference to the foremost problem in Russia, aroused expectations everywhere that emancipation would be forthcoming. Already the climate was changing, the censorship was relaxed, and Russians looked forward, as they had at the accession of Alexander I, to an era of change and progress. "Whoever was not alive in Russia in 1856," said Leo Tolstoy, "does not know what life is."

At the close of the Crimean War in 1856, the population of Russia was in the neighborhood of 70,000,000, of whom approximately 47,000,000 continued to exist under some form of serfdom. These included about 20,000,000 crown peasants, free in all but name, who had become dependents of the state by the process of redemption (see page 110). There were 4,700,000 peasants on appanages, or *udyely,* who largely managed their own affairs in accordance with tradition in their own communities. The cancerous sore in the system of serfdom lay in the ownership by individual landlords of some 22,400,000 peasants, of whom about 1,400,000 were lowly house serfs (*dvorovie* or *kholopy*). The solution of this problem was of crucial importance.

Fears of Revolt. The Crimean War undoubtedly accelerated the internal changes for which Catherine II, Alexander I, and Nicholas I, through their numerous committees to study agrarian problems, had laid some foundation. There is every indication that the motivating factor underlying emancipation was fear of revolution from below. Between 1801 and 1861 there were reported to be 1,467 peasants' uprisings in Russia, 474 of which occurred after the accession of Alexander II. Called upon to reassure the Moscow nobility of the perpetuation of their existing rights and privileges, Alexander bluntly informed them on March 30, 1856, that changes must come, since it was "better that serfdom should be abolished from above than from below"—the very statement Radishchev had put in the mouth of his imaginary tsar seventy years earlier.

Some members of the Russian nobility were prepared to sacrifice their own economic well being for security. The Crimean War had accentuated their fears that the suppressed peasantry might join forces with an enemy invader to put an end to serfdom. In general, however, Alexander's warning to the Moscow nobility, news of which spread like wildfire throughout the country, elicited no important response from the landlords. Even when they were convinced that serfdom was economically unprofitable and incompatible with up-to-date agricultural techniques, the landowners scarcely knew where to begin. Those who secured a profitable income from serfs working under the *obrok* system in factories or at some trade found it to their advantage to resist any change. Most landowners were concerned about the compensation they would receive for the loss of serf labor and land. Without compensation, they faced destitution.

Preparation for Emancipation. Since the landowners failed to take the initiative, Alexander in January, 1857, appointed a committee of high bureaucrats, who were also landowners, to draft the basic principles of emancipation. After further prodding by the emperor this committee, which set no deadline for action, recommended that the emancipation be accomplished in three main stages: first, that information be collected; second, that a period of transition should follow; and third, that the system of serfdom should be liquidated.

In October, 1857, V. A. Nazimov, governor-general of the Lithuanian province of Vilna, Grodno, and Kovno, requested permission to free the serfs of that area, without land. This solution was popular with many landlords who hoped to retain their property intact. Nevertheless Alexander vetoed any program, comparable to that carried out in the Baltic provinces, 1816–1819, which would have created throughout Russia a vast landless proletariat.

The Imperial Rescript of November 20, 1857, which constituted Alexander's reply to Nazimov, forecast some of the main provisions of the emancipation edict of 1861. It called for the establishment of a committee to draft plans for emancipation; recognized the landowners' possession of the land; recommended that peasants continue to occupy their homesteads while provision was made for purchase; insisted that peasants be provided with enough land to make a living; proposed that the peasants be organized in communes (*mirs*) instead of becoming private owners; implied that the landowners would retain police powers; and that provision should be made for the collection of taxes from the peasantry. For their guidance and emulation, copies of this rescript and of a subsequent one to the governor-general of St. Petersburg *guberniya* were sent to all provincial governors and marshals of the nobility. The landowners sensed that the die was cast and that some action must be forthcoming.

In 1858, forty-eight provincial committees were elected, with a total of 1,377 members, to draft recommendations for the conditions of emancipation. Alexander had already demonstrated that he had no intention of abolishing serfdom solely by fiat. He needed the support of the landowners for this purpose, which his father had never succeeded in getting, and he soon proved himself to be a first-class campaigner. Anticipating that they would, as heretofore, stall or even sabotage the project, Alexander literally "stumped" the northern and central *guberniyas* in a supreme effort to rally their support. At times he electrified his audience, practically convincing them that they were the crusaders in a holy cause prodding him to take action, instead of the reverse. He appealed to their fears, never far beneath the surface, of another Pugachev Revolt; to their reason, by emphasizing serfdom's responsibility for Russia's economic backwardness; and to their patriotism, which demanded great sacrifices for their country. These rallies, which ended with a resounding rendition of the national anthem, even if they failed to produce unanimity in subsequent sessions, nevertheless set the stage for positive consideration of the problem of serfdom. To those committees he could not visit in person, Alexander sent quantities of literature for their education and guidance.

Issues. Although there were wide differences of opinion on important issues—including the amount of land essential for serfs to eke out a living, the continuation of the *obrok* and *barshchina,* the size of redemption payments, and so on—not one of the 1,377 members of the provincial committees came out in defense of the old order. Times had changed since 1842, when only three landowners responded to the edict of Nicholas I, permitting them to free their peasants with land on the basis of agreements reached in common. There were protests, warnings of disaster to come, and efforts to obviate the disadvantages of emancipation, but there were also indications of a readiness to make sacrifices. Sir Donald Mackenzie Wallace, an acute observer of Russian conditions who visited Russia following the emancipation, found that many landowners regarded themselves "as the self-sacrificing victims of a great and necessary patriotic reform."[1]

As might be expected, Russian intellectuals hailed with joy these signs of emancipation to come. The reading public, including Alexander, according to his own admission, had already been profoundly impressed by the publication in 1852 of *The Memoirs of a Sportsman* by Ivan Turgenev. This series of apparently harmless sketches, depicting with artistry, insight, and objectivity the plight of Russian serfs oppressed by greedy, often vulgar, shallow masters, aroused the Russian conscience and prepared men's minds for emancipation. Alexander Herzen, in his new periodical, *Kolokol* (*The Bell*), first published

1. Sir Donald Mackenzie Wallace, *Russia on the Eve of War and Revolution,* ed. by Cyril E. Black (New York: Vintage Books, 1961), p. 162.

on July 1, 1857, jubilantly welcomed the preparations for the liberation of the serfs, with the headline: "Thou hast conquered, Galilean!" It was not long, however, before Herzen, Nikolai Chernyshevsky (1828–1889), and other Russian literary critics were levelling sharp criticism at the proposed terms of emancipation.

Among the peasants, rumor was rife, although every effort was made officially to preserve secrecy as to the terms of their liberation. There was increasing tension and restlessness among them. Figures on peasant uprisings during these years vary, depending on whether the source was the Ministry of the Interior, the Third Division, or local records. Eighty-six disturbances were reported in 1858, 90 in 1859, and 108 in 1860. During the Pugachev Revolt, 1773–1775, the crucial issue for the peasant was his personal freedom from his landlord. In the reign of Alexander II, however, when many landlords were prepared to free them *from* the land, the peasants were determined to secure freedom *with* land. The plight of peasants already freed without land was well known. In March, 1858, when a landowner by the name of Izvekov from Orlov *guberniya* tried to free his peasants without land, they refused to accept under these conditions. The problem of land continued to dominate the peasant issue at least until 1917.

Emancipation Edict. In January, 1858, Alexander II transformed his earlier committee into the Main Committee for Peasant Affairs and authorized it to review the reports now being submitted from the provinces. Under the chairmanship of General Ya. I. Rostovtsev (1803–1860), who had made a special study of German experience on emancipation, two editing commissions were set up, composed of equal numbers of landlords and bureaucrats, to edit the proposals and prepare the emancipation edict. N. A. Miliutin, the nephew of Count Kiselev, who had served Nicholas I as his agent for peasant affairs, now deputy minister of the interior, was the guiding spirit of the government's revised program. The heart of this program was freedom for the peasant with land, to be redeemed with government aid; a short period of transition for the perfection of arrangements, during which the peasants were to continue to fulfill their obligations to their landlords; and the organization of peasant communes.

After seventeen months of arduous and continuous labor, during which Rostovtsev died of overwork and was succeeded by Count Panin, the emancipation draft was ready by October, 1860. It bridged the Main Committee, not without a struggle but without significant change. The Imperial Council, however, added a provision which proved to be a stumbling block to peasant self-sufficiency in the years to come. Landowners, willing to accept the cancellation of all further peasant obligations, were allowed to provide only one-quarter of the land required by law. In anticipation of a negative reaction from the peasantry, the government held up the emancipation edict until March 3, 1861, the Sunday before Lent, at which time it was read in all the churches.

In their churches on Sunday, March 3, 1861, the Russian people received
the news of the emancipation of the serfs. This print shows Alexander II
announcing the emancipation edict to his court.

To insure the success of the manifesto, Alexander II astutely based his
action on the forces of history, on Christian principles, on the self-sacrificing
idealism of the nobility, and on the understanding and gratitude of the serfs:

> Thus We have become convinced that the matter of ameliorating the
> plight of the serfs is for Us a legacy from Our Predecessors and, due to the
> course of events, the lot assigned to Us by the hand of Providence. We
> entered upon this business with an act demonstrating Our confidence in the
> Russian nobility, who have evinced in practice their great devotion to the
> Throne and their readiness to make sacrifices for the sake of the Fatherland.
> . . . Russia will not forget that, induced solely by respect for the dignity of
> man and Christian love for his neighbor, it [the nobility] voluntarily rejected
> serfdom which has now been abolished and laid the foundation of a new
> economic future for the peasants. . . .
>
> And now We hopefully anticipate that the serfs for whom a new future
> has been opened up will comprehend and accept with gratitude the im-
> portant sacrifice made by the nobility for the improvement of their daily
> lives.[2]

2. For an English translation of this Emancipation Manifesto, see Ivar Spector and
Marion Spector, eds., *Readings in Russian History and Culture* (Boston: Allyn and
Bacon, 1965), pp. 170–176.

The four hundred printed pages of the complex and sometimes contradictory emancipation edict declared the peasants to be free, but effectively circumscribed that freedom. For a two-year period, while arrangements and surveys were being completed, the peasants were to continue their customary payments to their landlords. Thereafter, they became "temporarily obligated," until such time as they could redeem their holdings. If the peasant could provide 20 per cent of the purchase price of his land allotment, the government would advance the remaining 80 per cent to the landlord, in the expectation of recovering this credit from the peasant over a period of forty-nine years.

The actual terms of emancipation varied in different parts of the Empire. In general, however, especially in Great Russia, the land was turned over, not to the individual peasant, but to a local peasant commune (*mir*), which assumed responsibility for his redemption payments, for taxes, obligatory services, and law and order. In other words, the peasant, for reasons of security, was not given freedom of action. He had to purchase the holdings (sometimes more, sometimes less) that he had occupied and tilled, and until he had done so, not only was he obligated to the landowner, but supervised by the commune. The appanage peasants and state peasants, who did not come under the terms of the original emancipation edict, were liberated—the latter under more generous terms—between 1861 and 1866. In the Transcaucasus, the abolition of serfdom was carried out from 1863 to 1870. Here the allotments were often so small and the conditions so onerous that the temporary status of the peasants was perpetuated until 1912.

A Flawed Solution. Thus, in its final form, the emancipation edict was a compromise settlement. By rear-guard action, the landowners, to their own advantage, had whittled down the benefits originally intended for the peasantry. As was to be expected, the peasants were bitterly disappointed at having to pay for their holdings, often at more than the market value of the land and on high rental terms. Although conditions varied and allotments normally were larger in the north and west, many peasants emerged with less land than before the emancipation. The crown peasant received an average allotment of twenty-three acres, the appanage peasant one of fifteen acres, and the serf under private ownership nine acres.

The inadequacy of the allotments became only too apparent in subsequent years, especially for peasants deprived of pasturage, forest land, and a water supply. Although the transfer of the land should have been accompanied by the consolidation of the antiquated strip holdings, in the majority of cases this was not done. Several hundred thousand peasants, in order to settle matters directly with the landowner and avoid further obligations, accepted the pittance of one-quarter of the land provided by law. Little wonder that some of them, as recorded in Serge Stepniak's account, *The Russian Peasantry,* concluded that this was a phony manifesto, substituted for the real one by corrupt landlords, bureaucrats, and priests. The more than two thousand peasant disturbances that occured, 1861–1863, were ruthlessly suppressed

by the military. Peasants were flogged, shot, and exiled, and order was restored. Alexander Herzen bitterly commented that a new form of serfdom had
replaced the old.

Unfortunately, the masses of Russian peasants, reaching out for individual
freedom and private ownership, were forced, due to the landowners' concern
for their property, into the mould of communal ownership. Although each
peasant member of the commune assumed responsibility for payment of the
purchase price of the land, none of it became his private possession. In other
words, for an individual master (the landowner), there was substituted a
collective master (the commune). The arrangement approached that of the
Soviet *kolkhoz,* or collective farm, in the years immediately following the
Russian Revolution, and in fact, served as a training ground for Soviet
economic practices.

The historian, George Vernadsky,[3] has contended that either of two solutions of the problem of serfdom might have prevented subsequent disaster in
the revolutions of 1905 and 1917. The government might have given the
peasants their personal freedom and aided them as individuals rather than as
communes to purchase their allotments; or it might have taken over the land
from the owners, compensated them, and redistributed it to the peasants as
individuals. In either case Russia by 1914 might have been peopled, not by
millions of *peasants* but by millions of *farmers,* who would have constituted
an agricultural middle class with an important stake in the existing regime. As
it was, the emancipation was incomplete. It was the objective of Prime
Minister Peter Stolypin to complete the emancipation of 1861 by the reforms
of 1906 to 1911. The abolition of the peasant commune in favor of private
ownership and the consolidation of peasant holdings would, in time, have
created the conditions essential to the development of a nation of independent
farmers. Unfortunately, by then it was too late.

ADDITIONAL GOVERNMENTAL REFORMS

Local Government: Zemstvos. Emancipation, which had upset the existing
administrative and judicial order, necessarily brought in its wake a series of
other reforms. At no time did Alexander II regard the emancipation of the
serfs as a step toward the curbing of the power of the autocracy. The official
transformation of the landlord-peasant relationship, however, required the
reconstruction of local self-government. Under the old system, the nobility
governed all freemen resident in a province. The new regime appeared to
require representation on an all-class basis (nobility, townsmen, and peasants). This was accomplished, in spite of objections, by the new *Zemstvo* law

3. George Vernadsky, *A History of Russia* (New Haven, Conn.: Yale University
Press, 1930), pp. 154–155.

of January, 1864, which provided for district and provincial *zemstvos* (councils), elected for three-year terms, and responsible for many functions and services hitherto largely non-existent in Russian rural life. The original plan, which would have given equal rights of representation to nobility, townsmen, and peasants, was transformed into a system of indirect voting in three separate curias, which tipped the balance in favor of the nobility. Nevertheless, the *zemstvo* was a representative body in which the aristocracy no longer had exclusive power. Beginning with thirty provinces, *zemstvos* were introduced gradually throughout European Russia. In 1870, a similar system was provided for town government under *dumas* elected for four years on the basis of property qualifications.

The *zemstvos* served as a valuable training ground for public service for men of all classes. They were authorized to raise taxes for specific local purposes. They exercised supervision over roads, primary schools, public charity, and public health, including many hospitals. Through hired veterinarians and agronomists, they sought to improve agricultural methods, stock, and equipment. Many civic-minded gentry worked effectively through the *zemstvos* to improve rural conditions. Unfortunately, provincial governors and bureaucrats often interfered with their free operation, especially in regard to the primary schools, which were notably more liberal than the government desired. The institution was sometimes powerful enough to resist reactionary government pressure. By 1914, *zemstvo* expenditures in forty-three provinces amounted to around 400,000,000 rubles, of which 106,000,000 were allocated to public education. In 50,000 *zemstvo* primary schools, 80,000 teachers were providing instruction to 3,000,000 children. The *zemstvos* continued to make a significant contribution to the progress and development of Russia until the Revolution of 1917.

The Courts. Emancipation also made possible many long-needed reforms of Russian legal institutions to achieve what Alexander II termed "a fast, just, and merciful" court. Under the supervision of Minister of Justice D. M. Zamiatnin (1805–1881) a notable reform of the Russian law courts, based largely on French practice, was undertaken in 1864. New lower courts were required to replace the landowner, who, among his other functions, had served as local magistrate. Justices of the peace, elected by the *zemstvos* and *dumas,* handled petty cases. In the regional courts, greater independence of judges was assured by their appointment for life. The reforms corrected many longstanding sources of corruption and abuse of justice by the introduction of open trials; the organization of lawyers in a formal bar; the introduction of trial by jury in most criminal cases; recognition of the right of the accused to be represented by an attorney; and acknowledgment, at least in principle, of the equality of all citizens before the law. Peasants, it is true, still remained under the special jurisdiction of the commune and were tried in commune (*volost*) courts. During the years of reaction that followed the attempted assassination of Alexander II in 1866, there were encroachments on the new-found independence of the courts through arbitrary bureaucratic and police action. The legal reforms, however, contributed greatly to the rise of a remarkably able and articulate legal profession in Russia.

Military Reform. Under the guidance of Minister of War Dmitry Miliutin brother of Nicholas Miliutin who had shepherded the emancipation program through the editing process, a number of important military reforms were introduced in Russia. In the Crimean War, Russia's army of 2,000,000 men had been defeated by an Anglo-French-Turkish invading force of some 70,000, noted for its tactical blunders, including the famous "Charge of the Light Brigade." In the Russian army, the war had revealed a dearth of leadership, endless corruption, and a lack of administrative efficiency. Miliutin's objective was to modernize the armed forces on the Prussian model, to improve and humanize military training, and to provide up-to-date equipment. Even the judicial branch of the army was reorganized and the worst forms of corporal punishment abolished. The reforms culminated in 1874 in the adoption of a system of universal compulsory military service, which provided for exemptions on the basis of family ties and responsibilities. The former twenty-five-year military "sentence" was reduced to a six-year term in the regular army, followed by nine years in the reserve. Since the higher the educational qualifications of the recruit the lower his term of service, it is not surprising that the literacy rate rose rapidly. This was further encouraged in 1875 by army provision for literacy training, which helped to compensate for the inadequacy of the primary educational system.

The Narodniki. Under Alexander II, the government had assumed the initiative in social, legal, and military reforms. If there must be reform, the government was determined to be identified with it rather than to confront revolution from below. There were many Russian intellectuals who wanted to help or were dissatisfied with the government's reform measures. They sought, through voluntary organizations, to repay their debt to the suffering masses by joining the fight for social justice. They wanted reform to emanate, not from the government alone, but from the popular masses. As the articulate representatives of the people, these intellectuals planned to provide guidance for reform from below. University students, in particular, were attracted to the cause, which soon came to be known as the *Narodniki* (Populist) movement.

This movement had its beginning in 1869 when Mark Natanson formed a club, or circle, of students in St. Petersburg, organized on a communal basis. Its purpose was to establish other circles and to distribute illegal literature for "the liberation of the people." Under the impact of the Paris Commune (1871), another circle was organized by A. V. Dolgushin in 1872 in St. Petersburg; this group soon transferred its activities to Moscow and its environs. It had its own secret printing shop, and it published and distributed leaflets to members of the intelligentsia and to workers. This handful of intellectuals, not all of whom were peacefully inclined, was dedicated to the spread of populist ideals. *Narodniki* circles sprang up in Central Russia, the

Ukraine, White Russia, Georgia, Armenia, and the northern Caucasus. Their main task was to locate and indoctrinate others to work for the cause.

In the spring and summer of 1874 all this activity erupted in what was termed "Going to the People." The *Narodniki* left their books and their circles to join and identify themselves with the masses, especially with the peasants. Their object was to get a first-hand knowledge of the people whose conditions they hoped to ameliorate. They had no clearly defined program, other than the uplifting of the people. Some taught peasants to read. Others took them soap. They joined work gangs, became farmhands, lived with the peasants, ate and dressed like them. Avrahm Yarmolinsky has labelled this another "Children's Crusade."

The *Narodniki* movement was, in essence, a kind of Russian Peace Corps, on an unofficial rather than a governmental basis. In reality, the government regarded them as a subversive element, hampering and even sabotaging its own reform program. Their efforts were directed toward the improvement of conditions, not in foreign lands, nor even among their own minorities, but among Russians of the same color, nationality, religion, and language as their own. According to Yarmolinsky, this was "the first approach to a mass movement in the history of Russian radicalism."[4] It was a combination of the Salvation Army, the Peace Corps, and revolutionists of every color. Its members served as "missionaries" intent upon improving the lot of the downtrodden and destitute. In fact, most of its leaders, at least in the beginning, were imbued with Christian principles, and many were the sons or grandsons of priests.

Had there been a modicum of political freedom in Russia, they might have sparked a spiritual revival, as the Methodists did in England and the Pietists in Germany. As it was, they experienced persecution, arrest, and imprisonment, from which many emerged as atheists, anarchists, nihilists, and even regicides. One of their leaders, Peter L. Lavrov (1823–1900), admitted that the movement was more comparable to a religious sect than to a political party. The principal apologist for the *Narodniki* in the United States, Mark Slonim, claims, however, that Russian political parties have their origin in Russian Populism.

Ostensibly, the *Narodniki* movement was a failure. The people its members idealized and sought to help distrusted them or were not prepared for their message. They discovered that they had overestimated the "people's" intelligence and maturity, or "consciousness." The soil must be prepared for revolution. The government carried on an effective propaganda campaign against their efforts, declared the movement illegal, and arrested about one thousand of these Russian "peace corps" workers.

One of the best descriptions of the *Narodniki* in action is to be found in

4. Avrahm Yarmolinsky, *The Road to Revolution* (New York: Macmillan, 1959), p. 189.

Ivan Turgenev's last novel, *Virgin Soil* (1876). According to Turgenev, it was not through Nezhdanov, the *Narodnik,* but through Salomin, the practical businessman and representative of the new industrial age, that Russia's salvation would come. Through his mouthpiece, Salomin, Turgenev advocated a slower, but surer and more practical method of reform by painstaking education of the people and by gradual evolution rather than by violent revolution.

FOREIGN POLICY: CENTRAL ASIA AND THE FAR EAST

During the Crimean War, Fyodor Dostoyevsky, still a young Russian writer, whose exile to Siberia for association with the Petrashevists had made him Asia-conscious, published a poem, "On European Events." In this poem, he asserted that it was God's will for Russia to go to Asia under the banner of the White Tsar and the Orthodox Church to bring about a renaissance of the Asian peoples. As Russia proceeded to carve out for herself a vast Asian empire, this same Dostoyevsky, twenty-seven years older and at the peak of his literary career, reemphasized in 1881 in his *Diary of a Writer* the significance of Asia for Russia's future development:

> . . . By turning to Asia, with our new concept of her, our country may experience something akin to what happened in Europe when America was discovered. For, in truth, Asia to us is like the then undiscovered America. With Asia as our aim, our spirit and forces will be regenerated. . . . In Europe we were hangers-on and slaves, but we shall go to Asia as masters. To the Europeans, we were Tatars, whereas in Asia, we, too, are Europeans. Our civilizing mission in Asia will serve as a bribe to our spirit and will lure us thither.

This new orientation of Russia toward Asia was necessary, according to Dostoyevsky, "because Russia is not only in Europe but also in Asia; because the Russian is not only a European but also an Asian."

In 1856, shortly after the end of the Crimean War, Prince Alexander Gortchakov, Russian minister of foreign affairs, presented a memorandum to Alexander II which convinced the emperor that in Europe Russia confronted no major problems; that in Asia, on the other hand, there was in store for her an enormous field of activity; and that, in fact, "the future of Russia lies in Asia." The emperor's notation on the memorandum read: "I am in complete agreement with this."

Asian Department. The tsarist government in the nineteenth century was becoming more Asia-minded. Already, in the reign of Emperor Paul, on February 26, 1797, a special Asian Department had been set up in the Foreign Ministry to handle Asian matters. It soon became autonomous. Nicholas I had created a separate Asian Department parallel to the Central Ministerial Chancery, which at times rivalled the latter in influence. It had its own specialists to handle Near and Middle Eastern affairs and displayed a tendency to evolve its own foreign policy, based on Panslavism and expansionism.[5] The Asian Department became one of three departments of the Ministry of Foreign Affairs. Toward the close of the nineteenth century, it included the following sections: one on political affairs pertaining to the Orient; a second handling all correspondence with Asian governments, Russian diplomatic and consular agents, and various Russians living in the Orient or Asians resident in Russia; and a third handling translations of official documents and other materials. In this section, a school for Oriental languages was established to train interpreters for Russian missions in the Orient.

Increased interest in Asian affairs had also been manifested by the establishment of an Asian Museum on November 11 (O.S.), 1818, under the auspices of the St. Petersburg Academy of Sciences. The president of the Academy, S. S. Uvarov, had been instrumental in securing a substantial collection of Arab manuscripts, which, together with Asian materials acquired since the time of Peter the Great, formed the nucleus of the collection.

Prior to the Revolution of 1917, the museum was divided into the following sections: 1. A library of books about Asia in European languages. 2. Books in Far Eastern languages (Chinese, Japanese, Manchu, Tibetan, and Mongol). 3. Books in Sanskrit, the languages of India and Indo-China. 4. Arab, Persian, and Turko-Tatar books. 5. Books in Armenian and Georgian. 6. Hebrew books, and 7. Syrian books. All manuscripts were divided as follows: 1. Muslim manuscripts (Arab, Persian, Turko-Tatar, Afghan, and Kurd). 2. Manuscripts in other Eastern languages, Syrian, Hebrew, and Coptic. There was also a collection of Oriental coins. In 1930 the Asian Museum, together with other Oriental institutions, became an integral part of the Institute of Oriental Studies of the Academy of Sciences of the USSR.

From 1861 to 1864 the Asian Department was under Count Nikolai P. Ignatyev (1832–1908), a militant Panslavist who had several diplomatic successes to his credit. At the Congress of Paris, 1856, he had wrested from the Western powers some concessions for defeated Russia. Shortly thereafter he went to China to reaffirm the Treaty of Aigun (1858) and to conclude the Treaty of Peking (1860), which brought Russia vast territorial acquisitions and established his own personal prestige. Under such leadership, and with Alexander II's green light for an Asian orientation, the generals in the field had every right to expect strong backing from the government for their strategic aspirations in Asia.

Peoples of Central Asia. After the Crimean War, therefore, Russia expanded into the vast area of Central Asia: stretching eastward from the Caspian Sea and the lower Volga to the frontiers of China; and southward from Siberia to Iran and Afghanistan. Today the Soviet Socialist Republics of

5. Robert M. Slusser, "The Role of the Foreign Ministry," in Ivo. J. Lederer, ed., *Russian Foreign Policy: Essays in Historical Perspective* (New Haven, Conn. and London: Yale University Press, 1962), pp. 202–203.

Kazakhstan, Kirghizia, Uzbekistan, Turkmenistan, and Tadjikistan occupy this land. The area comprises 1,500,000 square miles or about one-half the size of the United States, but without irrigation the greater part of the land is desert.

Over the centuries, Central Asia had been subject to a series of invasions—by the Greeks, Persians, Arabs, Turkic tribes, and Mongols—with the result that the original largely Iranian stock became mixed with a variety of races and ethnic groups, differing in language and culture. The Kazakhs, a Turkic-Mongol people living a pastoral nomadic life, numbered about 2,500,000 in the mid-nineteenth century. The Kirghiz, closely related to the Kazakhs, inhabiting the mountainous region of Ala-Tau and the area around Lake Issyk-Kul, possibly included 300,000 at that time. The Turkmen, primarily a pastoral people located in the desert steppe from the Syr-Daria to the Caspian Sea, also numbered about 300,000. Approximately 3,500,000 Uzbeks, originally of Iranian stock, occupied the Khanates of Khiva and Kokand, as well as the emirate of Bukhara. The Tadjiks, also of Iranian origin and numbering about 100,000, occupied the valleys and slopes of the Pamir mountains. About 100,000 Turkic Kara-Kalpaks lived in the Amu-Darya region and west of the Aral Sea. Central Asia also acquired some recent arrivals from Chinese Turkestan—the Turkic Taranchi (about 50,000) and the Chinese Muslim Dungans (about 15,000), who migrated to Russian territory when their rebellions were suppressed by the Chinese during the 1860's.

Almost all the native peoples of Central Asia were Muslims of the Sunnite sect, although the Kazakhs, where Islam arrived late, failed to observe the Shariat and other Muslim observances. Except for the use of firearms, the mode of living for most of these peoples had not changed materially in the past thousand years. Although in general they were nomadic and organized in clans or tribes, the Uzbeks were a sedentary people, engaged primarily in agriculture. In the nineteenth century the area was beset by local feuds and internecine strife. Its glorious past of the days of Timur was but a romantic memory: the former lucrative trade routes, the elaborate network of irrigation canals, and the great monuments had fallen into decay. The peoples of Central Asia had lost touch with the modern world. This was an area, contiguous to Russia, which seemed unlikely to offer a serious obstacle to the experienced and better equipped Russian forces.

Rationale for Expansion. There were several reasons for Russian expansion into Central Asia following the Crimean conflict. First, the Russian army required action, decorations, and promotions for the restoration of its badly damaged prestige. After the completion of the conquest of the Caucasus in 1859, it moved on to the lands east of the Caspian. For thirty years Russian military leaders prodded the government into one Central Asian adventure after another. Second, after Russian expansion was blocked in the Balkans, Central Asia presented itself, especially to the Panslavists, as an appropriate detour to Constantinople and the Straits.

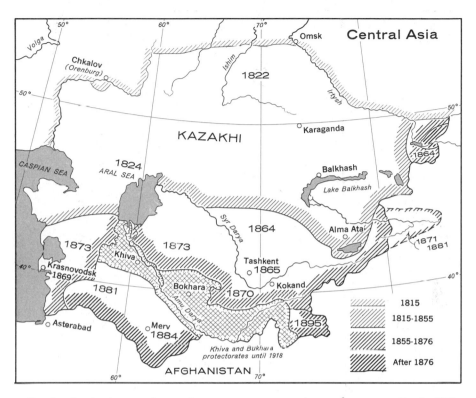

In the beginning, at least, the great powers expressed comparatively little concern or awareness about Russian expansion in the Asian area. The European attitude toward the fulfillment of Russia's "mission" in Asia, especially in Muslim Asia, was effectively explained by Nicholas Danilevsky (1822–1885), the creator of scientific Slavophilism, in his influential book, *Russia and Europe* (1869):

> What role on the universal stage does Europe assign us, her adopted children? To be the bearers and propagators of her civilization in the East— that is the lofty mission allotted to us, the task in which Europe will sympathize, which she will advance with her blessings, her best wishes, her applause, to the edification and delight of our humanitarian progressivists. Very well. Eastward-ho! then. But stop—*what* East? We had thought to begin with Turkey. What could be better? There live our brethren, in blood and spirit,—live in agonies and yearn for deliverance. "Whither away? You have no business there," thunders Europe; "that is not the East for *you;* there's more Slavic trash there than I like, and I'm going to manage them. My Germans have done such work before. Clear out of there."—We tackled the Caucasus—that's a sort of East too. Mamma got very mad: "Don't dare to touch the noble paladins of freedom! Much it becomes you to meddle with

them. Hands off!"—For once, thank goodness, we did not obey, and forgot
our Europeanism. There is Persia now; something might be done there in
the way of sowing the seeds of European civilization. The Germans would
not have minded; their *Drang nach Osten* [Eastward Push] scarcely would
reach so far; but out of respect to England we had to be checked: "Too
near India. Move on!"—to China, perhaps?—"Well, no. Is it tea you need?
We'll bring you all you want from Canton. China is a wealthy country—we
can teach her without your help. She is smoking our Indian opium like a
charm—let her alone."—But, for mercy's sake, where is *our* East, the East
which it is our sacred mission to civilize?—"Central. Asia, that's the place
for you, and do not forget it. We could not get there anyhow, besides it
would not pay. There lies your sacred historical mission. . . ."—So then we
shall have gone through a thousand years of labor streaming with sweat and
blood; we shall have built up an empire of a hundred million souls (of
which sixty millions of one race and blood, a thing unequalled in the world,
except in China),—all to tender the blessing of European civilization to five
or six millions of tatterdemalions, the denizens of Kokand, Khiva, and
Bokhara, with two or three millions of Mongolian nomads thrown in—for that
is what the high-sounding phrase about bearing European civilization into
the heart of the Asiatic continent really amounts to,—an enviable lot indeed, and a mission to be proud of. In sooth, *Parturiunt montes, nascitur
ridiculus mus.* . . .

Soviet scholars have attributed Russian penetration of Central Asia largely
to economic factors—as a source of important raw materials; of new land to
serve as the basis for cotton production for the Russian textile industry; and
as a market for Russian products. Actually, the strategic and military reasons
seem to outweigh the economic. As Russian penetration progressed, Russian
generals, like Skobolev, emphasized the need to keep the region out of British
hands; "It is the English," he said, "who have impelled us into Asia." Russian
Foreign Minister Gortchakov, in a circular note of assurance to the great
powers on November 24 (O.S.), 1864, emphasized Russia's need to protect
her borders against lawless tribes of "savages;" to secure defensible frontiers;
and to manifest a position of strength to Asians, after which the Russian
advance would stop.

Advance of the Russian Army. In Central Asia, however, there were no
geographical frontiers short of the mountainous borders of China and Afghanistan. Russian forces advanced, consolidated their gains, and proceeded to
establish new outposts, which served as stepping stones to other moves.
Expressions of concern from England inevitably evoked Russian denials of
further expansion or of any threat to India—the channels of diplomacy
proved useless in halting the Russian advance in Asia.

In a rapid succession of victories, the Russian army seized the Uzbek city
of Tashkent (1865), which became the capital of the new Russian province
of Turkestan; took possession of Tamerlane's capital, Samarkand (1868);

and established a protectorate over the Emirate of Bukhara (1868). At Heidelberg, in September, 1869, the British and Russian foreign ministers discussed the creation of a buffer zone between Russia and India—a solution much desired by England—but nothing definitive was accomplished. In the same year, the Russians occupied Qizil-Su (Krasnovodsk), in Transcaspia, as a jumping-off point for the advance on the Khanate of Khiva. Khiva was taken in May, 1873, followed by the annexation of the Khanate of Kokand (1876) as the Fergana *oblast*.

The worried British were assured that Afghanistan would provide a neutral zone between Russia and India. Alexander, after his generals had given the Afghans reason to expect Russian aid against England, refused to risk war with the British during the Second Anglo-Afghan War (1878–1881). Instead, the Russian forces, in 1878–1879, following the conflict with Turkey, began the subjugation of the warlike Turkoman tribes in the Transcaspian region near the borders of Iran and Afghanistan. In 1880 the great fortress of Geok-Tepe fell to a Russian army of eleven thousand men. This broke the back of Turkmenian resistance, and in January, 1881, Colonel A. N. Kuropatkin occupied Askhabad (Ashkhabad). A few months later Transcaspia was declared a Russian *oblast*.

Thus, the Russian army carved out a vast Asian empire. In all the Central Asian campaigns from 1847 to 1874, it claimed to have lost fewer than 400 men killed and slightly more than 1,600 wounded. Merchants and traders followed in the wake of the army. Although world opinion was virtually unanimous that it could not be done, Russian engineers built the first railroad in Central Asia—from Krasnovodsk to the east, through hot, waterless, and sandy wastes. Soon, American cotton was under cultivation in Central Asia. The future of Russian relations with Persia was forecast in 1878 by the shah's request for Russian aid to train the Persian armed forces.

The Far East. The Crimean War also demonstrated to the Russian government the need to provide for the security of the Russian Far East. The Anglo-French attack on Petropavlovsk in Kamtchatka served as a portent of further intervention by powers already engrossed in securing concessions from China. In Russian ruling circles there was a group that regarded the Far East as a possible source of Russian enrichment and of Russian retaliation for Sevastopol. In the years from 1858 to 1860 Russian expansion in the Far East led to the acquisition of a vast and thinly populated area of around 400,000 square miles, equal in size to Germany and France combined.

In 1847, prior to the Crimean conflict, Nicholas I had sent to the Far East one of Russia's great empire builders, Nicholas N. (later Count) Muraviev (1809–1881), to conduct a campaign that would block Anglo-French designs in that area. Muraviev was to spend fourteen years in the Russian Far East, during which time he set the pattern for Russian foreign policy in the Pacific, based on the premises of friendship toward the United States and expansion at the expense of China and Japan. Under his auspices, the first great Russian

After his appointment as governor-general of eastern Siberia in 1847, Nicholas Muraviev encouraged pioneering peasants to settle on the banks of the Amur River. Since the territory was not ceded to Russia until 1858, these settlements were technically violations of the Treaty of Nertchinsk.

drive to the Far East was conducted. Muraviev was ably abetted in his objectives by Captain (later Admiral) Gennadi I. Nevelskoy (1803–1876), whose exploratory expeditions in 1849 and 1850 revealed to the West that Sakhalin was an island, not a peninsula, and that the Amur estuary was navigable. In 1850 Muraviev, with Chinese consent, established on the lower Amur the first Russian settlement, which later became the city of Nikolaevsk. In 1853 Sakhalin, where the Russian flag had first been hoisted in 1806, was placed under the management of the Russian-American Company, with orders to prevent alien (Japanese) settlements.

Chinese Treaties: Aigun, Tientsin, Peking. Taking advantage of the fact that the Chinese were hard pressed by England and France to the south, Nikolai Ignatyev on May 28 (O.S.), 1858, by the Treaty of Aigun, secured for Russia the left bank of the Amur River, from the Argun to the estuary. Thus, Russia regained the Amur region lost by the Treaty of Nertchinsk in 1689. Pending a more definitive frontier settlement, the region between the Ussuri River and the Sea of Japan was declared open to joint occupation, with Russian and Chinese vessels sharing freedom of navigation of the Amur, Sungari, and Ussuri rivers.

Almost immediately thereafter, on June 18 (O.S.), 1858, Admiral Yefim V. Putyatin (1803–1883) concluded with the Chinese the Treaty of Tientsin, by which Russia gained access to Chinese ports already open to the other great powers, and was permitted to establish consulates there. Within two years of the Treaty of Aigun the hard-pressed Chinese government, ostensibly to keep out the English and French, transferred to Russia by the Treaty of Peking (1860) the jointly occupied Ussuri region, henceforth known as Russia's Maritime Province. By this treaty, Urgu, Kalgan, and Kushgui were opened to Russian trade. Muraviev, enamored of the fine natural port on the Bay of the Golden Horn in the Gulf of Peter the Great, in 1860 established there the military outpost which became the city of Vladivostok ("Ruler of the East"). From two other settlements on the Amur in the late 1850's sprang the cities of Blagoveshchensk and Khabarovsk.

By the Treaty of Peking the boundaries of Turkestan were also redrawn to Russian advantage, with another loss to China of some 350,000 square miles. Still more territory was surrendered by the Chinese in 1881, when the Russians secured about 15,000 square miles of Sinkiang along the Kazakhstan border south of Lake Balkhash. In 1914 St. Petersburg rounded out its possessions in this area by the annexation of Tanna Tuva, near Altai, now a Soviet autonomous region bordering Outer Mongolia. In March, 1963, as the Sino-Soviet ideological dispute waxed strong, the Red Chinese press cited among other examples of "unbridled aggression" against China, the three principal Russian "imposed" treaties which deprived China of such vast areas of land, and which neither the Chinese Communists nor the Chinese Nationalists appear to have recognized as irrevocable.

Treaty with Japan. In August, 1853, in the wake of Commodore Perry, Admiral Putyatin arrived in the Japanese port of Nagasaki, not to trade but to effect a boundary settlement with Japan. His secretary, the Russian novelist Ivan Alexandrovitch Gontcharov, has provided a choice description of this Japanese venture in *Frigate Pallas* (1856–1857).

After some delay, Putyatin concluded a treaty with the Japanese in Simoda in February, 1855, which established diplomatic relations between Russia and Japan, opened certain Japanese ports to Russian vessels, defined the rights of Russians in Japan, and reached a rather inconclusive boundary settlement. Under this treaty, the Kurile Islands, with the exception of the southernmost island of Iturup, were recognized as Russian.

Since the contracting parties failed to agree on the disposition of the Island of Sakhalin, it remained "undivided" between Japan and Russia. The Japanese wished to colonize the southern part of the island, but the Russians, aware of its strategic importance for the defense of the Amur and Ussuri areas, were determined to hold out for the entire island. In 1867, a condominium was established over Sakhalin, with joint occupation permitted. To populate the area, and thereby enhance their own claim to it, the Russians founded a convict settlement there. In 1875, amid threats of a Franco-German conflict in Europe, a compromise was reached, whereby Russia surrendered the Kurile Islands to Japan in return for the Island of Sakhalin. The Japanese retained the right to fish in Sakhalin waters.

The population of the Russian Far East was but 15,000 in 1860, 65,000 in 1867, and 108,000 in 1879. To secure the area against future Chinese encroachment, the Russian government had to develop and populate its new possessions. Few Russians went to this hard land voluntarily. Convicts who had served sentences for major crimes in Siberia and "Cossack armies" were settled along the Amur and Ussuri. From the beginning, the government provided financial aid to settlers, but without striking results. By 1897, the Russian Far East boasted only 310,000 settlers.

Relations with the United States. Russia's decision to concentrate on the development of the Russian Far East was a major factor in the disposal of her American possessions to the United States. In spite of their widely divergent political structures, the United States and Russia shared some common social and international problems, which fostered a *rapprochement* between them in the reign of Alexander II. In the emancipation of serfs and slaves, the two countries contended with a somewhat similar social problem at virtually the same time. In international affairs, both had reason to distrust and oppose England.

During the Crimean War, the United States had offered moral support by demonstrating its good will toward Russia. The Russians returned the favor during the American Civil War by demonstrations of support for the Union cause. The dispatch of Russian fleet units to New York and San Francisco in the fall of 1863 when England and France were contemplating active intervention in favor of the South, although shrouded in American-made myths,[6] appears to have been due more to Russian self-interest than to Russian zeal for the Union. With the threat of Anglo-French intervention in the Polish insurrection of 1863, the Russian fleet was safer abroad on neutral ground than bottled up in the Baltic. Nevertheless, the end result was an outpouring of American good will, which led Gideon Wells, secretary of the navy, to exclaim wholeheartedly: "God bless the Russians." There was even speculation about a full-fledged Russian-American alliance.

Sale of Alaska. As early as January, 1853, Nicholas Muraviev, Russia's empire builder in the Far East, had recommended the cession of Russian America (except Alaska) to the United States, because it was indefensible without a powerful Russian navy in Alaskan waters, and because its surrender would serve as a guarantee of continued good relations with the Americans. It was his opinion that the United States and Russia would eventually dominate the North Pacific, and that they should reach an amicable agreement to partition this area. Between 1859 and 1862, the United States more than once broached the question of the annexation of Alaska. The Civil War in the United States, however, served to postpone action on this issue. Alaska, in truth, had become a frozen asset to the Russian government, which was about to fall heir to the problems created by its economic mismanagement at the hands of the Russian-American Company. Only recognition of the "neutrality" of Russian America during the Crimean War had prevented its seizure by the vastly superior Anglo-French forces. An Alaskan gold rush, comparable to that in British Columbia, promised to lead to an American migration that might, in any event, turn the tide of possession in America's favor. Last, but by no means least, the Russian government had decided to focus on the development of its contiguous and more defensible possessions in the Far East.

The Russian government, for these reasons, rather than for sentiment, decided to sell Alaska to the United States while such a sale was still feasible and profitable. Pro-Russian sentiment in the Union played an important role in William H. Seward's purchase of Alaska for $7,200,000 in gold on March 30 (N.S.), 1867. Seward was as much an American, as Muraviev was a Russian, believer in Manifest Destiny. Alexander II, as F. A. Golder has pointed out, would under pressure even have parted with "Walrussia," land of walruses and icebergs for $5,000,000.[7] The United States also obtained the papers and archives of the Russian-American Company. This, it may be said, was the only occasion when Russia voluntarily ceded to a foreign power, even at a price, a territory comparable in area to Alaska. A Soviet textbook on

6. Thomas A. Bailey, *America Faces Russia* (Ithaca, N.Y.: Cornell University Press, 1950), especially Chapter VIII, "The Russian Fleet Myth," pp. 81–94.

7. F. A. Golder, "The Purchase of Alaska," *American Historical Review,* XXV (April 1920), pp. 419–420.

Russian history, widely used in higher educational institutions, now calls this treaty "the defeat of Russia in the Pacific."

FOREIGN POLICY: THE NEAR EAST

With the pursuit of an aggressive policy in Asia, the Near East could not long remain dormant. Prince Alexander Gortchakov, who succeeded Nesselrode in 1856 as foreign minister, was a diplomat, not a warmonger. His first objective was to restore Russia's international position in Europe by the abrogation at the first opportunity of the unrealistic provisions of the Treaty of Paris that excluded the Russian fleet from the Black Sea and the mouth of the Danube, and banned the construction of Russian fortifications along the coast. With more than one thousand miles of Black Sea coastline, the Russian government had no intention of permanently accepting such "intolerable" restrictions. In this respect, Alexander and his foreign minister were in complete accord.

Straits Question. Changes in the balance of power in Europe after 1856 contributed to the disintegration of the Crimean peace settlement. The Anglo-French-Italian wartime coalition, as so many other wartime alliances have done before and since, broke down in peacetime. In England, Gladstone, departing from the Palmerstonian tradition, had no wish to fight the Crimean War all over again. Bismarck, moving toward the unification of Germany, betrayed no concern whatsoever about the preservation of the *status quo* at the Straits. Even Austrian attention was focused on her expansionist German neighbor rather than on Russia. From 1866 to 1869 nine minor Russian infractions of the Straits settlement occurred, which brought protests to the sultan. By 1870 even Turkey was disposed toward some revision of the treaty provisions. It was clear that the Crimean system had provided no lasting solution in the Near East.

Opportunity for unilateral revision on the question of the Straits soon presented itself in the shape of the Franco-Prussian War (1870–1871), which diverted the attention of the major powers from the Ottoman Empire. The reorganization of Germany being wrought by Bismarck in the Austro-Prussian War (1866) and Franco-Prussian War placed the tsarist regime, the traditional friend of both Austria and Prussia, in a difficult position. As a reward for Russian neutrality, Bismarck placed the stamp of his approval on the abrogation of the Pontus clause of the Paris Congress. In October, 1870, Gortchakov thereupon issued a unilateral denunciation of the obnoxious Black Sea clauses, a move which was formally sanctioned by the London Conference of 1871.

Balkan Policies. The appointment of Count Ignatyev in 1864 as Russian ambassador in Constantinople heralded the renewal of a more aggressive Russian policy in the Near East. From Constantinople, where he remained until

1877, Ignatyev fomented Panslav agitation in the Balkans and encouraged Russian societies in the Holy Land and Middle East. Through his control of numerous consular agencies in the Slavic centers of the Ottoman Empire, Ignatyev first supported a Serbian-led Balkan federation for a united Slav front against the Turks and subsequently Bulgarian leadership at Serbian expense. The Russian purpose, of course, remained the control of Constantinople and the Straits. Russian involvement in local Balkan politics was scarcely calculated to promote unity. It stirred up animosity and rivalry among Greeks, Bulgars, and Serbs over the possession of Macedonia. This was especially true after 1870, when Russia intervened in Ottoman affairs to secure the establishment of the exarchate of Bulgaria, the most strategically situated Balkan state for the promotion of Russian goals. Even Balkan nationals predisposed in favor of Russia began to suspect that the emperor was using the Slavic minorities in the Turkish Empire to promote Russian rather than Slavic interest.

Three Emperors' League. There is reason to believe that Gortchakov did not see eye to eye with Ignatyev and his backers in the Asian Department on the matter of Balkan politics. As a diplomat, he had no desire to arouse the opposition of Austria and the Western powers over Turkey. Much of his diplomatic experience had been gained in the German courts and at Vienna. In 1873, moreover, Alexander II concluded a convention with Austria, which proved to be the initial step in the formation of the Three Emperors' League (Austria, Germany, and Russia) for the preservation of monarchical conservatism in Eastern Europe. This revival of the policy of Nicholas I as "gendarme of Europe" remained a basic factor in Bismarck's diplomacy. Its effectiveness, however, at least as far as Austria-Hungary was concerned, depended on Russian readiness to maintain the *status quo* in the Balkans. After 1866 Austria, excluded from German affairs, had only one possible outlet for expansion—toward the Balkans. She therefore became increasingly concerned about Russian intervention in that area.

Crisis. The Near Eastern crisis deepened in 1875 with the outbreak of disturbances in protest against Ottoman oppression, first in the Turkish provinces of Bosnia and Herzogovina and later in Bulgaria. Although public opinion in Europe, especially in England and Russia, was stirred to fever heat by the Bulgarian atrocities, the governments of the major powers failed to take joint action under the Treaty of Paris. Bismarck, in retaliation for Russian intervention to prevent a renewal of conflict between Germany and France in 1875—a move requested by Queen Victoria—refused to support Alexander II at the expense of Austria. Even when the Serbs and Montenegrins, in anticipation of Russian aid, declared war on Turkey, the tsarist government, afraid to risk unilateral action, sacrificed Serbia to an inconclusive agreement with the Hapsburgs in July, 1876, for the future disposition of the Balkan possessions of the Ottoman Empire. This agreement was incorporated in the Treaty of Budapest (1877).

War with Turkey. To assure Austrian neutrality in the rapidly approaching conflict with Turkey, Alexander II made important commitments to the Hapsburgs. In February and March, 1877, Ignatyev was dispatched to Berlin, London, Paris, and Vienna to obtain a clarification of the position of the major powers in the event of war with Turkey. As in the case of Nicholas I before the Crimean War, Alexander II must have felt that he had covered all eventualities and that the road was clear. Spectacular Russian successes in Asia may have produced over-confidence in Russian ruling circles. There had been two years of ineffectual diplomatic maneuvering, during which Bismarck had rejected Gortchakov's appeal for a European conference.

Confronted by the imminent collapse of Serbia, Russia on April 24, 1877, unilaterally declared war on Turkey. Europe waited until the victorious Russian army approached the vicinity of Constantinople. At San Stefano, the Russians encountered a British naval force, which had entered the Sea of Marmora to defend the Turks, even if England were compelled to fight alone. Austria, in spite of the Treaty of Budapest, threatened to break diplomatic relations if Russian troops entered Constantinople. On March 3, 1878, the triumphant Ignatyev dictated the Peace of San Stefano to the prostrate Turks.

Peace of San Stefano. The main provision of this treaty was the creation of a large Bulgaria, stretching from the Danube to the Aegean, and from the Black Sea to Lake Ohrid, and including disputed Macedonia. The new Bulgaria was placed under Russian occupation and supervision for two years, in a fashion which indicated it was fated to become a Russian satellite and an advance Russian outpost for further penetration of the Balkans. The treaty likewise recognized the independence of Montenegro, Rumania, and Serbia, and prescribed administrative reforms for Bosnia and Herzogovina. Russia retrieved her position at the mouth of the Danube along with Batum, Kars, and Ardahan in Transcaucasia, and exacted a financial indemnity from Turkey. Although Ignatyev demanded much more, the treaty opened the Straits in peace and war to neutral merchant ships bound to or from Russia.

The Treaty of San Stefano amounted to a significant Russian victory and was a clear portent of further Russian expansion to come. Thus, it aroused the fears of the other interested powers—those of England for the future of the Straits, and those of Austria, whose route to the Balkans was effectively blocked. The treaty rested on the assumption—a false one, as events soon proved—that Russia would be permitted to settle Balkan problems herself through bilateral agreement with Turkey. Austrian Foreign Minister Andrassy protested the breach of the Treaty of Budapest, which had specified that no large Slavic state was to be created in the Balkans and that Austria would receive compensation in Bosnia and Herzegovina. Under threat of war with England and Austria-Hungary, Russia yielded to pressure for a review of the Treaty of San Stefano by a European conference.

Congress of Berlin. The Congress of Berlin, under the chairmanship of Bismarck, the "honest broker," convened from June 13 to July 13, 1878.

Many of the major decisions had already been reached before the delegates assembled. The aging Gortchakov, who had long anticipated a European conference as the apex of his career, now confronted the dominant Bismarck. Gortchakov's associate, D. A. Miliutin, minister of war, 1878–1882, was a realist, opposed to an adventurist foreign policy, and prepared to sacrifice San Stefano rather than risk a European conflict. Alexander II, who had foreseen no serious opposition to the war with Turkey, expressed bitter disillusionment over the existence of an anti-Russian European coalition, which included Austria and Germany, his allies in the Three Emperors' League.

The Congress of Berlin dismembered Bulgaria, which lost its Macedonian territory to Turkey and its access to the Aegean Sea, and was partitioned into two states, Bulgaria and Eastern Rumelia, separated in general by the Balkan Mountains. Thus greatly reduced in size and strategic importance, the new Bulgaria was recognized as a Russian satellite, to be occupied for nine months by Russian troops. The San Stefano provisions regarding Bessarabia, Dobruja, and the independence of Serbia, Montenegro, and Rumania were allowed to stand. Eastern Rumelia, removed entirely from Russian control, was granted autonomy under the sultan, subject to supervision by the powers. The British, for their protection of the Turks, returned home boasting of peace with Cyprus. Finally Austria, which had not fired a shot, greatly extended her power in the Balkans by the occupation of Bosnia and Herzogovina, as well as the Sanjak of Novi Bazar.

The Russian diplomatic defeat at the conference table after decisive military victory on the battlefield provoked a virulent Russian press campaign against the West, especially against Germany. Constantinople and the Straits, virtually within the Russian grasp at San Stefano, were snatched from Russian control at Berlin. Once again Russia had lost face in Europe. Bismarck proceeded to fashion the Triple Alliance of Germany, Austria, and Italy, to which Rumania was added in 1883. Serbia, distrustful of Russia and isolated from Russian support, looked for a time to the Austrian orbit. After the Congress of Berlin, Russia was diplomatically adrift, but still defiant. This defiance was best expressed by Dostoyevsky in 1881, shortly before his death:

> Yes, the Golden Horn and Constantinople—all this will be ours. . . . In the first place, this will come to pass of its own accord, precisely because the time has come, and even if it has not yet arrived, indeed it is already near at hand; all signs point to this. This is the natural solution, the word of nature herself, so to speak. If it has not occurred before this, it has been precisely because the time was not yet ripe. . . . No matter what happens there—peace, or new concessions on the part of Russia—sooner or later, Constantinople will be ours. . . .
>
> Yes, it must be ours, not only because it is a famous port, because of the Straits, "the center of the universe," "the navel of the earth;" not from the

standpoint of the long-conceived necessity for a tremendous giant like Russia to emerge at last from his locked room, in which he has already grown up to the ceiling, into the open spaces where he may breathe the free air of the seas and oceans. . . . Our task is deeper, immeasurably deeper. We, Russia, are really indispensable and inevitable, both to all Eastern Christianity and to the whole future of Orthodoxy on earth, in order to achieve its unity. This was always understood to be so by our people and their Tsars. . . .

In brief, this dreadful Eastern Question constitutes almost our whole future destiny. Therein lie, as it were, all our problems, and what is most important—our only exit into the plenitude of history. Therein lies also our final conflict with Europe and our ultimate union with her, but only upon new, mighty and fruitful foundations. Oh, how can Europe at this time grasp the fateful, vital importance to us alone of the solution to this question?—In a word, no matter what may be the outcome of the present, perhaps quite indispensable diplomatic agreements and negotiations in Europe, nevertheless, sooner or later, *Constantinople must be ours,* even if it should take another century!

Tragic Aftermath. Defeat abroad had its inevitable repercussions on the Russian domestic scene. Discontent with government policy emanated from the two extremes—the Right and the Left. The conservative Right attributed Russia's loss of prestige abroad to the domestic reforms of Alexander II,

On March 13, 1881, Alexander II approved the constitution drawn up by Loris-Melikov and authorized him to call a General Commission to finalize the plans. On that same day the tsar was assassinated by a terrorist organization whose object was the overthrow of the imperial government.

which were said to have undermined the very foundations of the government. The radical Left, on the other hand, accused the government of procrastination in instituting reforms, which, when they came proved to be halfway measures. For them no alternative remained but revolution. In 1879 an attempt was made to assassinate the emperor. When word reached the authorities that the tsar had been condemned to death by a radical secret society, the government resorted to violent counter measures throughout the country.

Too late, Alexander approved a so-called constitution for Russia, on which Count Loris-Melikov (1825–1888), as head of a Preparatory Committee, had been working since 1880. On March 13, 1881, the emperor was assassinated by a member of a widespread terrorist organization called "The Will of the People." Alexander III, his son and heir, promptly rescinded the constitution, which had been signed but never proclaimed, and inaugurated a period of outright reaction in Russia.

8

Alexander III: Isolation and

Industrialization, 1881-1894

THE CIRCUMSTANCES surrounding Alexander III's accession to the throne not only shocked the nation, but raised the question as to what course should be pursued in the future in domestic and foreign policy. His father's reform measures, which were expected to strengthen the monarchy and add to its popularity, had resulted in increased subversive activity which culminated in the assassination of Alexander II, the Liberator and Reformer. The country, instead of prospering in the wake of the reforms, was confronted with severe economic depression (1880–1885)—an aftermath of the European slump of 1876—which led to a series of industrial strikes of weavers, railwaymen, and dockers. Among the principal victims of the depression was the landowning nobility, many of whom were forced to sell their estates and trek to the cities. The uprooted and injured joined in a rising chorus of denunciation of the reform policies which were blamed for existing circumstances. They demanded the reassertion of autocracy, the removal of all liberal ministers, and the abandonment of all liberal reforms. Nothing was said of military defeat, economic setbacks, and uprisings under the most autocratic of tsars, Nicholas I. Those who might have pointed out the parallels were silenced by reaction.

RETURN TO AUTOCRACY

Alexander III, the second son of Alexander II, who ascended the throne at the age of thirty-six, lost no time in announcing his own position on domestic and foreign policies. In his Manifesto of April 29 (O.S.), 1881, he proclaimed his determination to maintain law and order, to observe justice in the economy, to return to basic Russian principles, and to preserve Russian interests abroad by a firm stand in Central Asia and Bulgaria. He replaced Loris-Melikov as minister of the interior with Count Ignatyev, the militant Slavophile, who was regarded as a "safe" reactionary. When Ignatyev sponsored some Slavophile reforms, including a consultative assembly based on the sixteenth-century *Zemsky Sobor,* he in turn was replaced in 1882 by Count Dmitry Tolstoy, a former minister of education and a pronounced conservative.

154

The person who exercised the greatest influence over Alexander III, however, was his former tutor, Constantine Pobyedonostsev (1827–1907),[1] procurator of the Holy Synod from 1880 to 1905. A jurist of some repute and a former professor of civil law at the University of Moscow, Pobyedonostsev was strongly reactionary in his political philosophy and completely opposed to constitutional government, which he labelled "the greatest lie of our time." For him revolution spelled "the doom of the government and the doom of Russia." Under Pobyedonostsev, church and state once again worked in close alliance for the preservation of autocracy. He was the chief agent of Alexander III in the implementation of the government's decision to fight terror with terror.

Reign of Terror. A reign of terror was instituted on both political and religious grounds. A new law of 1881 dealing with political offenses was directed against all radical and terrorist organizations, such as "The Will of the People," responsible for the assassination of Alexander II, and they were driven underground. All such conspirators against the emperor and the government were to be "deprived of civil rights and condemned to death" (Section 249). All those having knowledge of such conspiracies who failed to inform the authorities thereof were subject to the same penalty. Even persons guilty of organizing a society to change the existing form of government in the future by peaceful means were subject to drastic penalties:

SECTION 250. If the guilty persons have not manifested an intention to resort to violence, but have organized a society or association intended to attain, at a more or less remote time in the future, the objects set forth in Section 249, or have joined such an association, they shall be sentenced, according to the degree of their criminality, either to from four to six years of penal servitude, with deprivation of all civil rights (including exile to Siberia for life) . . . or to colonization in Siberia (without penal servitude), or to imprisonment in a fortress from one year and four months to four years.[2]

The principle of guilt by association thus established brought exile to parents whose children became involved in revolutionary societies. It banished the popular Russian novelist Vladimir Korolenko (1853–1921) to Siberia for refusing to betray friends and acquaintances opposed to the government. So notorious did the police system become that George Kennan, an American, was persuaded to undertake for *The Century Magazine* a complete study of the exile system. His classic two-volume report (*Siberia and the Exile System,* New York, 1891) created such a stir in the West that some reforms were initiated in Siberia.

1. See Robert F. Byrnes, *Pobedonostsev: His Life and Thought* (Bloomington: Indiana University Press, 1968).
2. See George Kennan, *Siberia and the Exile System,* Vol. II (New York, 1891), p. 509.

Police Controls. Under Count Dmitry Tolstoy, measures were taken to strengthen the police system. Rigid censorship was enforced in August, 1882. Until 1901, newspapers warned three times by the censor were henceforth required to submit proofs to censorship the day prior to publication. In 1882 a Special Conference, comprised of the ministers of the Interior, Justice, and Education, and the procurator of the Holy Synod, was given power to suspend or suppress any "specially harmful" magazine. In 1884 this Conference banned the popular periodical, *Annals of the Fatherland,* and no liberal dared to protest. For the next decade, with the exception of *Russkie Vedomosti,* published in Moscow, the liberal press in Russia was virtually nonexistent. Public libraries and reading rooms, especially those frequented by the lower classes, were also subjected to special regulations which resulted in the banning of many books. The authorities encouraged only the use of those books which would preserve the "religious and moral convictions" of the people.

In 1884 the universities were subjected to a new statute, which restricted their autonomy, required the appointment of the rector by the minister of education, and the deans by the curators. Students, too, confronted more state supervision and inspection. The enrollment at St. Petersburg University was curtailed almost 12 per cent, and tuition fees were increased 500 per cent. Higher education for women met with official disapproval. In 1882 the enrollment of women in the only medical school open to them, the Nikolayev Military Hospital, was banned. In 1886 all courses of higher education for women were suspended, although this ban was relaxed somewhat in St. Petersburg in 1889 and again in 1897.

The new found freedom of the courts, especially in regard to the independence of judges and the jury system, was curtailed. In spite of controls over thought and action, which exceeded even those instituted by Nicholas I, a plot by *Narodniki* terrorists to assassinate Alexander III was uncovered in 1887. Among the leaders of the conspiracy who were executed was Alexander Ulyanov, eldest brother of Vladimir Ilyitch Lenin.

Religious Persecution. In addition to repressive political and educational measures, the government, under the guise of Russification, resorted to a program of religious persecution. It was often difficult to draw a line of demarcation between political and religious oppression. In the interests of conformity and Russification, the liberties of Roman Catholics and Protestants were curtailed. In Poland, additional restrictions were placed on the acquisition of land by Poles and the Bank of Poland was replaced by the Bank of Russia. In the Baltic Province, efforts were made from the close of the 1880's to eradicate German cultural influences and to replace the German language by Russian in courts and schools. This was done in spite of the traditional loyalty of the Baltic Germans to the monarchy. Even in Finland the impact of Russification was felt at the close of the century. Tatars and Georgians in the Caucasus were subjected to comparable restrictions. In Central Asia, Buddhists and Mongols encountered severe oppression.

Although all forms of dissent suffered from this campaign, it was the Jews who bore the brunt of the government's officially inspired hostility. Anti-Semitism had begun to grow in the latter part of the reign of Alexander II. Some Jewish youths had belonged to secret revolutionary organizations, whose aim was to overthrow the autocracy. Under Alexander III, the government gave free rein to anti-Semitism. It incited pogroms against the Jews, irrespective of their guilt or innocence, with the object of demonstrating popular fury against all revolutionaries and enemies of the emperor. Within a few weeks of Alexander's accession atrocities occurred in 170 places in South Russia. They were particularly violent in Kiev, Elizavetgrad, Warsaw, and Odessa. Regulations issued by Ignatyev in 1882 once again prohibited Jews from settling in rural areas. Beginning in 1887 only certain percentages of the Jewish children were permitted to enroll in the middle and higher schools—10 per cent in the Jewish Pale of Settlement, 5 per cent outside the Pale, and 3 per cent in the capitals. A sudden, mass expulsion of Jews from Moscow occurred in 1891. The result of this policy of discrimination was the increased exodus of Jews to the West, especially to the United States, and the departure of a smaller number to Palestine.

Privileged Nobility. One aspect of the return to basic Russian principles was the restoration of the privileged position of the Russian nobility. A special manifesto issued on the centenary of Catherine II's "privileges" reaffirmed their primacy in the armed forces, local administration, and justice courts, and anticipated the "diffusion by their own example of the rules of faith and loyalty and the sound principles of national education." In 1889 land captains (*zemskie natchalniki*), who acquired broad authority over the peasant communes, were appointed from the ranks of the nobility. They also assumed the functions of justices of the peace—a decisive blow to the reformation of the legal system under Alexander II. Finally in 1890 under I. N. Durnovo (1830–1903), successor to Tolstoy as minister of the interior, the law pertaining to *zemstvos* was revised to restrict their autonomy and to curtail and control the participation of peasant delegates.

Economic Improvements. While using a club to ensure political subservience, Alexander III at the same time undertook many measures to improve the Russian economy. One of his teachers had been Professor Tchivilev, a well-known economist at Moscow University. According to Count Witte, "Neither in the Imperial family nor among the nobility was there anyone who better appreciated the value of a ruble or a kopeck than Emperor Alexander III."[3] The economic progress of Russia attested to the positive character of the emperor's economic policies. To restore the economic position of the landowners, a Special Nobles' Bank was established in 1885, which provided loans on very favorable terms. By 1904 more than one-third of the land remaining to the nobility was mortgaged. Comparable measures

3. Avrahm Yarmolinsky, ed. & trans., *Memoirs of Count Witte* (Garden City, N.Y.: Doubleday, Page & Co., 1921), p. 39.

were launched to improve the economic condition of the peasants, already far in arrears in redemption payments to the state. A Peasants' Land Bank was created in 1883, through which peasants could borrow money to purchase additional land. By 1905, they had obtained, largely with its aid, 23,000,000 *desyatins* (62,100,000 acres) of land.

THE RISE OF RUSSIAN INDUSTRY

In industry a Russian version of the industrial revolution was already in the making. Emancipation for a time hurt some industries run by serf labor, such as the iron industry of the Urals, the woolen industry, and various craft industries. Soon, however, the foundations of heavy industry were laid in the Donets Basin, rich in coal resources, which in 1884 was linked by rail with Krivoi Rog, an important iron ore center on the Dnieper. The decline of industry in the Urals and the development of metallurgy in the Ukraine led to the rise of cities such as Kharkov, Ekaterinoslav (Dniepropetrovsk), and Rostov. From 1886 to 1895 the Russian production of pig iron increased 178 per cent. Russian heavy industry was greatly assisted by foreign investments in Russia, which more than doubled from 1881 to 1892. The oil industry, based on the Baku oilfields, was soon dominated by Nobel, Rothschild, and Manteshev interests. There was a spectacular rise in the production of crude oil, which in 1875 amounted to 5,000,000 *puds,* in 1885 to 116,000,000, and in 1895 to 345,000,000. By the close of the century Russia ranked first in oil extraction. Even more kerosene was exported abroad than could be afforded by Russians for domestic consumption.

Industrial Combines. During this period a trend could be observed toward the concentration of Russian industry in large enterprises or combines. In 1884 a Congress of Petrol Industrialists was held. Three years later the Permanent Consultative Office of Iron Industrialists, representing foundries throughout Russia, was established. In the development of Russian industry, highly profitable state contracts for the equipment of the armed forces and for railroad and port construction played an enormous role. The production of iron, coal, and cotton was also promoted by the policy of tariff protectionism inaugurated in 1891 by Professor Ivan Vyshnegradsky (1831–1895), minister of finance, 1888–1892, to free the country from economic dependence on Germany.

Count Witte: Monetary Reforms. Industrial development in the reign of Alexander III was the prelude to the greatest industrial upsurge in the history of Imperial Russia, which occurred from 1893 to 1900. These years also witnessed the greatest influx of foreign capital, especially from France, Belgium, and England, in tsarist history. By 1900 two hundred and sixty-nine foreign companies had invested in Russian industry, all but sixteen of which had been founded since 1888. Count Sergei Witte (1849–1915) succeeded Vyshnegradsky as minister of finance in 1892. Witte's monetary reforms,

First acquired during the reign of Peter the Great, the Baku region became the center of Russian oil industry. This print shows the oilfields at Balakhani, near Baku, in 1886.

which substantially increased Russia's gold reserves and made it possible to put Russia on the gold standard in 1897, established greater confidence abroad in the strength of the Russian economy. Witte, of Russified Baltic German extraction, had spent a number of years in railroad business; as a result, Alexander III appointed him to the important post of director of the Department of Railway Communications in the Ministry of Finance. From this position he rose to minister of communications in February 1892, and minister of finance in August of the same year. Serving in this last capacity until 1903, he exerted strong influence on the development of industry, railroad construction, and banking.

Planned Economy. Witte, who has been rated as Russia's leading industrial promoter and Westernizer prior to the Russian Revolution of 1917,[4] was influenced by Friedrich List's *National System of Political Economy,* which prescribed industrialization as the prerequisite to the development of a strong national state. Determined that Russia should equal, if not surpass, the Western powers, Britain, France, and Germany, Witte planned to exploit the country's vast mineral resources and industrial potential, first by expanding the railway network to open up a domestic market of great magnitude. The significance of Asia as an important source of Russia's power and riches, and as a potential market for Russia's industrial products was not lost upon Witte.

4. T. H. Von Laue, *Sergei Witte and the Industrialization of Russia* (New York: Columbia University Press, 1963).

To compensate for her two centuries of "economic sleep," he insisted that time was of the essence, that "railroadification" and industrialization must be achieved under pressure by every available means. The so-called Witte system emphasized, in addition to railroad expansion, higher taxes to produce income for capital investment; the protective tariffs introduced by Vyshnegradsky in 1891; greater influx of foreign capital to which the state had been committed since the reign of Alexander II; and an increase in the Russian worker's labor productivity. His model was Bismarck's Germany, where industrialization was combined with a strong centralized government and a powerful bureaucracy. Witte received strong backing from Alexander III, for whom he undertook to construct the Trans-Siberian Railway; and to a lesser extent from his successor, Nicholas II, at least until 1903. The power he wielded with the support of the autocracy enabled him to do his job with efficiency and probably contributed to his own assumption that industrialization could be combined with absolutism.

Agrarian Opposition. The Witte program, however, encountered bitter and continuous opposition in Russia—still basically an agrarian country—from all agricultural interests, including the *Narodniki,* the *Zemstvo* liberals, the grain exporters, and others. The Russian landowners were not industrially minded. In spite of the economic predicament in which they found themselves toward the end of the nineteenth century, they did not transfer what remained of their fortunes to industry. Insisting that agriculture should and would remain the permanent basis of the Russian economy, they bitterly opposed the higher taxes and high tariffs which affected them adversely, the import of foreign capital which affronted their national pride, and the huge investment in railroads at the expense of much-needed rural improvements. Not only did they dislike the tempo of industrialization accomplished by "artificial means," but they feared, with reason, that peasants lured by the prospect of better wages would leave the land for the factory.

One of the chief centers of opposition to Witte was the political *salon* of Konstantin Fedorovitch Golovin, a moderately liberal landowner and nobleman, where there congregated men such as Count P. I. Heiden, president of the Free Imperial Economic Society, and V. I. Gurko, head of the Peasant Section under Plehve in the Ministry of the Interior. They insisted that Witte had put the cart before the horse, that flourishing villages were the prerequisite to industrial development. They bemoaned the fact that poor peasants drawn from the villages to become factory proletarians were deprived of human dignity and creativity; that foreign capitalists were concerned only about making their fortunes in Russia and not about the economic improvement of the country. They repeatedly attacked Witte's claims as to the success of his program of industrialization. A. P. Izvolsky, Russian foreign minister, 1906–1910, who admired Witte's efficiency but resented his vast power, accused him of gradually building up "a state within a state."

Necessity for Industrialization. The agricultural depression at the end of the century, resulting from the crop failures of 1897 and 1898, convinced Witte more than ever that rapid industrialization, which would create a greater demand for agricultural products, was essential to the stability of the Russian economy. Without it, Russia's position would continue to be precarious, subject to the vagaries of climatic conditions. In March, 1899, he presented a report to the Council of Ministers, the first held under Nicholas II, which amounted to a "Five-Year Plan" designed to gear the Russian economy to industrialization.[5] This document summed up and defended his by then familiar program of tariff protection, the use of foreign capital, and higher taxes to insure successful national economic planning. Witte's recognition of the privation and sacrifices involved, especially on the part of the rural population, in order to attain greater benefits in the future, is reminiscent of Soviet pressure tactics during the Soviet Five-Year Plans.

Witte, of necessity, achieved only partial success in his introduction into Russia of a planned economy. Circumstances beyond his control—the famine of 1891 and its aftermath, the crop failures of 1897 and 1898, the Russo-Japanese War, and the Russian Revolution of 1905—obstructed his efforts. His numerous enemies succeeded in bringing about his downfall in 1903 while his program was still under way. He did, however, create an effervescent atmosphere in favor of industry and elevated business to a respectable profession. The gold standard, which evoked such bitter opposition, made Russia financially respectable abroad. His emphasis on industrialization did lead to the rise of a skilled labor class, which, however, formed the basis of the Social Democratic party from which the Bolsheviks emerged. The railroad expansion he sponsored, although in Russia's vast expanses it continued to require government subsidies, made a permanent economic and strategic contribution to the country's development.

Railroad Construction. As compared with the 1860's and 1870's, railroad construction under Alexander III was sharply curtailed, due in large part to the effects of the Turkish War of 1877–1878 on the national economy. Already by 1889, however, the railroad had crossed the Volga and reached the Urals. From 1893 to 1900 construction amounted to 2,500 *versts* (1657.25 miles) per year. In 1890, 76 per cent of Russian trackage (21,000 *versts*) was in the hands of forty-two private owners, and only 24 per cent under state enterprise. Within the next decade, however, the Russian government for strategic reasons took over most of the main railroad lines.

The decision to construct the Trans-Siberian Railroad—"one of the most cherished dreams of Alexander III," and the outstanding material achievement of the end of the century—was reached in 1885. Construction, delayed

5. For this revealing document, see T. H. Von Laue, "Sergei Witte and the Industrialization of Imperial Russia," *Journal of Modern History* (March 1954), pp. 64–74.

by failure to agree on a suitable route through the Urals, began from both Chelyabinsk and Vladivostok in 1891, following rumors that the English had undertaken a railway project in China. By 1900 the road had reached Lake Baikal, a section not finally completed until the Russo-Japanese War. In the Far East the line from Khabarovsk to Lake Baikal was linked by the Chinese Eastern Railroad, built by Russia on Chinese territory. The Trans-Siberian Railroad, conceived at first as an economic enterprise, but after 1891 regarded from the standpoint of its strategic significance, was built by the state at a cost of 400,000,000 rubles. As construction proceeded, new cities sprang up along the line. The city which came to be known as Novosibirsk became the economic center for all of western Siberia. In reality, the railroad made Siberia an integral part of Russia. By providing a direct land route to the Far East, it outflanked the British fleet in the Pacific.

Population Increase. The population of Russia, which in 1860 was 70,000,000 (without Finland), had reached 133,000,000 in 1900, an increase of 80 per cent in forty years. The heavy increase was due largely to the acquisition of vast areas of territory in Central Asia and the Far East. Russia's urban population, promoted by railroad construction, increased at a faster rate than rural population. From 1863 to 1897 the city population increased 97 per cent as compared with 48.5 per cent in rural areas. Even at this rate, the population of European Russia was but 12.8 per cent urban. Among the country's larger cities, St. Petersburg led with 1,270,000 inhabitants; Moscow followed with 1,036,000; Odessa had 405,000; Riga, 282,-000; and Kiev, 247,000.

Labor Legislation. The rise of Russian industry and the development of urban life resulted in a substantial increase in the number of industrial workers. Their number in 1896 was estimated to be 2,200,000; by 1900, perhaps 3,000,000 (550,000 in textiles, 500,000 in metallurgy, and 400,000 in railroad construction). In the last two decades of the nineteenth century, the government took modest steps to limit the exploitation of workers by means of labor legislation. In 1882, Bunge, minister of finance, prohibited the labor of children under twelve, prescribed an eight-hour day for children from twelve to fifteen, and made provision for their schooling. Factory inspectors were provided to supervise the enforcement of the legislation. Additional laws, 1884–1885, forbade night work for women and adolescents in the cotton, linen, and woolen factories. Labor unrest found expression in 1885 in a strike in the Morozov factory near Moscow, for which prison sentences were meted out to workers and their leaders. From 1881 to 1886 it is estimated that about eighty thousand workers participated in forty-eight strikes. Trade unions had been declared illegal by a law of 1874 in the reign of Alexander II. It was not until 1897, following the St. Petersburg textile strikes, that an eleven and one-half hour day (ten hours for night shifts) was introduced for all workers, irrespective of age or sex. In labor disturbances, the Russian

REAPPRAISAL OF FOREIGN POLICY

police frequently collaborated with the industrialists to maintain order. In serious labor disputes, the Cossacks were employed for the same purpose.

At the accession of Alexander III, Russian foreign policy, like Russian domestic policy, required a reappraisal. Following the Congress of Berlin, Russo-German relations deteriorated. In the delimitation of Balkan boundaries in 1879, Russian nationalists felt that Germany assumed an anti-Russian position in favor of Austria. A German ban on the import of all Russian cattle on the pretext of a plague epidemic in Astrakhan created additional friction. Both Germany and Russia indulged in violent press wars, with the Germans emphasizing the Russian threat to German national security and spreading rumors of a secret Franco-Russian alliance. In October, 1879, Bismarck concluded the secret Dual Alliance with Austria-Hungary, which in 1882 was transformed into the Triple Alliance by the addition of Italy. Russia, dangerously isolated in Europe, confronted a hostile England at the Straits and in Asia.

Nicholas K. Giers. Although the ailing Foreign Minister Gortchakov was not formally replaced until 1882, from 1879 his second in command and ultimately his successor, Nicholas K. Giers (1820–1895),[6] was in reality in charge of Russian foreign affairs. Of Swedish Protestant background, Giers was a modest, conciliatory person, far removed from adventurous Panslavism. He entered the Asian Department in 1838 and served as its director from 1875 to 1882. Prior to that time, he had had broad experience in diplomatic affairs at Russian embassies in Jassa, Constantinople, Bucharest, Teheran, Berlin, and Stockholm. His marriage to Gortchakov's niece promoted his status in the Ministry of Foreign Affairs.

In spite of his lack of wealth and aristocratic position, he managed to continue as foreign minister throughout the reign of Alexander III, and thereafter until his death in 1895. In general, the emperor and Giers saw eye to eye on major foreign-policy decisions. The two other men whose influence was felt on the reappraisal of Russian foreign policy were P. A. Saburov (1835–1893), Russian minister to Athens, 1870–1879, and Russian ambassador to Berlin beginning in January, 1880; and D. A. Miliutin, minister of war in 1879.

The key to Giers' diplomatic maneuvers was his emphasis on security in Europe and the Near East. To offset English intervention in the Ottoman Empire and the growing possibility of Anglo-Austrian collaboration at the Straits, he strongly supported a German *rapprochement*. It was for this

6. See Charles and Barbara Jelavich, eds., *The Education of a Russian Statesman: The Memoirs of Nicholas Karlovich Giers* (Berkeley and Los Angeles: University of California Press, 1962).

purpose that Saburov was sent to Berlin in 1880. Giers placed Russian interests above those of the South Slavs and was therefore prepared to accept a compromise solution of troublesome Balkan problems. Saburov saw in a European settlement the opportunity for an aggressive Russian policy in Asia.

Renewal of the Three Emperors' League. The outcome of the reappraisal of Russia's international position was the renewal on June 18, 1881, of the Three Emperors' League (*Dreikaiserbund*) of 1873. It differed from the original agreement concluded by Alexander II, which called for consultation in time of crisis, in that it provided for the "benevolent neutrality" of the signatories if any one of them was involved in war with a fourth power. A reluctant Austria was prevailed upon by Bismarck to accept the Russian interpretation of the closure of the Straits to the warships of other foreign powers. The agreement covered a war with Turkey, in the event that the three powers had reached a prior understanding as to the outcome of such a conflict. Thus it virtually guaranteed the *status quo* in the Balkans, barring consent to change it. A special protocol defined the spheres of influence of Russia and Austria in the Balkans, with Bosnia, Herzogovina, and Macedonia in the Austrian sphere and Bulgaria and Eastern Rumelia in the Russian.

Anglo-Russian Rivalry: Afghanistan. The revival of the *Dreikaiserbund* did strengthen Russia's international position vis-à-vis England and set the tone for Russian foreign policy in Europe and the Near East until 1887. Protected in the west, the Russians were in a position to renew their advance in Asia, with the occupation of Serakhs and the oasis of Merv in 1884 and Kushka in 1885. As the alarmed British advanced toward Herat on the route to India, Queen Victoria personally appealed to Alexander III to avert a conflict. Confronted by the possibility of an Anglo-Russian war over Afghanistan, Russia invoked the Straits agreement, calling for collective action to keep foreign (English) warships out of the Dardanelles. From 1885 to 1887, now that the vacuum between them was practically filled, England and Russia resorted to diplomacy, rather than war, to settle the boundaries of Afghanistan from Iran to the Amu-Darya. This agreement prescribed the limits of Russian expansion in Central Asia. Russia rounded out her possessions by the annexation of the Pamir region in 1895.

Colonialism in Bulgaria. The Bulgarian crisis of 1885 to 1887 resulted in a rift in the *Dreikaiserbund*. After 1878 the Russian government pursued in Bulgaria a typical "colonial" policy which alienated even the most pro-Russian among this Slavic population. Although the Russians had appealed to Bulgarian nationalism in the struggle against Turkey, they completely failed to understand that the Bulgars would react toward Russian domination as they did toward Turkish rule.

A succession of Russian civil and military representatives, men of mediocre caliber, handled Bulgaria as if it were a Russian province and a military outpost against the Ottoman Empire. Moreover, Russian policy toward the Bulgars was far from consistent. It fluctuated from support of the Bulgarian constitu-

tion to its abrogation; from collaboration with Prince Alexander of Batten-
berg, the new country's first ruler, to his forced removal in 1885 on the eve of
the reunion of Bulgaria and Eastern Rumelia. In the crisis produced by this
interference in Bulgarian internal affairs, Alexander III—a realist rather than
a Panslavist—bluntly announced: "The Slavs must serve Russia and not we
them." The Russian government displayed its iron hand by sending General
N. V. Kaulbars to Bulgaria to secure a government favorable to Russia. His
high-handed tactics provoked nationwide criticism.

Bulgaria's alienation from Russia brought to the Bulgarian throne in June,
1887, a German prince, Ferdinand of Coburg, who henceforth pursued a pro-
Austrian policy. By their ineptitude the Russians had forfeited their position
in Bulgaria, which now blocked rather than opened the Russian route to the
Straits. Having lost Bulgaria, the Russian government, in order to reestablish
its influence in the Balkans, was forced to revive its ties with Serbia, a policy
certain to antagonize Austria-Hungary.

Reinsurance Treaty. As a result of the Bulgarian crisis, Austria refused to
renew the *Driekaiserbund* in 1887. Bismarck papered over the cracks by
concluding the Reinsurance Treaty of June 18, 1887, by which Russia agreed
to observe neutrality only in the event of a French attack on Germany, and
Germany undertook to remain neutral in the Balkans only if Austria committed aggression against Russia. Even this remaining link in the Three
Emperors' League was permitted to lapse after the fall of Bismarck in 1890.

Relations with France. The growing coolness between Germany and Russia
following the Congress of Berlin, which was accompanied by German economic reprisals against Russian grain imports and the rejection of Russian
bonds as collateral security for Russian loans, provided an opportunity for
France. The reorientation toward republican France of Russian foreign policy,
traditionally based on close relations with Germany and Austria, was slow in
developing.

In the 1880's an important Russian faction came out in opposition to the
pro-German policy of Foreign Minister Giers and demanded a reappraisal. It
included landowners and members of the bourgeoisie, who felt the pinch of
German economic pressure. Its mouthpiece was Katkov, publisher of the
nationalist *Moskovskie Vedomosti.* In 1886 he conducted a press campaign
against Giers and demanded a *rapprochement* with France. In 1887, the
conservative paper, *Novoe Vremya,* joined the campaign, as did many leading
Russian figures, including Count Ignatyev, Dmitry Tolstoy, General N. I.
Obrutchev (1830–1904), head of the Imperial General Staff, 1881 to 1896,
and O. V. Gurko (1828–1900), governor-general at Warsaw.

Meanwhile, a group of French bankers took advantage of Germany's
negative position on loans to Russia to float a series of Russian loans in Paris,
1887 to 1889. Strategy entered the picture in 1889, when the French agreed
to manufacture 500,000 rifles for the Russian army. In May, 1890, the
French minister of the interior risked domestic repercussions by the arrest of

a number of *Narodniki* terrorists, Russian political émigrés in Paris, thereby earning the gratitude of Alexander III. In a period when Russian attention was focused on domestic issues, however, it was easier to secure support for a policy of non-alignment with Germany than one for an alliance with republican France.

In the final analysis, it was the changing international situation following the rise of Germany as a major power, rather than domestic or economic factors, that produced the dramatic reversal of Russian foreign policy in the 1890's. It was Germany that accorded primacy to its relations with the Hapsburgs after 1871 and finally broke the line to Moscow in 1890. It was France, isolated and increasingly alarmed by the rapid growth of German might, that initiated first economic and then military and diplomatic ties with autocratic Russia. Russian domestic politics did not require the diplomatic *volte-face*.

Dual Alliance. Although Giers rejected the first French proposal for a Franco-Russian alliance in 1891, the renewal in the same year of the Triple Alliance of Germany, Austria, and Italy, forced his hand. A French naval force received an enthusiastic reception at Kronstadt at its first entry into Russian waters since the Crimean conflict—a reception which culminated in the rendition of the French national anthem, the *Marseillaise,* hitherto strictly banned in Russia. On August 27 (N.S.), 1891, the Dual Alliance of France and Russia was signed to offset the threat to both countries of the Triple Alliance of the Central Powers.

The Franco-Russian alliance ended the isolation of both Russia and France in Europe. Both powers agreed to confer and to take concerted action in the event of any threat of aggression. A military convention of 1893 defined the terms of aid, thus putting teeth into the alliance. This measure of security in the West and the continued availability of French capital for the construction of the Trans-Siberian Railroad and other enterprises, enabled Russia to turn to the East, to Asia. In Europe, the Franco-Russian Alliance contributed to the division of the continent into two armed camps which eventually clashed in 1914 in World War I.

Anglo-Russian Rivalry: Persia. Persia, like Central Asia, was an important scene of Anglo-Russian rivalry. Although Russian tactics here differed from those employed to the East, the objective was similar. Many Russians, including Count Witte, regarded northern Persia as a future acquisition or at least a protectorate of Russia. The Cossack Brigade, a well-disciplined corps organized under Russian officers at the shah's request in 1879, was regarded as the vanguard of the Russian advance into Persia. The Russian government intended to follow up this entering wedge by the construction of railroads. Having failed, however, to win concessions, it exacted a pledge from the shah to ban all railways for the decade 1890 to 1900.

It was chiefly through its economic policy that Russia sought to check British penetration. If the English organized a bank or secured a concession, the Russians followed suit. In 1888 Russia acquired a fishing monopoly on the shores of the Caspian Sea, which led to infiltration in Enzeli, Mazandaran, and Gilan. Russians also secured important forest concessions in northern Iran. A certain Lazar Polyakov, a Russian with widespread business interests in Central Asia, in 1890 applied for a mammoth concession to run a bank, refine oil, manufacture paper, open an insurance company, and deal in opium, part of which he succeeded in getting. In the stormy reaction to the Talbot (British) tobacco concession in Persia in 1890, the Russians learned how to incite the city mobs to promote disorder, with the result that the concession was cancelled.

It was Sir Robert Morier, British ambassador to St. Petersburg, who in 1889 showed uncanny insight into the motives behind Russian policy toward Persia—a policy carried out by tsars and Soviets. He informed Lord Salisbury confidentially that the Russian purpose was to bring all the attributes of civilization to Central Asia, and to create there a kind of Russian Utopia, which would serve as a magnet to other adjacent Asian peoples and eventually win them for the Empire.[7]

7. Firuz Kazemzadeh, "Russia and the Middle East," in Ivo J. Lederer, ed., *Russian Foreign Policy* (New Haven, Conn.: Yale University Press, 1962), p. 514.

9

A Century of Russian

Arts and Sciences, 1815-1917

THE NINETEENTH CENTURY witnessed a remarkable flourishing of Russian literature, music, art, and the sciences. Although the foundations of this cultural renaissance were laid in the eighteenth century, it made gigantic strides in the reigns of Nicholas I and Alexander II. Prior to the nineteenth century, with few exceptions, the Russian arts and sciences were imitations, adaptations, and elongations of their Western counterparts—French, English, German, or Italian. As an outgrowth of the Napoleonic Wars and the rise of Russian national consciousness, the arts and sciences ceased to be largely derivative and foreign oriented. They became more creative and more characteristically Russian.

LITERATURE[1]

Whatever may be said of Russian backwardness, illiteracy, cruelty, for which the landowning nobility was largely responsible, the redeeming page in the Russian past was its literature. It was the literature, especially that of the nineteenth century, that made the nobility conscience-stricken over the plight of the downtrodden and underprivileged. Russian literature contributed substantially to the abolition of serfdom and to the amelioration of the people's lot.

Authors of the Nobility. For the most part, this literature was produced by the nobility and for the nobility, or at least for a very small intellectual class. The vast majority of the people could neither read nor write. These noblemen turned authors ordinarily were not professional writers but dilettantes, and for this reason Russian literature, by and large, was noncommercial.

In the eighteenth century, the term nobility was sometimes given the same connotation as that accorded to intelligentsia in the nineteenth century. Although the terms *intelligentsia* and *intellectuals* are often used synonymously in the West, in tsarist Russia the intelligentsia did not embrace all

1. In this section the writer has drawn extensively upon his book *The Golden Age of Russian Literature* (Caldwell, Idaho: Caxton, 1952).

168

intellectuals. The Russian intelligentsia as such represented no party or profession, but rather the conscience of the people. It was not the monopoly of university scholars, writers, composers, and artists, although many of them belonged to it. Generally speaking, its members were *idealists*. Many twentieth-century intellectuals who have claimed to speak for the masses actually represented political parties—in the case of the Bolsheviks, one party: the Communist Party. These intellectuals were materialists and *ideologists* rather than *idealists*. Actually, it was the Bolshevik intellectuals who put an end to the leading role of the idealistic Russian intelligentsia.

Denis Ivanovitch Fonvisin (1742–1792). Perhaps the first attempt in Russian literature to differentiate between an intellectual and a true member of the intelligentsia (although this term was not yet in use) was made by Denis Ivanovitch Fonvisin in his play *The Teen-Ager* (also translated as *The Minor* or *The Young Hopeful*), published in 1782. Through his mouthpiece, Starodum (Mr. Wisdom), Fonvisin presents a definition of nobility (intelligentsia) and continues to distinguish intellect from nobility:

> . . . The ranks of nobility I count by the number of deeds which the distinguished man has performed for his fatherland, and not by the amount of work he has taken on himself because of his arrogance; not by the number of servants idling in his hall, but by the number of people pleased with his work and conduct. My nobleman is, of course, happy. And my rich man too. In my reckoning that man is not rich who counts his money merely to lay it away in his coffers—rather the man who sets aside his surplus in order to help those who are in want. . . .
>
> . . . Intellect, if it is naught but intellect, is merely a trifle. We see bad husbands, bad fathers, bad citizens endowed with acute intellects. The value of the mind depends upon virtue (idealism). Without virtue, without morals, a clever man is a monster. Virtue is incomparably higher than any acuteness of the mind. This is easily understood by anybody who really thinks about such things. There are many, many different kinds of intellect. A clever man may be easily excused if he lacks a certain quality of intellect; but an honorable man cannot be forgiven if any one property of soul is missing from his heart. He simply must have all of them. The merit of one's heart is indivisible. An honorable man must be absolutely honorable. . . .
>
> . . . A nobleman, for instance, would deem it most dishonorable to do nothing when there is so much to be done, when there are people in need of help, when there is the fatherland which needs his service. Then there would be no nobleman whose nobility was buried, so to speak, with his ancestors. A nobleman! Unworthy of his name! I do not know anything in the whole world more vile!

Alexander N. Radishchev (1749–1802). If Fonvisin was the first to define the Russian intelligentsia, it was the fate of his contemporary, Alexander N. Radishchev, whose book *A Journey from St. Petersburg to Moscow* (1790) voiced the author's strong protest against serfdom and autocracy, that marked the birth of that intelligentsia. In the foreward to his *Journey,* Radishchev expressed the profound concern for human welfare which motivated the Russian intelligentsia throughout the nineteenth century:

> . . . I looked around me—my soul was troubled by the sufferings of humanity. . . . I felt that everyone could strive to help his fellowmen. . . .

For his temerity in so doing Radishchev was penalized by prison and exile. His martyrdom served as an example to the Russian intelligentsia.

Nineteenth-Century Literary Renaissance. The Russian literary renaissance of the nineteenth century was a product of many factors and literary influences. It received its immediate impetus, however, from two major forces: one cultural, the other political. The first was the appearance in the year 1800 of the manuscript of the *Tale of the Host of Igor,* which created a stir in Russian literary circles, and which inspired Russian authors to cast aside their foreign models in order to emulate the quality of work produced by their ancestors. In the second place Russian literature owed a great deal to the upsurge of nationalism which resulted from the Napoleonic invasion of Russia. During the French invasion there came a strong reaction against foreign influence in general—against French influence in particular. In spite of the fact that the Russian officers who fought Napoleon spoke French among themselves, the bulk of the Russian people despised it. Following the trend of popular opinion, and stimulated by the discovery of ancient manuscripts, Russian authors chose Russian themes as their literary medium during the golden age.

Realistic Novel. Unlike other literatures, where poetry occupies the most prominent place, prose, especially the novel, is foremost in Russian literature. For various reasons, the Russian genius expressed itself much better in prose. The majority of Russian writers considered poetry as entertaining literature— but Russian literature, regarded in its entirety, is not entertaining. It is closely interwoven with current events and deals with problems of utmost importance to the individual, to the nation, or to society as a whole. Much material, which in other countries would have found its way into scientific or theological journals, in Russia found an outlet in fiction. The censorship that existed in Russia during the period in question made it impossible, for example, to have the same debates and discussions over the condition of the serfs in Russia as occurred in the United States over the abolition of slavery. Russian champions of emancipation had to resort to fiction—to novels and short stories in which they discussed the pros and cons of the problem. It will suffice to mention Gogol's *Dead Souls* or Turgenev's *Memoirs of a Sportsman.* In the light of this situation there is perhaps no such thing as Russian fiction (as the term is usually understood), for each novel dealt with the burning issues of the day. In other words, if one were to substitute the real names for the fictitious names, one could easily reproduce an important part of Russian history in the nineteenth century. In this connection it is well to remember that the reading public in Russia during the period, although small in proportion to the total population, was, generally speaking, a highly intelligent group, capable of grasping the underlying facts behind the so-called fiction.

Drama. Although the novel occupies the most prominent place in Russian literature, we can hardly afford to overlook the role of the drama. Briefly, classical Russian drama is a purely secular institution. Unlike the drama of Western Europe, whose beginnings are traceable to the church, the Russian classical drama was founded and developed outside the church; in fact, it was established and flourished in spite of the church.

Although the novel afforded a medium for the highest expression of Russian tragedy, the genius of Russian drama lay in the comedy. For this reason, in Russian literature the novel and the play are closely interwoven and inseparable—the one complementing the other. Closer examination reveals, moreover, that the technical structure of the best Russian fiction was based upon the play. In view of these facts it is not surprising to find that practically every Russian novelist of renown was also a playwright and *vice versa.*

The novel reflected life as it was too often in Russia at this time—a tale of frustrations and defeat. Strictly speaking, the comedy interpreted the novel; that is, by exposing the corruption prevalent among public officials and by holding up to ridicule their mismanagement of public affairs, the comedy often revealed the source of the tragedy in Russian life. In a country where universal education did not yet exist, and where the majority of the ruling class could scarcely be called literary-minded, the stage had, potentially at least, a wider audience than the novel. This may partially explain why the censor was more lenient with the novel than with the play and why the novel became the main channel of expression in Russian literature.

Alexander Sergeyevitch Pushkin (1799–1837). The founder and the most outstanding leader of this Russian national literary renaissance was Alexander Sergeyevitch Pushkin. Pushkin has done more for the Russian language than Shakespeare for the English. As Peter the Great, in the time of one short life, sought to bridge the gap created by the Mongolian invasions, Pushkin cherished the same dream for Russian literature and the Russian language. He found it a rough, uncut diamond with great potentialities, and he left it a polished medium of expression unsurpassed by other modern languages. Even into the foreign words he borrowed, he breathed a new spirit. In the Russian language he was able to give expression to the pent-up thoughts and emotions of a previous generation as well as of his own contemporaries. He gave wings to the Russian language in poetry.

Pushkin's liberal leanings, radical associates, and revolutionary poems and epigrams, directed even against the highest functionaries of the government, including the tsar, soon rendered him suspect. His *Ode to Liberty* (1817), which constituted a summons to revolt against an unregenerate autocracy, *The Village,* which depicted the evils of serfdom, and other Pushkin poems

The year 1949 was the 150th anniversary of Pushkin's birth. This poster was painted by V. Zelensky for the Soviet Union's jubilee commemorating the great poet.

were widely circulated in manuscript form among his friends. Alexander I, antagonized by the rash young poet's boldness in deluging the country with shocking verses, banished him to South Russia in 1820. Although ostensibly he made his peace with autocracy under Nicholas I, his *Message to Siberia* (1827) revealed the poet's strong sympathy for the exiled Decembrists.

Until Pushkin, Russian writers were for the most part of the dilettante type—for it was an unwritten tradition that each outstanding noble family should produce at least one manuscript of merit in each generation. Pushkin, however, in addition to his other contributions, made a profession of writing.

Pushkin transmitted to others the inspiration and ambition to continue that which he himself was not able to complete in the brief span of his own life. His influence is clearly discernible throughout the entire period, many ideas being directly traceable to him. For instance, his *Eugene Onegin,* a novel in verse, provided the pattern for all subsequent novelists in Russia. His *Dubrovsky* forms an excellent background for Turgenev's *Memoirs of a Sportsman.* Tolstoy's *War and Peace* was patterned after Pushkin's *The Captain's Daughter,* while *The Queen of Spades* by Pushkin may have inspired Dostoyevsky's *Crime and Punishment.* To be sure, Dostoyevsky always acknowledged his indebtedness to Pushkin. For it was he who made Pushkin famous by evincing his admiration for *The Prophet.* If Belinsky, the Russian Lessing, was chiefly responsible for discovering Pushkin's talent, it fell to the lot of Dostoyevsky to proclaim him the greatest poet of the world and the national poet laureate of Russia.

As the first writer of Russian tragedies, foreign in form but Russian in content, Pushkin also made his contribution to the field of drama. Of these the best example is *Boris Godunov,* upon which Mussorgsky later based his opera of the same name. But Pushkin's real genius lay in poetry. It was through his verse that the young poet voiced the true sentiment of literary Russia. His greatest achievement, and one which alone would have ensured for him the literary immortality he sought, was the incomparable *Eugene Onegin.*

Few poets can claim to have exerted such an influence on their country's music as did Pushkin. His dramatic poems and fairy tales provided themes for most of the outstanding Russian composers of the nineteenth and twentieth centuries. The impressive list includes the best-known Russian operas, such as Glinka's *Ruslan and Lyudmila;* Dargomyzhsky's *The Stone Guest;* Mussorgsky's *Boris Godunov* (as revised by Rimsky-Korsakov); Tchaikovsky's *Eugene Onegin, Mazeppa* (*Poltava*), and *The Queen of Spades;* Rimsky-Korsakov's *Tale of the Tsar Saltan, The Golden Cockerel,* and *Mozart and Salieri;* Rachmaninov's *Aleko* (*The Gypsies*) and *The Avaricious Knight;* and the ballets of the Soviet composer Asafyev, based on *The Fountain of Bakhchisarai* and *The Prisoner of the Caucasus.*

Mikhail Yurevitch Lermontov (*1814–1841*). Next in importance to Pushkin was Mikhail Yurevitch Lermontov, whose fame rests primarily on his poems *The Demon, The Angel, On the Death of a Poet,* and on his prose novel, *The Hero of Our Times.* Unlike Pushkin, whose writings reflect the past and present of Russia and afford a glimpse into her future, Lermontov is primarily the poet of the Caucasus. He first visited this region as a lad, and was twice banished there—a punishment which proved to be a blessing in disguise. The prerequisite for a full appreciation of Lermontov's poetry is a knowledge of the Caucasus region as it was in the early nineteenth century. The Caucasus made of Lermontov more than a mere successor to Pushkin. It was due to the scenic grandeur of that environment that he inaugurated the age of romanticism in Russian literature.

His main contribution to Russian literature was that he revealed a new world in the Caucasus, a hitherto comparatively unknown region then in the process of conquest by the Russians. The Caucasus, in those days, stood in much the same relation to Russia as the Wild West to the Eastern states in America. The Cossacks were the Russian cowboys and the native tribesmen their Indians, who carried on an unrelenting guerrilla warfare against Russia for 137 years.

Lermontov was the first Russian poet to depict not only the magnificent grandeur of Caucasian scenery, but also to describe Caucasian culture, itself an elongation of the Near East, and to record the hitherto unwritten folk tales and ballads of the native peoples. In this light, his contribution was not only to Russian literature but to Oriental studies in general; for, although the Caucasus has long belonged to Russia, it has remained linguistically and culturally Near Eastern. During recent years when the Soviet government has encouraged a real renaissance of Caucasian culture, the inspiration and value of Lermontov's work have become even more apparent.

It is in part due to Lermontov that Russian literature—a literature in which the East and West meet—has such a fascination. Pushkin primarily interpreted western Russia to the Eastern world, whereas Lermontov, through the Caucasus, interpreted the East to western Russia and the world.

Alexander Sergeyevitch Griboyedov (1795–1829). One of the outstanding dramatists of this period, a contemporary of Pushkin and Lermontov, was Alexander Sergeyevitch Griboyedov. His masterpiece, and the most widely discussed comedy in the Russia of his time, was *The Misfortune of Being Clever.* The chief character was Tchatsky, who voiced the sentiment of a considerable part of the intelligentsia against the foreign influences which permeated the Russian ruling classes, and who advocated reform in preference to violent revolution. However, Tchatsky's "tirades," after a period of crystallization, reached their climax in the abortive Decembrist revolt of 1825—the first Russian revolution.

The influence of this play did not end with the Decembrist revolt. Subsequent Russian writers and leaders studied its verses by heart. Its influence is clearly discernible in Dostoyevsky's work. Tchatsky was undoubtedly a model for Dostoveysky's Prince Myshkin in *The Idiot.*

In brief, *The Misfortune of Being Clever* was written for the elite. It was both a confession of and a protest against the corruption of the official world and the excesses of the younger generation. The shadow of Tchatsky hovered over Russian literature almost to the outbreak of the Russian Revolution of 1917. Its great, although indirect, influence on the latter event can hardly be overestimated.

Nikolai Vasilyevitch Gogol (1809–1852). In the history of Russian literature, 1842 should be hailed as a red-letter year. For the appearance of *Dead Souls* by Nikolai Vasilyevitch Gogol in that year marked the birth of the genuinely realistic Russian novel, thereby inaugurating the age of prose in

Russian literature. Gogol was the father of the Russian novel, and, as previously stated, it was the novel which occupied the most prominent place in the field of Russian letters.

Although Gogol's work reflected Russian life as a whole, we immediately associate it with South Russia. Just as when we speak of Lermontov we visualize the Caucasus, when we turn to Gogol we think chiefly in terms of the Ukraine. Gogol first attained popularity by his sketches of Ukrainian life. These sketches were widely read, not because of their rich content, but chiefly because they revealed a new world to the people of Great Russia. The North Russians of the period in question looked upon Southern Russia as the Americans for many years regarded the West. Just as the stories of the "Wild West," real or fictitious, made a tremendous appeal to men in the more settled parts of the United States, so Gogol's early sketches of Ukrainian life, present or past, stirred the imagination of Russians elsewhere. His historical novel, *Taras Bulba,* became the first and foremost classic on the Russian Cossacks. The sixteenth-century Cossacks depicted in this novel held the same appeal for the Russian reader as the exploits of the Western cowboys for Americans. These tales hold the key to Gogol's widespread popularity.

Gogol's famous story *The Cloak* also broke new ground in Russian letters. *The Cloak* is not the best story in Russian literature, as some critics claim, but it was the most epoch-making literary production. Here, for the first time, the sad plight of the low-salaried chancery clerk attracted the attention of Russian society. Prior to this, the Akaky Akakiyevitches, if they were ever mentioned, received only incidental recognition and never captured a leading role. There were thousands of them in Russia, toiling for a mere pittance, yet striving to maintain the standard of living demanded of them. In *The Cloak* they received for the first time a new recognition when Gogol relegated the titled bureaucracy to the background in a story which was essentially economic and social. He therefore gave a new tone to Russian literature. That note of sympathy for the oppressed, so characteristic of later Russian writers, who selected now one group, now another, as the object of their concern, reached its zenith under Dostoyevsky. Gogol, in addition to arousing the public conscience, laid the foundations for a new literary school in which many of his successors were trained. It is hardly an exaggeration to say in the words of one great Russian author, Dostoyevsky, that all Russian literature emanated from that cloak! So great was its influence that Russian literary critics have enumerated about two hundred stories written in the same vein.

Gogol wrote many plays, but the best of all was *The Revizor* (*The Inspector-General*). *The Revizor* is the national comedy of Russia, and ever since its initial performance it has retained its crown of popularity. Because it holds up corruption and inefficient bureaucracy to ridicule, it is a play that will endure under any regime. Although some Western critics who approach the analysis of Russian plays with Western tools have maintained that there is no such thing as Russian drama, they have failed to realize that the Russian playwright, consciously or unconsciously, stresses character protrayal at the expense of action and other technicalities that loom so large to the Western mind. In the typical Russian play the plot evolves from and is an outgrowth of character portrayal. The same is true, not only of Russian drama, but of Russian literature in general. Russians emphasize the *who,* not the *what.* With reference to *The Revizor,* however, it is universally conceded that even technically speaking the play measures up to the standards of a Western drama.

The Revizor has done more to effect a bureaucratic housecleaning than any number of serious articles directed against a corrupt officialdom. The fact that Emperor Nicholas I himself overruled the censor and granted permission to stage the play was sufficient to stir up some activity in the various chancelleries of autocratic Russia. The emperor's position in this matter was obvious. He wanted to show a corrupt officialdom that he was aware of what was going on in Russia.

A closer analysis of *The Revizor* reveals that Gogol, in spite of his merciless exposure of the bureaucracy, did not attack the institution of autocracy. He merely pointed out the incongruity between the office and the behavior of its incumbent, between duty and abuse of power or privilege. Gogol's criticism was constructive rather than destructive. Constructive criticism is indispensable in every field of human endeavor, particularly in the state. For this reason Nicholas I, the most autocratic tsar of the nineteenth century, permitted the staging of *The Revizor.*

Whereas the scene of *The Revizor* was laid in a small locality, its message was national. Encouraged by the emperor's support and by the elite of Russian society—in spite of the bitter criticism of officials at whom the play was aimed—Gogol conceived a new work, almost a sequel to *The Revizor,* which was destined to play a greater role in the history of Russia, and which dealt a severe blow to the institution of serfdom. The work in question, which has come to be of the utmost historical importance, was later called *Dead Souls.*

Whereas the action of *The Revizor* took place in a single town and was confined to one restricted group of people among whom there was not a single redeeming feature—worse than Sodom and Gomorrah—the setting for *Dead Souls* was Russia in miniature. It embraced various classes and social strata, officials and civilians, landowners and serfs, who pass before the reader as on a literary screen. These characters had their prototypes in real life. *Dead Souls* may therefore be termed the first genuinely realistic Russian novel, because it dealt with Russian life *per se,* with a burning issue which occupied the best minds of Russia throughout the nineteenth century—the problem of serfdom—a parallel to which, against a different background, may be found in the United States. The chief difference is that the Russian serfs, unlike the American Negroes, were of the same stock and the same religion as their masters.

To understand Gogol, one must remember that his criticism was constructive. He aimed at individuals—not at the body politic. He held up corruption
to ridicule but did not question the divine authority of autocracy. He rather
aimed at those who by their very abuse of power undermined it, as subsequent
events were to show. In the light of his constructive criticism and profound
knowledge of Russian institutions *Dead Souls* represented the accurate diagnosis of a competent physician; the appellation *Dead Souls* can be attributed
not only to the deceased serfs in the novel, but to Russia as a whole. A
combination of ignorance, superstition, corruption, inefficiency, graft, and
abuse of power produced an environment in Russia only for dead souls—not
for the living. Gogol called the child by its name. Small wonder that when
Pushkin first heard the book read he cried: "God, what a sad country Russia
is!"

Dead Souls was the most mature and the most profound work that Gogol
produced—the crown of his creative imagination. As in the case of *The
Brothers Karamazov* by Dostoyevsky, Gogol's masterpiece remained unfinished. Although, technically speaking, *Dead Souls* is a novel without a plot,
the character of Tchitchikov binds all its separate parts together. The various
chapters are like distinct sections of one big department store.

Before Gogol only individual protests were voiced against existing corruption and the misery of the underprivileged classes. Gogol not only summed
these up but diagnosed the disease. His successors suggested remedies—
remedies which fell into two main categories—Westernization and Slavophilism.

Ivan Alexandrovitch Gontcharov (1812–1891). *Oblomov*, the classical
Russian novel produced by Ivan Alexandrovitch Gontcharov, was an elongation of, if not a sequel to, *Dead Souls*. In abridged form it might have served
as an additional chapter in that plotless novel. Both Gogol and Gontcharov
diagnosed the national distemper—one labeled it *dead souls,* the other
Oblomovism. However, in spite of Gontcharov's emphasis upon the negative
side of human nature, *Oblomov* is not so gloomy as *Dead Souls,* and the
atmosphere is fresher. When his novel first appeared, it made a tremendous
impression, for the Oblomovs were more familiar to the reading public than
the Tchitchikovs, and many a Russian recognized himself in Oblomov as in a
mirror. As Turgenev once said, "As long as there remains one Russian,
Oblomov will be remembered."

At the same time *Oblomov* paved the way for practically all of Turgenev's
novels. All Turgenev's negative masculine types found their prototype in Ilya
Oblomov, while Olga, Gontcharov's heroine, became the pattern for all the
active feminine characters of Turgenev. It occasioned no surprise to many
Russians when Gontcharov hurled the accusation of plagiarism against the
great novelist of the century—Ivan Turgenev. But instead of being condemned, Turgenev was completely exonerated from this literary heresy—and
justly so. The similarity of their ideas was a mere coincidence, for both

novelists belonged to the same class, were confronted with similar problems, and in the course of everyday life came into actual contact with the types whom they portrayed.

In the classical novel *Oblomov,* Gontcharov depicted the life of the idle-rich nobility of the middle of the nineteenth century from the cradle to the grave. No other author in Russian literature known to us has ever given such a vivid and faithful portrait of Russia's Oblomovs. Oblomov spent the better part of his life in dressing gown and slippers—the outward symbols of the mental and physical stagnation of the wearer—and it took Gontcharov an entire chapter to get him out of bed! It is very difficult to give in English the exact connotation of the Russian word *pokoy,* which implies *repose, seclusion,* and *unruffled peace.* Oblomov sacrificed everything to gain *pokoy.* This word supplies the key to Oblomov's character and to Oblomovism. *Pokoy* occupies the same prominent place in *Oblomov* as *smirenie* in the work of Dostoyevsky. *Smirenie* was a sublimation of *pokoy.* Both were distinctly Slavic traits, particularly characteristic of those directly or indirectly attached to the land. It was natural, therefore, that Oblomov and Oblomovism should become household words throughout Russia, just as Tartuffe in France, Pecksniff in England, and Babbitt in America. From this time on the idle-rich nobility became a legitimate target for attack, and many Russian authors were not slow to avail themselves of this opportunity.

In *Oblomov* Gontcharov depicts the clash between tradition and innovation in nineteenth-century Russia—between the old patriarchal landowners and the new industrial bourgeoisie represented by the successful and enterprising businessman; between rural life and urbanization; between culture and civilization. In this respect Gontcharov may be considered a forerunner of Tchekhov, whose own version of Oblomovism is to be found in all his plays. Throughout Tchekhov's works—and this is particularly true of *The Cherry Orchard*—there runs like a scarlet thread the same clash between the old and the new in Russia. Ranevsky in *The Cherry Orchard* was Tchekhov's version of Oblomov, and Lopakhin his version of Stolz. Tchekhov skilfully wove the problem of ruralism versus urbanization into the texture of this play.

Oblomov at his best was, as we have seen, a true representative of a declining patriarchal society whose roots were fixed firmly in the past. It took many generations to achieve the society of which Oblomov was, perhaps, the last representative. Gontcharov's novel was therefore in a sense a monument to that past. Until the dawn of the "practical age" Oblomovism represented an ideal devoutly to be wished. When Gontcharov wrote, *pokoy,* the *summum bonum* of life to every Oblomov, was rapidly becoming a lost horizon. When the age of industry began to encroach upon patriarchal society, in protest against the hustle-bustle of the practical businessman, the Oblomovs turned their backs upon it all and defied the world in dressing gown and slippers. They clung till the last ditch to what they believed to be the Russian heritage.

Gontcharov, himself a *barin* (nobleman), dealt with Oblomov sympathetically. He did not condemn everything in Oblomovism, and upon Oblomov himself he bestowed more positive than negative traits. It was not even Gontcharov's purpose to deprive the Oblomovs entirely of *pokoy,* for he was never an enemy of the existing order—but rather to place a price upon it. He wanted to purge Oblomovism of its less desirable attributes, laziness and neglect, and to add to it a new meaning. *Pokoy* as the reward of labor and the exercise of practical ability was his ideal.

In Stolz, Gontcharov attempted to portray the practical and enterprising businessman—the antithesis of Oblomov—whom he prophetically recognized as the leader of the new age. Gontcharov seems to have realized that it would take many Stolzes under Russian names to change the inherent characteristics of the Oblomovs. He would like to have seen Oblomov cooperate with Stolz. But Oblomov could not bring himself to adopt a mode of life which necessitated work and action, as well as everyday contact with the seamy side of life from which he held himself aloof, and he turned a deaf ear to Stolz's dreams of the approaching age of industrialism. There remained, therefore, only a choice between Oblomovism and Stolzism, and, as we have seen, Gontcharov predicted the triumph of the latter. He could only hope that victory would not come at the expense of the strong points of Oblomov's generation. In these two characters, Oblomov and Stolz, we find the forerunners of the nation-wide controversy between the Slavophiles and the Westernizers. Oblomov's better traits were the source of Slavophilism. Stolz's ideas were echoed again and again by the Westernizers.

In the person of Olga, Gontcharov has drawn a portrait of the new woman in Russia who began to wrestle with Oblomovism. Herself a member of the St. Petersburg nobility, she was, nevertheless, ahead of her contemporaries. She was active and persistent, with a fine mind, yet deep and tender feelings. She was also honest, decent, and sincere. As yet she had not acquired an established outlook on life or settled convictions but she was in search of them. Because of her love for Oblomov, she tried to expose his weak traits, to arouse him from his inertia, and to induce him to assume his responsibilities. She did not dwell at length upon his positive features, but it was because of these that she loved him. Like Gontcharov, she believed that if Oblomov could be cured of these negative qualities, he could continue to play a leading role in Russian society without resigning his place to the Stolzes. Unfortunately Olga failed. Turgenev's heroines met the same fate of frustration when they sought to eradicate the Oblomovism of their time in their lovers. Next to Pushkin's Tatyana, Olga represented the best in Russian womanhood until the appearance of Turgenev's Liza.

In the person of Zahar, Gontcharov represented the eternal serf, loyal as a dog to his master, yet dishonest in trifles, inefficient, and incurably lazy. Although he does not contribute a great deal to the novel, he was an indispensable fixture in the structure of the society of his time.

All in all we may say that *Oblomov* from a historical standpoint, and more especially as a sociological study of Russia in the middle of the nineteenth century, is almost indispensable. Without *Oblomov* one cannot understand Turgenev and Tchekhov.

Of considerable historical interest even today is Gontcharov's account of his world tour (1852–1854), as recorded in *Frigate Pallada* (1855–1857). The volume on *The Russians in Japan at the Beginning of 1853 and the End of 1854* (1855) throws considerable light on Admiral Y. V. Putyatin's efforts to open Japan, which parallel those of the United States through Commodore Perry.

Ivan Sergeyevitch Turgenev (1818–1883). Russian writers of the mid-nineteenth century became engulfed in a bitter controversy over Slavophilism and Westernism (see also page 113). The foremost literary exponents of Westernism and Slavophilism were Turgenev and Dostoyevsky. Turgenev was the most articulate mouthpiece of the Westernizers and around him this whole movement centered. Dostoyevsky filled a similar role for the Slavophiles. Only in this light can we understand the novels of these two leaders. Each of Turgenev's novels has its counterpart in a work by Dostoyevsky—the one expressing the point of view of the Westernizers, the other of the Slavophiles.

The Memoirs of a Sportsman affords what may be termed a preview of Turgenev's novels. Outwardly speaking a series of harmless sketches, the *Memoirs* were, if indirectly, at least partially responsible for the abolition of serfdom in Russia, as Alexander II himself admitted on one occasion. These sketches, more than any other work in Russian literature, elicited sympathy for the plight of four-fifths of Russian humanity. While in *Dead Souls,* Gogol dealt indirectly with the institution of serfdom, describing for the most part its physical status, in *The Memoirs of a Sportsman,* Turgenev most artistically depicted, for the first time, the life of the serf at its best. In this work he revealed the soul of the serf—a soul which was not so different from his master's, at times even superior. The sketches displayed so much objectivity that they immediately won universal approbation and established Turgenev's reputation as an author.

Inasmuch as Turgenev read *Uncle Tom's Cabin* by Harriet Beecher Stowe, an allusion to which is found in his novel *Smoke,* some comparison between the American classic and *The Memoirs of a Sportsman* may be of interest. The institution of slavery began in America in 1619 when the first slave ship landed at Jamestown, Virginia, with slaves for the pioneer planters. Russian serfdom dates to 1581, in the reign of Ivan the Terrible, when the serfs were "affixed" to the soil for a period of years, and later for life. By the time of Catherine the Great (1762–1796) they had for all practical purposes become the personal property of Russian landed proprietors or of the Russian state. Thus in the nineteenth century America and Russia alike were faced with the problem of a subject people—in America a black people, but in Russia a people of the same race and religion as their masters. By the year 1852 slavery in America threatened to divide the Union, serfdom in Russia to upset the monarchy. In this year the two books mentioned above, both destined to play an important role in the abolitionist movement in their respective countries, were published.

These books were an "open sesame" to literary fame for both Turgenev and Mrs. Stowe. Turgenev was lifted from obscurity to the very first rank of Russian writers. For a time he had the distinction of being the only Russian novelist of international reputation. Through him Russian literature was introduced to France and the Western world.

The *Memoirs* revealed Turgenev's skill and delicacy in character analysis both of men and dogs. He depicted the peasants more sympathetically than the upper classes. His squires were invariably vulgar, cruel, or ineffective, whereas he took pains to emphasize the humanity, imaginativeness, intelligence, and dignity, as well as the poetic and artistic gifts of the peasants. Yet his characters were not overdrawn. Turgenev did not dwell on atrocities which were the exception rather than the rule, nor did he try to idealize his serfs. By painting life-portraits of sensible, reasoning, and affectionate human beings bowed down by the yoke of serfdom, side by side with life-portraits of their mean and shallow masters, the landed proprietors, he, in a wholly unobtrusive manner, awakened in his readers a consciousness of the injustice and ineptitude of serfdom.

Turgenev's novels may be regarded as sketches on a larger scale than those which composed *The Memoirs of a Sportsman,* and they dealt with different problems. The novels span a period of twenty years, from 1856 to 1876, a period which practically coincided with the reign of Alexander II. The era was one of relative freedom in Russia, during which serfdom was abolished, *zemstvos* were established, trial by jury introduced, the term of military service reduced, and many unpopular laws repealed or mitigated.

The reign of Alexander II may be called Russia's Victorian Age—an age in which liberalism kept pace with industrialism and in which the rights of the individual were respected and guaranteed. It was, moreover, the zenith of the golden age of Russian literature and art. To offset England's rostrum of famous writers, her Tennyson and Browning, Carlyle, Dickens, and Thackeray, the Alexandrian age produced Turgenev, Dostoyevsky, Tolstoy, and many other poets and thinkers of the first rank. But behind superficial resemblances there is a profound difference between the relative positions of Russia and Great Britain. In the England of Tennyson freedom had broadened slowly from precedent to precedent. Culture was the mellow fruit of a literary heritage based upon Chaucerian, Elizabethan, and eighteenth-century traditions. Russia bridged the gap from barbarism to culture within the brief span of a few decades. In England's golden age the loyalty of the masses to the throne reached its climax. In Russia the relaxation of the censorship let loose forces directed toward the destruction of the Romanov dynasty, among them Nihilism, which later amalgamated with the more positive but equally destructive Marxism.

Turgenev was chiefly responsible for making the novel of the Alexandrian age the vehicle for the expression of opinions on and criticism of the foremost political, social, and economic issues of the day. Each of his novels had its thesis, relevant to one or more of the specific problems which faced his contemporaries. When Turgenev became a convinced Westernizer he realized that simply to diagnose Russia's ills in the manner of Gogol or Gontcharov would never provide an adequate solution of her problems. He must go beyond constructive criticism and suggest a remedy. The remedy which he believed would solve all Russia's problems for generations to come was the substitution of constitutional for autocratic government. In his novels beginning with *Rudin* and ending with *Virgin Soil,* Turgenev carried on his search for a leader capable of achieving that aim. Only in this light can we understand the trend of thought revealed in these works. They form the best background for the history of the Russian Revolution, for, in his search for a leader, Turgenev parades before us in review his various candidates for the task, most of whom are failures. It took him twenty years to locate his leader, who emerged from his last novel, *Virgin Soil,* not in the role of the leading character, Nezhdanov, but in the person of Solomin, a representative of the middle class. Turgenev's remedy for Russian political, economic, and social problems was a strong middle class.

It was not until 1906 that the Russian government began to take cognizance of this class and to sponsor it. Under the premiership of Stolypin, 1906–1911, several million peasants were given the opportunity to form the nucleus of a middle class in Russia. Although Turgenev intended this class to champion reform—to aid in the creation of a liberal constitutional government in Russia—the tsarist government used it to strengthen the position of the monarchy. As a result the majority of this group was dispossessed by the Soviet government during the first years of the Five-Year Plan.

When Turgenev looked about for a leader he naturally turned first in *Rudin* (originally *A Natural Genius*), to the student body. Many of his contemporaries thought that in the person of Dmitri Rudin, he described his friend and classmate at Berlin University, Michael Bakunin, the political anarchist. Others held that Rudin was a projection of Turgenev himself during his student days. But Rudin did not measure up to Turgenev's expectations. By nature he was more of an Oblomov than a man of action. When he finally decided to act he met death in a foreign cause, somewhere in France, and even for that he received no credit, for those who located his dead body believed him to be a Pole. In brief, in the person of Rudin, Turgenev has given us a most faithful and vivid portrait of the "superfluous" or "undesirable" man, who "speaks like a giant" but "acts like a pigmy."

Turgenev, after this denouement, was advised to abandon his search for a leader among the student youth and to seek him instead among the nobility proper. This he did in *A House of Gentlefolk* (also *A Nobleman's Nest*), which established his reputation as a novelist. Although the heroine, Liza

Kalitin, stole the show in this novel, Turgenev's interest centered in Fyodor Lavretsky, a character who combined traits favorable both to the Westernizers and the Slavophiles, and who, therefore, had no enemies in Russia. But Lavretsky in practice symbolized the decadence of the landed aristocracy, as, with a sigh of resignation, he abandoned his task and passed the torch to the new generation in which he had great faith.

After this second frustration, Turgenev either lost faith in Russian characters or, more likely, he wished to delegate ideas, which would not have been popular with the authorities if uttered by a Russian, to a Bulgarian. For this purpose he chose the Bulgarian Insarov, who became the hero of his third novel, *On the Eve*. Turgenev acknowledged that he owed the theme of this novel to V. Karatayev, a friend who was killed in the Crimean War. In *On the Eve* it was Turgenev's purpose to encourage all Russian liberals to emulate Insarov. Although Insarov's cause was, on the surface, national, in that he dreamed of the liberation of Bulgaria from the Turkish yoke, Turgenev's contemporaries were expected to read between the lines and, by substituting liberalism or constitutionalism for nationalism, to discover the real cause— the liberation of Russia from autocracy.

Turgenev's ruse calls to mind a similar expedient of the author of the Book of Job, who, when he wished to voice a protest against the world order of Jehovah and the plight of the people of Israel, selected a non-Jewish spokesman in the person of Job and permitted him to express statements which, from a Jew, would never have been tolerated. Turgenev's purpose was essentially the same, only the setting was different. Very few understood that purpose, and because Insarov was the only positive male character among Turgenev's heroes, Turgenev himself was condemned by many critics for conferring such an honor upon a foreigner whom he had dragged from the Bulgarian marshes.

When Insarov was rejected, Turgenev set out to prove that a Russian character was even more capable of assuming leadership than a Bulgarian. Bazarov, the hero of *Fathers and Children,* was supposed to be Turgenev's ideal type, stronger even than Insarov. Strange as it may seem, however, no sooner did he select a Russian character than that character proved a weakling whose every project met with frustration. Bazarov came to be known as a Nihilist. By setting forth the tenets of Nihilism, Turgenev, like Gogol and Gontcharov, assumed the role of diagnostician instead of supplying the remedy. Nihilism joined "dead souls" and "Oblomovism" in the list of Russian household words.

Strictly speaking, if we are to judge by the spirit of the work, Turgenev did not preach Nihilism in this novel. Nor did he create Bazarov—he discovered him. It was Turgenev's purpose to direct the attention of the authorities to this new movement which was rapidly taking root in Russian soil. Far from preaching violence or Nihilism through Bazarov, Turgenev sounded a warning against this dangerous newcomer, as if he would say—"Your type of government gave birth to this type of man. Mend your ways by introducing more and better reforms before it is too late. Do you not hear the threats of Bazarov?" Instead of heeding the warning, however, most of the authorities and conservative society, in general, were displeased with Bazarov and condemned Turgenev accordingly. Many members of higher Russian society chose to regard his novel as a serious attempt to negate the "culture of the nobility." On the other hand, the liberals, particularly the Westernizers, thought that, in Bazarov, Turgenev defeated his own purpose. *Fathers and Children* became, therefore, the most controversial and the most widely discussed novel in Russia and has remained so. The impression was given that Turgenev became frightened of his own creation: that he gave Bazarov a chance to expound his ideas, but when he reached the point where he was ready to translate those ideas into action, Turgenev, the *deus ex machina,* fearing that his hero might become a Frankenstein or a Golem, stepped into the arena in person and brought Bazarov's life to a premature end.

This novel likewise reflects the clash between the sciences and the humanities during the period in question. Very few are aware of the fact that Russian Nihilism, strictly speaking, was not so much a product of industrialism as of German science which invaded Russia in the form of an "ism" in the middle of the nineteenth century. The brothers Kirsanov represent the old traditional generation brought up on the humanities. Bazarov, the leading character in this classic novel is the forerunner of the new scientific age. The Nihilism of Bazarov was the result of science minus the humanities. Everything that savored of art and culture in the traditional sense was taboo to Bazarov, that prototype of Nihilism in its various forms. The duel between Bazarov and Pavel Kirsanov, ostensibly over Fenitchka, actually symbolized the clash between the two ideologies.

One of the few to understand the message of *Fathers and Children* was Dostoyevsky, who wrote what may be called its sequel from the Slavophile point of view in his novel *The Possessed.* Dostoyevsky began where Turgenev left off, by depicting the Bazarovs in action, with startling results. After reading *The Possessed* we are less likely to condemn Turgenev for the annihilation of his own creature.

When the furore over *Fathers and Children* died down, Turgenev produced *Smoke.* This novel, strictly speaking, was a rebuttal to the criticisms of those authorities and conservatives who misconstrued his message in *Fathers and Children.* He held up many of their ideas to ridicule and indirectly implied that they were incapable of grasping this message or the liberal recommendations of the Westernizers because they wasted their time on trivialities or, as he said, in trying to hypnotize a turtle.

Smoke was followed by *Spring Freshets,* in which, although it does not deal with the background of current events in Russia proper, Turgenev produced another negative type in the person of Sanin, who met with frustration in both love and business. In 1880 Turgenev omitted *Spring Freshets* from a volume containing his other six novels because he considered that he had not been sufficiently objective in his treatment of Sanin and the other characters. To Turgenev, objectivity was one of the most indispensable elements in any novel, and, since this one did not measure up to his own standards, he classified it as a separate story. Nevertheless *Spring Freshets* is an important link in the chain of Turgenev's novels. In the first place, many critics regarded Sanin as a self-portrait of Turgenev. In the second place, the novel caused some international repercussions. The German press, in Germany as well as in Russia, began a campaign against Turgenev because of his portrayal of the German character, Kluber, and the German officers, Baron von Dongof and Von Richter. After the publication of *Fathers and Children* and *Smoke,* Turgenev lost many Russian friends and followers; *Spring Freshets* likewise deprived him of his German friends and sympathizers.

As has been indicated previously, it was not until his last novel, *Virgin Soil,* the most mature of all, that Turgenev finally reached his goal. Moroeever, it was not his leading character, Nezhdanov, who measured up to the author's requirements for leadership, but Solomin, the practical factory manager and highly respected representative of the new industrial age. It was during this period that industry began to develop rapidly in Russia, and the businessman began to assert himself as in any industrial country. The practical man who talked seldom but acted often and with decision came into vogue. Solomin was Turgenev's version of Stolz in *Oblomov.*

We must remember that Turgenev was seeking political change rather than social revolution. Solomin, too, hoped that the new era could be inaugurated by evolutionary means rather than by violent revolutions. Although, as we have seen heretofore, Turgenev was at times inclined to side even with the revolutionists to effect the downfall of autocracy, either his aristocratic lineage or his native sagacity finally led him to distrust the leadership of the Bazarovs. Solomin was a man of different caliber—one who appealed to the majority of constructive liberals in Russia.

Virgin Soil is based chiefly on the *Narodniki* movement ("Going to the People"), which came into vogue among the radicals at this time. Instead of working longer in the dark among small groups of adherents, the young revolutionists determined to popularize their message by carrying it directly to the people at large. They wanted to get a firsthand knowledge of the people whose conditions they hoped to ameliorate. As a result they discovered that they had overestimated the "People's" intelligence and maturity, or "consciousness." The soil must be prepared for revolution. Turgenev diagnosed the situation by calling his novel *Virgin Soil,* and he recommended through his mouthpiece, Solomin, a slower but a surer and more practical method of reform, by painstaking education of the people and by gradual evolution, rather than by sudden and violent revolution. History proves that both his diagnosis and his remedy were correct.

The study of Turgenev's novels, therefore, clearly indicates how closely interwoven Russian literature is with current events. His novels faithfully reflected Russian life and the controversial issues of the day. If we had no history whatever of the period in question we could still reproduce it in part from Turgenev's novels.

Although Turgenev is better known for his sketches and novels, his contribution to drama should not be overlooked. His ten plays (1843–1852) were written almost concurrently with the *Memoirs of a Sportsman*. One of them *A Month in the Country,* has become a permanent part of the repertoire of the Russian theatre. In spite of the fact that it belongs to the pre-emancipation era, with the exception of a cursory reference to the 320 serfs belonging to Bolshintsov, Vera's unwelcome suitor, it might readily be included in a collection of Tchekhov's plays. In its portrayal of the inertia and boredom of country life, it has much in common with *The Three Sisters, Uncle Vanya,* and even with *The Cherry Orchard.*

Fyodor Mikhailovitch Dostoyevsky (1821–1881). As already stated, each of Turgenev's novels has its counterpart in a work by Fyodor Mikhailovitch Dostoyevsky. To understand the difference between Turgenev and Dostoyevsky is to comprehend the sharp distinction between culture and civilization. By culture is meant something organic and inherent. By civilization is understood something mechanical and artificial. Culture depends upon a certain locality and is, therefore, the natural outgrowth of a particular soil or environment. Civilization, on the other hand, does not necessarily depend upon geographical phenomena. It may appear everywhere or anywhere. Culture implies birth and growth; civilization calls to mind inventions and material betterment. For instance, if a person wishes to fly, he invents an airplane. That represents civilization. But, if the same person could grow wings on his body, that would denote culture. Character is culture; manners, civilization. If a person lacks character, nobody can give it to him. A character cannot be acquired, but good manners can be taught to anyone, even to an animal. To illustrate further, music is culture, the science of music is civilization. Anyone can study music, but not everyone can be a musician. Emerson represents American culture; Edison and Ford—American civilization. Culture is static; civilization, dynamic. Culture is feeling or emotion; civilization, rationalism and analysis. Culture is lyric; civilization, epic. We can tame or civilize practically every living thing; but we can cultivate only certain of them. We cultivate plants, but we do not civilize them. Thus a person may be highly cultured and possess little civilization, or *vice versa.* The East stressed culture—the West emphasized civilization. Civilization is the more objective, while culture is subjective. Culture stresses the heart; civilization the mind. The ancient Hebrews, for instance, were primarily a cultured people—the Romans predominantly a civilized nation; whereas the Greeks were fortunate in possessing both culture and civilization.

The novels of Dostoyevsky faithfully represent Russian character at its best and at its worst. In the works of Turgenev civilization predominates. In other words, the Slavophiles, whose most outstanding literary exponent was Dostoyevsky, consciously or unconsciously voiced the sentiment of Russian culture; while the Westernizers, whose principal champion was Turgenev, represented civilization—more specifically Western civilization. Only in this light can we grasp the underlying motives of these two great novelists.

Although he refrained from calling the child by its real name, Dostoyevsky always vigorously opposed the importation of foreign culture at the expense of Russian culture. In his own words, "No nation on earth, no society with a certain measure of stability, has been developed to order, on the lines of a program imported from abroad." This does not mean that Dostoyevsky blindly opposed everything foreign merely because it was alien. He was against foreign ideas when they threatened to supplant native influences. He had no objection to the introduction of foreign technique, mechanical equipment, inventions, and so forth. In other words, he was not antagonistic to the importation of civilization because that is transferable and changeable and does not depend on local environment. What he valiantly and consistently condemned was the importation of foreign "isms," that is, foreign culture, for he believed that culture could only be transplanted at the expense of native characteristics. Culture must grow like a tree.

There is no doubt but that most of the Westernizers were as good Russian patriots as the staunchest of Slavophiles; the difference was that the Westernizers for the most part exposed the shortcomings of the Russian character and the backwardness of their country in contrast to the rapid material progress and advanced ideas of the West. They presented the negative side of the picture, while the Slavophiles expressed their patriotism, rightly or wrongly, by advancing the strong points of Russian character and Russian culture in general—the positive side of the picture.

Dostoyevsky's method of characterization was the exact opposite of Turgenev's. Where Turgenev discovered his characters, Dostoyevsky for the most part created them. Turgenev's artistry stopped when the individual was completely drawn; Dostoyevsky's artistry began when the individual, having been almost scientifically portrayed, began to act and, although beset by seemingly insuperable obstacles, moved sincerely and artistically through a lifetime of climax. This incidentally throws an interesting light on the fact that Dostoyevsky's short stories were never so successful as his novels; while Turgenev's short sketches were greater works of art than his novels.

Turgenev was not great enough to control the characters he portrayed and to follow them through to their logical end—hence, the frustrations. In this respect Dostoyevsky proved himself the greater genius. Turgenev's characters differ from Dostoyevsky's principally in the degree of their individuality and stature. Turgenev's characters formed the loom on which Dostoyevsky's were woven. The latter are potentially similar to the former, but Dostoyevsky begins where Turgenev left off. He intensifies what conflict there is already and adds so much more that the proportion of adversity to normality becomes contorted to a degree which is invariably responsible for the insanity of the character in question. At this point Dostoyevsky is ready to begin the significant portion of his novel.

A few of Turgenev's characters might have been used to advantage and even with great profit by Dostoyevsky. He could have incorporated Lavretsky into his novels, after intensification to the point of abnormality. Bazarov, before his death, would have been an interesting figure for Dostoyevsky to begin with, and Bazarov's parents would have fitted admirably into one of his novels. "For such people as they are not to be found in your grand society even in the daytime with a light" (Bazarov). Of them all, perhaps Fenitchka, the mistress of the elder Kirsanov, came closer than the rest to being a creation of Dostoyevsky. Bazarov once said of her: "She'll go to destruction probably. Well, she'll extricate herself somehow or other." This was the nearest that Turgenev ever came to Dostoyevsky in the field of characterization.

Turgenev considered foreigners superior to most Russians (Insarov), and his more or less positive Russian types spoke at least a foreign tongue (Solomin). On the other hand, Dostoyevsky considered most Russians superior to most foreigners. Every one of his admirable characters was of pure Russian descent. In fact, according to Dostoyevsky, there were no bad Russians. They became so only when they came into contact with alien "isms." Even Sonya, the prostitute, he implies, was better than all the foreigners. In other words, according to Dostoyevsky, Russians are essentially good, if they remain Russians.

In brief, Dostoyevsky was a genius, while Turgenev, was an artist. Turgenev achieved his mark through restraint—Dostoyevsky through the absence of restraint. Turgenev was vivid through expression, Dostoyevsky through passion. Turgenev was a man of the world, Dostoyevsky an innocent. Turgenev wrote like an innocent, and Dostoyevsky like a man of the world.

In the light of the foregoing explanation, Dostoyevsky's major novels may seem more intelligible to Western readers. Let us consider briefly his first short novelette, *Poor People.* An outsider, on reading this novel in letters, may well wonder why it created such a sensation in the Russian literary world, even prior to its publication in 1846. Why did leading critics predict the rise of a new Gogol? In the first place, Dostoyevsky revealed in this novel a remarkable maturity of thought for a young man barely twenty-four years of age. Moreover, his literary style was both powerful and polished, not by any means inferior to the work of the best writers of his generation. Finally, and most important of all, without detracting from the originality of *Poor People,* Dostoyevsky enlarged upon Gogol's *Cloak,* which had already become a classic, and which had been extensively imitated. The literary exponents of the Russian poor enjoyed great popularity, and in consequence, their books were best-sellers, although this was not their purpose. The title of Dostoyevsky's small novel might be applied to an entire library of works produced by his contemporaries on the plight of the Russian poor. Later critics discovered in *Poor People* the germs of a philosophy which permeated all Dostoyevsky's subsequent novels—just as *Sevastopol* supplied a preview to the rest of Tolstoy's works.

Although the most popular of Dostoyevsky's novels among foreigners in general has a gruesome plot, *Crime and Punishment* was never meant to be a glorified detective story. Russian literature was not written for the entertainment of its readers, and the plot of *Crime and Punishment* is of secondary importance. The main idea, which runs like a scarlet thread through this and through his three subsequent novels, is the clash beteen the Slavophiles and the Westernizers. With *Crime and Punishment,* the controversy between these two camps began in earnest. The novel served both as a rebuttal to Turgenev and as an exposition of the Slavophile point of view on political, economic, and social matters. The reader must be warned again not to approach Dostoyevsky's major novels with Western tools. If Dostoyevsky had written his novels in the West, he might never have secured a publisher.

Crime and Punishment marks the breach between Dostoyevsky and the radicals. Like Turgenev he was in search of a leader, and, like him, he turned first to the student body. Raskolnikov is a much more interesting person, however, than Turgenev's Rudin or even Bazarov. Even the choice of his name served a particular purpose. The etymological derivation of Raskolnikov is *raskol,* meaning schism, rift, break, or detachment. It is another name for *bezpotchvenik,* a word coined by the Russian critic Grigorovitch, and extensively employed by the Slavophiles when they referred to the Westernizers. In free translation a *bezpotchvenik* is one who is detached from the soil, in contrast to one who is rooted in the soil. The name of Raskolnikov thus supplies the key to the entire novel. Before he was captivated by the rationalism of the West, our hero was decent and led a useful life. From the time he became a "Raskolnikov," he entered upon the path which led to crime.

Raskolnikov may be regarded as Turgenev's Rudin or Nezhdanov in action, presented from the Slavophile standpoint. His crime was the result of rationalism and cold logic, no feelings being involved. Not that Raskolnikov had no heart or emotions. But, according to Dostoyevsky, the science of the West, which was based on facts and laws, obliterated all human feeling. In *Crime and Punishment,* as in his three subsequent novels, Dostoyevsky emphasizes the struggle for supremacy between the heart and the mind. When the mind takes the upper hand, the result is crime; but when the heart prevails resurrection follows. As long as Raskolnikov remained under the influence of Western intellectualism, his life was miserable, and he became a detriment to society. When his Russian heart (soul) reasserted itself, he became a new man.

In other words, it was Dostoyevsky's conviction that the mind without the heart was like a body without a soul. Greek culture included both; Plato stressed the mind, Aristotle the heart. Greek culture would have been less interesting if either had dominated to the exclusion of the other. This, too, was the genius of Christianity—that it appealed both to the heart and to the mind, although the former predominated.

What was true of Raskolnikov may be applied to Sonya. She was not as well educated as he, but, according to Dostoyevsky, her thinking reflected the rationalism of the West. She became a prostitute, not from preference, but to save her family from starvation. The result was that she saved neither her family nor herself. When her Russian heart reasserted itself, she experienced a resurrection, breathed new life into Raskolnikov, and became a source of comfort and consolation to others. By way of digression, Dostoyevsky was the first author in Russian literature to lift a prostitute from degradation and contempt and to place her on a par with the most virtuous heroines of world literature. She became the moral force in the tragedy, and she served as a warning against a social order which was the product of Western rationalism.

It may be of interest to observe that Dostoyevsky dealt with his criminals as the prophet of the Old Testament dealt with the erring members of his flock. They passed through four stages: sin (crime), punishment (suffering), repentance (resurrection), and forgiveness (love). It may seem strange that Dostoyevsky, who was imbued with the teachings of the New Testament, where forgiveness is not necessarily dependent upon punishment, should subject his heroes to this purge. This becomes clear when the reader bears in mind that to Dostoyevsky, Love, the greatest thing in the world, evolved only from suffering. It would be erroneous to accept the dictum of many critics who maintain that he made a religion or a fetish of suffering. He did not advocate suffering for the sake of suffering, but rather as a price which the individual, society, or nation must pay in life for the *summum bonum*.

Although the main issue in *Crime and Punishment* is political, an ethical problem also exists. Was it ethical for Raskolnikov to murder the wretched pawnbroker, whom he regarded as a social parasite, so that he might use the blood money to complete his education and thereby become a useful member of society? Furthermore, was it ethical for his sister, Dunya, to marry a man she despised in order to finance her brother's education and assure his future? Finally, was it ethical on the part of Sonya to subject herself to humiliation, suffering, disgrace, and danger in order to feed a drunken father and a starving family? In Western Europe at that time many writers condoned as well as commended such a sacrifice of self. The individual thinking of the age might be transferred to the class. Was it ethical for one class or group, by implication the Westernizers, to destroy another in order to produce what they thought would be a better world?

In brief, Dostoyevsky's main purpose in *Crime and Punishment* was to show that Raskolnikov and his followers, when they fell victims to the imported "isms" of the West, became criminals; but after going through certain processes which restored them to their own culture and soil, they reasserted themselves and became useful members of society. All Dostoyevsky's criminals needed was a new start in life, and for this he felt that they required no assistance or enlightenment from the West. All that was necessary was for them to rediscover the potentialities of Russian culture and to develop them accordingly.

Crime and Punishment not only reflects the controversy between the Slavophiles and the Westernizers, but it is closely connected with economic conditions current in Russia in 1865; for in that year there was a severe economic depression in Russia. Money was so scarce that even persons with good security found it difficult or impossible to borrow the funds they required. There were many foreclosures on mortgages. Even Dostoyevsky himself was threatened with foreclosure on June 6, 1865, if he did not pay the lawyer Pavel Lyzhin a debt of 450 rubles. Possibly Dostoyevsky had this lawyer in mind when he described Dunya's unethical fiancé, Luzhin, in this novel. It has been suggested that Dostoyevsky might have called the book "1865" instead of *Crime and Punishment.*

It is likewise interesting to note that the plot of *Crime and Punishment* was undoubtedly suggested to Dostoyevsky by the notorious case of the merchant's son, Gerasim Tchistov, who in the spring of 1865 killed two women with an axe, after robbing them of 11,260 rubles. Russian newspapers of that day made the most of this sensational case.

Although Dostoyevsky did not kill Raskolnikov as Turgenev did Rudin, he was through with him, once his resurrection was assured. In his next novel, he sought a more ideal type—one far removed from the poverty-stricken student. Like Turgenev he went to his "house of gentlefolk" for Prince Myshkin, the hero of *The Idiot.*

Prince Myshkin, Dostoyevsky's new candidate for leadership, differed materially from Turgenev's Lavretsky. He had a magnetic personality which immediately commanded attention. People who agreed or disagreed with him, whether wise or flippant, adults or children, of whatever rank or station, listened to what the prince had to say. No one hated him. It seemed as if he were about to assume leadership and settle all their problems by Peace. However, like Christ, whom Myshkin in certain scenes distinctly resembles, he was crucified by the mob who termed him an idiot. The action of the mob abruptly terminated Myshkin's career, although it was apparent that he was much wiser than they. At times it almost seems that the idiot is a projection of the author himself, for it is a well-established fact that the Westernizers not infrequently hurled the epithet of idiot or that of epileptic at Dostoyevsky. In this novel he takes pains to prove that the idiot is wiser and saner than all of them, that, in fact, they themselves are the idiots, and it is he who suffers for their transgressions.

Psychopathologists and criminologists have paid homage to the remarkable contribution of Dostoyevsky in *The Idiot,* in which he anticipated with a great degree of accuracy many modern scientific developments in these fields. Far from being distressed by his epileptic condition, Prince Myshkin, voicing the sentiment of Dostoyevsky, regarded this disease as an asset rather than a liability. In fact, he implied that his talent or genius was directly attributable to his infirmity. It is interesting to note that a number of historical figures have been victims of epilepsy. Theologians or scholars, as the case may be, have advanced the theory that the prophet Ezekiel, St. Paul, Mohammed, Caesar, Constantine the Great, Catherine the Great, Alexander I of Russia, Napoleon, and Dostoyevsky all suffered from this disease.

While the controversy still raged over Turgenev's *Fathers and Children,* Dostoyevsky, instead of continuing his hitherto fruitless search for a leader, wrote a sequel to Turgenev's novel, which he called *The Possessed (The Devils).* Strictly speaking, in *The Possessed* Dostoyevsky portrayed the Bazarovs in action. When the novel appeared in 1873 it shook Russian society profoundly, particularly the Western camp. Many of Dostoyevsky's adversaries branded him again as an idiot and an epileptic who exaggerated and defamed the liberal and socialist movements. Even as late as 1913 Maxim Gorky published a protest against the production of *The Possessed* by the Moscow Art Theatre. In spite of the anger of the Westernizers, this novel crowned Dostoyevsky as the prophet of Russia. Within a few years of its completion the violence of the anarchists afforded convincing proof of the validity of his contentions. Although it may be true that *The Possessed* did not reflect the actual conditions of the time in which it was written, Dostoyevsky's keen psychological insight into the minds of the extreme radicals of his day enabled him to visualize the logical outcome of their thinking and activities.

The Possessed and *Fathers and Children* represent the best and perhaps the first primary literary sources on the Age of Nihilism in Europe. *Fathers and Children,* as already indicated, was the first to break new ground in this field by introducing the term *Nihilism* in its modern connotation. In Turgenev's main character, Bazarov, we have the prototype of the typical Russian Nihilist. On the other hand, *The Possessed,* published a decade later, not only reflects Russian Nihilism but is even more representative of German Nazism. Alfred Rosenberg, the Russian-born philosopher of National Socialism and father of Neo-Paganism in Germany, drew heavily upon *The Possessed* for his new mythology, although his interpretation betrays the immaturity and superficiality of his analysis. Although Dostoyevsky was obviously not in any position to foresee the actual circumstances of the rise of Nazism, the Nazis were undoubtedly influenced by Dostoyevsky's exponents of a "new order" as characterized in *The Possessed.*

Dostoyevsky's analysis of the theories of Shigalev, one of the characters of *The Possessed* (see especially Part II, Chapter VIII), provides the best possible background for the ideology expounded in Hitler's *Mein Kampf* and Rosenberg's *The Myth of the Twentieth Century.* Shigalevism, in brief, is an attempt to establish a perfect social order. It starts with the principle of absolute freedom and reaches the paradoxical conclusion of absolute slavery for nine-tenths of the human race. The remaining one-tenth constitute the directors with absolute power who demand absolute submission from the rest. In this new order, where everything must be reduced to a common denominator, and where the masses must be on the same level (Shigalev's interpretation of equality), there is no room for great minds, for genius, and for culture. Cicero would have his tongue cut out, Copernicus would be blinded, and Shakespeare stoned. All must work, however, and render obedience to the extent of submerging their individuality completely in the group. They must have no desires of their own.

To maintain rigid discipline and thereby preserve the new order for one thousand years, Shigalev invented a system of spying in which it became the duty of the slaves to spy upon one another. He even advocated the use of lies, legends (rumors), slander, incendiarism, murder, and "incredible corruption" to maintain the regime. To eliminate "boredom" and to hold the masses in terror, he worked out the idea of the purge (letting of fresh blood) as a regularly recurring shock. This, in Shigalev's opinion, would maintain a state of mental vacuum and prevent the organization of any subversive movements which were the product of a latent benevolence. Much of the theory and technique of Nazism can be found in Shigalevism.

Dostoyevsky implies that the characters of *The Possessed,* even the notorious Pyotr Verkhovensky, were essentially good, but for the fact that their energies had been directed into improper channels. Using Shatov as his mouthpiece, he maintained that they could only be redeemed by driving out the devils and making room for the healing properties of the Orthodox faith. By Orthodoxy, Dostoyevsky meant the ideal church, the church as conceived by Solovyov, Berdyaev, and Bulgakov—a church of freedom of the spirit and high religious devotion. No matter what "ism" people professed, no matter what cause they espoused even to the extent of self-sacrifice, without religious faith Dostoyevsky believed that they built their foundation upon the sand. In other words, the foundation of all foundations, the philosophy of all philosophies, the cause of all causes, was religion—the Orthodox faith, without which people became "possessed."

Arriving at this conclusion, Dostoyevsky ventured another prophecy that Russia would eventually become the savior of Christian civilization. Since the Russian church was dogmatically nearer to the Protestant church and ritualistically closer to the Roman Catholic, he believed that it was destined to become the bridge which would eventually unite the three. In his opinion the Russian Orthodox church was the only one which had retained its purity, since, in the West, science had practically eclipsed Protestantism, and the merits of Roman Catholicism were obscured by too much organization and temporal power. Although at times Dostoyevsky virulently attacked the Roman Catholic church, especially in the chapter of *The Brothers Karamazov* entitled "The Grand Inquisitor," on the other hand, he paid great homage to certain virtues which are distinctly characteristic of Roman Catholicism. For this reason many Catholic critics have found him inconsistent and consider that he defeated his own purpose.

Since he believed Russia would be saved by a spiritual leader rather than by a statesman or revolutionist, Dostoyevsky sought the fulfillment of his dream in the person of Alyosha, one of the Brothers Karamazov. Unfortunately this, his final novel, remained unfinished, and his ideal hero, Alyosha, undeveloped. Whether or not Dostoyevsky planned to write four or five volumes on *The Brothers Karamazov* cannot be established with certainty in spite of certain allusions to the contrary. Whether, on the spur of the moment, he was tempted to change the nature of Alyosha and to transform him into a villain remains equally obscure. Following the spirit of the novel, it would seem that Dostoyevsky wished to make of Alyosha a Redeemer and a Russian leader. At times it appears that he lost faith even in Alyosha, believing that only a miracle could save Russia. Alyosha, coming as he did from the family of the Karamazovs, might well be considered a miracle.

The story of *The Brothers Karamazov* is, in many respects, an epic of Russian life. Each member of the family represented a slice of Russian society. Dimitri was an uncultured and unconscious Slavophile, whereas Ivan, the brain of the trio, directly or indirectly represented the Westernizers. Smerdyakov, the illegitimate son, stood for the imitative mob which follows the leader and becomes a tool in the hands of the theoreticians. His father, Fyodor Karamazov, belonged to the sensuous, indifferent, reactionary group of the old generation. Alyosha was destined to reconcile the classes represented by Dimitri and Ivan. If, as some critics maintain, Dostoyevsky possessed in turn the traits of each of the Karamazovs, this would merely tend to substantiate the fact that he more than any other Russian author truthfully reflected the Russian people at their best and at their worst.

It seems clear from the very outset that Dostoyevsky felt more sympathy for Dimitri than for Ivan. Dimitri, in spite of his shortcomings, was essentially good at heart. Purged by suffering for a crime which he did not commit, he might have been redeemed, might have become a normal being—an eventuality which was hardly possible in the case of Ivan. With his desire to dominate, it was very difficult for Ivan to bow even to circumstances. When he was forced to do so, he became mentally unbalanced. Although the actual murder of Fyodor Karamazov must be laid at Smerdyakov's door, it was Ivan's brain that engineered the crime. Dostoyevsky clearly suggests that Smerdyakov had Ivan's sanction to murder his father. Since Dostoyevsky's philosophy of life was almost identical with that of the Near East, where the motive of the sinner or criminal as a rule receives greater consideration than the actual deed, he therefore blamed Ivan for the crime and labeled Smerdyakov his blind tool.

In this novel, even more than in *The Possessed,* Dostoyevsky asserted the necessity of religion and faith in the Christ. In spite of his conviction that the Christian church would eventually save Russia and make of it a model nation, whose light would radiate to the four corners of the earth, in this work he did not shut his eyes to the abuses and superstitions within the church. Through churchmen of the caliber of Father Zosima and Alyosha he hoped to remedy its faults.

In *The Brothers Karamazov,* Dostoyevsky made the most earnest attempt ever made in Russian literature to iron out the various controversial issues which confronted his countrymen. For this reason it is surprising to find that in this first volume he devoted more space to the arguments of his opponents than to his own rebuttal. No Westernizer ever presented his case more convincingly than Ivan in *The Brothers Karamazov.* No Westernizer has provided an equally clear analysis of the fundamental principles of Slavophilism. In fact, the Westernizers seem tacitly to have agreed to maintain a sort of censorship against Slavophilism in their writings, whereas Dostoyevsky, whom they termed a dogmatic Slavophile, was broad-minded enough to open his columns to his adversaries and to present the case of the Westernizers on the social order and on religion in a most articulate manner. No wonder Pobyedonostsev and his fellow-reactionaries were both frightened and shocked by the religious discussions between Ivan and Alyosha! They were only pacified when Dostoyevsky assured them of a rebuttal in the second volume. Death intervened before he could fulfill that promise, and Dostoyevsky died like a true Christian, turning the other cheek. Perhaps, for this reason, his message was all the more powerful.

To sum up, Dostoyevsky's novels are the noblest expression of nineteenth-century Slavophilism. Placing the heart above the intellect, he opposed all manifestations of foreign "isms" whose purpose was to supplant or eclipse Russian virtues, which were the product of many centuries of Russian joy and sorrow. In the field of "enlightenment" he felt that the West had nothing to offer Russia, since Russia possessed all the elements necessary for her own redemption—in particular, the Russian Orthodox church. While he was against the encroachment of Western "isms," he readily acknowledged Western accomplishments in the field of invention and technique which benefited humanity as a whole, opposing only the importation and adaptation of things intrinsically cultural.

Dostoyevsky had still another reason for urging the Russian people to turn their backs on Western Europe. It was his belief, as expressed in his *Diary of a Writer* in 1881 (see page 138), that Europe must inevitably fall a prey to "degrading Communism," whereas Asia offered the greatest potentialities for Russia's future development and for the release of Russian energy. Dostoyevsky's conception of Russia's Asiatic mission dates back to his exile in Siberia, when in 1854 during the Crimean War he composed the little-known poem, "On European Events." Within a century Soviet leaders were going to Asia, not for the tsar and Orthodoxy as Dostoyevsky demanded in his poem, but in the name of Communism and atheism.

During World War II Soviet literary critics ostensibly became enamored of Dostoyevsky, and the impression was given that he had been entirely redeemed and retrieved. In recent years, however, they have rediscovered in him a formidable, potential foe of the Soviet regime and system. With the defeat of Nazi Germany, the discerning Soviet reader now inevitably sees as Russian, not German, the radical element that Dostoyevsky portrays so unfavorably, and he is likely to find its counterpart in the Soviet government. Whereas the Soviet Union proclaims itself the first and foremost socialist state, Dostoyevsky denounces socialism (Marxian socialism), based on materialism, in no uncertain terms as a danger to the world. According to Dostoyevsky, the salvation of Russia will come through a rejuvenated Orthodox church. Although the present Soviet government may not be averse to using the Orthhodox church as a tool or weapon to further its own interests, needless to say it has no intention of setting it up as a rival or successor. Finally, the Soviet government, anxious to exalt the contemporary Soviet man, finds in Dostoyevsky only characters that are abnormal misfits who provide no worthy example for the emulation of the "contemporary man."

In the final analysis, Dostoyevsky's gallery of characters was composed of lunatics, perverts, epileptics, prostitutes, drunkards, and swindlers—the scum of society, afflicted with all manner of mental diseases. Most of them lived in the city slums or in the provincial metropolis. Dostoyevsky assembled them all, demonstrated their plight, expressed their thought, aroused sympathy in their behalf, subjected them to a spiritual bath, and started them out all over again. To a certain extent he played for them the role of the Salvation Army, emphasizing their spiritual welfare rather than their physical necessity.

The same controversy, which is reflected in the works of Dostoyevsky and Turgenev, has been rehearsed in Russia today under a somewhat different nomenclature. The existing clash of opinions between the Right and the Left in the Soviet Union, between those who demanded a nationalist orientation ("Nationalist in form, socialist in content."—Stalin), and those who advocated an international platform, constituted a revival of the struggle between the Slavophiles and the Westernizers. At present—in partial fulfilment of Dostoyevsky's prophecy—the former seem to be gaining ground.[2]

The current vogue of existentialism is tempting many writers to draw comparisons between Dostoyevsky and Soeren Kierkegaard or Jean-Paul Sartre, two of the leading exponents of that philosophy. Of the two, there appears to be much more in common between Dostoyevsky and the nineteenth-century Danish philosopher, Kierkegaard, for whom the "arrogance" of rationalism spelled destruction to European civilization and Jesus Christ afforded proof of the existence of God. But if Dostoyevsky is to be ranked as a religious existentialist, Leo Tolstoy, in our opinion, merits even greater consideration.

Lyev Nikolayevitch Tolstoy (1828–1910). Whereas Dostoyevsky introduced the slums and the middle class into Russian literature, Lyev (Leo)

2. For the Soviet attitude towards Dostoyevsky following World War II, see V. Yermilov, "F. M. Dostoyevsky and Our Critics," *Soviet Press Translations,* Vol. III (No. 5, March 1, 1948), pp. 155–160.

Nikolayevitch Tolstoy confined himself to green pastures, to the nobility, and the peasantry. The one deified the Russian people, the other lauded to the skies the virtues of the Russian peasant. In this respect Tolstoy has more in common with Turgenev, for he began where Turgenev left off in his *Memoirs of a Sportsman.* But Tolstoy treated the peasants subjectively, whereas Turgenev viewed their most vital problem, that of serfdom, with remarkable objectivity.

Tolstoy's characters are simple, like the country folk he admired so greatly; Dostoyevsky's are complex. Tolstoy wrote, for the most part, of the sane, the healthy, and the normal individual; Dostoyevsky, of the criminal, the diseased, the insane, and the abnormal. In spite of his dynamic power, Dostoyevsky wrote like a humble man; Tolstoy with authority. "I say unto you" is the predominant tone of Tolstoy's work, particularly in later years. Dostoyevsky underestimated his own greatness. Tolstoy was not only aware of his creative genius but, by implication, boldly announced to the world his opinion of himself. His ego defied even his own earnest attempts at humility, led him to project his personality into most of his works, many portions of which are autobiographical. Dostoyevsky rarely resorted to autobiography, an exception being his *Memoirs from a Dead House,* although he revealed his own Slavophile views in the person of Shatov and his own epileptic condition in the experiences of Prince Myshkin.

Tolstoy regarded himself as the foremost prophet and teacher of his generation, whereas Dostoyevsky in reality was both. The former raised disciples; the latter, imitators. Tolstoy was both a great teacher and philosopher; Dostoyevsky, a disciple of Christ and a psychologist. Tolstoy emerged unscathed from his "mission," whereas Dostoyevsky was "crucified" as an idiot and an epileptic. Even posthumously Tolstoy has fared better than his great contemporary. His works were the first of the Russian classics to stage a comeback after the Revolution, while Dostoyevsky's works were belatedly recognized. This is in spite of the fact that the New Russia reflects, under a new nomenclature, more of Dostoyevsky's philosophy than of Tolstoy's.

Whereas Turgenev was a Westernizer and Dostoyevsky a Slavophile, Tolstoy for a time combined the ideologies of both, until at length he established a teaching of his own known as Tolstoyism. In methodology, he was nearer Turgenev, but dogmatically and ideologically he was closer to Dostoyevsky. Like the latter, he repudiated Western civilization and, in particular, Western materialism. The philosophy of each was Oriental, the difference being that Dostoyevsky's was more of an elongation of the Near East plus Russia, whereas Tolstoy's was Russian plus the Taoism of the Far East. Tolstoy wrote extensively of Reason in his later years, often identifying Reason with God and with Knowledge, but the Reason he described emanated from the heart rather than from the head; for Tolstoy finds that Reason is inherent in every man, although often obscured or eclipsed by other factors. In order to reassert that Reason, it was only necessary, in his opinion, to listen to and obey the inner voice of conscience—which is again closer to the heart than to the mind. In brief, Tolstoy's Reason must not be identified with the Practical Reason of Kant. His is Russian Reason, grafted upon Oriental philosophy. In other words, it represents a combination of heart and mind, at times almost constituting an answer to Dostoyevsky's dream.

A significant factor in Dostoyevsky's Slavophilism was the Russian Orthodox church. To Tolstoy, the church—and by the church he meant the Orthodox or Catholic churches—distorted, institutionalized, particularized, obscured, and debased the Gospel of Christ, and he predicted its downfall. Dostoyevsky, although he admitted certain abuses and shortcomings (*The Idiot, The Brothers Karamazov,* and *Raw Youth*), believed that a rejuvenated Orthodox church constituted the only hope for the salvation of Russia and of the world, and he predicted its ultimate triumph. Tolstoy was nearer the Protestant church; Dostoyevsky, in spite of his attacks on Roman Catholicism, was nearer to it than he realized. Dostoyevsky dreamed of the universal application of Russian Christianity; Tolstoy of a universal religion, which would become the creed of Russia—a Christianity minus churchianity. Tolstoy put to the test most of the world's leading religions. Like Nietzsche, he did not discard Christianity but became jealous of the Christ and established a creed of his own—*Tolstoyism.*

Tolstoyism belongs to the later years of Tolstoy's life, from 1879 to 1910, that is, from the time of his conversion until his death. These years are sometimes known as the period of "preaching" or the age of Tolstoy the Apostle. The essence of Tolstoyism is to be found in *Confession* and in his subsequent work, most of which is summed up in *Resurrection.* In fact, all the later works of Tolstoy, even his dramas, may be termed "confessions"— either confessions about himself, about the Russian nobility, authorities and institutions, or in particular about the Russian church from which he was excommunicated in 1901.

Tolstoyism teaches that there is no God, other than the moral law inside man. Instead of being motivated by outward inducement, that moral law moves in obedience to an inward spontaneity. The inner life underlies the universe. The end or the goal of inner action is inner peace (happiness). By peace, Tolstoy does not imply Epicureanism but the doctrine of imperturbability or *quietism,* the essence of which is Taoism. In Tolstoyism, as well as in Taoism, there are elements of defeatism and anarchism, and also of domination. The *withdrawal* of the senses to a point where one no longer sees the things perceived implies all this. The idea that "to a mind that is still the whole universe *surrenders*" suggests domination—subjugation, rather than resignation. Thus, in spite of Tolstoy's later ethical teachings, in which "Resist no evil" occupies the most prominent place, he himself barely practiced it. In fact, Tolstoy recognized no authority above himself, for he was neither a disciple nor a follower. He was the founder of Tolstoyism—another creed.

Tolstoy is always more the moralist than the philosopher. He demands that everyone else see the light in the Tolstoyan way. Looking toward the Christian ideal of world brotherhood, he addresses his doctrine to every man. He has a positive energy which cannot be found in the quietly aloof spirit of the Taoist, who, after all, writes only for the few.

Taoism goes beyond Tolstoyism, historically and otherwise. Its truths, if truths they be, are more fundamental, for Tao is the Natural Way. Tolstoy loses sight of Tao when he sets up a code of morality, for morality comes into existence only when Tao is lost. Because the Tolstoyan's reason tells him to, he pursues his ideal, his way. About the Taoist philosophy there is something more elemental, more pliable, more "limpid" as Orientalist Arthur Waley terms it. It is quite intangible; one can't see it; and yet, if he once hits upon it there is an inexhaustible source of power, which also is indescribable, but even more potent because of its formlessness, its lack of definition. The Tolstoyan ideal is something one consciously attempts to reach, and there are definite rules for getting there. But the Taoist ideal of nothingness and complete harmony and mergence with the universe is something upon which one just falls.

The essential ideals are the same—the results are the same. Whether one reaches Tao or the Heavenly Kingdom is immaterial. Both are merely symbols of an inner, spiritual peace. Tolstoy has only modernized the route, putting up appropriate signposts along the way. Even with his better than average understanding of the philosophical ideals of the East, however, he is unable to make use of them in unadulterated form; hence with them he combines the Western ideals; not wholly Western either, because Christianity, too, is an Eastern philosophy. It is Tolstoy's plan to give us the basic truths of Christianity which find their complement and likeness in the great truths of the Far East. And in such a combined form, he gives the Eastern beliefs, meant in the first place only for a select few, a universality which makes them accessible to the whole of mankind.

In brief, Taoism is esoteric in nature, its fundamental premise being that the *summum bonum* in life is to lose oneself in the world through non-action. On the other hand, Tolstoyism has a wide, popular appeal, teaching, as it does, that the *summum bonum* in life is to find oneself in a world in which non-action is only a prelude to action.

The most representative work Tolstoy produced during the first period of his literary career, 1852 to 1862, was *The Cossacks*. Although this novel was published in January, 1863, he first projected it in 1852, wrote it in 1860, and added the finishing touches to it in 1862, prior to his marriage. Tolstoy had no intention of publishing this work for some time. It would, perhaps, have shared the fate of *Hadji Murad,* which appeared posthumously in 1911, had Tolstoy not used it to settle a gambling debt at a time when he was otherwise short of funds.

The Cossacks ranks next in importance to Gogol's *Taras Bulba.* Gogol's narrative was historical, but Tolstoy wrote of the Cossacks of his own day whom he knew in person. Gogol's work was a tale of adventure; Tolstoy's was philosophical in tone. *Taras Bulba* has its vivid climax, leaving the reader a glorious picture of triumphant fierceness of exaltation in the face of actual death. *The Cossacks* closes with an anticlimax, when Olenin returns to his former empty life, without Maryanna, and without having found the "inner peace" he sought in the Caucasus. Gogol's work was epic in tone, whereas Tolstoy's is lyric. Olenin also proved to be a new version of Petchorin in *The Hero of Our Times.*

Tolstoy's greatest contribution in *The Cossacks* was that he revealed the everyday life of the Caucasians, presenting their strong rather than their weak points, against a magnificent scenic background. His was a sympathetic account and an appreciative understanding of customs which were strange to the Russian people as a whole. Maryanna, Lukashka, and Yeroshka were soon as familiar to Russians as Turgenev's characters in his *Memoirs of a Sportsman.* Tales of the Caucasus have always held a certain fascination for the Russian people. The greatest Russian poets and a few outstanding writers received their literary baptism amid the scenic grandeur and the picturesque customs of the Caucasus. As we shall see, F. A. Korsh, the founder of the first private theatre in Moscow, was a native of the Caucasus; and V. I. Nemirovitch-Dantchenko, who established the Moscow Art Theatre, came from the same region.

In *The Cossacks* we can detect the symptoms of Tolstoy's later philosophy, particularly his preference for the simple life close to nature. In the person of Olenin we find that same restlessness which pursued Tolstoy all his days. For in this autobiographical novel he was just beginning his search for an answer to the riddle of life.

Tolstoy's three sketches, entitled *Sevastopol* (December 1854, May 1855, and August 1855), also belong to the first period of his literary career. Written while he was on active service at Sevastopol during the Crimean War, these sketches marked Tolstoy's first attack on war in general, particularly upon war between Christians. His descriptions of the horrors of war and his discrimination between real and false heroes were only excelled in his later masterpiece *War and Peace.* In *Sevastopol,* Tolstoy did for the common soldier what Turgenev in his *Memoirs* did for the serf. He directed attention to the services rendered by the ordinary soldier, who, more often than not, received no recognition of his sacrifice, since all the glory and honor went to false heroes. In Tolstoy's estimation, the common soldier was more patriotic than his superiors who spent most of their time talking about promotion. The army never forgave Tolstoy for this exposure, regarding him as a renegade from his own class.

The bulky novel *War and Peace,* together with *Anna Karenina,* may be termed the product of the "honeymoon period." After his marriage in 1862, Tolstoy conceived plans for writing works of an historical nature. Had it not been for the countess, however, he would never have been able to give to the world these two masterpieces. In her own handwriting she painstakingly copied and recopied the manuscripts of both novels many times.

Originally Tolstoy intended to write a history or a novel of the Decembrist Movement of 1825, which shook Russian profoundly. This first revolutionary attempt to secure a constitutional government involved the flower of the Russian nobility. Many paid for this revolt with their lives; others were exiled to Siberia, where they laid a foundation for culture in that remote region. The stories and legends about them which circulated throughout Russia, especially among the nobility, provided ideal subject matter for a novel. Tolstoy had only published three chapters of *The Decembrists,* however, when he became absorbed in the reign of Alexander I. His interest gradually focused on the Napoleonic campaigns, and he abandoned the Decembrists for *War and Peace,* a novel which was five years in the making. Tolstoy intended this novel as an introduction and background to the Decembrist Movement—a purpose which it fulfills to the letter, since *War and Peace* ends where the Decembrist Movement begins. It appeared first as a serial and later in book form in 1869.

War and Peace is justly called the national novel of Russia. It is a colossal prose epic, reflecting the whole range of Russian life at the beginning of the nineteenth century. Once again Tolstoy paid homage to the simplicity and strength of the common people in contrast to the artificiality of the upper classes. Being an officer himself, it was natural that he should devote more space to descriptions of battles than to other phases of Russian life. Nevertheless, one finds here a true reflection of the life of the various classes in Russia—of their life during peace and war, as well as during the aftermath of war; of the various superstitions and beliefs which were the product of war, as well as of the positive benefits arising from a just struggle.

In this novel, even more than in the Sevastopol sketches, Tolstoy denounced war as an instrument for the settlement of disputes between nations. He tried his level best to minimize the sagacity of the strategists and the heroic exploits of the superior officers. Some critics have seen in this approach the recurrence of an old fatalism in a new guise. But this was not fatalism. Tolstoy merely sought to minimize the achievements of the war lords and the glory of war. Perhaps here, too, he had already acquired a habit, which became more pronounced in after years, of consciously or unconsciously minimizing the achievements of others in his own field—in this case, the army.

Although Tolstoy's main purpose was to strip war, particularly imperialistic war, of its vain glory and to discourage men from seeking a military career, some critics feel that he accomplished just the reverse. Unintentionally, *War and Peace* became the text for patriotism in Russia, and the battles so vividly described and so artistically delineated, served rather as an inducement for men to enter the army than as a deterrent to military service. In spite of his antiwar message, Tolstoy, in this book, said practically nothing in opposition to defensive wars. It was not until later, after his conversion, that he advocated a literal application of the Christian doctrine, "Resist no evil." In this novel, Tolstoy was more objective than in his previous or in his subsequent works. Absorbed in others, for the first time he left himself, with a few exceptions, out of the picture. In *War and Peace* there are several heroes of equal importance, none of whom is Tolstoy, although Prince Andrey and Pierre Bezukhov no doubt reveal Tolstoy's outlook at that time.

There is a feeling of spaciousness in this novel. It leaves the reader with the impression of being part of a vast audience, watching a performance of the epic of a nation, in which Russians from one end of the country to the other flit across the stage before his eyes.

Although *Anna Karenina* was based upon an actual incident which took place not far from Tolstoy's estate, its central idea was a natural outgrowth of *War and Peace*. While Vronsky and Anna, so far as the plot goes, are the main characters, Levin was the soul of the novel so far as Tolstoy was concerned. In fact, Levin was Tolstoy himself—the transitional Tolstoy of the period between *War and Peace* and *Confession*. Levin's ideas on labor and the social order incurred all the hostility from members of the nobility that Tolstoy himself experienced from his own people—even from his own wife, the countess. Levin, in a rather artificial fashion, put into practice some of his ideas, which Tolstoy himself never succeeded in doing. In studying the personality of Tolstoy and his philosophy, especially after 1879, much attention should be paid to the character of Levin and even to Kitty, his wife. One almost infers that, at times, Tolstoy would have preferred a wife like Kitty to the countess.

Although Levin is the personification of Tolstoy, there is much of Tolstoy in Vronsky too. Before he met Anna, Vronsky was just a man in a uniform, *"un homme comme il faut";* from the bureaucratic standpoint, a man with a chequered past, not unlike Tolstoy prior to his marriage. This was the first time that Vronsky had actually fallen in love. Although an illicit love, it was nevertheless the real thing. Tolstoy shows that even an illicit love might prove a resurrection for a Vronsky, while it meant death for Anna. From the time Vronsky met Anna, his star began to rise, hers to decline. He was resurrected because of her love, and when she had done everything for him within her power, she gave him the last she had to offer—her life. There are indications that Vronsky's love for Anna began to grow cold—not so Anna's. Having given up everything in the world for him, she made Vronsky the center of her universe, and her love became a jealous passion. When she realized that her attitude would only bring him unhappiness, she took her own life.

In this novel, as in *War and Peace,* Tolstoy swung his lash at the military class with its unbalanced code of morals. He did for Anna what Dostoyevsky did for Sonya, although they belonged to different classes. One thing they had in common—adultery. Whereas Dostoyevsky gave Sonya a new start in life,

Anna Karenina, because of her position, character, and culture, and the conventional attitude of her class, could not begin life anew. Although Tolstoy himself disapproved of Anna's action, he portrayed her in such a fashion that her sin was almost obscured and eclipsed by her charm and courage. He presented her fall from grace in a most natural manner, as something which might happen to anyone, irrespective of background, rank, or station. As a warning to those who might presume to pass judgment upon one who paid a heavy price for her sin, he prefaced his book with the Biblical injunction, "Vengeance is Mine. I will repay!"

Subsequent to the publication of a few other works, a drastic change took place in Tolstoy's life. In 1879 he began his *Confession,* in which, for the first time, he preached his new creed of Tolstoyism. This is a theological treatise, in which Tolstoy openly voiced his opinion of the Orthodox church, and his personal recollections of the inconsistency of his own upbringing with the actual teachings of Christ, although those who reared him posed as Christians. He asserted, here as elsewhere, that the influence of the church upon true Christianity was detrimental, implying that the church did for Christianity what Buddhism did for Taoism. Just as Taoism degenerated into superstition and mysticism until it consisted of a debased ritual which bore no resemblance to the original teaching of Lao-Tzu, so the ritualistic and other functions of the Christian church, in his opinion, distorted and degraded the ethical teachings of Christ. In other words, it was in this book that Tolstoy for the first time openly advocated a Christianity minus Churchianity.

After another interval, during which additional publications appeared, Tolstoy produced *The Kreutzer Sonata* in 1889, followed by his explanatory *Afterword* to it in 1890. This short novel caused a sensation not only in Russia but throughout Europe. For a time it was even banned in the United States. Without going into details, it may be mentioned that this was the first sex novel in Russian literature. Tolstoy wrote two novels on sex. The other was *The Devil,* published posthumously in 1911. Strangely enough, in this novel, as in *War and Peace,* his achievement was in direct opposition to his intentions. *War and Peace* was intended to discourage the glorification of army life, but it served rather as an inducement to that very thing. The same was true of *The Kreutzer Sonata.* It was a didactic work, a moral novel, against "conventional" marriages. It opened the door to a stream of sex literature in Russia. It seems strange that Tolstoy, the moralist, should pave the way for writers like Artzibashev (*Sanine*), in whom this crude, licentious, abusive approach to the sex problem reached its culmination. *Sanine* was in more ways than one "a Russian tragedy." When *The Kreutzer Sonata* was first published, it was regarded as an attack on all marriage—which was not true. Tolstoy's attack was directed at light marriages, which he termed legal prostitution.

Tolstoy's last great novel, *Resurrection,* was written in 1899, and sold to the highest bidder to defray in part the expenses of the migration of the persecuted Dukhobors (Christian communists) to Canada. It was the most loosely constructed novel that Tolstoy has written. He himself acknowledged that he obtained the idea for this work from the resurrection of Raskolnikov, recorded in the epilogue of Dostoyevsky's *Crime and Punishment*. Tolstoy's *Resurrection* is a working out of the regeneration Raskolnikov achieved through Sonya's great love, but with an entirely new character, a different crime, and much the same setting.

Dostoyevsky's *Crime and Punishment* was a psychological study of the criminal mind. *Resurrection* is a sociological study of prisons and prisoners. Tolstoy began where Dostoyevsky left off. A consecutive reading of *Crime and Punishment* and *Resurrection* leaves one with two very moving, but quite distinct, experiences—the first a glimpse into the mind of a man; the second, into his heart. Both novels were concerned with criminals. Fundamentally the idea of both novelists was the same—that persons who commit crimes are normal people not unlike ourselves, but who, because of the injustice and inequalities of their social environment and certain ideologies, run counter to the law and to the legal machinery set up to ensnare them. *Resurrection* tells us much about the prison system and so-called criminal justice, but nothing of the mental and spiritual anguish to which the individual is subjected before his punishment is meted out to him. *Crime and Punishment,* on the other hand, tells what goes on in the mind of one man before and after he commits his crime, but next to nothing about his life in prison. Dostoyevsky brought out the "inner good" in Raskolnikov; Tolstoy related Nekhludov's search for "inner peace." In *Crime and Punishment,* the individual is the center of attention; in *Resurrection,* society predominates. Both novelists revealed some understanding of Russian society: Dostoyevsky, of the lower stratum; Tolstoy, of both the upper and the lower classes.

Resurrection summed up Tolstoy's "confessions." In this final novel, he not only advocated a theory, but through Nekhludov he put his own theories into practice. Tolstoy accepted as gospel truth the old Oriental adage that "The greatest hero is he who can overcome himself," and he believed that the only prerequisite to the practical application of his theories was courage.

In spite of the fact that Nekhludov is Tolstoy himself, he does not hesitate to reveal the limitations of Nekhludov even after his resurrection. It is strongly suggested that all Nekhludov's sacrifices were made from an egotistical motive—in order to achieve inner peace. His trip to Siberia with the convicts and his proposed marriage with Katusha Maslova were the price he expected to pay for this inner peace. There was nothing altruistic about it.

Katusha Maslova was infinitely superior to Nekhludov. Although of peasant origin, she had greater moral and spiritual stamina than the prince. His resurrection was the product of remorse—hers, of love. None of the many criticisms of Katusha do justice to her. Her love was a Russian love, the kind which is difficult for the Westerner to grasp—just as it is difficult for him to understand Anna's final sacrifice for Vronsky. When Katusha rejected

Nekhludov's proposal of marriage, she did it because she loved him, because she knew he did not love her, and because of the social gulf that separated them. Hers was an unselfish renunciation. He, knowing that she loved him, was obviously relieved at her decision, which he accepted with alacrity at its face value. Nekhludov found "inner peace" at Katusha's expense.

A member of the higher nobility himself, Leo Tolstoy was perhaps the most famous and the most popular portrayer of aristocratic life in Russia. Reared in a cultured environment and accustomed to consort with the elite, he was thoroughly acquainted with the best as well as with the worst traits of his class. In describing the life of the nobility, he confined himself to three groups: the first consisted of statesmen and prominent officeholders—men like Karenin, Oblonsky, and Shtcherbatsky; the second included military officers, such as Vronsky and Nekhludov; and the third was composed of rich landowners, represented by Nekhludov and Levin.

To the casual observer the Russian nobility was a gay, witty people whose time was spent in search of pleasure. Tolstoy gives us a vivid picture of a class, which in Russia no longer exists, and of which there remain only a few last representatives in exile. In the painting of such scenes he had no superior in Russia.

Tolstoy depicted this class at work and at play. He described their formal balls, as in *Anna Karenina,* where, against a background of beautiful gowns, smart uniforms, gay music, and graceful dances, the love between Anna and Vronsky was born before the very eyes of the distressed Kitty. Time and again he described their intimate informal parties, where at dinners, at homes, and musical evenings, groups of close friends gathered to discuss the latest scandals, political and war news, philosophical questions, literature, music, art, in fact, almost every conceivable subject which was not of an ultra-serious nature. Where gossip and light conversation became a fine art, the accomplished hostess dreaded a moment's awkward silence for fear it might ruin the entire evening. Tolstoy's novels covered the entire range of the normal activities of his class—not only the balls, but the skating party, where Levin renewed his acquaintance with Kitty; the horse races frequented especially by the officers; the hunting expeditions, which were an integral part of the curriculum of every nobleman; and even the new vogue for tennis.

In Tolstoy's novels we can follow the noble from youth to old age, for he described the education of both men and women of his class. Like himself, the majority of the men attended university for a time even if they did not graduate. They tasted the discipline of army life and observed its rigid code of honor. Their women were educated for marriage, learning, in addition, music, dancing, drawing, French literature, and languages. It was imperative for the Russian woman of aristocratic origin to marry as soon as possible, with the question of love a minor problem to be settled as satisfactorily as possible after the wedding. Before marriage they met men in society under strained, artificial conditions that did not lead to a real knowledge of character. As

Tolstoy indicates in the case of Kitty, it was the height of humiliation and social disgrace for a woman to be dropped by a young man who had paid her any noticeable attention. Both men and women were proficient linguists, and they all spoke French, the smart language of society, although German and English were popular. It was the custom at the evening salons Tolstoy described so well for both men and women to intersperse foreign words and phrases in their ordinary conversation.

In *Anna Karenina,* perhaps better than elsewhere, Tolstoy revealed the double moral standard for Russian men and women of the aristocracy. The typical nobleman, like Vronsky, was permitted, even expected, to have as many affairs as possible. The more women who fell in love with him, the more popular he became. The typical officer, like Vronsky, or like Olenin in *The Cossacks,* drank too much, gambled for high stakes, conquered as many women's hearts as possible, and in general lived a reckless and extravagant life.

The married aristocrat had to be more discreet about his affairs, when he chose to leave the straight and narrow path, especially if the object of his devotion was a woman of a lower class. In *Anna Karenina,* when Stiva had an affair with the former governess of his children, his wife Dolly could not forgive him, not because he had an affair, but because he had one with a woman of an inferior class.

A woman's affairs, even if she were married, were not particularly condemned as long as they did not become a topic for common gossip, and as long as her husband's professional reputation was not injured. When Karenin found out that Anna was unfaithful, he thought not of the immorality of the situation but only of his own reputation, fearing that this might cost him his career in politics. Anna's friends continued to accept her, even though they suspected her guilt, until she and Vronsky openly admitted their relationship to the world by going off and living together. Then they refused to associate with her any longer. Her women friends were more harsh in their uncompromising condemnation than the men, who might have forgiven her. Vronsky, however, was in a better position than Anna. He lost no respect and no friends, and had he given her up and returned to the army, he could have started again just where he had left off, with as good a chance for advancement as before.

In brief, Tolstoy, on the one hand, showed the life of the nobility at its best—its glamor, excitement, luxury, culture, and brilliant social life. The *raison d'être* of the nobility depicted in his major novels was ably summed up by Oblonsky in *Anna Karenina:* "The aim of civilization is enjoyment." But Tolstoy was among the first of the outstanding Russian authors to have the temerity to point out the corrupt and degenerate mode of living tacitly accepted by its members—as constructive criticism. He revealed its shallowness, its incongruous moral code, its extravagance, its unbalanced sense of values, the amount of valuable time wasted on ridiculous pastimes. In his novels he showed that the artificiality, restlessness, and boredom of the average noble demanded a far heavier price than he lavished on his own entertainment. Levin and Nekhludov bore witness to the serious problem of land management which faced the rural nobility; Karenin and Oblonsky, to the political wire-pulling necessary in order that the city official might not only retain his position but secure a better one.

Finally, Tolstoy exposed to the light of day the unhappy condition of any country where a small percentage of the population did none of the labor, yet lived in the lap of luxury, while the vast majority who did all the work lived in miserable poverty, with no educational opportunities and barely enough to eat. Of the three representative groups of the nobility with whom he dealt— the prominent officeholders, the military officers, and the rich landowners— Tolstoy pinned his hopes on the third, believing that they might be instrumental in bringing a new era to the Russian peasantry.

Although Tolstoy painted a vivid portrait of the nobility of his day and generation, the peasants were dearer to his heart, at least in his later years, than any members of his own class. Tolstoy approached the peasants from a different angle than Gogol or Turgenev. He not only regarded them as human beings, but he was not satisfied until he had placed them on a pedestal, until, in fact, he had almost deified them. Not only did he describe sympathetically

Sovfoto

Ilya Repin was the most influential realist painter in Russia. His "Leo Tolstoy on the Ploughfield" captures Tolstoy's feeling for peasant life.

their physical conditions but also their philosophy of life, their ideas, emotions, and opinions, in such a way that he left no doubt that he was their personal champion. Tolstoy, in other words, approached the peasants subjectively, with the result that one finds a better appreciation of them in his works than in those of any other Russian writer.

In the chapters about Levin and the management of his estate (*Anna Karenina*), Tolstoy revealed the peasant as an intelligent human being with a quick mind and a fine character. Simple living and hard manual labor had made of him a noble superior creature of lofty thoughts and strong character. Tolstoy believed that luxurious, artificial, idle living weakened a man's character and destroyed his peace of soul: that the most admirable type of existence was one of simplicity and hard work coupled with brotherly love and the practice of the Golden Rule. He thought the peasants came much nearer this ideal of perfection than the aristocracy. Therefore, he wanted to follow Christ's injunction to the rich young ruler, that is, to give up all that he had and become a peasant himself. He believed that since the peasants had more of the inner peace which comes from the attainment of these ideals than the aristocracy, they found greater favor in the eyes of God.

Levin, in *Anna Karenina,* who is really Tolstoy himself, voices his philosophy and thoughts. He has the distinction of being the most ideal landowner in Russian fiction. In his attempt to find some meaning in life, he associated with the peasants at harvest time, working side by side with them on an equal footing. During the dinner hour, he ate with an old man, and they became good friends. Tolstoy says that Levin "felt much nearer to the old man than to his own brother, and could not help smiling at the affection he felt for him." That night, after a hard day's work, Levin felt more at peace with himself than he had for a long time, and he reached the decision that it was more important to be a competent farmer than a rich but idle nobleman. In this passage, Tolstoy's account of the peasants swinging their scythes is typical of his fine descriptive powers.

Levin did not join the peasants at harvest in any spirit of condescension. The reader feels that he regarded them with an envy and admiration which were entirely new in Russian literature. Because he believed that the life of the peasant was an ideal life—not one to be pitied—he wanted them to be free to acquire land of their own, provided they themselves did not have serfs. Levin, or in reality Tolstoy, was a complete democrat in this respect. Serfdom was already abolished when he wrote *Anna Karenina;* it only remained for the aristocratic landowner to share his spoil with the peasants on an equal footing.

In *Resurrection,* Nekhludov attained this aim, by parceling out his land among his peasants. Unfortunately, Nekhludov's peasants had been subjugated and cheated so often by their landlords that they simply failed to understand that he was actually giving them the land, and they regarded his scheme as merely another ruse to extract money from them. It was almost impossible for them to realize that he was doing something for them at no profit to himself, and at first they bluntly refused to accept his offer. Such were the peasants with whom Tolstoy himself had to deal and whose conditions he sought to alleviate.

Tolstoy's idealization of and preoccupation with the peasants and peasant life go far to explain his attitude toward Shakespeare's work, which he never liked. To Tolstoy, any writer or artist who failed to appreciate the fundamental importance of the agricultural worker, or who depicted him as a clown for the sole purpose of entertaining an audience, failed to merit the laurels which the world had bestowed upon him. In fact, even writers who overlooked, while they did not disparage, the peasants lost caste with Tolstoy. This may well explain his negative attitude toward Leonid Andreyev.

To sum up, Tolstoy's literary career is one of the most absorbing in the history of Russian literature. His life was practically coincident with the Golden Age. His literary activity spanned a period of some fifty-eight years, from 1852 to 1910. In versatility, he was unexcelled by any writer of his time. He was not only a novelist, but a short-story writer, an essayist, a dramatist, a theologian, a philosopher, an artist, a preacher, and the founder of a creed of his own. No writer surpassed him in describing the life of the nobility in pre-Revolutionary Russia, or in appreciation of the Russian peasantry. His works reflected all the ideas and ideals that prevailed in the Russia of his day and generation. He was the only author in Russian literature who could speak with authority even to his rulers, who could prophesy their downfall, and yet emerge unscathed. In Tolstoy one visualizes the patriarch of old, who raised his powerful voice in protest against the injustice and corruption of his time. In short, Tolstoy was an institution by himself in the Golden Age of Russian literature.

Alexander Nikolayevitch Ostrovsky (1823–1886). Although in the study of Russian literature the novel occupies the most prominent place, an understanding of Russian life as revealed through that literature would scarcely be complete without some consideration of Alexander Nikolayevitch Ostrovsky, the dramatist. While, in the novel, Turgenev and Tolstoy were depicting the life of the Russian nobility or peasantry, and only incidentally referring to other slices of Russian society, a new class was making a niche for itself in the drama—namely, the Russian merchant (*kupetchestvo*). Whereas, in the literature we have already discussed, the underlying motives were political, social, philosophical, and idealistic, in the plays of Ostrovsky the economic factor predominates.

If Russian drama may be defined as "life relived," as a genuine transmigration of the souls of characters portrayed, then Ostrovsky is the most representative Russian dramatist. He placed the drama on a par with the novel. What Turgenev did for the serf, and Tolstoy for the nobility and peasantry, Ostrovsky did for the merchant. For almost half a century he dominated the Russian stage. He produced more than fifty plays, forty-seven of which he wrote himself, five in collaboration with others, while twelve were translations and adaptations for the Russian stage.

In spite of his popularity in Russia, Ostrovsky's plays are the most difficult to stage abroad. One reason for this is that his language was the vernacular, both regional and local, of the merchant class, and as such it often defies translation. As a result much of the content of his plays has been misconstrued or has failed to be appreciated in the West. In recent years a few of his plays have been translated, but the translator has sometimes departed so far from the original text that his final product contains little or nothing of Ostrovsky. Some translators have felt constrained to transform Ostrovsky's Russian merchants into American Rockefellers, American Babbitts, or American workers.

Three-quarters of Ostrovsky's plays deal with the everyday life of the merchant class, with their strong as well as with their weak points. Ostrovsky's approach was clearly revealed in one of his letters:

> Let the Russian be gay rather than sad when he sees himself reproduced on the stage. Let others assume the role of reformers if they wish. In order to claim the right to correct the shortcomings of a person without insulting him, it is essential to prove that you are also aware of his strong points. That is exactly what I am trying to do in my comedies.

This approach is particularly well illustrated in his two plays *The Sleigh* and *Poverty Is No Crime*. Because he adopted this methodology even in his comedies, stressing not only the incongruities but also the positive qualities of the Russian merchant class, many Westernizers accused Ostrovsky of Slavophilism. Such was the fate of any writer who attempted to portray the better qualities of Russian individuals or classes. On the other hand, when Ostrovsky had the temerity to champion the cause of the liberal merchant in his struggle with the hidebound traditionalists, many Slavophiles branded him as a Westernizer. As a matter of fact, Ostrovsky belonged to neither political camp. His purpose was to describe the life of the class of which he himself was a product, as it actually was—realistically and naturally. Inasmuch as any group has its merits and defects, it was therefore natural that the rival political camps alternately suspected him of partiality to one or the other.

Ostrovsky's merchant class, from the Russian standpoint, was neither a middle nor an upper class, but comprised the representatives of many classes. Within its ranks were to be found destitute members of the nobility, who, as a last resort, sought to retrieve their fortunes in the business world rather than by the management of their estates. It included the *nouveau riche,* the merchant capitalist, whose success only served to convince him of the power of the Almighty Ruble. Here, too, were to be found many ex-peasants, who had transferred their activities from the seasonal occupation of the farm to the more lucrative world of business, not to mention innumerable clerks and office employees who were the hangers-on of commerce and business. To the nobility described by Turgenev and Tolstoy, the running of an estate or the management of a business was usually a last resort, only to be undertaken in the face of desperate financial reverses, or when life held nothing but bitterness, disillusionment, and defeat. Ostrovsky's merchant class, on the other hand, devoted their lives to business management, and, far from regarding it as a disgrace, they elevated it to an art.

This class had its Russian Rockefellers as well as its Russian Babbitts. When Ostrovsky wrote, the merchant class was mainly responsible for the support of various social and cultural institutions, including art galleries. Its members not only subsidized talented writers, artists, dancers, and musicians, but produced them within their own ranks—as in the case of Ostrovsky himself. They helped to raise the standard of living not only for their own class but for others. In fact, their contribution to Russian culture and civilization has never received due recognition. On the other hand, they were also responsible for much bribery and corruption, prostitution, and vice, and for making a god of the Almighty Ruble.

In general, Ostrovsky voiced the sentiment of the liberal merchant. The plays which reflect this best are *The Storm* and *The Poor Bride*. *The Storm*, by general consensus, is considered one of the best, if not the best, of his many works. Here, as nowhere else, he presented the clash between the older generation of traditionalist merchants, the *samodurs* (domestic tyrants or bullies) like Madame Kabanova and Dikoy, whose roots were fixed in the feudal society of the past, and the younger and more liberal group (Katerina, Boris, Kuligin, Varvara), who strove for freedom of expression, liberty of action, and a more equitable division of authority. Balked by the *samodurs* from finding any legitimate outlet for their feelings, they sometimes, as in the case of Katerina and Boris, mistook license for liberty and indulged in serious lapses from the conventions. Even Tikhon, once he was beyond the reach of his mother's caustic tongue, cast everything else to the winds, in order to crowd as much pleasure as possible into a fortnight of freedom.

In *The Storm* it was the domestic tyranny of Martha Kabanova and Dikoy which bred license—a tyranny which demanded blind, unreasoning obedience from the younger members of the family. This tyranny produced both mental and physical suffering. Not only did Katerina have to submit to the constant nagging of her shrewish mother-in-law, but she had to endure a beating at the hands of her husband in accordance with her mother-in-law's orders—a beating which was supposed to make her a better wife. She was forced to kneel before her husband on the eve of his departure on a business trip and promise not to look at other men during his absence—just as he had to kneel before his domineering mother and pay heed to her countless instructions.

The chief object of Ostrovsky's dramas, particularly of this one, was the destruction of the *samodur,* and the triumph of honesty, moderation, and genuine goodness. Unlike Tolstoy, who practically sought to transform the nobility into a peasantry, or Tchekhov, who sought to supplant the nobility by a middle class, Ostrovsky was not seeking the destruction of the merchant class. He merely wished to rid it of its more undesirable elements, to eliminate the *samodurs*—in fact, to ethicize the business profession.

In *The Poor Bride* the power of the ruble is ably illustrated. In the first place a bride without a dowry was a frozen asset in a merchant's family, especially if she lacked beauty. If she were good looking, she could still hope to be sold to the highest bidder—to some rough, uncouth, and none too respectable merchant like Benevolensky. Anna Petrovna Nezabudkina was a product of the older traditionalist generation, for whom wealth covered up a multitude of sins, and who could unhesitatingly sacrifice her daughter to a man like Benevolensky in order to improve her financial position. Marya, representing the younger generation, accepts her mother's choice reluctantly, but unselfishly, in a fine spirit. On the one hand, Ostrovsky shows greed, selfishness, and disregard for human values; on the other, love and self-sacrifice.

Ostrovsky gave a faithful description of the practical, materialistic merchant class, which was about to supplant the idealistic nobility. The final triumph of this class is reflected in Tchekhov's plays, particularly in *The Cherry Orchard.*

Anton Pavlovitch Tchekhov (1860–1904). Although Anton Pavlovitch Tchekhov was a prolific writer of short stories, novels, and plays, practically all his ideas are summed up in his last drama, *The Cherry Orchard,* A Comedy in Four Acts, published in 1904. Technically speaking, and from a universal standpoint, *The Three Sisters* (1900) is perhaps his masterpiece; but from an historical point of view *The Cherry Orchard* is much more significant. For that reason we have confined our discussion to this play.

In general, *The Cherry Orchard* was more popular and more widely discussed than any of Tchekhov's previous writings. The main reason for its phenomenal success was that it voiced the prevailing political, economic, and social sentiment of the Russian people. This play appeared during the Russo-Japanese War, and almost on the eve of the Revolution of 1905, when the common platform of all political parties was the urbanization (industrialization) of Russia. By general consensus there were far too many villages and "cherry orchards" in Russia, when what the country actually needed was cities, factories, railroads, machinery, and a vast program of industrial development.

It should be pointed out that the Russian village of the period in question was not like a European village or an American farming community. Many of them were several hundred miles from a railroad station, and the roads leading to them were unpaved and often impassable. There were no libraries, no clubs, no daily newspapers, and very little connection with the outside world. In such an atmosphere people vegetated in boredom. A stranger from town, more particularly from Moscow, was sure to become an absorbing center of interest for the entire community. Most of the enterprising people marooned in these villages, like the "Three Sisters," spent their time planning how to get out, how to get to Moscow, the land of dreams. Some left of their own free will—others, because of the mismanagement of their estates, were forced out by the Lopakhins. To understand Tchekhov better, one should read Turgenev's *A Month in the Country,* where the theme—the negative side of country life—is the same, minus the Lopakhins, who have not yet appeared on the scene.

Tolstoy idealized the peasant and the simple naturalness of village life. In Tchekhov we see that too much village life retards the material progress of Russia. His plays mark a distinct reaction against the idealism of Tolstoy—a reaction which expressed the general sentiment of the people. In *The Cherry Orchard* more than in any other contemporaneous work, this clash between ruralism and urbanization, between the impractical, traditionalist, and often impoverished members of the nobility, and the impatient, ruthless business-man, is faithfully depicted. Tchekhov makes it quite apparent that a new era is beginning, and that the architect of the industrial age is the merchant capitalist.

In this play Madame Ranevskaya and her brother Gayev represent the unbusinesslike, impractical, decadent members of the "House of Gentlefolk," who have retained only the shadow of the former glamor which surrounded the nobility of *Anna Karenina,* and who contribute to the vegetation and stagnation of other classes by supporting "superfluous people" in idleness. On the other hand, Lopakhin, who seems to have stepped out of the pages of Ostrovsky, stands for the new, prosperous merchant class, not far removed from serfdom, which inherits the family estates of the Ranevskys, destroys the cherry orchards, together with all that they stood for symbolically and other-wise, and replaces them with suburban villas, the symbol of the new age.

In *The Cherry Orchard* the star of the Lopakhins is in the ascendancy—that of the Ranevskys is setting. The reader is confronted with a clash be-tween sentimentalism on the one hand, and dollars and cents on the other; between static life and dynamic life; between culture and civilization; between that which was old and familiar and that which is new and unknown. The new way had a stronger appeal because the old way had been tried and found wanting. The new way promised concrete returns in the shape of higher wages, shorter hours, better living conditions, popular education, and so on, at the expense of the Oblomovs, dilapidated manors, and run-down cherry orchards. The dissatisfied elements, therefore, pinned their hopes on indus-trialization or, as they called it, urbanization, which promised all this in return for the sacrifice of a group which was numerically insignificant.

Although it seems apparent that Tchekhov's sympathies lay with the Lopakhins, of which class he himself was a product, nevertheless, he was fair enough and objective enough to lay bare the strong and the weak points of both sides in the struggle. The crude methods of Lopakhin reveal the destruc-tive element latent in him. At times his coarseness assumes such proportions that one wonders which the merchant capitalist wanted more—a new world of his own making or revenge for the injustice and inequalities of the past—perhaps both. On the other hand, the sentimental Ranevskys, who cherished every stick and stone of the ancient and decrepit manor house, thoughtlessly abandoned the eighty-seven-year-old footman, Firs, who had served the family for forty years. When Firs discovered his predicament, his first thought was not for himself but for his master and whether he had remembered to wear his fur coat. Like Turgenev, Tchekhov, perhaps consciously, points out that the serf may reveal a nobler spirit than his master.

In *The Cherry Orchard,* the clash between the old and the new ends with the defeat of the old and the triumph of the new. The merchant capitalist, whose victory was foreseen by Gontcharov, whose leadership was sought by Turgenev, and whose representatives take precedence in the works of Ostrovsky, finally in *The Cherry Orchard* displaces the old nobility. The triumph of Lopakhin is also the triumph of the Stolzes and the Solomins, whereas the defeat of the Ranevskys is likewise the defeat of the Oblomovs and the Lavretskys.

The merchant capitalist dealt his death-blow with the axe that cut down the cherry orchard—a blow that was heard throughout Russia—and which proved to be the first signal of the approaching revolution. For the Revolution of 1905 was not, in the final analysis, a social revolution. It put the merchant capitalist in the saddle, where he remained until 1917. Strangely enough, it was his children who provided the leaders for the 1917 revolution; and it was this very class, which, by its contributions to the revolutionary money chests, blindly dug its own grave. The merchant capitalists were ousted, not by the axe, but by firing squads and "liquidation."

Abroad, and particularly in England, Tchekhov became the most popular of the Russian dramatists—even upon occasion a rival of Shakespeare. There are several reasons for this. In the first place, Tchekhov, with his humorous short story, broke new ground in Russian literature from the standpoint of the foreigner. By showing that the Russian could laugh as well as sigh, he was for them like a ray of light in "the monotonous gloom" of Russian literature. In Europe, moreover, the short story enjoyed an immense popularity, and in Russia, where it had reached its nadir, Tchekhov elevated it to an art. Furthermore, his dramas, although less amusing, expressed a reaction against sentimentality which coincided with English taste at the beginning of the twentieth century. The attention of the English public may have been attracted to the denouement of his plays, particularly in the case of *The Three Sisters* and *Uncle Vanya,* which are somewhat reminiscent of Goldsmith's *Deserted Village.* To be sure, in Goldsmith, the depopulation of the countryside was bemoaned as a tragedy, whereas in Tchekhov it is welcomed, but the milieu is the same. Finally, the merchant capitalist, depicted by Tchekhov, was an even more familiar figure in the industrial centers of Western Europe than in Russia itself. To the Englishman, as well as to Tchekhov, he was a practical man who stood for material progress.

Although *The Cherry Orchard* is for Americans undoubtedly the best-known Russian play, it may in the future, because of the popularity of Margaret Mitchell's *Gone With the Wind,* be even better understood and appreciated. For both works deal with the passing of a traditional way of life, based upon a landowning aristocracy and the institution of serfdom or slavery.

Tara meant to Scarlett what the cherry orchard meant to Madame Ranevskaya. Both women faced the loss of their property to men who, from their standpoint, were upstarts or white trash. Lopakhin, a product of the new industrial capitalism, insisted on buying the cherry orchard, where his father had been a serf. Jonas Wilkerson, the typical carpetbagger of the post-Civil War era, sought to buy Tara, where he had once served as an overseer, prior to his discharge on moral grounds.

Both women refused to capitulate to the new social and economic order. But Madame Ranevskaya, who was more of a sentimentalist, expected a miracle to save her. Scarlett, in whom the materialist prevailed, was ready to go to any length, even to sell herself to a man she did not love, in order to save Tara, that she might never be hungry again. Although Madame Ranevskaya lost her cherry orchard, she remained an aristocrat. Scarlett kept Tara, but in doing so she stooped to the level of the white trash she so utterly despised. A parallel reading of *The Cherry Orchard* and *Gone With the Wind* suggests further comparisons between Gayev and Ashley Wilkes, neither of whom was fitted to cope with the new way of life.

In brief, Tchekhov's works, especially *The Cherry Orchard,* mark the transition between the downfall of the "House of Gentlefolk" and the advent of the proletariat—sometimes called Russia's "Twilight Period."

Maxim Gorky (1868–1936). Maxim Gorky, like Tchekhov, believed that the future of Russia lay in further industrialization rather than in agricultural development. Both writers resented Tolstoy's idealization of the peasantry and traced much of the wretchedness and misery in Russia to peasant influence. Tchekhov, however, hitched his chariot to the merchant capitalist, as his agent for urbanization, whereas Gorky lined himself up with the urban workers—the proletariat. Moreover, Gorky, unlike his contemporaries, demanded a change through revolution rather than by education and evolution. In literature he did for the urban "serf" what Turgenev did for the rural serf.

Although Gorky is better known as the classic interpreter of Russian proletarian culture, he evinced his real talent in the portrayal of the Russian underworld. In his idealization of the underworld Gorky undoubtedly sounded a new note in Russian literature. He was the uncrowned king of the Russian *bosyak* (tramp or hobo) before he became the writer-laureate of the proletariat. Not all of his works—and he was a prolific writer—reflect Gorky. The Gorky who found a niche for himself among the writers of the classical age was the Gorky who championed the underworld and interpreted the prewar

Russian proletariat. Although this Gorky belongs essentially to the Golden Age, he was not a genius of the same caliber as Turgenev, Dostoyevsky, and Tolstoy. He was a man of great talent.

No other author, prior to Gorky, has given us such a characteristic and sympathetic description of the Russian *bosyak*. Gorky's tramps differ sharply from the members of the American underworld, or from those of any other country, except perhaps Germany and Italy. This partly explains the popularity of his works in these two countries. The Russian underworld described in *The Lower Depths* was not made up of racketeers, gunmen, and bootleggers, driving high-powered automobiles and wearing tuxedos and dress shirts. It was composed rather of "creatures that once were men." For the most part these human derelicts were victims of the social order rather than violators of the law. Their chief weapon was their fists—or, as a last resort, a knife. They were invariably penniless. Money, when they had it, burned holes in their pockets. Except for thieves and robbers, this underworld constituted an army of unemployed and unskilled laborers, who wandered from place to place in search of work. So true to life was Gorky's portrayal of this slice of Russian society that his name became a byword in the mouth of every tramp, and he was recognized as the patron of the underworld. To upbraid a hobo for his laziness might well bring the retort: "You never can tell—I might become a Gorky!"

By assembling the various types of the Russian underworld in a basement night lodging, Gorky in his play *The Lower Depths* was able to sum up his ideas concerning them. Although of diverse antecedents, barons, Tatar princes, thieves, prostitutes, or card-sharpers, they have this in common—that they are the victims of the social order, and they meet here on a plane of equality. Such a play, for the majority of people, broke new ground in Russian drama.

Originally this play was entitled *Na Dnye Zhizni* (The Lower Depths of Life); but, at the suggestion of V. I. Nemirovitch-Dantchenko, Gorky dropped the last Russian word. The play was first produced at the Moscow Art Theatre on December 31, 1902, and its thirty-fifth jubilee was held at the close of 1937. Germany, especially, went wild over the play. From 1903 to 1904 it enjoyed an uninterrupted run of five hundred nights in Berlin alone. English translations have appeared under various titles: *In the Depths, A Night Shelter, Submerged, Down and Out,* as well as *The Lower Depths.*

Whereas in Tchekhov's plays, the idle-rich nobility and other "superfluous" people vegetate in boredom in the Russian village, Gorky's hoboes vegetate in idleness and trivialities, sometimes reluctantly, in the dark damp basements where they seek a temporary lodging. In spite of their sordid surroundings, Gorky's heroes still have faith in a better future. They do not spend their time cursing the system or lamenting their misfortunes. The pinnacle of their discussion, as led by Luka, the vagabond pilgrim, and his interpreter Satin the cardsharper, is "the better man." Far from being crushed in spirit, some of them regard their wretched conditions as the price of their freedom. To Tchekhov's idle rich, life spelled boredom; although physically better off than Gorky's tramps, they were spiritually crushed. The human failures of Gorky's underworld, in spite of their environment, are spiritually the stronger of the two. They still have hope; they take life as it comes, sometimes in happy-go-lucky fashion; they sing, and they keep their faith in humanity. Man to them is the norm. Whether he turns out to be a carpenter, a cardsharper, a Napoleon, or a Mohammed, he is still a man, free and deserving of respect. Strangely enough they would prefer "a better man," even a better underworld. Gorky's philosophy of "the better man," expressed by Luka and Satin, almost approaches Tolstoy's "inner peace."

In other words, Gorky discovered a world in the underworld. His implication is clear enough—that tramps or hoboes with such beautiful souls should not be lost to humanity because they are the victims of an unjust social order. In this field Gorky had no predecessor, and herein lies his chief contribution to Russian literature.

Less artistic, but of greater political significance, was his proletarian novel *Mother*. This was the first novel subsequent to the 1905 revolution to portray the life of the urban worker in the factory, at home, at political meetings, on parade, and so forth. Although it truly reflects the life of the proletariat during the period in question, there were few mothers like Pelagueya Vlasova. It seems quite evident that Gorky wished other mothers to emulate her, but he has given us a portrait of the ideal, rather than of the real, proletarian mother.

If we did not know that Gorky's novel was produced in Russia in 1906, we could never guess that it ran the gauntlet of the world's most rigid censorship. This novel was an open challenge to the government—an appeal to the worker to emulate the Vlasovs and, by force or revolution, to bring about the new social order. Gorky did not mince words in the appeals of his agitators. In a country where freedom of speech exists, speeches like those of Pavel would be regarded as soapbox oratory or casually dismissed as Red propaganda. But in Russia during the period in question, the activities of the Vlasovs and their supporters constituted a serious menace to the old regime. Yet this book could be found in every library, accessible to anyone capable of reading it. This was chiefly due to the efforts of the Russian intelligentsia, in welcoming into Russian literature a real proletarian novel, without altogether subscribing to the ideas expressed in it.

Gorky's *Mother* is by no means a work of art. It is rather a political document of the tumultuous years 1905 and 1906. As we have already intimated, Gorky is really at home only in the underworld. In the world he is less of an artist and more of a propagandist. *The Lower Depths* is a sociological study—*Mother*, a political tract.

For a better appreciation of Gorky, American readers should turn to John Steinbeck. Of all American writers, Steinbeck is the one who most nearly approaches Gorky. There is a great deal of the Gorky philosophy in the works of Eugene O'Neill and in Erskine Caldwell's *Tobacco Road,* not to mention others, but Steinbeck is the American version of Gorky.

Both Gorky and Steinbeck succeeded in awakening the general public and the authorities to the existence of a class of people living under conditions almost beyond their comprehension. Both writers championed the cause of these lower depths and presented their characters in such a light that the public realized they were, after all, human beings, albeit tramps or migrants.

Gorky in *Lower Depths* and Steinbeck in *Grapes of Wrath* not only succeeded in gaining recognition of the plight of the Satins, the Lukas, and the Joads, but they made the public lament such a great waste of valuable human material. People not only wondered what could be done for these lower depths, but what they, in a better environment, could do for their countries. In other words, what could the Satins and Lukas do for Russia? What could the Joads do for America?

Any comparison of Gorky and Steinbeck should not overlook the fact that, although both were out-and-out realists, Gorky, always the artist, attained the same effects without the crudeness and profanity found in Steinbeck. In this respect, Steinbeck has more in common with the contemporary Soviet writer Mikhail Sholokhov than with Gorky.

In short, Gorky did for the tramp and for the proletarian what Tolstoy did for the peasant, Andreyev for the Jew, and Turgenev for the serf. He idealized him. The impression derived from a study of his works is that he stands at the head of a great mass of humanity, seeking recognition and a new life. With Gorky began the era of the domination of the proletariat.

The Symbolist Movement. This summary of Russian literature would not be complete without reference to the Symbolist movement, which began in the 1890's and came especially to the fore in Russia after 1905. Its most outstanding representatives were Leonid Andreyev (1871–1919), Vyacheslav Ivanov (1866–1949), Andrei Bely (1880–1934), and Alexander Blok (1880–1921). The Symbolist movement projected itself into what was a virtual vacuum in the Russian literary world, when after the 1880's no outstanding novels were being produced. It matured and became more articulate after 1905, as a result of widespread disillusionment over the achievements of the revolution in that year. At first the Symbolists attributed the chaotic state in the political and social life of Russia to what they alleged were wrong emphases in nineteenth century Russian literature, especially to overemphasis on social problems. In the process of their revaluation and reinterpretation of that literature, however, most of them became enamored of it and emerged as its staunch supporters. In particular, the Symbolists were responsible for the rediscovery of Dostoyevsky, whose works they made extremely popular. Indeed they found in Dostoyevsky, as in no other novelist, substantiation of their own distrust of and reaction against industrialism, materialism, and atheism. The Symbolists provided an important link between the Golden Age and Soviet literature. Their ideas and their experiments in technique influenced many Soviet writers, especially in the 1920's.

LITERARY CRITICISM

It is very difficult to provide non-Russians with a concise and yet comprehensive definition of a Russian critic or of Russian literary criticism. Ostensibly the critics interpreted Russian literature. Actually, because of the very nature of that literature, the scope of their work was much greater. Because the great writers of the Golden Age championed the cause of political freedom and social reform, the Russian critics devoted their articles mainly to an analysis of the great questions at issue in their time and to the remedies advanced. Their greatness lies in the fact that they did it boldly and at the risk not only of their careers but of their very lives. The history of Russian literary criticism is a record of martyrdom.

Although by the outside world most of these critics were regarded as atheists because of their attack upon organized religion, they actually took many of their ideas of social justice from Christianity. In other words, like the French philosophers of the eighteenth century, they attacked churchianity, not Christianity, as Belinsky's *Letter to Gogol* so clearly demonstrates. Many of these critics were the children or grandchildren of priests and had themselves attended a theological seminary. It was because of this background that they became conscious of the gulf between Christian principles and the practice of the official church, which in Russia had become a tool of the state, thereby constituting a reactionary force which impeded progress. In their denunciation of corruption in the Orthodox church, the Russian critics performed much the same role from without that the Reformers achieved from within the Catholic church during the era of the Reformation in Western Europe. For in nineteenth-century Russia the church as an institution never did champion the cause of the serfs or take a stand for the betterment of their position. That Christian task, strange as it may seem, had to be taken up through secular channels by writers and critics—the so-called atheistic intelligentsia.

It stands to reason, therefore, that the Russian critics had to do far more than analyze books from the standpoint of art and technique. Their outlook had to be broad, their understanding deep, and their courage unflinching. As political and social reformers they had to face the antagonism of both church and state. The Russian critic had to assume in turn the role of a Protestant Reformer, a French Encyclopedist, an American Revolutionist of the 1776 variety, and a contemporary columnist.

It is not surprising that the Russian critics have been very popular with the leaders of the new regime in Russia. By and large, both critics and revolutionary leaders shared the same fate of imprisonment and exile on behalf of their ideals. N. K. Krupskaya, the wife of Lenin, for example, testified to her husband's great affection for Tchernyshevsky and to the frequent references he made to the great critic in his writings. The most important contribution of the Soviet regime in this respect is that it has republished the works of the critics and has made them popular. Especially since the adoption of the new constitution in 1936 and the Pushkin Centennial in 1937, several works about the critics have appeared. To date, strictly speaking however, only a beginning has been made. The study of Russian literary criticism is still a virgin field.

Although there were many Russian literary critics during the Golden Age, three of the greatest among them will suffice here to represent their role in Russian literature and their chief contributions. These are Belinsky, Tchernyshevsky, and Dobrolyubov.

Vissarion Grigoryevitch Belinsky (1811–1848). Vissarion Grigoryevitch Belinsky was the founder of literary criticism in Russia. In fact he elevated it to an art and a science. He was practically the first who dared to criticize established writers in various fields. Before his time, writers were held in high esteem, and there was such respect for the printed word that hardly anyone had the temerity to criticize prominent authors. In his "Literary Reflections" Belinsky appealed to Russians to follow the example of West European critics and to point out the weak as well as the strong points of a writer's work, irrespective of his position. The impression is that he, himself, wished to set an example for others in this respect, for in this same work, while presenting a survey of Russian writers from Lomonosov to Pushkin, he went so far as to assert that there was still no such thing as Russian literature.

The importance of Belinsky's stand in favor of literary criticism should not be overlooked. It did have the salutary effect of inducing many writers to be more careful about what they wrote. Especially during the life of Belinsky, Russian writers became critic-conscious, fully aware that what they wrote could never escape his watchful eye. Belinsky left his imprint on Russian readers as well as upon Russian writers; the limited but select circle of Russian readers was a highly intelligent group who often paid as much attention to the critic as to the author. The reader of Belinsky's works inevitably gains the impression that he wrote with authority. Only one Russian writer excelled him in this respect and he was Leo Tolstoy. Belinsky's bid for criticism, however, did in practice open the door to the mediocre critic and encouraged a tendency on the part of Russian critics in general to expose the weak points rather than to commend the strong points of the work whose value they assessed.

Belinsky's indictment of Russian literature emanated from his failure to discover a single genius in that field. Although he found many great talents, he did not believe that any of them, with the exception of Pushkin, revealed even a spark of genius. A talented person—Belinsky implied in his essay—is at best only an artisan, whereas a genius is an artist. An artisan merely recreates, whereas an artist actually creates. It seems that the main purpose of Belinsky in writing his "Literary Reflections" was to reconnoiter the field in order to discover a genius. But Pushkin was the only man of great promise he found. His main reasons for elevating Pushkin above the rest were, first, that Pushkin's work reflected the national qualities of the Russian people and, second, that his poetry was free from any motivation.

With regard to Pushkin's place in world literature, Belinsky in his "Survey of Russian Literature in 1841" said that Pushkin stood in the same relation to the great European poets as Russia did to Europe, and vice versa.

Belinsky attributed the absence of any genius in the field of Russian literature to the lack of a national (*narodnaya*) literature. Too many Russian writers, he complained, had merely imitated the works of foreign writers. Belinsky's article in reality constituted an appeal for such a national literature, for he conceived the cosmos as a unit, comprised of national entities, each of which was destined to make its own distinctive contribution.

The real prerequisite to the understanding of Belinsky and the other leading Russian criticis is not only a knowledge of the political and social system extant in Russia during the period in question, including the ritual and dogma of the Orthodox church, as well as a comprehensive background of Russian and comparative literature, but also some familiarity with the ideas of the leading German philosophers of the eighteenth and nineteenth centuries.

Writers on Belinsky have ordinarily divided his literary career into several well-marked stages, according to the influence upon him of Schelling, Fichte, and Hegel. The consensus is that the Schelling period was ushered in by the appearance of the "Literary Reflections" in *Molva* in 1834. Judging by this work, Belinsky understood Schelling to mean that the universe is permeated with one eternal idea; that in the course of history this idea manifests itself in the life of peoples, each of which must express one aspect of the universal idea; and that this manifestation is the only justification of a people's existence. In art Belinsky found the best expression of the unique qualities of a people. At the time he wrote, Belinsky felt that Russian literature did not yet express the national qualities of the Russian people.

Following the Fichte period, which lasted for only a brief interlude (1836–1837), came the Hegelian period (1837–1840). As in Europe, so in Russia, Hegelian philosophy was subject to many interpretations by Conservatives (Rightists) and Liberals (Leftists). To Russians in these years it was summed up in a nutshell by the assumption that whatever was real was rational and should be accepted. The Slavophiles in Russia interpreted this to mean acceptance of Orthodoxy and Autocracy as they existed, but the Westernizers contended that, since life was dynamic, change must be accepted as reality. Belinsky, although fundamentally a Westernizer, came very near at times to voicing the interpretation of the Slavophiles as regards Orthodoxy, Autocracy, and Nationality.

As a result, Belinsky at times enjoyed the plaudits of both Westernizers and Slavophiles. His influence upon Dostoyevsky, the foremost literary exponent of Slavophilism, was particularly great. From the "Literary Reflections," Dostoyevsky undoubtedly derived his concept of the mission of the Russian people.

Belinsky also took cognizance of the comparative dearth of juvenile literature in Russia during his lifetime. In his article on "Two Books for Children" in 1840, he made a strong appeal for greater effort in this field. Too many Russians, he felt, looked upon children's books with contempt and bought them mainly for their colorful illustrations. Belinsky was aware of the importance of good literature for children. Far from believing that anyone could write books for children, he pointed out that only a genius could fill this gap. Turgenev was the first among Russia's great writers to take this admonition seriously with the publication of *Byezhin Prairie* (*Memoirs of a Sportsman,* 1852). He was the first in Russia to produce what may be termed standard juvenile literature.

As early as 1843 Belinsky was already in a position to announce the existence of a Russian literature. This was a far cry from his first survey in 1834, when he denied that there was such a thing as Russian literature. The progress of a decade led him to conclude that Russian literature was no longer confined to Pushkin but included a whole roster of outstanding writers. By 1847 ("Russian Literature in 1847") he admitted that even Russian literary criticism had been established on a sound basis.

In his survey of Russian literature in 1846, however, Belinsky warned his readers that they should not approach the field with the same gauge they used to approach other literatures. Just as the history of Russia did not follow the same pattern as the history of other countries, he pointed out that Russian literature, too, was unique. Unless this were borne in mind, he insisted that Russian literature would remain a riddle and a mystery.

To sum up, it may be said that Belinsky was largely instrumental in producing a national Russian literature and in laying the foundations of Russian literary criticism. He likewise made another outstanding contribution by interpreting standard European literature to the Russians, both through European and Russian glasses. In this respect, he therefore paved the way for comparative literary criticism in Russia, which flourished in the nineteenth century. Furthermore, in the interpretation of Belinsky's role in Russian literature, greater stress should be laid in the future on two aspects of his achievement. First, it is important to note the extent to which, in spite of his reputation as a Westernizer, Belinsky reflected the age of Nicholas I, with its growing emphasis on nationalization and Russification. This is particularly evident in his annual surveys of Russian literature from 1834 to 1847. Not only was Belinsky at his best in these surveys, but they provide a first-hand history of Russian national literature during its most formative years. Second, the influence of Belinsky on Dostoyevsky should no longer be overlooked.

Nikolai Gavrilovitch Tchernyshevsky (*1828–1889*). Nikolai Gavrilovitch Techernyshevsky has done for Gogol what Belinsky did for Pushkin. He correctly interpreted the historical significance of the Gogol period of the 1830's and 1840's in Russian literature. Although like Belinsky, Tchernyshevsky also recognized the genius of Pushkin, he found in Gogol's satirical sketches, which were themselves replete with criticism and analysis of the existing social system, the spark which produced modern Russian literary criticism. The implication is that both Tchernyshevsky and Belinsky, in laying the foundations of Russian literary criticism, derived much inspiration from Gogol.

Tchernyshevsky was not only a critic of Russian writers; he was also a critic of Russian critics, especially of Belinsky. This was done at a time when the mere mention of Belinsky in print was forbidden. In his *Essays on Russian Literature in the Days of Gogol,* Tchernyshevsky returned Russian criticism to the tradition of Belinsky.

With Tchernyschevsky began the attack on the Russian intelligentsia as weaklings. Although the repudiation of the intelligentsia really emerged first in Turgenev's novels, where the characters he portrayed as leaders for the founding of the new social order turned out to be weaklings and failures, it was Tchernyshevsky who was responsible for classifying all such progressives as typical representatives of the Russian intelligentsia, and who made them the butt of criticism and ridicule for their inability to achieve positive results. The attack on the Russian intelligentsia continued practically without respite until the 1930's.

A study of Tchernyshevsky's works reveals that in general he advocated reform by a gradual evolutionary process rather than by revolution. For he believed that any fundamental improvement in the Russian social system depended upon increased enlightenment and education for the illiterate, inarticulate, and unorganized masses (*narod*), who comprised four-fifths of the nation, as well as upon the ability of the intelligentsia to convince the rulers of Russia that reforms were necessary and should come voluntarily from above rather than by force from below.

Just as Belinsky was influenced by Hegel, Tchernyshevsky came under the spell of the German philosopher Ludwig Feuerbach (1804–1872). This in itself marks a change in outlook on the part of the intelligentsia from idealism and mysticism to materialism, as well as from the philosophy of reconciliation to a realization that concrete action must be taken to bring about a change in existing conditions. Just as Feuerbach put man at the center of the universe and insisted that everything should be done for man and through man, so Tchernyshevsky put the people (*narod*) first and claimed that everything should be done by the people and through the people.

As a careful perusal of his works indicates, Tchernyshevsky began as a philosopher, then turned to history, and finally to political economy. It is clear, however, that for him materialism was a means to an end rather than an end in itself. He reached the conclusion, however reluctantly, that materialism more than idealism would assist the revolutionary forces.

This transition from idealism to materialism is reflected in Tchernyshevsky's preference for Gogol, the realist, to Pushkin, the idealist. Whereas Belinsky had predicted that Pushkin would remain the model for Russian writers who sought to give expression to Russian genius, Tchernyshevsky, in his *Essays on Russian Literature in the Days of Gogol,* claimed that Gogol rather than Pushkin was the real founder of the school of national Russian writers. For Gogol, unlike Pushkin, was free from foreign influence. His works were devoted exclusively to a realistic portrayal of Russian life. Although his books were works of art, he was not motivated by art for art's sake, but rather by art for life's sake or for the sake of the *narod*. Since the *narod* was the center of his thinking, Tchernyshevsky placed the poet Nekrasov above Pushkin. In his judgment, Nekrasov was a product of the people, worked all his life for the people, and accomplished everything through the people.

Another reason why Gogol appealed particularly to Tchernyshevsky was that, unlike many other writers who blamed only individuals or specific groups or classes for the state of affairs in Russia, both men agreed in placing the blame upon the entire social structure. There were no redeeming characters belonging to any social stratum in either *The Revizor* or *Dead Souls*.

Tchernyshevsky subordinated writers like Griboyedov, Pushkin, Lermontov, and Koltsov to Gogol because none of them established a school of writers as Gogol did. It seems likely that Tchernyshevsky's elevation of Gogol contributed greatly to the advancement of Russian prose at the expense of poetry and made the novel, which was a more realistic medium than the poem, the true vehicle of the Golden Age of Russian literature. Among his own contemporaries, Tchernyshevsky preferred Tolstoy, for whom he predicted a great future, Nekrasov, and Dobrolyubov.

Nikolai Alexandrovitch Dobrolyubov (1836–1861). In spite of his premature death, the influence of Nikolai Alexandrovitch Dobrolyubov was such that by 1885 four editions of his works had been published. In Soviet Russia today, Dobrolyubov enjoys the same popularity as the other leading Russian critics.

The most striking feature of Dobrolyubov's political ideology is that, unlike most of his fellow-Westernizers, he advocated the American political system, in preference to any European model, to replace the existing autocratic regime in Russia. He favored the American system for many reasons, as outlined in an article written in 1859,[3] but mainly because he believed that it did more to advance the welfare of the people as a whole than any other system. Since Dobrolyubov worked for the good of the *narod,* it was natural that he should approve of America as the country which best served the interests of the people in contrast to most of Europe where the people were expected to serve the state. In fact, Dobrolyubov in 1859 grasped the spirit of America as it was reflected some years later in Lincoln's Gettysburg Address. "Government of the people, by the people, for the people" was exactly what Dobrolyubov and his fellow critics were crusading for at the risk of their lives in Russia. America had already achieved it.

The Puritanic principle, derived from the Old Testament (Leviticus 25:23), that all the land belonged to God and that any man was entitled to

3. A critical review by Dobrolyubov of *Travels in North America, Canada and the Island of Cuba* by Alexander Lakier, 2 Vols. (St. Petersburg, 1859).

the amount he could till, likewise appealed greatly to Dobrolyubov, who felt that it was carried into practice in America. In the process of westward expansion there was always land available for those Americans who were willing and able to till and exploit it. To the sponsors of the *narod* in Russia, confronted for the most part by a landless peasantry, in a country which was in 1859 still on the eve of the abolition of serfdom, the American example suggested an approach to near paradise on earth.

To most Europeans, because of the unusual absence of government interference, this freedom of the individual to go and take the land spelled anarchy. But Americans have termed it "rugged individualism." Strictly speaking, rugged individualism is the real essence of Russian idealistic anarchism, which has been so generally misinterpreted by Western scholars. If a critic like Dobrolyubov had lived in the United States in 1859 he would have qualified as a good American patriot and as a rugged individualist. In Russia he was denounced as a radical, undesirable citizen, and even as a venomous snake! Had he not, like Belinsky, died young, Dobrolyubov would undoubtedly have been exiled to Siberia, as were Tchernyshevsky and many others who displayed an active interest in the welfare of the people.

Dobrolyubov was a combination of Belinsky and Tchernyshevsky, but he surpassed them both in his impatience for immediate action to reform the Russian political and social system. In fact, he called as loudly for action as did his contemporary, Alexander Herzen (1812–1870), although Herzen, who left Russia in 1847, wrote from the safe vantage point of London, whereas Dobrolyubov dared to ring his bell inside Russia. Because he was conscience-stricken over the plight of his countrymen, Dobrolyubov, more than his fellow critics, belabored the intelligentsia, of which he himself was a member, for standing idly by and doing nothing. Dobrolyubov who, like Tchernyshevsky, was a strong believer in the strength and efficacy of public opinion, felt that where no other recourse was possible, the intelligentsia should at least take a stand, even though it meant assuming the cross of martyrdom. This protest against inaction explains Dobrolyubov's interest in Gontcharov's novel *Oblomov,* published in 1859.

What Belinsky did for Pushkin and Tchernyshevsky for Gogol, Dobrolyubov did for Gontcharov, with special emphasis on Oblomovism. To the average American the listless and parasitic Oblomov seems like an exaggerated version of the superfluous man. Dobrolyubov, on the contrary, felt that among the intelligentsia Oblomovism, to a greater or less degree, was unfortunately the rule rather than the exception. He compared the Russian intelligentsia, who were supposed to furnish leadership for the *narod,* to the Oblomovs who made flowery speeches full of promises, but who had neither the energy nor the courage to carry their promises into effect.

Next to Gontcharov, Dobrolyubov acclaimed Ostrovsky, in particular his play *The Storm,* with its revelation of the status of women and its portrayal of Katerina's struggle for freedom and self-expression. Of Turgenev's novels, he preferred *On the Eve* (1860), upon which he based his article, "When Will the Real Day Come?" It was natural that the energy and purposefulness of Insarov, the only dynamic character among Turgenev's men, should appeal to a lover of action like Dobrolyubov, although he was by no means satisfied with the way the novel ended—hence his query about when the real day would come. To a limited extent, it did come with the abolition of serfdom on March 3, 1861. Dobrolyubov died a few months later.

The Intelligentsia. Belinsky, Tchernyshevsky, and Dobrolyubov, this foremost trinity among the Russian literary critics of the Golden Age, were true representatives of the Russian intelligentsia of the nineteenth century. Intelligentsia is a term of Russian origin which is often translated into English as "the intellectuals," "the elite," or "the educated," sometimes even those with a modicum of education in contrast to the *narod,* who were mainly illiterate. Actually, it is as difficult to translate the Russian term *intelligentsia* into English as it is to translate the English word *gentleman,* with all its denotions and connotations into the Slavic and other continental European languages. Although many books and articles have been written about the Russian intelligentsia, it is doubtful if anyone has yet given a concise scientific definition of the term which would be universally accepted.

Irrespective of the definition that may eventually be coined, it is clear that the Russian intelligentsia did not consist only of Westernizers, as is sometimes implied, but also included Slavophiles and even Monarchists. It was no regimented group with but a single idea or a single solution for the betterment of existing conditions in Russia. Some of its members were purely doctrinaire in their approach to the burning issues of the day. Others preferred to present these problems to the public through the medium of fiction or drama. Still others were impatient with delay and hoped for the coming of a new political and social regime in the twinkling of an eye. In other words, some leaned heavily in the direction of evolutionary means to attain the ends in view, while others insisted on conducting a revolutionary crusade. But regardless of differences in outlook, the Russian intelligentsia were the leaders who molded and shaped Russian thinking in the nineteenth century. Inasmuch as their thoughts were focused upon ways and means for the betterment of the lot of Russians in general, they actually represented the conscience of the Russian people.

It is regrettable that the world outside Russia has derived a distorted impression of the Russian intelligentsia, especially of the Russian critics. Literary men abroad naturally preferred the restraint, the polished phrases, and the artistry of a novelist like Turgenev to what they called the sermonizing and the shrill, scolding tone of the critics. They have helped to perpetuate the impression that the Russian intelligentsia consisted of a group of hotheaded radicals of plebeian origin, mainly atheists and impractical idealists, who talked much and accomplished little. Englishmen and Americans who lived in countries where most of the reforms the Russian critics crusaded for had already been achieved often failed to observe the unselfishness of the motives of men like Belinsky, Tchernyshevsky, and Dobrolyubov, and their influence on the leading writers of the day. Writers abroad, unless they could read Russian, must have depended largely upon hearsay rather than upon a first-hand knowledge of the works of the critics, few of which had ever been translated. For the false impression that the intelligentsia were impotent and ineffectual the Russian critics, themselves members of the intelligentsia, were largely responsible. Conscience-stricken because of the condition of the *narod* and exasperated at their inability to achieve results as fast as they wished, they often scolded one another and voluntarily shouldered the blame for the limited progress that was made.

The intelligentsia as such represented no political party, but rather the conscience of the people as a whole. For the most part, its members were idealists. On the other hand, the intellectuals who claimed to represent the proletariat actually represented parties—in the case of the Bolsheviks, one party. They were ideologists rather than idealists. The Revolution of 1905 was led by the intelligentsia, with the participation of some party intellectuals. It was the Bolshevik intellectuals that devoured the Russian intelligentsia in the October Revolution of 1917.

After a careful study of the life and works of leading critics like Belinsky, Tchernyshevsky, and Dobrolyubov, one has to conclude, in view of the unselfishness of their motives and the Christian character of their objectives, that if they had been able to carry on their crusade for the *narod* inside the church, using theological terminology instead of scientific nomenclatures, the church would have revered them as martyrs and would undoubtedly have canonized them as saints.

MUSIC

There have been two great ages of Russian music: church music, introduced from Byzantium with the coming of Orthodox Christianity; and Russian nationalist music of the nineteenth and twentieth centuries. The liturgical chant which came from Byzantium was soon Russianized. The so-called *znamenny* chant, the principal chant of the Russian medieval church, existed for some centuries, at least until the church reforms introduced by Patriarch Nikon in the seventeenth century. It was entirely vocal, with no instrumental music, not even the organ. All the major Russian composers made use of church music and some, including Tchaikovsky, Rachmaninov, and Gretchaninov, composed complete liturgies.

Russian folk music dates back at least one thousand years, to the tenth century, but it did not become a fine art. The great collections of Russian folk songs were compiled in the eighteenth and nineteenth centuries under the impact of Russian nationalism. Secular music gained its first foothold in Russia about the middle of the seventeenth century, by way of the foreign colony in Moscow (*Nemetskaya sloboda*), in the reign (1645–1676) of Tsar Alexis Mikhailovitch, father of Peter the Great. The use of modern music notation likewise dates from this period. The three women empresses—Anna, Elizabeth, and Catherine the Great—were responsible for the introduction of opera (Italian, French, and German) at the Russian court. The earliest Russian operas of the eighteenth century were imitations and adaptations of Italian and French comic operas, often using Russian themes.

The growth of national consciousness that followed the Napoleonic invasion (1812) had a decisive impact on Russian music, as it did on literature. As in the case of the writers of the Golden Age, most Russian composers of the nineteenth century belonged to the ranks of the nobility and were dilettantes in the field of music, which may account for their lack of subservience to established Western musical traditions and techniques. Glinka was a zoologist and linguist; Borodin a professor of chemistry and military doctor; Mussorgsky a cavalry officer and government clerk; and Rimsky-Korsakov was a sailor.

According to Vladimir Vasilyevitch Stasov (1824–1906), the Belinsky of Russian musical criticism and head of the St. Petersburg Public Library (1872), several chief characteristics distinguished the new Russian musical school of the nineteenth century from other European schools of music: an urge for nationalism, revealed in the development of Russian themes; the use of folk songs and choral arrangements, and the creation of a new national opera. Closely associated with the emphasis on folk music was the impact of the Orient, which played a far greater role in Russian music than it did elsewhere in Europe. As in the case of Russian writers, the composers were strongly imbued with elements of the East as Russian expansion into the Caucasus and Central Asia progressed. Some of them, like Glinka and Balakirev, had lived in the Caucasus. The propensity for program music—as, for example, Glinka's *Kamarinskaya,* an orchestral composition based on a Russian folk song—was another trait strongly characteristic of Russian music. According to Stasov, Russian symphonic music, almost without exception, is program music. In this respect, Russian composers followed the general trend among nineteenth-century European musical circles.

Mikhail Glinka (1804–1857). The founder of national Russian music was Mikhail Glinka. He stands in the same relation to Russian music as Pushkin to Russian literature. In fact Glinka was a contemporary and friend of Pushkin and Gogol. His *Capriccio on Russian Themes* (1833), composed in Berlin, was one of the first fruits of his effort to write music in the Russian style. It was followed in 1836 by a Russian opera, *A Life for the Tsar* (originally entitled *Ivan Susanin*), which reflected the new nationalism by its glorification of the Romanov dynasty and won the composer the favor of Nicholas I. Strictly speaking, this opera, which dealt with the founder of the Romanov dynasty, began where Pushkin with his *Boris Godunov* (published 1831) left off. With the appearance of *A Life for the Tsar* Glinka gained recognition as the foremost composer in Russia. In his *Ruslan and Lyudmila* (1842), Glinka resorted to a Pushkin subject based on a popular fairy tale. The Oriental effect achieved by the inclusion of Tatar melodies in this opera exercised considerable influence over later Russian composers. *Kamarinskaya,* the symphonic dance which Glinka produced in 1848, became the model for Russian composers in the orchestration of Russian folk melodies. Tchaikovsky later wrote: "The present Russian symphonic school is all in *Kamarinskaya,* just as the whole oak is in the acorn." In other words, *Kamarinskaya* played much the same role for Russian music as Gogol's *The Cloak* for Russian literature. Since his death in 1857 Glinka has remained a national hero, revered alike by Slavophiles and Westernizers. Under the Soviet regime, *The Great Glinka,* a film based on his life, has been produced.

Mily Balakirev (1837–1910). Although Glinka is regarded as the founder of national Russian music, it was Mily Balakirev who became the head of the Russian national school of music. More important for his guidance of others than for his own compositions, Balakirev was the leader of the group known as "the mighty handful" or "the Big Five," which included César Cui, Borodin, Mussorgsky, and Rimsky-Korsakov. Balakirev prepared a collection of Russian folk songs, which appeared in 1866, and likewise collected Oriental themes in the Caucasus. He displayed a similar interest in the folk music of the other Slavic countries. In his emphasis upon folk music and Eastern themes he carried still further the development of the Russian-Oriental musical idiom which had begun to take form in the music of Glinka. Balakirev also played an important part in the establishment and activities of the Free School of Music (founded 1862) in St. Petersburg, which became a center for the national school.

Alexander Borodin (1833–1887). The first Russian composer to achieve an international reputation was Alexander Borodin, a physician and scientist as well as a composer. He is best known for his opera *Prince Igor,* based on a Russian epic which is as important to Russians as the Arthurian legends to the English. "The Polovetsky Dances" from Act II of this opera were based on authentic melodies collected among the tribes of Central Asia. These wild Eastern dances, with their intoxicating rhythms, and the Choral Finale of the opera have attained worldwide popularity. Borodin likewise broke new ground with his *Second Symphony* (1877), which has been called a panorama of Russian epical chronicles. In 1880 appeared his orchestral tone-picture, *In the Steppes of Central Asia,* which likewise bore the imprint of the Russian Orient and achieved success abroad. Although Borodin died before the completion of *Prince Igor,* this work was put into final form by Alexander Glazunov (1865–1936) and Rimsky-Korsakov. It is of interest that the Soviet government has honored Borodin for his medical services to the Russian people.

Modest Mussorgsky (1839–1881). The Russian composer who has emerged, with the passage of time, as the most outstanding representative of

Borodin's *Prince Igor* tells the story of Igor's defeat and capture by the Polovetsky. This scene, from the prologue, is from a Bol'shoi Theatre production of the opera.

Balakirev's "Big Five," is Modest Mussorgsky. A true successor of Alexander Dargomyzhsky (1813–1869) rather than of Glinka, Mussorgsky was an exponent of realism in Russian music. His close observation of old women and peasants, of the *muzhiks,* and the life they led, has made his operas and songs a reflection of the spirit of his time—especially of the Alexandrian Age. The liberation of the serfs had drawn the attention of the aristocracy and the intelligentsia to the common people. By going to the people in the field of music, Mussorgsky put into practice the precepts of the *Narodniki* movement.

Mussorgsky's *magnum opus* was his *Boris Godunov,* based on the Pushkin drama of that name. His first version of this opera, finished in 1870, in which he exalted the role of the people in several scenes, proved unacceptable to the authorities, and he was compelled to make a number of changes in it. Until recently this opera has been known to the public largely through the more polished version prepared by Rimsky-Korsakov, a version which sacrificed much of the flavor and "truth" of the original. In 1928, however, the Soviet government published the score of the original Mussorgsky version, which now appears to be gaining favor both in the Soviet Union and in the United States.

Khovanshchina (begun 1873), another of Mussorgsky's national operas which he left unfinished, was based on the story of the Old Believers of the seventeenth century. The Prelude, which describes daybreak over Moscow, is strongly national in tone. In *The Fair of Sorotchintsi* (begun 1874), a comic opera based on Gogol's story, Mussorgsky made use of Ukrainian folk songs. Another of Mussorgsky's works, the short opera *Marriage* (1868), was drawn from one of Gogol's plays. It is not remarkable that Gogol, the realist, was Mussorgsky's favorite author. Both men, one in literature, the other in music, had a deep understanding of the psychology of the Russian people. Both were Slavophiles. Mussorgsky's colorful *Pictures at an Exhibition* (1874), noted for its variety of characterization and humor, was based on an actual exhibit of the sketches, water-colors, and stage designs of Victor Hartmann, noted Russian architect and friend of the composer. Mussorgsky's *Nursery Cycle* and his numerous songs in themselves constituted a unique contribution to Russian music.

Nicholas Rimsky-Korsakov (1844–1908). The fame of Nicholas Rimsky-Korsakov, the last of the leaders of the nationalist school, rests on his numerous operas. His early works, including *Maid of Pskov* (1868) and *Sadko* (1894), show the influence of Glinka and the Balakirev circle. *Sadko* recalls *Prince Igor,* and *Maid of Pskov,* which tells of the efforts of Ivan the Terrible to humble the proud cities of Pskov and Novgorod, has been termed a lesser counterpart of *Boris Godunov.* Like other Russian composers, Rimsky-Korsakov often found his themes in the literary work of his day. *May Night* (1878), a comic opera, was based on one of Gogol's tales. Two of his operas, *Tsar Saltan* (1899–1900) and his final work, *The Golden Cockerel* (1907), were drawn from Pushkin's fairy tales. Rimsky-Korsakov revelled in Russian folklore and legends, which provided the inspiration for much of his music. This was true, not only of *Sadko* and *The Tsar's Bride* (1893), but of *The Snow Maiden* (1882), a truly national opera based on Ostrovsky's epic of the Slavonic legend of spring. Among his other well-known works are *Scheherazade* (1881) and the religious opera *The Invisible City of Kitezh* (1907).

Rimsky-Korsakov became a national martyr among Russian liberals when in 1905 he resigned his honorary membership in the Russian Musical Society in protest against the closing of the Conservatory by the authorities in their efforts to suppress student revolutionary activities. It was at this time that he orchestrated *Dubinushka,* one of the popular revolutionary songs of the day. A temporary ban on the performance of all Rimsky-Korsakov's compositions served only to increase their popularity. *The Golden Cockerel,* his final opera, which was in reality a satire on the stupidity of autocracy, came under the ban of the censor and was not produced during the composer's lifetime.

As professor at the St. Petersburg Conservatory of Music from 1871 to 1905, Rimsky-Korsakov helped to train a distinguished group of Russian musicians, including Alexander Glazunov, who carried on the traditions of the national school, Liadov, Arensky, Ippolitov-Ivanov, and Igor Stravinsky. Few Americans are likely to recall that it was in his capacity as a *gardemarine* on the Russian clipper *Almaz,* rather than as a musician, that Rimsky-Korsakov visited America with the Russian naval squadron which remained in American waters from October 1863 to April 1864, during the critical days of the Civil War.

Peter Ilitch Tchaikovsky (1840–1893). Peter Ilitch Tchaikovsky is undoubtedly the best-known Russian composer, and his works have enjoyed worldwide popularity. A prolific and highly versatile composer, Tchaikovsky has given the world ten operas, six symphonies, three ballets, four concertos, four suites, and twelve overtures, not to mention more than one hundred romances, an equal number of piano pieces, four string quartets, a piano trio, a string sextet, and several additional chamber works. Almost two-thirds of his music is still unknown in the United States.

Although he was not a member of the "Big Five," or the so-called national school, Tchaikovsky's music reflects the composer's love for the Russian landscape, the Russian past, and Russian customs, whereas some of his works, including his symphonies, especially the *Second Symphony* (Little Russian, 1872) and the popular *1812 Overture* (1880) have deep national roots. The Soviet composer, Dmitri Shostakovitch, calls him the founder of the great school of Russian music. In contrast to the "Big Five," however, his music was intensely subjective and introspective, reflecting man's struggle to overcome the blind elemental forces. Like the Greek tragedians, he was concerned primarily with the element of conflict, with a sense of the tragedy of life. Soviet musical critics, who refuse to consider him a pessimist, regard him as a great realist philosopher in the field of music.

In 1877 there began the unusual relationship between Tchaikovsky and the wealthy widow, Nadejda von Meck, whose generosity provided financial independence for the composer for some fourteen years and left him free to devote his entire time to musical composition.

Tchaikovsky is perhaps best known in the United States for his six symphonies, the last three of which are a standard part of the American concert repertory of all major American symphony orchestras. All his symphonies include song and dance themes and are marked by that lyrical quality so characteristic of Tchaikovsky and Glinka. His *Fourth, Fifth,* and *Sixth Symphonies* convey the same message, the tragic struggle of man against an inexorable fate. Among Tchaikovsky's program works, his finest symphonic poems, the *Romeo and Juliet* Fantasia—Overture (1869) and *Francesca da Rimini* (1876) are among the most powerful interpretations of Shakespeare and Dante in music.

Tchaikovsky's three best-known operas are *Eugene Onegin* (1878), *Mazeppa* (1884), and *The Queen of Spades* (1890), all based on Pushkin themes. In all his operas, Tchaikovsky was concerned primarily with the inner world of his heroes. This lyrico-psychological approach constituted his main contribution to world opera. In Russia, *Eugene Onegin* has become a permanent feature of the repertory of the famous Moscow Bolshoi Theatre, which in 1938 gave its eight hundredth performance of this opera.

In addition to his symphonies and operas, which reveal his predilection for dance melodies, Tchaikovsky contributed greatly to the revival and regeneration of ballet music in Russia. His three ballets, *The Swan Lake* (1876), the most popular ballet in the USSR, *The Sleeping Beauty* (1889) and *The Nutcracker* (1892), all concerned with the world of fantasy, have exerted a profound influence on the subsequent ballets of Glazunov, Stravinsky, Prokofiev, and Khatchaturian, among others.

Tchaikovsky did much to popularize chamber music, including the chamber ensemble, in Russia. His *First Quartet, Opus 11, in D-Major* (1871), contains the famous *Andante Cantabile,* with its stirring folk *motif,* which moved Leo Tolstoy, Tchaikovsky's favorite author, to tears when he first heard it. His *Trio for Piano, Violin, and Violoncello in A-Minor, Opus 50* (1862), was dedicated to the memory of Nikolai Rubinstein of the Moscow Conservatory. His chamber music is extensively performed in the USSR.

The music of Tchaikovsky dominated the last quarter of the nineteenth century. Since that time it has exerted a vast influence on world music. On his American tour in 1889 the composer himself discovered that he was "ten times more famous in America than in Europe." Tchaikovsky exerted a marked influence over the early works of the noted Bohemian composer Gustav Mahler (1860–1911), whose works have recently experienced a revival in the United States. Inside Russia Tchaikovsky has become as vital a part of the national consciousness in music as Pushkin in literature. Other Russian composers, including Arensky, Glazunov, Ippolitov-Ivanov, and especially Sergei Rachmaninov (1873–1946) owe much to the Tchaikovsky traditions of melody and harmony, while the Russian modernist Scriabin was influenced by Tchaikovsky in his treatment of philosophical and psychological problems. Under the Soviet regime, Tchaikovsky's reputation has waxed rather than waned. All the outstanding Soviet composers, including Shostakovitch, Myaskovsky, Khatchaturian, and Dzerzhinsky, have acknowledged their indebtedness to Peter Ilitch Tchaikovsky. Throughout the years, little or no adverse criticism of Tchaikovsky has come out of Russia.

Alexander Scriabin (1872–1915). The so-called modern school of Russian music (as distinguished from the Soviet) is best represented by Alexander Scriabin and Igor Stravinsky. Scriabin's best-known works are *The Divine Poem* (1903), *The Poem of Ecstasy* (1907–1908), and *The Poem of Fire* (*Prometheus,* 1909–1910). His technical innovations, which include the six-note or "mystic" chord and esoteric harmonies, are characteristic of modern music and they influenced later Russian composers. From 1900 on, Scriabin, strongly influenced by the Russian mystic philosopher Prince S. N. Trubetskoy, and by the philosophy of Nietzsche, began his efforts to fuse music with philosophy. Scriabin's experience in America in 1906, like that of Gorky, proved unfortunate, and he was forced to leave because of popular indignation concerning his private life.

Igor Stravinsky (1882–   ). Igor Stravinsky, onetime student of Rimsky-Korsakov, and the recognized leader of Western modernism, has spent much of his life abroad, having left Russia for France before World War I, and France for the United States in 1939. His well-known ballets, *The Fire-Bird*

(1910) and *Petrushka* (1911), both based on Russian folklore, were commissioned by Sergei Diaghelev for his *Ballet Russe* in Paris. Stravinsky's most revolutionary score, which best illustrates his disregard for conventional form and harmony, is *The Rites of Spring* (1913), based on the pagan rituals of Russia. His choral symphony, *Symphonie des psaumes* (1930) was commissioned by the Boston Symphony Orchestra and first performed in 1931. Even while abroad, Stravinsky has carried on the tradition of Russian national music.

Any study of Russian culture in the century between the Napoleonic wars and the Russian Revolution clearly reveals how intimately the literature and music were related to current events and to one another, and how all three reflected the underlying national current of that era.

ART AND ARCHITECTURE[4]

Russian art and architecture are less well known abroad than Russian literature and music, partly because over the centuries much was destroyed during the succession of invasions by Mongols, Turks, Poles, Swedes, French, and Germans. Those foreigners who have passed judgment on Russian art have sometimes claimed that it was not Russian, but rather a foreign importation. Igor Grabar, introducing his momumental *History of Russian Art* (in Russian, 1909), asked: "Has there ever been and is there now, great art in Russia?"—a question, however, which he answered unequivocally in the affirmative.

The two greatest art collections in Russia, which are becoming increasingly well known abroad, are the Hermitage Museum in Leningrad, repository of a magnificent collection of European art acquired by Catherine II and her successors, and the Tretyakov Gallery in Moscow, which has the world's largest collection of Russian paintings. The Hermitage galleries in 1965 housed some 2,300,000 art objects, including 14,000 paintings. The Tretyakov Gallery, begun in 1856 by the millionaire Moscow merchant P. M. Tretyakov, in accordance with the designs of the Russian artist, Victor Vasnetsov, was turned over to the City of Moscow in 1892. By 1965 it included over 35,000 works of art which attract approximately 1,300,000 visitors annually.

Byzantine Influence. Although the decorative arts in Russia can be traced by archeologists to 3000 B.C., Christian art dates from the period of Kievan

4. In addition to the general bibliography, see the following: Mikhail Alpatov, *Russian Impact on Art,* ed. by Martin L. Wolf, trans. by Ivy Litvinov; Alexandre Benois, *The Russian School of Painting* (London: T. Werner Laurie Ltd., 1916); David Douglas Duncan, *The Kremlin* (Greenwich, Conn.: New York Graphic Society, 1960); Camilla Grey, *The Great Experiment: Russian Art, 1863–1922* (New York: Abrams, 1962); and "Andrei Rublev: Icon Painter, 1360?–1430?" (Lazarev) and "P. M. Tretyakov and His Art Gallery" (Mudrogel), in Ivar and Marion Spector, eds., *Readings in Russian History and Culture* (Boston: Allyn & Bacon, 1965). *Life Magazine* (March 26, April 2, April 9, 1965) included a fine selection of masterpieces from The Hermitage.

Rūs (862–1240). Here, as in the case of literature and music, the influence of Byzantium on church architecture, icons, frescoes, and mosaics was strong. Russian art soon differed from that of Byzantium, especially in the number of bulbous domes used, the size of the iconostasis, the use of richer coloring in painting, and the humanization of the somewhat grim Byzantine conventionalized figures. The Cathedral of St. Sophia in Kiev boasted a large central dome, representing the Savior, and twelve smaller domes, standing for the twelve Apostles. Its baroque exterior was, of course, added later. In Novgorod, farther removed from Byzantium, the beginnings of a Russian national art can be discerned, especially in the depiction of Russian saints with Russian features, the use of folk ornamentation, and the introduction of the more practical sloping, instead of the vaulted, roof. Many wooden churches

The famous Cathedral of St. Sophia, built during the reign of Yaroslav, testifies to the relative sophistication of eleventh-century Kievan society. The interior of the cathedral is decorated with frescoes which depart from religious subjects to show scenes of secular life in medieval Russia.

were constructed in Russia, especially in the heavily forested north, with a tent-like superstructure to shed the winter snows. Most of these have disappeared, but some of those remaining are being restored by the Soviet government. One of the most beautiful monuments of this period is the church on the River Nerl near Vladimir, with its single bulb-like dome and simple but beautifully proportioned rectangular structure.

Moscow. With the rise of the Moscow state, a new and influential center of art and architecture developed. The Moscow Kremlin is the most noteworthy structure, including secular and religious buildings by Russian and foreign artists covering four centuries of Russian artistic development. The chief cathedrals—that of the Assumption (1479), for coronations and the issuance of state decrees; the Annunciation, for the royal family; the Archangel Michael, for the burial of Russian rulers until the time of Peter the Great; and the Bell Tower of Ivan the Great—are national monuments. Its Granovitaya Palace (Palace of Facets, 1491), designed by the Italians Solario and Ruffo, was the first stone building constructed in the Kremlin and remains the earliest surviving secular building in Moscow. The Senate Building belongs to the eighteenth century, the Grand Kremlin Palace (1849) to the nineteenth century, and the modern Palace of Congresses to the Soviet period. St. Basil's Church outside the Kremlin walls is, according to the Russian art historian Alpatov, the most Russian of all Russian churches.

Iconography. From the Moscow area, too, came Andrei Rublev (1360?–1430?), Russia's greatest religious painter. A noted icon painter, he worked mainly in the Moscow Kremlin and at the Troitse-Sergeyev Lavra (Zagorsk). He represents the golden age of iconography and influenced most of the outstanding painting during the fifteenth century. His masterpiece, *The Trinity,* in honor of Sergei Radonezh, founder of the Troitse-Sergeyev Monastery, is said to be the most famous single work of Russian art between the tenth and the eighteenth centuries, with the possible exception of *The Virgin of Vladimir,* brought to Kiev in the eleventh century from Byzantium and later transferred to Vladimir. Both works are now in the Tretyakov Gallery. The classical age of iconography came to an end in the sixteenth century, but icons continued to be produced in some Russian villages, such as Palekh (about 170 miles from Moscow), where, since the Revolution, artists have turned to the production of outstanding lacquer work using secular rather than religious themes.

St. Petersburg. The eighteenth century was one of the great ages of Russian architecture, marked by the construction of St. Petersburg and the preeminence of secular art. Peterburgian art and architecture are just as Russian as those of Moscow, but remarkably different. As in the case of Moscow and Kiev, St. Petersburg profited by the talent of foreign artists brought in by Peter the Great and his successors, and by Russians trained abroad. The foreign architects included Leblond (France), Rastrelli, Quarenghi, and Rossi (Italy), and Cameron (England). Many foreign artists caught the

Russian spirit and adapted the European classical and baroque styles they introduced to Russian tastes and environment. Their Russian counterparts were Ivan Starov, the first native Russian architect to graduate from the Academy of Fine Arts, Vassily Bazhenov, and Nikolai Lvov. St. Petersburg became a remarkable example of over-all city planning, characterized by a rectilinear layout; open squares; great boulevards; parks; broad, straight avenues; and granite quays. It was Peter's objective to catch up with and surpass European capitals. Peter himself preferred Dutch architecture, but was also greatly impressed by Versailles. His daughter Elizabeth leaned toward the rococo baroque. Catherine II reverted to the Roman classical style, which took deep root in Russia and is still popular under the Soviet regime. Alexander I chose the Greek classical style. All of this went into the making of St. Petersburg, which, by the nineteenth century had become one of the most beautiful cities in Europe.

Among the outstanding buildings constructed by these rulers were the Peterhof Palace, with its remarkable fountains and terraces descending to the sea, reminiscent of Versailles; the Winter Palace (1711–1732), Rastrelli's masterpiece, representing the fullest development of Russian baroque, which was characterized by immense frontages with rows and rows of windows, the monotony of which was relieved by columns and various sculptured decorations; the Palace of the Stroganovs, wealthy Russian aristocrats with rich mining interests in the Urals; the Admiralty; the Mining Institute; and the cathedrals, including Kazan Cathedral (with some resemblance to St. Peter's in Rome) and the Cathedral of St. Isaacs.

Portraiture. With the Petrine period of architecture came also the development of portrait painting, which had no traditions other than iconography to lean on in Russia, but in which Russian artists, both tsarist and Soviet, have excelled. Among the early portrait painters were Dmitry Levitsky, who produced the official portrait of Catherine the Great, Ivan Argunov, who in 1784 painted what appears to be the first peasant girl in Russian art, Ivan Nikitin, and Fyodr Rokotov.

The Nineteenth Century. The nineteenth century witnessed the decay of classicism in Russian art and the rise first of romanticism, followed in mid-century by the realist school. Typical of the Russian painters of the first half of the century were Alexei Venetsianov (1799–1847), sometimes called the first genuine Russian realist, Vassily Tropinin (1776–1859), who was born a serf ("The Lacemaker"), and Karl Bryullov (1799–1852), who liked to depict aristocratic women on horseback ("The Horsewoman").

The Travellers. What may be termed the national school of Russian art, paralleling that in music and the Slavophiles in literature, developed in the reign of Alexander II, following the great reforms. Its chief representatives were known as the Travellers (Wanderers, Itinerants, *Peredvizhniki*), who originally broke away from the Imperial Academy in order to depict Russian life as it was, rather than to devote their attention to allegorical themes, such as "Odin in Valhalla." The Travellers, so-called because of their travelling exhibits in various parts of the country, were nationalists, realists, and propagandists, who placed ideological content ahead of form and technique. They were profoundly interested in the social issues of the day—the sufferings of the peasants, bureaucratic corruption, religious superstition, and so on—and believed that art had a mission to perform to improve society. The Travellers were sponsored, not by the court, but by wealthy Russian merchants like P. M. Tretyakov.

Their ranks included many of Russia's outstanding artists and portrait painters. Among them were Ivan Kramskoi (1837–1887), who headed the Travellers for a decade in the 1870's; Vasili Perov (1833–1882), who produced some studies of peasant life and highly satiric paintings reflecting the shortcomings of the church; Ilya Repin (1844–1930), who, if not actually a member of the Travellers, was closely associated with them, and whose historical paintings and portraits were revelations of Russian national character; Vasili Surikov (1848–1916), who brought realism into Russian historical painting ("The Boyarina Morozova"); Victor Vasnetsov (1848–1926), son of a priest, likewise inspired by historical themes, and whose works included some that provided an authentic expression of religious art; Isaak Levitan (1861–1900), who introduced realism into Russian landscape painting, and whose later impressionistic works merited the label "poet of the Russian landscape."

Change in Motif. In the final decade of the nineteenth century, there occurred a strong reaction against the social message in art, which came to be

Sovfoto

Surikov's realistic treatment of historical subjects is evident in "Stepan Razin." Razin was the Don Cossack who led an uprising against Moscow in the seventeenth century. His army captured a number of garrisons on the Volga before the government forces were able to put down the revolt.

regarded with as much dislike as the Imperial Academy's "Odin in Valhalla" theme. The movement was characterized by a revival of religious and national motifs, inspired by ancient Russian art and eighteenth-century art. This new movement was akin to the Symbolist movement in literature. Some of the Travellers, such as Levitan and Vasnetsov, joined forces with it. Other representatives included Mikhail Vrubel (1856–1910), a strong individualist and mystic, who drew his inspiration from Lermontov ("The Demon"); M. V. Nesterov (1862–1942), who painted "The Vision of the Young Bartholomew"; A. Kuindzhi (1842–1910), whose landscapes were even more impressionistic than those of Levitan; and Valentine Serov (1865–1911), who persistently searched for "soul" in portraiture, and whose "Girl with Peaches" and "Girl in the Sunshine" are said to have created some of the brightest female images in Russian art.

World of Art Movement. At the turn of the century, many of these and other like-minded artists, musicians, poets, and dramatists, associated themselves with the World of Art Movement (*Mir Iskusstva*) and its magazine founded in 1899 by Alexandre Benois and Serge Diaghilev, whose name was later a byword for Russian ballet in Paris. These artists, who were strong exponents of "art for art's sake," encouraged the revival of iconography and folk art. They produced brilliant backdrops for ballet and opera, and became noted for their gay, frivolous subjects, bright colors, and exoticism. One of the objectives of the World of Art Movement was to make Russian art known to the West. Other members of the movement, whose work soon attracted attention, were Nicholas Roerich, Mikhail Larionov (b. 1881), Natalya Goncharova, and M. Dobuzhinsky, whose pupils included Mark Chagall and Yuon (b. 1875). Many of these younger artists were strongly influenced by Symbolism and some, even before the Revolution, were drifting toward cubism and futurism.

SCIENCE

Until recently, with very few exceptions, Russian science has been a *terra incognita* to the Western world. The launching of the first sputnik in 1957 marked the beginning of a better appreciation of the achievements of Russian science and scientists. There have been several reasons for this paucity of knowledge about the development of Russian science.

Until World War I, in Russian education the sciences were subordinated to the humanities. The emphasis was on literature and the arts. The Russian language was a major barrier to the dissemination of Russian scientific knowledge; classical Russian, with its elaborate grammatical structure, was an awkward medium for scientific exposition. Only those few works that were published in Western European languages became known abroad. Today many Western scientists study Russian in order to have first-hand access to

Soviet scientific publications. Abstracts and often complete English translations of Soviet scientific materials are published in this country. In tsarist times many Russian scientists regarded patents as too commercial and unbecoming to the scholarly profession. Their contributions are only recently being recorded by their Soviet successors.

Russian scientific research began in the eighteenth century in the reign of Peter the Great. Although some foundations for scientific progress were laid earlier, in the seventeenth century Russia had no great scientists or scientific associations. The Copernican theory, Euclid, and medical training were still unknown. It was not until 1682 that the first multiplication table was published in Russia. The first Russian arithmetic text was published in 1699 in Amsterdam, and the first multiplication table to use Arabic numerals was introduced in 1714.

At least two reasons can be advanced for the late beginnings of science in Russia. The Renaissance, which gave birth to modern science in Western Europe, did not reach Russia. The Orthodox church, with its Byzantine heritage, emphasized mysticism, was anti-rationalist, opposed secular education, and denounced the discoveries of Copernicus as "Satan's craft." Even in the early nineteenth century, for instance, geology was not studied in Russian educational institutions.

Academy of Sciences. The introduction of the sciences in Russia was an integral part of Peter the Great's program of Europeanization and secularization. The first step, encouraged by the German scientist, Gottfried von Leibniz, was the founding of the St. Petersburg Academy of Sciences, the plans for which were completed in 1724, although Peter died before they could be brought to fruition. His wife and successor, Catherine I, formally established the academy in December, 1725. No native scientists were available, and from 1725 to 1733 the academy was comprised of twenty Germans, five Swiss, two French, and one Russian scholar (Adadurov). It is significant that Peter made the Academy of Sciences a state institution, subject to government control, where it has remained ever since under both tsars and Soviets. Moreover, Peter, who was primarily concerned with the development of Russian military power and the Russian economy, had a "utilitarian" approach to science, as do the Soviets.

In spite of many handicaps and frustrations, the Russian Academy in its early years had important accomplishments to its credit. In 1725 an astronomical laboratory, one of the finest in Europe at the time, was located on Vasil'evskii Island. In 1728 the Academy secured its own press and was shortly thereafter equipped to publish material in Russian, Latin, German, Georgian, and Arabic. For some years, it published the country's only newspaper, the *St. Petersburg Gazette,* a source of Western ideas. The academy's workshops produced optical instruments, drafting tools, and precision equipment. Many foreign works, scientific and popular, were translated into Russian. The academy's cartographers produced Russia's first *Atlas*. It participated in the Great Northern Expedition to the Pacific planned by Peter and in subsequent voyages of exploration. It supervised an Academic Gymnasium (1727) and took over the Kunstkamera, a museum already rich in specimens of natural history and ethnography. Although there was much feuding among its members, foreign and Russian, and teaching was subordinated to private research, it did train many of Russia's first scientific scholars.

Mikhail Lomonosov (1711–1765). Russia's greatest scientist in the eighteenth century and one of her first Academicians, was Mikhail Lomonosov, a man of peasant origin. Lomonosov was not a specialist, but a person of encyclopedic knowledge—poet, chemist, physicist, geographer, philologist, astronomer, and historian—sometimes called Russia's Leonardo Da Vinci. His main contributions were in physical chemistry, including the establishment of the first chemical laboratory in Russia, and his efforts to create a Russian scientific terminology. He is also regarded as the founder of thermodynamics and the first scientist to find an atmosphere around the planet Venus. Lomonosov experimented with atmospheric electricity in the wake of Benjamin Franklin. A strong nationalist, however, he insisted on using the Russian language—a factor which obstructed the dissemination of his ideas abroad.

The Great Mathematicians. In the nineteenth century, Russia produced a galaxy of outstanding scientists. Perhaps the leading figure in mathematics was N. I. Lobatchevsky (1793–1856), sometimes called the Copernicus of geometry. His most important achievement was the discovery of non-Euclidean geometry (1826). His contemporary, P. L. Chebyshev (1821–1894) was believed to be the greatest Russian scholar in the field of applied mathematics; he made outstanding contributions to the theory of errors (1837–1841). He has been credited with making the first advances since Euclid on the theory of primes and developed the theory of approximate solutions. He laid the foundations for what came to be known as the St. Petersburg school of mathematics.

Dmitry I. Mendeleyev (1834–1907). Dmitry I. Mendeleyev, a professor at St. Petersburg University and one of Russia's better known scientists abroad, who worked with Bunsen, discovered and formulated the Periodic Law of the Atomic Weights (1869), acknowledged to be one of the greatest feats of nineteenth-century chemistry, and it remains basic to the present day. Although others were working in this field, Mendeleyev showed remarkable prescience in being able to predict and describe many new elements in advance of their discovery. Because he opposed the suppression of freedom of thought and assembly at St. Petersburg University, Mendeleyev was rejected for membership in the Academy of Sciences. In a sense, he summed up the classical age of chemistry.

I. M. Setchenov (1829–1905). The father of Russian physiology, according to Ivan Pavlov, was I. M. Setchenov, who created a school of Russian physiologists and performed great experiments on brain reflexes. As early as 1853 he claimed that the mechanical movements of the hands are subject to mathematical analysis and could be expressed by a formula. Many of his speculations in this area, regarded as heretical at the time, have been confirmed by the development of cybernetics in our own day.

Ilya Metchnikov (1845–1916). Of equal fame in the field of biology was Ilya Metchnikov, professor of zoology at the University of Odessa. His greatest discovery was the phagocyte, a type of white blood cell which engulfs and destroys foreign matter. Metchnikov subsequently left Russia and became head of the Pasteur Institute in Paris, where his work on immunity laid foundations for the study of aging and death.

Ivan P. Pavlov (1849–1936). Russia's world renowned physiologist was Ivan P. Pavlov, who won a Nobel Prize in 1904 for his research on digestive processes. His subsequent work on conditioned reflexes, the physiological foundations of psychological phenomena, were of outstanding theoretical significance and important to psychiatry. School children the world over have learned of his experiments with dogs.

Nikolai Pirogov (1810–1881). In the field of anatomy and medicine, Russia's scholar of outstanding stature in the nineteenth century was Nikolai Pirogov, who was associated with the Medical and Surgical Academy in St. Petersburg (founded 1798). His study of the pathological anatomy of cholera and his works on applied anatomy and clinical surgery brought him an international reputation. One of the founders of modern military medicine, he resorted to the use of ether as an anesthetic during Russia's wars in the Caucasus (1847), just a few months after this technique had been successfully demonstrated by the American dentist William T. G. Morton. Although Pirogov saw the need for scientific specialization, he strongly advocated that specialization should be preceded by a general, humanistic education.

Significant Inventors. In 1875–1876 P. N. Yablotchkov (1847–1894) invented an arc lamp using parallel carbons, which he patented in Paris (1876), and which went into production immediately. An even more significant inventor, A. N. Lodigin, a professor at the Naval Engineering School, created a filament lamp in 1873 in St. Petersburg, having discovered ahead of Thomas Edison the need for a vacuum in such globes. The General Electric Company took over Lodigin's patent on molybdenum and tungsten filaments in 1890.

In the Soviet Union Alexander S. Popov (1859–1905) is credited with the invention of wireless telegraphy, ahead of Marconi. It is claimed that he spelled out the message "Heinrich Hertz" by wireless signals, once in 1894 and again in 1896, over a distance of two hundred meters. He is just one of the many "firsts" the Soviet government has so persistently acclaimed. But in spite of the fact that Russia produced a number of outstanding scientists prior to the Revolution of 1917, the gulf between Russian achievement in this area and that of the West was a wide one.

Emphasis on Theoretical Science. The substantial achievements of Russian scientists in the nineteenth century were, for the most part, in theoretical rather than applied science. There were several reasons for this tendency. Russia was an underdeveloped country, with little industry, and most of that controlled by foreigners who had access to industrial laboratories abroad. Many Russian scientists, moreover, were disciples of German scholars, who were also enamored of pure science. With the industrialization of Russia in the early twentieth century, the pattern began to change, even before the Revolution. Basically, however, Russian scientific achievements were mainly in the field of theoretical science until the launching of the First Five-Year Plan in 1927.

Part Three

Imperial Russia, 1894-1917

10

Nicholas II and the Rise
of Political Parties

NICHOLAS II AS TSAR

Many opinions have been expressed about the character and stature of Nicholas II as ruler and diplomat. As yet, no authentic, scholarly biography has appeared on this, the last of the Romanovs. There are some traits, however, on which those who knew him well or were closely associated with him usually agree. Nicholas II was known as an unpretentious and courteous man of great personal charm. He was a good linguist and spoke several languages, some say with native facility. He was an exemplary husband, a devoted father, and was very much attached to other members of the royal family. Because of his early training in the shadow of Pobyedonostsev, he was strongly nationalist in outlook, prejudiced against minority groups, especially the Jews, and contemptuous of the mob. Unlike his father, he lacked strength of character, was inconsistent in policy and action, and often proved to be a poor judge of character in the selection of advisers. Most sources agree that his knowledge of the science of government was grossly inadequate.

The marriage of Nicholas in November, 1894, to the German Princess Alexandra of Hesse-Darmstadt subjected him to the influence of a narrow-minded, wilful, and uncompromising woman, who became an unqualified supporter of Orthodoxy and autocracy. The empress, who was unpopular with Russians, was known as "the funeral bride," because her first public appearances in Russia coincided with the funeral ceremonies of Alexander III. An unfortunate episode connected with the coronation festivities in May, 1896, in which the crowd broke through the police lines and about two thousand persons were stampeded to death by the troops at Khodynka Field in Moscow—an event which was not permitted to interrupt the coronation ball—provided an inauspicious beginning to the reign of Nicholas II.

Zemstvos. During his youth Nicholas II, perhaps because he liked to please others, gave some of his associates the impression that he was not wholly in accord with Pobyedonostsev's reactionary philosophy and would, therefore, be amenable to change. Upon his accession to the throne, there was some expectation, therefore, of the relaxation of his father's stern autocracy. For his coronation, a cross-section of the public, including the presidents of the *zemstvos,* who were not *persona grata* during the reign of Alexander III, were invited to participate in the ceremonies. It was in connection with the coronation that an address of congratulation from the *Zemstvo* of Tver, drafted by Fyodr Roditchev, one of the foremost barristers in Russia, expressed the hope that the *zemstvos* would be permitted to state their opinions on issues of concern to them, so that the throne might be apprised of the thinking of the Russian people. After a generation of experience in local self-government, many *zemstvo* leaders were ready and willing to exert their influence at the national level.

Preservation of Autocracy. Nicholas clearly revealed that he had no intention of permitting the *zemstvos* to participate in the administration of Russia. In response to this and to similar *zemstvo* requests, he unqualifiedly announced his intention to preserve "the principle of autocracy just as firmly and unflinchingly as my late, unforgettable father preserved it" (January 17 (O.S.), 1896). *Zemstvo* aspirations were dismissed as "senseless dreams." The door to political and constitutional reform having been slammed shut, the more radical supporters of change came to regard the overthrow of the monarchy as the prerequisite to reform. Shortly after his accession to the throne a *Narodniki* circle was formed with the express purpose of plotting the assassination of the emperor.

RISE OF POLITICAL PARTIES

The uncompromising stand of Nicholas II on the preservation of autocracy was greatly instrumental in bringing about the organization of Russian political parties. Such parties might have appeared earlier, but since the closing years of the reign of Alexander II, there had been outright suppression of all political movements and expression of political ideas at variance with those of the government. Toward the end of the century, there was a revival of some aspects of the *Narodniki* movement. For the most part, this was a revival in name rather than in spirit, for the idealism that marked the early stages of the movement was lacking. In the time of Nicholas II its objective was not so much "Going to the People," as taking over the people and using them as tools. Many members of the *Narodniki* were already infected with the Marxist virus. Under the guidance of professional leaders, idealism was replaced by ideology, and Christian principles by materialism and the desire for three square meals a day.

"Liberation of Labor." George Plekhanov (1857–1918), a former activist in "Land and Liberty,"[1] became disillusioned with the *Narodniki* movement.

---

1. An underground organization formed in St. Petersburg in 1876 for revolutionary propaganda among the peasantry.

During his sojourn in Switzerland, he was converted to Marxism, and together with his associate, P. B. Akselrod, in 1883 founded "Liberation of Labor," the first organized group of Russian Marxists. This group translated into Russian the works of Marx and Engels, which were surreptitiously distributed in Russia. Plekhanov, who exerted a strong influence on the Marxist movement abroad, produced two pamphlets in 1884 of significance for Russian political history. One was *Our Differences,* which stated the Marxist case against the *Narodniki* and emphasized that Russian socialism must be based on the industrial working class and not on the peasantry or bourgeoisie. In this pamphlet he discarded the village commune as an anachronism. In *Socialism and the Political Struggle,* Plekhanov stressed that socialists must not only train and organize workers for the coming revolution, but must engage directly in the struggle against autocracy.

"Social Democrats." A number of small Marxist groups, mainly study and discussion groups reminiscent of the early "circles" (*kruzhky*) of the Decembrists and *Narodniki,* was founded in St. Petersburg and other Russian cities in the 1880's. By 1893 they called themselves "Social Democrats," a term borrowed from Germany. One of these "Social Democrats" was Nikolai Lenin (Vladimir Ilitch Ulyanov, 1870–1924), who first joined the Marxists in Kazan as a university student. After his expulsion for subversive activities, he proceeded to St. Petersburg, where he became affiliated with a circle of the League of Struggle for the Emancipation of the Working Class.

The Marxist groups held their first congress in Minsk in February, 1898, to form the Russian Social Democratic Workers' Party (SD), which included representatives from the Jewish Socialist Party (the *Bund*). Most of the leaders of the new party inside Russia were quickly arrested by the police. It was left to those abroad, including Plekhanov's "Liberation of Labor" group, to develop the party organization and propaganda. Lenin edited the party's first newspaper, *Iskra* (*The Spark*), beginning in December, 1900. This revolutionary sheet was smuggled into Russia, where it was widely read among Marxist circles. Leon Trotsky (Lev Davidovitch Bronstein, 1879–1940) served on the editorial staff of *Iskra* in London. In 1902 Lenin's pamphlet *What Is to Be Done?,* its title borrowed from Tchernyshevsky's novel, called for a disciplined party of "professional revolutionaries," at first drawn mainly from the intelligentsia, to form a revolutionary vanguard for the education of the workers. "Give us an organization of revolutionaries," said Lenin, "and we will transform Russia."

To solve the disputes that soon arose among the Marxist groups abroad, a second congress was held in July, 1903, in Brussels and London. Here a rift developed over party organization and membership. The Jewish *Bund* seceded from the party and the Polish Social Democrats withdrew. The remaining members split into two parts: the *Mensheviks,* or minority, who contended that the prerequisite to social revolution was the intensive education of the masses for a democratic regime; and the *Bolsheviks,* or majority, who favored an early overthrow of the existing autocratic regime by force. The Bolshevik leader was Lenin, who founded a new party organ, *Vperyod* (*Forward*). Plekhanov, and for a time, Trotsky, threw in their lot with the Mensheviks. The rift between the Bolsheviks and Mensheviks continued to widen, until in 1912, at the party congress in Prague, the Mensheviks were expelled. In the same year the famous party organ, *Pravda* (*Truth*) was founded. By 1914 the Social Democrats in the Russian Empire numbered altogether about 150,000.

The Social Democrats used the strike as a weapon to achieve their objectives. Some favored permanent strikes. In the Russia of Nicholas II there was no freedom of assembly, especially for workers. Because of poverty and extremely long working hours, the workers did not belong to clubs or lodges. Once they went on strike, however, they assembled outside in the streets and exchanged ideas with other workers and with the unemployed. Thus the strike served several purposes in connection with the political agitation and education of the workers. No wonder that Soviet literature has constantly emphasized the number of strikes and workers involved in them. Moreover, an extended strike inevitably rendered the government unpopular for not having done anything about it. In general, however, the impact of strikes upon the masses and upon other strata of Russian society, especially upon the peasants, during these early years was negligible.

Social Revolutionary Party. The Social Revolutionary Party—a direct outgrowth of the *Narodniki* movement—was organized from 1901 to 1902, probably under the impact of the activities of the Social Democrats. Although they tried at first to appeal to the workers, the peasants, and the intelligentsia, their main emphasis was on the peasantry, in whom they sought to develop political consciousness. Like the *Narodniki,* they stood for the preservation of the peasant communes and the existing agrarian structure. In other words, they called for socialization of the land as against private ownership, but not for the communalization of production. They were not Marxists, but drew their chief inspiration from the works of Nicholas Tchernyshevsky, N. K. Mihailovsky, and Victor Chernov, as well as from those of the Utopian Socialists of France.

The SR's, as they were called, soon became the largest political party in Russia, and remained, in many respects, the most typically Russian. They developed no closely knit organization. As in the case of the SD's, the wide divergence of opinion in the membership of the Social Revolutionaries led to the development of "Left" and "Right" wings. From 1902 to 1905 the SR's published one illegal newspaper, *Revolyutsionnaya Rossiya* (*Revolutionary Russia*), printed in Finland, and three legal organs, *Narodnyi Vestnik* (*The People's Herald*), *Mysl* (*Thought*), and *Soznatel'naya Rossiya* (*Enlightened Russia*). Although their chief intellectual leader, Victor Chernov, was for moderation, some of the SR's resorted to terrorism as their weapon against the autocracy. The party's special "combat organization," headed for a time by the chemist Gershuni, was responsible for a series of political assassinations: Dmitry Sipyagin, minister of the interior, in April, 1902; the unpopular Plehve, his successor, in July, 1904; and Grand Duke Sergei, uncle of the tsar and governor-general of Moscow, in February, 1905. Their terrorist activities led to close surveillance on the part of the political police.

Although they differed as to objectives and methods, both the SR's and the majority of the SD's were revolutionary parties, bent upon the overthrow of the autocracy. The Marxists placed their faith in the industrial workers and counted on the rise of capitalism in Russia to provide the conditions essential for social revolution. The SR's discounted the power of capitalism and of the industrialized workers in the belief that social revolution must spring from the peasantry. Neither party was able to conduct its program openly inside Russia. Their leaders were subject to arrest and imprisonment, and spent much of their time in Siberian exile or abroad, mainly in Switzerland. Their membership was secret, and their party literature was for the most part produced abroad and distributed by underground channels inside Russia. Both parties were potentially strong, but actually during these years they were weak and divided.

The wave of strikes that accompanied the economic slump from 1899 to 1903 was grist for the mills of the revolutionary parties in Russia, especially for the Social Democrats. In November, 1902, a strike occurred in Rostov-on-the-Don, where workers demanded a nine-hour day. It developed into a general strike, and troops were called in to suppress the demonstrations. In July, 1903, a strike of oil workers in Baku, accompanied by riots and fires, was suppressed by similar means. Sympathy strikes spread throughout South Russia to Odessa, Kiev, Nikolayev, and Ekaterinoslav. In this wave of strikes some 225,000 workers from five hundred factories were involved.

Zubatovism. The government, in addition to suppressing the strikes, resorted to its own method to uncover revolutionary activities among the striking workers. This was known as Zubatovism, after its founder, Colonel Sergei Zubatov of the Gendarmes. Zubatov was an erstwhile revolutionary, who undertook to organize trade unions and even to conduct strikes in collaboration with the police. In 1901 the Jewish Independent Workers' Party, the objective of which was to divide the Jewish workers, was established by Zubatov sympathizers. On February 19 (O.S.), 1902, the anniversary of the Emancipation Decree, Zubatov workers staged a demonstration of loyalty before the statue of Alexander II. This episode was denounced by *Iskra,* and the Social Democrats proceeded to combat "police socialism." In 1904 what was commonly regarded as a police socialist organization was founded in St. Petersburg by Father George Gapon, whose name is associated with the outbreak of the Revolution of 1905.

As his response to the SD's, the SR's, and Zubatovism indicated, the Russian worker was primarily interested in a job, higher wages, and shorter hours. The experience of the reign of Alexander III showed that when he received concessions, he became more conservative. The Social Democrats, however, were interested not so much in the improvement of the condition of the workers as in the promotion of class struggle.

Constitutional Democrats. Under the impact of the organization of revolutionary parties in Russia, another party with liberal constitutional objectives was formed. The Constitutional Democrats, popularly known as Kadets or the KD's from the first letters of the Russian words for Constitutional Democrats, drew support from the conservative and liberal intelligentsia, liberal landowners, *zemstvo* leaders, and professional specialists, all of whom favored a constitutional regime. Its formation dates from 1904, when the Union of Liberation, an outgrowth of *zemstvo* constitutionalism, was established, but its formal organization as a party occurred at a constituent convention in October, 1905, which was in session when the October Manifesto (see page 270) was issued. The majority of the party stood for a gradual and peaceful transition from autocracy to constitutional monarchy, modelled upon the parliamentary system in England or France. Its broad platform also included universal suffrage, civil liberties, land reforms, a progressive income tax, and some social legislation, including health insurance for workers at the employer's expense.

Among the leaders of the Kadets were Paul N. Miliukov (1839–1943), a noted professor of history; Peter Struve (1870–1944), an economist and publicist; Ivan I. Petrunkevitch (1844–1928); and the lawyer V. L. Maklakov (1870–1957), the last two connected with the *zemstvos*. Their magazine, *Osvobozhdenie (Liberation)*, which was published abroad under the editorship of Struve, emphasized that the cultural and political liberation of Russia could not be the exclusive monopoly of one class, one party, or one teaching. In other words, they abjured the class struggle. The Kadets accepted as a starting point the political concessions of Nicholas II in the October Manifesto and played a leading role in the First and Second Dumas.

Octobrists. Various other parties to the right of the Constitutional Democrats appeared in Russia about the same time. Closest to the Kadets were the Octobrists, who were satisfied with the emperor's October Manifesto of 1905. Organized as a party in the fall of 1906, they responded vaguely to the quest for civil liberties, and were conservative in regard to land reform and concessions to minority groups. Their support came largely from the right wing of the *zemstvo* movement, the business class in Moscow and St. Petersburg, and from liberal bureaucrats.

Monarchist Parties. Since the new political parties in Russia appeared to be dedicated to the abolition of autocracy in favor of representative government or social revolution, the tsarist government sought to redress the balance in its favor through the organization of an extreme right which would support and uphold the monarchy. The Russian Monarchist Party, under the leadership of Vladimir A. Gringmut (1851–1907), editor of *Moskovskie Vedomosti (Moscow Journal)*, strongly supported the property rights of the landowners and solidly opposed popular representation. Other monarchist groups included the Union of Russian Men and the Union of the Russian People. The membership of the extreme right was drawn mainly from the ranks of the Orthodox clergy and from the most reactionary elements in the country. Some were sincere monarchists, but others resembled hoodlums and gangsters who, under the banner of the Black Hundred, a counter-revolutionary organization developed by the government and under government patronage, indulged in pogroms and other atrocities against the alleged enemies of the emperor. The Black Hundred incited the mob to reprisals against the non-Russian elements of the population, particularly against the Poles, Jews, and Armenians. The notorious Kishinev pogroms of 1903, which discredited Russia at home and abroad, must be laid at their door. Sincere monarchists, who deplored such extremism, were unable to influence Nicholas II and the empress to take remedial measures.

I I

The Russo-Japanese War, 1904-1905

TWO OUTSTANDING EVENTS during the opening years of the reign of Nicholas II had significant repercussions in Russia, Europe, and throughout Asia. These were the Russo-Japanese War and the Russian Revolution of 1905.

Prior to the Russian Revolution of 1905, the term "revolution" was associated mainly with Western Europe and the United States, especially with the American Revolution of 1776 and the French Revolution of 1789. The year 1905 marked a turning point in this respect. Since then, the term "revolution," albeit with a different denotation and connotation, has been affiliated with Russia. Its impact was especially felt throughout Asia. Before 1905 there was no significant ideological or cultural impact of Russia upon Asia. The countries adjacent to Russia feared tsarist aggressive designs at their expense. Tsarist Russia, however, had no "isms" or slogans comparable to "Liberté, Égalité, Fraternité" or "Life, Liberty, and the Pursuit of Happiness" to export to colonial or dependent peoples. The Revolution of 1905, as we shall see, contributed substantially to the awakening of nationalism and to the movement toward constitutional government in Asia.

Previous Russian revolutions and uprisings were carried out by army *coup d'états* or palace revolutions, or were initiated by discontented and oppressed minority groups. In its early stages, at least, the Revolution of 1905 amounted to a people's revolution, supported by a substantial and truly representative cross-section of the Russian people. Its real strength lay in the absence of any messianic zeal for the dissemination of its ideas abroad. It was the example of the struggle of the Russian people against tyranny that counted. The Russo-Japanese War and the Russian Revolution of 1905 were inextricably interwoven. Without the Revolution, Japan could not have won the conflict with Russia. Without the Russo-Japanese War, the Revolution in all probability would not have been launched, and in any event, would have been suppressed by the army without the extraction from Nicholas II of the October Manifesto of 1905.

FAR EASTERN POLICY

For almost a quarter of a century, from 1862 to 1885, Russia had neglected the Russian Far East. The expectations of Muraviev for a lucrative trade with China via the Amur failed to materialize. Such trade as there was

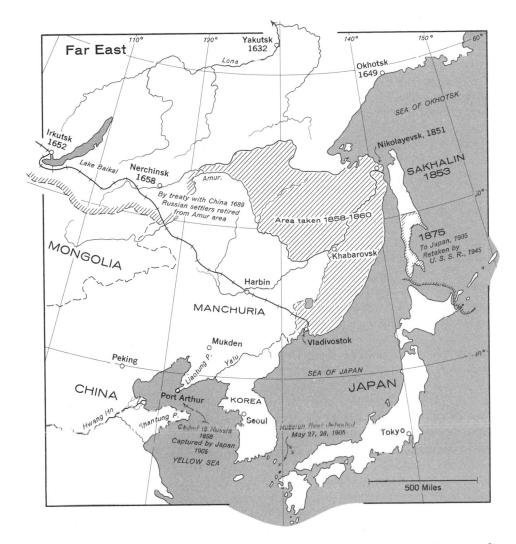

accrued mainly to Chinese, Japanese, and even American merchants and shipowners. The region was sparsely populated and communications were grossly inadequate. Lacking ice-free ports, adequate food supplies, and dock facilities, Russian naval strength deteriorated. The caliber of administrators in the region likewise suffered. Since Russia's strategic position remained precarious, the government failed to formulate a positive policy. It was 1879 before regular communications by sea were established from Odessa to Vladivostok. Until 1884, when a Treaty of Friendship and Commerce was signed, there was no serious effort to develop relations with Korea, with which Russia shared a common boundary. Prodded by two dynamic administrators, Baron A. N. Korf and Lieutenant General N. P. Ignatyev, Alexander III in

1886 agreed that "it was time" to promote the development of the Russian Far East.

Several factors combined to bring about a shift in Russian policy from Europe and the Middle East to the Far East after 1890. French loans were readily available for railroad construction in Siberia. Plans for railroad construction in Persia, which had delayed the Siberian program, were abandoned and a Russo-Persian agreement of 1890 prevented competition by England in this respect for at least a decade. The movement of Chinese into Manchuria, hitherto prohibited, aroused Russian apprehension that China was preparing for aggression against Russia. Russian Panslavists, rebuffed in Bulgaria by the failure of Russian policy from 1886 to 1888, gave way to a new but parallel school of thought which emphasized Russia's "mission" to disseminate Russian culture in the Orient.

Vostochniki. The *Vostochniki* (Easterners), as they were called, claimed that Russia had a closer affinity with the Orient than with Europe. A noted Russian explorer in Asia, General M. N. Prjevalskii, went so far as to claim that the Mongols and the Muslim Chinese of Sinkiang were just waiting for an opportunity to affiliate with tsarist Russia. Others stressed that the Russian advance in Asia was a boon to Western civilization, a contribution to the defense of Europe against the "yellow peril." Prince Esper Ukhtomsky, who was close to Nicholas II, was one of those who professed and expressed the views of the *Vostochniki.* Even Sergei Witte, although free from jingoism and brinkmanship, was in accord with the *Vostochniki* on the need for the economic development of Russia's Far East.

Nicholas II and the "Oriental Mission." Nicholas II, whose accession to the throne in 1894 coincided with the Sino-Japanese War, made Russians conscious of the Far East as no other Russian ruler had done before him. As heir apparent, from 1890 to 1892 he travelled widely in Asia, including Japan; during that time he was indoctrinated in Russia's "Oriental Mission" by Prince Ukhtomsky, publisher and editor of the St. Petersburg *News.* On his return, Nicholas laid the foundation stone for the eastern terminus of the Trans-Siberian Railway and subsequently became chairman of the committee on the construction of this road. Thus, he was the first Russian monarch to acquire first-hand information of Siberia and the Far East. This experience kindled his imagination and led him to subordinate the Near East to the Far East in pursuit of the goal of Russian territorial expansion.

Iranian Policy. As a result, the government of Nicholas II eased its pressure on Turkey and the Balkans prior to World War I. According to Count Witte, aggression against Turkey would inevitably precipitate a European war, for which Russia was not prepared. Russian foreign policy *vis-à-vis* the Balkans and the Middle East, with the exception of Iran, was therefore directed toward the preservation of the *status quo.* In Iran (see page 274) Russia vied openly with England for economic and political control. Russian capitalists made large investments in that country. The Russian-Iranian trade agreement of 1901 encouraged further economic penetration. Financially, the Iranian government became largely dependent upon Russia. In competition with Russia, England also strengthened her economic position in Iran, especially in the south in those areas adjacent to India. Russian activities in Iran and Russian imperialistic policy in the Far East paved the way for the conclusion in 1902 of an Anglo-Japanese Alliance directed against tsarist Russia.

Expansion in the Far East. The need for security in Europe, together with the completion of the conquest of Central Asia, left the Far East as the most feasible area for continued Russian expansion. Here, where Russian policy was still fluid, Nicholas II found an opportunity to assume the initiative, possibly in an effort to emancipate himself from the control of powerful ministers such as Witte and Kuropatkin, whose influence dated from the reign of Alexander III. He was able to circumvent Finance Minister Witte, who chose the alternative of economic penetration of the Far East in preference to outright territorial acquisition; to override War Minister Kuropatkin, who feared with some reason the effect upon domestic tranquility of the diversion of any substantial part of the Russian armed forces to the Pacific arena; and to ignore Foreign Minister Lamsdorff by the creation of an intimate cabal to support his personal foreign policy. The responsibility of Nicholas II for the outbreak of war with Japan cannot be overlooked. Russian public opinion, still preoccupied with European security and domestic issues, was in general indifferent or opposed to Russian expansion in the Far East.

General A. N. Kuropatkin (1848–1925), minister of war from 1898 to 1904 and commander-in-chief of the Russian armed forces during the Russo-Japanese War, confided to Witte early in 1903: "Our Sovereign [Nicholas II] has in his purview grandiose plans: the incorporation of Manchuria and the annexation of Korea; he is also entertaining the idea of extending Russian sovereignty over Tibet and Persia and of seizing not only the Bosphorus but also the Dardanelles." These so-called secret objectives of Nicholas II were fully shared by the expansionist ruling circles surrounding the emperor.

RELATIONS WITH CHINA

Sino-Japanese War. In the light of the above "grandiose plans," it is easy to understand why the tsarist government had rushed to the assistance of China when the latter was defeated by Japan in the war of 1894–1895; Japan had forestalled Russia by seizing the very territories coveted by Nicholas II and his associates.

Japan's victory over China thus threatened to undermine Russian designs upon the Far East and was largely instrumental in bringing about a coalition of Russia, France, and Germany in the Far East to thwart this emerging Pacific nation. Already by the conclusion of a political and military pact with

Russia (1891–1892), France had provided the tsarist government with a free hand in the Far East. Germany, anxious to offset the Franco-Russian alliance and to secure Russian support in the penetration of China while the time was still ripe, in 1894 concluded a trade agreement with Russia. With the defeat of China and Japanese seizure of part of Manchuria and the Liaotung Peninsula, Nicholas II, with the backing of Witte, secured the collaboration of Germany and France to force Japanese revision of the Treaty of Shimonoseki (1895) and the abandonment of Japanese conquests. On July 6, 1895, Russia and France loaned China 400,000,000 francs to pay the Japanese indemnity. England and Germany also made loans to China amounting to £ 16,000,000 each.

Treaty of Alliance. As a measure of her gratitude for Russian assistance, China was persuaded by Witte to conclude a treaty with Russia (June 3, 1896), permitting the latter to build railroads in Manchuria across the provinces of Heilung-Kiang and Kirin in the direction of Vladivostok. The Chinese Eastern Railway Company was organized and financed with the aid of France and Germany. According to the original plans, this railroad was to connect Chita (Tchita) and Vladivostok and to operate only in northern Manchuria. In return for this concession, Russia guaranteed to come to the assistance of China in the event that the latter was attacked by a third party. It was understood that this clause was aimed at Japan.

European Spheres of Influence. Thus Witte succeeded in laying the foundation for a "good neighbor" policy toward China, the main object of which was peaceful economic penetration. Had this policy continued, it might have redounded appreciably to Russia's economic advantage and spared the country a disastrous conflict with Japan. Unfortunately, the "grandiose plans" of Nicholas II and his advisers required more aggressive action.

In November, 1897, on the pretext of guaranteeing European financial interests, Germany seized the Chinese port of Kiaochow. In the wake of German initiative, Nicholas II, against the advice of Witte, took parallel action. Russian warships appeared at Port Arthur in December. On March 27, 1898, Russia wrested from China a twenty-five-year lease of the Liaotung Peninsula and adjacent islands—the very territory she had forced Japan to evacuate following the Treaty of Shimonoseki. France occupied Kwanchowan in the area adjacent to Indo-China, and Great Britain took Weihaiwei "for so long a period as Port Arthur shall remain in Russia's possession." As in the case of the Liaotung Peninsula, Weihaiwei had been occupied by Japan during the Sino-Japanese War, but was voluntarily relinquished thereafter. Within three years of the war with Japan, China granted some nineteen railroad concessions to the European powers. Japan was appeased at the expense of Korea. In April, 1898, Russia recognized the economic interests of Japan in that kingdom, thereby paving the way for its eventual annexation (1910). By the end of the nineteenth century there had taken place a virtual partition of China into spheres of influence among the great powers.

The painstaking efforts of Witte and his associates to befriend China and to benefit by peaceful penetration rather than by aggression were abandoned. Port Arthur was transformed into the main Russian naval base in the Pacific and the adjacent port of Dalny was declared open to the merchant vessels of all nations. Betrayed by all the major European powers, the Chinese were especially bitter toward Russia for her breach of friendship. The situation was aggravated in 1900 by the intervention of Russia and the other European countries in China to suppress the Boxer Rebellion (*I-ho T'uan,* 1899–1901). Fifty thousand Russian troops occupied Manchuria, with the intention of converting it into a Russian province, and they committed many acts of violence against the Chinese civilian population of the region. By this time Russia was so fully involved in the Far East that Wilhelm II of Germany referred to Nicholas II as "the Admiral of the Pacific."

Open Door Policy. The partition of China into spheres of influence led the United States to proclaim its Open Door policy, generally associated with John Hay and his celebrated "Open Door" circular addressed to the powers[1] on September 6, 1899. Although the European powers at that time were interested primarily in territorial acquisition, the main objective of the United States was commerce. The Open Door policy was intended to prevent the Europeans from claiming preferential rights in trade and commerce in their respective spheres of influence.

WAR WITH JAPAN

Anglo-Japanese Alliance. Among the great powers, only Russia rejected the Open Door policy, on the ground that it constituted a threat to Russian vital interests, especially those in Manchuria. In the United States, the tsarist government confronted a formidable opponent in the Far East, one which supported the Anglo-Japanese Alliance aimed at Russia. Prior to the formation of the Anglo-Japanese Alliance, the Japanese statesman Prince Ito in 1901 tried ineffectually to reach an understanding with Russia regarding Korea and Manchuria. When Russian military and naval forces, with strategic and imperialist considerations in mind, adamantly opposed all concessions to Japan, the Japanese turned to Great Britain. The construction of the Trans-Siberian Railroad in 1902 demonstrated to both England and Japan that Russia was determined to become a leading Pacific power—a situation they were anxious to prevent.

Manchuria. The Anglo-Japanese Alliance concluded and signed on January 30, 1902, forced the tsarist government to make concessions to China. By the Sino-Russian agreement of April 8, 1902, the Russians promised to evacuate their armed forces from Manchuria in three instalments within a period of eighteen months.

---

1. England, France, Italy, Germany, Russia, and Japan.

The cabinet of Nicholas II was sharply divided on the implementation of this new agreement. Both Witte, minister of finance, and V. N. Lamsdorff, minister of foreign affairs, favored a faithful observance of the terms of the pact. Nicholas himself was strongly influenced by the reactionary and expansionist cabal, which included Admiral E. I. Alexeyev, his viceroy in the Far East; A. M. Abaza; Grand Duke Alexander Mikhailovitch; and Alexander Bezobrazov, Secretary of State. Minister of the Interior Plehve, an opponent of Witte, who was attached to the tsar's cabal, is reputed to have said that what Russia needed was "a small, victorious war to forestall a revolution." This influential group, known as the Bezobrazov clique, as early as the fall of 1902 advocated Russian annexation of Manchuria, even at the risk of war. They succeeded in postponing the withdrawal of Russian forces from Manchuria.

In the spring of 1903 the Bezobrazov clique emerged victorious. It thereupon decreed the abandonment of Witte's policy of coexistence toward China and Japan, which they labelled appeasement (*ustupki*). Its first move was the dismissal of Witte. The military caste had never relished the presence of a civilian economist in a position where he could exert a strong influence on Russian foreign policy. Once Witte was removed, his opponents abandoned all pretense of troop withdrawals from Manchuria. Not only did they strengthen Russian military garrisons in the Far East, but they proceeded to occupy the region along the Yalu River, the site of important Russian concessions in which the Bezobrazov clique and the tsar's family were vitally interested. The activist policy supported by the tsar's cabal made war between Russia and Japan virtually inevitable.

When Russian "brinkmanship" threatened to erupt into open conflict, however, the tsarist government was ready to make substantial concessions, even in Manchuria. It first agreed to recognize the rights of Japan and other powers in Manchuria, barring the establishment of special settlements with extraterritorial rights. In its final reply to the Japanese, dispatched on January 21 (O.S.), 1904, it even abandoned this reservation.

Beginning of the War. By this time, however, the Japanese government was committed to a war policy and the Russian telegram was deliberately delayed by Japanese officials. Pursuing tactics strongly reminiscent of Pearl Harbor in 1941, Japanese naval forces, without a declaration of war, on January 24 (O.S.) attacked a squadron of the Russian fleet near Port Arthur, putting out of commission the battleships *Tsesarevitch* and *Retvizan* and the cruiser *Pallada*. A Russian declaration of war followed. Vice-Admiral S. O. Makarov, who arrived at Port Arthur on February 24, temporarily succeeded in reactivating the Russian fleet. Unfortunately for the Russians, he lost his life on the battleship *Petropavlovsk* when it was torpedoed by the Japanese on March 31. In this engagement, the famous Russian artist V. V. Vereshchagin (1842–1904) also perished. A few days later a Japanese force of around sixty thousand men equipped with 128 guns landed in Korea.

The war went badly for the Russians. Although General Kuropatkin superseded Alexeyev as commander-in-chief, the latter remained viceroy in the Far East, with the result that there was a lack of coordinated effort as compared to that demonstrated by the Japanese. The Russians suffered another important defeat in September, 1904, in the battle of Liaoyang. Having established their supremacy at sea, the Japanese unleashed their attack on Port Arthur.

Fall of Port Arthur. The siege of Port Arthur began on July 17, 1904, and lasted 157 days. Its garrison comprised 42,500 men and officers, not including marines. With the addition of Russian naval personnel it was about 50,000 strong, equipped with 646 guns and 62 machine guns. By August, 1904, the Japanese had assembled more than 70,000 troops and 400 guns. Although no aid from the outside reached the beleaguered Russians, the Japanese continuously received reinforcements. In four major attacks on the fortress, however, they failed to make an important breakthrough. On January 1, 1905, in a move approaching treason, General A. M. Stoessel, commander of the fortress, surrendered Port Arthur without summoning a Council of War. The blow to Russian prestige was irreparable.

From the safe vantage point of Western Europe, a still relatively unknown revolutionary, Vladimir Ilyitch Lenin, grasped the significance of the Russian defeat for tsarism and for Asia. For him, the capitulation of Port Arthur was but "the prologue to the capitulation of tsarism." Writing in *Vperyod* (January 1, 1905) on "The Fall of Port Arthur," he welcomed the Japanese triumph as the triumph of Asia over Europe:

> A progressive and advanced Asia has inflicted an irreparable blow on a backward and reactionary Europe. Russia held Port Arthur for six years, having spent hundreds and hundreds of millions of rubles on strategic railroads, on the construction of ports, on building new cities, on strengthening fortifications, which the whole mass of European papers, bribed by Russia, hailed as impregnable. Military writers say that in strength Port Arthur was equal to six Sevastopols. And behold, a small, hitherto universally despised Japan took possession of this citadel in eight months, whereas England and France together took a whole year to seize one Sevastopol.

The defense of Port Arthur cost the Russians more than 28,000 men and the Japanese over twice that number. With reinforcements from the fallen stronghold, the Japanese were able to win the Battle of Mukden in March, 1905. The Russo-Japanese war continued to be fought on Chinese and Korean territory. Throughout the conflict, Japan carefully avoided the disposition of her main forces against Vladivostok or any other part of Russian territory. In spite of the loss of Port Arthur, the tsarist government proceeded to dispatch Russian naval forces under Admiral Z. P. Rozhdestvensky and Rear-Admiral Nebogatov on an 18,000 mile trip from the Baltic to the Far

By 1904 warfare was taking on a distinctly modern appearance. Here,
Japanese observers are utilizing a balloon to estimate the effects of artillery
fire on Port Arthur.

East. En route the Russian squadron was detained for almost two and one-
half months on the Island of Madagascar. When he finally reached the Far
East after an interval of seven months, Rozhdestvensky was surprised,
outmaneuvered, and overwhelmingly defeated by Admiral Togo in the Battle
of the Tsushima Straits in May, 1905. Only the cruiser *Almaz* and the two

torpedo boats from a flotilla of forty-seven ships managed to reach Vladivostok.

American Attitude. Throughout the Russo-Japanese War, American public opinion remained overwhelmingly favorable to Japan. The presence in the United States of many Russian and non-Russian refugees from tsarist persecution contributed to the hostile American attitude toward Russia. Theodore Roosevelt's own pro-Japanese stand was clearly revealed in a letter to his friend Cecil Spring-Rice, British ambassador in St. Petersburg:

> As soon as this war broke out, I notified Germany and France in the most polite and discreet fashion that in the event of a combination against Japan to try to do what Russia, Germany, and France did to her in 1894 (*sic*) I would promptly side with Japan and proceed to whatever length was necessary on her behalf.[2]

The American press represented the Japanese war effort as a struggle for self-preservation against "a vicious despotism" and for the maintenance of the Open Door and integrity of China. The Japanese were largely dependent on Anglo-American loans to finance the war. As the conflict progressed, President Roosevelt became increasingly concerned lest a Japanese victory should lead to Japanese predominance in the Far East, thereby constituting as great a danger as Russia to American interests. In the expectation that Roosevelt would use his influence with Japan to secure reasonable peace terms, the tsarist government agreed to his mediation and to the holding of the peace conference in the United States. Japan, also at the point of exhaustion, asked President Roosevelt to arbitrate. A chastened Nicholas II, intent upon securing the best possible terms, appointed the previously discredited Witte as head of the Russian delegation, with instructions not to pay "a kopeck of indemnity or yield an inch of land."

Portsmouth Peace Conference. At the Portsmouth Peace Conference, the Japanese delegation led by Minister of Foreign Affairs Komura made the following demands upon Russia: an indemnity of $750,000,000; the entire Island of Sakhalin; the lease of the Liaotung Peninsula including Port Arthur; withdrawal from Manchuria and abandonment of all Russian concessions there; the use of the Chinese Eastern Railway for commercial purposes only; the limitation of Russian naval power in the Pacific; and "full rights" for Japanese fishermen in the Japanese, Okhotsk, and Bering Seas, as well as in adjacent rivers. The chief controversy revolved around the indemnity, the fate

2. Quoted in Edward H. Zabriskie, *American-Russian Rivalry in the Far East, 1895–1914* (Philadelphia: University of Pennsylvania Press, 1946), p. 104. For an interesting survey of American public opinion at this time, see Winston B. Thorson, "American Public Opinion and the Portsmouth Peace Conference," *American Historical Review*, LIII (No. 3, April 1948), pp. 439–464; and by the same author, "Pacific Northwest Opinion on the Russo-Japanese War of 1904–1905," *Pacific Northwest Quarterly*, XXXV (October 1944), pp. 305–322.

of Sakhalin, and the disposition of Russian warships which had taken refuge in neutral ports. Neither protagonist was in a position to secure additional loans for the resumption of the conflict. Roosevelt exerted pressure for a compromise settlement, but in spite of his efforts, the Russians obdurately refused to pay even a reasonable tribute to an Asian power.

By the final terms of the Peace of Portsmouth, Russia recognized the political and economic interest of Japan in Korea, transferred to Japan without compensation her lease of Port Arthur and Dalny, and surrendered the southern half of the Island of Sakhalin. Also the two belligerents agreed to evacuate Manchuria and return it to China. The Russians credited Witte for terms more favorable than their military defeat warranted, and he was given the title of "count." The Japanese believed, as in 1895 following their war with China, that they had been deprived of the just "fruits of victory." It was not long before they joined forces with Russia to curb American power in the Pacific.

The war with Japan is estimated to have cost the Russian treasury about 6,553,800,000 rubles, more than half of which (3,943,600,000 rubles) was paid out in interest on domestic and foreign loans. The sum expended on the conduct of the war amounted to no more than 434,100,000 rubles.

Aftermath of the War. The Russo-Japanese War was instrumental in precipitating the first people's revolution in Russia. Without the engagement of Russian armed forces in the Far East, the people could never have launched a revolution or secured the Manifesto of October 17/30, 1905, limiting the power of the autocracy. The Russian population was unarmed, and it would have been no match for a loyal army. Without the Russian Revolution of 1905, which forced the tsarist government to maintain an appreciable force within the country to combat the revolutionary forces, Japan in all probability could not have won the war. In other words, the Russo-Japanese War resulted in two victories; one for Japan, and one for the Russian people against autocratic rule.

12

The Revolution of 1905

and Its Impact Abroad

URBAN BEGINNINGS

Bloody Sunday. The first people's revolution of 1905, which Soviet historians have termed a "bourgeois democratic revolution," began on January 9/22, when Father George Gapon led a crowd of several thousand people, most of them factory workers, to the Winter Palace in St. Petersburg to petition Nicholas II to ameliorate their plight. Instead of receiving the petition, the Imperial Guard opened fire on the unarmed masses, killing and wounding many. According to Soviet sources, on that day more than one thousand dead were brought to the morgues and over five thousand injured to the hospitals. In Russian history, this day came to be known as Bloody Sunday. The revolution thus inaugurated with bloodshed in January continued until December 18–19, 1905, when the armed rebels who manned the barricades surrendered. Soviet scholars prefer to date the end of the revolution as June 3, 1907, when the tsar prorogued the Second Duma and the Social Democratic faction, numbering sixty-five deputies, was arrested and sent to Siberia.

Prior to Bloody Sunday, there was widespread discontent in Russia provoked by external and domestic conditions. The revolutionary groups, however, were small and unorganized. The unwarranted resort to violence by the palace against unarmed and loyal workers served as a spark to weld all dissident elements into one united front; Bloody Sunday transformed the uprising of January 9 into a people's revolution. Its goal was no longer confined to the improvement of economic conditions, but assumed a political character, with demands for a constitutional regime in Russia. The significance of Bloody Sunday was assessed with insight by the young revolutionary, V. I. Lenin, who wrote: "The revolutionary uprising of the proletariat accomplished in a single day what would have taken months and years under ordinary everyday living conditions of the downtrodden."

The fact that the uprising occurred in St. Petersburg, the capital, helps to account for the widespread repercussions that followed Bloody Sunday. In an absolutist regime, marked by centralization of political power, the capital set

265

the tone for the rest of the country. A Bloody Sunday in Kiev, Odessa, Baku, or Kharkov might have aroused protest, but in all probability it would not have ignited a revolution nation-wide in scope.

Father Gapon and the Workers' Petition. Father Gapon, the controversial priest whose name is identified with Bloody Sunday, was of Ukrainian Cossack peasant stock. Employed as chaplain at a deportation center for convicts, he became increasingly concerned about the role of the Orthodox church to act

Father Gapon stands beside the St. Petersburg chief of police at the opening of a workers' club. The picture was taken shortly before Bloody Sunday.

on behalf of the downtrodden in order to avert a violent revolution. As a result of his contacts with prominent government leaders and the police, he undertook, with their blessing, to organize Assemblies of the Workers of St. Petersburg, and to convince them to seek the amelioration of their plight by peaceful means and through cooperation with the authorities, rather than by violence. By the organization of the workers, by tearing down the wall between them and the tsar, he hoped to save the monarchy. Because he collaborated with the government and police, his opponents derided his efforts as police socialism, or Zubatovism.

The petition which Father Gapon and his workers intended to present to the tsar, with the object of breaking through the "Iron Curtain" of bureaucracy and big business, included a number of demands: a constituent assembly representative of all classes of Russian society; a system of free, universal education; guaranties of civil rights and equality before the law; separation of church and state; termination of the war with Japan; regulation of the relations between capital and labor; an eight-hour working day and minimum wage. As they appealed to the tsar for justice and protection, the tone of their petition was humble rather than arrogant and loyal rather than subversive:

> We, the workers and residents of the city of St. Petersburg, of various ranks and stations, our wives, children, and helpless old people—our parents, have come to you, Sire, to seek justice and protection. We have become destitute, we are being persecuted, we are overburdened with work, we are being insulted, we are not regarded as human beings, we are treated as slaves who must endure their bitter fate in silence. We have suffered, but even so we are being pushed more and more into the pool of poverty, disfranchisement, and ignorance. We are being stifled by despotism and arbitrary rule, and we are gasping for breath. We have no strength left, Sire. We have reached the limit of endurance. For us that terrible moment has arrived, when death is preferable to the continuance of unbearable torture.

The Intelligentsia. The Russian Revolution of 1905 was led, for the most part, by the Russian intelligentsia, not by professional revolutionaries. In a land where widespread illiteracy prevailed, the masses looked to the intellectuals for leadership. In the West, the terms *intelligentsia* and *intellectuals* are usually regarded as synonymous. Strictly speaking, in Russia not all intellectuals were classified with the intelligentsia, which was motivated by idealism and by humanitarian concepts. On the other hand, many revolutionary intellectuals were opportunists, who regarded revolution as an opportunity for self-agrandizement. They were ideologists rather than idealists. The Russian intelligentsia wanted to help the people, even at great personal sacrifice. Many party intellectuals sought to use the people for their own interests. The role of the intelligentsia in the Revolution of 1905 was substantiated by M. Pokrovsky, who, until his death in 1932, was the leading Soviet historian:

In spite of the fact that the problem of the workers' party already existed, and the party was taking shape, nevertheless, during the first revolution . . . there is no doubt, that ideologically, the leading role belonged to the intelligentsia. It could not be otherwise.

Role of Social Democrats. One reason the Revolution of 1905 was not led by Social Democrats was that the masses of Russian workers at that time were not revolutionary-minded. With few exceptions, they did not stand for the overthrow of the monarchy. Nor were they conscious of the class struggle. The chief contribution of the Social Democrats in 1905 was the organization and instigation of strikes in the cities. Even the Social Democratic leaders were still divided on whether to emphasize economic or political issues. The Bolsheviks now claim, that in contrast to the Mensheviks, they were the first to give priority to political factors in the revolution. Their impact upon the masses, however, was not significant.

Meaning. In a heterogeneous nation such as Russia, the Revolution of 1905 did not mean the same thing to all Russians. To the nobility, it involved the restoration of power to the aristocracy. To the factory workers, it meant higher wages, shorter hours, and improved working conditions. To the peasants, who constituted the bulk of the population, it meant more land and lower taxes. The rising middle class looked for a new economic deal and the growth of capital investment. The national and ethnic minorities envisaged independence or cultural autonomy. It was the intelligentsia that managed to convince these divergent groups that their respective goals could be achieved through a constitutional regime. The constitution, therefore, became the magnet toward which the aspirations of the people as a whole were directed.

EXPANSION OF THE REVOLUTION

As long as the Revolution of 1905 was confined to strikes and uprisings in the cities, where troops and police were quartered in substantial numbers, the Russian government was able to cope with the situation. When revolutionary violence, instigated by the Social Revolutionaries, extended to the countryside in the spring and summer of 1905 the forces at the government's disposal were inadequate. The peasant uprisings constituted a greater threat to the regime than did the urban strikes. The tsarist regime recognized that it had to contend with a war on two fronts—the one against Japan and the other against the Russian population. Since the armed forces were composed mainly of peasants, who might be trusted to fire at city workers but were less reliable against their own kind in the rural areas, Cossacks had to be used against the peasantry. There were not enough Cossacks to deal with the widespread peasant uprisings.

Bulygin Plan. At this juncture, Count Witte, as president of the Council of Ministers, offered Nicholas II two alternatives: (1) to grant a constitution; or

(2) to appoint a responsible authority, such as Grand Duke Nikolai Niko-layevitch, and invest him with dictatorial powers to crush all popular manifestations of discontent. Such an expedient would have multiplied the number of Bloody Sundays throughout the country. The grand duke, on the ground that the forces available in wartime were insufficient to quell internal revolution, came out in favor of a constitution as the lesser evil.

Under pressure from reverses at home and in the Far East, the reluctant tsar was prevailed upon to choose the lesser evil and grant a measure of political reform. The government on August 6/19, 1905, announced its own plan for an Imperial Duma, which proved to be a consultative rather than a legislative body, based mainly on the State Council, and chosen by indirect election on the basis of a highly restricted franchise. Since all the organs of government under the Russian autocracy were held accountable to the tsar, there was need for an institution to reflect the voice of the people. This government program, known as the Bulygin plan, after A. G. Bulygin, minister of the interior, failed to meet this need and appeased no one; as a result, the disturbances continued throughout Russia. Already they had extended to the armed forces, where in June the uprising on the Battleship *Potemkin,* one of the warships attached to the Black Sea fleet, shocked the nation.

October General Strike. Although peace with Japan was concluded on September 5, 1905, the return of the armed forces from the Far Eastern front to cope with domestic uprisings required months. In October, the country was faced with a general strike, which, according to Soviet sources, involved more than two million workers and employees, including doctors, railroad engineers, postal and telegraph operators, etc. The loss of the war to an Asian power; the widespread peasant uprisings; the general strike, involving not only workers but a representative cross-section of the people; and pressure from the landowners made further concessions as imperative as they had been after the Crimean debacle of 1856.

Count Witte: Advocate of Reform. Count Witte returned from the Portsmouth Peace Conference in time to confront the domestic constitutional crisis of October, 1905. Although he had long championed industrial progress, social and labor legislation, and peasant reform, especially the elimination of the peasant commune, Witte remained a staunch supporter of a strong centralized autocracy dedicated to the public welfare. The reforms needed to remold Russian society, in his opinion, should come from above, not even from representative institutions such as the *Zemstvo.* He had for some time deplored the government's lethargy in the face of growing opposition to the regime and complained to the arch-reactionary Pobyedonostsev that the administration had failed to win the loyalty and support of "thinking people."

Witte had helped to draft the *ukase* of December 12, 1904, which promised such concessions as freedom of speech, religious toleration, and local government. In the growing emergency created by the Russo-Japanese War, he even recommended a modest measure of popular representation, which was rejected. Confronted by the October crisis, Witte conceded that Russia had outgrown the existing regime. He came out in favor, not only of the "four freedoms," but of a representative Duma including workers and peasants, although he cautiously counterbalanced this new organ with a conservative State Council. As Witte explained years later to Bernard Pares and Samuel Harper during the Third Duma, he had a constitution in his head, but not in his heart. In 1905, however, Witte admitted that even conservatives advocated a constitution. He foresaw that the concessions made by Nicholas II would come as "a bolt from the blue," and insisted that the government must not only inaugurate the new era, but work tirelessly and with singleness of purpose to implement it.

October Manifesto. Nicholas II reluctantly capitulated, and on October 17/30, 1905, issued the following manifesto, which appeared to meet popular demands, and which, in all probability, temporarily saved the dynasty:

Unrest and disturbances in the capitals and in many parts of Our Empire fill Our heart with great and heavy grief. The welfare of the Russian Sovereign is inseparable from the welfare of the people, and the people's sorrow is His sorrow. The unrest, which now has made its appearance. may give rise to profound disaffection among the masses and become a menace to the integrity and unity of the Russian State. The great vow of Tsarist service enjoins Us to strive with all the might of Our reason and authority for the speediest cessation of unrest so perilous to the State. Having ordered the proper authorities to take measures to suppress the direct manifestations of disorder, rioting, and violence, and to insure the safety of peaceful people who seek to fulfill in peace the duties incumbent upon them, We, in order to carry out more successfully the measures designed by Us for the pacification of the State, have deemed it necessary to coordinate the activities of the higher Government agencies.

We impose upon the Government the obligation to carry out Our inflexible will:

1. To grant the population the unshakable foundations of civic freedom based on the principles of real personal inviolability, freedom of conscience, speech, assembly and association.

2. Without halting the scheduled elections to the State Duma, to admit to participation in the Duma, as far as is possible in the short space of time left before its summons, those classes of the population which at present are altogether deprived of the franchise, leaving the further development of the principle of universal suffrage to the newly established legislature (i.e., according to the law of August 6, 1905, to the Duma and Council of State).

3. To establish it as an unbreakable rule that no law can become effective without the sanction of the State Duma and that the people's elective representatives should be guaranteed an opportunity for actual participation in the supervision of the legality of the actions of authorities appointed by Us.

We call upon all the loyal sons of Russia to remember their duty to their country, to lend assistance in putting an end to the unprecedented disturbances, and together with Us to make every effort to restore peace and quiet in our native land.

In evaluating the effects of the Manifesto of October 17/30, 1905, Witte credited it with dividing the opposition, although temporarily, at least, it stimulated disorder on the part of those unprepared to accept it. Witte, chosen by Nicholas II to be the first prime minister under the new system, suspected with some reason that a constitution granted by the emperor in "a fit of panic" would subsequently be so manipulated as to become a "ghastly farce."

The October Manifesto, which granted the basic demands of the liberal and moderate elements in opposition to the government, was a decisive turning point in the Revolution of 1905. It marked the finest hour of the reign of Nicholas II. Although it failed to grant a constituent assembly, it did authorize a legislative body and a substantial measure of constitutional government and civil rights. Russians in all parts of the country spontaneously celebrated the end of the autocracy. The bulk of the population was still quite unprepared to demand the end of the monarchy. Only the extreme Left—the Bolsheviks and Social Revolutionaries demanded the overthrow of Nicholas II, and their program did not reflect the will of the people as a whole. Not only was the army war weary and in no mood for revolution, but the people, too, were weary of revolution. By granting the manifesto in time, Nicholas II effectively divided the opposition and provided the necessary respite to bring back the armed forces from the Far East to cope with continued disturbances incited by extremists.

Soviets. The creation of *soviets,* or councils of workers' deputies, was a direct outgrowth of the strikes that occurred during the Revolution of 1905, especially of the October general strike. Those established in St. Petersburg and Moscow served as a pattern for others throughout the country. In 1905 alone, approximately eighty soviets of workers' deputies were established, including a soviet of soldiers' deputies in Moscow and one of sailors', workers', and soldiers' deputies in Sevastopol. Although these soviets were not of Bolshevik origin, their creation helped to make the Revolution of 1905, in the words of Lenin, a "dress rehearsal" for the Russian Revolution of 1917.

Lenin's Evaluation. From the Revolution of 1905, especially from the abortive December uprising in Moscow which he had instigated, Lenin[1] drew important conclusions for the future of the revolutionary movement. For him, the greatest achievement of 1905 was the progression—from general strike to barricades to uprising. The Revolution revealed the inadequacy of the general strike. Instead of concluding that the December uprising was a mistake, he insisted that it should have been conducted with greater resolution

1. Lenin took no direct part in the early stages of the Revolution of 1905. He returned to Russia from Western Europe in November, in time to organize the general strike and prepare for the Moscow uprising.

and aggressiveness. In preparing for the future, Lenin emphasized the need for the indoctrination of the army and for an all-out effort to win the troops to the side of the revolution. He strongly recommended the development of new military tactics learned at the barricades and the seizure of adequate supplies of up-to-date military equipment. These were lessons that Lenin and the Bolsheviks implemented in 1917.

THE REACTION ABROAD

Europe. The revolution of 1905 had its impact, in differing degrees, in various parts of Europe and Asia. Among the labor and socialist movements already well established in Western Europe, it served to promote social unrest. German and Austro-Hungarian Social Democrats, as well as French and Italian Socialists, welcomed the blow to Russian autocracy, which they envisaged as a precursor to the eventual success of their own struggles against the ruling classes and reactionary forces in their own societies. Throughout Western Europe an epidemic of labor meetings and conferences heralded the achievements of Russian workers and roundly condemned tsarist policies. French Socialists, in particular, regarded the Revolution of 1905 as the most significant development since the Paris Commune of 1871. In Germany, France, Austria-Hungary, and Italy, a wave of strikes conducted by miners, textile workers, and railroad employees occurred in 1905 and 1906. Widespread peasant disorders erupted in agricultural Hungary, accompanied by political ferment among the Slavic minorities seeking national liberation. The pattern of events in revolutionary Russia was reproduced on a lesser scale in the Balkan states of Bulgaria, Serbia, and Rumania.

There were some specific indications of the reaction in various parts of Europe to the events of 1905 in Russia. On April 15, 1905, the workers of the city of Limoges in France erected barricades. Under the direct influence of the heroism of the *Potemkin*'s sailors, the crew of the German cruiser *Frauenlob* arrested all their officers in July, 1905, and threw overboard the locks of their guns. On September 15, on "Red Friday," more than 100,000 workers demonstrated in the streets of Budapest. On November 2 in Vienna and on November 4 in Prague, there were bloody clashes between demonstrators and the police. In January, 1906, the workers of Hamburg conducted the first political general strike in the history of Germany, coinciding with meetings held all over Germany on the first anniversary of "Bloody Sunday" in Russia. These various manifestations of unrest were, of course, an outgrowth of local conditions. The example of the Russian Revolution of 1905 increased the tempo and broadened the scope of the demonstrations.

Asian Reaction. In Asia the Revolution of 1905 stirred political and national, rather than social, unrest. As an imperialist power, Russia differed from Great Britain, France, and Germany, in that she had within her own

In June, 1905, the crew took control of the *Potemkin,* a battleship in the Black Sea Fleet. The mutineers planned to sail to Odessa and join the general strike. Other ships in the fleet intervened, however, and the *Potemkin* finally escaped to Romania.

borders Iranians, Turks, Armenians, Georgians, Chinese, Koreans, and Mongols. Events inside Russia, therefore, were bound to have repercussions across Asia. The politically conscious elements in Asian lands contiguous to Russia were already constitution-minded due to Western influence. The Russian Revolution of 1905 provided a practical demonstration on their own doorsteps that a constitution could be won from an autocratic monarch in a predominantly agrarian country where the masses were both heterogeneous in origin and largely illiterate. These conditions were close to Asian experience—closer by far than Western industrial democracy—and they could not fail to make a profound impression. The impact of the Russian Revolution of 1905 was greater and more direct in Asian countries contiguous to tsarist Russia, where cross-border communications were frequent, as in Iran, Turkey, and China.

Iran. Iran was the first to experience the full impact of the Revolution of 1905. The appreciable number of Iranian students in Russian universities, the traditionally close economic contacts between Russian and Iranian merchants, and the large Iranian labor force in the Russian Transcaucasus, especially in the oil center of Baku and in Tiflis, contributed greatly to the rapid dissemination in Iran of information about the events of 1905 in Russia. During the last decade of the nineteenth century from 15,000 to 30,000 migratory workers (*otkhodniki*) bearing passports crossed the border from Iranian Azerbaijan in search of employment in Russia. In 1905 alone, when Russian laborers were mobilized for service in the Russo-Japanese War, these migrants numbered 62,000. These figures do not include Iranians who slipped across the border without benefit of passport from Gilan and the other northern provinces of Iran.

In the autumn of 1904 a special Social Democratic Muslim party, known as *Gummet* (Power) was created in Baku for Muslims laboring in the oil fields. From Baku this organization spread rapidly to other localities throughout the Transcaucasus. In 1905 an organization of Iranian revolutionaries was established in Tiflis (Tblisi). As a result, when Iranian migratory workers returned to their homeland, they took with them revolutionary ideas, printed propaganda, and weapons to incite strikes and disturbances. It was only logical, therefore, that revolution in Iran should follow close on the heels of revolution in Russia.

As in Russia, however, the leadership of the Iranian Revolution, 1905–1911, was provided by the middle and upper classes—the clergy, the merchants, and the lesser bourgeoisie. Even according to Soviet admission, there was no independent peasant and worker's movement in Iran in 1905. The two revolutions followed a parallel course in other respects. Subsequent to the tsar's October Manifesto granting a constitution in Russia came the shah's decree of August, 1906, bestowing a constitution on Iran. The opening of the first Russian Duma on May 10, 1906, was followed a few months later by the first session of the Iranian Mejlis, which Soviet writers have hailed as "the first Parliament in the East." Even the caliber of representation in the Persian Mejlis approximated that in the Russian Duma. Real leadership in both countries was in the hands of men whose views were those of the Constitutional Democrats. Their immediate interest was in political change, in the limitation of autocracy by the inauguration of constitutional government, to be followed only gradually by social reform. Even the Caucasian revolutionaries who marched at the head of a mass demonstration in Tabriz on March 26, 1909, bearing the red flag, were content to use the slogan, "Long live the constitution!"

Anglo-Russian Entente. Following the suppression of internal revolt in Russia, the tsarist government, in August, 1907, entered into an entente with England, which served to strengthen the anti-revolutionary forces in Iran. Thereafter, the shah was able to confine Iranian revolutionary activity largely to the northern provinces. Like the tsar, who dissolved the first Duma on July 21, 1906, and the second Duma on March 5, 1907, the shah finally dissolved the Mejlis on June 23, 1908. The Anglo-Russian Entente accelerated the collapse of the Iranian Revolution of 1905. Its complete suppression was assured by Anglo-Russian occupation of the country in 1911.

The Anglo-Russian "partition" of Iran created a new problem. Instead of constitutional government and social reforms, the quest for national liberation from tsarist and English "domination" became the prime consideration. In 1912, at the height of the reaction in Iran, there was founded in Gilan an organization called Ittikhadi-Islam (Unity of Islam), the purpose of which was to combat foreign domination. One of its leaders, Mirza Kuchik Khan, became a prominent figure in the uprising in northern Iran (Gilan) following the Bolshevik Revolution of 1917. It was this preoccupation with national liberation that the Bolsheviks were able to take advantage of in 1917, when they proclaimed the abandonment of all tsarist rights and concessions in Iran, and temporarily, at least, diverted the ire of Iranian nationalists toward England.

Turkey and the Ottoman Empire. The Russian Revolution of 1905, followed by the Iranian Revolution, had repercussions in Turkey, where comparable conditions existed. Russian efforts to limit the power of the tsarist autocracy and Iranian demands for curbing the authority of the shah revived the aspirations of progressive Turks at home and abroad for the termination of the despotic rule of the sultan. As in the case of Russia and Iran, the leadership of the revolutionary movement in Turkey rested in the hands of the upper and middle classes—the military, the intelligentsia, and business. In contrast to Russia and Iran, where the objective of the revolutionary movement was the introduction of constitutional government, in Turkey, under the leadership of the Young Turk Party, the goal was the restoration of the constitution of 1876, abrogated by Sultan Abdul Hamid II shortly after his accession to the throne.

With the revival of opposition to the sultan, stimulated by the return of Turkish liberals from Paris and other centers abroad, the Young Turk movement spread throughout Macedonia, Armenia, and Anatolia, with uprisings occurring in Erzerum, Kastamonu, and Trebizond in 1906–1907. Caucasian newspapers from Azerbaijan, Armenia, and Georgia were circulated among the population in Anatolia, spreading news of events in Russia. In Russia the Revolution of 1905 had had serious repercussions among the Muslim minorities of Central Asia and the Caucasus, and the Turkish Revolution was likewise quickly felt among the minority groups of the Ottoman Empire, including the Arabs. Disturbances occurred from Albania to Yemen. On July 24, 1908, the sultan was forced to comply with the demands of the Young Turks by restoring the constitution. The promulgation of the Turkish constitution and the opening of the Turkish Parliament led to mass demonstrations in Cairo, with demands for the introduction of a parliamentary regime in Egypt. Failure to extend the privileges of new regime to the minorities led to an upsurge, especially in Egypt, in favor of national liberation from four hundred years of Turkish hegemony.

As in the case of Iran, the Young Turk Revolution was brought to a premature halt by the return of reaction at home and by a succession of international reverses. The Austro-Hungarian annexation of Bosnia and Herzegovina in 1908 was a blow, not only to the South Slavs, but to the Young Turks. This was followed by the unsuccessful war with Italy over Tripoli in 1911, and the Balkan Wars of 1912–1913.

China and India. The impact of the Russian Revolution of 1905 was felt even beyond the boundaries of the predominantly Muslim areas of Asia, especially in China and India. The downfall of the Manchu dynasty in the Chinese Revolution of 1911 was accelerated by the events of the Russo-

Japanese War and the Russian Revolution of 1905. According to Soviet sources, and to Chinese material in Russian translation, the main objective of Chinese revolutionary leaders from 1905 to 1911 was the establishment of constitutional government. Although China had experienced numerous revolts in the past, including the Taiping Rebellion, after 1905 it was the word "constitution" that served as a magnet. Even ultra-conservative monarchists sought to induce the empress-dowager to accept a constitution in order to save the monarchy. The newspapers *Min Pao* and *Tung Fang Tsa chih* published articles by Chinese monarchists, attributing the Japanese victory to the fact that Japan had a constitution, and Russian defeat to the absence of a Russian constitution.

In other areas of Asia that had not yet achieved independence, such as India, Indonesia, and Korea, the Russian Revolution of 1905 and its counterparts in Iran and Turkey served mainly to stimulate nationalist aspirations for freedom from a foreign "yoke," which manifested themselves in strikes or uprisings against the English, Dutch, and Japanese. Here, too, the leadership, as even the Soviets admit, was not proletarian, but came from the upper and middle classes, from the intelligentsia.

13

The Dumas and the Struggle
for the Peasantry, 1906-1914

THE FIRST DUMA, 1906

In accordance with the October Manifesto, the tsarist government proceeded with arrangements for the summoning of the first State Duma. The
term "Duma," a derivation of the verb "dumat," to think, was associated with
the traditions of the Russian past. The *Boyarskaya Duma,* for which Peter the
Great had substituted the Administrative Senate in 1711, had been a purely
consultative rather than a legislative body. Although Nicholas II undoubtedly
would have preferred a Duma with correspondingly restricted functions, the
exigencies of the times demanded greater concessions. The complicated
electoral law worked out by Witte provided for almost universal suffrage to
males twenty-five years of age. Soldiers, sailors, students, landless peasants,
farm laborers, and women were not given the franchise. The term of the
Duma was set at five years.

Restrictions. As the revolution subsided, the government resorted to last-
minute measures to curb the power of the new legislative body. On February
20 (O.S.), 1906, on the eve of the opening of the First Duma, the government violated the spirit, if not the letter, of the October Manifesto by exempt-
ing the army, navy, and foreign loans from the competence of the Duma,
thereby restricting its right of legislative initiative. Its authority over the
budget was likewise restricted. The autocratic power of the emperor was
reaffirmed. His ministers remained responsible to him alone, although the
Duma acquired the right to interpolate them. The State Council, set up by
Alexander I in 1801, was transformed into an upper house, with half of its
members appointed by the tsar. The government conferred upon it the veto
power over legislation passed by the Duma. The right of free assembly
granted by the October Manifesto was virtually cancelled in March, 1906,
thereby hampering the activities of Russian political parties. To strengthen the
government's financial position, Count Witte, acting for the administration,
successfully negotiated a French loan of 843,000,000 rubles, a foreign-aid
program which staved off economic bankruptcy and greatly reduced government dependence on the elected Duma. Altogether, in 1906, the tsarist regime

secured loans from English, French, and Belgian banks, amounting to 2,500,000,000 francs.

Composition. The revolution was already subsiding when elections to the First Duma were held in March and April, 1906. The trend in the direction of moderation was indicated by the failure of the Black Hundred to elect any of its candidates. Among the 478 members of the Duma, there were 187 Kadets, 85 representatives of the Moderate Labor Party (*Trudoviki*), and 204 peasants, only two of whom were recorded as illiterate. The radical socialist elements, the Social Democrats and Social Revolutionaries, very much in the minority, had decided to boycott the Duma to demonstrate the gulf between them and the other parties. This measure proved only partially effective, due to the defection of some of the Mensheviks. The vast majority of Russians eligible to vote, including the peasants, disregarded the call for a boycott and exercised the franchise. The first of the four Dumas, which convened on April 27 (O.S.), 1906, was opened by the emperor in person. The members who, according to Sir Bernard Pares constituted "the cream of the Russian intelligentsia,"[1] elected as president, S. M. Muromtsev, a member of the Kadets. The acknowledged leader of the Kadets, Professor Paul Miliukov, was excluded from the Duma on technical grounds.

Agrarian Problem. The first Duma confronted many highly controversial problems, including an amnesty for revolutionaries, the pogroms of the Black Hundred, the abolition of capital punishment, and the liquidation of the extraordinary courts and passport system. By far the most explosive and controversial issue, however, was the agrarian problem. In June, 1906, the Kadets introduced their own program for agrarian reform, calling for partial expropriation of the land, with adequate compensation to the owners, and making provision for its redistribution to the peasants. Since they did not demand outright confiscation of property, their plan elicited widespread support among the deputies. Nicholas II was unaccustomed to open criticism of government policies and unwilling to submit to an agrarian solution imposed by the Duma, which would antagonize many landowners. He was determined, like his grandfather Alexander II, that reform, if it must come, should come from above. He therefore hastily dissolved the Duma on July 9 (O.S.), 1906, after it had been in session only seventy-two days.

Stolypin Land Reforms

Having chosen reform from above, the government undertook to formulate its own solution of the agrarian problem. The government's program, usually labelled the Stolypin Land Reform, actually comprised a series of measures adopted by the imperial administration, 1905–1917. It was not hastily

---

1. Sir Bernard Pares, *The Fall of the Russian Monarchy* (New York: Alfred A. Knopf, 1939), p. 94 .

conceived to meet the needs of the revolutionary crisis. Agrarian reform had been in the planning stage since the 1880's. Sergei Witte, as minister of finance, had conducted a large-scale investigation of land problems, 1902 to 1904. As head of the Peasant Section of the Ministry of the Interior, V. I. Gurko had undertaken to draft plans for agricultural reform. Late in 1904 Peter Stolypin had called for the sale of new land to poor peasants.

The main aspects of the government's land reform program consisted of three decrees, of which only the third, drafted by Gurko, occurred during the Stolypin administration. Basically, it aimed at providing new land for needy peasants and envisaged the substitution of individual for collective ownership of village lands. The reform was carried out in European Russia, with the exception of the three Baltic provinces and Congress Poland.

Initial Reforms. Already, by the first decree of November 3, 1905, Sergei Witte, a foremost exponent of rural reform, sought to head off violence and appease the peasant masses by cutting in half the redemption dues for 1906 and cancelling all redemption payments thereafter. The second decree of March 4, 1906, drafted by A. Krivoshein, subsequently minister of agriculture and executive director of the land program, 1908–1915, set up local commissions to implement measures acceptable to the peasants. The government decrees were essentially experimental in nature, couched in general terms; the land commissioners were given wide latitude in accomplishing their work, due to the great complexity and diversity of customs and conditions prevailing in different parts of the country. The program was, therefore, modified as experience and the demands of the peasants dictated and was not something foisted upon them from above, irrespective of their wishes. Before the commissions began to function, however, there was little demand from the peasants for land consolidation. They were primarily interested in acquiring "free" land from the government.

Even prior to the dissolution of the First Duma, the government dispatched one of its officials, A. A. Kofod, to Western Europe to study other methods of agrarian reform. His report, *Agrarian Law in Russia and Other Countries,* published in 1906, served as a guide to government action. Following the dissolution of the First Duma, Peter A. Stolypin (1862–1911) was named chairman of the Council of Ministers; under his administration the implementation of the land program proceeded.

Viborg Manifesto. The Viborg Manifesto, issued from the safe vantage point of Finland by some two hundred Kadets and Labor deputies in protest against the arbitrary dissolution of the Duma, called for a campaign of civil disobedience to the government, including nonpayment of taxes and nonrecognition of loans contracted by the government without the consent of the Duma. To silence these protests and fill the vacuum created by the dissolution of the Duma, the government issued a summons for a second Duma. In the interval prior to its election, the government's program for land reform was launched.

Peter A. Stolypin. In charge of this program was Peter A. Stolypin, the son of Adjutant-General A. Stolypin, a wealthy landowner, and the Princess Gortchakova. A graduate of the University of St. Petersburg, he had advanced rapidly in the government bureaucracy by virtue of his family's influence. His practical political experience included service in the Ministries of the Interior and Agriculture. As governor of Saratov Province during the Revolution of 1905, he resorted to harsh measures tempered with justice to suppress the peasant uprisings. Appointed minister of the interior in 1906 and shortly thereafter chairman of the Council of Ministers, Stolypin continued as head of the tsarist government until September, 1911, when he was assassinated in Kiev by a certain Bogrov, a Social Revolutionary employed as an agent of the secret police. Although far from brilliant, Stolypin was a courageous, shrewd, honest, and ruthless man. Immediately following his appointment he took drastic measures to put an end to rural uprisings throughout Russia by the establishment of military courts (field courts martial) to handle terrorists. According to Thomas Masaryk, these courts executed 676 persons from August, 1906, to April, 1907. First peace and quiet, and then reform, was Stolypin's slogan.

Land Law. Stolypin's revolutionary Land Law, the official government reform program, and the third of the major decrees, was proclaimed by imperial *ukase* on November 9 (O.S.), 1906, under Article 87 of the Fundamental Law. This decree abolished the peasant commune, or *mir,* established in 1861, and substituted private ownership and the consolidation of peasant holdings. The Emancipation Edict of 1861 had driven the peasants into communes. During the Revolution of 1905 many of these same communes had served revolutionary purposes, facilitating the organization of the peasants for attacks on the landlords' estates. The object of the new measure was to replace landless peasants by well-to-do farmers under a system of private ownership. Together with the consolidation of peasant strips and termination of the open-field system, this would permit improved agricultural methods, including the use of farm machinery and fertilizers. The revision of the Peasant Land Bank, on November 16, 1906, was likewise designed to improve the conditions of the poorer peasants by facilitating loans for the purchase of land and equipment. The popularity of these measures among the peasantry was demonstrated in subsequent years by the receipt of 8,700,000 applications from peasant households for the delimitation and consolidation of their holdings. From November, 1906, to June 14, 1910, over 2,000,000 peasant households, or more than one-quarter of the whole, left the communes. Altogether, about 14,000,000 *desyatins* of land, or more than 30,000,000 acres, became the property of individual peasant families.

Peasant Migration. Peasants in the overcrowded agricultural areas were encouraged to migrate to Siberia. Whereas about 39,000 peasants took up land in Siberia in 1905, with the inauguration of the Stolypin program in 1906 the numbers increased to 141,000; in 1907 to 427,000; and in the record year of 1908 the figure reached 665,000. Although the numbers declined somewhat thereafter, they remained impressive. Some migrants even travelled to Kazakhstan in Russian Central Asia. Not only did these Siberian peasants open up vast grain-producing areas, but within a few years they were annually purchasing millions of rubles worth of agricultural equipment. Thus, their impact was felt on Russian industrial development.

THE SECOND DUMA, 1907

The second State Duma, convened on March 5, 1907, therefore confronted a *fait accompli* in the government's agrarian program. In composition, it was more radical than its predecessor, perhaps in protest against the government's arbitrary action toward the First Duma, its exclusion from the Second Duma of all deputies who signed the Viborg Manifesto, and also because of Lenin's decision in favor of Social Democratic participation in the work of the Second Duma. Of its 516 deputies, only 98 were Kadets, and approximately 180 were Socialists. In the Second Duma, there was not only a Kadet program for land reform, but also a Social Democratic program, both opposed to the government measures.

Social Democrats. The Revolution of 1905 had demonstrated to the Social Democrats that they had neither the numerical strength nor the influence to take over a revolution and bring about the overthrow of the tsarist regime. In 1905 the Bolshevik wing of the Social Democrats, which numbered only 8,500, was in no position to assume leadership of about 100,000,000 peasants. They had oases of strength among workers throughout the country, but not enough to assume a leading and decisive role. To achieve their objectives, they now realized that they must have not only the united support of the industrial workers (proletariat), but also that of the peasant masses. Most of their propaganda heretofore had been directed toward the urban workers. They had developed no effective means of reaching the peasants in the countryside and still lacked an intimate knowledge of peasant goals and thought processes. At the fourth united congress of the Russian Social Democratic Workers' Party in Stockholm, which convened on April 10, 1906, the Social Democrats had undertaken a hasty reappraisal of their position. Here Lenin proposed, as a bait to the peasantry, the confiscation of all land from the landlords, followed by the nationalization of all Russian land. The prerequisite for these changes was the overthrow of the tsarist regime and the establishment of the dictatorship of the proletariat *and* the peasantry. In other words, Lenin envisaged the use of the peasantry to achieve the goals of the Social Democrats.

The Social Democratic boycott of the First Duma made it impossible to advance this program among the deputies. Having accomplished nothing by the boycott, the Social Democrats prepared to redress this situation in the

Second Duma. Since their agrarian program was contingent upon the forcible overthrow of the monarchy, once it got wind of their intentions, the government promptly acted by dissolving the Second Duma on June 3, 1907, and arresting the sixty-five Social Democratic deputies, many of whom were exiled to Siberia. These drastic measures were taken, not because the government believed the Social Democrats could implement their program, but because it was apprehensive that their propaganda, from the tribunal of the Duma, would produce a recurrence of the agrarian unrest recently suppressed with such great effort.

Competition for Peasant Support. The Revolution of 1905 had made all political parties, and even the tsarist government cognizant of the significance of the Russian peasantry as the key to the country's political and economic future. This resulted in a competition for the support of the peasantry, which was reflected especially in the debates of the First and Second Dumas. If Russia was to operate on the basis of free elections, the peasants, who constituted the bulk of the population, would control the votes. The government's program for the distribution of the land to private owners would increase the number of peasant voters. The government gambled on the fact that once the peasants had a stake in the economic and political life of the country conferred upon them by the government, they would become a conservative force, opposed to socialism, and supporters of the monarchy. "The greenhorn [peasant] will save us," said Witte. Neither the Kadets nor the Social Democrats relished a government program of land reform, likely to produce such results. The peasants themselves were impressed by the fact that while the deputies of the Duma *talked,* the government *acted* in their favor with a program that liberated them from the communes.

THE THIRD DUMA, 1907–1912

A drastic revision of the electoral law, which on June 3, 1907, accompanied the dissolution of the Second Duma, vastly augmented the voting strength of the nobility and propertied classes at the expense of the peasants, urban workers, and national minorities. The Third Duma, which convened in the fall of 1907, was, according to Witte, *selected* rather than *elected.* This highly conservative Duma included about 191 landowners, 36 industrialists, 44 Orthodox clergy, 84 professional men (lawyers, engineers, doctors, etc.), 11 workers, and 66 peasants, some of whom were well-to-do. In other words, the government for the first time enjoyed substantial influence in the legislature.

Endorsement of Land Reforms. In spite of the process of selectivity, however, the Duma did represent a cross-section of the population. Among the chief supporters of Stolypin and the government were the Octobrists, with 150 representatives, whose strategic position in the Duma often enabled them to control important decisions. A succession of bumper crops after 1907 also added to the prestige of Stolypin and the land reforms. Under these circumstances, it is not surprising that the Third Duma, unlike its predecessors, completed its five-year term, and that it formally endorsed the Stolypin agrarian program launched by imperial *ukase* in 1906.

Primary Schools. Another of the Third Duma's positive achievements was legislation passed in 1908 designed to bring about universal primary education for children from eight to eleven years of age. By 1914 approximately half the children of school age were enrolled in the schools, and educational authorities estimated that by 1922 primary schools would be available for all children, and the end of Russian illiteracy would be in sight.

The Fourth Duma, 1912–1917

The election of the Fourth Duma in 1912 demonstrated an even greater disregard for the right of popular suffrage. Sabler, the reactionary procurator of the Holy Synod, was determined to increase the number of clergy serving as deputies in the Duma. To make their election certain, the minister of the interior resorted to gerrymandering. While the first Duma included 6 clergymen, and the Second Duma 13, two of whom were bishops, the Third had 45 and the Fourth 46. There can be no better indication of the willingness of the Orthodox church to cooperate with the government in restricting the liberties of the people. Nevertheless, the Fourth Duma startled the Russian people by overthrowing the Romanov dynasty.

Significance of Stolypin's Land Reforms. A complete reappraisal of the Stolypin agrarian program has been long overdue. In the Soviet Union, there has been a resurgence of interest in Stolypin, albeit from a Marxist point of view. Soviet scholars have admitted, however, that the success of his plans would have produced a nation of peasant capitalists rather than peasant communists. Indirectly, at least, they have recognized the impact of the land reforms on the growth of industry and on urban development in European Russia and Siberia. Renewed interest in Stolypin since World War II also stems from the vast land programs in developing nations, still basically agrarian in their economies. In the 1960's the shah of Iran, for instance, attempted a redistribution of the land, which affected the propertied classes in Iran in somewhat the same fashion as the Stolypin reforms affected the great Russian landowners.

In the final analysis, the Stolypin program was a twentieth-century government version of the nineteenth-century "Going to the People" movement. Whereas the Populists could do little but spread propaganda among the peasantry, the government had a practical program which it was in a position to implement. The transplanting of large numbers of peasants to other parts of the Russian empire, including Siberia, peasant satisfaction with the land reforms even in the Ukraine and Byelorussia, and the new schooling perhaps unintentionally contributed more to Russification than the consciously repressive policies of the eighteenth and nineteenth centuries.

The significance of the land reforms for the peasant was soon evident. As landowners enjoying the franchise, they straightened their backs, acquired a new outlook on Russian problems, and cast off the servility which was the aftermath of serfdom. Having achieved a stake in the regime, they defended it in World War I throughout several trying years in a fashion that was quite different from their response during the Russo-Japanese War. The Stolypin reforms also made the Russian peasantry more conscious of private ownership of land than ever before. The land they received whetted their appetites for more. There are those who claim that the Stolypin measures served as a bulwark against revolution and would have continued to do so had Stolypin himself not been killed in 1911, and had World War I, with its calamitous consequences, not intervened. After the holocaust, however, when Lenin offered the peasants land, many were prepared to follow him, at least in the crucial initial stages, until they discovered that collectivization rather than private ownership was the ultimate goal of the Bolsheviks.

Reaction. Stolypin's assassination precipitated a government crisis and a temporary reaction against his land reform. The extreme Right openly campaigned against Kokovtsev, chairman of the Council of Ministers and minister of finance, accusing him of providing inadequate state aid to ameliorate the predicament of the Russian nobility, and expressing dissatisfaction with Russian foreign policy toward Germany and the Entente. Kokovtsev was forced to resign on January 30, 1914. His successor, I. L. Goremykin, a representative of the extreme Right wing in Russian politics, pursued a reactionary, nationalistic policy, which resulted in further restrictions on the rights of the Duma.

The impression is given that Stolypin's death created a political vacuum during which liberals and conservatives indulged in mutual recriminations, and the Stolypin program lost momentum. Several attempts by the liberal forces to extricate themselves from their dilemma proved unsuccessful. This wrangling in government circles had its repercussions in the labor movement, with serious strikes in the oil center of Baku and elsewhere. The epidemic of strikes, involving more than one million workers, was comparable to that of the revolutionary year 1905. It reached its peak in July 1914, with sympathy strikes and demonstrations in Moscow, St. Petersburg, Riga, Kharkov, and other Russian industrial centers during the international crisis that culminated in World War I.

14

Russia and the European System

of Alliances, 1905-1914

ORIENTATION TOWARD EUROPE

After the Russo-Japanese War, Russia's desperate financial situation, together with the growing threat of German expansion in the vitally strategic Balkans and Ottoman Empire, forced the Russian government to orient its foreign policy toward the Anglo-French Entente. In April, 1906, in return for Russian support against Germany in Morocco during the Algeciras crisis (1906), the French government extended a huge loan of $400,000,000 to Russia, which greatly strengthened the ties between the two allies.

Rapprochement with England. Under the circumstances, a *rapprochement* with England seemed indispensable. A. P. Izvolsky, Russian foreign minister, was convinced that Russia could achieve her historic mission in the Near East—control of the Straits to provide free access to the Mediterranean—and the solution of vexatious problems in the Middle and Far East by agreement with England rather than by conflict with her. Economic factors likewise favored an Anglo-Russian understanding on the Straits question. Russian grain exports via the Straits had greatly increased the significance of this route. By 1907, 89 per cent of Russian grain exports were shipped through the Dardanelles. From 1903 to 1912 no less than 37 per cent of Russia's entire export trade used this route. A new orientation toward England was approved, therefore, by business interests and landowners, by the Kadets, and even by moderate Rightists. Many regarded it as the only solution of Russian problems in Europe and Asia.

German Ties. The understanding with England was not achieved, however, without strong resistance from the monarchy, which had close dynastic and traditional diplomatic ties with Germany. For Nicholas II, the Revolution of 1905 had emphasized the need for reliable ties with neighboring monarchies, capable of providing help to Russia in an emergency. Among the most influential Germanophiles close to the tsar were the empress, herself of German origin, Count Benckendorff, several members of the Council of Ministers and diplomatic corps, including Russian ambassadors such as Baron Rosen (United States), Bakhmetev (Japan), Count Osten-Sacken

(Germany), and Prince Urusov (Austria-Hungary). In the Duma the parties of the extreme Right feared and distrusted liberal ideas emanating from the French and English democracies. In July, 1905, during the Russo-Japanese War, the tsar reached a secret agreement at Bjorko with Wilhelm II of Germany, which virtually restored the German-Russian alliance, the nucleus of the former *Dreikaiserbund*. Pressure from his ministers forced Nicholas II to annul this "deal," which violated the Franco-Russian alliance.

Anglo-Russian Common Interests. Sir Arthur Nicholson, newly appointed British ambassador in St. Petersburg, seized the initiative in May, 1906, by proposing that negotiations for an Anglo-Russian understanding be undertaken without delay. According to Izvolsky, four main factors facilitated the Anglo-Russian *rapprochement*. (1) The rapid rise of Germany forced England to change her traditional policy toward Russia. (2) An understanding with England would make it easier for Russia to reach an agreement with Japan, already an ally of England. (3) The common fear of the development of national liberation movements in the Orient brought England and Russia closer together, since the impact of the Revolution of 1905 had spurred revolutionary activity in several Asian countries, especially in Iran. (4) England's fear that she might lose her colonies as a result of revolution, with the consequent loss of prestige involved, impelled her to make concessions to Russian absolutism and to enlist Russian support as a gendarme to help preserve order among Asian peoples. In brief, fear of revolution in the Orient and the growing strength of Germany in Europe confronted England and Russia with common problems and led to their collaboration in World War I.

The Russian Rightists were extremely reluctant to compromise with England on Iran, which they already regarded as a Russian preserve. Only when Sir Edward Grey, British foreign minister, in a special message of April, 1907, agreed to support the Russian position on the Straits as soon as conditions were feasible, did an agreement become possible. The Russo-Japanese trade agreement and fisheries convention, signed July 28 (N.S.), 1907, followed on July 30 by a general political agreement for the maintenance of the *status quo* in the Far East, was facilitated by Anglo-French support. The secret clauses of this agreement, providing for a Russian sphere of interest in northern Manchuria and Outer Mongolia and a Japanese sphere in southern Manchuria and Korea provided the pattern for the partition of Iran by England and Russia in August.

Anglo-Russian Entente. By the terms of the Anglo-Russian Entente of August, 1907, Russia restricted her territorial claims in Central Asia to abate English apprehension for the security of India. Afghanistan was recognized as part of the British sphere of influence. It was agreed that Tibet should serve as a buffer state, free from encroachment by both powers. Iran, however, was divided into two spheres of influence, with the Russians in the north and the British in the south. The English magazine *Punch,* in an appropriate cartoon, depicted the Russian bear and the British lion mauling the Persian cat.

THE HARMLESS NECESSARY CAT.

British Lion (to Russian Bear). "LOOK HERE! *YOU* CAN PLAY WITH HIS HEAD, AND *I* CAN PLAY WITH HIS TAIL, AND WE CAN *BOTH* STROKE THE SMALL OF HIS BACK."
Persian Cat. "I DON'T REMEMBER HAVING BEEN CONSULTED ABOUT THIS!"

Punch, October 3, 1907

Triple Entente. Inasmuch as the Russo-Japanese War had all but ruined Russian pretensions in the Far East, Great Britain gained most of her objectives, with the exception of Russian recognition of her claim to an exclusive position in the Persian Gulf. The way was paved for a better understanding between the two powers, and in the Russian Third Duma, on February 27, 1908, Paul Miliukov, leader of the liberal opposition to the government, warmly welcomed Foreign Minister Izvolsky's announcement of the conclusion of the Anglo-Russian Entente.

The alignment of England, France, and Russia in the Triple Entente—a strategic response to the Triple Alliance of Germany, Austria-Hungary, and Italy—partitioned Europe into two opposing military blocs which led to a series of international crises, 1908–1914, and culminated in the outbreak of World War I.

As long as he lived, Stolypin firmly opposed any Russian military move that might precipitate a war for which Russia was unprepared and which would interfere with his land reform program. The lesson of 1905, as he and his associates interpreted it, was that war would produce revolution in Russia, and that the government could not cope simultaneously with domestic uprisings and foreign enemies. The adventuresome Izvolsky, with the tsar's consent, was restrained from pursuing an aggressive policy abroad.

Hague Peace Conferences. The reluctance of the tsarist government to risk armed conflict with its military forces unprepared was reflected as early as

1898 in its call for an international conference on peace and disarmament. Today such conferences have ceased to be a novelty, but this was not the case at the close of the nineteenth century. The first Hague Peace Conference in 1899 was attended by twenty-six states. It succeeded in formulating some of the rules of war, but, like many of its successors, accomplished little in the way of disarmament. Russian initiative in calling the conference has been attributed largely to Russian military weakness at a time when the Hapsburgs were engaged at vast expense in the modernization of the Austrian military machine. In 1907, after Russia's military capacity had been seriously weakened in the Russo-Japanese War, a second Hague Conference was summoned at the invitation of Nicholas II; this time the suggestion came from Theodore Roosevelt. Unfortunately, the great powers were much too distrustful of one another to achieve productive results by declaring a moratorium on armaments.

Bosnia and Herzegovina. This Russian "appeasement" policy was tested in 1908, when Austria-Hungary by unilateral action abruptly annexed the Turkish provinces of Bosnia and Herzogovina which she had occupied by international agreement since 1878. The Young Turk Revolution of 1908 interfered with Austrian plans for railroad construction in the Balkans. The Austrian Foreign Minister Aehrenthal, in the hope of securing Russian support for the annexation of the two Macedonian provinces, entered into negotiations with Izvolsky on the reopening of the Straits to Russian warships. Izvolsky, prevented by his own government from assuming a strong stand, and no match diplomatically for the astute Aehrenthal, failed to secure a European convention for the negotiation of Austrian designs on Bosnia and Herzogovina. Their annexation—a major defeat for tsarist diplomacy in the Balkans—was followed by a German ultimatum of March 22 (N.S.), 1909, demanding Russian recognition of Austrian action. Due to Russian military unpreparedness and the belief that foreign war would precipitate domestic revolution, the Russian government, lacking promise of Allied support, accepted the Austrian *fait accompli.* The Right wing in Russian politics refused to forgive Izvolsky for the surrender of Bosnia and Herzegovina without equivalent compensation for Russia. He was removed from office and dispatched as Russian ambassador to Paris. His successor, S. D. Sazonov, supported close ties with the Entente.

TENSION IN THE ALLIANCE SYSTEM

Potsdam Agreement. In 1910, through resumption of negotiations with Russia on the Baghdad Railroad and the delimitation of Russo-German interests in Iran, Germany tried to break up the Anglo-Russian Entente. At the Potsdam meeting between Wilhelm II and Nicholas II in November, the Germans proposed a general agreement, by which Russia would refuse to back England's anti-German policy, in return for which Germany would detach herself from Austria-Hungary's aggressive policy in the Balkans. The Potsdam meeting aroused great concern in Paris and London, which feared a renewal of the traditional Russian line-up with the Central Powers. Business interests in Russia were alarmed lest German economic competition should push them out of Iran. The pressure on the tsarist government was so strong that all consideration of a general agreement with Germany, which would have abrogated the Triple Entente, was abandoned.

On August 19 (N.S.), 1911, a more limited Russo-German agreement on Iran provided that Germany would refrain from the development of transportation and communications projects in northern Iran. Russia, in her turn, agreed not to oppose German construction of the Baghdad Railroad and even to permit a line from Teheran to Haneke on the Turkish border. This agreement temporarily eased Russian relations with Germany. It did not prevent Russia from extending full support to France in the Agadir crisis in Morocco in the summer of 1911. On this occasion, the Germans were forced to accept a French protectorate in Morocco (November 4, 1911), for which France ceded them some 250,000 square kilometers in the northern Congo (German East Africa).

Crisis in Iran. The Anglo-Russian Entente barely survived another crisis over Iran in 1911, resulting from the appointment of Morgan Shuster, an American, as chief adviser to the Iranian government on finance. Shuster's efforts to achieve the financial rehabilitation of Iran, over which he exercised extensive control, included the appointment of an English tax collector. An Englishman was also appointed to collect taxes in the Russian sphere of Iranian Azerbaijan. The dispute over this situation led to Russian and British military occupation of their respective spheres of interest. In spite of Anglo-French threats to end the Entente, the Russian government refused to withdraw its military forces from Iran unless Shuster and his appointees were removed from office.

Renewal of the Straits Question. The threat of German hegemony in the Balkans and German domination of the straits, which increased following the Young Turk Revolution of 1908, led to renewed Russian efforts in October, 1911, to modify the existing Straits regime. The Russian government, confronted by a major threat to its security, wished to augment the Black Sea fleet. It was not yet technically equipped to accomplish this in its Black Sea ports. Nor could the Russians transfer warships from the Baltic or purchase them abroad, because of existing provisions barring the Straits to all military vessels. Taking advantage of the Italo-Turkish War and the French crisis at Agadir in 1911, the Russian government once again sought to reach a separate agreement with Turkey. Tcharykov, Russian ambassador in Constantinople, who conducted the negotiations, promised Russian support of the *status quo* in the Balkans and abandonment of Russian concessions obtained in 1900 for railroad construction in Turkey in areas adjacent to the Caucasus.

To dispel suspicion of tsarist designs on Turkey, the Russians proposed a Balkan federation to include the Turks.

These Russian negotiations came to naught. The Slavic states in the Balkans, which envisioned the partition among themselves of Turkey's remaining European possessions, found the preservation of the *status quo* entirely unacceptable. England, determined to keep the Straits open to all nations on a basis of equality, and France, fearful lest Russia's achievement of her historic goal should end her dependence on the Entente, strongly opposed the Russian program. The tsarist government hastily abandoned the negotiations, at the same time withdrawing Tcharykov from Constantinople. Having failed to eliminate the German threat to Russian security by unilateral action with Turkey, the Russians proceeded to achieve their goal by collaboration with the Slavic states in the Balkans.

The Balkan Wars. With Russian encouragement, Bulgaria and Serbia submerged their differences and formed an alliance in the spring of 1911, to which Greece adhered in the following year. In March, 1912, the Bulgars and Serbs signed a defensive treaty vis-à-vis Austria-Hungary and a secret offensive alliance against Turkey. The latter provided for the division of the Turkish spoils, or, in the event of disagreement, the submission of the dispute to Russian arbitration. The First Balkan War, conducted by Bulgaria, Serbia, and Greece against Turkey, 1912–1913, almost stripped the Ottoman Empire of its European territory. In the subsequent dissension among the victors, fomented in part by Austria and Germany, Bulgaria lined up with the Central Powers and the Serbs with Russia. In the Second Balkan War, 1913, Bulgaria was defeated by the combined action of Serbia, Greece, and Rumania.

The Balkan Wars of 1912–1913 greatly increased European international tensions. In November, 1912, Austrian troops were concentrated on the Serbian border and the Austrian fleet blockaded Duratsa on the Adriatic. The tsarist government exerted pressure on the Balkan states to avert the outbreak of a European conflict and rejected demands for partial mobilization of the Russian armed forces against Austria. Although on this occasion France and England supported Russia, once again the tsarist regime deliberately avoided aggressive moves while still militarily unprepared, for fear war would lead to revolution. At the request of Turkey, the Germans dispatched a military mission, headed by General Liman von Sanders, to reorganize the Turkish armed forces. The Balkans remained a powder keg, requiring no more than a pretext to provoke hostilities which were virtually certain to involve the major powers.

Arms Race. One result of the Balkan Wars was the acceleration of the armaments race. In 1913 the German Reichstag passed legislation to increase the size of the German army. France extended the period of military service from two to three years. Already in 1912 Winston Churchill had introduced legislation in the British Parliament designed to provide two dreadnoughts for every one built by Germany. Tsarist Russia, due to the military and naval defeats of the Russo-Japanese War, lagged behind in the armaments race. It was not until the close of 1913 that the Russians drafted a program for a 480,000-man increase in the Russian army by 1917, and for the restoration of the Baltic fleet destroyed at Tsushima. The Russian rearmament program was fully supported by the Third and Fourth Dumas. In 1914 the Fourth Duma approved the allocation of 100,000,000 rubles, 1914–1918, to accelerate the preparedness of the Black Sea fleet.

Prelude to War. In general, the Balkan crises strengthened Russian ties with the Entente powers and they stimulated the revival of Panslavism in Russia. The Russian press denounced the country's continued economic dependence on Germany. With the removal of Kokovtsev, the exponent of "appeasement," in January, 1914, the war party came to the fore in Russia. Its supporters regarded war as the last chance to save tsarism and avert revolution. They opposed any further concessions by Russia in subsequent crises. In a memorandum of February, 1914, P. N. Durnovo, president of the Council of State, made one last effort to shift Russian policy back to a pro-German orientation, on the ground that Germany would be more likely than England to accept Russian control of the Dardanelles. A war between Germany and Russia, in his opinion, could only result in European revolution which would engulf Russia. The warning went unheeded. The internal situation in Russia in the summer of 1914 even evoked warnings against saber-rattling from the pro-Entente Kadets. Since the Russo-Japanese conflict, the association of foreign war and domestic revolution was indelibly imprinted in the minds of responsible Russians. In the crisis of July-August, 1914, however, the lesson of 1905 was ignored.

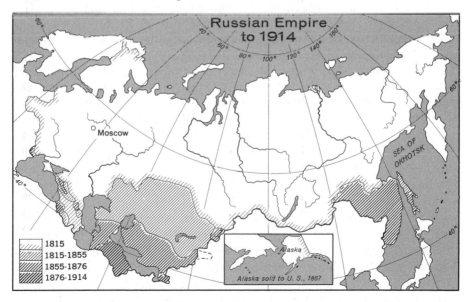

15

World War I and the Downfall of
the Romanov Dynasty, 1914-1917

WORLD WAR I: THE FIRST YEAR

Assessment of the responsibility of the great powers for the outbreak of World War I has fluctuated from pinning the war guilt label on the Central Powers—a logical wartime reaction of the members of the Triple Entente—to the almost complete exoneration of Germany during the first postwar decade. A more considered judgment of the international situation from 1878 to 1914 has resulted in an apportionment of the blame among all the major European participants.

French revanchism over the loss of Alsace-Lorraine to Germany in 1871, and Franco-German imperialist rivalry over African colonies embroiled these two countries in a major power struggle throughout the period in question. This was accentuated by Anglo-German economic competition as Germany's industrial revolution enabled her to outdistance England, and by Anglo-German imperialist and naval rivalry in Africa and the Pacific. The interests of imperial Russia after 1878 clashed increasingly with those of Austria-Hungary and Germany in the Balkans and at the Straits. Europe, by means of the Triple Alliance and Triple Entente, was divided into two hostile power blocs, each of which was intent upon securing armed superiority over the other. With international tensions rising, especially in the series of crises that beset Europe from 1908 to 1914, the likelihood of armed conflict increased; the only question was which incident would precipitate it.

Sarajevo. The immediate crisis which precipitated World War I was the murder of the Austrian Archduke Franz Ferdinand, heir to the Hapsburg Empire, by an unknown Serbian nationalist, Gavril Princip, in the remote Bosnian town of Sarajevo on June 28, 1914. Alleging that the Serbian government was implicated in the plot, Austria issued an ultimatum against Serbia on July 23, demanding among other things the right of Austrian officials to investigate the murder on Serbian soil. The German government, at least until the final stages of the crisis, fully supported Austrian measures which could only terminate in the loss of Serbian independence. The Serbs on July 25 accepted the major part of the Austrian ultimatum; confident of

Russian aid, however, they rejected any Austrian investigation on Serbian territory. On July 28 Austria-Hungary declared war on Serbia and invaded the country.

General Mobilization. With Europe divided into two armed camps, the chain reaction resulting from this incident led directly toward war. The localization of the conflict in a "brush-fire" war proved impossible. The Russians, with their vast military program no more than launched, were apprehensive that a delay in general mobilization of the Russian armed forces would redound to Austro-German advantage. Although Nicholas II, on receipt of a personal appeal from Wilhelm II, wavered on July 29, the decree for general mobilization followed on July 30. According to the terms of the Franco-Russian alliance, it was understood that general mobilization meant war. Due to parliamentary considerations, the English position during the Serbian crisis remained somewhat ambiguous. When it became clear, however, that France would be involved, England declared unequivocally that she would not stand idly by to witness the destruction of her ally.

The German government, which had counted, erroneously as it proved, on Russian unpreparedness and on English neutrality, exerted last-minute pressure on its ally, Austria, to make concessions. The German military command, however, was prepared for war, if necessary, against the combined forces of France and Russia. The Germans demanded of Sazonov that Russia halt general mobilization of her forces by noon on August 1. This time the Russians refused to accept a German ultimatum. On August 1, therefore, Germany declared war on Russia, followed by similar action against Russia's French ally on August 3. German violation of Belgian neutrality, guaranteed by an English "scrap of paper" since 1839, brought England into the war on August 4. England's Japanese ally followed suit on August 22. Austria-Hungary declared war on Russia August 6. On November 2, Turkey opened a new front against Russia by bombarding a Russian Black Sea squadron and closing the main Allied supply route to Russia. What began on June 28 as an incident in Bosnia thus ended in a conflict that eventually involved not only Europe, but also the major Asian powers and the United States.

Schlieffen-Moltke Plan. In spite of the entry of England into the war, the German High Command anticipated a speedy victory on the continent. Its immediate purpose was to destroy the French army and remove France from the war. To accomplish this, the Germans followed the Schlieffen-Moltke plan, which involved the immediate dispatch of the bulk of the German forces to France, three-quarters of them attacking the French right wing and the remainder using the weakly defended route through Belgium to confront the left wing. By the resulting pincer movement, the Germans expected to overwhelm the French in a *blitzkrieg* that would be completed before the Russian forces could undertake a major offensive on the eastern front. According to the German plan, the Austro-Hungarian armies would conduct the initial offensive against Russia from the Bug to the Vistula Rivers. Once France was defeated, the Germans would transfer their main forces to the east, defeat Russia, and bring the war to a victorious conclusion.

Russian Strategy. The Russian High Command was equally confident that the war would be of short duration. Its plans involved the speedy encirclement and defeat of the Austro-Hungarian forces in Galicia. This was to be followed by the seizure of East Prussia. The Russian army would then undertake two major offensives, one directed against Berlin and the other against Vienna. The Russian obligation to France to begin an offensive against Germany within fifteen days of the outbreak of war interfered with the original plan to defeat Austria first. Russia was not prepared for a prolonged conflict against a strong opponent. Although her army numbered 1,423,000 men prior to mobilization and 5,300,000 after mobilization, it was deficient in heavy field artillery, and lacked up-to-date military equipment and even sufficient quantities of rifles and guns. The supreme command was vested in Grand Duke Nikolai Nikolayevitch, cousin of the tsar.

The Germans, as compared to the Russians, had an army of 3,800,000 after mobilization, equipped with 9,388 field artillery. They were in a position to dispatch to the front lines 112 infantry and 11 cavalry divisions. The German High Command was of superior caliber to its Russian counterpart. Its weakness was over-confidence and an unwarranted sense of superiority over its opponents. The Germans were reinforced on the eastern front by the troops of their Austrian ally, which mobilized 2,300,000 men in 59.5 infantry and 11 cavalry divisions, equipped with 4,088 field guns. The Austrian army, which was multi-national and only 25 per cent Austrian, was inferior to the German armed forces. Its Slavic troops fought reluctantly, and many, including the Czechoslovaks, proved unreliable on the field of battle.

The Russian people, following the example of the Fourth Duma and the *zemstvos,* gave their unqualified support to the war effort during its initial stages. Many Russians, including radicals, appeared to be buoyed up by the hope that the Russian alliance with the Western democracies would serve the cause of democracy in Russia. Others wholeheartedly approved a struggle on behalf of the Serbs, their Slavic brothers and co-religionists. Few in Russia believed that the war would last indefinitely or that it would involve more than the regular army.

Second Front. With the German occupation of Belgium and the retreat of the French forces in the west, the Russian army assumed the offensive in the east. Under the command of General Rennenkampf, the First Russian Army, followed closely by the Second Russian Army under General Samsonov, entered East Prussia. This army of 200,000 men provided a "second front" for the hard-pressed French. They were the first forces of the Triple Entente to set foot on enemy soil, which gave them a great psychological advantage. Since they constituted a major threat to the German rear, the German High Command, in order to save East Prussia, was forced to dispatch General von Hindenburg to the eastern front to redeem the military situation. The Russian offensive forced the Germans to withdraw six infantry divisions and one cavalry division from the western front. It was this diversion of German forces which made it possible for the French to check the German advance on Paris at the first Battle of the Marne, thereby stalling the *blitzkrieg* and changing the course of the war.

Battle of Tannenburg. In the east, however, General von Hindenburg, by superior strategy, overwhelmingly defeated the flower of the Russian army at the Battle of Tannenburg, August 31, 1914. Driven into the Mazurian swamps of East Prussia, 30,000 Russians were drowned or slain, and 90,000 were taken prisoners. The blow to the Russian army was irreparable. General Samsonov committed suicide and General Rennenkampf, accused of treachery, was replaced by General Ruzsky.

Invasion of Austria-Hungary. Against Austria-Hungary the Russians were more successful. They launched four armies against the Austrians in 1914 and occupied Austrian Galicia. Although Russian losses in men and equipment were appreciable, the Austrians sacrificed almost 400,000 men and 400 guns. This effective blow to Germany's Austrian ally cancelled, at least in part, the German victory in East Prussia. Instead of depending on Austria to hold the eastern front, the Germans were forced to come to the aid of their ally.

Ottoman Empire. The Russians likewise carried the war to Turkish soil in 1914. Following the Turkish bombardment of Odessa, Sevastopol, Theodosia, and Novorosiisk, Russia declared war on the Ottoman Empire on November 21. While the English fleet blockaded the Dardanelles, the Russians in December defeated the Third Turkish Army, which lost 70,000 men in the Sarikamish operation. The establishment of a Russian Caucasian front against the Turks provided valuable assistance for the British forces under General Allenby in Iraq and at Suez.

War on Two Fronts. Thus, in the first year of World War I the German armies failed to win a decisive victory in the west by *blitzkrieg* tactics. The alternative proved to be a long war on two fronts, which in the west amounted to a war of position. Contrary to German plans, the Russian front immobilized appreciable German forces, and the Russian defeat of Austria necessitated a further diversion of German troops. The Russians, however, sustained heavy losses. Already they had expended their reserves of rifles, lacked equipment for new recruits, and were compelled to use manpower as a substitute for guns.

The Second Year

With the armies of France and England bogged down on the western front, the Germans in 1915 transferred their military forces from the west to Russia to save Austria-Hungary from destruction. The Russian position worsened when Bulgaria joined the Central Powers in October. A catastrophic lack of supplies forced the Russian armies to retreat with heavy losses from Galicia, Poland, Lithuania, part of Latvia, and White Russia. Russian morale suffered correspondingly. Since the beginning of World War I, Russian losses had amounted to almost 3,500,000 men. Russia's manifest unpreparedness for a major conflict led to cries of treason against tsarist generals. General Sukhomlinov, who was regarded as chiefly responsible for the woeful inadequacy of Russian equipment, was dismissed in August 1915. The emperor, however, refused to yield to the demands of the Duma for a new cabinet comprised of responsible leaders; he assumed the command of the Russian armed forces himself and transferred Grand Duke Nikolai Nikolayevitch to the Caucasian front.

Secret Agreements. Turkey's entry into the war on the side of the Central Powers, and Anglo-French apprehension about the possible withdrawal of Russia from the conflict, paved the way for important Allied concessions to Russia at the Straits in the spring of 1915. A so-called Secret Agreement in regard to Constantinople (March–April, 1915) was embodied in an exchange of letters among the three Entente powers. In a complete reversal of traditional Anglo-French policy on the Straits Question, this agreement officially recognized the right of Russia to Constantinople, and also provided for the transfer to her of the western part of the Bosphorus coast, the Sea of Marmora, and the Dardanelles; the southern part of Thrace along the line from Enos to Midea, as well as the coast of Asia Minor lying between the Bosphorus, the river Sakaria, and the Gulf of Ismid; and the islands of the Sea of Marmora, plus Imbros and Tenedos. This deal, together with the Sykes-Picot Agreement concluded between England and France in 1916, was tantamount to the dismemberment of Turkey. It was the price the Allies were prepared to pay to keep Russia in the war.

On July 3, 1916, tsarist Russia concluded a secret treaty with Japan which, strictly speaking, provided for the partition of China between Japan and Russia. Had it not been for the Revolution of 1917, the tsarist government would have emerged from World War I with enormous territorial acquisitions both in the Near and the Far East. A fate similar to that of Turkey was in store for China.

The Russian Role. In spite of heavy reverses, the Russians continued to play an important role in 1915, immobilizing more than half the forces of the Central Powers. In August there were 105 Austro-German divisions in the east as compared to 90 on the western front. In accordance with a Franco-Russian agreement of December 19, 1915, five Russian brigades were sent via the Chinese Eastern Railway and the Pacific port of Dairen to aid the Allies on the Western Front and at Salonika. Continued Russian participation in the war provided England and France with the breathing spell necessary to accumulate manpower and equipment for offensive action against the Germans.

The Entente plans for 1916 envisaged a Russian offensive in the east on June 15, followed by one in the west on July 1. These plans were forestalled by General Falckenhayn; he considered the Russian army incapable of an offensive, and on February 21 hurled the German forces against Verdun, where the historic siege continued for a month. To ease the pressure on France, the Russians were persuaded in March to stage an offensive in the direction of Kovno. Although this failed, once again Russian action forced the Germans to transfer forces to the east and to abandon the siege of Verdun.

Muslim Participation. In World War I there were approximately 1,500,000 Muslims of various ranks serving in the tsarist armies. Most of them proved loyal, at least until 1916, in spite of the fact that Russia was at war with the Ottoman Empire, the seat of the Caliphate. On June 25, 1916, however, the tsarist government was forced to mobilize all Kazakh, Uzbek, Kirghiz, Turkmenian, Uighur, and T'ungan males from the ages of nineteen to forty-three for labor service in the rear of the Russian forces. This produced widespread discontent directed against local Russian authorities, and resulted in a Muslim revolt throughout Central Asia, which was not crushed until September. This was the first manifestation of internal revolt during World War I.

THE LAST DAYS OF THE MONARCHY

Preliminary Peace Negotiations. The year 1916 marked a turning point in the war in favor of the Entente. In this year the Germans put out their initial feelers for peace, first approaching Russia, and later England and France. In the spring of 1916 A. D. Protopopov, later Russian minister of internal affairs, was reputed to have conducted secret negotiations in Stockholm for a separate peace between Russia and Germany. Inside Russia, those who backed a pro-German policy prevailed on the "monk" Rasputin to use his influence with the royal family to bring about the dismissal of Minister of Foreign Affairs Sazonov, who enjoyed the support of the pro-Allied forces, including the Russian Duma. His replacement by V. V. Sturmer, a well-known Germanophile, aroused a storm of discontent in the Fourth Duma. The insecurity of the monarchy in its continued clash with the Duma was marked by successive changes in the government, including the replacement of Sturmer by A. F. Trepov, and of Trepov by N. D. Golitsyn.

Rasputin. Gregory Rasputin (1872–1916) was a so-called "holy man," who acquired great personal influence over the imperial family, especially over the empress. She believed that he was gifted with healing powers which benefited the sickly crown prince Alexis, a victim of hemophilia. In spite of his personal magnetism, Rasputin was no more than a licentious adventurer, but he acquired great political ascendancy at court, particularly in regard to public appointments and foreign policy following the death of Stolypin. His success in placing his favorites, often weak and incompetent men, in high office made him hated by both the Left and the Right.

An ignorant but shrewd peasant, Rasputin was implicitly trusted by the tsarina, who referred to him as "Our Friend." He was fond of society gatherings, and the faith which the royal family placed in him did little to deter him from revealing confidential court business to his fellow party-goers.

Criticism of the Monarchy. During the winter of 1916–1917, feeling in the Duma against Nicholas II and the empress reached a new peak. Several speeches were made in November attacking the pernicious influence of the empress, who constantly admonished the emperor to defy the Duma and suppress the opposition. While he was at the front in 1916, one of her letters urged him to hang the premier and exile several other high officials to Siberia. Such was the deterioration of the position of the monarchy that members of the Right wing on December 29, 1916, assassinated Rasputin, in order to eliminate his baneful influence upon the royal family. When even this drastic action failed to produce concessions, proposals for the deposition of the emperor and his replacement by another member of the royal family were discussed in court circles, even by generals and members of the Duma. This would have amounted to another palace revolution similar to those which had overtaken the Romanov dynasty in the past. Neither military nor civilian leaders, however, appeared ready to take the initiative. Actually, the Duma sought concessions from Nicholas II in order to forestall a revolution from below. Rodzyanko, its president, begged the tsar to act before it was too late: "Save yourself!" he urged. "We are on the eve of great events, of which we cannot see the end. What do you want? To bring about a revolution in time of war?"

In the Duma, the speeches of two members of widely differing political philosophy demonstrated (February 28) the uninhibited criticism of the government and monarch that was risked, irrespective of consequences. Paul Miliukov, leader of the Kadets, a professor and moderate rather than a demagogue, warned his fellow deputies: "When the fruits of the great popular sacrifices are being jeopardized in the hands of an inefficient and ill-intentioned Government, then, gentlemen, even the man on the street becomes a citizen and declares that the homeland is in danger and that he wishes to take its fate into his own hands. Gentlemen, we are approaching this last limit."

On the same day Alexander Kerensky, a Trudovik who had veered to the position of the Social Revolutionaries and a man noted for his impassioned oratory, boldly threatened the tsar: "Have you finally understood that the root of evil is personal rule? . . . Have you understood that the historic task of the Russian people . . . is the abolition of the medieval regime immediately at any cost . . . ?"[1] Such utterances vastly increased the popularity and prestige of these two political leaders.

The Duma demanded the introduction of a parliamentary system of government, in which the appointment of the tsar's ministers would be subject to its confirmation. Its members rightly insisted that the sharing of responsibility by the tsar and the Duma would redound to the advantage of both. In the event of future reverses, neither the tsar nor the Duma could be held solely responsible for Russia's misfortunes. In other words, it would be a divided responsibility. The Duma also recommended an amnesty for political and religious prisoners, autonomy for Poland, and equality for all classes of Russian society. Nicholas, misinterpreting the significance of his concessions in 1905, stubbornly refused to form a new cabinet—a measure supported by his brother, Grand Duke Michael Alexandrovitch, as well as by the prime minister, Prince Golitsyn—to restore public confidence in the government.

Internal Problems. Thus, at the peak of a domestic and military crisis, the monarchy had lost the support of the people's representatives. The Russian army of approximately 15,000,000 men, including the reserves and the wounded, was war weary, discouraged by defeat and lack of equipment, and ripe for revolt. Many liberals and radicals had become desperate, convinced that their opposition to imperial policies would culminate in their exile or death as soon as the course of events permitted the emperor to give the matter his personal attention. Worst of all, there was a serious food shortage, rendered even more critical by the presence of some 2,500,000 refugees from the front. In the major cities, this situation produced an epidemic of strikes, reminiscent of 1905. Conditions were particularly serious in Petrograd (St. Petersburg), where the acute food shortage resulted on March 10, 1917, in crowds parading through the streets bearing red flags and shouting: "Down with the German woman [the empress]!" and "Down with the tsar!"

Prorogation of the Fourth Duma. With the country already on the brink of revolution, Nicholas II by his *ukase* on March 11 prorogued the Fourth Duma. He then ordered General Ivanov, who had suppressed the Kronstadt uprising in 1905, to use troops from the front to crush the disturbances in Petrograd.

The Duma, which met in "informal conference" the following day in defiance of the imperial *ukase,* was confronted by a dilemma. Some of its

---

1. Both statements are quoted in Robert Paul Browder and Alexander F. Kerensky, eds., *The Russian Provisional Government 1917: Documents* (Stanford, Calif.: Stanford University Press, 1961), Vol. I, p. 20.

members still hoped for an agreement with the tsarist government. The Duma, however, was forced to choose between assuming the leadership of the revolution or being consigned to the scrap heap along with tsardom. Supported by the troops of the Petrograd garrison, it chose to launch the revolution. It promptly established a twelve-man temporary committee to organize a Provisional government. The members of this committee were liberals and moderate conservatives, with the exception of two socialists— Alexander Kerensky (Trudovik turned Social Revolutionist) and Nicholas Tchkeidze, a Social Democratic (Menshevik) representative in the Duma. The latter promptly resigned in order to head the Petrograd Soviet. According to Kerensky, the Duma's weak-kneed refusal to continue in formal session on March 12 reduced it to the same level as other self-appointed organizations, such as the Petrograd Soviet, which soon emerged from the disorder and confusion prevailing in the capital.

The decision of the Duma came none too soon. A mob spirit, which the police were no longer able to control, reigned in Moscow and Petrograd. The mob itself proceeded to arrest unpopular officials and reactionary ministers, such as the gray-haired former minister of justice, I. G. Shcheglovitov, and former minister of war, V. A. Sukhomlinov. The Social Democrats were quick to take advantage of the prevalent disorder and confusion and to encourage its spread. Mindful of their defeat in 1905, they were conducting a successful campaign to urge the soldiers and Cossacks of the Petrograd garrison to join the revolution. On March 12, with military backing, they established a Soviet of Workers' Deputies on the 1905 model (renamed three days later the Soviet of Workers' and Soldiers' Deputies), with Tchkeidze as chairman and Kerensky as vice-chairman. It established its headquarters at the Duma and soon threatened to become the real master of the capital. In these initial stages, the Bolsheviks comprised only a small fraction in the Soviet.

Provisional Government. On March 14, the Duma's temporary committee formed a Provisional government, which was to serve until the election of a permanent government by a constituent assembly. The Provisional government, which was headed by Prince George E. Lvov, head of the Zemstvo Red Cross, included Alexander Gutchkov, an Octobrist, as minister of war; Professor Paul Miliukov, leader of the Kadets, as minister of foreign affairs; M. U. Tereshchenko, a sugar manufacturer, as minister of finance; and Alexander Kerensky as minister of justice. Although they represented the landowners and big business, all these men were of liberal persuasion. Events were moving too rapidly in Russia for the appointment of Rightists.

Fall of the Dynasty. The first act of the Provisional government was its demand for the abdication of the tsar. On March 15, 1917, Nicholas II passively abdicated in favor of his brother, Grand Duke Michael Alexandrovitch, who discreetly refused to accept. Thus the Romanov dynasty, which had ruled Russia for more than three hundred years, came to an abrupt end. Shortly thereafter, Nicholas II, the empress, and their children were arrested, imprisoned in the palace of Tsarskoe Selo near Petrograd, and exiled to Siberia in July, 1917. Early the following year, the Soviet government sent them to Ekaterinburg (Sverdlovsk), where they were murdered on July 16, 1918.

It was the Fourth Duma that launched the February-March Revolution of 1917 and its creature, the Provisional government, which overthrew the Romanov dynasty. As in 1905, the leadership came from the intelligentsia rather than from the Bolsheviks. Among Bolshevik leaders, Lenin was in Switzerland, Trotsky in America, Stalin, Molotov, and Kamenev in Siberia. The Provisional government, not the Bolshevik Party and the Bolshevik intellectuals, represented a real cross-section of the Russian intelligentsia. There were two revolutions in 1917—the February-March Revolution set in motion by the Duma and the October-November Revolution, sometimes referred to as a Party Revolution, launched by the Bolsheviks.

16

The Provisional Government,

March 12-November 7, 1917

AMONG THE PRINCIPLE FACTORS that contributed to the fall of the Romanov dynasty were extreme war fatigue; the unbridgeable rift between the emperor and the Fourth Duma; acute food shortages; a dearth of ammunition and munitions; rampant inflation; and the demoralizing Rasputin scandal. The most important, as we have seen, was war fatigue, combined with the fact that the end of the war was not in sight. Many Russian soldiers had spent three winters in primitive dugouts at the front, existing and fighting under appalling conditions, and during much of this period they were instructed to save ammunition at the expense of manpower. The shortage of bread was almost as significant as war weariness. In time of peace, the average Russian soldier consumed about one and one-half pounds of bread per day. In time of war, this was increased to three pounds per day. In the army, although the bread ration was cut, food was available. Among the civilian population, bread and flour shortages were more critical. Even when these staple items were obtainable, runaway inflation made prices prohibitive for the average worker whose wages did not increase proportionately. It was therefore natural that the main cry of crowds of street demonstrators in the capital was "Bread and Peace!"

For the masses of the people at home and at the front, there was no horizon left. The Duma had tried to persuade the emperor to create a horizon by making concessions and promising political reforms, especially the establishment of "a Ministry responsible to the Duma." When the Provisional government was established on March 14, the majority of the Russian people expected a dramatic change. In particular, they anticipated that peace would be concluded and that once again bread would become plentiful. Otherwise, for them the deposition of the tsar had no *raison d'être*.

CONFLICT: PROVISIONAL GOVERNMENT VERSUS PETROGRAD SOVIET

From its inception, however, the Provisional government confronted a paradoxical situation, due to the role assumed by the Petrograd Soviet of Workers' and Soldiers' Deputies, which virtually functioned as a government within a government. Following the abdication of Nicholas II, the Petrograd

Soviet was not in a position to take over the Russian government, even had its members wished to do so. Seizure of power by the Soviet, as N. N. Sukhanov has pointed out,[1] would have driven the moderate and liberal elements, as well as all propertied Russia, into the arms of the monarchy and against the revolution at a time when it was still threatened by hunger and disorder. The Petrograd Soviet could not have obtained the prompt recognition from the Allied powers which redounded to the prestige of the Provisional government. Moreover, the members of the Soviet, other than those connected with the Duma, having spent much time in prison and abroad, had a theoretical knowledge of, but no practical experience in, government. They had no well-defined program ready to meet the emergency, and they were hopelessly divided on ideological and other grounds. The Mensheviks among them, who assumed the leadership in the initial stages, were not even conditioned to assume the responsibilities of government, believing as they did that a "bourgeois" regime must succeed autocracy and that the country was not yet ripe for socialism.

For many reasons, therefore, the Petrograd Soviet held aloof, preferring neither to take over nor to join the Provisional government. It was with great difficulty that Miliukov succeeded in finding a *modus vivendi* with the Executive Committee of the Petrograd Soviet on a common platform, which included an amnesty for political prisoners, which, in truth, was already under way; the "four freedoms" of speech, press, assembly, and association, as well as the right to strike; equal rights for all citizens, irrespective of class, nationality, or religion; the establishment of a citizen militia to replace the tsarist police system; the preservation of military discipline for all soldiers on duty, and the age-old dream of Russian radicals, the calling of a Constituent Assembly.

Military Control. Although the Petrograd Soviet left the formal responsibility for civil affairs in the hands of the Provisional government, from the first it campaigned for the control of the military and of munitions. This was a result of the Revolution of 1905, which taught the socialists that they were defeated by lack of ammunition and by the return of the tsar's armies at the conclusion of the Russo-Japanese War. Their prerequisite for the salvation of the Revolution of 1917 was, therefore, the seizure of the arsenals and control of the armed forces. They were content, for the time being, to prod the Provisional government to implement their program of reform in civil affairs. The Provisional government, which was helpless to act without the approval of the Soviet on major issues, served as a "front," and bore responsibility for whatever action was taken.

In its relations with the armed forces, the Soviet on more than one occasion acted independently of the Provisional government. Its most arrogant asser-

1. N. N. Sukhanov, *The Russian Revolution 1917: A Personal Record,* trans., ed., and abridged by Joel Carmichael (London, New York, Toronto: Oxford University Press, 1955), p. 8.

tion of power was the famous Army Order No. 1 of March 14, ostensibly designed to strengthen military discipline, but which actually undermined it by concentrating military authority and the control of military weapons in "Soldiers' Committees." It specifically stated that whenever orders of the Military Commission of the Provisional government conflicted with those of the Soviet, only those of the Soviet were to be obeyed. In order to reassert its authority over the army, which was the backbone of the revolution, on May 22 Kerensky, by this time minister of war, had little alternative but to issue a Declaration of Soldiers' Rights, confirming the substance of Order No. 1 and even including additional concessions. This struggle between the Provisional government and the Soviet for the control of the military accelerated the demoralization of the armed forces already under way. Within a few months, the number of deserters had increased to two million. In the words of Lenin, the army "voted for peace with its legs."

Conduct of the War. Another area of basic disagreement between the Provisional government and the Petrograd Soviet concerned the conduct of the war and the substance of war aims. On March 22, 1917, the United States became the first major power to grant recognition to the Provisional government. Great Britain, France, and Italy followed suit. In April, the United States entered the conflict on the side of the Allies. This was an event of tremendous significance, not only in Russia, but throughout Europe. Association in a common cause with democratic America created a new horizon for the future of Russian democracy. It likewise forecast ultimate victory in the war. Russians now wanted to live for the revolution, not to die for it. Heretofore they believed they had borne the brunt of the war, and henceforth they expected that Americans would do the fighting. Many Russians, including some members of the Petrograd Soviet, felt that the time had come for the Provisional government to announce that Russia would no longer engage in active combat, but would keep her soldiers under arms until the end of the conflict, thereby immobilizing substantial German forces on the eastern front. Such a policy would have permitted the shaky Provisional government to concentrate on the preservation of internal order and the implementation of its reform program. Events were soon to prove that it could not continue active participation in the war and solve the domestic problems of a nation in revolution at the same time.

War Aims. A clash between the Provisional government and the Petrograd Soviet soon developed over war aims. Paul Miliukov, the minister of foreign affairs, whose goal was continuity in Russian foreign policy, at a meeting of the Allied representatives in Petrograd on March 18 committed the Provisional government to a continuation of active Russian participation in the war until peace was concluded. On April 5, he revealed to the public that Russia's reward, based on the secret agreements with the Allies in 1915, would be the acquisition of Constantinople and the Dardanelles. This placed the Provisional government in outright opposition to the Petrograd Soviet, which on March 27 had issued its Manifesto to the Peoples of the World, calling for a "peace without annexations or indemnities." Ignoring the signs of popular displeasure, Miliukov once again (May 1) reassured Russia's anxious Anglo-French Allies that Russia would continue to observe its obligations to carry on the war until victory was assured. This action precipitated the "May crisis" which forced the resignation of Gutchkov and Miliukov, two of the strongest members of the Provisional government.

THE COALITION GOVERNMENTS

First Coalition Government. Miliukov's ouster on May 15 paved the way for the first coalition government, which included representatives of both the Petrograd Soviet and the former Provisional government, under the nominal leadership of Prince Lvov, but with Alexander Kerensky, its most influential member, serving as minister of war. The price the Provisional government paid for the coalition was the abandonment of Miliukov's foreign policy for the Petrograd Soviet's program of a "peace without annexations or indemnities." Any expectation that the problems created by the "dual government" had been solved by coalition, however, soon proved to be an illusion.

Growing Bolshevik Strength. The dilemma confronted by the Provisional government in its relations with the Petrograd Soviet was aggravated in the spring of 1917 by the growing power of the Bolsheviks, whose leaders streamed back to the capital from foreign countries and from Siberia on the heels of the political amnesty. Lenin and a number of other Russian exiles, transported from Switzerland by the German government in a sealed railroad coach in the hope that they would disorganize the Russian war effort, reached Petrograd on April 16. Trotsky, who was soon to transfer his allegiance from the Mensheviks to the Bolsheviks, returned to Russia from the United States via England on May 15. They were joined by Nikolai Bukharin from New York, Maxim Gorky, the writer, from Capri, Vyatcheslav Molotov and Joseph Stalin (Joseph Vissarionovitch Dzhugashvili, 1879–1953) from Siberia, and many others.

Lenin, in particular, jolted his Bolshevik associates by demanding in his so-called "April Theses" that they should actively prepare for the overthrow of the Provisional government, or in other words, for the seizure of power from the "bourgeoisie." He uncompromisingly attacked the Provisional government and the Petrograd Soviet for procrastination in the termination of the war and the solution of the agrarian problem. Lenin's own solution, regarded as visionary by many of his followers, was peace, replacement of the Provisional government by the Soviet of Workers' Deputies (controlled, of course, by the Bolsheviks, not the Mensheviks), and nationalization of all large estates. These "April Theses," at first rejected by the Bolsheviks on the ground that

In April, 1917, Lenin arrived in Petrograd. This drawing was done in 1943, and although Stalin stands at Lenin's shoulder, the artist did not include Trotsky in the gathering.

Lenin was ignorant of actual conditions in Russia, soon became so popular with Lenin's audiences that the Communist Party accepted them at an All-Russian Congress of Bolsheviks in May. The Bolsheviks launched a strong propaganda program to encourage fraternization of Russian and German troops at the front and peasant seizure of estates from the landlords throughout the country without waiting for the Constituent Assembly.

July Offensive. Alexander Kerensky, the real force behind the first coalition government, although he had no intention of committing the same mistakes as Miliukov, nevertheless decided to work for peace by conducting a victorious offensive which would place Russia in a position of strength with the Allied powers. Military victory, it was hoped, would restore the prestige of the Provisional government with the armed forces. Russia's allies, pending the arrival of fresh American troops on the western front, strongly urged a Russian offensive, without giving adequate consideration to the effect such a step would have on the precarious position of the Provisional government. Kerensky himself personally campaigned in the front lines to inspire the weary and sceptical troops in the "struggle for freedom." To help regain the support and control of the army, he appointed the highly popular General A. A. Brusilov as commander-in-chief on May 26.

The *raison d'être* of the July offensive has remained something of an enigma for historians. Kerensky has claimed that domestic conditions required it,[2] although he neglected to elucidate in what respect this was true. In reality, the offensive represented one more attempt on the part of the Provisional government to reassert its authority over the armed forces. Unless the troops were kept busy at the front, progressive demoralization was to be expected from inactivity. Moreover, Bolshevik propaganda, if successful, could lead to the employment of the armed forces against the Provisional government rather than on its behalf. Had the victory Kerensky anticipated actually materialized, in all probability it would have restored military morale and associated the army more effectively with the Kerensky regime. The Petrograd Soviet, perhaps with these factors in mind, very reluctantly committed itself to the July offensive.

Second Coalition Government. On July 1 the Russian army launched its offensive against the Austrians in Galicia. When victory failed to materialize, the offensive ground to a halt on July 14. A German-Austrian counteroffensive, launched a few days later, almost transformed the Russian retreat into a rout and shattered all expectations of an early peace. In other words, while the Bolsheviks continued to agitate against an "imperialistic" war, the coalition government suffered a further loss of prestige, which it could ill afford, by conducting an offensive instead of working directly with its allies for a negotiated peace. Kerensky and the Provisional government now faced hostile popular demonstrations and an uprising of the Petrograd garrison, incited by the Bolsheviks under the slogan "All Power to the Soviets!" Although this Bolshevik effort to take over the Petrograd Soviet and force it to assume power was premature, the popular demonstrations culminated, as in the case of Miliukov, in another reorganization of the government on August 7, known as the second coalition, with Kerensky as prime minister at the head of a socialist majority.

Constituent Assembly. As early as March 14 the Provisional government and the Petrograd Soviet had agreed on the need to convene a Constituent Assembly in Petrograd at the "earliest possible" date. It was understood that the war would not, under any circumstances, be permitted to prevent the implementation of this decision. The Executive Committee of the Petrograd Soviet was particularly insistent on the speedy convocation of the Constituent Assembly in order that the all-important social reforms, especially the distribution of the land, could be achieved. In view of Bolshevik agitation among the troops and peasants urging them to take matters into their own hands, this was a problem that brooked no delay. It was even suggested in some quarters that the agrarian problem should be handled at once by decree, as Stolypin

---

2. See Richard E. Pipes, "Domestic Politics and Foreign Affairs," in Ivo J. Lederer, ed., *Russian Foreign Policy* (New Haven, Conn. and London: Yale University Press, 1962), pp. 159–160; and Alexander F. Kerensky, *The Catastrophe* (New York, London: Appleton-Century-Crofts, 1927), pp. 207–212. Pipes claims that if Kerensky's statement was true this is one of the rare instances of the impact of domestic politics on Russian foreign policy.

had done, with ratification to follow when the Constituent Assembly convened. The Provisional government, fearing the label of dictatorship, however, insisted that action on the land problem, in order to be legal, must await
the Constituent Assembly. Thus it subordinated the omnipresent social problem to a political issue, the working out of a perfected electoral system.

Civil Reforms. The details of the new electoral law presented many difficulties, especially since the old electoral districts had to be revised, and
arrangements made for soldiers and for voters of the sparsely populated Asian
areas to participate in the elections. An additional problem was the introduction of a complicated system of proportional representation. Although it was
originally planned to convene the Constituent Assembly in midsummer, which
the Petrograd Soviet considered too late, on June 15 the elections were set for
September 17, with the Assembly convening on September 30. In August the
elections were still further postponed until November 12, with the summoning
of the Constituent Assembly on November 28.

It is often claimed that the Provisional government passed as little legislation as possible. It did carry out an important program of civil rights and an
amnesty of political prisoners. It abolished the death penalty and deportation
to Siberia and inaugurated a program of penal reform. It also legislated
against restrictions based on nationality, religion, and class. Lenin claimed
that Russians had more freedom than existed in wartime among Russia's
Western allies. A lawyer by profession, it was natural that Kerensky should
take cognizance first of legal and penal reforms and civil rights. These, however, were not of fundamental importance to land-hungry peasants and war-
weary soldiers. Moreover, the Provisional government's emphasis on the four
freedoms and the wholesale release of prisoners, admirable as was its purpose
to correct injustice, opened wide the door for criminals to pursue their search
for loot and booty and for the avowed opponents of the regime to plot its
destruction.

Kornilov Affair. The Provisional government had barely recovered from
the disorders of the "July days," when it suffered an almost mortal blow from
the Kornilov "affair." General Lavr Kornilov, son of a Cossack peasant, was
a dashing officer who had won renown by his daring escape from the Austrian
enemy forces. He was appointed by Kerensky on July 31 as commander-in-
chief to replace General A. A. Brusilov, who did not agree with the prime
minister on the conduct of the war. In Russia a civilian government was not
popular with the armed forces, which had been accustomed to a military
regime. Kerensky undoubtedly expected Kornilov to support him and his
policies, the task which Brusilov had not carried out. He certainly did not
appoint Kornilov in order that the latter might succeed him as military
dictator. Kerensky was too much wedded to democratic ideals for that. The
folly of the appointment, however, soon became apparent.

Immensely popular with the army, especially with the Cossacks, Kornilov
restored a modicum of order at the front following the collapse of the ill-fated

Galician offensive. He was, however, unable to save Riga, which the Germans captured on September 3. Known as an uncompromising anti-socialist, Kornilov readily responded in August to the request of Boris Savinkov, minister of war, to dispatch a Cossack cavalry corps to the vicinity of Petrograd as insurance against a Bolshevik uprising. Convinced that something must be done to save Russia from the Bolsheviks, and that he was the man to do it, Kornilov entered into a conspiracy to liberate the Provisional government from the power of the Petrograd Soviet. In this he was supported by V. N. Lvov, former procurator of the Holy Synod, and even Kerensky was approached. When Kornilov addressed the Moscow State Conference, which the Kerensky government had summoned, August 25–28, to demonstrate the unity of the country behind its program, he received a jubilant welcome from the forces of the Right, which showered him with flowers, while at the same time it displayed cold hostility toward Kerensky. Men of such high reputation as Rodzyanko, Miliukov, and other former Duma members, appeared ready to rally behind Kornilov as the one man who could save the country from the Bolsheviks. Banking and industrial leaders collected funds to be placed at Kornilov's disposal at the proper moment.

A dispute over leadership soon developed between General Kornilov and Kerensky. When it became apparent that Kornilov planned to supersede Kerensky, the latter promptly arrested Lvov and dismissed his rival. On August 29, with the authorization of the Provisional government, Kerensky announced to "All the Country" the dismissal of Kornilov, the establishment of martial law in the city and county of Petrograd, and appealed to all citizens, military and civilian, to rally to the defense of Russia Kornilov's response was the dispatch of troops, including Cossacks and the Caucasian "Wild Division," to seize Petrograd. In his proclamation to the Russian people, he declared that "the Provisional Government, under the pressure of the Bolshevik majority in the Soviets, is acting in complete harmony with the German General Staff and . . . is killing the army and shaking the country."[3] He appealed to all Russians "to save their dying land."

Thus, in the midst of a foreign war Kornilov launched against the Provisional government a civil war which had all the earmarks of a counter revolution. A military dictatorship imposed by the army would crush the revolution. Some Russians again recalled 1905 and the return of the tsar's armies from Japan. In 1917, however, not even Kornilov's Cossacks and the Caucasian "Wild Division," which struck fear in the hearts of all but the extreme Right, could bring about a counterrevolution. By this time the Petrograd Soviet was well equipped with troops and ammunition. Without waiting for Kerensky to act, it arrested thousands of suspected Kornilov collaborators in Petrograd, forestalling any possibility of an uprising in the capital. Railroad workers, at the behest of their unions, impeded the advance of the Kornilov forces by

3. Frank A. Golder, *Documents of Russian History: 1914–1917* (New York: Appleton-Century, 1927), pp. 521–522.

cutting telegraph wires, overturning locomotives, and blocking the railroad route to the capital. Fear of counterrevolution drove the Petrograd Soviet to welcome Bolshevik collaboration, with the result that the Bolshevik Red Guard of the "July Days" was reconstituted, and the Soviet and the Bolsheviks presented a united front. Soviet propagandists infiltrated the ranks of the Kornilov forces, even those of the "Wild Division," who had been led to believe that they were en route to quell a Bolshevik uprising in Petrograd. When they understood that they were expected to overthrow the Provisional government, the troops and even the generals began to desert the Kornilov movement. General Denikin was arrested, and General Krymov committed suicide after a stormy interview with Kerensky. In four days the attempted Kornilov coup collapsed. Kornilov himself was arrested on September 14 by his erstwhile supporter, now his successor as commander-in-chief, General Alexeyev.

Third Coalition Government. The aftermath of the Kornilov affair was more lasting. It permanently weakened the position of Kerensky and the Provisional government, which now owed their continued existence to the Perograd Soviet and the Bolsheviks, who had formed a united front in the emergency. Many members of the Soviet completely distrusted Kerensky thereafter, in the belief that he was implicated in the disgraceful Kornilov affair. His failure to capitalize on the collapse of the Right aroused even more suspicion of his ultimate intentions of overthrowing the revolutionary regime. The Kadets, too, some of whom had helped to finance the Kornilov movement, had compromised their position vis-à-vis the revolution. The abortive Kornilov coup once again accelerated the demoralization of the armed forces, leaving troops unable or unwilling to trust their officers. Nor did the Allied cause profit from the participation of a British unit of armored cars in Kornilov's advance on Petrograd. The Provisional government likewise faced another reorganization. On September 14 Kerensky set up a Directory of Five, with himself as head, and Russia was declared a republic. The third coalition government, which was not finally established until October 8, still included a majority of socialists.

Bolshevik Control. The well-organized Bolsheviks were not slow to capitalize on the crisis and the growing unpopularity of the Kerensky government. Many members of the Petrograd Soviet joined forces with them, in the belief that Kerensky was no longer capable of saving the revolution. Even some aristocrats gave aid and comfort to the Bolsheviks in order to regain their former power by the overthrow of the Kerensky regime. Only six days after the collapse of the Kornilov movement the Bolsheviks gained control of the Petrograd Soviet. In October, they elected Trotsky as its president. The Moscow Soviet also went over to the Bolsheviks on September 18, and many provincial soviets followed suit. Bolshevik propaganda blaming Kerensky for his failure to secure peace and for the prolonged delay in summoning a Constituent Assembly was proving highly effective. Bolshevism was becoming

Kerensky had hoped to hold the Provisional Government together until the Constituent Assembly met in December. This photograph shows him, in uniform, making a last-minute appeal for support.

synonymous with peace. For Lenin the lesson of the Kornilov insurrection was clear. The time was ripe for the Bolshevik seizure of power. The slogan "All Power to the Soviets," which had been abandoned in July, was revived now that the Soviets were in Bolshevik control.

The Provisional government was dealt one more blow when a German naval squadron entered the Gulf of Riga on October 23, attacked the weak remnant of the Baltic fleet, and for a time threatened Petrograd. The attempt of Kerensky and the Provisional government to abandon the capital in the emergency led the Bolsheviks to raise the cry of treason. On October 30, with conditions in the capital and throughout the country rapidly deteriorating, the unhappy Kerensky confided to the American journalist, John Reed: "The Russian people are suffering from economic fatigue—and from disillusionment with the Allies! The world thinks that the Russian Revolution is at an end. Do not be mistaken. The Russian Revolution is just beginning."[4]

4. John Reed, *Ten Days That Shook the World* (New York: Modern Library), p. 39.

Coup d'État. The Bolsheviks could not afford to wait another month until the Constituent Assembly was in session. They summoned an All-Russian Congress of Soviets for November 7 in Petrograd. That very night their troops seized control of the chief government buildings in the capital. The next morning Russians found the city placarded with the announcement of the establishment of the Soviet regime. Unlike Kornilov's venture, the Bolshevik coup worked. Kerensky fled, and the Provisional government collapsed like a house of cards.

Evaluation of Kerensky. Kerensky's role in the Russian Revolution has remained a major subject of controversy. Many of those who disliked him most and held him responsible for the Bolshevik victory have recognized his honesty and sincerity in working for the best interests of the country as he understood them. It seems doubtful, however, that he really understood the Russian people. Both the military and civilian population had been accustomed to strong military discipline. Kerensky, although a popular leader in the beginning, was a civilian head of government and by no means a disciplinarian. Complete freedom was something the Russian people were not prepared to cope with, especially in the midst of a world war and with disorder running rampant at home.

In subsequent years, Kerensky stated that his continuance in power was contingent upon his doing what the Bolsheviks did: conclude a separate peace with the Central Powers and make himself a dictator. He said that he was constitutionally incapable of doing either. In response to the accusation that he was weak and that he handled the opposition with kid gloves, Kerensky pointed to Denikin and Kolchak, so-called strong men who authorized atrocities against their Bolshevik opponents, received aid and military support from Great Britain, France, Japan, and the United States, and nevertheless went down to defeat.

Part Four

Soviet Russia, 1917-1941

17

The Bolshevik Revolution:

A New Definition

THE SEIZURE OF POWER by the Bolsheviks in Petrograd on October 25/November 7 ended the nine-month struggle to establish a Russian democratic regime. The Bolsheviks, a small minority within a socialist minority, which coasted into power in Petrograd in the midst of revolutionary disorder, still had to gain recognition throughout the country. During the first weeks following the take-over, its position was extremely precarious. Most of the Mensheviks and Social Revolutionaries resigned from the Second All-Russian Congress of Soviets in protest over the overthrow of the Provisional government. At the City Duma they joined forces with the Council of the Republic and the former Central Executive Committee to establish a Committee for the Salvation of the Fatherland and the Revolution. Kerensky, having escaped the Bolshevik net in a borrowed American legation car, had gone to seek military aid from General P. N. Krasnov to suppress the Bolshevik uprising. Even Lenin was sufficiently uncertain of the position of the Congress of Soviets that he failed to attend the opening session, convened at eleven o'clock on the evening of November 7. Many Russians were confident that the new Bolshevik regime would prove transitory.

CONGRESS OF SOVIETS

In spite of Lenin's doubts, the Congress of Soviets on November 7 ratified the Bolshevik insurrection by the relatively narrow margin of 390 votes out of 650. Before the historic session was over, Chairman Kamenev was able to announce the seizure of the Winter Palace and the complete overthrow of the Provisional government. The Congress, after a stormy interlude, proclaimed to "All Workers, Soldiers, and Peasants" its resolve "to take governmental power into its own hands." It promised immediate action to secure an armistice on all fronts and a democratic peace, the transfer of all land to peasant committees, and the convocation of the oft-postponed Constituent Assembly.

Peace Decree. When Lenin appeared before the Congress of Soviets on November 8 he received a great ovation. He lost no time in presenting to the

In early November, 1917, the Red Guards awaited their instructions on the steps of the Smolny Institute in Petrograd. Inside, the Bolshevik leaders were finalizing the plan of action.

assembled delegates his "Appeal to the peoples and governments of all warring countries" for the conclusion of "an immediate peace without annexations or indemnities," to be achieved through "open diplomacy." His decree promised the immediate publication of the tsarist secret treaties with the Allies, at the same time proclaiming their annulment. Pending the conclusion of peace, Lenin called upon all the belligerents for an immediate three-months' armistice. This decree on peace was adopted with tremendous enthusiasm by the Congress of Soviets.

Land Decree. Lenin then presented his "Decree on the Land" as an immediate and indispensable panacea for the peasantry. It provided for the abolition of all private landholding without compensation and for the transfer of all private, crown, and church lands to peasant committees pending the convocation of the Constituent Assembly. In the emergency, Lenin simply appropriated the land program of the Social Revolutionary Party, which envisaged a mass of small peasant farms rather than the Bolshevik plan for the nationalization of all the land. This decree even stipulated that the "land of ordinary peasants and ordinary Cossacks shall not be confiscated." Lenin managed to convince the Congress of Soviets that it was vital for the peasants to know at once that landlordism had been liquidated and that henceforth they were free to manage their own lives. With only one negative vote and eight abstentions the Congress of Soviets followed Lenin's leadership and approved the land decree. Obviously this measure was intended to win the support of the peasant masses for the new Bolshevik regime. Unlike the

Provisional government, the Bolsheviks did not make the mistake of post-poning the entire solution of agrarian problems until the Constituent Assembly convened. As in the case of Stolypin, they acted by decree, leaving final confirmation to the forthcoming legislative body.

One-Party Regime. The organization by the Congress of Soviets of a new "provisional" government presented some difficulty. The remaining Social Revolutionaries and Mensheviks, as well as some Bolsheviks, and the representatives of the railwaymen's union favored a socialist coalition government. Chairman Kamenev presented a proposal for a Council of People's Commissars (*Sovnarkom*), which would hold power, subject to the Congress of Soviets or its Executive Committee, until the Constituent Assembly convened. Kamenev's proposed list of commissars, headed by Lenin, without exception proved to be Bolsheviks. This attempt to superimpose a one-party regime met with vigorous protest from the supporters of a coalition government, the railwaymen even threatening to cut off rail communications to the capital if it were accepted. Since such a coalition government could hardly be accomplished by a "rump" congress, and time was of the essence, Kamenev's decree was adopted without a roll call. A Central Executive Committee, the legislative organ to which the Council of People's Commissars was responsible, was confirmed, with sixty-two Bolsheviks among its 101 members. Lenin emerged as president of the new Council of People's Commissars, which included Leon Trotsky as commissar of foreign affairs, Alexei Rykov as commissar of the interior, the not-so-well-known Joseph Stalin as commissar of nationalities, and Anatole Lunacharsky as commissar of education.

Lenin's insistence that the time was ripe for a Bolshevik seizure of power appeared to be justified. The All-Russian Congress of Soviets of Workers' and Soldiers' Deputies came to a close on November 9, leaving the Bolsheviks with a semblance of legal authority. With almost prophetic insight, prominent Menshevik, B. V. Avilov, had warned the Congress of Soviets that Lenin's "Provisional" government would be no more successful than its predecessors in solving the problems of peace, bread, and land, which could not be accomplished merely by passing decrees.

THE CONSTITUENT ASSEMBLY

Elections. When the Bolsheviks seized power in Russia on November 7, the election campaign for the Constituent Assembly was already under way. The repeated postponement of the assembly was one of the chief Bolshevik clubs for belaboring the Provisional government. Once in power, however, Lenin and his associates were confronted by a dilemma. The Constituent Assembly had been projected prior to the socialist revolution. The Bolsheviks now had their own organ, the All-Russian Congress of Soviets of Workers' and Soldiers' Deputies, which had accepted the Bolshevik program. They had good reason to know that country-wide elections would not produce a Bolshevik majority in the Constituent Assembly, and they had no intention of permitting the enactment of a program counter to their own. As a result of their promises and propaganda, they were not in a position to call off the elections. There was every reason to expect, however, that if the Constituent Assembly failed to rubber stamp the Bolshevik program it would be treated at least as summarily as Nicholas II had handled the Duma.

In the elections, as was anticipated, the Bolsheviks and their sympathizers captured 175 votes of the 707 registered at the Tauride Palace. The Social Revolutionaries, who dominated the countryside, emerged with 410 delegates, although 40 of these belonged to the Left wing, which so far sided with the Bolsheviks. Victor Chernov, the leader of the SR's, was elected chairman of the assembly by a two-thirds majority. The Kadets (many of whom were in prison) elected only 17 delegates, and the Mensheviks 16.

A Single Meeting. The Constituent Assembly, which a few months earlier was expected to solve Russia's major national problems, convened for the first and last time on January 18. It passed three measures: one declaring Russia a democratic federative republic; a second transferring the land to the peasants; and the third calling for an international socialist conference to achieve a "general democratic peace." To stem the tide of opposition, Iraklii Tseretelli, an eminent Menshevik, warned that the destruction of the assembly would bring "the protracted anarchy of civil war" and the eventual overthrow of the Russian revolution. The Bolsheviks nevertheless prevented the assembly from meeting the following day. On January 20 the Council of People's Commissars announced its dissolution on the ground that it had refused to recognize the Bolshevik program. Thus ended the democratic revolution in Russia. Strangely enough, the abrupt demise of a legislative organ of which so much had been expected caused little more than a ripple of protest. The hungry and war-weary masses were not concerned about the process of democracy. There are some who contend that the results might have been different had the assembly been held, as originally planned, in the summer of 1917.

With the passing of the Constituent Assembly, no political forum remained for the opponents of Bolshevism. Nor was any to be permitted. On December 20, 1917, Lenin ordered the creation of a Special Commission for the Suppression of Counter-Revolution, Sabotage, and Profiteering, better known as the Cheka, of which the Polish Bolshevik Felix Dzherzhinsky was named head.

BOLSHEVIK STRATEGY IN THE EAST

Realizing that as yet they did not have the wholehearted support of the Russian population, especially of the Slavic element, nor tangible backing from the European proletariat, the Bolsheviks turned to the East, in particular to the Muslim East inside and outside the Russian borders. Although ostensibly anticipating a revolution in the West, they turned their heavy propaganda artillery toward the East, where they expected more tangible results. Although many European workers sympathized with the Bolshevik Revolution, they were not ready to submit themselves to Russian leadership. In the Orient, however, the Bolsheviks sensed their opportunity to assume command. Indeed, within a month of their seizure of power, on December 5 (November 22 O.S.), 1917, the Council of People's Commissars of the Bolshevik regime issued a highly significant "Appeal to the Muslims of Russia and the East."

"Appeal" to the Muslims. This Appeal (see below) amounted to a new definition of the October Revolution. Although Lenin had long foreseen a revolution in Europe and in the European colonial world, the Bolsheviks had heretofore emphasized Europe. This document, however, stated that the main purpose of the revolution was the liberation of the Orient, especially the adjacent Muslim Orient, with Russia's Muslims serving as the vanguard. Although the Bolsheviks had successfully seized power, they lacked the military might to impose their revolution upon the Great Powers or even to render substantial aid to European proletariats in a class struggle. Subversion was their chief weapon, and even this they sensed could be used more effectively in Asia. With the armed might of the Allies and Central Powers concentrated in Europe, the peripheral areas of their empires and their traditional spheres of influence were exposed. Lenin and his followers, who direly needed help from any available source, envisaged the possibility of rallying the subject peoples of the colonial world to their side, of assuming leadership among them, and using them to weaken and eventually overthrow the capitalist world. In other words, they proclaimed their intention of joining forces with dependent peoples who were even more backward than Russia to achieve their new world order. In December 1917, their appeal to the Muslims of the Orient was tantamount to the creation of a second front against the West in Germany's favor, and the agitation it promoted may have accelerated the Allied, especially the British, intervention in Russia.

Appeal to the Muslims of Russia and the East

Comrades! Brothers!

Great events are taking place in Russia. The end of the sanguinary war, begun over the partitioning of foreign lands, is drawing near. Under the blows of the Russian Revolution, the old edifice of slavery and serfdom is crumbling. The world of arbitrary rule and oppression is approaching its last days. A new world is being born, a world of the toilers and the liberated. At the head of this revolution stands the workers' and peasants' government of Russia, the Council of People's Commissars.

All Russia is dotted with revolutionary councils of workers', soldiers', and peasants' deputies. Power in the country is in the hands of the people. The laboring people of Russia are burning with the single desire to achieve an honorable peace and to help the downtrodden peoples of the world to win their freedom.

In this sacred cause, Russia does not stand alone. The mighty call to freedom sounded by the Russian Revolution is being taken up by all the toilers of the West and East. Exhausted by the war, the peoples of Europe are already stretching out their hands to us, working for peace. The workers and soldiers of the West are already rallying under the banner of socialism, storming the strongholds of imperialism. Even far-off India, the very country which has been oppressed for centuries by "enlightened" European plunderers, has already raised the standard of revolt, organizing its councils of deputies, casting off from its shoulders the hated yoke of slavery, and summoning the peoples of the East to the struggle and to liberation.

The empire of capitalist plunder and violence is crumbling. The ground under the feet of the imperialist plunderers is on fire.

In the face of these great events, we turn to you, the toiling and underprivileged Muslims of Russia and the East.

Muslims of Russia, Tatars of the Volga and the Crimea, Kirghiz and Sarts of Siberia and Turkestan, Turks and Tatars of Transcaucasia, Chechens and Caucasian mountaineers—all you, whose mosques and shrines, whose faiths and customs have been violated by the Tsars and oppressors of Russia!

Henceforth your beliefs and customs, your national and cultural institutions, are decreed free and inviolable! Build your national life freely and without hindrance. You have the right to do it. Know that your rights, like those of all the peoples of Russia, are being protected by all the might of the Revolution, and by its organs, the councils of workers', soldiers', and peasants' deputies.

Therefore support this Revolution and its authorized government!

Muslims of the East, Persians, Turks, Arabs, and Hindus! All you in whose lives and property, in whose freedom and native land the rapacious European plunderers have for centuries traded! All you whose countries the robbers who began the war now desire to partition!

We declare that the secret treaties of the dethroned Tsar regarding the seizure of Constantinople, which was confirmed by the deposed Kerensky, now are null and void. The Russian Republic and its government, the Council of People's Commissars, are against the seizure of foreign territories. Constantinople must remain in the hands of the Muslims.

We declare that the treaty for the partition of Persia is null and void. As soon as military operations cease, the armed forces will be withdrawn from Persia and the Persians will be guaranteed the right of free determination of their own destiny.

We declare that the treaty for the partition of Turkey, which was to deprive her of Armenia, is null and void. As soon as military operations cease, the Armenians will be guaranteed the right of free determination of their political destiny.

It is not from Russia and her revolutionary government that enslavement awaits you, but from the European imperialist robbers, from those who have transformed your native land into a "colony" to be plundered and robbed.

Overthrow these robbers and enslavers of your countries! Now, when war and desolation are demolishing the pillars of the old order, when the whole world is blazing with indignation against the imperialist usurpers, when any spark of indignation is transformed into a mighty flame of revolution, when even the Indian Muslims, oppressed and tormented by the foreign yoke, are rising in revolt against their subjugators—now, it is impossible to remain silent. Lose no time in throwing off the yoke of the ancient oppressors of your lands! Let them no longer rob your hearths! You yourselves must build your own life in your own way and in your own likeness. You have the right to do this, for your destiny is in your own hands!

Comrades! Brothers!

Let us advance together firmly and resolutely towards a just and democratic peace.

Our banners bring liberation to the oppressed peoples of the world.

Muslims of Russia!

Muslims of the East!

On this road to the regeneration of the world, we look to you for sympathy and support.

DZHUGASHVILI STALIN, People's Commissar for National Affairs.

V. ULYANOV (Lenin), President of the People's Commissars.

A careful analysis of the "Appeal to the Muslims" and of other literature pertaining to the period suggests that the Soviet government believed the success of the Bolshevik Revolution to be contingent upon its alliance with the Muslim Orient. In other words, the success of the October Revolution and the liberation of the Muslim world were regarded as inseparable and interdependent. One could not be achieved or endure without the other.

In retrospect, we may safely say that the main purpose of the Council of Commissars in 1917 was to create the impression that the Bolshevik Revolution, as distinguished from the March Revolution, had as its mission the liberation of the Oreint, in particular the Muslim Orient. In fact, the Bolsheviks made many of their own Muslims believe, at least temporarily, that it was the hand of Providence that brought about the Bolshevik Revolution. Russian Muslims even spread propaganda to the effect that the Soviet regime would be established on the principles of the Koran and the Shariat. Many ignorant Muslims compared Muhammed with Lenin and the Koran with the teachings of Bolshevism.

The "Appeal" of the Council of People's Commissars likewise marked a turning point in the attitude of Muslims toward Russia. As a result of Bolshevik denunciation of tsarist imperialism and renunciation of tsarist claims on Constantinople and the Straits, as well as of all treaties that infringed on the sovereign rights of adjacent Muslim states, Muslim hatred of Russia was mitigated, at least temporarily. As commissar of nationalities, Stalin was particularly concerned with the problems of colonial and dependent peoples; he emphasized this in an article in *Pravda,* November 7, 1923, on "The October Revolution and the Question of the Middle Strata":

> . . . the fact that Russia, which formerly served as the symbol of oppression in the eyes of the oppressed nationalities, has now, after it has become socialist, been transformed into a symbol of liberation, cannot be described as a mere chance. Nor is it accidental that the name of Comrade Lenin, the leader of the October Revolution, is now the most cherished name of the downtrodden, browbeaten peasants and revolutionary intelligentsia of the colonial and semienfranchised countries. If formerly Christianity was considered an anchor of salvation among the oppressed and downtrodden slaves of the vast Roman Empire, now things are heading towards a point where socialism can serve (and is already beginning to serve!) as a banner of liberation for the many millions in the vast colonial states of imperialism.

By denouncing all tsarist special privileges and territorial claims on the countries of the Muslim world temporarily, at least, Russia became "a symbol of liberation" for the oppressed colonial and semicolonial peoples. It was logical, therefore, that England in the eyes of many Muslims should supersede Russia as "the symbol of oppression." Prior to World War I, England controlled the largest area of Muslims; at the conclusion of that conflict she appreciably extended rather than diminished the area, which stretched from Egypt to India. It stands to reason, therefore, that England became the main target of Soviet propaganda. This propaganda took deep root among Muslims and other Asians.

New Definition of the Eastern Question. In view of their identification of the Bolshevik Revolution with Muslim liberation, Soviet leaders revised the traditional concept of the Eastern Question; to the average person under the tsarist regime this had meant the partition of the Ottoman Empire, including the Russian threat to Constantinople, the Dardanelles, and the Bosphorus. Not only did the Soviet government publicly renounce the secret treaties by which the tsarist regime paved the way for further annexations, but it redefined the Eastern Question as one which involved Soviet aid for the liberation of enslaved peoples from domination by "England, France, the United States, and other capitalist countries." Moscow was to become "the Mecca and Medina of all enslaved peoples." Moreover, the Soviets broadened still further the scope of the Eastern Question, by including therein the problems of oppressed colonial peoples everywhere—not merely in Asia:

> The Orient is not only the oppressed Asiatic world. The Orient is the entire colonial world, the world of oppressed peoples, not only in Asia, but also in Africa and South America; in short, the entire world on whose exploitation rests the might of capitalist society in Europe and the United States. European and American capitalism draws its chief strength, not from industrial European countries, but from their colonial possessions.

The extent to which the Soviet government identified the interests of the Soviet regime with those of the new Orient was clearly indicated by M. Pavlovitch, when he said: "A war against any of these countries of the Orient is a war against the USSR, just as a war against the USSR is a war against the Orient." Thus in the Soviet interpretation of the October Revolution one can easily detect the signs of a new Soviet imperialism, which later developed on a global scale, and which constituted a threat not only to the West but to the Orient itself.

Complications. Subsequent events prevented the Bolsheviks from taking effective measures to implement this call to revolution. Early in 1918 the German-dictated Treaty of Brest-Litovsk (see also page 326), which recognized the independence of the Ukraine, Poland, Finland, Esthonia, Latvia, Lithuania, and Georgia, and surrendered to Turkey the Transcaucasian provinces of Kars and Ardahan, including Batum, virtually dismembered Russia in Europe. Immediately thereafter the Bolsheviks were placed on the defensive by the intervention of Great Britain, France, the United States, Turkey, and Japan to stem the tide of revolution and to support the White Russian armies engaged in civil war with the Communists. The counter-revolutionary forces of Denikin and Kolchak, as well as those of the British and French invaders, made regular communication with the Muslim East impossible for some time.

Impact of the October Revolution. The significance of the October Revolution as the first revolution among the underdeveloped countries, pointing the way to a succession of others in Asia and Africa, was not grasped in 1917. Nor was this surprising. The October *coup d'état* itself was not generally recognized at the time as one of the major events of the twentieth century, the event which would transform backward Russia and the minorities on her southern periphery before midcentury into one of the world's leading industrial powers.

Nor was Bolshevik interpretation of the real goal of the October Revolution—the liberation of the colonial, especially the Muslim, world under Russian leadership—understood in the West. Amid the vicissitudes that followed, Lenin and his followers soon learned that they must first transform backward Russia by the process of modernization and industrialization before they could hope to rally the still more backward colonial world in support of revolution. Years later, when the movement for the national liberation of dependent peoples was well under way, the significance of the new Soviet definition of the October Revolution became clarified and the Soviet regime sought once again to capitalize upon it.

18

Peace, Civil War, and Foreign

Intervention, 1918-1921

PEACE

A Separate Peace. The first major foreign policy issue confronted by the new Soviet regime was the conclusion of peace with the Central Powers. Lenin's "Decree on Peace" of November 8 had called on all the belligerents to negotiate a peace without annexations and indemnities. It stated without equivocation that revolutionary Russia was through with the traditional methods of secret diplomacy. When neither the Allied nor the enemy powers responded to this Bolshevik overture, the Soviet regime on November 21 directed General Dukhonin, Russian commander-in-chief, to enter into direct negotiations with the Germans for an armistice. On the following day Leon Trotsky notified the Allied ambassadors in Petrograd of the Soviet peace move and called for an armistice on all fronts, preparatory to the negotiation of a general peace. Hard pressed on the western front, Russia's allies bitterly rejected Trotsky's proposal. They ignored the timely warning of Sir George Buchanan, British ambassador in Petrograd, that Allied opposition to the conclusion of a separate peace by the Bolsheviks was likely to redound to the advantage of the Germans.[1] General Dukhonin, who, to his own undoing, followed Allied advice and defied Soviet orders to seek an armistice, was lynched by Russian soldiers. Shortly thereafter Adolph A. Joffe (Yoffe) succeeded in arranging an armistice effective December 17.

Treaty of Brest-Litovsk. The members of the Bolshevik peace delegation which met at Brest-Litovsk conducted themselves as revolutionists rather than as negotiators. Reluctant to conform to the traditional procedures of diplomacy, they rejected all social contacts with their German counterparts, perhaps hoping thereby to make a favorable impression on the German proletariat. The Russian bargaining position vis-à-vis the Germans was extremely weak. Although German Foreign Minister von Kühlmann yielded to Bolshevik pressure for a peace without annexations, he did so on condition that all the belligerent powers follow suit. General Max von Hoffman of the German High Command soon forced the Bolshevik delegation to confront the

---

1. Sir George Buchanan, *My Mission to Russia,* 2 Vols. (Boston, 1923), pp. 225 ff.

cold reality of German military power by interpreting "self-determination" to mean German annexation of any occupied Russian territories whose peoples expressed a preference to join Germany. Trotsky, who joined the Russian peace delegation on January 7, 1918, admitted that the Bolsheviks pursued stalling tactics with the intent of using the negotiations to incite an uprising of the German and Austro-Hungarian proletariats, which would obviate the necessity of a formal treaty.[2] The anticipated European revolutions, however, failed to materialize on schedule. On January 18, General von Hoffman presented Germany's terms—acceptance of the existing boundary between German and Russian forces, which detached from Russia all Poland, Lithuania, and western Latvia, including Riga, and left the Ukrainian boundary to' be settled by the Germans and the Ukraine. A stunned but angry Trotsky returned to Petrograd to confer with his associates.

Russian Reaction. The Russian people, who were content to demand peace at any price, had no concept of what that price would be. The harshness of the German terms precipitated a serious dispute among Bolshevik leaders as to the course to be pursued. Unlike the tsars, whose prerogatives included the making of arbitrary foreign-policy decisions, Lenin was in no position to assume that responsibility. Following the Bolshevik Revolution important foreign-policy matters, as the Treaty of Brest-Litovsk clearly demonstrated, were not even made by the Council of People's Commissars, but by the Central Committee of the Communist Party. Lenin was a master in the art of persuasion, and in the final analysis, he could exert intolerable pressure by threatening to resign. His major task, however, was to convince his associates of the rightness of his position in favor of the acceptance of the German peace terms. In this respect, he had the backing of Kamenev, Zinoviev, and Stalin. Trotsky, who found the humiliating terms intolerable, favored continued procrastination, by one means or another, until the anticipated revolution occurred in Germany. If all else failed, he contended that Russia should withdraw unilaterally from the war and pursue a policy of "neither war nor peace." Nikolai Bukharin, an extremist, called for outright rejection of the German terms, followed by the proclamation of "a revolutionary war." His intransigeance appealed to the Party's Left wing, especially to Joffe, Dzherzhinsky, and Radek.

Convinced that any continuation of the war would strengthen the "imperialist" democracies and further postpone revolution in the West, Lenin continued to hammer away at the impossibility of conducting a military offensive and the indispensability of a breathing spell for the establishment of the socialist revolution in Russia. The reorganization and consolidation of the new regime, bolstered by the creation of a Red Army of peasants and workers, would make socialism invincible at home and abroad. Both Lenin and Trotsky anticipated a revolution in Germany. Lenin, the more realistic,

2. Leon Trotsky, *Lenin* (London, 1921), p. 128.

expected it to follow rather than to precede the collapse of the German armed forces.

Trotsky's Compromise. On January 30, however, Trotsky returned to Brest-Litovsk with the Party's authorization to try out his compromise plan. The Soviet position deteriorated on February 9, when the Germans concluded a separate peace with the Ukrainian *Rada* just as Bolshevik forces occupied Kiev. Trotsky's bombshell, the announcement of Russia's unilateral withdrawal from the conflict to pursue "neither war nor peace" failed to work. The German army began its advance into Russia on February 18, meeting little or no resistance from the demoralized Russian forces. Bolshevik recruitment of men for the Red Army had barely begun. Although the Russian forces rallied on February 21 when Lenin proclaimed that the "Socialist Fatherland was in danger," the situation was untenable. With Petrograd so close to the frontier, the capital of Peter the Great was abandoned for Moscow, where it has since remained. The Russians had no alternative but to resume normal diplomatic negotiations with the Germans and to accept their terms, although German military leaders raised the price of peace.

Ratification. With Petrograd in danger, Lenin refused to "play with war any longer." There was no sign of an imminent German revolution. The Russian situation was fast deteriorating, especially in the south where opposition to the Soviet regime was increasing. He set out to convince his associates that the German-dictated peace—in his terms, a Tilsit peace—would in reality be nothing more than a truce, which could be broken as soon as revolution occurred in the West. He demanded a retreat on the foreign front in order to preserve the Bolshevik power at home. Unless the terms were accepted, he threatened to resign. The unhappy Social Revolutionaries and Mensheviks, who had backed Lenin's domestic program, protested this decision with great bitterness and withdrew their support from the government. Lenin's ultimatum was nevertheless accepted. Trotsky was soon shifted to the post of commissar of war, and a new commisar of foreign affairs, G. V. Chicherin, was dispatched to Brest-Litovsk. On March 3, 1918, the Bolshevik delegation signed the Treaty of Brest-Litovsk as if it were an ultimatum, without further discussion of the terms, in order to halt the German advance into Russia. It was ratified by the Congress of Soviets, March 16, by a vote of 784 to 261. In its official history, the Communist Party credited Lenin with teaching it how to retreat in good order against superior enemy forces, in order to devote its energies to a new offensive.[3] In this respect, the Treaty of Brest-Litovsk may be regarded as a "model" decision in Soviet foreign policy.[4]

Results of the Treaty. Under the terms of this treaty, Russia was compelled to recognize the independence of the Ukraine, Poland, Finland, Esthonia,

---

3. *History of the Communist Party of the Soviet Union (Bolsheviks) Short Course* (New York: International Publishers, 1939), p. 219.
4. Richard Pipes, "Domestic Politics and Foreign Affairs," in Ivo Lederer, ed., *Russian Foreign Policy* (New Haven, Conn.: Yale University Press, 1962), p. 166.

Latvia, and Lithuania, and to surrender, at the last minute, the Provinces of Kars and Ardahan in Transcaucasia to Turkey. In a subsequent treaty between the Central Powers and Rumania on March 9 the Russians lost Bessarabia.

To secure peace at any price the Bolsheviks thus sacrificed almost 522,676 square miles of territory with a population of about 66,000,000 people. At one fell stroke, the treaty deprived Russia of nearly all the territory acquired since the accession of Peter the Great, including the window on the Baltic. In specific terms, Russia lost 34 per cent of her population, 32 per cent of her

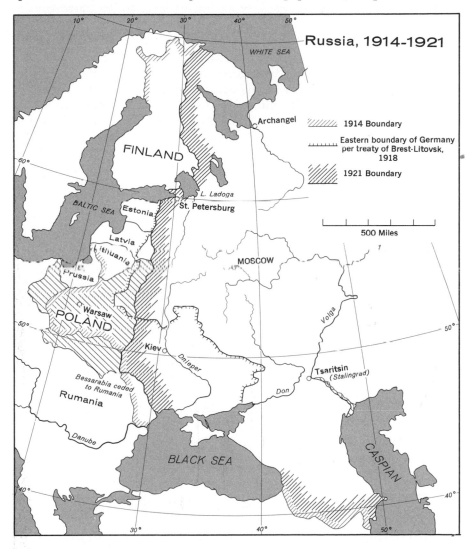

agricultural land, 85 per cent of her sugar-beet land, 54 per cent of her industrial enterprises, and 89 per cent of her coal mines. The Ukraine was the Russian breadbasket and the center of Russian heavy industry. By a codicil to the treaty in August, 1918, the Bolsheviks further agreed to the demobilization of the Russian army and fleet, the payment of an indemnity of six million marks, and some additional German commercial rights in Russia.

This German "peace by violence" appeared to reduce Russia to a German satellite, or at least a colonial hinterland for German exploitation—a prospect which greatly alarmed Russia's former allies. The unconditional Bolshevik repudiation on February 10, 1918, of all foreign loans to the tsarist government greatly reduced the chance of a reconciliation between the revolutionary regime and the Western powers. There were tentative contacts between Trotsky and three semi-official representatives of the Allied powers: Colonel Raymond B. Robins, head of the American Red Cross Mission to Russia; R. H. Bruce Lockhart, British special agent; and Captain Jacques Sadoul of the French Military Mission in Petrograd. As late as March 5 Trotsky sounded out Colonel Robins as to possible American reaction to a Soviet rejection of the treaty, but there was no response. These men were not in a position to make a specific offer, and time was pressing.

The Fourteen Points. President Wilson's famous Fourteen Points, issued on January 8, were in one sense a response to the Russian predicament. The sixth point called for the "evacuation of all Russian territory," assurance to Russia of "a sincere welcome into the society of free nations under institutions of her own choosing," and assistance "of every kind that she may need and may herself desire." No immediate steps were taken, however, to implement the Wilsonian program, and the Bolshevik leaders had no faith in the prompt remittance of substantial allied aid. In a message addressed to President Wilson, October 24, 1918, Foreign Commissar Chicherin pointedly remarked that although the Fourteen Points specified independence for Poland, Serbia, Belgium, and the peoples of Austria-Hungary, they omitted any reference to freedom for Ireland, Egypt, India, or even to liberation of the Philippines, in which the Soviet government was equally interested.

Within five days of the Russian ratification of the Treaty of Brest-Litovsk the Germans launched their 1918 spring offensive on the western front, which very nearly ended in catastrophe for the Allies. No sooner had the Soviet regime established diplomatic relations with the German victor on the eastern front than it proceeded, under the cloak of diplomatic immunity, to spread Communist propaganda to undermine the German government.

CIVIL WAR AND INTERVENTION

There were many reasons for the outbreak of civil war in Russia, but the greatest of these was the Peace of Brest-Litovsk. By accepting the German terms the Bolsheviks, even at the risk of the disruption of the Party, had redeemed their pledge to the Russian people. Peace with dismemberment, however, could have been achieved under the tsarist and Kerensky regimes. Lenin's decision was highly unpopular among many Russians who felt that the price of peace was too high. The Soviet regime still confronted the problem of supplying the population with bread, a task rendered virtually impossible by the loss of the Ukraine, Russia's principal breadbasket.

Food Rationing. The Soviet government did not increase its popularity by the measures undertaken to end the food shortages. Its first concern was to meet the needs of the urban areas, where both its staunchest supporters and bitterest enemies were to be found. Confronting a shortage of practically all the necessities of life, the government on June 28, 1918, nationalized large-scale industry and requisitioned available food supplies. The following November private trade was outlawed, with the intention of substituting state and cooperative stories. Private banks were likewise nationalized, although this alone did nothing to stem the tide of inflation. A system of rationing was instituted, with the twofold purpose of providing food for all and insuring support for the government, since opponents of the regime could be deprived of ration cards, which, under existing conditions, amounted to a sentence to starvation. The amount of food a citizen could obtain was in direct proportion to his rating by the Soviet regime. The city population was classified in several categories: Communists, government employees, craftsmen, and unemployed. Members of the former nobility, bourgeoisie, and intelligentsia were among the "declassed" or unproductive element who received no ration cards. Theirs was a sad plight indeed, and sufficient cause for their joining organized forces committed to the overthrow of the Soviet regime.

In Russia, where bread was literally the staff of life, a ration card providing only about half a pound per day—about half the normal consumption—was wholly inadequate. The other items comprising a well-filled dinner plate— meat, herring, vegetables, and dairy products—had either disappeared from the market or were extremely scarce and expensive. The shortage of bread alone was sufficient to make any government unpopular. In many provincial towns the excessive zeal of some local commissars in confiscating surplus suits, coats, shirts, chairs, and sundry household articles, which came under the heading of "disrobing the bourgeoisie," increased popular discontent.

Nor did all the measures taken by the government to ration food in the cities end the shortages. It was therefore compelled to seek new sources of food supply from the rural population, comprising almost four-fifths of the nation. Having responded with avidity to Bolshevik propaganda during the Kerensky regime, the peasants had appropriated the property of the large landed estates and crown lands to satisfy their land hunger. They now displayed little or no interest in providing farm produce for the urban population, which had little but worthless paper money to offer in exchange.

"Food Battalions." Since the peasants were not to be persuaded, the Soviet government, impelled by sheer economic desperation, resorted to force to secure compliance, by dispatching "Food Battalions" to villages to requisition

farm products. These tactics quickly led to organized resistance on the part of entire villages, assisted by armed peasant war veterans who had taken advantage of the disintegration of the armed forces to return home and secure land for themselves. Some villages even managed to acquire artillery to emphasize their defiance. Peasant liquidation of the "Food Battalions" led to Soviet destruction of their villages, some of which were literally razed to the ground.

Population Classification. To combat unified opposition in the villages, the Soviet regime sought to induce a *Klassenkampf* (class struggle) by classifying the rural population in line with the policy already pursued in the towns and cities. The peasants were divided into *kulaki,* or rich peasants, whose income exceeded $88 per anum; *seredniaki,* or middle peasants, who earned about $46 per year; *bedniaki,* or poor peasants, whose earnings amounted to no more than $39 per year; and *batraki,* or hired farm laborers. The *bedniaki,* organized into Committees of the Poor, were authorized to seize surplus grain and cattle from their well-to-do neighbors. Meanwhile, the government substituted a state grain monopoly for private trade in that commodity. In spite of the bitter class war in the villages, which impeded their program, the Soviets managed to introduce a few state and collective farms during this period.

By such measures the government restored a modicum of order to city and rural areas under its control. The class struggle in the countryside, however, propelled the Social Revolutionaries into open and organized opposition to the Soviet regime. Resorting once again to acts of terrorism, on July 6, 1918, they assassinated Count Mirbach-Harff, the German ambassador in Moscow, followed on July 30 by the assassination of the German commander in the Ukraine, Field Marshal Hermann von Eichorn.

Finland. Although the Peace of Brest-Litovsk ended the conflict with the Central Powers, the Soviet regime continued to confront a hostile world. On March 7, 1918, the German government made peace with an anti-Soviet regime in Finland, which was engaged in bitter conflict with a Finnish Socialist government supported by Moscow. Shortly thereafter a German army under General von der Goltz was dispatched to Finland to suppress the revolutionary forces. German intervention was a determining factor in the victory of Baron Mannerheim's anti-Soviet regime. The Germans also occupied the entire Ukraine and even pushed beyond it to the Crimea, much to the distress of the Soviet government, which ordered the scuttling of the Black Sea fleet to prevent its seizure.

Repudiation of Debts. The German threat, however, was soon superseded by the hostile attitude of Russia's former allies, based upon Soviet conclusion of a separate peace with Germany, repudiation of all foreign debts, Soviet propaganda for world revolution, and the persecution of religion. Today, with the advantage of hindsight, it is clear that the Soviet government's repudiation of foreign debts, incurred by the tsarist and Kerensky regimes, was one of the first and greatest blunders of the new revolutionary regime. This hasty action created for the Bolsheviks a lasting reputation for unreliability throughout the capitalist world, especially in France, where Russian bonds for tsarist loans were widely distributed among the population. The only hope such investors had of retrieving their losses was the overthrow of the revolutionary regime, and they were tempted to support any kind of movement designed to achieve this end. Repudiation of debts was, of course, a Bolshevik means of defying the capitalist world, which, in any event, was not expected to survive. As Communists, the Soviet leaders were not concerned about maintaining Soviet integrity in the eyes of capitalist regimes. Even a token payment, or a request for a moratorium, might have restrained the business interests of creditor nations from backing the military intervention of their governments in Russia. In subsequent years, neither the Hitler nor the Mussolini regimes committed this mistake.

The Red Army. The Peace of Brest-Litvosk demonstrated the appalling military impotence of the Soviet regime. The Bolsheviks had reaped the fruit of their propaganda campaign for the destruction of the remnants of morale in the imperial army. On February 23, the Council of People's Commissars proclaimed the establishment of a Red Army of Workers and Peasants, based on the volunteer principle. Its nucleus was the reliable Red Guard, supplemented by some foreign battalions of Letts, Chinese, Finns, and German prisoners of war. In April, when it was evident that the "voluntary" forces were inadequate to defend the new regime, Leon Trotsky as commissar of war undertook to organize the Red Army as a well-disciplined military force of regular troops. The election of commanding officers was scrapped, and compulsory military service was introduced by stages. Because of the dearth of officers available to the Bolshevik cause, many of those who served the old regime were conscripted. To improve discipline the death penalty was restored and deserters were shot upon capture. For propaganda purposes and for the surveillance of the officer corps, Trotsky initiated the practice of appointing political commissars in the army. By September, 1918, after conscription was extended throughout Bolshevik-controlled territory, the Red Army had increased to 450,000, and by the end of the year it reached 790,000. During the Civil War it was probably unable to place more than 600,000 troops in action at any one time. Its forces, which had the strategic advantage of inner lines of communication, were nevertheless poorly clad, underfed, and inadequately equipped with arms and ammunition inherited from the old regime. Among its most outstanding officers were Semyon Budënny, Klementy Voroshilov, and Joseph Stalin, the last two of whom rose to fame in the Red Army's defense of Tsaritsyn (Stalingrad, now Volgograd) in the fall of 1918.

The organization of the Red Army came none too soon. In the spring of 1918 the Soviet regime had a firm grip on part of central and northern Russia. The rest of the country was split among various anti-Bolshevik warlords and governments. A Polish legion was active in the northeast, a Czechoslovak legion in the south. Ukrainians and Cossacks offered armed resistance to the Soviets in the Don and Kuban areas, in the Urals, and in Siberia. Many alienated tsarist officers, some of whom had been involved in the Kornilov mutiny, gravitated to south Russia in the hope of rescuing the country from the disgrace of the Treaty of Brest-Litovsk and the grip of the Bolsheviks. In Georgia the Mensheviks established their own regime in Tiflis. Victor Chernov and his outlawed Social Revolutionaries formed another nucleus on the lower Volga. In the Transbaikal, Ataman Gregory Semenov, an unscrupulous monarchist known for his brutality, seized control. In Manchuria, General Horvath, a conservative of the old regime, was entrenched at Harbin, defending the Chinese Eastern Railway. For a time the SR's held Vladivostok.

The White Army. In south Russia, which was to become the main theatre of resistance to the Soviets, General M. V. Alexeyev and General Kornilov organized a Volunteer Army to restore the Empire. They appealed for recruits in the name of resistance to the "German-Bolshevik" invasion, the defense of liberty, and the Constituent Assembly. Out of more than 300,000 former officers, it is estimated that fewer than 3,000 joined the Volunteer Army. Its strength came from its organization and the military experience of its personnel, as well as from its zeal in combatting Communism. At times, however, its numbers sank to no more than 1,000 men. Under General Anton Denikin, Kornilov's successor, it emerged as the chief threat to the Soviet regime.

The miscellaneous forces that organized to overthrow Bolshevism came to be known as the "White" armies, not because there was any connection between them and the geographical area of White Russia, but merely to distinguish them from the Red Army which they fought from 1918 to 1920. Had these splintered forces ever combined, they might have overcome the Red Army, but this they never succeeded in doing. The principal divisions of the White armies were those led by General Anton Denikin in south Russia, General Nicholas Yudenitch in the Baltic region, and Admiral Alexander Kolchak in the north and in Siberia. Kolchak, the former commander of the Black Sea Fleet, enjoyed the prestige with the Allies which was a prerequisite to military assistance. Following a *coup d'état* in Omsk, Siberia, in November, 1918, he was installed as "Supreme Ruler" of all Russian military and naval forces. His leadership was accepted by the other commanders, including General Denikin. It was through Kolchak that the Allied War Council in Paris arranged for military aid to the White armies. When Kolchak met death at the hands of the Soviets in February, 1920, White leadership passed to Denikin.

Terrorism. Both the Red and White armies, alternately advancing and retreating across the European and Asian countryside of the former Russian Empire, committed unbelievable atrocities which alienated the Russian population. In some areas, especially in those beyond the surveillance of foreign consuls, the White terror exceeded the Red terror. After seizing a city their troops, many of them Cossacks, were given *carte blanche* to ravage and pillage the place for from one to three days. They went on a rampage for loot and booty, often seizing both the possessions of the local inhabitants and their women. On the Don the Red forces slew White prisoners and wounded soldiers, in retaliation for which the White volunteers staged mass executions. In Siberia, Kolchak's prestige was irreparably damaged by such notorious bandits as Kalmykov, Semënov, Annenkov, and Rozanov. One of the most notorious was the fanatical Baron Ungern Sternberg, of Baltic descent, whose efforts to create a large Mongolia and to become a new Attila resulted in atrocities which rivaled those of Genghis Khan. Such uncontrolled bestiality, especially from forces which claimed to be fighting for the salvation of Russia, impelled many disillusioned Russians to switch to the Soviet side.

W. S. Woytinsky, reporting in his memoirs of the revolution the tale of a shocked and disillusioned White Army soldier in Georgia, has reflected the impact of both Red and White atrocities on the common man:

> ". . . We took a village. The Reds fled. I came to the church. Its door stood wide open. I went in. In front of the altar lay dead men, their skulls shattered by butts, their brains blown out. Among them was the priest, an old man in a black cassock. The door of the altar was broken to bits. The altar itself was filthy and stinking; it had been used as a privy. Is this not a sacrilege?"
>
> I nodded. He went on looking past me, as if speaking to himself. "A sacrilege! But across the green, in front of the church, was the house of the village council. A man had been nailed to the boards of the fence. Naked, dead, his hands and feet pierced by nails, as if crucified. His toes charred. The remains of a fire on the ground beneath him. And over his head a board with a single word scribbled in large letters: *Commie*. Our men had done that. Russian, Christian men! Is that not also a sacrilege? What hope is left to us? . . ."[5]

Readers of Mikhail Sholokhov's best-selling Soviet novel, *The Silent Don,* will recall the plight of Gregory Melekhov, who transferred his allegiance from the Reds to the Whites and back to the Reds, but emerged from it all with no horizon left.

Czechoslovak Legion. One of the strangest and most remarkable episodes of the Civil War was the participation in the struggle of the Czechoslovak Legion, originally created by the tsarist regime from the ranks of Austro-Hungarian prisoners of war with the object of liberating the Czechs from Austrian rule. They were used effectively by Kerensky in his offensive on the German front, after which they were permitted to organize as a separate unit and were billeted in the Ukraine. After the Bolshevik Revolution this Czech corps, numbering approximately forty thousand, remained for some time the

5. W. S. Woytinsky, *Stormy Passage: A Personal History Through Two Russian Revolutions to Democracy and Freedom: 1905–1960* (New York: Vanguard Press, 1961), p. 417.

only well-organized military force in Russia. It received its instructions from the Czech National Council in Paris, headed by Professor Thomas Masaryk (later the first president of the Czechoslovak Republic), who had been instrumental in setting up the corps.

After Brest-Litovsk, the Czechs sought and obtained permission from the Soviet regime to evacuate their forces to France by sea from Vladivostok, and by May, 1918, some ten thousand reached the Pacific. About this time the Germans put pressure on the Council of People's Commissars to halt the evacuation. Either for this reason, or because of local incidents between the Czechs and Soviet supporters, on May 25 Trotsky ordered them to surrender their arms or be shot. The prospect of disarmament and internment precipitated hostilities between the Czechs and the Red forces. Having seized Samara (Kuibyshev) on the Volga on June 21, the Czech corps spread rapidly eastward by way of the Trans-Siberian Railway from the Volga to Vladivostok, successfully seizing control of the principal cities along the route. They reached Ekaterinburg just a week too late to save the imperial family from execution by the Bolsheviks. The Allied Powers, who had good reason to be impressed by the remarkable military feats of the Czech corps, which increased to about sixty thousand en route to Vladivostok, laid plans to use it as the nucleus of a new eastern front against the Germans. The pretext of safeguarding the Czechs was one of the chief reasons advanced for Anglo-French-Japanese-American intervention in Russia.

Allied Intervention. Originally, the idea of foreign intervention in Russia was directed not so much against the Soviet regime as it was toward the reconstitution of the eastern front against the Germans. Apprehensive lest substantial stores of Allied arms and ammunition located at Murmansk, Vladivostok, and Harbin should fall into the hands of the Germans following the Peace of Brest-Litovsk, the English and French, in particular, began to support the landing of Allied troops. Small forces of Allied and American marines were landed in Murmansk as early as March, 1918, without opposition from local Soviet authorities or from the central government. The success of the Czechoslovak corps, which occupied Vladivostok on June 29, precipitated further action.

Due to divergent motives, the Allied Powers were sharply divided on the subject of intervention. For some, intervention offered a splendid opportunity to carve out new spheres of influence of great economic and strategic advantage. All were concerned about the collapse of the eastern front and its implications for the Allied offensive in the west. The French viewed intervention as a means of overthrowing the radical socialist Soviet regime. The Japanese, who benefited most from the collapse of the Russian Empire and who had high hopes of exploiting the forest and mineral resources of eastern Siberia, were willing and anxious to take the initiative. The use of Japanese troops to bolster the sagging eastern front during World War I had received strong support from the French, but was opposed by the United States on the ground that the "old enemy of 1905" would be unwelcome. Following the successful seizure of Far Eastern centers by some local soviets, the Japanese, on April 5, 1918, quickly landed a token force at Vladivostok. The English and French immediately exerted pressure on a reluctant United States to convert unilateral into inter-allied action. Here was a new version of the historic Straits Question, where unilateral intervention by Russia had invariably been opposed by the great powers.

In European Russia and Siberia President Wilson's objective was to prevail upon the Allies to subordinate expediency and strategy to idealism and morality. In Russia's dire extremity, he felt they should act as trustees of her territorial integrity, irrespective of the regime in power. Although some Americans already in the Far East and others, such as George Kennan, specialist on the Siberian prison system, actively and persistently called for intervention, Wilson's stand was corroborated by his cabinet and by American military personnel, including Major General William S. Graves, later commander of the American expeditionary force in Siberia. The policy of the major powers toward the new Soviet regime during these years was somewhat ambivalent, and the United States was no exception. Popular response in favor of aid for the embattled Czechs and the concern of American leaders for the containment of Japanese imperialistic designs on Siberia and Manchuria —a threat to the open door—enabled the Allies to overcome American resistance to intervention. In August, 1918, over 70,000 Japanese (whose troops were readily available) and smaller contingents of American and Allied troops landed at Vladivostok. Substantial forces also occupied Archangel on August 2. In December, following the armistice on the western front, the French sent a naval and military expedition to occupy Odessa on the Black Sea. The intervention, which soon resulted in substantial military aid to the White armies, amounted to an undeclared war against the Soviet regime.

British Policy. Meanwhile, the British government viewed the German-Turkish advance toward the Caucasus as a threat to British power in Iran, Afghanistan, and India. With the disintegration of the imperial armed forces during the Revolution, Russian columns withdrew from Iran, and Russian troops literally abandoned their weapons and equipment on the Turkish front. After the Treaty of Brest-Litovsk, the Germans advanced to Poti in the Caucasus and the Turks, having occupied Kars and Batum, crossed Armenia to Azerbaijan and northwestern Iran. With 35,000 Austro-Hungarian prisoners east of the Caspian in Turkestan, the Allies confronted the possibility that the Central Powers might acquire possession of Russian oil resources at Baku and Russian cotton production in Central Asia. To forestall such an eventuality, the British government in January, 1918, dispatched the Dunsterforce Mission (under Major-General L. C. Dunsterville) to Enzeli in northern Iran and later to Baku to keep the Turks under surveillance. A second small mission under Major-General W. Malleson proceeded under great difficulty from India to Krasnovodsk in Transcaspia (August, 1918) to maintain peace and order in Turkestan. Both missions were too small to prevent the Turks, prior to their collapse, from temporarily seizing Baku. Soviet propaganda, however, has accused England of supporting counter-revolution throughout the area and of planning the permanent occupation of Turkestan. The murder of the twenty-six commissars during the British retreat from Krasnovodsk, to all intents and purposes carried out by local Ashkhabad authorities, but attributed to Malleson, has become a Soviet revolutionary epic—a subject for poetry and drama. Following the collapse of their Turkish-German opponents, the British withdrew from the area. Early in 1920 the Soviets took Krasnovodsk, completing the reoccupation of Transcaspia. The dramatic intervention in the Russian Middle East proved to be just another instance of Allied effort to achieve major goals through the medium of heroic but wholly inadequate forces.

In colorful but extravagant terminology, Lenin described the Soviet power during these months as "an oasis in a raging sea of imperialist banditry." The remarkable fact about the Civil War and Intervention is that the Soviet regime, encircled by White armies aided by fourteen foreign powers located at strategic points on the Russian periphery in Europe and Asia, not only survived but emerged victorious. Some of the reasons were quite apparent.

Weakness of the Whites. One of the most striking weaknesses of the White forces was their failure to unite on a common platform for the postwar period, other than the overthrow of the Communist regime. In August, 1919, General Denikin did proclaim his intention of calling a Constituent Assembly, but his Cossack associate, General Shkuro, in this writer's presence repudiated the proclamation and asserted that as soon as they reached Moscow Denikin would disappear. The White leaders made no firm promises of land reform and gave no guarantees of the rights of minorities. In some instances, extremists in their midst took back land that had already been appropriated by the peasants. Others instigated pogroms against the Jews in the Ukraine and elsewhere. The foremost slogan of the White armies, "Russia: One and Indivisible," although it appealed to the majority of the Great Russians, aroused fear and hostility in the ranks of the minorities along the borderlands to whom it spelled a return to the Russification policies of Nicholas I and Alexander III. As already indicated, White atrocities contributed greatly to the alienation of the Russian population.

As had happened so often in Russia's past, the insurgent forces from the borderlands lost much of their effectiveness as they approached the heart of Great Russia. The very fact that the White armies belonged to the camp of the foreign interventionists aroused suspicions of further concessions to come at Russian expense. It gave the Red Army the appearance of fighting for Russia against foreign invaders. The Soviet regime, like its opponents, fought for a united Russia, but its promises of local autonomy and the right of self-determination, even when implemented only on paper, were less objectionable than the prospect of integration in "Russia: One and Indivisible." Moreoever, the Soviet government, which had not yet resorted to forced collectivization, had encouraged and sanctioned the distribution of the land to the peasantry. In contrast to the Whites whose military efforts lacked integration, the Soviet regime survived by mobilizing industry, agriculture, and manpower, in other words, by conducting "the first total war of the twentieth century."[6]

Polish Invasion of the Ukraine. One of the fatal errors of Denikin's successor, Baron Peter Wrangel, was his invitation to the Poles to join the struggle in south Russia for the overthrow of the Soviet regime. Under the leadership of Joseph Pilsudski, they invaded the Ukraine on April 20, 1920, and occupied Kiev. Many opponents of the Soviets, their nationalist sentiment outraged by Polish action, transferred their allegiance to the revolutionary regime. Even General Brusilov, who had remained in retirement in Mogilev following his dismissal by Kerensky, issued a call to all Russians to rally to the defense of their country and expel the invaders. The Red Army, buoyed up by its new popularity, drove the Poles from Kiev on July 6 and pursued them to the environs of Warsaw. Only Anglo-French threats of reprisals, together with the fact that the Red Army's lines were dangerously over-extended, brought about a retreat almost to Minsk in the face of Polish forces led by the French General Weygand. The Soviet government accepted an armistice agreement with Poland on September 12, followed by a preliminary peace in October. On March 18, 1921, the final peace was signed at Riga. This treaty remained in effect until the Hitler-Stalin Pact of September, 1939.

Evaluation of the Intervention. The principal interventionist powers never mounted an offensive capable of defeating the Red Army. At no time did they conduct an all-out war or provide all-out aid. With only limited forces of their own available, they relied on the White armies to defeat the Reds. Since their motives were so much at variance, they often displayed as much distrust of one another as of the Soviet regime. The French and the Japanese called for the extension of intervention, whereas the United States exerted pressure to contain it and resisted interference with the internal affairs of the revolutionary regime. Once the armistice was signed on November 11, 1918, the need for a new eastern front ceased to exist. Troops at Archangel, Vladivostok, and Odessa proved to be as anxious to return home as those on the western front.

Comintern. Peace in Europe also led to the creation of the Communist International, or Comintern, under Soviet auspices, March 2–6, 1919, with Gregory Zinoviev as president. Comintern policy accelerated the end of the intervention. The First International (1864) and the Second International (1889), comprised of Socialists of many ideological shades who focused on the improvement of the lot of the working masses, were largely defensive, even pacifist in character. The Comintern, on the other hand, comprised exclusively of Communists, was designed both for purposes of aggression and

6. F. L. Schuman, *Soviet Politics at Home and Abroad* (New York: Alfred A. Knopf, 1946), p. 160.

defense. Established at a time of dire peril for the Soviet regime when its isolation was virtually complete, the Comintern launched an ideological offensive. Its purpose was to set in action at the international level the same kind of subversive and demoralizing campaign as the Bolsheviks had carried out at home against the Kerensky regime. It was essentially defensive in nature, for it was intended to prevent the capitalist countries from further intervention in Soviet affairs by keeping them busy at home. The White armies, to their disadvantage, never did resort to such political and psychological warfare. The Soviets, who initated it, soon found it an asset to their survival. Soviet tracts and journals were dropped by airplane over enemy lines. In March, 1919, Soviet propaganda among Allied troops in the Archangel area incited minor mutinies among the French, British, and American forces stationed there, and led to their early withdrawal from north Russia. Soviet subversive tactics among the French sailors and troops located in Odessa and other Black Sea ports led to the hoisting of the Red flag, which was an important factor in the evacuation of French forces in April. Nor were the ranks of the White armies immune from Soviet infiltration, with the result that desertions steadily increased in number.

Time of Greatest Peril. During the Civil War, the three periods of greatest peril for the Red regime occurred in the summer and autumn of 1918 prior to the end of World War I, while the Red Army was still undergoing training; in May, 1919, when Kolchak's army was poised for a drive to the heart of Russia; and in October of the same year, when Denikin pushed north within 250 miles of Moscow and from the west Yudenitch reached the suburbs of Petrograd. Peace in Europe in November, 1918, and the subsequent outbreak of socialist revolutions in Germany and Hungary, broke the ring of encirclement on the Soviet government's western front. The end of the Allied intervention in Europe followed in the summer of 1919. In Siberia, it proved easier for the Allied powers to enter than to leave. At the beginning of 1920, after the collapse of the Kolchak forces and the evacuation of a substantial part of the Czechs, the United States suddenly decided to withdraw from Siberia, on the ground that American troops were no longer needed and that continued intervention threatened to involve Americans in conflict with the Bolshevik forces advancing into western Siberia. On April 1, 1920, the last contingent of American troops withdrew from Vladivostok, leaving the Japanese still entrenched in eastern Siberia. The *Literary Digest* somewhat tartly summed up America's role in the intervention, when it commented that "some might have liked us less if we had intervened more, but that, having concluded that we intended to intervene no more nor no less than we actually did, nobody had any use for us at all."[7]

Far Eastern Republic of Siberia. Within a few days of the American depature there was established (April 6) at Verkhne-Udinsk, with the advice and consent of Lenin, the Far Eastern Republic of Siberia, under the

7. *Literary Digest,* LXII (September 6, 1919), p. 60.

presidency of Krasnoshchekov, erstwhile Chicago lawyer who supported the Soviet cause. The new republic, whose capital was subsequently transferred to Chita, extended from Lake Baikal to the Japanese-occupied Maritime Province. Far from being a Communist state, the Far Eastern Republic recognized private property, freedom of the press, universal popular suffrage, and other attributes of democracy. With the tacit consent of the Soviets and Japanese, both of whom granted the Republic formal recognition, it served as a buffer state between them. Although it failed to secure recognition from the other Allied powers, the Republic was represented unofficially by a trade delegation at the Washington Conference on Disarmament, 1921–1922. Not until the end of October, 1922, after repeated protests from the United States and other powers, did Japan finally withdraw from the Siberian mainland, although she continued in possession of northern Sakhalin until 1925. Once Japanese forces had withdrawn from Siberia, the Far Eastern Republic lost its *raison d'être* as a buffer state. On November 13 this ephemeral Soviet puppet voluntarily merged with the Russian Federation of Soviet Republics.

A few years later, and in the following incisive terms, Winston Churchill pronounced judgment upon the Allied intervention in Russia:

> As it was, enough foreign troops entered Russia to incur all the objections which were patent against intervention, but not enough to break the then gimcrack structure of the Soviet power. When we observe the amazing exploits of the Czech Army Corps, it seems certain that a resolute effort by a comparatively small number of trustworthy American or Japanese troops would have enabled Moscow to be occupied by National Russian and Allied forces even before the German collapse took place. Divided counsels and cross-purposes among the Allies, American mistrust of Japan, and the personal opposition of President Wilson, reduced Allied intervention in Russia during the war to exactly the point where it did the utmost harm and gained the least advantage.[8]

Intervention Complex. The Soviet government and people emerged from the Civil War with an intervention complex. Encircled largely by hostile powers, Soviet foreign policy henceforth reflected the fear of renewed foreign intervention. In spite of its ultimate failure, the Intervention intensified traditional Russian distrust and suspicion of the motives of foreign powers. It left its indelible stamp on Soviet political organization, which was molded and shaped under the abnormal conditions of a life-and-death struggle against domestic strife and foreign encroachment.

Soviet historiography has reflected this intervention complex by gross distortion of the motives that fostered it. For some years, Soviet historians, especially M. N. Pokrovsky, distinguished between American intervention and that of the other Allied powers, admitting that the United States joined the

8. Winston Churchill, *The World Crisis,* Vol. V, *The Aftermath* (New York: Scribner, 1929), p. 285.

movement largely to check Japanese imperialist designs on Siberia. France, in these years, was the chief interventionist villain. In times of international stress, in particular during the Stalin regime, whenever England, Japan, or Nazi Germany appeared to threaten Soviet interests or Soviet security, the interventionist bogey was aired again. With the advent of the Cold War after World War II, the United States emerged as the "chief instigator" of intervention, which was interpreted as "one of the bloodiest and most infamous acts of imperialist America." Several Soviet novels and plays, including Nikitin's *Aurora Borealis* and *Unforgettable 1919,* both awarded Stalin Prizes, reinforced for popular consumption the anti-American trend. The virulence of these attacks has diminished somewhat since Stalin's death in 1953.

19

The Asian Orientation of

Soviet Foreign Policy, 1917-1921

THE BAKU CONGRESS

The "Appeal." The first "Appeal to the Muslims of Russia and the East" was issued on December 5, 1917, by the new Soviet revolutionary government (Council of People's Commissars). The summons to the Baku Congress of September, 1920, came from the Second Congress of the Communist International (Comintern). The main purpose of the government's "Appeal" was to identify the October Revolution with the national interests of the peoples of the Orient. According to Bolshevik leaders, the success of the October Revolution depended on the peoples of the East and the national liberation of the Orient was inextricably linked with the new Soviet regime. As early as 1917, Lenin and Stalin, who affixed their signatures to the first "Appeal," grasped the significance of the awakening nationalist movements in Asia. Thus they supported these movements in order to achieve a Communist objective.

Comintern Sponsorship. The shift in sponsorship in 1920 from the Soviet regime to the Comintern occurred for at least two reasons: 1. The Soviet government, having emerged from the Civil War with an intervention complex, was apprehensive that outright Soviet intervention in the Orient would lead to a renewal of foreign intervention in Russia. If the Sovietization of the Orient were handled by the Comintern, however, the Soviet government could disclaim all responsibility for it, other than its role as host for the Congress. 2. Bolshevik Russia had just been invaded by fourteen countries. Although the Soviet regime as yet had no allies abroad, the Comintern was able to claim that its summons represented the workers and peasants of eleven countries.

By July, 1920, the Soviet government was confident of victory over the White armies and foreign interventionists and reasonably sure that the war-weary Russians were in no position to offer a serious challenge to Soviet authority. The first Congress of the Third International had been summoned in 1919, at a time of dire emergency for the Bolshevik regime, to devise ways and means for the successful defense against counter-revolution and foreign invasion. The second congress, summoned in July, 1920, as a result of foreign withdrawal and the disintegration of domestic opposition was ready to assume the offensive. In Turkey, the "revolutionary core" of the East, the Nationalist forces of Kemal Pasha were already challenging the Entente powers. In neighboring Iran, a Soviet republic had been established in Gilan, and there was upheaval in Khorassan. Georgia, although its independence was recognized by a treaty signed with the Soviets on May 7, 1920, was still regarded as the "kept mistress of the Entente," and the Bolsheviks feared that the theater of Entente military operations had been removed from Russia proper only to be reestablished in Transcaucasia.

The second congress of the Comintern thereupon determined, first, to instigate strikes, riots, and subversion in Europe and America, especially in those countries that had led the foreign intervention, in order to discourage any repetition of the invasion of Russia. Second, it planned to attack the colonial periphery, "the Achilles' heel of imperialism," to deprive the Entente of its sources of raw materials and fuel. The summons to Baku was therefore a summons to the Muslim world to organize a counterattack against the foreign invaders of Russia, in order to expel them from the lands adjacent to the Soviet republics, including Turkey, Iran, Armenia, and Mesopotamia.

Rival Plans. The idea of convening a Muslim congress originated with A. Zeki Velidi Togan (Velidov), a prominent Bashkir from Muslim Central Asia, who in 1919 was with Karl Radek, a well-known Bolshevik intellectual, and a group of Turkish officers in Moscow. According to Togan, this congress was to have been summoned by the Muslim peoples themselves, not by the Russians or the Third International, and in accordance with his recommendation, it was to be held in Baku. General Ali Fuat Cebesoy, the first ambassador of the Turkish Republic in the Soviet Union, credits Radek with the plan for a Muslim congress, to be held in Moscow. Radek, with the object of arousing the leaders of the Muslim world against the West, planned to use the former Turkish leaders of the Sultanate, including Enver Pasha and Jamal Pasha, to entice Muslim delegates to Moscow. General Cebesoy managed to convince Enver Pasha that the congress should be held in Ankara, Turkey, far removed from Soviet pressure. Before any agreement was reached with Ankara, the impatient Bolshevik leaders summoned Muslim delegates to Moscow, some of whom responded, but failed to locate Enver Pasha, and nothing was accomplished. Faced with this debacle, Radek and his associates appear to have selected Baku as a compromise gesture. The Bolsheviks then stole the show by having the Third International summon the Muslim peoples to the Baku Congress, with the result that neither Togan, the Bashkir leader, nor Enver Pasha participated officially in the proceedings.

Baku: Strategic Location. No doubt one reason Baku was chosen for the congress was its ready accessibility to the Muslim peoples of Soviet Russia, and to the Persians, Turks, and Arabs to the south. What Zinoviev failed to mention was that the Soviet government undoubtedly hoped by this means to consolidate Soviet power among the Muslim minorities, much of whose territory had been occupied without difficulty by the English, French, and Turks during the period of foreign intervention. There was still widespread disaffection among anti-Soviet forces in the area. Indeed, in the city of Baku itself, Communist power had been reestablished as recently as April, 1920. Even while the congress was in session at Baku a serious revolt erupted in Daghestan.

Invitations. The Executive Committee of the Communist International published its summons to the "Enslaved Peoples of Persia, Armenia, and Turkey" in *Izvestia,* July 3, 1920. It called upon the "workers and peasants" of these countries to join those of Europe and America to accelerate the destruction of world capitalism and to liberate workers and peasants throughout the world. A specific appeal was addressed to the peoples of Mesopotamia, Syria, Arabia, and Anatolia, because these areas were at the time subject to foreign occupation. A blanket invitation was extended to representatives of oppressed peoples from remote areas, including those of India and the Muslim peoples allied with Soviet Russia (Central Asia and the Caucasus). The Russians, having defeated the English, French, and American interventionists in their own country, were now prepared to show other peoples how to organize and drive out their occupation forces. The Executive Committee of the Comintern promised to join the thousands of delegates expected in Baku on September 2 to discuss the question of united action for the struggle against "the common enemy:"

> You formerly went through deserts to the holy places; you now cross mountains, rivers, forests, and deserts, in order to meet one another, to discuss how to free yourselves from the chains of slavery, to form a fraternal union, and to begin a free, equal, and brotherly life.

Delegates. According to Bolshevik claims, and their figures are subject to question, 1,891 delegates answered the summons. Of these, 1,273 were said to be Communists, 266 nonparty, 100 failed to indicate their affiliation, and 55 were women. All the Muslim peoples of Soviet Russia and those linked by treaty relations with it were represented. In addition to the Turks (235 delegates), Persians (192), and Armenians (157), specifically summoned by the Third International, there were Chinese (8), Kurds (8), and Arabs (3), as well as Georgians (100). Some of the delegates representing other Muslim countries were already in Soviet Russia as exiles, including Mustapha Subhi, a member of the Presidium, and Enver Pasha of Turkey, who did not appear in person before the congress. It was in all a motley assembly, too heterogeneous for effective action. With the exception of the Muslims of Russia, very few of the delegates were workers and peasants. Those who did come from abroad were representatives of the upper and middle classes, including some mullahs. The workers and peasants of these lands were illiterate and could not read the summons. Nor did they have the wherewithal to travel. Three official languages—Russian, Azerbaijani-Turkish, and Persian—proved altogether inadequate, and additional translations into standard Turkish, Kalmyk, Uzbek, Chechen, etc., were necessary. The three official delegates of the Third International, Grigory Zinoviev, Comintern president who served as chairman, Karl Radek, and Bela Kun, erstwhile leader of the short-lived Communist regime in Hungary, set the tone of the conference.

Call to a Jihad. The high watermark of unity among the delegates appears to have been reached during Zinoviev's fiery summons of the Muslims to a jihad, or holy war—primarily against English imperialism—which was delivered as the keynote speech at the opening of the congress. A holy war against English imperialism was something that Arabs, Turks, Persians, and other Muslims could understand and which they could wholeheartedly endorse. The record indicates that the Zinoviev address was punctuated by "stormy applause" and "prolonged hurrahs." The aroused Muslims, convinced by Zinoviev that they were participating in one of the most important events in history, in a frenzy of excitement rose from their seats, and brandishing their swords, daggers, and revolvers, swore to undertake the fight against imperialism. The one delegate to sound an anti-American note at Baku was the American John Reed of the state of Oregon, best known as the author of *Ten Days That Shook the World.* In his attack on United States policy in the Philippines, Central America, and the Caribbean Islands, he undertook to warn the assembled delegates that "the peoples of the East, the peoples of Asia, had not yet experienced the power of America." The Baku delegates, especially those from other countries who responded with such enthusiasm to Zinoviev's address, were eager for a political revolution—one which would oust existing governments, expel imperial occupation forces, and enable them to become rulers. They were, on the whole, not members of the proletariat, and knew and cared little or nothing about communism. Since a social revolution would have to be accomplished at their expense, this was definitely not in their purview.

Proceedings. If the official record is not distorted, the three representatives of the Comintern held the whip hand at the congress. A plethora of speeches, for the most part prepared in advance of the sessions, and involving endless repetition of Comintern principles, gave a cut-and-dried aspect to the performance and left little opportunity for discussion, even if the babel of languages had permitted the free interplay of ideas. Indeed, there was more than one indication that the Comintern leadership railroaded its decisions through the congress. When the list of forty-eight candidates for the proposed Council of Action and Propaganda in the East, intended to carry on the work of the congress after the delegates dispersed, was presented, a lone Persian delegate raised his voice in protest, but it was drowned in the ensuing hubbub, and the list was declared to have been passed "unanimously." The two manifestoes issued by the congress, "To the Peoples of the East" and "To the Workers of Europe, America, and Japan," were approved "in principle," without the delegates having any opportunity to see or discuss the text of the messages. Zeki Velidi Togan, later protested to Lenin, Stalin, and Trotsky that Zinoviev and Radek treated the representatives of the Eastern nations "like anti-revolutionary peasants." Togan, who was present incognito in Baku, and who wished to salvage something from the congress for his fellow Muslims, busied himself behind the scenes by formulating resolutions for the delegates. According to him, Zinoviev recognized that someone was providing resolutions with uncanny regularity, but remained ignorant of their real authorship.

Gospel of Revolution. The Baku Congress afforded an opportunity for the recruitment of revolutionary forces designed to spearhead the Communist revolution in other Muslim lands. Mustapha Subhi, who had organized Communist Turkish prisoners of war for the Central Bureau of Eastern Peoples, a subdivision of the Commissariat of Nationalities, after the sovietization of Azerbaijan moved his headquarters to Baku in May, 1920, in advance of the congress. He set up a central bureau of the Turkish Communist organizations in Baku to unite various factions from Anatolia and Constantinople. In September he organized special courses to train Turks as propagandists and mobilized a Turkish Communist regiment to aid Kemal Pasha against the Greeks. Subhi and his cohorts entered Turkey in November, ostensibly to join the Turkish struggle for liberation in Anatolia, but actually to promote communism there. Armenian Communists were likewise accused of using the congress to gain adherents, who shortly thereafter went to Armenia to displace the Dashnak (Nationalist) government already established there. Little wonder that on their return to their respective countries many of the delegates were cast into prison as Communist agitators and had no opportunity to disseminate the Baku gospel!

Attack on Islam. To the president of the Third International, as he faced this large assembly of the "old decrepit East," hitherto of no concern either to Kazbek or to the Western bourgeoisie but now assembled and working in apparent harmony under Communist leadership, it appeared that a miracle had occurred—the East had awakened and was organized. Ostensibly this was a great achievement and it could well have marked a turning point in Soviet-Muslim relations, had the Third International not made the fatal mistake of attacking Islam and Muslim religious institutions. It was one thing to attack organized religion in the Soviet Union, but quite another to apply the same epithets and slogans to the Muslim world in 1920. Even the most stalwart Muslim adherents of the Third International were not yet conditioned for an attack on their faith. Thus the achievements of the Baku Congress were virtually annulled by Zinoviev when under his chairmanship delegate Skatchko labeled the Muslim clergy parasites and oppressors who should be deprived of their lands.

Although Lenin, Stalin, and others had warned the representatives of the Third International to be cautious in their approach to the Muslims, especially in regard to religious issues, these warnings were ignored at the Baku Congress. Zinoviev, president of the Executive Committee of the Third International, evinced very little knowledge of the Muslim Orient. His utterances revealed more heat than light on the subject. Casting caution to the winds, he brushed aside likewise the warning of K. Troyanovsky who in 1918 in his book, *Vostok i Revolyutsia,* explained that "Muslim unity consists, not in territorial or other ethnographic foundations. It rests almost exclusively on spiritual and cultural foundations, on religion, which for the Muslim is theology, ethics, jurisprudence, and the supreme terrestrial power that is the state. Islam is an extraterritorial power." Hence any attack on Islam is an attack on Muslim life as a whole.

Criticism of Turkey. Zinoviev not only attacked Islam, directly and indirectly, as well as its leaders and institutions, but he committed another unpardonable blunder. He attacked Turkey, which the Soviet government intended to use as its key agent to win over the rest of the Muslim world, especially the Near and Middle East. To win adherents to the Turkish cause, Kemal Pasha had promised the masses that Turkey was waging its war to retain the caliph. But at the Baku Congress, Zinoviev, referring to Turkey, complained: "What the government of Kemal is doing in Turkey is not communism. You must not support the power of the Sultans . . . On the contrary, you must break up and destroy the faith in the Sultan, just as the Russian peasants destroyed the faith in the Tsar. The same thing will happen in Turkey and throughout the Orient when the real black soil peasant revolution breaks out."

Revival of Muslim Suspicions. This, in no uncertain terms, was an appeal for a Soviet revolution in the Muslim world, with all its implications. The importance of the Baku Congress is that it marked a turning point by reviving the suspicions of Muslims against the Soviet Union, which the Soviet government had been taking such pains to eradicate. Zinoviev not only alienated the Muslim elements, but in his unbridled zeal he antagonized Turkey, without which the Soviet Union could never expect to win the Muslim world. The Baku Congress did accomplish its purpose of stirring up the Muslim peoples, but not in the manner envisaged by the Soviets. It destroyed the illusion that the Soviet Union might become the Mecca and Medina of the Muslims. The threat to Islam was clear, even to the most ignorant mullahs, who had been comparing Lenin and Marx with Muhammed. No matter how much Muslims outside Russia detested colonialism and all it stood for, they feared even more the antireligious propaganda that emanated from the Baku Congress. A few Muslims may have been conditioned for this, but not the bulk of the delegates, and these few upon their return found that they were unpopular among their own people. Thus the Baku Congress served as an eye opener to the most "progressive" Muslims on the kind of "liberation" the Third International had in store for them.

Records of the Congress. Accurate information concerning the Baku

Congress is exceedingly limited. The basic primary sources are the steno-graphic record of the sessions, together with the manifestoes and other material published following the congress in the official journal of the Comintern. The Soviet press, no doubt for very good reasons, practically ignored the congress. In all probability, the Soviet government, which was on the eve of emerging victorious from the Civil War and foreign intervention, preferred to leave to the Third International the summoning of the Muslim and Armenian peoples to a counterattack against the invaders. Foreign newspaper reports on the congress need to be handled with caution, since they were in no wise firsthand accounts of the sessions. The world's journalists were not invited to cover a congress devoted to the incitement of social revolution in colonial and semicolonial countries and to the struggle for national liberation on the part of Muslim countries, whose lands, as in the case of Turkey, were occupied by English, French, Greek, Italian, or other foreign armies. Finally, the vast majority of the delegates to the congress, still far from being articulate on the broader issues involved, were not the kind who kept diaries and published memoirs. They came to listen and to get their instructions from the leaders of the Third International. The columns of their home newspapers were ordinarily closed to them, and as previously indicated, many landed in jail, instead of returning as heroes to their native lands.

The Baku Congress approved in principle the issuing of an "Appeal (Manifesto) to the Peoples of the East," the text of which was not passed by the delegates or included in the official records of the congress. In brief, this manifesto urged the Faithful to substitute the red flag of revolution for the green banner of the Prophet, the Third International for Islam, Lenin for Muhammed. The price of liberation from England was the repudiation of religion—of Islam.

Far Eastern Congress. Smarting under the failure sustained at the Baku Congress of 1920, which was primarily a gathering of Soviet Muslims and those of the Middle East, the Comintern a year later turned to the Far East. During the third congress of the Communist International (June–July, 1921) the decision was reached to hold a Congress of the Toilers of the Far East. Whereas the invitation to Baku was issued by the Third International and signed, for the most part, by its European members, the summons to the Far Eastern congress was issued by the Asians themselves. Its preliminary sessions were held in Irkutsk in November, but the congress proper took place January 21–27, 1922, in Moscow and Petrograd. As at Baku, Zinoviev on January 23, delivered the keynote address to the assembled delegates, this time tactfully admitting Comintern ignorance of the Orient. Since this congress coincided with the Washington Conference (1921–1922), from which the Soviets were excluded, the latter became the main object of attack. Whereas at Baku the main target was England, in Moscow it was the United States. Either because the Comintern had learned its lesson at Baku, or because religion did not occupy the same place among the peoples of the Far

East as it did among the Muslims, Zinoviev and his cohorts did not mar the congress by virulent antireligious propaganda.

Contrast: Bandung Conference, 1955. Thirty-five years after Baku, the next congress of the peoples of the East—the Asian-African Conference in Bandung, Indonesia, in April, 1955—was held without benefit of the Communist International or the Western democracies. The delegates of the twenty-nine independent nations were in striking contrast to those of the motley assembly of colonial, semicolonial, and strife-torn countries represented at Baku in 1920. Although much water had run under the bridge between Baku and Bandung, some major issues remained the same, namely, colonialism and religion. It is significant that the Bandung delegates, like those at Baku, were unanimous in their opposition to colonialism. In the Muslim environment of Indonesia, however, there was no attack on religion, only an appeal for tolerance. On the contrary, the numerous references to religion in the plenary sessions by President Sukarno of Indonesia, Sir John Kotelwala, prime minister of Ceylon, and others, indicate that the Bandung assembly was fully conscious of the significance of religion in the Orient. Even the premier of Red China, Chou En-lai, whose delegation included a pious Imam representative of the millions of Chinese Muslims, expressed the hope that "those with religious beliefs will respect those without," and announced that the days of instigating religious strife should have passed. In this connection, it should be noted that in 1956 when President Sukarno of Indonesia visited the Soviet Union, he openly affirmed in his speech to the Uzbeks of Central Asia that one of the five principles on which the Indonesian state was founded was "belief in God and respect for all religions."

In the light of the treatment of the religious issue at Bandung, we can better appreciate Zinoviev's fatal mistake at Baku, which sounded the death-knell to the schemes of the Third International in the East. It was perhaps symbolic that the Baku Congress closed with a funeral ceremony.[1] Although the delegates intended to make it an annual event, actually it had no successor. Due in part to the blunders at Baku and to the course of subsequent events, this was the first and last Congress of the Peoples of the Middle East to be held under the auspices of the Third International.

Soviet-Turkish Rapprochement

The Turkish Revolution. The Turkish Revolution, 1918–1922, of which Mustapha Kemal Pasha (Atatürk) became the recognized leader, was a direct outgrowth of Turkey's military defeat in World War I, of foreign occupation by English, French, and Greek troops, and of the October Revolution

---

1. The funeral ceremony for the twenty-six Baku commissars, whose bodies had just been returned to Baku after being put to death by the "Whites," allegedly at the instigation of the English, caused a sensation in Baku.

in Russia. The October Revolution, accompanied by the Soviet decree on peace, publication of the Allied Secret Agreements, and Soviet announced abandonment of all tsarist territorial claims on Turkey, opened up the prospect of an early end of the war and a peace without dismemberment for the hard-pressed Turks.

When news of the Turkish Revolution reached the Soviet regime, the Soviet government and the official Soviet press regarded it as a counterpart and an elongation of the October (Bolshevik) Revolution. It was welcomed with enthusiasm by the editor of *Izvestia* "as the first Soviet Revolution in Asia." Of immediate importance to the Soviet government, then confronted by civil war and foreign intervention, was the strategic position of Turkey. Revolutionary Turkey was expected to protect the exposed Russian flank in the Caucasus and to serve as a bulwark likewise for revolutionary Hungary. Even more important, however, was the fact that Soviet leaders appear to have sensed an opportunity to make use of revolutionary Turkey, not only as an ally against the Entente powers, but as the vanguard of Bolshevik Revolution in the Muslim world, especially in the Near and Middle East.

In its "Appeal to the Muslims of Russia and the East" on December 5, 1917 (see page 319), the Soviet government completely abandoned all Russian claims to Turkish territory: "We declare that the secret treaties of the dethroned Tsar regarding the seizure of Constantinople, which was confirmed by the deposed Kerensky, now are null and void. The Russian Republic and its government, the Council of People's Commissars, are against the seizure of foreign territories. Constantinople must remain in the hands of the Muslims." Although Soviet leaders reiterated this renunciation time and again and even boasted about it, at least until 1947, there is reason to believe that the Turkish Revolution of 1918–1922 produced a sudden "about-face" in their attitude. Of special interest to the historian and diplomat is an article by Yu. Steklov on "The Turkish Revolution," published in the official government newspaper *Izvestia* on April 23, 1919, which has been completely overlooked in the evaluation of Soviet-Muslim relations:

> The famous question of the Dardanelles now assumes a somewhat different color. Russian imperialism of the Tsarist and bourgeois period continually dreamed about these Dardanelles, German imperialism intended to seize these Dardanelles. But actually it was Anglo-French imperialism that took possession of them. And recently we learned that American imperialism is stretching out its greedy hand for them. Now the Turkish Revolution is returning the Dardanelles to the Turkish masses and through them to the world proletariat, which includes also the Russian. Thus, what Russian imperialism failed to realize by virtue of centuries of intrigue, now as a ripe plum will fall to the Russian working class.

Whether the Turks knew of or simply overlooked the public acknowledgment of Soviet designs in the Soviet press, it is difficult to say. They were undoubtedly aware of Communist propaganda in Turkey, the purpose of which was the ultimate overthrow of Kemal Pasha's regime.

Turkish prisoners of war returning from Russia following the Bolshevik seizure of power were already indoctrinated with the Communist virus, while those returning from Germany were influenced by Spartacist ideology. They helped to organize trade-unions in Istanbul. Mustapha Subhi, who had been interned in Russia during World War I, played a prominent role in the indoctrination of "thousands" of Turkish prisoners of war.

No doubt the Turkish government was forced to put up with Soviet subversive propaganda, for the time being, even when it was explicitly and openly acknowledged in the Soviet press, or when Soviet leaders like Chicherin blatantly interfered in the domestic affairs of the country to promote a Soviet revolution. Confronted by foreign occupation and the prospect of the dismemberment of their country by the Entente victors, the Turks may have regarded Communist infiltration as the lesser evil, to be dealt with under more favorable circumstances. In retrospect we may safely say that during the Turkish Revolution and for some time thereafter, the character of Turkish relations with the Soviet government was contingent upon the policy of the Entente toward Turkey. In other words, whenever the Turks were hard-pressed by the Entente and threatened with dismemberment of their country, they turned inevitably, even though reluctantly, to the Soviet Union for support. On the other hand, in proportion as the Entente powers eased their pressure and displayed a willingness to compromise, the Soviet-Turkish rapprochement cooled off appreciably.

In order to suppress the Turkish Revolution, English troops occupied Constantinople in force on March 16, 1920. Cutting himself aloof from the Ottoman government in Constantinople, Kemal Pasha called for the election of a Turkish Grand National Assembly, which held its opening session in Ankara on April 23, 1920. Henceforth, to all intents and purposes, there existed two Turkish governments, that of the sultan in Constantinople, and that of Kemal Pasha at Ankara. According to the Turkish leader, "the first decision arrived at by the Grand National Assembly of Turkey was to send an Embassy to Moscow." On April 26, Kemal Pasha hastily dispatched a note to Lenin asking for the establishment of diplomatic relations and appealing for Soviet aid to revolutionary Turkey in its struggle against imperialism.

If the Soviet government and the Comintern had not interfered in Turkish internal affairs by spreading subversive Communist propaganda, a Soviet-Turkish alliance might then have been effected, which would have been the equivalent of an alliance between the Soviet Union and the Muslim world. The Turks stood in dire need of Soviet assistance to preserve Turkish independence and defy the Treaty of Sèvres. By this treaty, concluded in August, 1920, between Turkey and the Allied Powers, the government of Sultan Muhammed VI gave up all claims to non-Turkish territory. The Turks made use of the Soviets until they were able to wring concessions from the

Western Allies at the Lausanne Conference of 1923. Neither country trusted the other, although circumstances forced them to collaborate on the international scene. Barely two months after his appeal to Chicherin in January, 1921, Kemal Pasha took steps to rid himself of the Communist menace at home by seizing the notorious Subhi and sixteen members of his Communist cohort at Erzerum. They were cast into the Black Sea off Trebizond, as a warning of the fate that awaited others of their persuasion. Chicherin's inquiries merely produced word that the Communists had possibly met with an accident at sea. Not even this incident produced a breach between Turkey and Soviet Russia, when it was manifestly in the interests of both countries to reach an agreement.

Moscow Treaty. On March 16, 1921, Turkey and the RSFSR,[2] recognizing that they shared certain principles of "the brotherhood of nations and national self-determination, taking note of their solidarity in the struggle against imperialism, as well as of the fact that any difficulty created for one of the two nations worsens the position of the other," finally signed a "treaty of friendship and fraternity." This treaty established a boundary settlement between the two countries, by which Kars, Ardahan, and Artvin were ceded to Turkey and Batum was restored to Russia (Georgian SSR). It included a pledge by each contracting party against interference in the internal affairs of the other (Article VIII). Taking cognizance of "the points in common between the movement of the Eastern peoples for national emancipation and the struggle of the workers of Russia for a new social order," Turkey and Russia agreed to recognize "the right of these peoples to freedom and independence" and to a government of their own choosing (Article IV). The troublesome Straits Question was to be settled by a conference of the Black Sea powers, with the proviso that there should be no infringement of Turkish sovereignty and that Constantinople should remain in Turkish hands. In brief, the Moscow Treaty normalized relations between Turkey and the RSFSR, although contrary to opinion in some quarters, it contained no pledge of joint action against the Entente powers. The Soviet government took steps toward the conclusion of similar treaties between Turkey and the Transcaucasian Soviet Republics (Armenia, Azerbaijan, and Georgia); the treaties were signed on October 13, 1921. On January 2, 1922, during M. V. Frunze's mission to Ankara, the Ukrainian SSR likewise entered into treaty arrangements with Turkey.

In spite of their criticism of the Kemalist government, Soviet leaders recognized that this treaty strengthened the international position of the Soviet government. From the Soviet point of view, this treaty, together with similar treaties concluded with Persia and Afghanistan in the same year, was greatly instrumental in strengthening the cause of peace, encouraged the national liberation movement in the Near and Middle East (Article IV), "paralyzed"

2. Russian Soviet Federative Socialist Republic which preceded the USSR.

The Russian right to sail through the Bosphorus was part of the long-standing Straits controversy. This photograph, taken from Asia, looks across to
the European shore near Istanbul.

the Allied intervention in Transcaucasia, and in general weakened the position of the Allied camp. Even when Soviet leaders suspected that the Turks
were using the RSFSR in order to make better terms with the Entente, they
justified the military aid extended to Turkey on the ground that the Turks
were fighting Soviet battles and that Turkish defeat of the Greeks spread
dissension among the Allies. These were the two factors which, in their
estimation, brought about a rapprochement between Turkey and the RSFSR,
and led to the treaty of March 16, 1921. The Moscow Treaty likewise
strengthened the Turkish position vis-à-vis Greece and the Entente powers,
thereby making it possible for the Turks to make a better deal with England
and France at Lausanne.

Cebesoy's Mission to Moscow. The decisive role in the conclusion of a
"treaty of friendship and fraternity" between Turkey and the Soviet regime
was played by General Ali Fuat Cebesoy. Commander-in-chief of the Turkish
armies on the western front and deputy for Ankara in the Grand National
Assembly, he was appointed first ambassador of the Turkish Republic in
Moscow, November 21, 1920. Cebesoy arrived in Moscow on February 27,
1921, accompanied by his fluent Russian-speaking secretary, Aziz Bey, only
to find the negotiations hopelessly deadlocked by a boundary dispute involv-

ing the disposition of Kars, Ardahan, and Batum, all three of which were claimed by the Turks. According to Cebesoy, Soviet minister of foreign affairs Chicherin was adamantly opposed to yielding any of these points, and the Turks were equally determined to secure them. During an evening meeting between Stalin and Cebesoy, arranged at the invitation of the former, Stalin advanced a compromise recommendation that the Russians keep Batum, to which the Turks had no access by road in any event, in return for Kars, Ardahan, and Arpaçayi (Oats River). Thus the deadlock was broken.

Cebesoy's experience throws new light on the significance of Stalin, whose role during the early years of the Soviet regime appears to have been underrated. As ambassador in Moscow, February 27, 1921, to May 22, 1922, Cebesoy had contacts with Lenin, Trotsky, Stalin, Radek, Zinoviev, Chicherin, Kalinin, Karakhan, Frunze, and Voroshilov. According to his estimate, Stalin was more important than all the rest of Lenin's associates. When Cebesoy, upon his arrival, asked to see Trotsky, who as commissar of war was the leading Soviet figure in military affairs, Lenin sent him instead to Stalin, who handled the entire arrangements for the treaty with Turkey. Trotsky, according to Cebesoy, was already at odds with Stalin and his power was on the wane. Lenin placed more trust in Stalin than in Trotsky and delegated more authority to the former.

Another particularly important phase of Cebesoy's mission to Moscow was the negotiation of Soviet military aid to the embattled Turkish Republic, the terms of which were outlined in secret clauses attached to the treaty of March 16, 1921. Only token Soviet aid had reached the Turks prior to this treaty. By its terms, Soviet Russia provided the beleaguered Turks with substantial aid: ten million gold rubles, thirty thousand Russian rifles with one thousand rounds of ammunition for each rifle, thirty thousand bayonets, from two hundred and fifty to three hundred machine guns with ten thousand cartridges for each gun, some cavalry swords, from twenty to twenty-five mountain cannon, and a large number of hand grenades. Altogether, according to the general, the Soviets supplied enough arms to equip three Turkish divisions. Among other things, the Soviet government deposited in Berlin one million Russian rubles to the credit of the Turks, who were thereby enabled to secure replacements for German weapons obtained before and during the First World War. In 1916, when the Germans took large numbers of Russian prisoners on the eastern front, they provided their Turkish allies with from fifty to sixty thousand weapons seized from these prisoners. Kemal Pasha's forces later obtained from Soviet Russia the necessary replacements for these Russian weapons. General Cebesoy and Rauf Orbay, the first prime minister of the Turkish Republic, agreed that Soviet aid helped the Turkish revolutionaries both materially and psychologically, but that it was not available in sufficient quantities to prove decisive. Tsarist arms abandoned by the retreating White armies, according to them, went to the sultan's forces, and were of no use to Kemal Pasha.

Communist Partisans in Turkey. Although, on the one hand, the Soviets appear to have rendered moral and material aid to the Turkish Nationalists, on the other hand, they disseminated Communist propaganda hostile to the Kemalist regime and organized Communist detachments, or partisans led by Communist sympathizers, to harass the Turkish armed forces. At one moment, the Kemalists feared the dismemberment of Turkey by Greece and the Entente powers, and the next moment they faced being stabbed in the back by pro-Soviet partisans. This is somewhat reminiscent of the position of the Soviet regime during and after the Revolution, when it confronted foreign intervention and civil war at one and the same time. Both countries faced foreign intervention, in part from the same sources. The domestic opposition to the Soviets was directed toward the restoration of the tsarist regime or the establishment of a constitutional government, whereas Kemal faced the possibility of being superseded by the Communists and their sympathizers. According to Soviet sources, the Kemalist government at times had to use more soldiers against the partisans than against the Greek invader. It is not surprising that as soon as he was able to check the Greek advance, Kemal Pasha set about in earnest to remove the Communist menace. The ban on the Turkish Communists, which had been temporarily lifted from March to October, 1922, while Kemal Pasha was conducting a major campaign against the Greeks, was renewed once the Turks had driven the Greeks into the sea, and no longer stood in dire need of Soviet aid.

Lausanne Conference. Just as the Baku Congress of 1920, by attacking Islam and preaching the Bolshevization of the Near and Middle East, alienated the Muslim peoples from the Soviet regime, the Lausanne Conference of 1923 marked a decisive turning point in Soviet-Turkish relations. By scrapping the Treaty of Sèvres at Lausanne, England and France set Turkey free from impending bondage within the Soviet orbit. Although they did not meet all Turkish demands, they nevertheless removed the trap that Soviet diplomacy had carefully set for the Kemalist regime. By so doing, they were likewise greatly instrumental in stemming the tide of Militant Communism in Iran, Afghanistan, and the Arab countries. The blunders committed by the Third International at Baku, namely, the attack on Islam and the use of subversive propaganda, were repeated in Turkey. The loss of Turkey as the key Soviet agent for the spread of revolution in the East signified the loss of Soviet leadership in the Muslim world.

SOVIET BLUEPRINT FOR IRAN

In the minds of the leaders of the October Revolution, Iran ranked next to Turkey in importance. At times, because of its geographical location, Iran even took precedence over Turkey in Soviet strategy. In fact, prior to 1921, Turkey, Iran, and Afghanistan, because they were Muslim states and had a common frontier with Soviet Russia, and because all of them, for the time being, recognized England as a common enemy, were treated as a unit by Soviet diplomacy. The control of these three Muslim states was tantamount to the domination of the Near and Middle East and a threat to "colonialism" throughout Asia. Soviet leaders labored to create a chain of vassal states along the southern periphery of revolutionary Russia, both as a measure of defense against foreign intervention and as a prelude to the Bolshevization of India and the East.

Konstantin Troyanovsky's book *Vostok i Revolutsia,* published as early as 1918, clearly revealed the handwriting on the wall as far as Iran was concerned. This "natural basin" was for him a primary objective of Soviet policy because it was the gateway to India, "the citadel of revolution in the East," which only the Bolsheviks were in a position to open. According to Troyanovsky:

> The Persian revolution may become the key to the revolution of the whole Orient, just as Egypt and the Suez Canal are the key to English domination in the Orient. Persia is the "Suez Canal" of the revolution. By shifting the political center of gravity of the revolution to Persia, the entire strategic value of the Suez Canal is lost. . . . The political conquest of Persia, thanks to its peculiar geopolitical situation and significance for the liberation movement in the East, is what we must accomplish first of all. This precious key to all other revolutions in the Orient must be in our hands, come what may. Persia must be ours! Persia must belong to the revolution!

With the exception of the revolution, there was nothing new in the Soviet blueprint for Iran which had not been envisaged by Peter the Great, General Kuropatkin, and other Russian imperialists of the tsarist era. For a time it appeared that Lord Curzon's nightmare of Russian power established on the Persian Gulf might become reality under the Soviet regime.[3]

As far as Iran was concerned, the Soviet government inherited from tsarist Russia and the Provisional government the following situation: (1) the Anglo-Russian Treaty of 1907, which divided Iran into British and Russian spheres of influence, with a neutral zone between them; (2) the occupation during World War I of northwest Iran by Russian military forces; (3) the extraterritorial rights and other special privileges accorded Russian citizens by the Treaty of Turkmanchai in 1828; (4) numerous tsarist concessions in Iran; (5) restrictions on Iranian sovereignty in matters pertaining to the Caspian Sea.

Withdrawal of Russian Troops. The Bolshevik "Appeal to the Muslims of Russia and the East" condemned tsarist imperialism in Iran and declared that "the treaty partitioning Persia is null and void." It likewise promised that "as

3. Harold Nicolson, *Curzon: The Last Phase, 1919–1925* (London, 1934), pp. 119–148.

soon as military operations cease, the armed forces will be withdrawn from Persia, and the Persians will be guaranteed the right of free determination of their own destiny." Shortly thereafter, Trotsky, Soviet commissar of foreign affairs, in a note of December 19 (December 6, O.S.), to Assad Khan, Iranian *chargé d'affaires* in Petrograd, proposed immediate negotiations for the evacuation of imperial Russian troops from Iran, on condition that the Turks withdraw simultaneously. This was in line with the armistice agreement between the Central Powers and the Bolsheviks concluded at Brest-Litovsk on December 15 (December 2, O.S.). The Treaty of Brest-Litovsk later confirmed (Article VII) the "political and economic independence and the territorial integrity" of both Iran and Afghanistan.

On January 4 (December 23, 1917, O.S.), 1918, Trotsky informed the Iranian government of the Soviet evacuation program, which was to begin at once with the withdrawal of those Russian detachments that served no military purpose, and of the Russian military mission training the Iranian Cossack brigade. According to Trotsky, there should be no delay: "The greatest speed is necessary in this matter in order to wipe out as quickly as possible the effects of the acts of violence perpetrated by Tsarist and bourgeois Russian governments against the Persian people." On January 14 Trotsky officially reassured the Iranian government of Soviet renunciation of the Anglo-Russian Convention of 1907, and of all other conventions infringing upon the independence of Iran.

British Control. Having actually begun the evacuation of Russian troops from Iran in December, 1917, the Soviet government completed the withdrawal in the summer of 1918. The "vacuum" created by the departure of Russian and Turkish troops was promptly filled by the English who, ostensibly to forestall the Turks in Transcaucasia, included all of Iran in the British sphere, moved in limited numbers of British and White Russian troops, and intervened from this vantage point in revolutionary Transcaucasia. In June, 1918, the English occupied Resht and Enzeli (Pahlevi) in the Caspian area, overthrew the local Soviets, and occupied the oil center of Baku in advance of the approaching Turks.

Anglo-Iranian Treaty. The subsequent Anglo-Iranian Treaty of August 9, 1919, to all intents and purposes, transformed Iran into a British protectorate. According to this treaty, Great Britain obtained control over the key branches of the Iranian administration through the appointment of advisers to the Treasury, of officers to reorganize the army, of experts to revise the tariff, by assistance in the matter of railroad construction, and by a loan of £ 2,000,-000 sterling.

When the terms of this treaty became known, the Soviet government on August 30, 1919, appealed to the Iranian people over the head of the Iranian government of Vossuq-ed-Dowleh, by denouncing English policy and reaffirming Soviet renunciation of all tsarist infractions on Iranian sovereignty. Chicherin, in what may have been a rehearsal for his "notorious" appeal to the Turkish people two weeks later, made every effort to arouse the country against the English, representing Soviet Russia as the sole support and only friend of the Iranian people:

> At this moment when the triumphant victor, the English robber, is trying to lasso the Persian people into total slavery, the Soviet workers' and peasants' government of the Russian Republic solemnly declares that it does not recognize the Anglo-Persian Treaty which carries out this enslavement. . . . (It) regards as a scrap of paper the shameful Anglo-Persian Treaty by which your rulers have sold themselves and sold you to the English robbers, and will never recognize its legality.

Chicherin promised that the hour was near when the "valiant revolutionary Red Army will march across Red Turkestan to the frontiers of a still enslaved Persia."

The Anglo-Iranian Treaty was a "triumph" for the diplomacy of Lord Curzon, English foreign minister, who had long regarded Russian encroachment on Iran as a major threat to British possession of India. Sincere as he undoubtedly was, Curzon failed to understand what his biographer has taken pains to point out, that in 1919 the roles of Britain and Russia in regard to Iran were reversed. The Iranians were not, as in the closing decades of the nineteenth century, looking to England for support against the Russian enemy. For a time, at least, the Bolshevik Revolution, accompanied by the complete renunciation of Russian interests in Iran and the withdrawal of Russian troops, left the English, as the sole occupants of the country, the major threat to Iranian independence.

In spite of English pressure for the speedy ratification of the Anglo-Persian treaty, this Iranian version of the Treaty of Sèvres was never ratified by the Mejlis, due to widespread opposition from Iranian nationalists and effective Soviet propaganda. In protest against it the Iranians, like the Turks after the Treaty of Sèvres, turned to Soviet Russia for support against England and for a treaty based on "equality" of the signatories. With England in control of Iran, and Soviet Russia isolated from Iran by White Russian forces and those of the intervention, treaty arrangements were not possible. There were many difficulties in the way of establishing official contacts, the misadventures of Ivan Osipovitch Kolomiitsev being a case in point. Upon recommendation of the Soviet government that an official representative be dispatched to Teheran, Shaumyan, Soviet commissar extraordinary in the Caucasus, selected Kolomiitsev, who reached the Iranian capital on June 30, 1918. The Iranian government, allegedly under pressure from the English, refused to recognize the Soviet mission on the technical ground that Kolomiitsev had no documents signed in Moscow. In the summer of 1919, when Kolomiitsev, equipped with the appropriate documents, attempted to return to Teheran as the official Soviet representative, he was captured by White Russians and shot on the island of Ashurad. Widespread Communist activity in the northern provinces of Iran proved to be another obstacle toward the establishment of closer relations between Soviet Russia and Iran.

Liberation Movement. According to Soviet sources, under the impetus of the October Revolution there came an upsurge in the national liberation movement in Iran. In northern Iran, especially at Resht and Enzeli (Pahlevi), the shah's governors were removed and local soviets were established by Russian soldiers who had gone over to the side of the Revolution and by representatives of the local population. In connection with the Iranian Revolution (1917–1920), the importance of Central Asiatic Russia, and especially of Baku, should not be overlooked. At the second congress of the Comintern (July–August, 1920) Sultan-Zade, an Iranian delegate, maintained that the experiences of the Russian proletariat in Kirghizia and Turkestan showed what could be accomplished where no industrial proletariat existed, and that the same could be accomplished in Iran, Egypt, and India.

A'delyat. While there were undoubtedly many local factors contributing to the unrest in northern Iran, such as agrarian problems, bureaucratic corruption, and hostility to foreign occupation, the strongest impact emanated from Baku in adjacent Azerbaijan. Baku was a revolutionary school for workers, farm hands, and a miscellaneous assortment of people who went there to work in the oil fields. That is one reason why it was chosen by the Third International for the first Congress of the Muslims of the East in September, 1920. Iranian migrant workers, returning to Iran from Baku and Central Asia, where they had witnessed or even taken part in revolutionary activities, played an important role in the spread of Soviet ideas in their homeland. These migrants were responsible for the organization of the first so-called Iranian Proletarian Party, A'delyat (Justice), which in 1920 was transformed into the Communist Party of Iran. The choice of the name "Justice" was psychologically astute, since among the Muslims it was more powerful than any of the customary revolutionary slogans. To the average Muslim, justice is an all-inclusive term which symbolizes the solution of all problems, and it is a cardinal point in Islam.

A'delyat was organized by Kafar-Zade in Baku immediately following the overthrow of the Romanov dynasty (February, 1917) and quickly spread throughout Turkestan, the Caucasus, and into Iran. Upon the initiative of the Turkestan Regional Committee, the first A'delyat party congress was summoned at Enzeli on July 23, 1920, at which time its name was changed to that of the Communist Party of Persia. The Enzeli Congress was attended by forty-eight delegates from Iran, Turkestan, and the Caucasus. As at the Baku Congress several weeks later, the main target was England. Some of the delegates who had worked in revolutionary circles from ten to fifteen years expressed their preference, under existing circumstances, for the principles of the Russian Revolution of 1905 in the direction of constitutional government, instead of coming out for the doctrine of social transformation set forth by the

October Revolution. They likewise called for the exploitation of the national movement in Persia.

Sultan-Zade, a prominent delegate from Turkestan, who later attended the Baku Congress, explained during the second session in Enzeli why the Persian Revolution should be modeled after the 1905 Revolution rather than after the Bolshevik pattern. According to him, the October Revolution drew its main support from the Russian peasantry, which constituted nearly 90 per cent of the population. In Iran, however, out of a population of fifteen million, only about half were peasants. In addition there were around three million nomads, three million merchants, and approximately one million belonging to the nobility and clergy. Iran, he felt, was not yet ripe for the Soviet structure.

Bolshevik Revolution in Gilan. The revolutionary movement in the Iranian province of Gilan, under the leadership of Kuchik Khan, was in many respects typical of the course of the revolution elsewhere in northern Iran. No doubt Lenin, at the second congress of the Comintern (July–August, 1920) had Gilan in mind when he confidently asserted: "At the present moment the flag of the Soviet is beginning to be raised throughout the Orient, in Asia." The leadership of the rebellion was essentially middle-class rather than proletarian, including tradesmen, small landed proprietors, and intellectuals. Because of this composition and in order to secure a united front, the Communist program subordinated local issues in order to concentrate on the one objective common to all—the expulsion of the English from Iran. Once having achieved a modicum of unity by driving out the English, the next step was to be an attack on the feudal landowners—another issue on which there was general agreement among the middle-class leaders. The third step in the program was to be the capture of Teheran, the capital, and the overthrow of the shah's regime. This was, in a nutshell, the program outlined by the Third International for the revolution in the Near and Middle East. The real social revolution in Iran was to follow, and not to precede, these three prerequisites. However, under pressure from Ehsanullah Khan, Pishevari, and other extremist elements among the followers of Kuchik Khan, including Russian advisers who held key positions in his government, the revolutionaries ignored this basic program, which was prepared with backward Near Eastern conditions in mind, and tried to achieve everything at once. In other words, they tried to effect in Gilan a full-fledged Bolshevik program, with wholesale confiscation of enterprises, prohibition of private trade in the bazaars, attacks on the Muslim clergy and on Muslim social customs. There followed a virtual reign of terror against the middle class. This terrorist program broke the united front so painstakingly fostered among the leaders and led to the rejection of all revolutionary leadership by the more moderate and conservative elements, the most articulate members of the population.

Although the Third International was working hard to justify the Bolshevik regime in Russia, it was completely opposed to Bolshevik revolution in Iran at this stage. This was indicated at the Baku Conference, where "the traitorous policy of the Iranian Leftists" was criticized. Thereafter the Central Committee of the Communist Party of Iran was reorganized under the leadership of an Iranian member of the Baku Presidium, Haidar Khan Amouqli, a friend of Stalin, who had spent many years in the Baku oil fields, and who became one of the founders of the Communist Party of Iran. Since this change proved ineffective in winning the support of the moderates in Gilan, another reorganization took place in March, 1921, upon the initiative of the Central Committee of the Communist party in the city of Fumen. Ostensibly a reconciliation was effected at this congress among Kuchik Khan, Ehsanullah, and Haidar Amouqli. A new government was formed, in which Kuchik Khan became president of the Sovnarkom and commissar of finance, Haidar Amouqli assumed control of foreign affairs, and Hali Kurban became commissar of military affairs.

The main purpose of this reorganization was to appease the middle and upper classes, but it came too late. By this time Kuchik Khan was convinced that the Third International wished to use him only as a tool to effect the ultimate Bolshevization of Iran. Being a patriot, although not of the stature of Kemal Pasha in Turkey, he subordinated the welfare of the Party to the welfare of Iran. He definitely broke with his Bolshevik colleagues, foreign and native, on September 29, 1921; during a conference in Fumen, his forces attacked and routed them, putting a number of Communist leaders to death, including Haidar Amouqli. Kuchik Khan's detachments then destroyed the Communist regimes in Resht and Enzeli. Obviously, he was determined to wipe out communism in northern Iran. However, this interparty strife paved the way for action on the part of the shah's armies, which had no difficulty in occupying the whole of Gilan. Kuchik Khan himself, instead of being regarded as a hero, was put to death and his head presented to the shah. Essentially a supporter of the *via media,* Kuchik Khan in the end was regarded as a traitor by both the Communists and the Iranian government. Needless to say, a note of caution should be sounded as to the use of Soviet sources on the career of Kuchik Khan. Many works appearing in English have largely accepted the Soviet estimate of this Iranian nationalist. In this connection, it is significant that Major-General L. C. Dunsterville, who led an English expedition through Gilan to Enzeli in 1918, recognized Kuchik Khan as "a high-minded enthusiast," whose main objective was "Persia for the Persians."[4]

Soviet action in regard to Gilan affords one more indication of how the Soviet government failed to live up to its promises of "friendship" and "non-interference" in the internal affairs of other countries. Although the predicament of Iran was such that a Soviet-Iranian alliance against England was well within the realm of possibility, once again, as in the case of Turkey, the Bolshevik menace became even greater than the threat from the English

4. L. C. Dunsterville, "Military Mission to North-West Persia 1918," *Journal of the Royal Central Asian Society,* VIII, Part II (1921), p. 83.

invader. In reply to Iranian protests over Soviet incursions at Enzeli and in Gilan, Moscow disclaimed all responsibility, asserting that the new republic of Azerbaijan, over which it had no control, had acted on its own authority. Today, however, the Soviets attribute their failure in Gilan, Khorassan, and south Azerbaijan to provocative and tactless Leftist elements who took premature action in confiscating Iranian lands and attacking the Muslim religion.

Renewed Negotiations. In the spring of 1920, several factors contributed to the renewal of Soviet and Iranian efforts to reach an understanding. After the restoration of Soviet authority in Baku at the end of April, Iranian merchants began to insist on the resumption of trade and diplomatic relations with Soviet Russia. The withdrawal of the British in May from Enzeli and Resht in advance of Soviet troops weakened British prestige and rendered even less likely the ratification of the Anglo-Iranian Treaty of 1919. The advance of Soviet Azerbaijan forces into Gilan and the subsequent proclamation of the Soviet Republic of Gilan on May 20, 1920, aroused apprehension in Iranian government circles, but it may have indicated the need for an understanding, especially in view of the fact that Iranian protests to Moscow and to the League of Nations produced no results.

On May 5, 1920, Vossuq-ed-Dowleh asked the Soviet government to establish normal diplomatic and trade relations and to conclude an "equal" treaty based upon the earlier Moscow proposals. He was even ready to recognize the Soviet Republic of Azerbaijan. However, according to Soviet sources, the Iranian government refused to guarantee the safety of Soviet representatives upon their arrival in Iran. Not until the following October did the Iranian representative, Mushaver-ol-Mamalek, Iranian ambassador at Constantinople, arrive in Moscow to begin negotiations with the Russians.

Soviet-Iranian Treaty. Soviet-Iranian treaty negotiations, which began in November, 1920, were not completed until the advent of Reza Khan to power in February, 1921. Meanwhile, the special council summoned by the shah to expedite ratification of the Anglo-Iranian Treaty met on December 13, 1920. The English, already forced by the Communists to withdraw from Enzeli on the Caspian Sea, now threatened to abandon northern Iran entirely, leaving the country open to Soviet occupation, unless the Anglo-Iranian Treaty was speedily ratified. In spite of English pressure, the council postponed a decision on the Anglo-Iranian Treaty pending the outcome of Soviet-Iranian negotiations in Moscow, which were then nearing a successful conclusion. On December 3, the council approved the draft of the basic terms of the Soviet-Iranian Treaty, with minor amendments. News spread that the Soviet government had abandoned the capitulations, the restoration of which was stipulated in the unpopular Anglo-Iranian Treaty. English efforts to offset the Soviet-Iranian negotiations, under these circumstances, proved unavailing.

The Soviet-Iranian Treaty was concluded in Moscow on February 26, 1921, as the first official act of the new government of Seyyid Zia ed-Din and

Colonel Reza Khan, who had seized power by army *coup d'état* five days earlier. The new prime minister, Seyyid Zia, had been active in the preparation and conclusion of the Anglo-Iranian Treaty of 1919, and he praised this treaty in a brochure published in 1920 in Baku, where he was a member of the Iranian delegation which conducted negotiations with the anti-Soviet Mussavatist (Muslim Democratic) government in Baku prior to the restoration of Soviet authority. The main purpose of Reza Khan, an Iranian counterpart of Kemal Pasha, was to free Iran from both English and Soviet interference and to introduce drastic reforms, which in the Muslim world are known as secularization. Just as Kemal Pasha used the Russians to offset English and French encroachment, Reza Khan first used the English to help him consolidate his power. The treaty of friendship between Iran and the RSFSR on February 26, 1921, enabled him in turn to force a British withdrawal from Iran and to abandon the Anglo-Iranian Treaty of 1919. On the heels of the departure of the last British troops from Iran in May, 1921, Kuchik Khan's forces, with the support of Soviet advisers and reinforcements from Soviet Azerbaijan, began their march on Teheran, which failed miserably. Chicherin promptly repudiated any Soviet connection with this effort and according to Louis Fischer, Soviet leaders abandoned Kuchik Khan and withdrew their forces from Iran by September, 1921. The collapse of the Gilan Soviet Republic followed.

The second official act of the new regime was the repudiation of the treaty with England, on the pretext that the Mejlis had failed to ratify it. Soviet historians claim that Seyyid Zia did everything possible to prevent the ratification of the Soviet-Iranian Treaty. One even goes so far as to say that he annulled the Anglo-Iranian Treaty to create confusion, to paralyze the national democratic movement, and to prepare the ground for a new agreement with England.

The difference between the Soviet-Iranian Treaty of 1921 and the abortive Anglo-Iranian Treaty of 1919 was as great as that between Lausanne and Sèvres for the Turks. Having reiterated their intention of abandoning tsarist policies and declared once again that all tsarist treaties with Iran were null and void (Articles I and II), having restored the Russo-Iranian boundary of 1881 with minor adjustments on both sides, the RSFSR restored to Iran numerous concessions and properties of the tsarist government, including roads, railroads, telegraph and telephone lines, church properties, etc., and canceled tsarist loans. Each contracting party agreed to refrain from intervention in the internal affairs of the other and to prohibit hostile organizations and groups from operating on the territory of the other. The Iranians secured the right to free navigation on the Caspian Sea.

The full significance of Articles VI and XIII, which did infringe upon the territorial sovereignty of Iran, and constituted a serious potential threat to Iranian independence, was not apparent until World War II. Article VI provided as follows:

If a third party should attempt to carry out a policy of usurpation by means of armed intervention in Persia, or if such Power should desire to use Persian territory as a base of operations against Russia, or if a foreign Power should threaten the frontiers of Federal Russia or those of its allies, and if the Persian Government should not be able to put a stop to such menace after having been once called upon to do so by Russia, Russia shall have the right to advance her troops into the Persian interior for the purpose of carrying out the military operations necessary for its defense. Russia undertakes, however, to withdraw her troops from Persian territory as soon as the danger has been removed.

Article XIII further provided: "The Persian Government, for its part, promises not to cede to a third Power, or to its subjects, the concessions and property restored to Persia by virtue of the present Treaty, and to maintain those rights for the Persian Nation."

When the Iranian government in November, 1921, in apparent violation of Article XIII, granted an oil concession formerly held by a Georgian of Russian nationality to the Standard Oil Company of New Jersey in the five northern provinces of Iran, vehement protests from the Soviet government led to the annulment of the concession. The same fate befell the Sinclair Oil Company in a similar venture in 1923.

Iran protested the vagueness of the above-mentioned and other articles in an exchange of notes on December 12, 1921, and received assurance that Article VI applied only to "preparations for a considerable armed attack upon Russia or the Soviet Republics allied to her," such as might be organized by White Russian *émigrés*, with the active assistance of foreign powers, and not to verbal attacks on the Soviet Union by Russian *émigrés* or Persian groups. Article XIII, according to the Russians, was not intended "to place any restriction upon the progress and prosperity of Persia."

Article VI did serve as a basis for Soviet intervention in Iran, August 25, 1941, to forestall German occupation in World War II. Both articles nevertheless proved of direct service to Iran, Article VI by facilitating British withdrawal, and Article XIII by preventing the concessions and properties restored by Russia to Iran from reverting to any other foreign power.

One reason the Soviet government was prepared to make major concessions to Iran at this time was that the prevalence of famine made peace abroad a virtual necessity. These concessions came on the eve of the introduction of the New Economic Policy (NEP), which stemmed the tide of militant communism at home and abroad. The Russian treaties with Iran, Turkey, and Afghanistan were designed to erect an effective southern barrier against further English intervention. The text of the Iranian treaty, especially Article II, suggests that the Soviet leaders still hoped to make a lasting impression on the peoples of the Orient. This they might well have accomplished, had it not been for the subversive propaganda activities that belied the fine phrases of the treaties. This treaty nevertheless formed the basis for all later agreements between the USSR and Iran and served to restore peace and order in the midst of chaotic conditions on both sides of the border. The Soviet-Iranian Treaty, and those with Turkey and Afghanistan concluded in the same year, together with major religious, social, and economic concessions made by the Soviet government to the natives of Central Asia,[5] had a pacifying effect in a very troublesome area in the Soviet Union.

With the conclusion of the Soviet-Iranian Treaty, the Soviet government appears to have abandoned any immediate prospects for the establishment of a Soviet regime in Iran. According to the *Year Book of the Comintern* for 1923, which devoted more space to Iran than to any other Muslim state of the Near and Middle East, there were in 1922 no more than two thousand Communists and Socialists in Iran, only one Communist newspaper, and altogether only twenty thousand Iranians connected with trade-union organizations. This insignificant number, less than half of the 4,500 Communists Sultan-Zade had boasted of in *Pravda* in 1921, was a clear indication that communism had failed to make headway among the poverty-stricken masses in Iran. Even as early as October 22, 1920, according to Chicherin, the Central Committee of the Communist Party had resolved that an Iranian revolution would not be possible until the complete bourgeois development of the country had occurred.

Reaffirmation of the Treaty. On October 1, 1927, the Soviet Union and Iran signed a Treaty of Guarantee and Neutrality, which reaffirmed the provisions of the Soviet-Iranian Treaty of February 26, 1921. According to Soviet sources, this treaty enabled Iran to proceed with the abolition of the capitulations in 1928, as well as to pass legislation for an autonomous customs tariff.

AFGHANISTAN AND THE OCTOBER REVOLUTION

Amanullah and the October Revolution. The Soviet government and the Comintern lost no opportunity to convince the Soviet peoples and those of the Near East that not only Turkey and Iran, but likewise Afghanistan owed its freedom and independence to the October Revolution. In April, 1919, inspired in part, at least, by the Bolshevik Revolution, Amanullah and his "Young Afghans," who by means of a palace revolution had seized power the previous February, denounced Afghanistan's treaty obligations with England. Amanullah's first manifesto declared that Afghanistan must become a free and independent country, enjoying the rights of every sovereign state. Since the English government was by no means persuaded to accept the Afghan

---

5. Such as the *waqf* lands, previously confiscated for the benefit of the state, which were returned to the Muslims; the religious schools were reopened; the Shariat courts were brought back; and the NEP permitted the return of private trade.

coup d'état, Amanullah turned to Soviet Russia for assistance. The initial Afghan attitude toward the new Soviet regime may have been conditioned in part by a brochure on *Bolshevism in the Koran,* by the Hindu revolutionary leader Barkatulla, published in Persian, Afghan, and Arabic.

As a result of the Second Anglo-Afghan War of 1878–1881, Afghanistan had lost its independence. Thereafter its foreign policy was wholly directed by the British government through the British viceroy in India. In addition to this humiliating treaty arrangement, in 1893 Afghanistan, under British pressure, was forced to accept a modification of its boundary with India in favor of the latter, known as the Durand line. The culture and economy of the country remained at a low level. There were no railroads, only one major highway leading to India, one printing shop, and no factories other than a military arsenal. Amanullah, influenced no doubt by the "Young Turks" and the Iranian revolutionaries, as well as by the Russians, intended to cast off English domination and introduce many needed reforms in this backward country.

Confronting the threat of hostilities with Great Britain, Amanullah on April 7, 1919, addressed identical letters to Lenin and Chicherin, informing them of his accession to the throne and of the independence of Afghanistan. He proposed the establishment of diplomatic relations. On May 27 when Lenin and Chicherin replied, in line with the provisions of the Treaty of Brest-Litovsk, with unconditional recognition of the sovereign rights of Afghanistan to independence and indicated their willingness to establish diplomatic relations, the Third Afghan War (May–June, 1919) with England was already under way. As in the case of Iran and Turkey, the Soviets insist that Afghan success in this war was due to the October Revolution. Because of the removal of the Russian threat in the north, the Afghans were able to concentrate all their forces against the British. Actually the English were not defeated, but were handicapped by an uprising in the Punjab. Both sides appear to have been satisfied to terminate the conflict. On August 8, 1919, in Rawalpindi, India (now in Pakistan), an Anglo-Afghan truce was signed, by which England recognized the independence of Afghanistan in domestic and foreign relations. The Afghans were forced to accept the Indian boundary of 1893, which left some three million Afghans in India.

Negotiations with Russia. Although a Soviet representative, Ya. Z. Surits, arrived in Afghanistan during the summer of 1919, due to foreign intervention in Russia and Soviet difficulties in Central Asia, it was October before an Afghan mission, headed by Muhammed Vali Khan, arrived in Moscow to enter into treaty negotiations with Soviet Russia. An interview with Mirza Muhammed Khan, a member of this mission, by a *Pravda* reporter in 1955 during the much-publicized visit of Bulganin and Khrushchev in Kabul, throws additional light on the conditions under which Soviet-Afghan relations were established. According to Mirza Muhammed Khan, in 1919 it took the Afghan delegation thirteen days to travel from Tashkent to Moscow. With civil war raging on all sides, they had to tear down fences and old buildings to provide fuel for their locomotives. In Moscow the diplomatic corps consisted of the representatives of only three states which at that time recognized the Soviet regime. Nevertheless, as the Afghan delegate explained during his reminiscences, Soviet recognition of Afghanistan's independence constituted valuable moral support for his country at the very time England embarked on the Third Afghan War. In his unforgettable interview with Lenin, the Soviet leader expressed like appreciation for the friendly act of the Afghan government, which, according to him, was the first to recognize the Soviet regime.

In England, where the mission of Muhammed Vali Khan had gone first, the Afghans were told to negotiate directly with the British viceroy in India. An Afghan appeal to the recently established League of Nations produced no immediate results. The Soviet regime, on the other hand, received the Afghans warmly, and sensing its opportunity, entered into treaty negotiations without delay. As in the case of Turkey and Iran during the period of the intervention, Afghans infiltrated Central Asia, with the intent of extending the borders of Afghanistan. They caused sufficient trouble that the Soviets were willing to enter into treaty arrangements to put an end to border problems. Moreover, as Stalin pointed out, "The struggle of the Afghan Emir (Amanullah Khan) for the independence of Afghanistan is objectively a revolutionary struggle, in spite of the monarchical outlook of the Emir and his followers, for it weakens, disorganizes, and undermines imperialism."

Writing to Amanullah on November 27, 1919, Lenin called for trade and friendly agreements "for a joint struggle against the most rapacious imperialistic government on earth—Great Britain." Referring to Afghanistan as "the only independent Muslim state in the world," he indicated in phraseology that has a familiar ring in view of Soviet references to Turkey, that the Afghan people confronted "the great historic task of uniting about itself all enslaved Muslim peoples and leading them on the road to freedom and independence."

Soviet-Afghan Treaty. Actually Amanullah displayed no more haste in completing treaty relations with Soviet Russia than was shown by Kemal Pasha in Turkey. Afghan sympathy with the fate of Bokhara and Afghan designs on Turkestan were apparently among the factors which induced the emir to hesitate. Once the truce was signed with England, Afghanistan was under no pressure to come to terms with Moscow. Ivan Maisky, in his study of Soviet foreign policy during these years, has indicated that there was friction at this time between Afghanistan and the RSFSR. A Soviet source, which makes no attempt to account for the procrastination, states that the discovery in June, 1920, of an English plot to assassinate Amanullah Khan strengthened the desire of the Afghans for a rapprochement with Soviet Russia. It therefore appears that the renewed threat of English intervention revived Soviet-Afghan negotiations. On September 13, 1920, a preliminary draft of the Soviet-Afghan Treaty was signed in Kabul.

Alarmed by the turn of events in the latter part of 1920, the British government through one of its agents in Afghanistan tried, in January, 1921, to shelve the Soviet treaty by substituting for it the draft of an Anglo-Afghan

Treaty, which would have required the Afghans to accept certain English political demands and to restrict themselves to the establishment of trade relations with Soviet Russia. In spite of the efforts of the Afghan Anglophiles, the treaty between the RSFSR and Afghanistan was concluded on February 28, 1921, two days after the Soviet-Iranian Treaty, and was ratified in August of the same year.

The Soviet-Afghan treaty reaffirmed the independence of Afghanistan, provided for the establishment of regular diplomatic relations and the opening of consulates, promised Afghanistan "financial and other material assistance" and the restoration of frontier areas which belonged to Afghanistan in the nineteenth century. A supplementary article, of particular interest because it affords a preview of the tactics pursued on a much larger scale by the Soviet Union today in the Middle East, provided for Afghanistan an annual Soviet subsidy of one million rubles in gold or silver, the construction of a telegraph line on the Kushk-Herat-Kandahar-Kabul route, and Soviet technical experts and other specialists to assist the Afghan government.

Turko-Afghan Treaty. On March 1, immediately following the Soviet-Afghan Treaty and while negotiations were still in progress for the Soviet-Turkish Treaty, a Turko-Afghan Treaty was signed in Moscow; it was obviously designed to fit into the projected Soviet system of alliances with Muslim lands on the southern Soviet border. This treaty, a first-class propaganda instrument, having recognized that "thanks to the Almighty" the oriental world was at last awakening, credited Turkey with having been "the guide of Islam" and "an example" in regard to the Caliphate. The treaty recognized the complete independence of both Turkey and Afghanistan, as well as "the emancipation of all oriental nations and their right to freedom and independence." Each of the contracting parties undertook to support the other against "an imperialist state which follows the policy of invading and exploiting the East"—an obvious reference to England. It is significant that this treaty, too, no doubt in conformity with the wishes of Afghanistan, specifically recognized the independence of Khiva and Bokhara (Article II). It likewise provided for the establishment of diplomatic and consular relations, as well as for the sending of Turkish military and educational missions to Afghanistan for at least five years. The fact that this treaty was signed in Moscow under Soviet auspices indicated that all three countries involved had one objective in common—collaboration against English intervention.

Concessions from England. As in the case of Turkey and Iran, Soviet Russia made concessions to remove the threat to her southern frontier. The Soviet-Afghan Treaty placed the Afghans in a favorable position to secure like concessions from England. In the Anglo-Russian Trade Agreement of March 16, 1921, Afghanistan was referred to as "the independent state of Afghanistan." Alarmed by Soviet conquest of Bokhara and other Soviet successes in Central Asia, the Afghans signed a treaty with England, November 22, 1921, which recognized Afghan independence and existing Afghan boundaries and, like the Soviet treaty, provided for the exchange of diplomatic representatives and the establishment of British consulates in Afghanistan. The treaty prohibited the opening of Soviet consulates at Ghazni and Kandahar close to the Indian frontier—a setback for the Russians.

Anti-British Propaganda. The sending of Fedor Fedorovitch Raskolnikov (Ilin) as the first Soviet minister to Afghanistan, 1921–1923, clearly indicated that the Soviet government planned to make use of its treaty arrangements to establish in Kabul a key propaganda center for activity against the British in India. Raskolnikov, a Bolshevik since 1910, had been acting commissar of the Red Navy (1918) and commander of the Caspian flotilla (1919) which drove the British from Enzeli in northern Iran. Having some pretensions as a scholar, he became a member of the board of directors of the Scientific Association of Orientalists. Lord Curzon, in his ultimatum to Soviet Russia of May 2, 1923, accused Raskolnikov of "exceptional zeal" in conducting propaganda activities against the British in Afghanistan, as well as of supplying arms to the rebellious tribes of the Indian northwest frontier, and demanded his recall.

Pagman Treaty. Since the Afghans continued to take advantage of the *Basmatchi* revolt[6] against Soviet authority, the Soviet government on August 31, 1926, at Pagman, entered into a Treaty of Neutrality and Nonaggression with Afghanistan, by which each contracting party agreed to refrain from interference in the internal affairs of the other. This pact, according to Soviet interpretation, put an end to the frequent raids into Soviet territory on the part of Afghan sympathizers with the *Basmatchi* movement, and also marked a new step in strengthening friendly relations between the USSR and Afghanistan. The Pagman Treaty was renewed in 1931. During his European tour in 1928 Amanullah visited Soviet Russia, where this so-called "Socialist King" received a royal reception from the Soviet Socialist regime, and a gift of two tractors. Although shortly after his return to Kabul, Amanullah was overthrown, his successor pursued the policy of using Russia to offset English influence.

Ineffective Soviet Policies. The treaties concluded with the three Muslim states in 1921 proved conclusively the failure of Soviet propaganda to make any appreciable headway among the Muslims outside Soviet territory. The Soviet regime intended to make Central Asia the stepping stone from which to win over all Muslims to the Soviet side. In retrospect, we may safely say that the Baku Conference and the subsequent Soviet propaganda accomplished just the opposite. Instead of being on the offensive, the Soviets were forced to assume the defensive. The *Basmatchestvo* was not solely a local movement, but also a kind of counterattack inspired and guided from the outside, especially from Turkey and Afghanistan. In other words, the impact of the Muslims outside Soviet territory on the Muslims inside was much stronger and more effective than any impact of the Soviet Muslims abroad.

6. A counter-revolutionary revolt of the "downtrodden" (*Basmatchi*) or oppressed, which spread throughout Soviet Central Asia and plagued the Soviet government during the Civil War following the Bolshevik Revolution.

20

Reappraisal: Domestic
and Foreign, 1921-1928

In 1920, Soviet Russia emerged from the Civil War and Intervention exhausted and frustrated. The country had not known peace since 1914. Food supplies and other commodities were in extremely short supply because Soviet manpower had been absorbed, even after 1918, in the struggle against its White opponents, and arbitrary Soviet policies had discouraged production. Once the Civil War and Intervention subsided, the latent discontent evoked by War Communism manifested itself in serious agrarian revolts in the Kuban and Tambov regions and strikes in the cities. Bolshevik leaders had counted on world revolution, or at least on European revolution, but the latter, when it came in defeated Germany and Hungary, rejected Soviet leadership and proved to be transitory. At this critical juncture, the German Revolution had just experienced a disastrous setback with the suppression of insurrection and the general strike. At Baku, Soviet expectations of a revolution in the Muslim World had likewise met with frustration. Both at home and abroad a reappraisal became necessary.

Kronstadt Uprising. It was against this background that there suddenly occurred on March 2, 1921, a revolt at the naval fortress of Kronstadt against the Soviet regime. This was no ordinary uprising. The Kronstadt sailors were socialists who had played a decisive role in the *coup d'état* of November 7, 1917, which brought the Bolsheviks to power. Under the slogan, "The Soviet System Without Communists," they demanded the restoration of freedom of trade, freedom of the press, the secret ballot, and the election of new soviets. Some even asked for the return of the Constituent Assembly. With the exception of freedom of trade (private trade), these were much the same slogans the Bolsheviks had used prior to their seizure of power. In 1921, however, with the Soviet regime in the saddle, they had a counter-revolutionary ring, strongly reminiscent of the Mensheviks and Kadets.

The Kronstadt uprising, which was a severe blow to Soviet prestige at home and abroad, was a dilemma for the Soviet government. The Red sailors were the heroes of the Revolution. They could not be dismissed as capitalists and reactionary Whites, for they belonged to the proletariat. To dispatch regular

369

Soviet troops to suppress the revolt was a risky matter. They might refuse to fire on their comrades or might even find the struggle infectious and join them. The slogans of the sailors—especially freedom of trade to relieve conditions approaching famine—voiced the sentiments of many Russians at that time, even of some Bolsheviks. There still existed, moreover, a threat of renewed Polish intervention under Pilsudski, supported by French officers. Since the final treaty between Poland and the Soviet regime had not yet been signed, Petrograd was in an exposed strategic location. By this time, the Soviets were short of military manpower for the western front.

Tatar Regiments. At this juncture Joseph Stalin, with the consent of Lenin, approached General Ali Fuat Cebesoy, then ambassador of the Turkish Republic in Moscow, urging him to use his influence with the Tatar (Muslim) regiments to join in the suppression of the revolt. These Tatar regiments, organized in separate units because of the need for observance of dietary laws, had remained neutral during the Civil War, refusing to fight for either side. Since the Turks and Soviets were engaged in fighting a common enemy,

General Cebesoy was the first ambassador to Moscow appointed by the Turkish Republic. He had been instrumental in concluding the 1921 "treaty of friendship and fraternity" between the two nations.

the British and French, who, by the Treaty of Sèvres (August 10, 1920) had threatened the destruction of the Turkish Republic of Kemal Atatürk, Cebesoy was persuaded to come to the aid of the Soviet regime. The fact that the French were involved in the Polish struggle against Russia was a factor in his decision. It was, therefore, with the help of Tatar regiments, whose soldiers had no scruples about fighting Soviet sailors, that Commissar of War Trotsky was able to suppress the Kronstadt revolt. Whether or not it could have resulted in the overthrow of the Soviet government remains a matter of speculation. In the vicinity of Petrograd any uprising which reached substantial proportions—and this one was hopefully watched by all forces in opposition to the Bolsheviks—would have encouraged the Poles to exploit Soviet difficulties by continuing the conflict, instead of concluding peace as they did on March 18, 1921. General Cebesoy stated on August 29, 1963, in Istanbul, that had it not been for the Treaty of Sèvres he would never have consented to use his influence with the Tatar regiments on behalf of the Soviet regime.

THE NEW ECONOMIC POLICY

While these events were taking place, the Tenth Congress of the Communist Party convened in Moscow, March 8–16, 1921. This congress confronted the hard fact that while revolution was receding in the major European countries, it had survived in Russia—all of which was directly at variance with Communist theory. The important fact was that the Soviet regime should continue in power, no matter what the cost. Lenin, with his capacity for grasping essentials, was convinced that if the Party and Revolution were to survive, drastic measures must be taken to stem the tide of popular, and especially of peasant, discontent. He marshaled all his persuasive powers to secure from the congress concessions which marked a radical departure from the principles of Militant Communism. In brief, Lenin recommended a tactical retreat—the famous two steps backward in order to prepare for one step forward. His recommendations amounted to the introduction of a modicum of private trade to save the country from widespread famine. Avoiding capitalist nomenclature, however, Lenin labelled his program the New Economic Policy (NEP). The new program confronted strong opposition in the congress from Trotsky and other left-wing supporters of Militant Communism. Only the stature and prestige of Lenin led to its ratification. This Brest-Litovsk on the domestic level, as it was termed, was never intended to be a permanent retreat. It was no more than a truce to secure the survival of the Soviet regime and the Communist Party.

Resumption of Production. The introduction of the NEP served as a green light to the bulk of the population to resume production and normal business activity. Many food and consumer items that had been secreted immediately reappeared. A famous confectionary in the National Hotel in Moscow, which had been gathering cobwebs during the early years of the Revolution, was reopened and well stocked with white bread, pastry, and candy on the very morning the new economic policy was announced.

With the cancellation of the obnoxious grain requisitioning system (*prodrazvërstka*) and the substitution of a tax in kind, the middle-class concept stimulated by the Stolypin agrarian reforms soon reasserted itself. Once a peasant had met his obligation to the state, he was free to dispose of the balance of his surplus. Almost immediately products and household articles which had been carefully concealed during the war years made their appearance in the markets. Although key industries and the land remained nationalized and foreign trade continued to be a government monopoly, there was enough leeway to encourage private incentive in both industry and agriculture. The concession to the peasantry soon led to a loosening of the industrial straitjacket by further concessions to industry, much of which was decentralized under "trusts," some local and regional, and a few even national in scope. The first of these, established in July, 1921, by Samuel Liberman, was the Northern Timber Trust, the object of which was to restore lumber exports. By the summer of 1923 there were 478 trusts, embracing 3,561 enterprises employing about 1,000,000 workers, or 75 per cent of those involved in nationalized industry.[1] Many small industries were completely denationalized.

Drought and Famine: Foreign Assistance. Before the NEP concessions had a chance to bear fruit, a catastrophic drought in the summer of 1921 in Russia's major agricultural areas threatened the entire program with disaster. The severe famine conditions of 1921–1922, which stemmed not only from the drought but from the exigencies of the Civil War and Soviet grain-requisitioning policies, broke through the icy barrier between capitalism and communism. On July 13, 1921, Maxim Gorky, a Soviet writer already well known abroad, made a stirring appeal for bread and medicine, not for the land of "Communism," but for "the country of Tolstoy, Dostoyevsky, Mendeleyev, Pavlov, Mussorgsky, Glinka, and others." Although this appeal was undoubtedly instigated by the Soviet government, it evoked from the capitalist world a remarkable response on humanitarian grounds. The American Relief Administration, headed by Herbert Hoover, is estimated to have saved the lives of eleven million Russians, many of them helpless children and young people. Other foreign organizations, including the Swedish Red Cross, the German Red Cross, the Quakers, the Nansen Aid, and a Vatican relief mission, worked with a will, even at times competing with one another, to save the Russian people from starvation. A number of Jewish organizations, such as the Joint Distribution Committee and People's Relief, contributed over $40,000,000 to save their coreligionists in Russia. The Soviet govern-

---

1. Maurice Dobb, *Soviet Economic Development Since 1917* (New York: International Publishers, 1948), p. 135.

ment later claimed that this foreign aid was given, not from purely altruistic motives, but to secure first-hand information about Soviet domestic conditions (spying) and to dispose of American wheat surpluses in order to forestall a drop in grain prices. Even if, in some instances, the motives were mixed, nothing can detract from the fact that millions of Russian lives were saved by this basically humanitarian venture into the field of foreign aid. One rather bizarre sidelight on this aid program was that Vidkun Quisling, who betrayed Norway to the Nazis in World War II and whose name has become a household word with unpleasant connotations, served as a valuable member of the wholly altruistic Nansen mission.

Anti-Inflation Measures. Under the NEP, immediate steps were taken to combat runaway inflation, which had rendered Soviet currency so worthless that at the beginning of 1921 one gold ruble was worth 26,539 paper rubles. Toward the end of the year a State Bank was established which by June, 1924, had stabilized Russian currency on the basis of the *chervonetz,* valued at ten gold rubles, or a little more than $5.00. Metal coins began to replace the worthless paper in circulation.

Foreign Capital Investment. The complete reconstruction of the country's economy, however, was beyond the immediate capacity of the Soviet government. It required foreign loans, foreign capital equipment, and foreign technical assistance. To accelerate recovery, Lenin therefore invited foreign capital investment under close supervision of the Soviet regime. Foreign companies were given an opportunity to exploit some of Russia's rich natural resources in return for the indispensable equipment to accomplish the task. There was reason to doubt whether capitalist nations would respond to Lenin's invitation. Russia was in dire need of commodities of all kinds and capital equipment, for much of which credit would be required. Soviet credit, following the government's default on tsarist and Kerensky foreign debts, was by no means good. No substantial trade could be developed, moreover, until the Soviet government established diplomatic relations with capitalist powers —a situation it had never expected to confront.

In the years 1921 to 1928, somewhat to the amazement of Soviet leaders, 2,400 applications were received from foreign sources. Apprehensive lest the country should become dominated by foreign capitalists, the Soviet government proceeded with caution and granted only 178 contracts, of which 68 were still functioning on the eve of the First Five-Year Plan. These represented a capital investment of 61,000,000 rubles. One of the most outstanding was the American manganese concession at Chiaturi in the Transcaucasus, headed by W. Averill Harriman, who subsequently became American ambassador in Moscow. The British and Japanese also secured for a time important mining concessions in Siberia. The Germans set up the huge but not very successful "Mologales" timber concession on the Volga. Soviet suspicion of foreign enterprises presented serious obstacles to their profitable development. Although foreign capital investment never assumed major proportions in the Soviet economy, Soviet leaders regarded it as an insurance policy against any renewal of foreign intervention in Soviet Russia.

Success of Private Initiative. Largely due to the return of peace-time conditions, private initiative in agriculture and industry, and foreign capital investment under the NEP, food supplies increased, business conditions improved, and the Russian people enjoyed "relative" prosperity. By 1927 the Russian national economy had become a mixture of private and state capitalism, and production in some areas had risen to the 1913 level. By resorting to capitalist tools and other devices, the Soviet government and Communist Party engineered their own survival. The NEP established an important precedent. In the future, when the Soviet regime found itself face to face with economic emergency, as in the years following World War II, it resorted to private initiative. Even as late as 1963, Khrushchev did not hesitate to advise Soviet collective and state farmers to adopt whatever was useful from the American system.

The NEP concessions vastly increased Lenin's popularity in Soviet Russia with the people at large. Most of the articulate peasants and businessmen recognized that it was Lenin who wrested these concessions from Trotsky and other staunch supporters of Militant Communism. In the USSR today, Lenin's popularity is attributed to his Communist ideology. Actually, Lenin died during the retreat from Communism under the NEP, when one concession after another was made to private initiative. This was the time when he became endeared to the Russian people as "Vladimir Ilitch."

CREATION OF THE USSR

The return to normalcy made possible the establishment of a new political structure based on the federal principle. In December, 1922, the Russian, Ukrainian, White Russian, and Transcaucasian[2] Soviet republics became constituent members of the Union of Soviet Socialist Republics (USSR). To these were added in 1925 the Uzbek and Turkmenian republics, followed by the Tajik republic in 1929. This constitution, modelled on that of the Russian Socialist Federation of Soviet Republics (RSFSR), a 1918 product of Militant Communism, was adopted by the Central Executive Committee of the Union on July 6, 1923, and ratified by the Second All-Union Congress of Soviets on January 31, 1924.

Death of Lenin. The creation of the USSR was Lenin's last political achievement. He had suffered his first stroke in May, 1922, the month in which Stalin became general secretary of the Central Committee of the Communist Party, a second stroke in March, 1923, which deprived him of the power of speech, and a fatal third stroke on January 21, 1924. Lenin was

2. In 1936 the Transcaucasian federation was separated into the Armenian, Azerbaijan, and Georgian Soviet Socialist Republics.

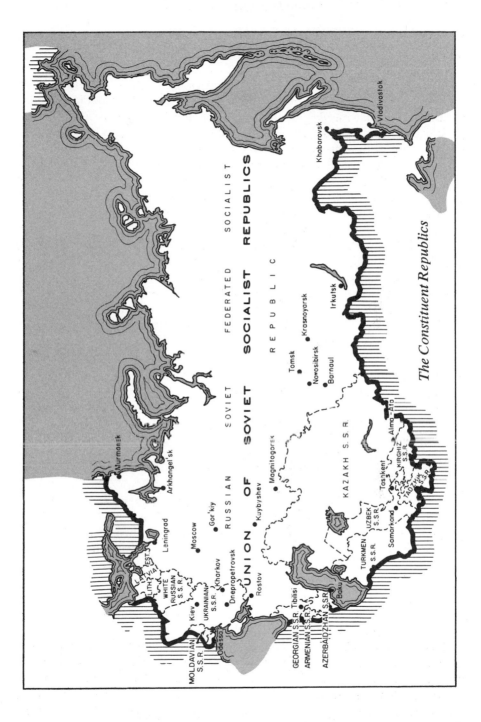

UNION OF SOVIET SOCIALIST REPUBLICS

RUSSIAN SOVIET FEDERATED SOCIALIST REPUBLIC

The Constituent Republics

Vladivostok

Khabarovsk

Irkutsk

Krasnoyarsk

Tomsk

Novosibirsk

Barnaul

Magnitogorsk

Alma-Ata

KIRGHIZ S.S.R.

KAZAKH S.S.R.

Tashkent

TADZHIK S.S.R.

UZBEK S.S.R.

Samarkand

TURKMEN S.S.R.

Murmansk

Arkhangel'sk

Gor'kiy

Leningrad

Moscow

Kuybyshev

LITH. EST.
LATVIA
WHITE RUSSIAN S.S.R.
Kharkov
Kiev
UKRAINIAN S.S.R.
Dnepropetrovsk
Rostov
Baku

MOLDAVIAN S.S.R.
Odessa

GEORGIAN S.S.R. Tbilisi
ARMENIAN S.S.R.
AZERBAIDZHAN S.S.R.

buried in the now familiar black granite tomb in Red Square, which has become a shrine for Communist pilgrims, comparable to that of Mecca for the Muslims and Bethlehem and Jerusalem for Christians.

Evaluation of Lenin. One of Lenin's biographers, Stefan Possony, while recognizing his intellectual ability, his capacity for work, his courage, and his selflessness, emphasizes his "dominant power urge" and labels him a "compulsive revolutionary." Bolshevism as a doctrine is conceded to be Lenin's contribution. Although revolution was his vocation and he fanatically opposed all enemies of Bolshevism, shedding the blood of the "class enemy" without compunction, Lenin was pragmatic rather than inflexible. This quality he demonstrated when he called for the acceptance of the Peace of Brest-Litovsk rather than continuation of the war against Germany, and when he undertook to retreat from Militant Communism by the adoption of the New Economic Policy. Winston Churchill once suggested that Lenin, had he lived, might have saved Russia from the extremes and violence of the Stalin era. Yet Lenin, in many respects, laid the foundations on which his successor's policies were based. Lenin believed in dictatorship, not in political freedom, as the instrument of revolution. He insisted on the principle of "democratic centralism" in the Party, with the expulsion of those who threatened Party unity by refusing to conform. This concept of dictatorship is strongly reminiscent of Shigalev's ideas in Dostoyevsky's novel *The Possessed.* Lenin also made the Third International, his own creation, a Bolshevik organ, although by so doing he split the world socialist movement. In spite of his professed dislike of bureaucracy, he strengthened the Party administrative apparatus, which Stalin then used as a stepping stone to power. In other words, as Trotsky observed, the apparatus created by Lenin created Stalin. Lenin likewise condoned terrorism as a useful and indispensable weapon for dealing with class enemies—the peasants, the bourgeoisie, the clergy, and the intelligentsia. The purge he undertook in 1921 involved the expulsion of 170,000 from the Party, one-quarter of its membership. Acting on the principle that the end justifies the means, he considered subversion, distortion of truth, and the use of slander justifiable in promoting revolution. He employed many men of dubious past, including Stalin, whose prowess as a bandit in the Caucasus served the purposes of the revolution. He even displayed the strength of character to collaborate with men he disliked, as in the case of Trotsky, believing him to be the proper person to build the Red Army and thus serve the cause of Bolshevism. It is hardly an exaggeration to say, on these grounds, that without Lenin there would have been no Stalin.

Diversity in the Communist Party. The men who composed the inner circle of the Communist Party following its seizure of power in 1917 were by no means of one mind on political and ideological issues. Nor did they comprise a congenial unit as personalities. Lenin, due to his personal magnetism, zeal, and sense of reality, emerged as their acknowledged leader. As long as he lived, his preeminence among them was recognized. Trotsky, although a late comer in the Bolshevik ranks, was a brilliant orator, derived prestige from his prolonged sojourn abroad, and in spite of his ignorance of the Russian grass roots and the Asian minorities, enjoyed wide popularity in the Party and throughout the country as the organizer of victory in the Civil War. Before he abandoned Menshevism, Trotsky forecast the ultimate end of Bolshevism: "The organization will replace the Party, the Central Committee will replace the Party organization and, finally, the dictator will replace the Central Committee." In the early years of Soviet rule, Stalin remained virtually unknown to the people at large, except in the East, where his role as commissar of nationalities brought him to the fore. Among the top leaders of the Party, however, he was well known for his organizational abilities. The experience with General Ali Fuat Cebesoy even indicates that Lenin placed more trust in him than in Trotsky and delegated to him greater authority.

The triumvirate that took over during Lenin's illness, which included Kamenev, chairman of the Moscow Soviet and vice-president of the Council of People's Commissars, Zinoviev, chairman of the Petrograd Soviet and head

Wide World

When this photograph was taken in 1925, Stalin, Rykov, who had succeeded Lenin as premier, Kamenev, and Zinoviev headed the Soviet government. By the end of 1927 the latter three had been removed from positions of power, and Stalin was in full control.

of the Comintern, and Stalin—all "old Bolsheviks"—did not include Trotsky, certainly an important signpost of his declining power. Before his death in January, 1924, however, Lenin reappraised his leading associates. Disturbed by Stalin's "rudeness," and by the enormous power already concentrated in his hands, Lenin in his will recommended that he be replaced as general secretary of the Party's Central Committee. No one appears to have anticipated at this time the emergence of Stalin as Lenin's successor.

Stalin's Rise to Power. Joseph Stalin, the shoemaker's son from Georgia, had a long record as a professional revolutionary. Time and again, from 1902 to 1917, he was arrested and exiled to Siberia. From the beginning of the split in the Social Democratic Party, he sided with the Bolsheviks against the Mensheviks. Lenin placed the stamp of his approval on Stalin's *Marxism and the National Question* (1913), regarding him henceforth as an authority in that field. Returning to Petrograd in March, 1917, Stalin became a member of the Presidium of the Central Committee and an editor of *Pravda*. Even as early as the summer of 1917, he challenged Preobrazhensky and others who insisted that revolution could not succeed in Russia without revolution in the West. Immediately following the October Revolution, with Lenin's blessing, he became people's commissar of nationalities and a member of the All-Union Executive Committee. During the Civil War, Stalin participated in the defense of Tsaritsyn (renamed Stalingrad in 1925). In 1922, in the midst of one of Lenin's periodic Party purges, Stalin, now a successful organization man, secured the highly strategic post of secretary-general of the Central Committee of the Communist Party, where he could easily place his own henchmen in key Party positions. Against the anti-Party groups, Stalin consistently supported Lenin. In 1924, when Lenin's reassessment of Stalin came before the Thirteenth Party Congress, Stalin was already effectively undermining the Trotskyites—no doubt one reason why he emerged unscathed. To some of Lenin's associates, Stalin may have appeared as a lesser evil than Trotsky.

Once the stabilizing influence of Lenin was removed, friction quickly developed among his successors. Although he had been at odds with Trotsky since Civil War days, Stalin astutely stood aside from the contest between Trotsky, on the one hand, and Zinoviev and Kamenev, on the other. By the time the three joined hands in opposition to Stalin, the latter had consolidated his position sufficiently that he was able to bring about their decline and fall.

One of the issues at stake was the continuance of the NEP. As early as the Eleventh Congress of the Communist Party in March, 1922, some delegates, alarmed at the resurgence of private enterprise, demanded that this "retreat on the economic front" be checked. The opposition increased at the Fourteenth Party Congress in the spring of 1925, when, upon Stalin's recommendation, the *kulaki,* or middle-class peasants, were permitted to lease land and hire labor. Trotsky, who had never abandoned his belief in "permanent revolution," regarded the NEP as a betrayal of the October Revolution (*Lessons of October,* 1924). His theory of permanent revolution was based on the premise that revolution in Russia could succeed only if accompanied by world revolution and to this end he devoted his efforts. He also viewed with great concern the growth under Stalin's guidance of a Soviet bureaucracy. Trotsky refused to forget the initial opposition of Zinoviev and Kamenev to Lenin's timing of the Bolshevik Revolution of 1917. They, in their turn, never permitted Trotsky to forget that he had been in the ranks of the opposition prior to 1917. Against Trotsky's stand on world revolution, Stalin advanced his own interpretation of Leninism, the theory of "socialism in one country." Soviet Russia, he claimed in *Problems of Leninism* (1924), was, strictly speaking, not one country. It was multi-national, composed of several republics, in fact a Soviet "League of Nations." It was a huge land which spanned a continent, with rich natural resources. Under these circumstances, according to Stalin, socialism could be achieved in Russia, irrespective of world revolution. Stalin was supported by Bukharin, editor of *Izvestia;* Rykov, premier of the Soviet Union; Tomsky; and others, who now represented the Right wing of the Communist Party.

Fall of Trotsky. The ideological and personal battle which followed led to the decline and fall of Trotsky, who, by degrees, was deprived of position and honors. His removal as war commissar in January, 1925, was followed by his ouster from the Politburo in October, 1926. In 1927, not only did he cease to be a member of the Party's Central Committee, but the Fifteenth Congress of the Communist Party in December deprived him of Party membership. To forestall any plots to reinstate him, the government exiled him to Alma Ata in Turkestan at the beginning of 1928. His continued opposition to the government's program led to his exile from the USSR in January, 1929. As he was shunted from one country to another—from Turkey to France, Norway, and Mexico, he remained the center of Trotskyite opposition to the Stalin regime. Stalin's final revenge came with Trotsky's death by assassination in Mexico City on August 21, 1940.

World events from 1921 to 1927 served to strengthen Stalin's position on the development of "socialism in one country." Communist attempts to stir up revolution in Germany in October, 1923, failed miserably. Not only had the prospects of world revolution receded in Europe, but in Italy communism produced Fascism under Mussolini. The neighboring Polish Republic was overthrown in May, 1926, by a military *coup d'état* under Pilsudski. In England, following a general strike, Baldwin's Conservative government severed relations with the Soviet Union in 1927. In April of the same year, Chiang Kai-shek's Kuomintang Party split with the Chinese Communists and expelled Soviet advisers from China. With world revolution out of the picture, at least for the foreseeable future, the only practical alternative was the building of socialism in Russia. Trotsky's thesis would have consigned the Russian Revolution to oblivion.

European Policy

In its struggle for production and survival, the Soviet government was forced to reappraise its position vis-à-vis the very capitalist powers whose demise its leaders had so confidently but vainly anticipated. In other words, it had to work for and practise coexistence at the same time that its Communist leaders and its agent, the Communist International, continued to preach and work clandestinely for the overthrow of all existing capitalist regimes. This anomalous situation handicapped Chicherin and his assistant, Maxim Litvinov, in their assiduous efforts to secure parity for Soviet Russia in the comity of nations. The Western powers, although prepared to normalize their relations with the Soviet government following the Intervention, refused to accept Soviet Russia as a great power. In fact, they reconstructed the international system at Versailles without Russia and continued to block her participation in major international conferences, including Lausanne, Washington, and Locarno.

Peace Treaties. Soviet Russia's economic revival and the retreat from Militant Communism did create a more favorable climate of opinion toward her in Europe and Asia. The impression was given, erroneously as it proved, that Russia by degrees was returning to the capitalist system. Even prior to the end of the Civil War, the Allied Supreme Council on January 16, 1920, had abandoned its blockade against the Soviet regime. In the same year, peace treaties were signed between Soviet Russia and the Baltic states of Esthonia (February 2), Lithuania (July 12), Latvia (August 3), and Finland (October 14). On March 18 the Treaty of Riga brought peace between Poland, on the one hand, and Soviet Russia and the Soviet Ukraine, on the other. Almost immediately following the lifting of the Allied blockade, Soviet and British representatives began tentative negotiations for the resumption of trade. After surmounting innumerable obstacles, an Anglo-Soviet agreement was reached on March 16, 1921, providing for *de facto* recognition of the Soviet government by Great Britain, and for a commercial convention.

Soviet-German Rapprochement. Perhaps the most significant development in Soviet Russia's relations with the West during the years of the NEP was her *rapprochement* with Germany, a move inadvertently facilitated by Russia's former allies. The severe reparations terms and military controls imposed on defeated Germany in 1920 by the Versailles settlement overcame initial German reluctance to establish closer contacts with the Soviet regime. As in the case of Turkey, Germany veered toward Soviet Russia in proportion to the pressure applied against her by the English and French victors. It was only logical, although Lloyd George's warning to this effect apparently failed to impress the treaty makers, that the two pariahs on the international scene, Germany and Soviet Russia, would gravitate toward one another. For the time being, both countries were excluded from the League of Nations.

The basis for a Soviet-German *rapprochement* was laid in April, 1920, with the conclusion of a Soviet-German agreement for the exchange of prisoners-of-war. This was followed in 1921 by a secret agreement between the two powers for military collaboration. This arrangement enabled the Reichswehr[3] to evade the crippling restrictions placed on German rearmament by the Treaty of Versailles, because it provided limited facilities for the training of German air force personnel and tank crews in Russia. Other benefits included a supply of ammunition from Soviet plants restored with German technical assistance, and construction of a few Junkers airplanes mainly useful for training purposes. The Red Army, in its turn, benefited from German instruction in the use of modern weapons and from the education of its high-ranking officers in German military schools. From the Soviet point of view, the strengthening of the Red Army was essential to assure the survival of the regime, and to this all other considerations were subordinated. The 1921 military agreement, which by no means constituted an alliance, proved useful to both participants for a decade until Hitler had assumed full control in Germany. Soviet historians later claimed that it was a product of Trotskyite treachery and that it provided the German armed forces with valuable military information about the USSR and its defenses, which was used to German advantage in World War II. Since that time, the Soviet government has been wary about entering into any system of international inspection of nuclear facilities which would equip foreign powers with important information about Soviet defenses.

Genoa Conference. The Soviet-German *rapprochement* made a significant forward step at the Genoa Conference of 1922, the first Western-sponsored international gathering in which the Soviet government participated. Here the vexatious matter of Russian war debts embittered discussions, especially when the Soviet delegation, headed by Chicherin, presented a bill for Soviet losses due to the Allied Intervention. Against Allied claims for $13,000,000,000 from Russia for tsarist and Kerensky debts and for property confiscated by Soviet nationalization, Chicherin advanced counter-claims for $60,000,000,-000 for damages resulting from the Intervention. Although the Soviet government at this time was prepared to settle Allied claims on the basis of token payments in return for new Allied loans to promote Soviet economic reconstruction, this maneuver was unqualifiedly rejected.

Rapallo Treaty. The Germans, who attended the Genoa Conference to secure some amelioration of their reparations payments, likewise met with frustration and ostracism. Nervous over the prospect of a Soviet deal with the West at their expense, they chose the alternative of reaching a prior deal with the Soviets, the groundwork for which had already been prepared by Chicherin in Berlin en route to the conference. The result was the conclusion on

---

3. Voluntary military force organized in Germany for the purpose of defending the realm.

April 16, 1922, of the Rapallo Treaty, by which Germany and Soviet Russia reestablished full diplomatic relations and accorded one another most-favored-nation treatment. According to Article 5, the German government promised to facilitate the business of German private firms in the development of the Soviet economy. Both countries wiped the state clean of all claims for damages resulting from the war, intervention, occupation, and Soviet nationalization.

Although the Rapallo Treaty envisaged no alliance, it afforded a demonstration of Soviet reversion to the paths of secret diplomacy. For the Soviets, as well as for the Germans, it constituted a breach in the wall of postwar isolation to which they had been consigned by the West. The treaty was a diplomatic triumph for Chicherin. It substituted for the Treaty of Brest-Litovsk, imposed by force, an arrangement providing for fruitful collaboration. The honeymoon in German-Soviet relations lasted until Germany improved her status with the West through the Dawes Plan for reparations in 1924 and the Locarno Pact of 1925. Recognition of Soviet Russia by Germany and the provision of German foreign aid paved the way for similar action on the part of the other Western powers. In 1924, Great Britain, Italy, Norway, Austria, Greece, Sweden, China, Denmark, Mexico, and France granted Soviet Russia *de jure* recognition, and Japan followed suit in 1925.

Lausanne Conference. During the balance of the NEP period, Soviet Russia's relations with the West remained unstable, even at times hostile, due in part to Communist interference in the internal affairs of other countries and Communist incitement of unrest in the colonial world. In May, 1923, Lord Curzon of Great Britain threatened to denounce the 1921 Trade Agreement unless anti-British propaganda in the Middle East were abandoned. At the Lausanne Conference in the same year, where Chicherin was admitted only to those sessions concerned with the Straits Settlement and excluded from those between the Entente Powers and Turkey, the Russians failed in their efforts to secure the closure of the Straits to outside powers and to confine the future discussion of the Straits Question to the Black Sea powers. Under Lord Curzon's indominitable leadership, the Straits were demilitarized, and with certain restrictions, remained open to the warships of outside powers. The Straits Convention was signed but never ratified by the Soviet Union.

Having refused to recognize the Versailles Peace Settlement, including the League of Nations, Soviet leaders watched with great concern the *rapprochement* between Germany and the West, which culminated in 1926 in Germany's admission to the League of Nations and which appeared to herald the end of the Rapallo policy. Although Soviet-German relations cooled, an important commercial treaty was signed between the two powers in 1925, followed by the "Berlin Treaty" of April 24, 1926, a neutrality pact which helped to assuage Soviet fears of renewed Allied intervention via German territory.

ASIAN POLICY

The treaties of 1921 between Soviet Russia and Turkey, Iran, and Afghanistan afforded clear and unmistakable proof of the failure of the Soviet government and the Third International in their efforts to Bolshevize the Muslim Orient. Before launching another attack on the citadel of Islam, the Soviet regime required a breathing spell in foreign, as in domestic, affairs. The above-mentioned treaties provided such a respite, in which Soviet leaders could take stock of the situation, account for their failure, and make more adequate preparations for the future.

Oriental Studies. Although many reasons were advanced to explain the failure of their mission to communize the East, including lack of organization, there was one which persisted throughout Soviet literature and the press, namely, Soviet ignorance of Asia in general and of the Muslim East in particular. To remedy this situation, it was decided to launch an extensive and intensive study of the Orient. Accordingly in January, 1922, acting upon the instructions of Lenin and Stalin, the All-Union Scientific Association of Oriental Studies was established in Moscow. Several periodicals soon made their appearance, devoted to the national and colonial problems of the East, the most important of which were *Novyi Vostok* (*The New Orient*), the official organ of the association; *Zhizn Natsionalnostei* (*The Life of the Nationalities*); *Revolyutsionnyi Vostok* (*The Revolutionary East*) and *Materialy po Kolonialnym i Natsionalnym Problemam* (*Materials on Colonial and National Problems*). Branches of the association were formed in such centers as Tashkent, Baku, Tiflis, and even abroad; the first foreign center was in Teheran. In addition to the Institute of Oriental Studies of the Academy of Sciences of the USSR established in Leningrad (transferred to Moscow in 1950), new centers for the study of oriental problems made their appearance, especially in Central Asia. Some leading orientalists of the tsarist regime took an active part in this educational venture, including Academicians V. V. Bartold, former editor of *Mir Islama*, B. Ya. Vladimirtsov, and I. Yu. Kratchkovsky.

University of the Toilers of the East. On a different level, but likewise designed to train Communist cadres for the revolution in the Orient, was the Communist University of the Toilers of the East, established in Moscow by Stalin under the auspices of the Commissariat of Nationalities in the spring of 1921. Here instruction was to be carried on in native languages. Students of heterogeneous background were gathered from the tundra, the taiga, from far-off Yakutia, the Caucasus, and Central Asia. Of the six hundred who registered in September, 1921, only four students had received any higher education. Most of them had only a grade-school background and some were illiterate. This unique "university" began with a seven months' training course in the principles of Marxism-Leninism. Within the next few years a four-year curriculum was developed, where Oriental students were indoctrinated in the principles of Marxism, received training in revolutionary tactics, and studied Eastern customs and languages. According to Stalin, the university served a dual purpose: the training of cadres for the soviet republics of the East and the preparation of other cadres for colonial and dependent countries. Although comprised largely of students from Soviet Russia, the student body included ten groups from colonial and dependent countries, who were being trained as revolutionary leaders for the liberation of their peoples. Branches of the university were established in Central Asia, especially in Tashkent, Irkutsk, and Baku. In 1923 it claimed an enrollment of almost nine hundred students, representing fifty-seven nationalities. The University of the Toilers of the East was the predecessor and in some respects served as a model for the University of the Friendship of Peoples (Lumumba University) in Moscow, where a revolutionary intelligentsia is being trained for Asia, Africa, and Latin America.

Change in Tactics. As a result of this intensive study of the Orient and the reexamination of colonial questions at the sixth congress of the Comintern in 1928, several conclusions were reached, which provided the basis for the new Communist programs for the Muslim world. Whereas in 1917 the Soviet government made one all-inclusive appeal to the Muslims of Russia and the East, they now discovered that the same yardstick would not suffice to measure the problems that confronted the variety of peoples, cultures, and economies of this vast area.

To insure the success of their struggle to win the colonial and dependent peoples of the East, Soviet leaders changed their tactics, and instead of a quick decisive victory they envisaged a prolonged struggle in which the revolutionary movement would pass through three distinct stages. (1) The colonizing power would be expelled by means of an intensive national liberation movement—in other words, a campaign against colonialism which, in their opinion, would create a united front of all classes except the direct agents of imperialism. (2) Once national independence was achieved, the local Communists must conduct a campaign among the workers and peasant masses to the effect that political sovereignty was not enough—that complete liberation involves a social as well as a political revolution. The liberated state must therefore pass to the control of the workers and peasants. (3) The final stage involved the seizure of power by the Communist Party.

The Documents: Blueprint for Middle East Communization. The results of approximately a decade of study of the Muslim East, with a view to the promotion of a successful Communist revolution there, are to be found in the *Documents of the Programs of the Communist Parties of the East.*[4] Because of their authenticity these *Documents* undoubtedly will reinforce the views then held by many scholars and statesmen as to the futility of relying on trea-

4. For a complete English translation of the Communist programs, see Ivar Spector, *The Soviet Union and the Muslim World: 1917–1958* (Seattle: University of Washington Press, 1959), pp. 111–180.

ties concluded with the Soviet Union, the basis of which is "co-existence." The best example is the Communist program for Turkey, an independent Muslim state, which had entered into a treaty of "friendship and fraternity" with Soviet Russia in 1921, in which each country promised to avoid interference in the internal affairs of the other. Nevertheless, the Communist program for Turkey (1931) outlines the very steps by which the regime of Kemal Pasha was to be undermined, ultimately overthrown, and the country taken over by the Communists.

Likewise the programs for the Arab countries, especially for Egypt, reveal the extent of the infiltration by Communist agents in that area. It would be of great benefit for the Arabs in general, and for the Egyptians in particular, to read and study this primary source material bearing upon the future prepared for them. The Palestine program should be of equal interest to contemporary Israel. The attack on Zionism and the emphasis on the Arabization of the Communist party of Palestine clearly indicate the handwriting on the wall as far as the Jewish state is concerned. In view of their experiences in the past, the Arab peoples have been prone to question the motives of the Western powers, especially those of England and France, but also those of the United States, in the Near and Middle East. These *Documents* leave no room for doubt as to the designs of the Soviet Union.

Irrespective of the future course of events in the Muslim world, these programs will remain a standard text on Soviet designs for the eventual inclusion of that world in the Soviet orbit. This is further substantiated by the report of Khalid Bakdash, the leader of the Arabic Communists, to the central command of the Communist Party of Syria and Lebanon in January, 1951. In an orgy of self-criticism, similar to that which was characteristic of Stalin's Russia in the same period, Bakdash bemoaned the general lack of theoretical knowledge of the principles of Marxism-Leninism, and admitted that the attention of the Arab Communists had been directed mainly toward the creation of "a lot of sound and fury" rather than toward the establishment of solid foundations among the workers and fellahin.[5] His program was in substance little more than a paraphrase of the 1934 documents.

Far East. After Soviet expansion in the direction of the Near and Middle East was blocked in the early 1920's by internal resistance on the part of Turkey, Iran, and Afghanistan, as well as by their counterattack against Soviet Russia as expressed in the *Basmatchi* revolt, the USSR met with another resounding defeat in the Far East with the loss of China in 1927. The Nanking government, with Anglo-American support, broke off diplomatic relations with the Soviet Union.

For some time the Soviet regime was cut off from the Far East by the Civil War and Intervention. Concentration on the Muslim East likewise led to procrastination in the development of normal relations in the Far East.

5. An Arab tiller of the land (farmer or peasant).

Beginning in the summer of 1919, several overtures were made to China and Mongolia for the establishment of diplomatic relations on the basis of the liquidation of tsarist secret treaties, concessions, and special privileges. The chief obstacles to an early solution of outstanding Soviet-Chinese problems proved to be the Soviet refusal to recognize the cession of the Chinese Eastern Railway to China and China's claim to sovereignty over Mongolia.

Mongolia. In Mongolia, where Soviet propaganda in favor of Mongolian independence was warmly welcomed, there appeared to be greater promise for Soviet success. A Mongolian People's Party, established toward the close of 1919, appealed for Soviet assistance for the eviction of the White forces under Baron Ungern Sternberg. In a pastoral country lacking a proletariat, Lenin was dubious about the possibility of transforming the Mongol People's Party into a Communist Party, when this matter was discussed following the Baku Congress. In July, 1920, however, with the aid of Red Army units, the Whites were driven from Urga and the Soviets thereafter reached a special agreement with the hutukhta (Living Buddha) on the establishment of a limited monarchy in Outer Mongolia. Soviet troops were asked to remain in Mongolia, which they did until 1925. In November, 1921, the Soviet government triumphantly restored diplomatic and friendly relations with the new Mongolian People's government. Soviet tactics of rendering assistance to a small group of Mongol revolutionaries in response to their appeal for aid had thus paid off. Here was an alternative to the Muslim route to the Orient—a Mongolian-Buddhist route via the Kalmuk steppes and the Altai to Mongolia, and from there to Tibet and India.[6]

"Russian" Period of the Kuomintang. Impatient over the reluctance of the Peking government to come to terms, the Soviet regime exploited the political chaos in China by establishing close relations with the much more amenable Kuomintang regime in south China, led by Sun Yat-sen, hero of China's Revolution of 1911 and a dedicated foe of Western "imperialism." In the fall of 1923 Michael Borodin, amply supplied with funds and with a troop of civilian and military experts in tow, was dispatched to Canton as adviser to the Kuomintang. The Soviet objective was to build up the revolutionary Kuomintang, which was neither Communist nor Socialist, along Soviet lines as a powerful political and military force, capable of overthrowing the Peking government and combatting Western, especially British, imperialism in the Far East. After their experience in the Near East, Soviet leaders were dubious about the prospect of producing a revolution of the 1917 Bolshevik vintage in agrarian China. They therefore concentrated, in spite of strong opposition from Trotsky, on a Chinese equivalent of the Russian Revolution of 1905, to be achieved in collaboration with the Chinese "bourgeois" nationalists.

Soviet assistance to the followers of Sun Yat-sen led the Peking government

6. Xenia Joukoff Eudin and Robert C. North, *Soviet Russia and the East, 1920–1927: A Documentary Survey* (Stanford, Calif.: Stanford University Press, 1957), p. 199.

—the only Chinese government enjoying international recognition—to enter into belated treaty arrangements with Soviet Russia. By the treaty of May 31, 1924, the Peking government granted full diplomatic recognition to the Soviet regime and agreed to joint (mainly Russian) provisional management of the strategic Chinese Eastern Railway. In return, the Soviets promised to withdraw their military forces from Outer Mongolia in recognition of Chinese sovereignty. With a Soviet-trained Mongolian People's Army on the spot this constituted no serious problem.

There is evidence in the Russian literature of the period that this sudden shift of emphasis from Europe to Asia did not meet with the unanimous approval of Soviet leaders. The best substantiation of this is to be found in a cartoon published in *Pravda* on January 30, 1925, following the dispatch of Borodin to China. This cartoon depicted a compass, accompanied by the reassuring message from the Narkomindel (People's Commissariat of Foreign Affairs), "The needle turns to the East. Don't worry, gentlemen. There is no anomaly here. Everything is in order." Apparently the sudden about-face in policy caught many Party members in the Soviet Union unprepared, and Party leaders took this somewhat unorthodox means of reassuring them. In spite of Soviet efforts to accomplish in the Far East what they had been unable to do in the Near and Middle East, and in spite of the millions of dollars in gold devoted to this objective at a time when the Russians could ill afford to spend it abroad, here as before the Soviet government failed to instigate a revolution.

During the so-called "Russian" period of the Kuomintang, 1923–1927, under Borodin's guidance many Chinese students were sent to Soviet Russia for training. Among them was Chiang Kai-shek, one of Sun Yat-sen's ablest aides and ultimately his successor, who spent several months in Moscow. The Whampoa Military Academy, established on the Soviet model by Chiang Kai-shek with the assistance of General Blücher (Galen) provided effective training facilities for the Kuomintang officer corps. The small and politically insignificant Chinese Communist Party, founded in 1921, was subordinated to the Kuomintang and, for all practical purposes, merged with it—a move which soon produced friction. Until his death in 1925, Sun Yat-sen, without sacrificing his own ideology, placed great faith in Soviet Russia and its top adviser, Borodin, as the means by which China could secure its national independence.

Partial Failure. Soviet policy appeared to be succeeding. By 1926 the Kuomintang at its own request was admitted to the Comintern as a "sympathizer-member," and the reorganized Kuomintang army was ready for its Northern Expedition against the Peking regime. It was at this stage that the Soviet regime lost control of the movement. Chiang-Kai-shek took decisive action to purge his party of Chinese Communists, who were expelled from the Kuomintang in 1927. Having succeeded in uniting China with the aid of the Communists, he broke with them completely. Borodin's mission collapsed, and he returned to the Soviet Union in July, 1927. Arrested by the Soviet government in February, 1949, he died in an eastern Siberian prison camp in 1953.

The collapse of Soviet efforts to bring about a Chinese revolution was a serious blow to Russian prestige at home and abroad. The denouement accelerated the fall of Trotsky, who had always opposed the deal with the Kuomintang. The diplomatic breach between Great Britain and the Soviet Union, which was not unrelated to the situation in China, created a climate of crisis in Soviet government circles, with renewed fears of intervention which failed to materialize. Having sacrificed the interests of the Chinese Communist Party to the "bourgeois nationalism" of the Kuomintang, the Soviet regime sowed seeds of distrust which in all probability were never entirely suppressed. Nevertheless, Soviet policy did lay the foundations for a Communist Party in China, especially in the countryside, which produced positive results in later years. Mao Tse-tung ultimately succeeded in moving the decimated ranks of the Chinese Communists to north China where, without benefit of Russian aid, they gradually renewed their strength.

2 1

The Stalin Regime, 1928-1941

BY 1927 IT BECAME CLEAR even to the most ardent anti-Trotskyites that the continuation of the New Economic Policy constituted a major threat to the Communist goals of the Soviet Union. The Nepmen, as they were called, had grown in numbers and riches. Although from time to time the acquisitions of some were confiscated, this had failed to discourage the majority. The NEP was only designed to get the economy functioning again, mainly through the restoration of agricultural production. Throughout the NEP period the Communist Party had devoted much thought and discussion to ways and means of industrializing underdeveloped Russia. Since its establishment in 1920, and especially after 1926, the State Planning Commission (Gosplan) had labored assiduously to prepare blueprints for an integrated program of industrial development. The concept of a planned economy was, therefore, no sudden innovation. As the NEP prospered beyond expectations, however, the question in Communist minds was, Where do we go from here? Should there be more of the NEP, as advocated by the Right wing, or did the industrialization of Soviet Russia require much greater investments in industry, transportation, housing, schools, medical care, etc., than the NEP was capable of insuring? And where was the Soviet Union to secure the resources for this industrial revolution? Surely not from the voluntary efforts of a nation of small peasant proprietors using medieval techniques! Comparable problems confront all the developing countries of Asia, Africa, and Latin America today.

THE FIRST FIVE-YEAR PLAN

The Fifteenth Congress of the Communist Party in December, 1927, the very one which expelled Trotsky from the Party, authorized Stalin to carry out a greatly accelerated program of industrialization and collectivization, commonly known as the Five-Year Plan (October 1, 1928–October 1, 1933), which included many of Trotsky's recommendations. One reason for resorting at this time to Trotsky's proposals for collectivization of agriculture was that the NEP had provided something to collectivize. At the close of the Civil War, there was such chaos in both industry and agriculture that there was virtually no base on which to build a collective economy. The decision represented a determination to secure rapid economic growth at any cost. The rationale of the Five-Year Plan was production. Its authors hopefully anticipated so much production in five years that the world would be flooded with Soviet exports, with resulting unemployment in capitalist countries which, in its turn, would pave the way for revolution. In other words, the Five-Year Plan, far from abandoning the Communist goal of world revolution, was expected to achieve it by surer methods than those Trotsky had advocated.

A Second Soviet Revolution. The year 1928 is sometimes said to have inaugurated a second Soviet revolution in Russia. If so, it was a revolution imposed from above rather than one emanating from the masses. It was the scope of the Five-Year Plan and the pace Stalin set for its accomplishment that were breathtaking. Every aspect of Soviet life, even the arts, was to be mobilized to insure its success. The entire literature of the period, from the kindergarten up, may be entitled Five-Year Plan literature. With the resources of the nation and its regimented manpower devoted to the program, the planners expected vast and often quite unrealistic improvements in agriculture, mining, transportation, fishing, forestry, education, public health, recreation, and so on. This millennium was to be achieved in one five-year period. Its fruits were therefore to be reaped by the generation that made the supreme sacrifices to attain its goals. In spite of the widespread opposition of those

Wide World

Peasants on a collective farm in the 1930's participate in the government's plan to banish illiteracy. Millions of books, magazines, and newspapers were sent to the villages to raise the cultural level of the peasants.

who had profited by free enterprise under the NEP, the Five-Year Plan offered a new horizon. Backward Russia was to overtake and surpass the capitalist countries of the West, a goal that has never since been abandoned. As late as 1963, Khrushchev was predicting that the Soviet Union would overtake and surpass the United States in seven years.

Forced Collectivization. Stalin's way out of Russia's dilemma (like that of Peter the Great) was a hard way for the Russian people, especially for the Russian peasantry. Through large-scale, collectivized farming he hoped to improve technical efficiency, which would increase production and at the same time release peasant labor for the new industries. Collectivization was also designed to stamp out peasant individualism and acquisitiveness. The initial rather modest agricultural goals were by no means commensurate with those for industry. In 1929 they had to be revised upward in favor of total collectivization, which destroyed the NEP alliance with the peasantry. The fact that over 14,000,000 households were collectivized by June, 1929, as compared to 1,000,000 in March, 1928, indicates the increased tempo. All *kulak* opposition was labelled counter-revolutionary and was suppressed with every means at the disposal of the government, including trusted city Communists, the army, and the secret police. There was some reason for comparing Stalin's ruthless policy toward the peasants with that of Ivan Grozny toward the boyars. It has been estimated that some 5,000,000 peasants were deported or shot for resistance or sabotage. Unskilled labor, which increased costs of production and reduced the quality of goods, too often proved to be inefficient labor. Many peasants, accused of wrecking and sabotage, were transferred to concentration camps, where they worked practically for nothing on vast government projects under what amounted to slave labor conditions.

The immediate result of forced collectivization of agriculture was chaos. The far from pliable peasants retaliated by the destruction of crops, horses, cattle, and buildings. Nevertheless, the collective farms produced grain for the cities, even when the peasants were left to starve. The Ukraine and the Kuban, the chief centers of opposition to collectivization, were literally depleted of food products. The result was the famine of 1931–1932, which is estimated to have brought death to about three million Ukrainians. The excess zeal of local authorities added greatly to the hardships of the peasantry. In the spring of 1930, on the ground that Party members were "dizzy with success," Stalin beat the drums of retreat. Numerous privileges and concessions were bestowed on the collective farms, which in some measure reduced the violence of discontent. By 1934, William Chamberlin, then an American reporter in the Soviet Union, found that there were 230,000 collective farms (*kolkhozi*) and from 5,000 to 6,000 state farms (*sovkhozi*) in the USSR, the latter mainly experimental farms for opening up new lands.[1] Three

---

1. William Henry Chamberlin, "The Ordeal of the Russian Peasantry," (April 1934), reprinted in *The Soviet Union, 1922–1962: A Foreign Affairs Reader,* edited by Philip E. Mosely (New York: Frederick A. Praeger, 1963), pp. 124–136.

huge tractor plants—the one at Rostov being the largest agricultural machinery works in Europe—were in operation and some 200,000 tractors were in use for large-scale farming. These tractors were concentrated at from 2,500 to 3,000 Machine Tractor Stations (MTS), which were expected to maintain their upkeep and control their distribution—an ingenious device for preserving discipline under the collective farm system.

"Socialist Competition" in Industry. In Soviet factories, a campaign for "socialist competition" among workers in different enterprises served to stimulate production without increasing wages. Soviet industries soon operated on a "continuous five-day week" (1929), in which a new shift took over where the previous one left off and the machines were kept in operation. Soviet "union" labor formed the nucleus of "shock brigades," which set a stiff pace for their comrades, and which sometimes failed in its goal for increased production. Unemployment in the Soviet Union, in the years corresponding to the height of economic depression in the West, was virtually liquidated by the transfer of idle peasants and workers to new industrial sites, many of them beyond the Urals. By such means, the volume of output of the means of production was vastly increased over previous levels, although not to the extent envisaged by the Five-Year Plan.

Foreign Skilled Labor and Equipment. As in the case of the NEP, the Soviet government encouraged the use of foreign skilled labor and the importation of foreign equipment to ease chronic Soviet shortages. As a result of the depression in the West, it became possible to secure labor for Russian factories from the ranks of the European unemployed. From Germany, in particular, technicians and engineers numbered in the hundreds or even thousands trekked to the Soviet Union in search of employment. German industry welcomed Soviet orders for various types of heavy machinery and other equipment, which in 1931 alone amounted in value to 919,200,000 reichsmarks. Several large German manufacturing firms are believed to have survived the depression years only by virtue of Soviet business. In the first half of 1932, according to figures provided by Gustav Hilger, second counsellor at the German Embassy in Moscow, the percentage of German exports purchased by Soviet Russia amounted to 50 per cent for cast iron and nickel products, 60 per cent for earth-moving equipment and dynamos, 70 per cent for metal-working machines, 80 per cent for cranes and sheet metals, and as high as 90 per cent for steam and gas turbines and steam presses.[2]

Shift in Emphasis. The authors of the Five-Year Plan had not envisaged any adverse changes in the international situation, which would obstruct its progress. Japanese occupation of Manchuria in 1931, regarded as a major threat to Siberia, forced the revamping of the original program to emphasize heavy industry at the expense of light industry and consumer goods. New emphasis was placed on construction in Asiatic, at the expense of European

2. G. Hilger and A. G. Meyer, *The Incompatible Allies: A Memoir-History of German-Soviet Relations, 1918–1941* (New York: Macmillan, 1953), p. 240.

Russia. The Japanese threat likewise forced the Soviet government to transfer large numbers of workers from industry and agriculture to expand its Far Eastern army (created in 1929) for purposes of defense. It was to make up for this shortage of labor that Stalin in 1931 introduced piecework on a large scale and encouraged overtime work. It was to feed the new army that the Ukraine in March, 1932, was denuded of two million tons of grain, to be delivered in thirty days.

THE SECOND FIVE-YEAR PLAN

By 1932, the Soviet government realized that due to changing circumstances, as well as to over-extended goals, very little of the original blueprint could be accomplished. It began to condition the Soviet public for a Second Five-Year Plan. With much fanfare, the Soviet press announced the completion of the First Five-Year Plan in four years. Whereas its main purpose had been to build heavy industry, the new plan, it was promised, would stress light industry.

Development of the Soviet Far East. Under the Second Five-Year Plan, huge sums of money and equipment were diverted to the Soviet Far East, the population of which numbered only 2,500,000. New coal mines were developed, metallurgical plants were established on the Amur River, and numerous power stations were constructed in the area. For strategic reasons, the Soviet government undertook to double-track the Trans-Siberian Railroad, and to begin construction on the Baikal-Amur line far removed from the exposed Manchurian border. To promote settlement in this dangerously underpopulated region, the government increased military compensation, encouraged army personnel to locate in the area at the conclusion of their terms of service, used large numbers of convicts on construction projects, and reduced taxes. According to the "Privileges of the Population of the Far Eastern Region," issued on December 11, 1933, collective farmers were granted ten years exemption from taxes on the staple commodities of grain and rice, and a 50 per cent reduction on other products. Even individual settlers secured a five-year exemption from grain and rice taxes.

Third Five-Year Plan: Reemphasis on Heavy Industry. As the Japanese threat disrupted the First Five-Year Plan, the Hitlerite menace forced the reshaping of the Second Five-Year Plan. The accession of Adolph Hitler to power as reichschancellor of Germany on January 30, 1933, marked a further deterioration of Soviet relations with Germany. Soviet planners ceased to be the masters of their fate. In the 1930's, instead of acting in accordance with their blueprints, they reacted to external threats by a reemphasis on heavy industry, the backbone of defense, while the hard-pressed Soviet population, poorly clothed and badly housed, continued to face excessive shortages of practically all consumer goods. The government fround the external threat a handy tool to justify its methods of production and repression at home. Its Third Five-Year Plan was disrupted by Hitler's precipitation of World War II in Europe.

Stakhanovism. In Soviet industrial enterprises, piecework and bonuses served as incentives to higher production. In August, 1935, Alexei Stakhanov, a Donetz coal miner, by combining team work and piecework overfulfilled his quota to such an extent (400 per cent) that he was hailed throughout the country as a national hero. In a nation-wide campaign, other workers were urged to emulate his example. It was not always possible to distinguish Stakhanovism from a speed-up system of production, with all the tensions arising from such practices. It nevertheless served to raise the norms of production under the Second Five-Year Plan and accelerated the drift away from egalitarianism in industry. He who worked more was paid more.

Industrial Expansion. Even the most uncompromising opponents of Soviet totalitarianism admit that the first three Five-Year Plans (1928–1941) resulted in vast industrial expansion in the USSR. Any resort to figures for purposes of comparison with tsarist production or that of foreign countries is likely to be misleading. Within a little more than a decade the Soviet Union had established the foundations of a great new metallurgical base east of the Urals to match the Donbas in the Ukraine. Here the coal of the Kuznetsk basin in Siberia was transported by the overloaded Trans-Siberian facilities to the iron center of Magnitogorsk in the south Urals for smelting. What seemed to many Americans like a highly uneconomic venture proved its strategic value in World War II. The story of the Ural-Kuznetsk Combine has been recorded by an American eye-witness, John Scott, in *Behind the Urals* (1942). Other highlights of Soviet industrial production at this time include the great tractor works at Stalingrad (Volgograd), Kharkov, and Chelyabinsk (in Siberia) designed to promote the mechanization and collectivization of Soviet agriculture. These tractor plants, together with the Molotov automobile works at Nizhny-Novgorod (Gorky) represented the first steps toward Stalin's goal of putting the USSR in cars and the *muzhik* on a tractor. Among Soviet hydro-electric projects, the prize exhibit was the Dnieprostroi Dam on the Dnieper, designed and supervised by Hugh L. Cooper, an American. Its power plants, with a capacity of 625,000 kilowatt hours, were designed by another American engineer, Alexander Vasilievitch Winter. The Moscow Subway (Metro) was also constructed during this period.

During the Second Five-Year Plan great efforts were made to exploit the rich mineral resoures of the USSR: copper in the Urals and at Lake Balkhash in Kazakhstan; lead at Chimkent, the Altai, the northern Caucasus, and the Far East; zinc in the Urals and at Kemerovo in Siberia; aluminum on the lower Dnieper, on the Volkhov east of Leningrad, and in the Urals at Kamensk; nickel in the Urals; tin in the Transbaikal and Kazakhstan; and magnesium on the Dnieper and in the northern Urals. The American mining engineer J. D. Littlepage, employed by the Gold Trust, 1928–1937, has left an interesting record of his search for gold in Siberia (*In Search of Soviet*

Gold, 1937). Among the new Soviet industries of the period were airplanes, heavy chemicals, plastics, artificial rubber, aluminum, copper, tin, and nickel. By 1938, on the eve of World War II, the USSR had become the world's largest producer of tractors and railway locomotives (Voroshilovgrad), and ranked second in oil, gold, and phosphate products.

Accelerated industrial development soon revealed the inadequacy of Soviet transportation facilities, especially of the Trans-Siberian Railroad. The Turkestan-Siberian (Turk-Sib) Railway, linking Tashkent, Alma-Ata, and Novosibirsk, was completed in 1930. In European Russia, the railroad network connecting the industrial Donbas with Leningrad, and Moscow with the Volga region, was double-tracked. To relieve pressure on the railroads, steps were taken to develop Russia's inland waterways by the construction of important canals linking the Moscow River with the Volga and by the widening of the old Mariinsky canal system to connect the Baltic via the Neva and Lake Onega with the Volga. A small beginning was made in the construction of automobile highways, connecting Moscow, Leningrad, Minsk, Kharkov, the Crimea, the Caucasus, and the Urals, as well as a direct route from Leningrad to Kiev.

Positive Results. In spite of the suffering and hardship endured by the Russian people, the positive results of planning should not be overlooked. The apocalyptic outlook of the early post-revolutionary years gave way to a constructive state of mind. At times, the zeal for the construction of the new industrial society proved as infectious as the drive for the destruction of the old regime during the era of Militant Communism. Achievement stimulated national patriotism. Soviet leaders soon discovered that married men, who had to provide for their families, often worked more assiduously than single men and women with less at stake. As a result, the family achieved a new status. With the reinstatement of the family, morality once again became fashionable, although it was called "the new morality." In matters of morals, the Communist Party was expected to set an example to the public at large. One of the women characters in Boris Pilnyak's novel *The Volga Falls to the Caspian Sea* (1930) announced that she would give her love only to one man *because* she was a Communist. It became equally clear that wherever private incentive existed or was encouraged, production correspondingly increased. In spite of the intensive drive for collectivization of agriculture, there still existed oases of private ownership. To spur production—always the major consideration—it became imperative to encourage private incentive, to provide legal outlets for individuals with energy and ambition who were willing to produce more if they could call even part of the output their own.

THE "STALIN" CONSTITUTION OF 1936

In 1935, the Seventh All-Union Congress of Soviets provided for a Constitutional Commission, over which Stalin presided, to revise the USSR Constitution of 1924 in the light of Soviet achievements in industry and agriculture.

The new Projected Constitution of the USSR was published on June 12, 1936. During the six months prior to its adoption on December 5, 1936, it was widely discussed throughout the country, some 43,000 changes were recommended, forty-three amendments were introduced, and the final draft was believed to represent the progress of the Soviet people in their march toward communism. In particular, it was said to reflect the end of class conflict, socialist ownership of the means of production, and the dictatorship of the workers under the continued "guidance" of the Communist Party. Although the Constitution itself made no mention of democracy, Stalin called it "the only democratic constitution in the world."

Democratic Façade. Certainly every effort was made to present to the world an outward façade of democracy. Like the Constitution of 1924, that of 1936 remained federal in form, with the addition of the right of constituent members to secede from the Union, a step never attempted to date. The Supreme Soviet, which replaced the Congress of Soviets, and which was declared "the highest organ of state power," was elected by direct, equal, universal, and secret suffrage, an apparent concession to the principles on which the Constituent Assembly was to have been based. In reality, however, this provision involved the democratic election of candidates nominated by organizations controlled and directed by the Communist Party. Like its predecessor, the Supreme Soviet remained a bicameral legislature, consisting of the Soviet of the Union, where representation was based on one deputy for every 300,000 voters, and the Soviet of Nationalities, which included 25 deputies from each of 11 constituent republics, 11 from each autonomous republic, etc. Although a simple majority decision was all that was required for the passage of legislation, in actual practice both houses have confirmed by unanimous vote the issues presented to them. The Supreme Soviet was given the authority to elect its own Presidium, the chairman of which serves as "president of the USSR," and to appoint the Council of Ministers. It also elects the Supreme Court and appoints the procurator general of the USSR.

Social Structure. Chapter I of the USSR Constitution provided an official definition of Soviet social structure. According to Article 1, the USSR is "a socialist state of workers and peasants." Thus, according to Soviet definition, the Soviet state is *socialist,* not *communist,* although its leadership is communist. Communism, as interpreted by Marx and Lenin remained the Soviet goal, but in actual fact it died in Soviet Russia during the period of the NEP. Those who incorrectly term the USSR a communist state attribute to communism successes which are not its due. It is also recognized as a class state of workers and peasants, no longer antagonistic to one another, since they work together toward the same goal. In 1963, the elimination of the phrase, "the dictatorship of the proletariat" from Article 2 was under consideration for the next revision of the Constitution, on the ground that the term "proletariat" suggests a class exploited by capitalists. Since the USSR has no more capitalists, there can no longer be a proletariat.

Private Incentive. To encourage increased production, the new constitution included substantial concessions to private initiative on Soviet collective farms. According to Article 7, in addition to its basic income from the common enterprises of the collective farm, every household was permitted "for its personal use a small plot of household land and, as its personal (private) property, a subsidiary husbandry on the plot, a dwelling house, livestock, poultry, and minor agricultural implements. . . ." Article 9 further indicated that the USSR officially recognized the existence of "the small private economy of individual peasants and handicraftsmen, based on their own labor," provided they did not exploit the labor of others. Still another concession to private property is to be found in Article 10, which guaranteed to citizens their incomes and savings from work, their homes, their household and personal property, as well as their right to inherit personal property.

Emphasis on Work. Since the Soviet Constitution was based on "existing reality," rather than on Communist goals, the final article of Chapter I (Article 12) bluntly prescribed work as a duty and honor for every able-bodied citizen, based upon the principle: "He who does not work, does not eat." Communism envisaged compensation according to "need." The principle of the socialist state read: "From each according to his ability, to each according to his work." Only by its emphasis on work could the Soviet state expect to transform a backward country into a progressive industrialized society.

A Bill of Rights. The heart of the new constitution, as far as the Soviet masses were concerned, was Chapter X, the Soviet Bill of Rights. Unlike the American Bill of Rights, however, it included not only the rights but also the obligations of the Soviet citizen. Among these rights were listed the right to work, rest, and leisure, to security in the event of old age or sickness, to education, and equal rights for women. Article 123 specifically guaranteed racial equality and proscribed all racial discrimination. Freedom of religious worship and of anti-religious propaganda were guaranteed by Article 124. No mention was made of the fact that in the Soviet Union anti-religious propaganda is heavily subsidized by the state, whereas religious institutions are discouraged and heavily taxed. From 1960 to 1963, for instance, 3,500 churches in the Soviet Union were closed "for lack of parishioners to support them." In the same year, only 10,000 Orthodox churches and 17 monasteries remained in the country. There were only two divinity schools (academies) and five seminaries for the training of priests. Even these were regarded as too many.

The Soviet System. Ostensibly the Soviet Constitution (Article 125) also guaranteed the four freedoms (speech, press, assembly, street processions and demonstrations). The last paragraph of this article, however, virtually cancelled the guarantees, since the facilities essential to their exercise remained at the disposal of the Soviet government. Similarly, Article 126 guaranteed to Soviet citizens the right to unite in trade unions, cooperative societies, youth organizations, sport and defense organizations, cultural, technical and scientific societies, with the proviso that they "voluntarily" accept the leadership of the Communist Party, the only recognized Party in the Soviet Union. It is significant that the USSR guaranteed the right of asylum (Article 129) not to individuals persecuted on grounds of race or religion—the two most prevalent forms of persecution—but to foreigners persecuted for defending the interests of the workers, for scientific activities, and to those struggling for national liberation.

Any analysis of the thirteen chapters of the Soviet Constitution (as revised, 1959) suggests that socially, according to Soviet definition, the USSR is a class rather than a classless society (Article 12). Politically, it is a totalitarian state under the dictatorship of one Party—the Communist Party. The existence of more than one party is said to reflect the class struggle. Economically, the Soviet system (especially since 1948) may be defined as state capitalism, since every state enterprise is required to show a profit, and profit is the soul of capitalism. Even the federal principle enunciated in the constitution is circumscribed with limitations. The constitution as amended in 1944 did grant each republic the right to conduct its own relations with foreign states (the basis for separate representation of the Ukraine and Byelorussia in the United Nations) and to maintain its own military formations. Nevertheless, the all-enveloping blanket of Communist control, centralized in Moscow, transcends republican boundaries and curbs republican autonomy. According to the constitution, a Union law supersedes a republican law at variance with it. In the USSR, the Presidium of the Supreme Soviet has the power to annul any action by a Union Republic (Article 49).

The Communist Party. In spite of the all-pervasive control of the Communist Party over Soviet life, only one specific reference was made to it in the constitution (Article 126). In the USSR, the Soviets represent the state and the Communist Party takes the place of the church, although its power in state affairs is far superior to that formerly exercised by the Orthodox church. Up to the present time in Soviet Russia, the Party (church) has controlled the state. Until the eve of World War II (May 6, 1941), when he became chairman of the Council of Ministers, Stalin occupied no official position in the Soviet government. He nevertheless ruled the country as secretary-general of the Communist Party. In other words, the Communist Party is the cement which holds the Supreme Soviet (legislative body) and the Council of Ministers (the executive branch) together. Every key position in the Soviet government has been occupied by a bonafide member of the Party.

Purges. In August, 1936, during the final stages of the preparation of the constitution, purges of leading Soviet Communists on an unprecedented scale were launched. One reason for these purges was a sharp split in the Communist Party in regard to Stalin's leadership, culminating in a plot to assassinate him. Although Stalin's leadership of the Party had been recognized since 1929, many of his associates had never fully accepted his domestic policy and his failure to react promptly and decisively against Fascism and Nazism abroad. Stalin, intent on "building socialism in one country," believed that the real road to Soviet security lay in the strengthening of Soviet defenses and Soviet military forces, rather than in intervention beyond Soviet boundaries. His intolerance of opposition and disposition toward totalitarianism left many of his erstwhile comrades restless and uneasy. Unquestionably, if Stalin was to rule the country, he had to secure his supremacy over the Party. The savage and seemingly indiscriminate purges of 1936–1938 were the result. The preparation for them dates back to the mysterious assassination of Stalin's friend and associate, Serge M. Kirov, secretary of the Leningrad Party organization, in December, 1934.

Those who were caught "red-handed" were summarily tried by the Supreme Military Tribunal of the USSR and executed. The first victims of the purge, which in the two years that followed comprised a virtual "Who's Who" of the Soviet Union, were Kamenev and Zinoviev, who had been under suspicion since the assassination of Kirov. The "Trial of the 17" in January, 1937, condemned a number of Trotskyites accused of conspiring with foreign powers to overthrow the Stalin regime. Among them were the Austrian-born Karl Radek, the most brilliant of Soviet journalists; G. Ya. Sokolnikov, commissar of finance during the NEP and one of the organizers of the Bolshevik coup of 1917; and Yuri L. Pyatakov, former commissar of heavy industry.

In June, 1937, following a secret trial, several prominent leaders of the Red Army were executed on grounds of treason and espionage for collaboration with a foreign power (presumably Germany) to overthrow the Stalin regime, in return for which they were said to have promised to relinquish the Ukraine. This galaxy of Soviet military commanders, topped by Marshal M. N. Tukhatchevsky, assistant commissar of defense and hero of the Soviet offensive against Poland in 1920, included seven Soviet generals. In the last of the great public purge trials, held in March, 1938, two leading Right-wing Communists, Nikolai Bukharin, editor of *Izvestia* and a member of the committee that drafted the 1936 Constitution, and Alexei Rykov, former premier of the USSR, were condemned for collusion with Trotsky and his supporters to bring about the overthrow of Stalin. G. G. Yagoda, former head of the OGPU[3] whose position had already been turned over to Stalin's protégé, N. I. Yezhov, confessed responsibility for numerous killings, including that of his predecessor Menzhinsky, Maxim Gorky, and V. V. Kuibyshev. In 1956, when he inaugurated his de-Stalinization campaign, Khrushchev confirmed that during the purges Stalin executed 98 out of 139 members and candidate-members of the Central Committee of the Communist Party elected by the Seventeenth Congress. These vacancies, and countless thousands of others occasioned by

---

3. The federal political police organization which succeeded the Cheka in 1922.

the purges, were filled by persons conditioned to become Stalin's tools, thereby enhancing his power.

Although the prominence of the men listed above made the purges spectacular, throughout Russia persons of high and low degree, numbered in tens of thousands, fell victims to this orgy of Communist bloodletting. To the astonishment of the Western world, the leaders abjectly confessed their guilt. With a few exceptions, as in the case of Radek who disappeared during the purges, they were promptly liquidated. Since the purges affected government, military, and Party officials of varying status, they terrorized Soviet officialdom. The masses of the people, on the contrary, often looked with some degree of satisfaction on the liquidation of officials who had caused them or their relatives and friends so much hardship and privation. In some respects, the purges had an even greater effect abroad than at home. The Western countries recoiled in horror and amazement at the savage terror unleashed upon Soviet officialdom. Journalists, scholars, and diplomats, who had written sympathetically of the Soviet "experiment," many of them former friends and acquaintances of the victims, quickly reversed themselves and denounced the Stalin regime for betraying the Russian Revolution. The purge of Soviet military leadership, in particular, contributed to a widespread belief in the weakness of the Red Army.

The Soviet purges of 1936–1938 have never ceased to be a subject for speculation beyond the borders of the Soviet Union. Although, basically, they appear to have been the outcome of internal Party dissension, they were not unrelated to foreign politics. George Kennan has seen a possible connection between the purges and the decision of the Party to intervene in the Spanish Civil War—a step undertaken during Stalin's absence in the Caucasus.[4] Gustav Hilger has interpreted the purges as an essential phase of Stalin's preparations for a German-Soviet alliance. Only a Party from which the Bukharins, Krestinskys, and Radeks had been eliminated, he claims, could have brooked the Nazi-Soviet Pact of August, 1939.[5]

FOREIGN POLICY

With Japanese occupation of Manchuria and the rise of Hitler in Germany, in the 1930's the USSR appeared to be caught in a pincer movement. Soviet leaders had reason to fear that Japan would take advantage of Soviet preoccupation with the Nazi threat in Europe to attack Soviet possessions in the Far East. These fears were not purely theoretical. Several skirmishes occurred along the Soviet-Manchurian border, as the Japanese probed for

4. George Kennan, *Russia and the West under Lenin and Stalin* (Boston: Little, Brown & Co., 1961), p. 310.
5. Hilger and Meyer, *The Incompatible Allies,* pp. 292–293.

Soviet military weakness, encouraged by White Russian officers still residing in the area.

United States Recognition. In the United States, the new administration of Franklin D. Roosevelt shared Soviet apprehension that Japan would seek territorial expansion in Siberia, in which event it might prove impossible to localize the resulting conflict. With the United States barely beginning the upward trend toward economic recovery, the government had no wish to become involved in a foreign war. In Europe, France, too, because of the rise of Nazism, had become favorably disposed toward better relations with Soviet Russia in the interests of French security. So great was public hostility to the Soviet regime, however, that the French government hesitated to take the initiative. Recognition of the Soviet Union by the United States was needed to ease the way for better Franco-Soviet relations.

Even prior to his election in 1932 Roosevelt indicated by sending William C. Bullitt as his personal emissary to Moscow that the time had come for the United States to abandon the policy of non-recognition of the USSR. Hope for improved business opportunities, as well as concern about Japanese aggressive designs in Asia, led the new Democratic administration to accord priority to this issue. In January, 1933, in a message to Roosevelt, eight hundred college presidents and professors supported the shift in American foreign policy because of tensions in the Orient. At the London Economic Conference in June, Soviet Foreign Minister Maxim Litvinov raised Western hopes of huge business transactions by stating that the USSR might soon agree to place orders abroad amounting to $1,000,000,000. At this conference, Litvinov entered into negotiations with American representatives, which paved the way for recognition. The United States recognized the USSR on November 16, 1933, sixteen years after the establishment of the Soviet regime. In the opinion of President Roosevelt, this action "strengthened the structure of peace" in the Far East. His conviction was shared by Joseph C. Grew, American ambassador in Japan, for whom recognition served as "a restraining influence, probably of greater effect than any other single integral."[6]

Japanese Conflict. Japan, suspecting that a secret Soviet-American understanding had been reached on issues pertaining to the Far East, did not risk further expansion at this time at the expense of the Soviet Union. The Soviet government therefore won a breathing spell to increase the defenses of Siberia. With Manchuria in Japanese hands, Soviet retention of the Chinese Eastern Railway became impracticable. The railway was virtually a Japanese hostage. Bowing to the inevitable, the Soviet government arranged for the sale of its stake in the Chinese Eastern to the Japanese puppet state of Manchukuo, 1933–1935, thereby abandoning all Russian gains in Manchuria since the construction of the Trans-Siberian Railroad. In 1938 the Japanese, emboldened by their success in China, attacked the Red Army in force at

6. Joseph C. Grew, *Ten Years in Japan* (New York: Simon and Schuster, 1944), p. 120.

Changkufeng (Khasan) near Posiet Bay on the Soviet-Korean-Manchurian border, the site of a new submarine and air base. The Japanese Kwantung Army then conducted the most intensive Russo-Japanese military engagement since the War of 1905 at Nomanhan (Khalkingol) on the Mongolian-Manchurian frontier from May to September, 1939. Soviet forces were ready for them. The Red Army inflicted two decisive defeats on the Japanese. After incurring 42,000 casualties, including some 20,000 killed at Nomanhan, the Japanese government reappraised any intention it may have had to attack the Soviet Union. Encouraged by the defenseless position of the Dutch East Indies following German occupation of the Netherlands in 1940, Japan turned instead to Southeast Asia.

The breathing spell that followed American recognition of the Soviet Union likewise enabled the United States to recover from the depression without confronting a serious foreign crisis in the far Pacific. The Soviet-American diplomatic *rapprochement* did not result in the anticipated economic gains for American business. The USSR was not in a position to import large quantites of American equipment without first securing substantial credits from the United States government. Congress interpreted the Johnson Act (April, 1934), which forbade foreign loans to governments which had defaulted on previous obligations, as being applicable to the Kerensky debts, and the necessary loans to Soviet Russia were not forthcoming. A trade treaty, signed in July, 1935, provided for Soviet purchases amounting to $30,000,000 within the next twelve months, a mere tidbit compared to previous expectations.

League of Nations Membership. Recognition by the United States also paved the way for a belated Soviet entry into the League of Nations. For years the USSR had uncompromisingly rejected the League as an agent of capitalist imperialism and as a possible source of collective action against Russia. With the emergence of the German and Japanese threats, however, the Soviet government was prepared to accept any measure of security offered by this international organization, in which it demonstrated little faith. Sponsored by France, which shared Soviet fears of Nazi Germany, the USSR entered the League of Nations on September 18, 1934, with permanent representation on the League Council. In spite of French Foreign Minister Louis Barthou's assiduous efforts to make the vote unanimous, Switzerland, the Netherlands, and Poland voted against Soviet admission. It was significant that the Soviet Union entered the League shortly after Germany (October, 1933) and Japan (March 1933) had withdrawn from it.

Defensive Alliance with France. Soviet Russia's new respectability on the international scene enabled the French government to subordinate anti-Soviet sentiment at home to strategy and security. A defensive alliance between France and Soviet Russia—a new version of the Franco-Russian Alliance of tsarist times directed against Germany—was ratified on May 2, 1935, followed by a pact with France's ally, Czechoslovakia, on May 16. The latter guaranteed Soviet military aid to the Czechs under circumstances requiring the implementation of the Franco-Czech Alliance. This "encirclement" of Nazi Germany shocked the Hitlerite regime, which had not anticipated a *rapprochement* between France and the Soviet Union. From its conclusion until the Munich crisis of 1938, Hitler's main objective was to break through this encirclement, which barred the way to German expansion. For this purpose, the Hitler regime expended large sums of money in France and exerted strong diplomatic pressure on England in what it termed the interests of peace.

Munich. During the Munich crisis of 1938, the Chamberlain government of England exerted great pressure on France and Czechoslovakia for Czech surrender of the German-populated Sudetenland to Germany. As compensation for this cession, England guaranteed the territorial integrity of the remainder of Czechoslovakia. Although by this action Chamberlain believed that he had insured "peace in our time," events soon proved he had no grasp of the political situation in Europe or of Nazi strategy. During the Munich crisis Soviet Russia, the ally of both France and Czechoslovakia, was not consulted. In the words of Chamberlain's successor, Winston Churchill, "Events took their course as if Soviet Russia did not exist."[7] President Benes of Czechoslovakia subsequently announced that the Soviet government had not only given him assurance of its intention to honor the terms of the alliance, but had offered to come to the aid of Czechoslovakia in the event of German invasion, irrespective of the action taken by France. The Munich "deal," concluded without Soviet Russia, effectively scrapped the Franco-Soviet-Czechoslovak system of alliances, the only serious obstacle to German expansion. When the Nazi armed forces occupied Prague in March, 1939, the Munich signatories took no action against Hitler for his destruction of Czechoslovakia. The legacy of Munich, as far as the Stalin regime was concerned, was that the Western democracies had no serious intent of stopping Hitler and that they might even endorse a German "Drang nach Osten" (Drive to the East) at Soviet expense.

Anglo-French-Soviet Negotiations. Immediately after the fall of Czechoslovakia, Foreign Minister Litvinov, in pursuit of Soviet security, called for an international conference of all nations opposed to aggression (German aggression), a step which was deemed "premature" by the Chamberlain government. The French government, finally aroused by the dénouement in Czechoslovakia, assumed the initative in arranging for Anglo-French-Soviet negotiations in Moscow for an agreement designed to stop Hitler. The abrupt replacement of Maxim Litvinov, staunch advocate of a Western alliance and of collective security, by Vyatcheslav Molotov as minister of foreign affairs in May, 1939, should have forewarned the Anglo-French negotiators of an

7. Winston Churchill, *The Second World War,* Vol. I, *The Gathering Storm* (Boston: Houghton Mifflin, 1948–1953), p. 305. See also Chapters 16 and 17, dealing with Churchill's own efforts to include Soviet Russia in the Munich negotiations.

imminent shift in Soviet foreign policy. Anthony Eden's offer to make of these negotiations a summit meeting by going himself to Moscow was turned down. England's representation by William Strang, a minor foreign office official, doomed the negotiations from the start. The Soviet government, confronted by the fact that Chamberlain himself went to Godesberg and Munich, but was content to send a representative of Strang's caliber to Moscow, could only conclude that England and France had no intention of conducting serious negotiations with Soviet Russia at this time. In subsequent years, the implication that a summit meeting was premature produced little or no commotion in Moscow. In the crisis atmosphere of 1938–1939, however, it resulted in a diplomatic *volte-face,* because the Soviet regime had a ready-made alternative.

German-Soviet Non-Aggression Pact. Negotiations were already under way with Germany to do as England and France had done in Munich—to make a deal with Nazi Germany. England's guarantee of Poland following Munich made it imperative for Hitler to reach an understanding with the USSR, or at least to forestall a Soviet deal with the Western democracies. He was in a position to offer Stalin a tempting sphere of influence in Eastern Europe. The English and the French, although they had sacrificed Czechoslovakia, were not prepared to follow the same policy in regard to the Baltic States, and the Poles were adamantly opposed to any agreement which would allow passage for Soviet troops through Poland in the event of conflict with Germany.

Until the last moment, the Stalin regime appears to have weighed the advantages to Soviet Russia of a pact with the West against those accruing from a deal with Nazi Germany. The Germans had more to offer. They promised to use their influence with Japan to improve Russo-Japanese relations. A pact with Germany also held the prospect of a breathing spell for the USSR while Germany fought in the West. During the process of negotiations with the West, the Soviets learned that England and France expected them to provide more than 300 divisions on the eastern front, as compared to 100 French, and, in the beginning, two English divisions in the West—a proposition which undoubtedly recalled to Soviet minds the conditions under which tsarist Russia fought in World War I. The exposure in London of an English plan to lend £1,000,000,000 to Nazi Germany,[8] which Soviet leaders interpreted as an offer to finance a German conflict with the USSR, ended any prospect of a Soviet agreement with the West.

England (September 30, 1938) and France (December 6, 1938) had concluded non-aggression pacts with Nazi Germany, in what they believed were the interests of peace in Europe. The conclusion of a German-Soviet non-aggression pact on August 23, 1939,[9] however, led to bitter accusations of

8. *New York Times,* July 21–25, 1939. See also Frederick L. Schuman, *Night Over Europe* (New York: Alfred A. Knopf, 1941), p. 204.

9. Copies of this pact will be found in Raymond James Sontag and James Stuart Beddie, eds., *Nazi-Soviet Relations 1939–1941: Documents from the Archives of the German Foreign Office* (Washington, D.C.: Department of State, 1948), pp. 76–78; or see George F. Kennan, *Soviet Foreign Policy, 1917–1941,* pp. 176–178.

betrayal on the part of England and France. Irrespective of the motives of the Soviet government the Nazi-Soviet Pact effectively severed Soviet Russia's last link with the West (Article IV). It scrapped the containment of Nazi Germany and served as a green light to Hitler to pursue his own aggressive designs in Europe. A secret protocol to the non-aggression pact defined the respective spheres of influence of Germany and Soviet Russia in Eastern Europe. The Russian sphere included the Baltic states of Finland, Esthonia, and Latvia, and in the south, Bessarabia. In the event of a partition of Poland, the Russian share included the area east of the rivers Narew, Vistula, and San. A subsequent agreement of September 28, 1939, allocated Lithuania to the Soviet sphere, with certain provisions for the repatriation of Germans, White Russians, and Ukrainians to their respective homelands.

In the Far East, the Moscow-Berlin Pact, together with the decisive Japanese defeat at Nomanhan, forced a reappraisal by the Japanese government of Soviet-Japanese relations. A truce concluded on September 15 put an end to military operations and established a border commission designed to end border incidents in the future.

Invasion of Poland. On September 1, 1939, eight days after the signing of the Hitler-Stalin non-aggression pact, the German panzer divisions invaded Poland. Two days later, to the surprise of both Hitler and Stalin, England and France, in keeping with their obligations to Poland, declared war on Nazi Germany. Within two weeks, and before any Allied aid was forthcoming, Polish resistance collapsed and the Polish government fled to Rumania. In spite of German encouragement, Stalin cautiously refrained from intervention as long as the Polish government resisted the German advance. On September 17, on the pretext of protecting Ukrainian and Byelorussian nationals in eastern and southern Poland, the Red Army advanced to meet the German forces, and a peaceful adjustment of the boundary, based mainly on the Curzon Line, was effected. Soviet acquisitions in Poland were annexed to the Ukrainian and Byelorussian Republics.

Soviet Bases in the Baltic. Determined to strengthen Soviet security in the Baltic States, where German influence was particularly strong, the Soviet government peremptorily demanded permission from Esthonia, Latvia, and Lithuania for the establishment of Soviet bases on their territory manned by Red Army garrisons. With no prospect of outside aid in sight, these three Baltic States yielded without armed resistance. The resulting mutual assistance pacts between Esthonia (September 28), Latvia (October 5), and Lithuania (October 10) and the USSR reduced their status to that of Soviet protectorates.

Trade Agreements. With the Germans involved in a major conflict with the Western democracies, the Stalin government felt secure in Europe. Stalin appears to have foreseen a war of position in the West, comparable to that of World War I, which would provide ample time for the strengthening of Soviet defenses. He was prepared to do business with the Germans on a large scale. In February, 1940, an extensive Soviet-German barter agreement was signed, which provided for the exchange of German industrial equipment for Soviet raw materials, including feed grains, cotton, phosphates, chromium ore, iron ore, scrap and pig iron, platinum, and other strategic materials essential to the German war effort, amounting to 600,000,000 reichsmarks. What England and France had feared in 1918, and had intervened in Russia to prevent, came to pass in 1940. It was impossible for Great Britain to impose an effective economic blockade on Germany as long as Soviet Russia provided the Nazis with the sinews of war. Nazi Germany continued to maintain contact with the outside world—with Iran, Afghanistan, Manchukuo, Japan, and even South America—as a result of Soviet neutrality.

Soviet-Finnish War. Since the spring of 1938 the Soviet government had been engaged in negotiations with Finland aimed at an adjustment of the Soviet-Finnish boundary to protect both Leningrad, which lay within artillery range of the Finnish border, and the Baltic-White Sea Canal. Although Soviet terms were relatively moderate and included territorial compensation for Finland, the Finnish government, with the example of the other Baltic States before it, stubbornly refused to yield. Unfortunately, the wholesale purge of the personnel of the Soviet Ministry of Foreign Affairs following the removal of Litvinov left delicate diplomatic arrangements in the hands of a new staff, unfamiliar with the processes of diplomacy and almost wholly ignorant of Europe. Apparently misled by Finnish Communists into thinking that the Red Army would encounter no more resistance than it had in Esthonia, Latvia, and Lithuania, the USSR abruptly invaded Finland on November 30, 1939, without even using its first-line troops. The initial Soviet reverses appeared to confirm the disastrous effect of the purge of the Red Army high command. World public opinion was wholly on the side of beleaguered Finland. In the West the Soviet Union was generally regarded as a colossus with feet of clay. In the minds of some Englishmen, Soviet reverses justified England's refusal to make a deal with the USSR in 1939. In the first flush of outrage over Soviet aggression, the USSR was expelled from the League of Nations (December 14, 1939) and from the International Labor Organization (February 5, 1940). England and France, deceived momentarily into thinking that heroic little Finland could resist giant Russia, once again laid plans for intervention against the Soviet Union, this time via Scandinavia and Turkey. Entirely aside from the moral issue involved, the establishment of Allied bases in Finland and the eastern Baltic would have been of strategic advantage to England and France in their struggle against Nazi Germany. The refusal of neutral Sweden to permit the passage of six English divisions and the sudden collapse of Finnish resistance were probably the only deterrents at that time to the outbreak of hostilities between the West and the USSR.

The Germans, in spite of their sympathy for the Finns, whom they had supported against Soviet Russia at the time of the foreign intervention, remained aloof from the Soviet-Finnish conflict. Finland had been assigned to the Soviet sphere of influence. Had they grasped the significance of the Red

Army's frontal breach of the supposedly impregnable Mannerheim Line—the Finnish equivalent of the Maginot Line—they might have hesitated before embarking on the invasion of the USSR in June, 1941. At the time of the Nuremburg trials following World War II, German military leaders complained that in Finland Soviet Russia deliberately tricked the Nazis into believing in Soviet military weakness!

The USSR emerged from the "Winter War" with Finland with a badly besmirched reputation abroad, but with important territorial acquisitions. Under the harsh terms provided, although Finland preserved her independence, she surrendered to the Soviet Union the Karelian Isthmus, including Viborg, the adjacent islands in the Gulf of Finland, a lease on the strategic Hango Peninsula, the northern and western shores of Lake Ladoga, a strip of Arctic territory in the vicinity of the Murmansk Railroad, and part of the Petsamo Peninsula, although the port of Petsamo itself was returned to the Finns. In July, 1940, the Soviet government established the Karelo-Finnish Soviet Republic.

Strengthening Security. Like many of his contemporaries, Stalin overestimated the strength of the French Maginot Line, which the Germans circum-

Wide World

In June, 1940, the Soviets accused Esthonia, Latvia, and Lithuania of violating the mutual assistance pacts of 1939 and demanded the formation of new governments. To ensure implementation of Soviet orders, the mighty Red Army, shown here in Latvia, occupied the three countries.

vented by invading the Netherlands and Belgium. The sudden collapse of France on June 18, 1940, dramatically altered the Soviet strategic position in Europe. Only the stubborn refusal of Great Britain to recognize defeat deprived Germany of a free hand in Eastern Europe. Almost immediately after the fall of France, the Stalin regime took additional steps to strengthen Soviet security. In August Esthonia, Latvia, and Lithuania (including the southwest corner reserved for Germany) were hastily incorporated into the USSR as Union Republics. With a display of ruthless realism, hundreds of thousands of the inhabitants of these countries, unreliable according to Soviet standards, were deported from the strategic coastal area to Siberia and other remote areas of the Soviet Union. Soviet annexation of the three Baltic States has never been formally recognized by Great Britain and the United States. Together with the Finnish War, it has continued to serve as a major impediment to improved Soviet relations with the West.

Soviet occupation of southern Poland in September, 1939, had served to delay the Nazi advance to the Balkans. Almost on the eve of German occupation of Rumania, the Soviet government in June, 1940, demanded from the Rumanian government the cession of Bessarabia, which Hitler had included in the Soviet sphere of influence, and for good measure, they also asked for northern Bukovina. Disregarding German protests over this violation of the Hitler-Stalin Pact, the USSR occupied these areas on June 28, 1940. Shortly thereafter, southern Bessarabia and northern Bukovina were incorporated into the Ukrainian Republic. Out of the rest of Bessarabia was created the Moldavian Republic, the thirteenth constituent member of the USSR.

Approaching Conflict. With Soviet annexations in the Baltic and the Balkans, the clash of German and Soviet interests came to the fore. Ironically, it was the Germans who had given the USSR the green light to recover territory, most of which had been lost by the Treaty of Brest-Litovsk and subsidiary treaties following the Bolshevik Revolution. The Stalin regime, without counting the consequences, now asserted its claims to a vital interest in Bulgaria and the Straits as an integral part of the Soviet security zone. Molotov protested the presence of German troops in Finland following the Nazi occupation of Norway. The Soviet government had good reason to be disappointed over the delay of German deliveries of machinery to the USSR, although it continued to furnish raw materials for the German war effort. After the fall of France Hitler, dizzy with success, was convinced that the German panzer divisions could conquer the world. He was neither prepared to listen to his generals nor to pay the increasing Soviet price for Soviet neutrality. On December 18, 1940, he issued orders for the preparation of "Operation Barbarossa"—a *blitzkrieg* against the USSR. In January, 1941, the German armed forces occupied Rumania. In April, the Soviet government entered into treaty arrangements with Yugoslavia—a step which is said to have made Hitler angrier than did the other Soviet moves in the Baltic and the Balkans, and one which failed to save the Yugoslavs from Nazi occupation.

In spite of these Soviet countermoves, Stalin had no wish to involve the Red Army, as yet no match for the victorious Germans who controlled most of Western Europe, in a conflict with Nazi Germany. Until the last moment he continued his policy of economic appeasement, and apparently refused to believe in the imminence of a German invasion of the Soviet Union. It was only in subsequent years that Soviet propaganda stressed Stalin's prescience in foreseeing and preparing for the German conflict.

SOVIET-MUSLIM RELATIONS

In general, from 1927 to 1941, there was no direct Soviet action on a large scale in the Muslim countries of the Near East. Soviet activities, for the most part, were restricted to the blueprint for communism, represented by the Communist programs presented in the previous chapter, and to instructions and guidance to local Communist groups, which were weak and inarticulate, and which, in most cases, had been driven underground.

Communism Versus Fascism. There are several major reasons for the comparative lull in Soviet-Muslim relations in the Near East. The rise of Fascism was the strongest deterrent to communism in Europe. Fascism represented middle-class reaction against disruptive Communist tactics in Western European countries. It likewise reflected the disillusionment of Western European Socialists and workers over Soviet treatment of Russian Social Revolutionaries and Mensheviki inside the Soviet Union. Fascism accomplished in Europe the same results in regard to the Soviet Union that Islam achieved in 1921, when it forestalled Soviet expansion in the Near and Middle East. The rise of Hitler in Germany and the expansion of Japan on the Chinese mainland in the early 1930's threatened the USSR with a possible pincer movement. The Soviet government, facing danger on two fronts, had to concentrate its efforts on defense and had little opportunity for adventures in the Muslim world. Although the Nazi brand of Fascism eventually proved more dangerous than communism, for the time being it served to divert Soviet attention from the Near East and to save the Muslim world from the Soviet orbit.

Domestic Priorities. The desperate economic situation on the Soviet domestic front, with the famine that accompanied the first Five-Year Plan, and frantic Soviet efforts in the direction of industrialization, deterred the Soviet government from engaging in activities that would unduly antagonize the major colonial powers, England and France, especially in India and the Near East. The vigilance of the colonial powers themselves in the mandatory areas and in Egypt was sufficient to offset the feeble and spasmodic attempts of local Communist parties to upset the stability of established governments. Moreover, the national liberation movements against colonialism in Muslim countries, certainly among the Arabic peoples, were in the hands of the bourgeoisie and upper classes, as the Communists themselves admitted in their own programs. In Egypt, for instance, the Wafd Party was a counterpart of the Kadets in tsarist Russia.

Soviet Rationale. Even as late as 1954, B. N. Zakhoder, head of the department of Near and Middle Eastern history and economics of the Institute of Oriental Studies at the Academy of Sciences of the USSR, declared that the reason why the national revolutionary struggle was successful (1949) in the Far East—the non-Muslim world—and failed in the Near and Middle East—the Muslim world—was that in the Far East it was led by the working class, which alone guaranteed victory, whereas in the Near and Middle East it was led by the national bourgeoisie, who invariably failed to take decisive action at the opportune moment. Soviet historians and leaders, including Stalin, likewise attributed the failure of the Taiping Rebellion in China (1850–1864) to the lack of proletarian leadership. According to Soviet thinking the view still prevails that a revolution, even in predominantly agrarian countries, to be successful must be controlled by the working class, even if it constitutes a minority.

Montreux Convention. Typical of the Soviet policy of normalizing relations with neighboring countries during this period was the alacrity with which the Soviet government responded (April 16) to the Turkish note of April 11, 1936, calling for the revision of the Lausanne Treaty of 1923, in particular for the abrogation of those clauses providing for the demilitarization of the Straits. Turkish action was a direct outgrowth of Turkish fear of the growing strength of Fascist Italy in the eastern Mediterranean and of the inability of the League of Nations to take prompt and decisive action to stop the Italian invasion of Abyssinia in 1935. At the subsequent conference at Montreux, Switzerland, June 22 to July 29, the focal point of disagreement between England and the USSR concerned first, the right of free passage of the warships of the Black Sea powers through the Straits into the Mediterranean and second, the right of entry into the Black Sea of the fleets of non-Black Sea powers. The compromise reached was in many respects favorable to the Soviet Union.

The Montreux Convention, signed on July 20, granted complete freedom of transit through the Straits for the commercial vessels of all nations. It permitted the Russians unlimited egress for surface vessels and tankers in peacetime, subject to the proviso that warships of more than fifteen thousand tons must proceed singly through the Straits. Soviet submarines were likewise permitted to pass singly through the Straits by day when returning to their Black Sea bases or en route to dockyards located elsewhere. The control of transit for the vessels of the non-Black Sea powers was achieved by restricting the aggregate tonnage, admitting only "light warships," and limiting the length of their stay. In the event of a conflict in which Turkey remained neutral, the warships of belligerents were permitted passage to aid a victim of aggression, provided such assistance resulted from action taken under the League of

Nations Covenant or under a treaty of mutual assistance signed by Turkey and concluded within the framework of the Covenant. The convention granted Turkey complete sovereignty over the Straits, permitting her to close them to the warships of all nations in the interests of her own security when she herself was a belligerent or in imminent danger of war, subject to League of Nations action.

The Soviet Union was in many respects well satisfied with the Montreux Convention, which safeguarded Soviet exit to the Mediterranean and restricted the naval power of potential enemies in the Black Sea. The standard Soviet history of diplomacy as late as 1945 conceded that, "In spite of some shortcomings in the Convention, its acceptance was of great positive significance and it was a tremendous victory for Soviet diplomacy." At the end of World War II, however, the Soviet government demanded the revision of the Montreux Convention on the ground that its disadvantages outweighed the advantages, due to the fact that it conferred on Turkey the exclusive right to control the Straits, to interpret the convention, and to implement it unilaterally. Since the powers concerned failed to agree on the nature of the "revision," the Montreux Convention continued to determine the use of the Straits after World War II.

Saadabad Pact. The decline of Soviet influence in the Near and Middle East in this period can be measured by the fact that the very states Soviet Russia had counted upon to spread communism throughout the Muslim world—Turkey, Iran, and Afghanistan—joined with Iraq on July 8, 1937, in Teheran to conclude the Saadabad Pact, the main provisions of which had been agreed upon in 1935, although the pact was held up pending the settlement of the Iran-Iraq boundary dispute. Although the Turks, who initiated proceedings for this "Near Eastern Entente," may have been impelled by fear of Italian expansion in the Mediterranean under Mussolini, the other Middle Eastern states had no immediate cause for concern from this quarter. The Soviet government viewed the pact as a British scheme to create a chain of alliances along the southern Soviet border directed against the USSR and to insure joint action on the part of member countries to stamp out the national liberation movement in this Muslim area (Clause VII). Although the Saadabad Pact remained in effect a scrap of paper, it appears to have served as a pattern for the Baghdad Pact of 1955, which was likewise intended to establish an effective barrier to Soviet expansion to the south.

Nazism in Iran. In the 1930's communism had still another competitor in the Near and Middle East—namely, Nazism. This was particularly true of Egypt and Iran, not to mention the growing strength of German influence in Turkey. According to Soviet sources, by 1941 there were about four thousand German secret agents operating in Iran, approximately one thousand of them in Teheran. Some of these agents were located in the vicinity of the borders of Soviet Turkestan, with the alleged object of creating bases in Iran for an ultimate attack on the USSR. In Teheran and in some provincial cities, Nazi organizations were established, in many cases under the guise of tourist camps. All these Nazi activities were directed by the German ambassador, Von Ettelen, and by the German consuls in Iran, with inspection from time to time by such top Nazi leaders as Hjalmar Schacht, the financial wizard, and Baldur von Schirach, a Nazi youth leader. Extensive Nazi propaganda, aimed especially at the Soviet Union, was conducted through the press, radio, cinema, and "cultural" societies. From 1933 to 1937 the Nazis published a paper *Irane-Bastan* (*Ancient Iran*) and a monthly magazine, both in the Persian language. As late as 1940 they even organized a "Brown House" in Teheran and began construction of the Nazi-Abada (Nazi city), which was to become the Nazi center of Iran.

Whereas the Bolsheviks had sought to disseminate communism in Iran, Nazi propagandists appealed to the people on the basis of their Aryan origins, that is, on the ground of racial superiority. This approach had greater appeal for the Iranian nationalists than did Soviet propaganda, since nationalism was stronger in Iran than the *Klassenkampf*.

Because of Iran's proximity to the Soviet Union and because it was the gateway to Baku and Central Asia, the Nazis concentrated their efforts in that country over a more extended period of time. Nazi anti-Communist propaganda was likewise strong in the Arab countries, especially in Egypt and Iraq. Their emphasis among the Arabs was on Islam as the enemy of atheistic communism. Nazi propaganda appealed to the Muslim world to join forces with the Nazis under the leadership of the führer against the Comintern. As in Soviet Russia after the Baku Congress, the Germans entered upon an intensive study of the Islamic world from the standpoint of Nazi interests and possible Nazi infiltration. Just as the Communists before them had sought to identify Lenin with Muhammed and communism with the Koran, the Germans proceeded to link Hitler with Muhammed and Kemal Pasha, and Nazism with Islam.

The success of the Nazi propaganda campaign was reflected in the spectacular increase in German-Iranian trade and the parallel slump in Soviet-Iranian trade. Whereas from 1936 to 1937 the USSR accounted for 35.5 per cent of all Iranian foreign trade, by 1939–1940 the Soviet share was only 0.5 per cent. By 1938–1939 Germany, which had previously done very little business with Iran, occupied first place, with more than 40 per cent of the entire foreign trade of Iran.

In spite of the strength of anti-Nazi sentiment in England at this time, British colonial authorities appear to have evinced a considerable degree of tolerance toward the Nazis under their jurisdiction and influence. The best explanation appears to be that in the colonies and mandates the British regarded the Soviet Union as a greater potential threat than the Germans and even hoped to use the Nazis as tools to rid them of communism.

The Soviet Muslim Republics. Just as Turkey, Iran, and the Arab states tried to suppress the Communist movement among their peoples, in the Soviet

Middle East during this period the Soviet government made every effort to counteract Western and Muslim propaganda emanating from Muslim countries outside the USSR. The various manifestoes and appeals of the newborn Soviet regime to the Muslim peoples for national self-determination proved to be a two-edged sword. Strictly speaking, the application of self-determination to the Muslim minorities inside the Russian borders would have meant the dismemberment of Russia in the East on a scale equivalent to that effected in European Russia by the Treaty of Brest-Litovsk (1918). Like any other colonial power, the Soviet government expected to assume control of this movement, at least during its early stages. It soon discovered, however, especially during the *Basmatchestvo* revolt, that this was easier said than done. As a result, the Soviet government required time to reassert Soviet authority in this irredentist area. The Turks, Iranians, and Afghans all had claims on Soviet Central Asia, and Turkic, Iranian, and Afghan peoples were to be found on both sides of the border.

On May 1, 1918, within a few months of the establishment of the Bolshevik regime, the fifth All-Turkestan Congress of Soviets proclaimed the Turkestan Autonomous Soviet Socialist Republic (TASSR) in what was formerly Russian Turkestan. The bitter resistance of Muslim leaders to Soviet rule, together with the widespread nature of the *Basmatchi* insurrection in Central Asia, soon led the beleaguered Soviet government to divide the TASSR into a number of separate republics, thereby weakening the opposition forces. The partition of the Soviet Middle East began in August, 1921, to the tune of a high-pressure propaganda drive, emphasizing the desirability of creating independent republics along ethnic, national, and linguistic lines—the Soviet version of a national liberation movement. The effectiveness of this propaganda, even among the Muslims it was designed to weaken, was demonstrated shortly after the establishment of the Republic of Uzbekistan. On December 15, 1924, an assembly of Muslim spiritual leaders in Tashkent issued "An Appeal to All the Muslim Peoples of the East": "Turn your eyes, Muslim peoples, to the land of the Soviet Republics, where there live many free Muslim peoples. In contrast to the imperialists, who for hundreds of years have blocked the development of the native population, the Soviet Government with all its strength assists the growth of the Muslim peoples."

This Soviet policy of "divide and rule," which is still in effect, has served at least a twofold purpose. As already indicated, it divided and weakened Islamic authority, the chief unifying factor in Soviet Central Asia, while at the same time the satisfaction over "national liberation" took much of the wind from the *Basmatchi* sails. In the second place, it served until World War II as an important propaganda weapon abroad, where the Muslims of the Arab world, India, and Indonesia, were still subjected to the Western "colonialism" of England, France, and the Netherlands.

Census-taking in Muslim countries has always proved to be a difficult task. The same situation prevailed in Central Asiatic Russia. According to M. S.

Rybakov, as of January 1, 1912 there were in tsarist Russia 16,226,073 Muslims, of whom 4,635,000 lived in European Russia, 7,955,000 in Central Asia, 3,335,000 in the Caucasus, and 120,000 in Siberia. François de Romainville in 1947 claimed that there were 20,000,000 Muslims in the USSR: "Avec vingt millions d'âmes; le groupe musulman constitue la minorité la plus importante de l'URSS." S. Maksudov, a member of the provisional Central Bureau of the Russian Muslims, speaking in 1917 before the Kadet Congress declared that there were 30,000,000 Muslims in Russia. Today there are between 25,000,000 and 30,000,000 Muslims in the Soviet Union. Although major and periodic population shifts in the USSR do not make for stability in the location of the Muslim peoples, there are six so-called Muslim republics: Azerbaijan (capital, Baku), Uzbekistan (capital, Tashkent), Kazakhstan (capital, Alma Ata), Turkmenistan (capital, Ashkhabad), Tadjikistan (capital, Stalinabad), Kirghizia (capital, Frunze). Four other republics, the Crimean, Ingush, Chechen, and Balkar, were almost liquidated in 1944. The remnants of these minorities were absolved in 1956 of charges of collaboration with the Germans, and in the following year the Soviet government restored their right of autonomous rule.

From the standpoint of religious administration, the Sunni Muslim community has been organized since World War II, at least since 1948, under four administrative councils, each headed by a mufti, as follows: (1) Russia in Europe and Siberia; (2) Central Asia; (3) Transcaucasia; and (4) Daghestan and North Caucasia. The Shi'is in Baku have been placed under a sheikh ul-Islam.

The primary task of the Soviet government was to reconcile Soviet Muslims, who constituted from 10 to 12 per cent of the population, to the Soviet regime and to counteract the impact of the independent Muslim states of Turkey, Iran, Afghanistan, and Iraq (1936) on the Soviet frontier. Thus the Soviet government, having established the six Muslim republics, at least on paper, with a modicum of cultural and political autonomy, sought to offset the independent Muslim states of the Middle East. Likewise to counteract the Zionist homeland, it created the autonomous region of Birobidjan in 1934.

Soviet propaganda in the Muslim republics then sought to convince Soviet Muslims that they were already far ahead of foreign Muslims and could learn nothing from their experience. Soviet Muslims were assured that they were superior, culturally and economically, to their Muslim neighbors. They were told that by the establishment of the six Muslim republics, their national liberation movement was complete, that they had not only achieved political independence but had installed working-class governments. The Muslims outside the USSR, on the other hand, either remained under the domination of "the imperialist colonizers," or had achieved only the first stage of national liberation, political independence minus social revolution, and were still subject to the internal yoke—the bourgeois domestic regime.

To symbolize the leadership of Soviet Muslims among the peoples of the

East, erected throughout Central Asia and the Caucasus were monuments to Lenin, in which the Soviet leader, with his right hand uplifted, pointed to the East. On the pedestal, in Arabic and in Russian, appeared the inscription, "Leninism leads to the emancipation of the peoples of the East." The Soviet government by every possible means sought to instill into the minds of Soviet Muslims that their republics were the models for the Orient.

Soviet leaders proceeded with caution to break traditional or existing cultural ties between the Soviet Muslims and those abroad. As in the case of Turkey, where Kemal Pasha had substituted the Latin for the Arabic script, the Soviet government began its attack on the Islamic character of the Muslim languages at the Congress of Turcology in Baku in 1926. The decision reached at this congress to substitute the Latin instead of the Cyrillic alphabet for the Arabic was designed to prevent all semblance of "Russification" of the Muslim East. It was not until March 13, 1938, that the decree was issued making Russian the second compulsory language of the Soviet Muslim republics. The replacement of the Latin alphabet by the Cyrillic took place, beginning in 1939.

To sum up, we may safely say that during the period under consideration the Muslims inside the USSR and those outside exercised no appreciable influence upon each other. The Soviet government effectively sealed off the Soviet Muslims from contact with the outside world. Both inside and outside the USSR the Muslim states were mainly absorbed in their own domestic problems. That these problems remained basically unsolved seems clear from the fact that Muslim states on both sides of the Soviet border were by no means immune to Nazi penetration and propaganda in World War II. In Egypt, North Africa, and Iran, Nazism constituted a major threat to the Western Allies, and it was strong enough to bring Turkey to the brink of war with the Soviet Union during the period of German military successes. Inside the USSR, with the advance of Nazi armies to the Caucasus, many Muslims collaborated with the Germans, with the result that in 1944 the Soviet government deported the entire Muslim population of four autonomous Muslim republics—the Crimean, Ingush, Chechen, and Balkar—to unspecified destinations east of the Volga.

Policy Shift to the West. The comparative lull in Soviet-Muslim relations in the Near and Middle East may be attributed in large measure to the threat of Hitlerite Germany. In the 1930's the Soviets, in spite of the rising Japanese menace, began to subordinate Asia to Europe in order to meet the Nazi threat. The entire regime was mobilized for this purpose. In the clash between the Red Army forces and the Japanese at Khasan in 1938 and at Nomanhan in 1939, Soviet action remained defensive, confined to the repulse of the Japanese attacks, and Soviet leaders resisted every temptation to become involved in an aggressive campaign in the Far East.

This shift in emphasis in Soviet foreign policy from the East back to the West became effective during the purges of 1936 to 1937, which revealed the

existence of a fifth column in the Red Army officer corps. Since Soviet literature and the arts are the best barometer of Soviet domestic and foreign
policies, it is logical that the Soviet government should have sought to
interpret the Soviet policy shift to the West and to justify it to the Soviet
public through the medium of a film—the Serge Eisenstein film *Alexander
Nevsky,* produced in the record time of little more than a year. The purpose
of this film was to convince the Soviet peoples that the German threat loomed
larger than the Japanese, that the Germans had been in the past and still
could be defeated by the Russians, and that the Russians, confronted simultaneously by invasion from the East and West, must as in the past forego
retaliation in the Orient. In other words, the East must be subordinated to the
West and "the Mongols can wait." Under these conditions, the Bolshevization
of the Near and Middle East likewise had to wait for more propitious circumstances, soon to be provided by World War II.

Part Five

The Soviet Union, 1941-1968

22

The USSR in World War II,

1941-1945

Warnings Disregarded. Early in June, 1941, the Soviet government was warned by the United States and Great Britain that a vast German onslaught upon the USSR was imminent. German, Chinese, and even Soviet sources confirmed the warnings. Even the precise day of the attack, June 22, 1941, had been transmitted to Moscow. Stalin, to be sure, had received a succession of warnings about a Nazi invasion of the Ukraine ever since Hitler came to power. When these predictions failed to materialize, he interpreted such warnings as Western machinations to involve the Soviet Union in a conflict with Germany for the benefit of England and France. Up to the very moment of invasion, Stalin refused to believe that Hitler would risk war with the USSR while he was still involved in a conflict with the West. Hitler had loudly condemned the kaiser for involving Germany in a two-front war in 1914.

Soviet leaders, however, clearly failed to understand to what extent the Red Army purges and the Finnish campaign had damaged Soviet military prestige abroad. It was their assumption that if Germany had intended to invade the Soviet Union, this would have been done in 1939, with the tacit approval of the Western democracies. Once Hitler became involved in a conflict against England and France, it was against all logic that he should invade the USSR, the major source of his strategic raw materials for the conduct of the war. As late as June 14, Stalin publicly announced that rumors of an impending attack on the Soviet Union were groundless. To avoid border incidents which might provoke hostilities, the main Red Army defense forces, consisting of 170 divisions, were stationed from eight to twenty kilometers inside the border. Fifteen years later, in his secret report to the Twentieth Congress of the Communist Party (1956), Nikita Khrushchev denounced Stalin for failing to heed the impressive body of evidence on the imminent Nazi invasion of the USSR, for neglecting to alert the armed forces to the emergency, and for his failure to provide adequately for the defense of the new frontier. Thus Stalin was held "criminally responsible" for the initial Nazi successes and the wholesale Red Army retreat.

German Viewpoint. What Stalin failed to recognize was that in 1941 Germany was much stronger vis-à-vis the Soviet Union than she was in 1939. After June 1940, the only active opponent Hitler confronted in the West was Great Britain, a country in no position to conduct an offensive against Nazi Germany. The Nazis, moreover, had practically all Europe under their jurisdiction, from Norway and Finland in the north to the Balkans in the south. At their disposal were some 130,000,000 people from satellite countries to produce food, run factories, and swell their military manpower. It was not, therefore, a case of 70,000,000 Germans facing about 193,000,000 Russians.

Hitler knew that ultimate victory depended on the defeat of England. If he challenged British air and naval power in an all-out effort to cross the English Channel, however, he was apprehensive that the Soviet Union, which had already taken advantage of German involvement in the West to expand Soviet frontiers in the East, would stab him in the back. As he admitted to Mussolini on the eve of the German invasion of the USSR, he would be prepared to risk throwing his entire air force against England "if, aside from all other conditions, I at least possessed the one certainty that I will not then suddenly be attacked or even threatened from the East." He was loathe to place himself in any position in which he would have to yield to Russia's "strategy of extortion" in the south and the north. Winston Churchill was quick to sense that it was the danger from the East that led Hitler in 1941, like Napoleon in 1804, to recoil from the invasion of England.[1]

After the fall of France, Hitler's judgment was warped by success. Having obviated even the "impregnable" Maginot Line against the advice of his generals, he was in no frame of mind to heed their warnings against the invasion of the Soviet Union. Among those who opposed Germany's expansion to the East at this time were Admiral Raeder, commander-in-chief of the German navy, who urged that Germany's entire war potential be directed against England, numerous German military commanders, members of the diplomatic corps, economic experts who believed that more could be obtained from the USSR under the Nazi-Soviet Pact than by war, and even Rudolf Hess, Hitler's deputy, who undertook a fantastic flight to England in the hope of terminating the war in the West.

"Operation Barbarossa." Hitler had long regarded Russia as a German "Lebensraum" (living space)—as Germany's "India" for colonial expansion. Once Germany had in her possession the fabulous natural resources of the Urals, the Siberian forests, and the vast wheatfields of the Ukraine, he believed that the country would have all it needed "to swim in plenty." As early as July, 1940, Hitler decided in favor of eastward expansion, and campaign preparations were set in motion. Military considerations made an invasion of Russia in the fall of 1940 impractical. It was therefore postponed

1. Winston Churchill, *The Second World War,* Vol. I, *Their Finest Hour* (Boston: Houghton Mifflin, 1948–1953), p. 577.

until May, 1941. The transfer of German troops from the West to the Soviet border began in August, 1940. On December 18, during the Moscow-Berlin negotiations for a Four-Power Alliance (Germany, Italy, Japan, and the USSR), Hitler issued his top-secret order launching "Operation Barbarossa," the code name for the invasion of the Soviet Union. In April, 1941, when Hitler found it expedient "to clean up" the Balkans by direct intervention in the Italo-Greek War and the occupation of Yugoslavia, a crucial decision was made to postpone the invasion of the USSR from May 15 to June 22, reducing by five weeks the time available for the completion of the German *Blitzkrieg* before the advent of the Russian winter.

BLITZKRIEG AGAINST THE USSR

On June 22, 1941, the anniversary of Napoleon's crossing of the Niemen and one year to the day after Marshal Petain's government was forced to come to terms with Adolph Hitler, 3,300,000 German troops suddenly and without any declaration of war launched the German *Blitzkrieg* against the USSR. It was a surprise attack on a front stretching from Finland to Rumania, a German version of Pearl Harbor on a gigantic scale. According to Soviet sources, Hitler's invading army constituted 87 per cent of the German land forces (3,800,000 men) and included 80 per cent of Germany's air fleet, as well as four tank groups. Altogether, including forces from the satellite states, Hitler hurled 190 divisions against the Soviet Union, with the intention of destroying the Red Army and seizing both Moscow and Leningrad within six weeks. German military strategy called for an all-out frontal assault conducted by three army groups: one in the north under Field Marshal von Leeb following the line from Pskov to Leningrad; one in the center under Field Marshal von Bock along the Minsk-Smolensk route to Moscow; and a third in the south under Field Marshal von Rundstedt converging on the Ukrainian capital of Kiev.

Initial Russian Retreat. The precipitate retreat of the Red Army amounted in some instances to a rout. In just four days Manstein's Panzer Corps crossed the Dvina, some two hundred miles from the border. In less than three weeks Leeb's northern army, supported by Field Marshal Mannerheim's Finnish forces, had penetrated the borders of Leningrad Province. By mid-July Guderian's armored columns were in the vicinity of Smolensk and Rundstedt's southern forces had reached the outer defenses of Kiev. Within three weeks the German invaders, advancing at approximately twenty-five miles per day, had pierced Soviet defenses all along the front and had advanced five hundred miles into the interior.[2]

Delayed Drive to Moscow. At this critical juncture Hitler made what may well have been one of the fateful decisions of World War II. Instead of

2. Matthew P. Gallagher, *The Soviet History of World War II: Myths, Memories, and Realities* (New York: Frederick A. Praeger, 1963), p. 7.

Visiting the Red Army near the front in 1941 was the novelist Mikhail Sholokhov. Winner of the Nobel Prize for Literature in 1965, Sholokhov is famous for his realistic stories and novels about the Don Cossacks.

yielding to the advice of Bock and Guderian, who urged an all-out drive to Moscow, he dispersed his armored divisions to the north and south to accelerate the drives toward Leningrad and Kiev. The result was the encirclement—but not the fall—of Leningrad and the capture of Kiev, together with 600,000 Soviet troops commanded by Marshal Budënny. Within four months Rundstedt had occupied virtually all of the Ukraine as far as Kharkov and Taganrog on the Sea of Azov. Although these gains were impressive, they were made at the expense of the main drive toward Moscow, which was delayed until October 2. By the time the central army reached Mozhaisk, sixty-five miles west of Moscow, the Russian winter had begun. When the German advance guards reached the suburbs of Moscow on December 2, the ill-equipped German army was in no position to cope with a winter offensive, nor would Hitler, for psychological reasons, permit its withdrawal. Hitler's perverse military strategy cost him the services of his foremost field generals, Rundstedt, Bock, Leeb, and of Brauchitsch, the commander-in-chief. Hitler dismissed Guderian and assumed the command of the German armed forces.

Soviet Losses. During this first phase of the *Blitzkrieg,* according to official Soviet statistics, the USSR lost 490,000 killed, 520,000 missing (prisoners), and 1,112,000 wounded—a total loss of 2,100,000 from June 22, 1941, until the German advance was stemmed before Moscow on December 6. During these critical months, the Red Army depended almost entirely on its own resources, without substantial help from abroad. With the replacement of Marshal Semyon Timoshenko by General (later Marshal) Zhukov in October, the main objective of Soviet military leaders was to regain the strategic initiative. Their first step in this direction was achieved before Moscow in December, 1941; their second at Stalingrad (Volgograd) in the winter of 1942–1943; and their third at Kursk in July, 1943.

By November, 1941, the Soviet Union had lost 63 per cent of its coal mines, 68 per cent of its cast-iron production, 58 per cent of its steel production, and 68 per cent of its aluminum production. Nevertheless, after a hasty reorganization and the full utilization of its Siberian facilities, in 1942 the country was able to produce 25,000 planes, 23,500 tanks, and 34,000 field guns.

Treatment of Soviet Minorities. The German *Blitzkrieg* was most successful in the Soviet borderlands, where Soviet minorities from the Baltic States, Byelorussia, and the Ukraine, hostile to the Soviet regime, at first welcomed the invaders. In the Ukraine, in particular, where the German occupation of 1918 had left a favorable impression, the people looked forward to liberation from Soviet rule. In some instances, they greeted the German troops with flowers. Many Ukrainian churches were reopened and many Soviet collective farms were voluntarily liquidated. When the German forces reached Great Russia proper, the resistance stiffened. The people of Leningrad, in spite of the loss of 750,000 inhabitants from starvation and artillery bombardment, indomitably resisted the German invaders until the siege was broken by the Red Army in January, 1943. A tenuous Soviet link with the beleaguered city was kept open over the frozen waters of Lake Ladoga.

One of the great mistakes of German occupation policy in the USSR was its failure to make any serious effort to win the support of the population. This was in line with the Nazi concept of "a master race," which depicted the Slavic peoples as *Untermensch* (subhuman) and as "a conglomeration of animals," whose future role would be to serve the Germans in menial capacities. Although the German propaganda machine directed every effort toward the subversion of the Red Army, the Hitler regime made no real effort to treat the captured peoples on a basis of equality, or to appeal to their national aspirations for self-government, civil liberties, and private ownership of land.[3] Heinrich Himmler's Storm Troops (*Sturm Abteilung*) and the Gestapo must bear the chief responsibility for the reign of terror in the occupied lands. German army leaders, more realistic in their concern for military considerations in the midst of the offensive, were less disposed toward brutality. Although Alfred Rosenberg envisaged concessions to the Soviet minorities, especially to the Ukrainians, to insure their voluntary support of the German reich, wartime confusion and dissension among the various German occupation agencies prevented the application of his theories.

Thus the German treatment of Soviet minorities was a tactical error of great magnitude. The Red Army soon learned that conditions in German-

3. See Alexander Dallin, *German Rule in Russia, 1941–1945: A Study of Occupation Policies* (London: Macmillan, 1957).

occupied lands belied German propaganda, that Soviet prisoners-of-war were badly abused, that Jews and commissars were exterminated, that mass deportations of civilians and the shooting of non-communist hostages were instituted in retaliation for local sabotage, that the population was being exploited mercilessly to German advantage, and that a veritable reign of terror existed. In the first year of the occupation alone, the Germans were said to have liquidated 90,000 men, women, and children.

Partisan Movement. Of course, German terrorism boomeranged. It revitalized the Soviet partisan movement in the rear of the German front lines, which harassed the German war effort, and eventually welcomed the returning Red Army forces with the same zeal originally displayed toward the invaders. Although Soviet partisans were not regarded with particular favor when the German invasion began, and proved largely ineffective in its initial stages, within a year the situation had changed. The partisans, who took to the forests, represented a sizeable force, more than 100,000 strong, which Stalin termed a second front in the enemy's rear. Composed in the beginning largely of Red Army stragglers and escapees, thanks to German occupation policies the partisan movement soon attracted large numbers of the peasant population, both men and women, and beginning with the winter of 1941–1942, it received substantial Soviet aid and leadership. In the course of the war, the number of partisans increased to 700,000.

THE SOVIET COUNTEROFFENSIVE

What most impressed the outside world, which had expected an early Soviet collapse, was the ability of the Red Army, under the leadership of General Zhukov, to reorganize and to launch a major counteroffensive on December 6, 1941, the eve of Pearl Harbor, without giving the cold and exhausted Germans any opportunity to recuperate. In its first winter offensive lasting until March, 1942, the Red Army, paying the price of another 434,000 men killed and wounded, drove back the fifty German divisions to positions 100 miles west of Tikhvin and 240 miles west of Moscow. The Soviet capital, the political and communications hub of the USSR, was saved. Instead of being comfortably housed in Moscow and Leningrad for the winter, Hitler's legions were badly mauled by the Red Army offensive and incurred heavy losses in manpower and equipment.

British-Soviet Mutual Aid Agreement. Immediately following the invasion of the USSR, Great Britain welcomed Soviet Russia as an ally against Hitlerite Germany. "If Hitler invaded Hell," Winston Churchill, the British prime minister, once stated, "I would make at least a favourable reference to the Devil in the House of Commons." On this basis, he was prepared to deal with Stalin, erstwhile his sworn enemy. Churchill had already conditioned the United States government for his support of the USSR. Eight days prior to

Hitler's invasion he informed President Roosevelt that England would provide all possible aid to Russia on the ground that every measure should be taken to defeat the main foe, Nazi Germany.[4] In view of public hostility toward the USSR in England and the United States as a result of the Russo-Finnish War, it was not an easy matter for the Western democracies to accept the Soviet regime as an ally. When the conflict began, the political and military authorities of the Western world expected Soviet resistance to last from two to six weeks. Many American military and naval experts made the same miscalculation of Japanese strength following Pearl Harbor. On the basis of such an hypothesis, there seemed to be little logic in providing substantial aid to the Soviet war effort, since supplies dispatched to the USSR would soon fall into the hands of Nazi Germany. Nevertheless, within three weeks of the invasion, Great Britain and the Soviet Union on July 12, 1941, concluded a mutal aid agreement, with the following provisions:

    1. The two governments mutually undertake to render each other assistance and support of all kinds in the present war against Hitlerite Germany.

    2. They further undertake that during this war they will neither negotiate nor conclude an armistice or treaty of peace except by mutual agreement.

Atlantic Charter. The United States, although still officially neutral in the struggle against Hitler, responded to the British lead. In July President Roosevelt dispatched his trusted associate, Harry Hopkins, to Moscow to secure an estimate of Soviet military needs. He released Soviet blocked funds in the United States and refrained from enforcing the Neutrality Act against the Soviet Union. In fact, on August 2, in an exchange of letters between Acting Under-Secretary of State Sumner Welles and Soviet Ambassador Oumansky, the United States promised the USSR "all economic assistance practicable" to strengthen its resistance against the aggressor. At the Atlantic Conference between Roosevelt and Churchill in August, to which Stalin was not invited, Harry Hopkins presented an optimistic report on the prospects of continued Soviet resistance to Hitler and strongly supported Lend-Lease aid to the USSR. At the same conference, Churchill made his bid for the lion's share of American aid, on the ground that Moscow was certain to fall to the Germans, thereby terminating Soviet resistance. In spite of their doubts, Roosevelt and Churchill on August 13 agreed to provide the Soviet Union "with the very maximum of supplies" most urgently needed, and announced that many shiploads were already en route to Russia. The Soviet government had asked in particular for early shipments of antiaircraft and antitank guns.

    Although Soviet leaders later protested the failure to consult them prior to the Atlantic Conference, they did subscribe in principle to the terms of the

    4. See *The Memoirs of Cordell Hull,* Vol. II (New York: Macmillan, 1948), pp. 972 ff.

Atlantic Charter. According to Churchill, this was a conditional support, based upon the restoration to the USSR of territories incorporated following the Nazi-Soviet Pact of 1939, in particular, of the Baltic States, and parts of Finland, Poland, and Rumania.

American Lend-Lease Aid. To facilitate the passage of Lend-Lease appropriations in Congress—a difficult matter at best due to the hostility toward the Soviet Union of several politically influential minorities in the United States—President Roosevelt, according to Secretary of State Cordell Hull, urged that the USSR publicize in the United States its policy toward freedom of religion, guaranteed by the Soviet Constitution of 1936. It was no accident, therefore, that within a few months the first Soviet publication on religion in the USSR, *Pravda o religii v rossii* (*The Truth About Religion in Russia*), produced on fine paper and profusely illustrated, was issued by the Moscow Patriarchate in 1942 and widely distributed among Russian-speaking minorities and refugees in the United States. This book, which was exclusively the work of Russian clergymen, denied any persecution of the Orthodox church in the USSR and emphasized German atrocities and German destruction of Russian churches during the war. It demonstrated the patriotism of the Russian Orthodox church in wartime.

The American military aid program was launched by token provision through the Reconstruction Finance Corporation for a credit-barter agreement amounting to $75,000,000. Following Averill Harriman's mission to Moscow, September 29 to October 1, 1941, the Roosevelt administration, on the ground that the defense of the Soviet Union was essential to the defense of the United States, provided initial Lend-Lease aid to the USSR amounting to a five-year credit of $1,000,000,000.

Anglo-Soviet Treaty of Alliance. Anglo-Soviet negotiations for a treaty of alliance were protracted by Soviet insistence on the specific recognition of Soviet boundaries as they existed at the moment of the German invasion. In December, 1941, on the very eve of Pearl Harbor, Anthony Eden was dispatched to Moscow to clarify Anglo-Soviet relations during and after the war. Although the Churchill government was disposed to accede to Soviet demands, the United States opposed the conclusion of any specific secret territorial agreements prior to the victorious conclusion of the war. Soviet security, according to Cordell Hull, could best be obtained through a strong postwar peace organization and by a disarmed Germany as called for in the Atlantic Charter. The Stalin regime, involved in a titanic struggle with Nazi Germany, needed above all to retain the moral as well as the material support of the Western democracies in order to strengthen its position vis-à-vis the Russian people. It was, therefore, forced to make concessions. To resolve the deadlock, a twenty-year Anglo-Soviet treaty of alliance, minus any territorial provisions, was signed in London by Foreign Commissar Molotov on May 26, 1942. According to the terms of this alliance, Great Britain and the Soviet Union pledged themselves "to afford one another military and other assistance and support of all kinds" in the war against Germany and her satellites, agreed not to conclude a separate peace, or to participate in any alliance or coalition directed against one or the other high contracting party. Thus the Soviet boundary issue was postponed to the end of the war, when it was assumed by the Western democracies that a fair and just settlement was more likely to be obtained. By that time, however, the USSR had recovered the areas claimed and had no intention of parting with them.

Second-Front Controversy. The major wartime controversy between the USSR, on the one hand, and Great Britain and the United States on the other, concerned the establishment of a second front in Europe. This issue was first raised by the Soviet government during the initial retreat of the Red Army in the summer of 1941. Almost a year passed, however, before a joint communiqué was issued in London on June 11, 1942, to the effect that a "full understanding was reached with regard to the urgent task of creating a second front in Europe in 1942." The Soviet text was more forceful, more obligatory, but the rather vague wording of the English text led to misinterpretation and misunderstanding that marred wartime relations among the Allies. Foreign Commissar Molotov had discussed the second front issue in both London and Washington during the negotiations for the Anglo-Soviet alliance.

It seems clear that Molotov left Washington convinced that the Roosevelt administration strongly supported the opening of a second front in Western Europe in 1942, as the most effective means of assisting the Red Army to stem the tide of the German advance in Russia and of shortening the war. In London, however, where Molotov argued for a second front that would divert at least forty German divisions from the Soviet front, Churchill and his military advisers raised numerous obstacles to the achievement of such an objective in 1942. Churchill, a "naval person," as he was fond of calling himself, emphasized the difficulty of overseas invasion, the lack of special landing craft to transport large numbers of men and tanks, and the danger of failure as long as German airpower was in a position to oppose such a landing in force on the other side of the English Channel. When the joint communiqué was issued on June 11, the British government presented to Molotov an *aide-memoire,* which explicitly stated that it could "give no promise" to open a second front in 1942.

When the Soviet government evinced great uneasiness over the failure of its Western allies to implement a second front in 1942, Churchill flew to Moscow in August to explain its postponement until 1943 and to inform Stalin of the alternate plan for "Torch," an Anglo-American landing in North Africa. Although Churchill presented his case in masterly fashion, for the Russians there was no satisfactory alternative to a cross-Channel invasion. On November 6, 1942, on the eve of the twenty-fifth anniversary of the Bolshevik Revolution and of the Allied landings in North Africa, Stalin announced that England was immobilizing only four German and eleven Italian divisions in Egypt and Libya, as compared to the concentration of two hundred and forty

German divisions on the Russian front. It was later revealed that President Roosevelt, General Marshall, and General Eisenhower on strategic grounds preferred a second front in Europe in 1942 to a landing in North Africa, but they were unable to overcome Churchill's opposition. Churchill remained strongly disposed to an attack on "the soft underbelly of Europe," preferably through the Balkans. At the Quebec Conference of August, 1943, he accepted "in principle" a cross-Channel invasion. Although he reluctantly agreed to an invasion of Western Europe in 1944, he would have preferred to postpone it once again until 1945.

Unfortunately, Soviet leaders came to regard the repeated postponement of the second front in Europe as a breach of faith on the part of the Western democracies, especially Great Britain. After the Allied landing in Italy in 1943, Stalin reported to the Supreme Soviet (November 6, 1943):

> Of course, the present actions of the Allied armies in the south of Europe cannot yet be regarded as a second front. But still it is something like a second front. Obviously the opening of a real second front in Europe, which is not so distant, will considerably hasten the victory over Hitlerite Germany and will consolidate even more the fighting partnership of the Allied countries. . . .

As late as 1963 popular thinking and Soviet textbooks revealed that Soviet resentment on the second-front issue had not subsided. Soviet historians have recognized the significance of the Anglo-American bombing of Germany as a factor which seriously undermined German civilian morale. They nevertheless continue to claim that until June, 1944, the Red Army was mainly responsible for the depletion of German military manpower. The second-front controversy had serious repercussions on subsequent negotiations between the Soviet Union and the Western democracies for a peaceful settlement of postwar problems.

Second German Offensive. The second German summer offensive against the Red Army was launched on June 13, 1942. During the first year of the war, German casualties on the eastern front numbered 1,292,656 men and 39,821 officers, including 277,000 killed. By comparison, Hitler's conquest of Western Europe in two years of conflict had resulted in only 97,136 men killed and taken prisoner. To bolster the 171 understrength German divisions in the USSR for the 1942 summer offensive, Hitler raised 69 satellite divisions—27 Rumanian, 9 Italian, 13 Hungarian, 17 Finnish, 1 Spanish, and 2 Slovak. In spite of warnings from his generals to the contrary, Hitler was sure that this army was sufficient for the accomplishment of his main objective—the conquest of Stalingrad on the Volga to cut Moscow's communications with the south and with the Iranian supply route, and a major drive to the Caucasus to secure additional oil resources and to command the route to the Middle East and India. Hitler's ultimate objective was the encirclement and capture of Moscow which, with the success of this campaign, would have become feasible. Since the death of Stalin in 1953, Soviet historians have reevaluated their original contention that Hitler's primary objective in 1942 was the outflanking and capture of Moscow. General von Paulus, German commander at Stalingrad, however, substantiated the original Soviet interpretation that Moscow was the chief objective.

Winston Churchill was primarily concerned about the German conquest of the Caucasus, with its ultimate threat to India and the Near East. During his visit to Moscow in August, 1942, Stalin assured him that Soviet Russia's twenty-five divisions in the Caucasus would prevent a breakthrough. Soviet leaders were more concerned about the threat to Moscow.

Battle of Stalingrad. In the summer offensive of 1942, the German army extended its occupation of Soviet territory to its maximum of 580,000 square miles. When this offensive finally ground to a halt at Stalingrad on November 10, the Germans had advanced from Kursk to Voronezh on the central front and from Taganrog on the Sea of Azov to the vicinity of the Grozny oilfields in the Caucasus. The possession of Stalingrad, as Hitler belatedly discovered, was the key to continued German occupation of the Caucasus. The city was subjected to a five-month siege, beginning August 22, in what became one of the most crucial battles of World War II. The historic battle, which reduced the city to rubble as the fighting was waged street by street and building by building, has been graphically depicted in Konstantin Simonov's novel *Days and Nights* and Theodore Plievier's *Stalingrad.* The significance of this siege, both for the Soviet Union and for the Middle East, was recognized in the Western democracies, where prayers were offered regularly in the churches for the success of the Red Army defenders. The advent of winter found Hitler's troops ill-clad and ill-equipped to cope with the cold. Against the advice of his generals, Hitler obdurately refused to withdraw the Sixth Army from Stalingrad while yet there was time. On November 19 the Red Army, drawing upon its Siberian forces, began its counteroffensive. By a giant pincer movement it encircled the Germans and forced the surrender of General von Paulus and the twenty-two divisions (330,000 men) of the German Sixth Army by February 2, 1943. In the process, the Red Army fell heir to vast quantities of usable German equipment.

The Battle of Stalingrad marked an important psychological turning point in World War II. It destroyed Hitler's reputation for infallibility and invincibility. The loss of the city forced the Germans to abandon the Caucasus, which was promptly reoccupied by the Red Army. The Soviet victory may have kept the Turks from entering the war on the side of the Axis powers.

As Hitler's victorious armies approached Stalingrad and entered the Caucasus, rumors circulated that Turkey was about to declare war against the USSR. Soviet historians have since confirmed Turkish plans for intervention. In 1947 a former member of the Turkish cabinet, writing in the American magazine *PM,* claimed that Turkish Premier Ismet Inönü was on the point of announcing the Turkish decision to join the Axis, when Franz von Papen, German ambassador in Ankara, forestalled this by revealing the encirclement and defeat of the German armies at Stalingrad. In Moscow Churchill had promised Stalin to use all Britain's influence to persuade the Turks to preserve their neutrality.

At the height of the Battle of Stalingrad, when the disposition of Red Army forces encouraged Soviet leaders to anticipate a victorious finale, Stalin dispatched a message to General Ali Fuat Cebesoy, then Turkish minister of communications, whom he had known and respected since 1917, asking for his opinion on the outcome of the battle. Stalin apparently assumed that the Turkish decision on entering the conflict depended on Soviet defeat or victory at Stalingrad. In any event, he was sufficiently confident of the result to provide the Turkish general with a map disclosing the disposition of the Red Army. When General Cebesoy thereupon predicted a Soviet victory within fifteen days, the Soviet leader must have been satisfied that Turkey would not join the Axis. Following the victory, Stalin notified Cebesoy that he had always trusted his military judgment, now more than ever. Whether or not General Cebesoy's influence helped to keep Turkey out of the war at this time is not known. He appears to have performed an important role at two crucial periods in Soviet history—the Kronstadt Mutiny and the Battle of Stalingrad.

Red Army Successes. Before the second Soviet winter offensive came to an end on March 31, 1943, the Red Army had retrieved 184,000 square miles of German-occupied territory. On a front stretching from Leningrad to the Caucasus, they advanced as much as four hundred miles in some sectors. On January 18, the Red Army successfully lifted the sixteen-month siege of Leningrad. This was followed by the capture of Voronezh (January 25), of Krasnodar in the northern Caucasus (February 13), as well as of Rostov on the Don and Voroshilovgrad (February 15). Although Kharkov was temporarily liberated (February 18), the Germans by the transfer of thirty new divisions from Western Europe, recaptured the city on March 14 and recovered large areas in the Don Basin. In his order of the day for February 23, 1943, the twenty-fifth anniversary of the founding of the Red Army, Stalin observed, "In view of the absence of a second front in Europe the Red Army alone is bearing the whole weight of the war." The significance of the Soviet victory was grasped by Winston Churchill who, on May 19, 1943, announced that "Russia has already inflicted injuries upon the German military organism which will, I believe, prove ultimately fatal."

Kursk-Belgorod: Third German Offensive. Smarting under the smashing defeat of the German forces at Stalingrad which badly undermined his prestige at home and abroad, Hitler in 1943 determined to gamble his last card on a third summer offensive designed to break through Red Army defenses on the Kursk-Belgorod salient of the central front. For this purpose, he assembled near Kursk an army of unprecedented size, consisting of 70 divisions (900,000 officers and men), 10,000 artillery pieces, 27,000 tanks and self-propelled guns. Commanding this army were some of Hitler's best strategists—Field Marshals Manstein and Kluge, as well as Generals Model, Got, Kemper, and others. When the Germans launched their offensive on July 5, the Red Army, profiting by the strategic lessons learned at Stalingrad, was ready for them. The recovery of vast areas of Soviet territory following the Battle of Stalingrad had provided Red Army troops with a first-hand demonstration of the brutality and destruction perpetrated by the Nazis during the years of German occupation. The incensed Soviet soldiers were psychologically prepared to exert every effort to expel the Germans from Soviet territory.

Soviet Field Marshal Pavel Rotmistrov, commander of the Fifth Guards Tank Army at the village of Prokhorovka—the decisive battle of the Kursk Bulge—has termed this "the biggest battle of armor in history." The Germans lost upwards of 3,000 tanks, 1,400 airplanes, over 1,000 guns and 70,000 troops. Before the encounter at Kursk, the Germans as well as the Western democracies assumed that the Red Army could only conduct a winter offensive. In the summer of 1943, however, "General Winter" was not around to take the credit for the gigantic offensive launched by the Red Army on July 12, which by the end of September advanced to the Dnieper and liberated 115,000 square miles of territory in two months. The very rapidity of the German retreat, which at times amounted to a rout, stirred speculation in the United States about "a deal" between the Soviets and the Nazis. The Red Army even crossed the Dnieper to recover Dnepropetrovsk (October 25) and the historic Ukrainian capital of Kiev (November 6).

The Germans never retrieved the losses sustained in the Battle of Kursk and the offensive which followed. According to German sources, in fifty days of fighting, they lost over half a million officers and men. After the Kursk battle, according to Field Marshal Manstein, "The initiative went over irretrievably to the Soviet side." The Soviet objective of 1941 had been accomplished. This battle likewise forced the Germans to move large forces from Italy to the eastern front, thereby depriving Mussolini of much-needed German support to the advantage of the Allied cause. If any further evidence was needed after Stalingrad to demonstrate that the Germans could not win the war against Russia, it was provided by the Battle of Kursk and the Red Army summer offensive of 1943.

RAPPROCHEMENT WITH WESTERN ALLIES

Extent of the Lend-Lease. In spite of the absence of a second front in Europe until June, 1944, the West, and especially the United States, made a direct and important contribution to Soviet victory through Lend-Lease aid, often provided at the expense of the Allied war effort in other areas. Whether Moscow, Leningrad, and Stalingrad could have been saved without American aid remains a subject for speculation. The margin between success and failure in those battles was narrow, and even limited quantities of aid in vitally important categories may have been an important factor in turning the tide. President Roosevelt accorded priority to United States shipments to the Soviet Union. Nor were any "strings" attached to that aid by the American government. By the late spring of 1943 mass quantities of Lend-Lease materials were reaching the USSR.

American equipment was shipped to the Soviet Union by three routes, via Murmansk in the Arctic, Iran in the south, and Vladivostok in the Pacific. With the establishment of Nazi air and submarine bases in Norway and northern Finland, the Murmansk route became the most dangerous. In 1942 twelve ships out of every hundred sailing for the USSR were sunk. These losses were reduced in 1943 to one ship out of one hundred. During the siege of Stalingrad the United States army assumed the main responsibility for the Iranian supply route, serviced earlier by Great Britain. By May, 1943, military and miscellaneous supplies amounting to 100,000 tons per month were being handled over this route. Throughout the Lend-Lease period, however, more than 50 per cent of American shipments continued to use the safer Pacific route to Vladivostok.

According to American sources, United States Lend-Lease shipments to the Soviet Union in World War II amounted to $11,141,470,000, or 23 per cent of this country's total Lend-Lease aid of $49,096,000,000, of which the British Empire obtained more than 60 per cent. The Soviet Union also received substantial aid from American private relief and from Great Britain. During the first year alone, the USSR obtained under Lend-Lease 3,052 airplanes, 4,084 tanks, 30,031 vehicles, and 831,000 tons of miscellaneous supplies. Based on Soviet figures of wartime airplane production, American-supplied aircraft is estimated to have amounted to approximately 10 per cent of Soviet production.

General John R. Deane, head of the United States Military Mission in Moscow, whose responsibility it was to coordinate the Lend-Lease program, has provided some impressive statistics that reveal the magnitude of American aid to the USSR. From October 1, 1941, to May 1, 1945, he reports that 2,660 ships carrying 16,529,791 tons of supplies were sent to Russia, of which 15,234,791 long tons reached their destination. In evaluating the importance of thousands of items provided through Lend-Lease, General Deane placed truck transportation and combat vehicles first. The United States delivered 427,284 trucks, 13,303 combat vehicles, 35,170 motorcycles, and 2,328 ordnance vehicles. From his own personal observation, General Deane was able to verify the extensive use of these vehicles on the Soviet front. Next in order, he placed petroleum products, food, and railroad equipment. Under Lend-Lease the USSR received 1,900 steam locomotives, 66 diesel locomotives, 9,920 flatcars, 1,000 dump cars, 120 tank cars, and 35 heavy machinery cars. Since more than half of American Lend-Lease shipments utilized the Pacific route, this railroad equipment must have helped greatly in the transportation of more than 7,000,000 tons of supplies via the Trans-Siberian network.

As the USSR increased its own production of military weapons, Lend-Lease shipments included more machine tools, industrial plants (one entire rubber plant was shipped from the United States), raw materials, medical supplies, steel, aluminum, copper, clothing, bedding, food, and seeds. Although the Soviet administrator of the aid program, Commissar of Foreign Trade A. I. Mikoyan, was careful to confine Soviet requirements to dire necessities while the USSR was on the defensive, toward the end of the war more and more items of importance for postwar reconstruction were included. General Deane, who reported himself "in high dudgeon" most of the time due to lack of Soviet cooperation, was inclined to feel that Soviet officialdom assumed that American aid was prompted by expediency rather than by generosity. During the war there was formal, if not overly appreciative, recognition of Lend-Lease aid in the Soviet press. Front-line troops appear to have been enthusiastic about American materiel, especially about American motorized equipment. Undoubtedly more effective aid could have been provided had American personnel been permitted freely to visit Soviet plants and battle areas where this equipment was being utilized. In one of his rare tributes to American Lend-Lease shipments, Stalin informed President Truman in 1945 that they had contributed "to a substantial degree" to Soviet victory. According to Soviet sources for the period, 1941 to 1945, the total aid received by the USSR from her allies did not exceed 4 per cent of Soviet production, but this was acknowledged to have played "a positive role."

In spite of frequent clashes over wartime objectives and the conduct of the war, relations between the USSR and the Western democracies had appreciably improved since 1941. Soviet leaders attributed much of the credit for the semblance of cordiality to President Roosevelt. No doubt it was due in part to the shelving of some highly controversial issues, such as the determination of the western borders of the Soviet Union, until the end of the conflict, in the expectation that they could be solved more equitably at that time, or so American leaders thought.

Dissolution of Comintern. On May 22, 1943, the Stalin regime made what was then regarded as a further gesture of good will by officially dissolving the Third International, or Comintern. This move, according to Stalin, was intended to allay Allied fears of any Soviet intent to "Bolshevize" the peoples of other countries, and to strengthen unity among all forces fighting against Hitlerism. On the domestic front, and especially for Soviet communists, this step was justified on the ground that thousands of former German communists were caught red-handed committing atrocities against Russian workers, peasants, and communists comparable to those perpetrated by the Nazis. The Second International had been discarded in World War I because of its ineffectiveness. The Third International shared the same fate in World War II, essentially for the same reason. The European proletariat and even its communist members had fought the Soviet proletariat, and tortured and slaughtered its communists. Irrespective of Stalin's motives, the dissolution of the Comintern created a better international atmosphere, especially between the United States and the USSR. Only much later was it disclosed that Stalin retained the Comintern apparatus intact, although its curtailed activities were conducted with the greatest secrecy.

Differences of Opinion. What marred the Anglo-American-Soviet *rapprochement* was the repeated tendency of the USSR and the Western democracies to approach wartime and postwar problems, each from its own experience. The Soviet Union, with 240 German divisions on its territory, was concerned primarily about the ways and means of expelling them in the shortest possible time. England, which had been bombed but not otherwise invaded, and the United States were concerned, not only about the conduct of the war, but also about its outcome and the postwar settlement. If their peoples had to suffer, British and American leaders wanted it to be in the interests of a better world in the future. By 1943 it was no longer possible to shelve the second front indefinitely or to postpone all consideration of the fate of Germany, Poland, and other basic issues. These matters were discussed in a series of important wartime conferences in Moscow, Teheran, Yalta, and Potsdam, the last of which was held following the end of the war in Europe.

Moscow Conference. The main objectives of the Moscow Conference of Foreign Ministers, October 19–30, 1943, were to resolve the differences among the Allies on the conduct of the war, to create a postwar horizon, and to pave the way for a future summit conference of heads of state. When it became clear to Soviet leaders that the second front was not the main issue under consideration in Moscow, they manifested reluctance about attending further conferences, including the forthcoming conference in Teheran (Iran) for which Stalin would have to leave the USSR. As an inducement to Stalin to participate in the summit conference, Allied representatives promised to set the date at that time for the opening of a second front. Only then did Secretary of State Cordell Hull secure Soviet consent for the Big Three meeting in Teheran. For Cordell Hull the outstanding achievement of the Moscow conference was the "Four-Power Declaration," in which China was included, which called for united action against the enemy, unanimity on the terms of surrender, the need to establish an international organization (the beginning of the United Nations), and continued postwar collaboration. Upon the insistence of the Soviet Union, the conferees issued a declaration denouncing Fascism and supporting the punishment of war criminals. It was in Moscow that the joint occupation and postwar control of Germany were first considered. Although no decision was reached, the dismemberment of Germany was strongly favored as the solution most likely to forestall future aggression. Soviet demands for Allied pressure to force the entry of Turkey into the war, and thereby divert fifteen German divisions from the Soviet front, received no support from the British and American delegates on the ground that subsequent aid to the Turks would deplete supplies needed for the second front, the Italian campaign, and the Pacific war.

Teheran Conference. The Teheran Conference, November 28–December 1, 1943, attended by Roosevelt, Stalin, and Churchill, marked the first real effort at coordinated planning of the conduct of the war. As the first summit conference of the Big Three, the world's attention and the world's hopes for the future were focused upon every bit of news, mostly of social events, that filtered through the tight censorship. It was in Teheran that President Roosevelt had his first opportunity to meet Stalin face to face, and he used all his personal magnetism in an effort to win the friendship of the Soviet leader, on the assumption that this would facilitate a more satisfactory postwar settlement. Aware that Roosevelt and United States military leaders were concerned about Soviet participation in the Pacific war, Stalin won their cooperation by officially committing the Soviet Union to entering the war against Japan when the conflict in Europe was over. Once this commitment was made, the United States had a vested interest in the opening of the second front, in order to accelerate the end of the war with Germany. Churchill's strong preference for an extension of the Mediterranean front in northern Italy, Rhodes, or the Balkans, was vetoed in favor of the oft-postponed cross-Channel invasion, set for May, 1944, on the understanding that a Red Army offensive on the eastern front would be timed to coincide with the offensive in the west. The only concession to Churchill's preoccupation with the Mediterranean was the proposed invasion of southern France, an area far removed from the Red Army's military activities, in conjunction with "Overlord," the cross-Channel invasion. At Teheran, in line with Soviet demands, the Curzon line was accepted as the future Soviet-Polish boundary, thereby assuring the USSR of part of its acquisitions under the Nazi-Soviet Pact. The lengthy discussion of a broad range of topics led one participant in the Teheran Conference to conclude that if Soviet views prevailed at the peace table the USSR would emerge as the only important military and political force on the European continent.

Allied Victories. The Allied military situation following the Teheran Conference brightened considerably. The year 1944 was marked by a rapid succession of Allied victories. The Red Army's swift recovery of Soviet territory foreshadowed the outlines of the peace to come, at least on the Soviet boundary. In January, when Soviet forces crossed the former Polish frontier, the USSR came out in favor of "a strong, independent Polish state," with compensation in the west at German expense for territory lost to Russia east of the Curzon line. On April 2, as the Red Army approached the Rumanian frontier, a comparable declaration of Rumania's independence was issued, with specific reference, however, to the Soviet-Rumanian frontier of 1941, which substantiated Stalin's intent to retain Bessarabia.

Benefits of the Second Front. By D-Day on June 6, 1944, when the long-awaited Anglo-American-Canadian expeditionary force under the command of General Dwight D. Eisenhower made the second front a reality, the USSR had liberated virtually all of Soviet territory, with the exception of the Baltic fringe, eastern Poland, and Bessarabia. The second front in Western Europe, upon which the Stalin regime had placed such store, therefore came too late to exert any decisive influence on the recovery of Soviet territory from the Germans, although the devastating Anglo-American air raids on German cities like Cologne, Frankfurt, Hamburg, and Berlin, together with the Italian campaign and United States Lend-Lease aid, had undoubtedly accelerated the Red Army's westward advance. Four days after the Allied landings in Normandy, the promised Soviet eastern offensive was set in motion, first in the north against Finland and the Baltic States, then in Poland, and finally in Rumania. With Nazi reserves at the point of exhaustion, Russian manpower already exceeded that of Germany three to one. The Red Army was in a position to choose its objectives at will.

Having effected a breach in the Finnish Mannerheim Line in June, the Red Army captured Minsk (July 3), Vilna (July 13), and crossed the historic Niemen River on July 17. With his flair for colorful language, Winston Churchill (August 2) credited the Red forces with having accomplished "the main work of tearing the guts out of the German army." The troops of Marshal Rokossovsky swept westward across Poland until, on August 15, they reached the Warsaw suburb of Praga on the east bank of the Vistula, where they remained while the non-Communist uprising of General Tadeusz Bor-Komorowski was crushed by the Nazis and Warsaw was destroyed. As the Soviet advance in Poland came to a halt, the Red Army offensive swept rapidly across Rumania, Bucharest was captured on August 31, and the Rumanian army joined the Soviets for the invasion of Hungary. By early September, Soviet troops had entered Yugoslavia and East Prussia and reached the Czechoslovak border. Hostilities with Finland were terminated by the armistice of September 19, which provided for the withdrawal of Finnish troops beyond the Soviet-Finnish border line of March 12, 1940, the cession to Russia of Petsamo in the Arctic and of a naval base at Porkkala-Udd, and reparations payments of $300,000,000 over a five-year period. Although the terms were severe, Finland's independence was assured without Soviet military occupation and the Soviet lease of the Hangoe Peninsula was ended. Following a Soviet declaration of war on Bulgaria (September 5), the Red Army entered Sofia, the capital, on September 16, and the Bulgarians joined the Soviets in the expulsion of the Germans from the rest of the Balkans. In October, as German resistance began to crumble in the Baltic States, Soviet forces seized the strategic port of Riga. By early November all Soviet territory from the Barents to the Black Sea, with the exception of a small German pocket in western Latvia, had been cleared of enemy forces. By the end of the year the Red Army had encircled Budapest.

On the eve of the triumphant celebration of the twenty-seventh anniversary of the Bolshevik Revolution (November 6, 1944) Stalin paid public tribute to the significance of the second front in Western Europe:

There can be no doubt that without the organization of the second front in Europe, which pinned down 75 divisions of the Germans, our troops would not have been able in so short a time to break down the resistance of the German troops and drive them from the confines of the Soviet Union. Thus it is equally without doubt that without the mighty operations of the Red Army in the summer of this year, which pinned down some 200 German divisions, the troops of our allies would not have been able so quickly to deal with the German troops, and thrown them out of the area of middle Italy, France and Belgium.

In spite of its successes, the Red Army still faced 180 German and 24 Hungarian divisions on the eastern front.

THE YALTA CONFERENCE

The military situation on the eve of the Yalta Conference was far different from what it had been at Teheran. Allied troops were preparing to cross the Rhine. In its final winter offensive, launched on January 12, 1945, the Red Army had regained Warsaw (January 17), reached the German border of Silesia (January 19), captured Tannenberg in East Prussia (January 21), and invaded Germany proper as far as the Oder River, where it was poised for the attack on Berlin, some forty miles distant. In brief, the USSR already occupied the greater part of Eastern Europe. Both the Allies and the Soviets were so busy occupying territory that they neglected to draw any line of demarcation limiting the advance of their respective forces.

It was against this backdrop of military realities that the Big Three met for the second and last time at Yalta in the Crimea, February 4–11, 1945, to reconsider the problems of the war and the post-war world. Winston Churchill unhappily commented that ten years of research could not have resulted in a more unsuitable locale for the discussions. With the imminent collapse of Germany, the USSR had suddenly emerged as the most powerful country in Europe—a position that Russia had not held since the defeat of Napoleon in the reign of Alexander I. At Yalta Stalin was therefore able, for the first time, to negotiate from what is now popularly called "a position of strength." According to Secretary of State James F. Byrnes, the Yalta Conference marked the "high tide of Big Three unity." Although in one sense this was true, the repercussions from the Yalta decisions provoked violent and continuing disagreement in the Western world, especially in the United States. In this sense, Yalta became the most controversial of the wartime conferences.

Dismemberment of Germany. At Yalta the Big Three confronted head-on the problem of what was to be done with Nazi Germany. Although no agree-

US Office of War Information

Yalta in the Crimea was the scene of the last wartime conference between
Stalin, Roosevelt, and Churchill. In July when the Allies met at Potsdam
to plan the European settlement, of the original Big Three, only Stalin
remained.

ment was reached on the partition of Germany into a number of small states,
it was agreed to include "dismemberment" in the surrender terms as a means
of insuring "future peace and security." The division of Germany into three
occupation zones under an Allied Control Council, with provision for a fourth
French zone to be carved out of the English and American occupied areas, for
all practical purposes constituted partition, although such was not the intention of the conferees at the time. Although Berlin was accepted as the headquarters of the Allied Control Council, the actual boundaries of the occupation zones were not defined at Yalta and no mention appears to have been
made of British and American access to Berlin in the Soviet zone. President
Roosevelt, from the vantage point of Yalta, did not expect American occupation forces to remain in Germany longer than two years.

Reparations Payments. The chief concern of the USSR in regard to
Germany at Yalta, according to Secretary of State Byrnes, was reparations
payments. The Soviet government asked that the German reparations total be
set at $20,000,000,000, half of which would go to the Soviet Union, with
$8,000,000,000 for Great Britain and the United States, and $2,000,000,000
for the remaining Allied countries. Although Churchill strongly opposed the
setting of any reparations figure on the ground of the ignominious failure of
the reparations system following World War I, President Roosevelt, to avoid

a deadlock at the conference, agreed to accept the twenty billion figure "as a basis" for discussion—a decision which proved to be a source of serious misunderstanding later. The Russians henceforth assumed that their reparations total was a *fait accompli*.

In view of the tremendous Soviet losses in World War II, it was only logical that the Soviet government should seek reparations compensation from Germany, as it did from Finland. Some two years later, in 1947, Molotov informed the Council of Foreign Ministers that the cost to the USSR of the war against Germany and Japan amounted to $357,000,000,000, to which he added the costs of destruction resulting from German invasion and occupation amounting to $128,000,000,000, making a total cost of $485,000,000,000. According to Molotov, 1,710 towns and workers' settlements, 70,000 villages and hamlets, and 6,000,000 buildings were destroyed, leaving 25,000,000 Soviet citizens homeless. Further losses included 35,000 factories and plants, and 40,000 hospitals. More recent statistics have pointed to the destruction of 98,000 *kolkhozi,* 1,876 *sovkhozi,* and 2,890 Machine Tractor Stations (MTS). Against this background, the Soviet government did not feel that its demands were exorbitant. The final settlement of reparations, however, was left for the Potsdam Conference.

Polish Issue. Of all the controversial issues considered at Yalta, perhaps the most trying was that of Poland. According to Churchill, its impact was felt in seven out of the eight plenary sessions of the conference. Disagreement focused not so much on the Polish border settlement as upon the character of the Polish government. The whole issue was complicated by the existence of two Polish governments, one comprised of Polish exiles resident in London, and the other of the communist-oriented Lublin government, established under Soviet sponsorship, and recognized on January 1, 1945, as the "legitimate" Polish government. The Anglo-Polish Alliance of 1939 and the presence in the United States of a large and articulate Polish minority of anti-communist persuasion gave both England and America serious cause for concern about the future of Poland. The Stalin regime, on the other hand, mindful of Polish hostility in the past, was determined to insure the presence of a "friendly" (meaning the Lublin) Polish government. With the Red Army already occupying Polish territory, Roosevelt and Churchill were confronted by military realities. In what the Soviet government regarded as a concession to its Western allies, agreement was reached on the reorganization of the existing Lublin Provisional government "on a broader democratic basis," to include representatives of the Polish government in exile in London. Stalin made it clear, however, that from his point of view the Lublin government was as broadly democratic already as was the French government of De Gaulle, supported by the Western democracies without blessing of elections. When the Polish decision became public, England and the United States were bitterly accused of betraying Polish democracy. The genuinely free Polish elections envisaged at Yalta, as events were to prove, were something that

Stalin was not prepared to risk. According to General John R. Deane, who was present at Yalta, the acrimonious disputes arising out of the Polish discussions adversely affected the implementation of all Anglo-American agreements for joint collaboration on Soviet soil in the war against Japan. The Polish dispute is generally conceded to have accelerated the disintegration of the wartime alliance.

United Nations. Another Yalta decision that gave rise to much future misunderstanding and recriminations pertained to the exercise of the veto power in the Security Council of the United Nations. The "veto right" came to be regarded by many Americans as a special concession to the Soviet Union. Actually, although it was the excessive use of the veto by the USSR that brought it into disrepute, both England and the United States were in hearty accord on the veto provision, as long as it was not used for procedural matters—a limitation readily accepted at Yalta by the Soviet delegation. The real concession made at Yalta in regard to the United Nations was the one by which the United States and Great Britain agreed to support the applications of Byelorussia and the Ukraine for separate membership. The British Empire, with its dominions enjoying separate representation, was scarcely in a position to protest.

Secret Protocol on Japan. A top-secret protocol to the Yalta Agreement, which was not released to the public until February, 1946, outlined the conditions under which the Soviet Union was expected to enter the war against Japan. Even at Teheran there had been some informal consideration of Soviet territorial objectives in the Far East, including Soviet interest in Dairen and Port Arthur, Southern Sakhalin, and the Kurile Islands, but no definite decision was reached. The agreement finally signed and sealed at Yalta contained the following provisions: 1. The preservation of the *status quo* in Outer Mongolia (the Mongolian People's Republic). 2. The restoration to Soviet Russia of tsarist rights lost to Japan by the Russo-Japanese War, namely, of Southern Sakhalin and the Kurile Islands, together with the lease of the Port Arthur naval base and the internationalization of the port of Dairen, and of former Russian rights in Manchuria, including joint Soviet-Chinese management of the Chinese Eastern Railway. President Roosevelt promised to obtain the concurrence of the Nationalist government of Chiang Kai-shek to the provisions pertaining to China.

Public furore over this "secret" agreement stemmed in part from the "sellout" of China, which had not been consulted in advance on Soviet territorial expansion, and to what was regarded as the excessive price paid for the Soviet entry into the Pacific war. Secrecy was, of course, of prime importance at the time to prevent a premature Japanese invasion of the USSR before the conclusion of the war in Europe. Objections to Soviet entry into the conflict with Japan materialized only after the sudden collapse of that country in August, 1945. At Yalta, when the war in the Pacific was expected to last another eighteen months and when the invasion of Japan was expected to cost a million American casualties, it was the American chiefs of staff and General Douglas MacArthur who exerted the strongest pressure to bring the USSR into the war at any cost. Much of the disillusionment, which was the aftermath of World War II, was a product of the underestimation by political and military experts of Soviet strength and stamina and the overestimation of Japanese powers of endurance.

End of the War in Europe. Following the Yalta Conference, events in Europe moved swiftly toward a climax. On April 13 Vienna was completely occupied by the Red Army. The troops of Marshals Zhukov and Konev pierced the Berlin defenses on April 21 and encircled the city. On April 25 American troops from General Courtney Hodges' First Army joined those of Marshal Konev's First Ukrainian Army near Torgau on the River Elbe. Berlin fell to the Red Army on May 2. When the German armed forces accepted Allied terms of unconditional surrender at Rheims on May 7, followed one day later by their final capitulation in Berlin, the war in Europe was over.

Victory, however, did not promote unity in the Allied camp. The stress and strain of military problems gave way to political issues on which wide disagreement was soon manifested. Even before the death of President Roosevelt (April 12, 1945), the United States repeatedly protested the open and frequent violation of agreements reached at Yalta, especially those in respect to the Polish and Balkan governments. The Stalin regime displayed no serious intention of altering the Polish Lublin government which represented those Poles who had fought side by side with the Red Army against the Germans. It even arrested fourteen Polish leaders in exile who proceeded under safe-conduct to Moscow to discuss Polish national issues. In February the Soviets forced Rumania to accept the Communist hireling, Petr Groza, as prime minister. At the San Francisco Conference, where the Charter of the United Nations was being drafted, Molotov and Western delegates clashed over the admission of Argentina, the composition of the Polish government, the application of the veto power to procedural matters in the Security Council (supposedly settled at Yalta), and other issues.

In an effort to salvage a fast deteriorating situation, President Truman hastily dispatched the ailing Harry Hopkins to Moscow. Stalin than yielded to American pressure on the veto question and made a gesture of conciliation on Poland by including Stanislaw Mikolajczyk, Polish Peasant Party leader, in the Warsaw government. Anglo-American diplomatic recognition of the Polish government followed, together with Polish membership in the United Nations.

Stalin's obdurate insistence on "friendly," that is, subservient Communist regimes on the western periphery of the USSR did not stem from any fear of Poland, Rumania, or Bulgaria. It was the possibility of these states acting in conjunction with a major foreign power against the Soviet Union that concerned him. The presence of a weak but unfriendly Communist Cuba ninety miles from American shores, acting in conjunction with the USSR, in subsequent years presented what was in some respects a similar problem for the United States.

THE POTSDAM CONFERENCE

The Potsdam Conference, July 17 to August 2, 1945, summoned to pave the way for an equitable European settlement, reflected the growing dissension among the victorious Allied powers. Had it not been for the prospect of Soviet entry into the Pacific war, which the United States still considered indispensable to an early victory, relations might conceivably have reached the breaking point. Before the conference was finished, Stalin was the only remaining member of the original Big Three. President Truman had already succeeded Roosevelt. During the course of the conference, a British election, which swept a Labor government into power, forced the replacement of Churchill and Anthony Eden by the mild-mannered Clement Attlee and the blunt-speaking Ernest Bevin. Although these changes involved personalities rather than policies, they did remove the two men who had had wartime experience in dealing with the Soviet Union.

At Potsdam, discussion ranged over a wide variety of topics: supervision of free elections in Poland, Bulgaria, and Rumania; Allied policy in Greece, which came under attack by Stalin; the disposition of the Italian colonies, with Stalin demanding, but not getting, a trusteeship over one of them; unilateral action by the USSR in turning over to Poland for administration that part of East Prussia east of the Neisse River, disposition of which was left by the Yalta Agreement for the peace conference (which never materialized); revision of the Montreux Convention to insure free passage through the Straits of Soviet naval and merchant ships in peace and war—a situation the Soviet Union would have preferred to control unilaterally with Turkey; and deportation under "humane" conditions of Germans from Poland, Czechoslovakia, and Hungary to the four zones of occupied Germany.

Reparations Question. The first decision approved at Potsdam was the creation of a Council of Foreign Ministers charged with the preparation of the peace treaties, with priority given to those for Italy and the Balkans. On the touchy reparations question, no final settlement was reached. The American and British delegations were nonplussed by Soviet removal of large quantities of Germany property and equipment to the USSR prior to the conference. The International Telephone and Telegraph Company's Berlin plant, as reported by Secretary of State Byrnes, had been stripped of its machinery, as had other rayon, ice, and optical instruments plants in the Berlin area. As at Yalta, the British and American delegations refused to consider any payment of reparations out of current production, at least until such time as German exports covered the cost of German imports, thereby making American loans unnecessary. This Western position on reparations was a direct outgrowth of

British experience following World War I. After having raised once again the $20,000,000,000 figure accepted at Yalta as a basis for discussion, Stalin avoided an open rupture by agreeing to an American proposal that each of the occupying powers should satisfy its reparations needs from its own zone. The USSR was also assigned 10 per cent of the war-industrial equipment of the three Western zones, with the opportunity of securing an additional 15 per cent in return for Soviet food and raw materials. This arrangement, intended to be permanent, was soon abandoned. Within a year Molotov was once again demanding $10,000,000,000 in reparations from Germany's current production.

Limited Agreement on Germany. Although the delimitation of Poland's western frontier was left to the anticipated peace conference, the British and American delegates were in agreement on the transfer of Koenigsberg, the capital of East Prussia, to the Soviet Union and promised to give it their full support. They also accepted Soviet proposals for the equal division of the German fleet and merchant marine among the Big Three powers. The strictly limited agreements reached at Potsdam on Germany were no substitute for a German peace treaty. As a result of the postponement of an over-all settlement with Germany, decisions which were intended to be temporary, such as the four occupation zones, became part of a frozen structure that proved unsatisfactory to all concerned.

Declaration on Japan. Although the Potsdam Conference was concerned primarily with Europe, the war in the Pacific was inevitably injected into the discussions. Prior to and during the conference, the USSR was approached by Japan and asked to serve as mediator in bringing the Pacific war to an end. These overtures were promptly rejected and the other delegations notified accordingly. Once again, Stalin committed the USSR to entry into the Pacific war, possibly late in August, 1945. President Truman took advantage of this opportunity to inform Stalin of America's possession of the atomic bomb and the possibility of its use to shorten the Pacific war. Although Stalin showed no indication of comprehending the revolutionary potential of this new strategic weapon, he and the other conferees agreed to issue first a Potsdam Declaration, based upon one previously issued at Cairo in 1943, which prescribed the main outlines on which any peace with Japan must be based. These revised terms included the expulsion of Japan from all islands acquired since 1914 and from all other possessions obtained by "violence and greed," an obvious reference to territories taken from Russia in 1905; the return to the Republic of China of Manchuria, Formosa, and the Pescadores; independence for Korea; the restriction of Japanese territory to the four home islands; Japanese military and industrial disarmament; the trial of Japanese war criminals; and the military occupation of Japan. Promises were made to the Japanese people of democratic institutions and the continuation of Japan as a national state, with access to essential raw materials. Had the Japanese government accepted these terms without delay, it is possible that the war in the Pacific might have ended without the entry of the USSR or the bombing of Japan. Japan hesitated and was lost.

The Potsdam Conference, according to Secretary of State Byrnes, ended in "good spirit," although the delegates emerged less "sanguine" than at Yalta, and aware that agreements recorded on paper "must be hammered out on the hard anvil of experience." There still existed some optimism about the possibility of postwar collaboration with the Soviet Union. Neither Byrnes nor the others appear to have had any premonition that it would take another sixteen months to conclude the first peace treaties with Italy and the Balkan states. In spite of disagreements, the conference was pronounced a "success," and a step on the road to the "early restoration of stability in Europe."

The Soviet Role in the Pacific

Immediately after Potsdam, the USSR confronted an early entry into the war in the Pacific. This entry was precipitated by the first atomic bombing of Japan (Hiroshima) on August 6. Two days later, and exactly three months after the conclusion of the European conflict, the Soviet Union declared war on Japan. Stalin, claiming that he had waited forty years to remove the "blemish" of 1905, disregarded the fact that the Social Democrats of that day loudly applauded the defeat of tsardom. Bomb or no bomb, it is practically certain that Stalin would have entered the Pacific war in order to reap the benefits of the Yalta Agreement. Already in April, 1945, the USSR had notified Japan that the Soviet-Japanese neutrality agreement of 1941 (still in force) would not be renewed in 1946. From the Japanese occupation of Manchuria in 1931 until the signing of the neutrality agreement just prior to the Hitlerite invasion, the Soviet Union had been involved in intermittent border hostilities with Japan, some of which developed into major engagements. Throughout World War II, according to Soviet claims, the USSR was forced to maintain forty Red Army divisions in the Soviet Far East to offset any possible Japanese threat to Siberia. By so doing, Soviet leaders believed that they had made an important contribution to the war in the Pacific. They had immoblized the formidable Kwantung Army (admittedly reduced in strength during the war period), or at least the major part of it. The Stalin regime readily admitted that the United States had borne the major brunt of the war in the Pacific, especially against the Japanese navy. The core of the Japanese land power and part of the Japanese air fleet remained in northeast, central, and southern China, and in the Japanese Islands.

Invasion of Japanese Territory. Under the command of Marshal Vasilevsky, the Soviet invasion of Manchuria, Korea, and Southern Sakhalin launched on August 9, rapidly overwhelmed the Japanese forces. When Japan surrendered on August 14, the Red Army continued its offensive on the ground that Japanese troops had not been instructed to lay down their arms. Although the Kwantung Army capitulated on August 19, Soviet airborne troops landed at Dairen, Port Arthur, and the Kurile Islands on August 22. The headlong Soviet drive was not halted until September 2, the date of the Japanese surrender to General Douglas MacArthur aboard the battleship *Missouri,* where General Derevyanko represented the Soviet Union. The USSR was unsuccessful in securing an occupation zone on the Japanese Island of Hokkaido. Marshal Vasilevsky nevertheless reigned supreme in Manchuria. Soviet Russia was accorded nominal representation on the Allied Council for Japan in Tokyo.

Significance. The last-minute entry of the Soviet Union into the Pacific war has led most Western historians to discount completely the significance of Soviet participation on the outcome. With benefit of hindsight, it is now evident that Japan had exhausted herself by prolonged conflict in China and the South Pacific. There are some who contend that as a result, neither the atomic bomb nor Soviet entry into the war was a decisive factor in the sudden Japanese surrender. Japanese peace overtures had coincided with the Potsdam Conference. Peace overtures, however, are not equivalent to surrender, as was proved by Japanese silence in the face of the Potsdam Declaration. In all probability, Japanese surrender could not have been long delayed. Whether Japanese resistance on the Chinese mainland would have ceased without the Soviet entry must remain a matter for speculation. Soviet casualties in the month-long Soviet campaign and its aftermath are said to have been 8,219 killed and 22,264 wounded. Those of Japan, according to Soviet statistics, amounted to 80,000 killed, 20,000 wounded, and 594,000 taken prisoner, including 148 generals. The military experts who overestimated Japanese strength as late as the Potsdam Conference may well have swung to the opposite extreme following surrender. Meanwhile, the Soviets continue to claim that it was the Soviet entry rather than the atomic bomb that triggered the Japanese capitulation.

In Retrospect. The sudden collapse of Japan in 1945 does raise the question as to whether the United States should have subordinated the Pacific to the European front, where no major offensive was staged for two and one-half years; or whether priority to the Pacific theater of operations might not have enabled General MacArthur to finish the war against Japan in time for the shift to the second front in Europe. Under such circumstances, the controversial concessions to the Soviet Union at Yalta need not have been made.

The Soviet Union fought World War II as a struggle for national survival. Both during and since the conflict, the war has been labelled *Otetchestvennaya Voina,* the Patriotic War (War for the Fatherland). This misled many persons into thinking that the USSR was on the verge of abandoning communism for nationalism. Soviet textbooks published in 1962, however, reinterpreted the Patriotic War, not as a struggle between two armies or two states, but as an ideological struggle between two social systems—that of socialism, as represented by the Soviet Union, and that of reactionary capitalist imperialism in Nazi Germany.

23

Soviet-American Confrontation

in the Balkans and

Middle East, 1941-1947

WORLD WAR II provided a second opportunity for the USSR to seek ideological and territorial expansion in the Balkans and the Middle East at the expense
of Iran and Turkey. The war brought to an end what George Lenczowski has
called the "Period of Armed Truce" between the Soviet Union and Iran
(1922–1939). It raised once again Soviet hopes of wresting from the Western
Allies the bases at the Dardanelles for which Stalin had been negotiating with
Hitler. At the end of World War II the USSR emerged with substantial
acquisitions of territory both in Europe and the Far East. The Soviet government had every expectation of pursuing the same course in the Balkans and
the Middle East.

IRAN

Anglo-Soviet Occupation. The Iranian government issued a formal declaration of neutrality on September 4, 1939, following the outbreak of hostilities
in Europe, and again on June 26, 1941, on the heels of the German attack on
the USSR. The Soviet government, in view of German machinations in Iran,
nevertheless feared the opening up of a second German-Iranian front aimed at
the Soviet Muslim areas of the Caucasus and Central Asia. In three successive
notes of June 26, July 19, and August 16, 1941, it protested against German
activity in Iran and called upon the Iranian government to evict German
agents. The British government took parallel action. Either because Iranian
leaders failed to foresee that Anglo-Soviet action was imminent or because the
Germans were too well entrenched in important official posts in more than
fifty Iranian departments to permit freedom of action, they neglected to
comply with the ultimatums. On August 25 at four o'clock in the morning,
following the presentation of their final notes to the Iranian government,
Soviet and British forces invaded Iran. Encountering no appreciable re-

sistance from the population, the Red Army entered Teheran on September 17, with the English one day behind them. On September 16, as the Red Army approached the capital, Reza Shah, founder of the Pahlevi dynasty, who successfully stemmed the tide of the Soviet advance in 1921 and reached a *modus vivendi* with the Russians the same year, abdicated in favor of his twenty-three-year-old son Muhammed Reza. Afghanistan profited by the fate of her Iranian neighbor and in October, 1941, acceded to Anglo-Soviet requests for the expulsion of Axis agents.

Foreign Minister Molotov's note of August 25, after a summation of Soviet concessions to Iran, 1918 to 1921, and of the violation of Soviet-Iranian treaty obligations resulting from German intrigue in Iran, justified the Soviet occupation of northern Iran by citing Article VI of the Soviet-Iranian Treaty of February 26, 1921 (reaffirmed in 1927). This famous article provided for Soviet entry into Iran in the event that a third country attempted to seize Iran or to make of it a base for the military invasion of Soviet Russia.

Secretary of State Cordell Hull, who condoned the Anglo-Soviet occupation of Iran for strategic reasons, nevertheless urged the British and Russians to publicize their intentions to withdraw as early as military conditions permitted, on the ground that such an assurance would have "a very healthy and wholesome effect" throughout the Muslim world. It was upon American initiative, therefore, that such public commitments were made.

Tripartite Treaty of Alliance. Negotiations for a Tripartite Treaty of Alliance on the part of the USSR, Great Britain, and Iran, begun in September, 1941, were concluded on January 29, 1942. By this treaty, the USSR and Great Britain guaranteed the territorial integrity and political independence of Iran (Article I) and provided for the withdrawal of Soviet and English forces six months after the end of the war. In order to protect the vital supply line to beleaguered Russia, Iran conceded to her allies the use and military control of the Iranian communications system. Stalin expressed his satisfaction with the provisions of this treaty in a telegram to M. A. Furuqi, prime minister of Iran. It was not until September 9, 1943, after the German retreat from Russia was well under way, that Iran declared war on Germany.

Soviet Activity in Iran. No sooner did the Red Army enter Iran than it became clear that elaborate Soviet preparations had been made for just such an eventuality. The Soviet government incorporated the northern provinces within its own security zone, appropriated all available food supplies, and made every attempt to exclude British and American, not to mention Iranian, representatives from the area. Soviet propaganda was extensively and effectively organized. Soviet embassy personnel included representatives of the Muslim peoples of Central Asia and the Caucasus, well-versed in the Persian language and in the languages of the Turkic, Armenian, and other Iranian minorities. Soviet press representatives, under the leadership of Danil S. Komissarov, press attaché at the Soviet Embassy, by devious means obtained full coverage of TASS (Soviet news agency) dispatches in Iranian news-

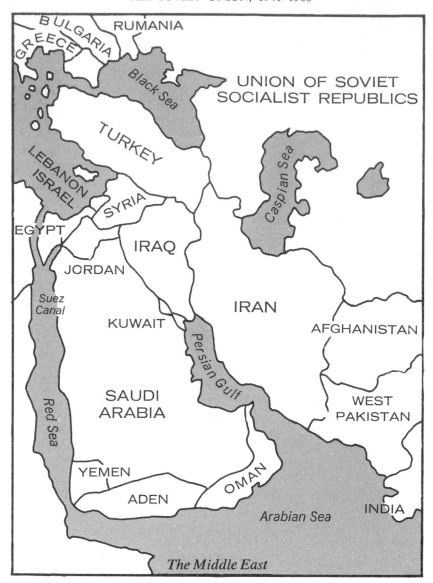

The Middle East

papers. In Teheran the "People's Party," a Soviet front headed by Suleiman Mirza, was organized during the first month of the occupation. The amnesty which accompanied the Soviet entry released a horde of Communists and Communist sympathizers from Iranian jails to lend support to Soviet propaganda activities. The People's Party established newspapers, such as *Rahbar* (*The Leader*), edited by Iraj Iskandari, and *Mardom* (*The People*), edited by

Dr. Reza Radmanesh of well-known Communist background. During the war years political activity mushroomed. By 1944 in Teheran alone there were 103 newspapers and 29 journals reflecting widely diverse shades of opinion. Even the small town of Isfahan boasted eleven newspapers.

Tudeh Party. The Tudeh Party (The Masses), officially organized in January, 1942, emanated from the People's Party. Among its founders were Reza Rusta, recently released from jail, and Jafar Pishevari (alias Seyyid Jafar Badku Bayi and Sultan-Zade), a veteran Communist and Comintern agent. Pishevari, a native of Iranian Azerbaijan who lived for fourteen years in Baku (1904–1918), had played a leading role in the short-lived Gilan Republic, returning to Soviet Russia following its collapse in 1921. There he remained until 1936 when, together with a band of apparently destitute refugees who claimed to have been deported by the Soviet secret police, he reentered Iran. Released from Iranian custody by the 1941 amnesty, he became the leading instrument of Soviet tactics in Azerbaijan. The Tudeh Party remained a minority, but a well-organized minority, variously estimated at from three thousand to two hundred thousand members. The hard core of this party, which in all probability never exceeded fifty thousand, included many of the Iranian Azerbaijani who crossed the border as "refugees" in 1936 and others who followed in the wake of the Red Army in 1941. Tudeh supporters infiltrated Iranian trade-unions and scattered throughout the country, instigating strife even in the English-occupied area in the south. The Tudeh Party held its first national congress in August, 1944, in which year it won eight seats in the Parliamentary elections. As a result of Soviet financial and military backing, it became for a time the largest of all the Near Eastern Communist parties.

Irano-Soviet Society for Cultural Relations. One of the most effective Soviet propaganda organs was the Irano-Soviet Society for Cultural Relations, founded in the fall of 1943, which included in its membership many outstanding Iranian scholars and scientists, such as Professor Said Nafisy, secretary-general of the Iranian Academy of Arts and Letters; and Madame Fatima Sayah, professor at the University of Teheran and founder of a women's party, who edited the society's publication *Payam-i-No* (*The New Messenger*), established in August, 1944. The society was active in the distribution of Soviet literature, newspapers, and films, held lavish parties and receptions, and through the Soviet Hospital distributed much-needed drugs and vaccines for Iranian patients. During the remaining years of the Soviet occupation, its influence was widely felt. In the winter of 1944–1945 it arranged the visit of an Iranian delegation, including Professor Nafisy, to Soviet Uzbekistan to help celebrate the twentieth anniversary of that republic, and incidentally to witness the development that had occurred there under the Soviet regime.

Oil Concessions. By 1944, when Red Army victories on the eastern front and the Allied landing in Normandy assured an early Allied victory in

Europe, there were indications that Soviet interest in Iran was not confined to culture and the transport of military supplies. In September of that year a large delegation of diplomatic and technical experts headed by Sergei Kavtaradze, an assistant commissar for foreign affairs, arrived in Iran to negotiate for an oil concession. The Soviet mission was preceded in the fall of 1943 by representatives of the British Shell Company and in the spring of 1944 by those of two American companies—Standard Vacuum Oil Company and Sinclair Oil Company—likewise interested in oil concessions. Whether the Kavtaradze mission entered the picture at this particular time in order to secure for the USSR its share of the oil resources of Iran or merely to frustrate the designs of the competing English and American companies, the announcement of a Soviet demand for an omnibus concession in the five northern provinces aroused consternation. The Iranian government on October 16 rejected all Soviet, English, and American bids for oil concessions.

Inefficacy of the Conferences. At the Teheran Conference, the Big Three had reaffirmed the intention of the great powers to maintain the independence of Iran. Alarmed by Soviet pressure for Iranian oil concessions in 1944, Edward R. Stettinius at the Yalta Conference tried in vain to secure from Molotov a specific date for the withdrawal of Soviet troops from that country. President Roosevelt's discussion of an American plan for the reforestation of Iran, to serve as an example of what could be done for an underdeveloped country by "an unselfish American policy," was certainly not designed to allay Soviet suspicions of future United States intervention. The Potsdam Conference passed also without any settlement of troop withdrawals from Iran.

Violation of Tripartite Treaty. Although Article V of the Tripartite Treaty of January 29, 1942, provided that the USSR and Great Britain should withdraw their forces from Iranian territory not later than six months following the end of hostilities, that is by March 2, 1946, the Soviet Union did not comply until the beginning of May and did so then only under pressure from the United States and the United Nations. The Soviet government rejected both a British proposal of September 19, 1945, for joint Anglo-Soviet withdrawal from Iran by mid-December and an American proposal of November 24, for the evacuation of all American, British, and Soviet troops from Iran by January 1, 1946. The United States government, which had already reduced its forces from a maximum of approximately twenty-eight thousand to fewer than six thousand, completed its unilateral withdrawal of the remainder by January 1. British troops observed the prescribed treaty deadline of March 2, 1946. Only the Red Army remained.

Azerbaijan "Adventure." The main reason for Soviet violation of the Tripartite Treaty of 1942 was the situation in Iranian Azerbaijan. Of all the areas in Iran, Azerbaijan provided the most fertile soil for Soviet (Communist) activites. During the years of occupation, the Red Army had dismantled border military, customs, and police posts, virtually extending the

USSR frontier south to include Azerbaijan. The local Tudeh Party, with the help of the Red Army, played a significant role in arousing the agrarian population to demand local autonomy amounting to secession and sovietization. The impression is given that the Soviets wished to accomplish as a result of World War II what they had failed to achieve in 1921—the conquest of Iran by the installment plan.

Following what appears to have been a premature effort to seize power in Azerbaijan in August, 1945, the Tudeh Party in that province assumed the alias of Democratic Party and intensified its activity, supported by an influx of Soviet troops. By December, 1945, preparations for the "national liberation" of Azerbaijan were complete. On December 12 the provincial "National Assembly" meeting in Tabriz proclaimed the Autonomous Republic of Azerbaijan and selected as premier none other than the veteran Communist Jafar Pishevari. The "People's Army" of Azerbaijan, armed with Iranian rifles produced for the Red Army at the Teheran arsenal during the war, was infested with Soviet agents of Caucasian, Armenian, and Iranian origin. Although the new regime avoided outright separation from Iran, its administration and police system were organized in the Soviet image, with Turkish rather than Persian as the official language. It undertook an extensive land distribution scheme and the nationalization of banks. Red Army troops occupying Azerbaijan prevented units of the Iranian army from entering the area to come to the rescue of the dispossessed. The spread of the revolutionary virus led to the establishment of a Kurdish People's Republic with its capital at Mahabad in western Azerbaijan on December 15, 1945, which entered into a military alliance with Azerbaijan the following April. This was but the prelude to an irredentist movement among the Kurdish minorities in northern Iraq and eastern Turkey.

Appeals to the UN. With the empire disintegrating, the Iranian government turned to the newly organized United Nations for support. On January 19, 1946, the Iranian delegate, Seyyid Hasan Taqi-zadeh, protested to the United Nations Security Council against Soviet interference in the internal affairs of Iran and called for an investigation. As in the case of the League of Nations a quarter of a century earlier, the Security Council on January 30 recommended direct negotiations between Iran and the Soviet Union. Iranian Premier Qavam Sultaneh, known to be pro-Tudeh in his orientation, thereupon headed an Iranian mission to Moscow, February 19 to March 11, only to find that the Soviet government demanded Iranian recognition of the autonomy of the Soviet puppet regime in Azerbaijan, the continued occupation of parts of Iran by Soviet troops, and the establishment of a Soviet-Iranian joint-stock oil company, in which the USSR would control 51 per cent of the shares.

Soviet Withdrawal. When the March 2 deadline for Soviet withdrawal produced no more than a Soviet announcement in *Izvestia* to the effect that the government contemplated withdrawal from certain specific areas— Khorassan, Shahrud, and Semnan—but would remain elsewhere until the situation was "clarified," Great Britain (March 4) and the United States (March 8) joined with Premier Qavam in formally protesting this treaty violation. Since the Soviet government, instead of withdrawing, dispatched additional troops and tanks to northern Iran thereby threatening a military *coup d'état,* the Iranian government through its ambassador in the United States, Hussein Ala, appealed a second time to the United Nations, this time about the breach of the treaty deadline. The storm of adverse publicity in the United States and throughout the Western world apparently convinced Soviet leaders of the desirability of reaching a solution. On March 26 Andrei Gromyko notified the Security Council that the Soviet government had reached an agreement with Iran providing for Soviet evacuation six weeks after March 24. The Soviet-Iranian agreement signed by Premier Qavam and Soviet Ambassador Sadtchikov on April 4 specified this deadline, announced the forthcoming establishment (seven months after March 24) of a Soviet-Iranian Joint-Stock Oil Company, subject to ratification by the Mejlis, and provided that Azerbaijan and Iran should reach a peaceful settlement. With premier Qavam at the helm, the prospect of an oil concession, and the growing strength of the Communist regime in Azerbaijan, Soviet leaders probably felt that Soviet forces could be withdrawn from Iran without sacrificing vital Soviet interests. In this respect they were outmaneuvered by the shrewdness of Qavam.

According to Robert Rossow, Jr., who was in charge of the United States Consulate in Tabriz from December, 1945, to June, 1946, and thereafter chief of the political section of the United States Embassy in Teheran until January, 1947, the "battle of Azerbaijan" was not an isolated incident. It was rather a part of a Soviet pincer movement, aimed at the reduction of Turkey and Greece on the west and Azerbaijan on the east, which was stopped cold by United States action in a move that anticipated by precisely one year American policy under the Truman Doctrine.

The fact that Azerbaijan had been sacrificed for the second time on the altar of Soviet interests was unmistakable. With the final withdrawal of Soviet troops in May, 1946, the days of the Azerbaijan and Kurdish autonomous regimes were numbered. To appease the USSR, the Teheran government reached a temporary agreement with the Azerbaijan Autonomous Republic in June, and the following August included three Tudeh members in the Iranian Cabinet. Tudeh-inspired violence in the Abadan oil refinery strike during the summer and Tudeh truculence in politics antagonized popular opinion. In late 1946 and 1947 the Iranian government of Qavam es Sultaneh suppressed the revolution in northern Iran by force of arms. As in 1921, so in 1946 the Iranian revolutionaries proved no match for the Iranian troops, once Soviet forces were withdrawn. The Iranian Mejlis, with apparent backing from the United States, on October 22, 1947, rejected the Soviet demand for a Soviet-controlled joint-stock company to prospect for oil in northern Iran.

The Soviet press gave full vent to Soviet indignation over the failure to gain access to the oil resources of northern Iran. An article in *Trud* in November, 1947, entitled "Representatives of the Iranian People, or American Lackeys?" by I. Belov, attributed the postponement by the Mejlis of a decision on the oil question in October, 1946, to direct intervention of the American ambassador George Allen. It further alleged that "acting upon the orders of the American ambassador, the clause on the extension of Iranian sovereignty to the Bahrein Islands and the Persian Gulf (where the American oil concessions are to be found) was stricken from the original text of the bill." The prospect of Iranian entry into the American orbit as the outcome of Soviet aggression in Iran was a bitter pill for Soviet leaders to swallow. Henceforth the United States replaced England as the chief butt of Soviet attacks on imperialistic colonizers.

Results of Soviet Occupation. By the Azerbaijan "adventure," the Soviet government proved that it had not profited by its experience in Gilan following World War I. When the Red Army entered Iran in 1941, the impression was given, in spite of Soviet propaganda activities, that the USSR wished to blot out the past, to allay Iranian fears of sovietization, and to lay the foundation for better Soviet-Iranian relations in the postwar era. During the war years, as we have seen, it did make appreciable headway among all strata of the Iranian population. By violating the treaty deadline of March 2, 1946, by actively promoting the dismemberment of Iran through the establishment of the "autonomous" republics of Azerbaijan and Kurdistan, and by seeking to grab control of the oil resources of northern Iran, the Soviet government undid everything it had accomplished previously and demonstrated to Iran and the world at large that its policy more than matched that of the so-called "imperialist" powers it was constantly denouncing. Thus vis-à-vis Iran, the Soviet Union was in the same position in 1946 as it was a quarter of a century before, in 1921. It had learned nothing and accomplished nothing. In 1946, however, it was the Americans rather than the English who played the most important part in the defeat of Soviet expansionist aims in Iran.

TURKEY

As in the case of Iran, the Soviet government expected, as a result of World War II, to advance Soviet interests in Turkey, where pro-German and anti-Soviet sentiment was sufficiently strong to prevent the Turks from joining the Allied camp until the end of the conflict was in sight on February 23, 1945. Unlike Iran, the Soviet government did not have the advantage of Red Army occupation of Turkish territory during the war years. Prior to the Nazi invasion of the USSR in 1941, while Nazi and Soviet leaders were still drafting plans to divide the world between them, the Soviet government, as we have seen, vigorously asserted that Turkey and Bulgaria fell within the Soviet security zone and demanded a Soviet base at the Dardanelles. It sought, first from the Germans and later from the Allies, a decision in favor of the complete revision of the Montreux Convention of 1936 in regard to the Straits.

Turkish Neutrality. On the eve of World War II, Soviet-Turkish negotiations for a mutual assistance pact (September–October, 1939) proved fruitless, due in part to Soviet reluctance to exempt Turkey from any obligation to participate in hostilities against England and France, to German pressure on the Soviet Union to secure the neutralization of Turkey, so as to insure that the latter would under no circumstances fight Germany, and Soviet pressure on the Turks for a modification of the Straits Convention. On October 19, two days after the lapse of Soviet-Turkish negotiations, the Turks signed a fifteen-year tripartite treaty of mutual assistance with England and France. The Turks had wrung from them the concession that "the obligations undertaken by Turkey in virtue of the above-mentioned treaty cannot compel that country to take action having as its effect or involving as its consequence armed conflict with the USSR." The Turks were striving to steer a neutral course in the stormy international waters ahead of them.

During the war years, especially during the successful advance of the German armies toward Moscow and Stalingrad, the officially neutral Turks entered into a closer rapprochement with the Germans, under the expert guidance of Franz von Papen, Nazi ambassador in Constantinople after the death of Kemal Pasha. The war resulted in a great increase in German-Turkish trade, under the trade agreements of July, 1940, and October, 1941, which were reinforced by a German-Turkish pact of "friendship and non-aggression" on June 18, 1941, four days prior to the German invasion of the Soviet Union. The initial success of the Germans in Western Europe, the Balkans, and the USSR evoked a revival of Pan-Turkism, which led many Turks to anticipate a favorable readjustment of Soviet-Turkish boundaries, the possible establishment of Turkish puppet regimes in the Crimea and the Caucasus, and perhaps even the outright acquisition of Soviet Azerbaijan and Baku.

German revelation as early as March, 1941, of Soviet designs on the Straits was not calculated to dispel Turkish suspicions of the USSR. In spite of Anglo-Soviet declarations on August 10 as to "the scrupulous observance of the territorial integrity of Turkey," Anglo-Soviet occupation of Iran by the end of the same month proved anything but reassuring to the Turks, whose fears of the revival of the Secret Agreements of 1915 to 1916 were encouraged by the Germans. Turko-Soviet relations were strained by the attempted assassination on February 24, 1942, of von Papen in Constantinople, allegedly by Omer Tokat, a Muslim Madeconian Communist, and the subsequent trial and conviction by the Turkish courts of two Russians attached to the Soviet trade mission. The services of the British and United States ambassadors in Constantinople were required before tension between Turkey and the Soviet Union was alleviated.

In the fall of 1942, with the German descent upon the Caucasus and in anticipation of the fall of Stalingrad, the Turks concentrated considerable forces on the Caucasian boundary, and the anti-Soviet press campaign in Turkey reached a new peak. Subsequent publication of the secret documents of the German Ministry of Foreign Affairs pertaining to Turkey lends substantiation to Soviet suspicions that Turkish leaders were jubilant about the approaching "annihilation of the Russian colossus," and that they were interpreting Turkish neutrality to the advantage of the Axis rather than to the advantage of the Allies. Soviet historians have contended that in the fall of 1942 Turkey was on the brink of declaring war against the Soviet Union.

In fact, the cautious Turks, in spite of German pressure and German propaganda, exercised a remarkable degree of restraint, refusing to be precipated into war during the years of German victory. After Stalingrad, and especially from the time of the Cairo Conference of 1943, the Turks veered again in the direction of England and France. Although England and the Soviet Union both brought pressure upon the Turks to abandon their neutrality, and Stalin at the Teheran Conference in November was reported by Churchill to be in favor of bringing them in "by the scruff of the neck if necessary," the Turks resisted them with as much tenacity as they had the Germans. They eventually joined the Allies in 1945 in time to insure their participation in the San Francisco Conference.

Continuation of the Straits Question. This fortuitous Turkish about-face by no means appeased the Soviet government, which had watched with concern the occasional use of the Straits during the war years by German and Italian warships, in what it alleged was a violation of the Montreux Convention of 1936. The United States and Great Britain were forewarned at the wartime Big-Three conferences as to subsequent Soviet tactics in regard to the Straits. At Teheran in 1943 and again during the final plenary session at Yalta on February 10, 1945, Stalin raised the question of the revision of the Montreux Convention to remove Turkey's "hand on Russia's throat" without detriment to Turkey's legitimate interests. On March 19, 1945, within a month of the Turkish entry into World War II, the Soviet government denounced the Soviet-Turkish Treaty of Friendship, Neutrality, and Nonaggression of 1925 (renewed in 1935 and due to expire November 7, 1945), together with all protocols and extensions pertaining thereto, as "no longer in accord with present conditions." At the Potsdam Conference of the three great powers— the United States, England, and the USSR—in July and August, 1945, the Soviet government pressed its case for the return of the districts of Kars and Ardahan, ceded by the RSFSR to Turkey in 1921, but had to be satisfied with recognition from its allies of the necessity for the revision of the Montreux Convention of 1936 on the ground that it was no longer in accord with present conditions. The three powers agreed to undertake separate and direct negotiations with Turkey toward the attainment of this objective. The Turkish government was, to all intents and purposes, prepared to discuss the Straits regime and to negotiate a new treaty of friendship and nonaggression with the

Soviet Union, providing such negotiations did not involve the sacrifice of Turkish rights and Turkish integrity. Soviet occupation of the Balkans had brought the Russians uncomfortably close.

In June, 1945, however, Soviet Foreign Minister Molotov notified the Turkish ambassador in Moscow that "revision" involved Turkish cession to the USSR of a Soviet base on the Black Sea Straits, together with the districts of Kars and Ardahan, in return for which the Turks might look for compensation from Syria in the form of the city and railway junction of Aleppo. These demands, as might be expected, touched off a press campaign of more than ordinary bitterness and invective. The Turks, after consultation with Anthony Eden in July, fell back on the logical line of defense that the Montreux Convention was a multilateral agreement which could not, therefore, be revised by Turkey and the USSR alone.

In seeking the return of Kars and Ardahan, the Soviet government appeared to be in search of a more defensible frontier along the Armenian border. Although the RSFSR had transferred these districts to Turkey in 1921 without expressing any solicitude for the rights of the Armenians, the Soviet press in the summer of 1945 gave extensive support to the Armenian claims, which dovetailed nicely with the Soviet program (announced December 2, 1945) for the repatriation of Armenians abroad.

Montreux Convention: Proposed Revision. The basic tenets of the American recommendations for the revision of the Montreux Convention were submitted to the Turkish government in a note of November 2, 1945. They provided that (1) the Straits should be open to commercial vessels at all times; (2) they should likewise be open at all times to warships of the Black Sea powers; (3) with the exception of an agreed limited tonnage in peacetime, the passage of the Straits should be denied to warships of non-Black Sea powers, unless with the consent of the Black Sea powers or when acting under the UN; and (4) the United Nations organization should replace the League of Nations under the Montreux Convention, and Japan should be eliminated as a signatory. These proposals were welcomed by the Turkish government, which soon had reason to fall back upon them in its dispute with Soviet Russia over the administration of the Straits.

Rejection of Soviet Program. Soviet activities in Iran following the termination of hostilities in August, 1945, and the disposition of Red Army troops in Iranian Azerbaijan occasioned grave concern among the Turks. On January 6, 1946, Prime Minister Sucru Saracoglu officially rejected Soviet claims to Kars and Ardahan, which the Soviet government had voluntarily transferred to Turkey in 1921. Alarmed by the trend of events and by Soviet intrigue among the Turkish Armenians and Kurds, the Turkish government first looked to the Arab world for support. On March 29, 1946, Turkey and Iraq signed in Ankara a pact of mutual assistance on the question of public order, designed to prevent further Soviet encroachment.

Blocked in its designs on Iran, from which the Red Army was forced to retire in May, 1946, the Soviet government at once turned its full attention to

Turkey and the Straits. In a vigorous note of August 8 (7), 1946, Foreign Minister Molotov outlined the alleged wartime violations of the Montreux Convention, the decisions of the Potsdam Conference, and presented a program for the revision of the Straits regime, designed to place that strategic area under the control of the Black Sea powers, with Turkey and the USSR jointly responsible for the defense of the Straits. Well aware that such a proposition, which excluded the other great powers from a share in the control of the Straits, would in fact establish Soviet control at the expense of the Turks, the Turkish government on August 22 flatly rejected this part of the program. A second Soviet note of September 24 reiterated the Soviet position in regard to the revision of the Montreux Convention and called for Soviet-Turkish talks prior to any general conference on the issue. In spite of the arrogant tone of the Soviet communications, which clearly indicated that the Russians would regard continued Turkish rejection of the Soviet program as a threat to Soviet security in the Black Sea, the Turks staunchly refused to be drawn into bilateral negotiations which would have violated the Montreux Convention. Turkish-Soviet relations had reached a new low, and the Turkish armed forces were alerted to resist a possible Soviet attack.

The Turks were undoubtedly encouraged to take a firm stand in opposition to the Soviet program in the knowledge that their position was fully supported by the United States and England. The United States, by virtue of the Potsdam Protocol, received a copy of the Soviet note of August 7, and thereafter claimed the right to participate in any revision of the Montreux Convention. Secretary of State Dean Acheson on August 19 in no uncertain terms rejected the idea of the control of the Straits by the Black Sea powers, contending that this implied not a revision of the Montreux Convention "but rather the establishment of a new regime. . . ." He likewise objected to joint Soviet-Turkish defense of the Straits on the ground that any threat of aggression there must be a matter for action on the part of the UN Security Council, which the Russians had failed even to mention. As if to indicate that the United States would fight to defend Turkey, Secretary of the Navy Forrestal announced on September 30 that American naval forces would remain at full strength in the eastern Mediterranean.

The Soviet government, expecting in all probability to outflank Turkey by the establishment of a Communist regime in Greece and knowing from past experience that the Turks would fight, gave vent to its displeasure in an anti-Turkish press campaign and in military maneuvers along the Caucasian border. If it had expected that the United States and England would permit the USSR to have a free hand at the Straits, it was already fully disillusioned on that score. As in Iran, so in Turkey, the United States took the lead in opposing Soviet expansion.

Truman Doctrine. The United States government, alarmed by Communist efforts in Greece and by the prospect of early English withdrawal from that beleaguered country, as well as by Soviet designs on the Straits, on March 12, 1947, officially announced the extension of American aid to Greece and

Turkey—the so-called "Truman Doctrine." The Soviet government promptly labeled the Truman pronouncement "a scarcely concealed declaration of preparation for war against the USSR." From this moment, according to I. F. Miller, a Soviet authority on Turkey, "Turkey in fact fell under the tutelage of the United States of America."

Even prior to the enunciation of the Truman Doctrine, the United States had begun to provide aid to Turkey, including a $25,000,000 credit from the Export-Import Bank, $10,000,000 in credit for the purchase of surplus military equipment, and another $5,000,000 for the purchase of American merchant ships. Once the decision was reached, no time was lost. On March 24, Dean Acheson informed the House Committee on Foreign Affairs that $100,000,000 were required for Turkey, another $150,000,000 for Greece. On the same day the Turkish navy took over eight former United States minesweepers lent to England during World War II under the Lend-Lease program. The British government revealed on April 9 that some five hundred British "Spitfires," "Mosquitoes" and other types of planes had been sold to Turkey and were in the process of delivery. In May an American military mission headed by Major-General Lunsford Oliver arrived in Ankara to confer with Turkish officials. On July 12 the American and Turkish governments signed the agreement to implement Congressional authorization of the $100,000,000 for Turkish aid, of which $80,000,000 were earmarked for the modernization of the Turkish armed forces and the balance for the construction of strategic roads and ports. According to Soviet sources, which maintained a close scrutiny of these unwelcome developments, during the second half of 1947 Turkey received more than twenty different American commissions, delegations, and missions to advise on all types of issues ranging from military and economic aid to press, radio, and information services.

Communism Contained. Thus, not only were Greece and Turkey saved from Stalin's clutches, but the tide of Soviet expansion was likewise stemmed throughout the Middle East. In 1921 Turkey, Iran, and Afghanistan stopped the march of communism with some help from the outside, at a time when Soviet Russia was weak and exhausted as a result of the Revolution and Civil War. In 1947 Turkey and Iran were in no position to cope alone with the victorious forces of the Red Army. They were saved only by the decisive intervention of the United States and the possibility of action by the United Nations. Since the crisis that evoked the Truman Doctrine, the United States has superseded France and Britain in the historic role of defending Turkey from the Russians. By reaching for a base at the Dardanelles, the return of Kars and Ardahan, and the five northern provinces of Iran, the Soviet Union lost the opportunity to secure a modification of the Straits regime. Neither by abandoning the tsarist claims in 1917 nor by advancing its own in 1945, did the Soviet regime achieve its objectives. Contained in the Near and Middle East, the USSR once again turned to the Far East, where Soviet policy met with unprecedented success.

24

Stalin the Great: De-Europeanization
and Industrialization, 1945-1953

THE "CULT OF PERSONALITY"

Although the Soviet Union emerged from World War II the strongest land power in Europe and Asia, its economy was badly shaken and its peoples disillusioned by the terrific human and property losses resulting from the Nazi invasion and occupation. The immediate objective of the Stalin regime was the justification of the tremendous sacrifices endured by the Russian people. Since the Communist Party was responsible for Soviet foreign policy and the conduct of the war—and the Party was infallible—every effort was made to prove that its prescience and wisdom had been above reproach. The prestige of the Party was restored and exalted, even at the expense of the illustrious marshals and generals whose worldwide military reputations had been established through decorations bestowed by Stalin himself. Henceforth, all the major Soviet victories and the winning of the war were attributed to Stalin, the head of the Communist Party. Stalin, the "architect of victory," had foreseen the invasion and had even planned the large scale strategic retreats before the Nazi invaders in order to prepare for the great counteroffensives that drove the Germans from Soviet soil.

Velikii Stalin. Thus began the "cult of personality," which made Stalin the first Soviet leader to bear the title "the Great," *Velikii Stalin.* The personality of Stalin came to occupy an altogether unique place in the Soviet press. A veritable avalanche of articles, editorials, and poems lauded the genius, infallibility, and omniscience of the leader (*vozhd*). Pictures, busts, and statues of Stalin kept his name and image ever in the spotlight. If his picture failed to appear on the front page of newspapers and magazines, there were certain to be numerous references to his "concern" for the welfare of the people, to his initiation of major achievements in science, strategy, or technology, and there would be ample quotations from his speeches and writing, which carried the weight of holy writ. The history of the Party was based on his individual accomplishments, with some credit, of course, going to Lenin, who was dead and could not compete for power in the turbulent postwar present. Outstanding mathematicians, chemists, archeologists, biologists, and military strategists invariably acknowledged their indebtedness to Stalin, and their books ordinarily began and ended with him and quoted him at length. On Stalin's seventieth birthday, December 21, 1949, even Nikita S. Khrushchev contributed one of many laudatory articles, attributing to him every possible virtue. Although this idolatrous praise provoked ridicule in the outside world, in the USSR it did serve to restore the unity and prestige of the Party. Russians were historically conditioned to the exaltation of the tsar. They responded likewise to the virtual deification of Stalin.

Territorial Expansion. As in the case of his "great" tsarist predecessors, Stalin owed his title *Velikii* in part at least to the recovery of Soviet lands on

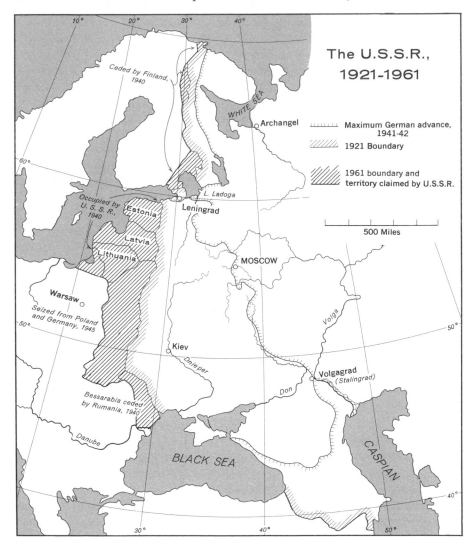

the western periphery and the Far East, to the acquisition of new territory from Germany, Austria, and the Czech and Polish satellites, and to Red Army military occupation of most of Eastern Europe, Manchuria, and North Korea. Territorial aggrandizement, always an important factor in basically agrarian Russia, helped to atone to some extent for the sufferings and privations of the war years.

European Reaction. After the defeat of Nazism and Fascism, Europe was not conditioned for the rise of another "infallible" leader. The halos were gone from Hitler and Mussolini, whose mistakes were revealed in numerous books and articles in all parts of the Western world. Since the exposure of Soviet scholars and leaders to this "debunking" process might be expected to produce repercussions at home, contacts with the West were quickly discouraged. Stalin's estrangement from the West was accelerated by the abrupt end of American Lend-Lease in 1945, failure to secure a huge loan from the United States for reconstruction purposes, the unceremonious scuttling of the Soviet reparations demands, and the Marshall Plan, with strings attached, which gave England the lion's share of American postwar aid. Stalin proceeded, therefore, to turn his back on Europe and looked to Asia, a continent more conditioned to the exaltation of the ruler. Winston Churchill, who was quick to recognize Soviet reaction against Europe and the West, gave public expression to what had already happened in his memorable Fulton, Missouri, address of March, 1946: "From Stettin in the Baltic to Trieste in the Adriatic an iron curtain has descended across the continent."

DE-EUROPEANIZATION POLICIES

Linguistic Controversy. Until his death in 1953, Stalin pursued a policy of gradual de-Europeanization of the USSR. Under the tsarist regime, and even during the years immediately following the Bolshevik Revolution, Europeanization denoted progress and civilization to Russians, with the exception of the most extreme Slavophiles and revolutionists. Soviet scholars, writers, artists, and engineers, who actively prepared to resume their European contacts at the end of the war, were among the first victims of this reaction against all things European (Western). The well-known linguistic scholar, V. V. Vinogradov, author of *The Russian Language,* was castigated for "the absence of a militant, patriotic spirit, and for exaggerating the contribution of foreign linguistics. . . ." To avoid adverse criticism, writers were even forced to abandon words of foreign (Western) origin and to eliminate references to or quotations from Western sources. The historian B. A. Rybakov, who in 1948 published a lengthy volume on *Arts and Crafts in Ancient Russia* served as an example to Soviet writers because he literally coined Russian words where none existed in preference to "marring" his book with European terminology. A host of foreign terms introduced in the Soviet Union during the Five-Year Plans underwent hasty Russianization. In the columns of *The Literary Gazette* Professor E. Agayan, who demanded the ideological purity of Soviet linguistics, even questioned the Indo-European origin of the languages of the USSR. It had taken Russian and Western scholars many years to establish Russian as an Indo-European language. Soviet linguists now stressed its autochthonic character or claimed that it had more in common with Asian languages than with European. In 1950, after a series of articles pro and con in *Pravda,* Stalin himself contributed the final word, "On Soviet Linguistics," which at one fell stroke toppled from his pedestal the late Academician N. Ya. Marr, heretofore the uncrowned king of Soviet philologists. Instead of being "national in form, socialist in content," the criterion applied during the 1930's to the entire Soviet educational program, Marr's thesis was found to be cosmopolitan (Western) in form, national in content, and therefore erroneous. The linguistic controversy went so far that in the summer of 1950 Soviet tourists were upbraided for using the terms "Russian Riviera" and "Russian Switzerland" to describe popular Soviet resort areas. *The Literary Gazette* complained that "no one has yet extolled the beauty of the shores of Lake Baikal and the banks of the Lena and Yenisei Rivers, before which all the beauty of Europe pales into insignificance."

Orientation Toward China. Instead of making the Soviet people Europe-conscious, the Soviet press proceeded to make them China-conscious. A rapid succession of books, articles, and pamphlets on Asia, particularly on China, poured from daily and weekly newspapers, periodicals, and even from Soviet academic quarterlies. One of the most significant of these publications, which serves to illustrate the process of de-Europeanization on the academic level, was S. V. Kiselev's *The Ancient History of Southern Siberia* (1949), used in all higher institutions of learning in the USSR. Kiselev went out of his way to establish similarities between the history and development of early societies in Russia and Asia. These and other examples served to illustrate the spiritual withdrawal of the USSR from Europe and from all that Western civilization connoted. Soviet Russia was being purposefully oriented away from Europe and toward Asia, especially toward the China of Mao-Tse-tung. Historically speaking, whenever Russia pursued an isolationist policy vis-à-vis Western Europe, reaction and absolutism triumphed at home. Stalin's de-Europeanization program became the symbol of reactionary totalitarianism during his closing years.

Soviet Theory of Biological Science. The East-West breach was clearly demonstrated, as far as science was concerned, by the publication of *The State of Biological Science,* the stenographic record of a session of the V. I. Lenin All-Union Academy of Agricultural Sciences (July 31–August 7, 1948). From this conference, Academician Trofim D. Lysenko, leader of the I. V. Mitchurin school of biological science, emerged triumphant over other Soviet scientists who were disciples of the Western theory of genetics as developed by J. G. Mendel (Czech), August Weismann (German), and

Thomas H. Morgan (American). In line with the principles of dialectical materialism, Mitchurin biological science claimed that environment determined "the origin and development of the living organism, changes in its heredity, and the acquisition by it of new features and characteristics, which are thereupon transmitted through heredity. This theory was diametrically opposed to the thesis of most Western biologists, who have maintained that heredity is primarily determined by genes transmitted from one generation to the next, which are completely independent of the living conditions of plants and animals. When Stalin and the Party placed the stamp of their approval on the Lysenko theory, outstanding Western scientists, including H. V. Muller, president of the Genetics Society of America, and Henry Dale, president of the Royal Society of Great Britain, denounced this new and unsubstantiated Soviet dogma and resigned their memberships in the Soviet Academy of Sciences. Lysenko, whose doctrine was officially adopted by the Presidium of the Soviet Academy of Medicine, became for a few years the virtual dictator of Soviet science. His theories on heredity were popularized in 1949 in the widely distributed technicolor film *Mitchurin*. As long as Stalin lived, science bowed to politics. Soon after his death, however, the party organ, *Kommunist,* began to downgrade Lysenko, no doubt because his theories failed to transform Soviet agriculture and make of the USSR a land of milk and honey (see also page 522).

Nationalism. Another problem confronted by the Soviet government after the war was nationalism, which had transcended the bounds of Party ideology. In World War II, Russians had fought, not for the tenets of Marxism-Leninism-Stalinism, but for the "Motherland" (*Rodina*). In his first address to the nation after the invasion began (July 3, 1941), it was in the name of the "Motherland" that Stalin summoned the people to resist and to pursue a scorched earth policy. To stoke the fires of patriotism all the great Russian military heroes of the past were exhumed and Soviet war heroes were lionized. The atheistic Kremlin even entered into an alliance with the Russian Orthodox church to promote national unity. Once the war was over, however, these departures from the Party line were subjected to reappraisal. National communism (socialism in one country) was one thing. Except in time of national crisis, traditional nationalism was incompatible with communist ideology. The Stalin regime had no intention of discarding patriotism, which had proved to be a highly useful and effective tool in wartime. Its objective was to transmute it to national pride in the socialist system which had emerged victorious.

From the standpoint of the Party, it was the nationalism of the Soviet minorities that constituted the greatest threat to ideology and unity. The loyalty of many of them to the Soviet system was highly questionable, as the mass defections to Hitler indicated. Those who remained under Soviet rule had taken advantage of the patriotic license of wartime to rediscover and reemphasize the historic past of their respective minorities, ignoring the relationship between their political, material, and cultural progress and the

Russian (Soviet) connection. If the nationalism of the minorities continued to burgeon, the Kremlin feared that it would eventually contribute to separatism (independence) and the destruction of the Soviet Union. After the war, therefore, the history of each minority was rewritten under Soviet tutelage. Its historians complied with instructions to demonstrate that its achievements were due to association with Great Russia, that without Russia its fate would have been comparable to that of the "exploited" native colonies of the Western "imperialists." Soviet neocolonialism was a new version of the white man's burden under socialist nomenclature.

The threat of minority obstruction of the Soviet program was partially solved by the dispersal of "unreliable" national entities in other parts of the USSR. Following the precedent of the deportation of the Volga Germans (400,000) in August, 1941, the Crimean Tatars and Chechen Ingush, the Kalmyks of the West Caspian and the Balkars were liquidated as political and national units in 1944 and their peoples scattered to the far reaches of the Soviet state, mainly to Soviet Asia. In 1949, more than a quarter of the allegedly pro-German inhabitants of the Baltic States, especially the educated and the spiritual leaders, shared the same fate. The non-Slavic republics of the Union were subjected to mass colonization by Russians and Ukrainians.

Monetary Reform. Among its efforts "to liquidate the aftermath of World War II," the Soviet government on December 16, 1947, resorted to monetary reform to pave the way for the end of wartime rationing of food and consumer goods. The inflation of Soviet currency during the war, the circulation of large quantities of counterfeit money following the German occupation, and widespread speculation in scarce commodities, all pointed to the revaluation of the ruble. The exchange of one new ruble for ten of the old represented a substantial gain for workers with bank savings accounts which retained their original value up to 3,000 rubles. For speculators and peasants, who hoarded their savings in their own private strongboxes, this "reform" was tantamount to confiscation. Subsequent rumors of the devaluation of the ruble circulated after Stalin's death in 1953 produced a virtual stampede for the exchange of Soviet currency for durable goods.

INDUSTRIALIZATION

The end of World War II brought no respite or relaxation to the war-weary Soviet population, desperately in need of housing, food, and almost all types of consumer goods. The Party was determined to reinstate discipline and to strengthen the economy without delay. As the Nazi armies were rolled back in European Russia, reconstruction began. Even before the war was over, thousands of industrial enterprises had been restored in the occupied lands, as well as over 1,800 *sovkhozi* and 3,000 MTS, 85,000 *kolkhozi,* about 6,000 hospitals and over 70,000 schools. When Soviet forces occupied the border states and East Germany, Manchuria, and North Korea, they stripped these areas of machinery and equipment to replace what had been destroyed in the USSR. In deference to the Western Allies, they held tight rein over the Red Army to prevent the wholesale slaughter of Germans in retaliation for what had been done in Russia. In plays and films, the troops and people were conditioned to prefer repayment, not in blood, but in labor by German prisoners and others guilty of maltreatment of Russians. Soviet prisoners in Germany, many of them turned over to the USSR by the advancing Allies, were subjected to reindoctrination and dispatched to labor camps to contribute their share to reconstruction.

Labor Force. In the USSR the pressure for greater production continued without letup. Wartime labor legislation, including the forty-eight-hour week, remained in force. Soviet workers were urged "to volunteer" labor even beyond that requirement. As a result of the loss of Soviet manpower during the war, approximately half of the urban labor force consisted of women, who

Wide World

In building, as well as in other heavy labor, women worked side by side with men. Here, a Russian woman lays bricks on a construction job on Gorky Street, near the Kremlin.

were used on the roads as well as at heavy jobs in factories. Once again Stakhanovites, earning from 5,000 to 10,000 rubles per month as compared with the average worker's pay of from 700 to 800 rubles, became the models for other workers to emulate. Typical headlines in the Soviet press during the postwar years read, as follows: "Steadily Increase the Capacity of Every Enterprise"; "Speedily Improve the Quality of Our Products!" "Steadily Increase the Tempo of Production"; "Ural Miners Will Increase the Output of Coal"; "Some Questions on Raising the Labor Productivity of Women Workers"; and so on, *ad infinitum.*

State Capitalism. In 1948 the Soviet government introduced a high-pressure campaign for profits which proved as effective in spurring production as the earlier introduction of piecework in 1931. Just one hundred years after the publication of Karl Marx's *Communist Manifesto,* the Stalin regime required every Soviet enterprise to show a profit, the bigger the better. The demand for profits spurred Soviet efforts to reduce the costs of production, led to emphasis on intraplant cost accounting, the publication of texts on economics, and the training of more economic specialists, state planners, and accountants. Business efficiency, monetary reform, and profits were processes understood and approved in the capitalist world. Once again many onlookers from abroad envisaged the possibility of a common meeting ground for the capitalist and socialist systems as a result of the development of "state capitalism" in the Soviet Union. To compete with the capitalist West, the Soviet system was obliged to resort to capitalist "tools."

Faced with disgrace and removal if they failed to show a substantial profit, and well regarded when they did, many Soviet managers resorted, either with the government's consent or on their own initiative, to gross infractions of the labor laws in order to increase production and cut down waste. By the fall of 1949 the situation was out of hand and the government was forced to step in, ostensibly as the champion of the workers who had been so severely exploited in the implementation of the state program. An editorial in the Soviet labor paper *Trud,* entitled "Strictly Observe the Laws on Working Time," revealed the whole sordid story only too clearly. Soviet trade unions were warned to enforce the labor laws, and told that it was "high time to put an end to the illegal use of overtime hours, to the postponement and cancellation of off-days, as well as to the shortening of the dinner hour." In spite of this warning, the high-pressure campaign for greater production and better quality continued throughout the summer of 1950, as indicated by an editorial in *Trud* headlined "Persistently Fight for an Increase in the Productivity of Labor," and another in the same paper entitled "Step Up the Campaign for Quality Production." To the question as to whether there was any limit to such demands on the strength and will power of the Soviet people in the battle for production the Soviet novelist, A. Voloshin, in his 1950 Stalin Prize novel *Kuznetsk Land,* gave a decisive answer: "No, there are no such limits!" The postwar tempo of production has been depicted in the 1963 film *Russkoe Chudo (The Russian Miracle).*

Method for Recovery. Soviet postwar recovery was not accomplished by voluntary labor, as in America, or by a remarkable degree of self-discipline and self-denial, as in England, but by means of an all-out pressure campaign on the part of the Soviet government and the Communist Party which led to sweatshop labor conditions, by the arbitrary transfer of "surplus" labor from one part of the country to another in the overall interests of the Soviet state, and in part by the use of "slave labor" and prisoners-of-war. Under the jurisdiction of the MVD (political police), slave laborers variously estimated at from two to twenty millions worked on a wide variety of construction projects, in forests and mines, drilling oil wells, building hydroelectric plants and military installations. Evidence obtained from escapees and other sources was sufficiently reliable to elicit strong protests from the Economic and Social Commission of the United Nations.

Fourth Five-Year Plan. The Fourth Stalin Five-Year Plan (1946–1950), launched in March, 1946, was expected to lay the foundations for the transition from a socialist to a communist society which would mature in the next fifteen years. Its immediate objective was the restoration of the economy to its prewar levels in industry and agriculture by 1948, with substantial increases in new production thereafter. The Soviet peoples were conditioned for still more sacrifices under a program emphasizing heavy industry (iron and steel, fuel, and machine tools, etc.) and railway transport, as well as equipment for the mechanization and electrification of agricultural production, and irrigation. According to Nikolai A. Voznesensky, chairman of the State Planning Commission, the object was "to carry out industrial production twice as rapidly as after the termination of the First World War and the Civil War." For the better distribution of industry throughout the country—a strategic lesson of World War II—the construction of new enterprises in Moscow, Leningrad, Kiev, Kharkov, Rostov, Gorky, and Sverdlovsk was restricted. Some provision was made in the plan for the cultural and material needs of the Russian people: more schools, kindergartens, hospitals, and recreation facilities. They were promised that the end of rationing of food and consumer goods would come in 1946 and 1947 with increased production.

Some of the major reconstruction projects in European Russia were the Dnieper Dam, the Zaporozhe Steel Plant, the mines of the Donbas, the Baltic-White Sea Canal, the Sevastopol Naval Base, and the rebuilding of the ruined cities of Stalingrad and Minsk. Other cities, such as Leningrad, Kiev, Odessa, Kharkov, and Pskov, had also been extensively damaged during World War II. Essential railroad reconstruction included the Moscow-Leningrad, the Moscow-Minsk-Brest, and the Moscow-Kiev-Odessa trunk lines.

Private Construction. Because of the drastic shortage of housing, not only in European Russia but in the areas of pioneer construction in Siberia, the USSR, as in the past, resorted to private initiative to accomplish what could not be done by socialist construction alone. The Fourth Five-Year Plan provided for individual tenant-builders to secure state credits for the construction of private housing. When the volume of private construction failed to meet expectations, Soviet enterprises and trade unions were harshly criticized in the labor organ, *Trud,* for lack of cooperation and for procrastination in securing the necessary loans and materials for prospective builders. According to *Trud,*

> In some enterprises private construction is still regarded as a task of minor importance, one whose performance may be postponed because it is a secondary issue. Is it necessary to demonstrate the impropriety and harmfulness of such a viewpoint?
>
> Helping the worker to provide himself with his own house and substantially improving housing conditions will insure the creation of permanent cadres in industrial enterprises.

This emphasis on private construction sounded a strange note in the Soviet "socialist" state. On August 29, 1948, the Presidium of the Supreme Soviet authorized Soviet citizens to construct private homes of not more than five rooms in size or two stories in height, providing they did not exploit the labor of others, and granted them perpetual use, but not ownership, of the building sites. In the city of Kiev, 80 per cent of which was destroyed or heavily damaged during the war, it was disclosed in 1953 that over six thousand private homes were constructed by workers with loans provided by the government. As late as 1963 a neon sign on the Kreshchatik, the main street of Kiev, advertised government loans at 3 per cent. According to Soviet admission, approximately one-third of the city's population was housed in private homes, long lines of which extended east of the Dnieper en route to the airport.

Transformation of Nature. As the USSR made rapid strides toward economic recovery, the Soviet government devised a vast program for the transformation of nature in the Soviet Union, which provided a new horizon that gripped the imagination of the Soviet people and afforded new outlets for the release of Soviet energy. This program was launched in the fall of 1948 with the decision of the Party and government for a fifteen-year blueprint for the establishment of eight forest shelter belts in the steppes and forested steppes of European Russia to hold back the dry winds from Central Asia and the Pre-Caspian desert, and thereby protect Russia's basic grain regions from drought. This program for "the containment" of the desert was followed by one designed "to liquidate" desert and drought conditions. In the USSR, upwards of 14 per cent of the land, or almost three million square kilometers, consists of dry steppe and desert. Soviet troops returning from the offensive against Nazi Germany were encouraged to conduct a new offensive against the desert. It was better, from the standpoint of the Stalin regime, that they should work off their discontent and belligerency against the desert than against the government. In 1950, the Council of Ministers of the USSR made a number of decisions of great significance for the transformation of the dry steppes and deserts of the Soviet Union through the construction of great hydroelectric stations on the Volga, the Dnieper, the Amu-Darya, and the Don, and provided at the same time for irrigation systems for the Povolga, Don, southern Ukraine, northern Crimea, as well as for the Pre-Caspian, Turkmenian, and Kara-Kalpak deserts. On July 12, 1952, the Soviet government announced the completion of the V. I. Lenin Volga–Don Navigation Canal, the dream of Peter the Great. Another unit in the project, the Tsimlyanskaya Hydroelectric Plant on the Lower Don also went into operation. Other projects under construction included the Stalingrad and Kuibyshev Hydroelectric Stations, those at Gorky on the Volga and Molotov on the Kama, as well as the Turkmenian Irrigation Canal, stretching from the Caspian to the Aral Sea.

The challange of the transformation of nature perhaps found its best expression in the speech of engineer M. Davydov at the Moscow Power Institute at the close of 1948—a speech which elicited wide response at home and abroad. What Davydov outlined was the diversion of the waters of the great Siberian rivers from the frozen tundra of the Arctic by way of their ancient riverbeds to the torrid sands of Uzbekistan and the subtropical belts of Central Asia:

> Let us turn our attention to the tremendous incongruity between the geographical location of our rivers and the potentialities nature provides for their economic utilization. Take a good look at the map! In the European part of the Union there is a rather limited water supply. The southeastern part of the country is exceedingly arid—under the burning sun lie sandy deserts—but nevertheless, these deserts could become blooming paradises if water were available. On the other hand, Siberia, through which flow the greatest rivers of the world—the Ob, the Yenisei, and the Lena—is abundantly supplied with water. But the waters of Siberia pass through the *taiga,* through swamps, through the tundra, and through the land of perpetual frost to the Arctic Ocean. A considerable part of the waters of Siberia flows away without being utilized. These waters are of practically no service to us. This geographical incongruity must be rectified! Soviet man can reshape nature to fit the needs of the national economy, and he has boldly embarked upon a path leading to the transformation of his country.[1]

As part of the Fifth Stalin Five-Year Plan (1950–1955), one phase of Davydov's program was carried out—the construction of the vast Ust-Kamenogorsk Hydroelectric Station on the Irtysh River in Siberia, which provided a great new source of power for eastern Kazakhstan, with its rich deposits of Altai ores, its potentialities for sheep herding and irrigated agriculture. Other phases of the program initiated by Stalin were continued by

---

1. Vladimir Yurezansky, "Orchards to Bloom in the Desert," *Literaturnaya Gazeta* January 1, 1949, trans. in Ivar Spector, ed., *Soviet Press Translations,* IV (No. 8, April 15, 1949), pp. 246–248.

Khrushchev. In March, 1963, came the announcement that after six years of construction the blocking of the Yenisei, Russia's biggest river, at Krasnoyarsk had been accomplished, in preparation for the construction (in an area formerly inhabited by a few hermit monks) of a five-million-kilowatt hydroelectric station. When completed, this plant is expected to provide energy for additional aluminum, magnesium, and chemical industries, with surplus power available for transmission to European Russia, still the heart of the Soviet economy. In December, 1963, a huge Siberian electric power grid spanning three time zones went into operation, when the Bratsk Hydroelectric Station on the Angara River (a tributary of the Yenisei) was linked with Kemorovo, the industrial center of the Kuznetsk Basin. This enabled the Soviet power industry to shunt current between the time zones in accordance with peak consumption requirements. The construction of a third Angara station at Ust-Ilim, to follow the completion of the Bratsk project, is intended to make the Angara River navigable throughout its entire length. It will be possible to travel by ship from London to Lake Baikal ("Holy Sea") in the heart of Siberia, where heavy deposits of gold, mica, coal, and manganese are being mined. Of this lake Chekhov once wrote: "I myself saw depths with cliffs and mountains sunk in the turquoise waters that made my skin creep."

Progress in Siberia. During the Soviet period the transformation of Siberia has outdistanced all that was accomplished in centuries of tsarist rule. Perhaps one reason for this was that Soviet leaders, most of whom had spent years of exile in that area, had a first-hand knowledge of its potentialities. In the years following the Revolution, there was extensive exploration of Siberia's natural resources, on which the industrial development of the pre-war Five-Year Plans was based. During World War II, in advance of German occupation, as many as 455 factories were moved to the Urals, 665 to Siberia proper, and many others to Soviet Central Asia. A substantial number remained in Asiatic Russia after the war, serving to boost industrial production there. By 1950 it was estimated that Siberia's share of total Soviet production was between 15 and 20 per cent.

The remarkable progress of Siberia in the twentieth century can be illustrated by the development of Novosibirsk on the River Ob, where the Trans-Siberian Railway crosses the lines from the Kuznetsk Basin to the Altai Mountains and Central Asia. A small trading center at the beginning of the century, Novosibirsk has become an industrial metropolis with a population of 1,000,000 (1963), where large metal-working and machine-building plants are located. Its opera house rivals, if it does not excel, those of Moscow and Leningrad. The city is Siberia's big scientific and cultural center, site of a Siberian branch of the Academy of Sciences. Between 1960 and 1962 a new scientific city was carved out of the virgin forest in the Zolotaya Valley suburb of Novosibirsk, which soon boasted new apartment houses and research laboratories. As of 1963, the Novosibirsk branch of the USSR Academy of Sciences had ten academicians and thirty corresponding members, eighty-five Doctors and about eight hundred Masters of Science. Altogether, east of the Urals, there were located thirty-one institutes, three affiliated branches of the Soviet Academy of Sciences, four complex scientific research establishments, and the Central Siberian Botanical Gardens.

The experience of Novosibirsk was duplicated more or less in other parts of Siberia, the Soviet Maritime Province of the Far East, and Central Asia, with the typical juxtaposition of heavy industry and pioneer living conditions. Since World War II had demonstrated that industrial centers provided better bases of resistance to enemy invasion than the broad expanses of rural Russia, the construction of such centers along the Asian periphery became an integral part of the Soviet defense program. With all the industrial achievements in Soviet Asia during and after the war, its potential resources were just beginning to be tapped. The postwar economic recovery of the USSR was attributed mainly to reconstruction in European Russia.

STRUGGLE FOR THE SUCCESSION

The closing years of Stalin's rule witnessed a struggle for power among his associates in line for the succession. All members of the Politburo were legitimate candidates to succeed Stalin the Great. Until the death of Kalinin (replaced by Voznesensky) in 1946, the membership of the Politburo had remained relatively stable since 1939 (Stalin, Molotov, Voroshilov, Kalinin, Kaganovitch, Andreyev, Mikoyan, Zhdanov, and Khrushchev). Malenkov and Beria became full-fledged members only in 1946. Marshal Nicholas Bulganin was added in 1948 and A. N. Kosygin in 1949. Irrespective of the contest for power within the top echelons of the Communist Party, the Soviet public until the last moment was conditioned for the succession of Molotov, whose portrait on placards throughout the country regularly accompanied that of Stalin. This situation calls to mind the public's expectation in the 1920's that Trotsky would succeed Lenin. The death in 1948 of Andrei Zhdanov, celebrated for launching in 1946 an all-out campaign for ideological conformity among Soviet writers, composers, and artists, removed one of the leading contenders from the scene. Malenkov's purge of Zhdanov followers in the mysterious "Leningrad affair"[2] has been repeatedly denounced by Khrushchev. There followed on March 5, 1949, the removal of Nikolai A. Voznesensky, the USSR's top economic planner, and his execution a year later (Voznesensky was posthumously honored by Khrushchev in November, 1963). The two emerging political leaders were Georgi M. Malenkov and Nikita S. Khrushchev who in 1949 moved from the post of Communist Party boss in the Ukraine to head the Moscow Party organization close to the center of power. Stalin's replacement of the eleven-man Politburo by a

2. In 1934 Serge Kirov, head of the Communist Party in Leningrad, was mysteriously assassinated. His death resulted in widespread purges.

Presidium of twenty-five members during the Nineteenth Congress of the Party in October, 1952, evoked much curiosity as to the purpose of this dilution of power.

Death of Stalin. For some months prior to Stalin's death, there was much speculation in the European, and especially in the American press, about the successorship. In the United States, Malenkov appeared to American journalists to be the most likely candidate. More than rumor seems to have been involved in the impact their selection was said to have made on Lavrenti P. Beria, head of the dread secret police (MVD). In any event, Beria knew that he could not dominate the old-time Bolshevik, Molotov, any more than he did Stalin, and that he might even be removed from office in the event of Molotov's succession. His chances of handling the younger and more amiable Malenkov were much better. Beria is believed to have encouraged Malenkov to make a bid for the succession, backed by the powerful authority of the MVD. There were rumors, too, that Stalin's death on March 5, 1953, was expedited by Beria, perhaps to forestall another Stalin purge, comparable to the *Yezhovshchina* of 1936–1938. The unveiling of the "doctors' plot" against Zhdanov and other Soviet leaders, with its anti-Semitic overtones (six doctors were Jews), in January, 1953, offered further substantiation of a purge in the making.[3] Subsequent statements in 1967 by Svetlana Alliluyeva, Stalin's daughter, following her arrival in the United States, tend to refute the rumors of any effort on the part of his cohorts to assassinate him. With much pomp and ceremony, Stalin was buried in the Lenin Mausoleum on March 9, his embalmed corpse placed alongside that of his renowned predecessor. Malenkov, Beria, and Molotov eulogized the "man of steel," and Khrushchev has since admitted that there were sincere tears in his eyes on this occasion.

Evaluation. In many respects, Stalin was what he claimed to be—a true disciple of Lenin, reared on Lenin's theories and methods. Even in the *Bol'shaya Sovetskaya Entsiklopediya* he is acknowledged to be "an outstanding theoretician of Marxism-Leninism."[4] He is credited with an important role in the organization of the Russian proletariat against tsarism, in the preparation and carrying out of the October Revolution, in the Soviet struggle against the White Armies and Interventionists, in the realization of the Lenin program for the industrialization of the USSR and the collectivization of agriculture, the struggle for the building of socialism, the preservation of Soviet independence, and the maintenance of peace. His services in the contest against the Left and Right deviationists who opposed the Lenin program have been readily acknowledged. Both Lenin and Stalin believed in the

3. In January, 1953, a TASS dispatch in the Soviet press alleged that a terrorist group of doctors, most of whom were affiliated with the international Jewish organization JOINT, had conspired to bring about the death of Soviet leaders Andrei Zhdanov and A. S. Shcherbakov. Although in April the charges aganist the doctors were repudiated, the tone of the accusations clearly indicated that anti-Semitism was by no means dead in the USSR.

4. Second edition, 1957.

ultimate victory of communism throughout the world, but resorted to strategic retreat when expediency so dictated. Whereas Lenin used terrorism against class enemies, Stalin applied Lenin's methods to eliminate all who opposed his dictatorship, including the liquidation of large numbers of Communists in the top echelons of the Party and the Red Army. Whereas Lenin upon occasion humbly acknowledged his mistakes and shortcomings, Stalin welcomed adulation and came to believe in his own infallibility. He encouraged the cult of his own person, and especially during the final years of his life, carried this to such extremes that he resembled an Oriental potentate more than a practitioner of socialism.

Fall of Beria. With the actual crisis over the succession confronting them, and no successor of Stalin's stature at hand, the leading contestants postponed the showdown and agreed to bridge the vacuum by sharing the power, at least temporarily. Malenkov assumed the premiership, but surrendered the strategic post of secretary of the Communist Party to Nikita Khrushchev (1894–   ). Beria emerged as deputy premier and minister of internal affairs, while Molotov, also a deputy premier, resumed his old post as minister of foreign affairs. In the struggle for power that followed, the first victim was the unpopular Beria, whose arrest was announced on July 10, 1953, and who was subsequently executed, together with six of his lieutenants. Beria, who had deployed his MVD legions at strategic points throughout Moscow immediately following Stalin's death, exposed the phony "doctors' plot," and placed some of his henchmen in prominent positions in the non-Russian Republics, was clearly a threat to his rivals and had to be removed. Ironically, he was accused of having been a British agent since 1919, an accusation worthy of Stalin himself.

25

The Cold War: Strategy

Versus Diplomacy, 1947-1965

THE TRUMAN DOCTRINE of March 12, 1947, not only saved Greece and Tur-
key from the expansionist aims of the Stalin regime, but it appreciably slowed
Soviet penetration in the Near and Middle East. The growing estrangement of
the Soviet Union and the United States henceforth assumed the proportions of
a "cold war." Soviet leaders had not foreseen American intervention in
Turkey on the doorstep of the Soviet Union. Their search for a base in the
Americas on the United States periphery dates from the Truman Doctrine.
They intensified their propaganda in South America and eventually achieved
their objective, at least temporarily, in Cuba.

In the USSR, changes in foreign and domestic policies are frequently indicated in Soviet literature. Even prior to the Truman Doctrine, the well-known
Soviet author Konstantin Simonov produced a play, *The Russian Question*
(1946), which attacked "not the America of Washington, Lincoln, and
Roosevelt," but a so-called reactionary minority in the United States which
demanded of an American correspondent that he produce an anti-Soviet
book. In this country, however, the satire was interpreted as "anti-American."
In 1948 and 1949 a series of plays much more inimical to the United States
and the West made their appearance, including *The Foreign Shadow* by
Simonov; *The Voice of America* by Boris Lavrenev; *I Want to Go Home* by
Sergei Mikhalkov; and to top them all, *The Ill-Starred Haberdasher,* a crude
travesty on President Truman, by Anatoly Surov. The tone of these plays was
sarcastic, the language coarse and hostile. They indicated to the Soviet public
that the Soviet-American wartime partnership had been dissolved.

RELIANCE ON STRATEGY

In Soviet-American relations, 1947 to 1960, the impression is given that
diplomacy gave way to strategy. The term "strategy" became part of the
American way of thinking, as illustrated by the familiar headlines: "Strategy
of Peace," "Strategy of Annihilation," "Strategy for a Nuclear Age," "Tariff
Strategy," and even "Diplomatic Strategy." Although diplomacy may, and
usually does, involve strategy, basically it implies the settlement of disputes,

or efforts to settle them, through negotiation and mutual compromise. No one is likely to define diplomacy better than an Englishman, for England has had a long and varied experience in diplomacy. Baron Strang, a member of the British Foreign Service who served in Moscow in the 1930's and headed the British Foreign Office, 1949–1953, has provided a suitable definition:

> Diplomacy, as traditionally understood, is the method by which governments talk and write to each other and make agreements with each other. One of the essential purposes of diplomacy is negotiation. One of its main objectives is the reaching of accommodations or agreements.[1]

Diplomacy, in other words, does not look for "unconditional surrender" or "nothing less than victory." It seeks a settlement that will endure.

Definition. Strategy (generalship), on the other hand, is a military term, implying a plan of action against an opponent. It calls to mind a chess game, in which one contestant moves and the other promptly seeks to checkmate that move, the outcome being victory for one of the contestants or deadlock between them. In brief, when diplomacy takes precedence, the parties involved talk, but do not move, at least not until they have reached an understanding. When strategy prevails, each contestant moves first to offset a prior move of the other, and if they talk, it is often to threaten and upbraid one another.

Following World War II, the key to American foreign policy was the use of strategy "to contain" the Soviet orbit, while the United States established "a position of strength." Once that objective was achieved, it was believed that diplomacy could take over and bring about a settlement of disputes in our favor. In other words, the United States divorced strategy from diplomacy, assuming that one succeeded the other.

Sino-Soviet Alliance. Smarting under the American policy of "containment" (Iran, Greece, and Turkey) in the Near and Middle East, the Stalin government turned to the Far East where, in violation of its commitments to the government of Chiang Kai-shek, it helped the Chinese Communist forces of Mao Tse-tung drive the Chinese Nationalists from the mainland, 1948–1949. The much publicized Berlin blockade of 1948 served as an effective smoke-screen to divert the attention of the United States and the West from the Far East while the expulsion of the supporters of Chiang Kai-shek was in process. When the dust finally settled, and the United States government jubilantly announced that it had saved Berlin, it became clear that this was accomplished at the expense of the loss of China. Without further delay the USSR concluded an "unbreakable" defensive alliance with Red China, February 14, 1950, which upset the balance of power in Europe and Asia. Further expansion of the Moscow-Peking orbit in the direction of Southeast Asia threatened to outflank the Near and Middle East and ultimately Europe.

1. *New York Times,* April 15, 1962. Magazine Section, p. 27.

Korean War. The Sino-Soviet Alliance was not consummated in order to preserve the *status quo* in the Far East. Its immediate objective was the expulsion of the Americans from Korea, which in turn was to provide the stepping stone for the termination of the United States occupation of Japan. Once successful in Korea, the USSR expected to use substantial numbers of Japanese prisoners-of-war, already undergoing indoctrination in Siberia, "to liberate" Japan under the slogan "Remember Hiroshima! Remember Nagasaki!" The Sino-Soviet timetable for the achievement of this goal was upset by the entrance of the United States and the United Nations into the Korean War in 1950 to stem the tide of Communist aggression. Although the United Nations, due to Red Chinese intervention, was unable to impose its terms on North Korea, it did succeed in preventing South Korea and possibly Japan from being reduced to Sino-Soviet satellites. By retarding the Sino-Soviet advance to Southeast Asia, it provided three years for the buildup of Western defenses. With the signing of the Korean truce on July 26, 1953, the pace of Communist aggression in Indo-China was stepped up.

In spite of the Korean War, the treaty with Japan, and defensive pacts with Australia, New Zealand, and the Philippines, until 1953 American foreign policy subordinated the Orient to Western Europe. During the same period, in spite of American activity in Europe, Soviet foreign policy subordinated Europe to Asia. Although the Eisenhower administration made the United States Asia-conscious, with China lost, India "neutral," and Indo-China partitioned, it faced the problem of creating an effective system of Asian alliances to counterbalance the eight hundred million population of the Sino-Soviet axis. To make American alliances in Asia really effective, they had to be bolstered by large reserves of Asian manpower.

American Initiative in Asia. It was now the American turn to assume the strategic initiative. The American government realized that the only effective means of securing Asian manpower was the extension of its system of alliances to include the countries of the Muslim world. The leading Muslim nations were strategically located along the soft underbelly of the USSR in Asia, and they had the manpower to enable the West to balance, if not to outnumber, the thickly populated countries of the Moscow-Peking orbit. Since some Muslim peoples were still inordinately distrustful of the Western powers, it became the task of American diplomacy to convince them that the United States did not approach them as masters or as "colonizers," but as equals, with mutual interests at stake. Conscious only of the threat of Western domination, the Arab states often failed to realize the imminent danger of their being submerged physically and spiritually by the non-Muslim Asian world—a fate far worse than that imposed by the Western colonizers under whom they retained their national identity and religious faith, not to mention the improvement of their economic status. As Soviet policy in Iran and Turkey after World War II fully demonstrated, the Muslim world could not hope to contain non-Muslim Asian aggression without the United States. Likewise, without the Muslim world, the United States could not build an effective system of alliances to block the expansion of the Red axis. It was, therefore, to their mutual advantage to join forces without delay.

Many other difficulties confronted the United States in its efforts to win the Muslim world for the Western orbit. Non-Muslim Asia, led by Red China and the Soviet Union, was growing rapidly in strength, whereas the Muslim world as yet lacked organization. It had no well-defined aims and objectives. Unfortunately, very few Muslims understood the need for Western-Muslim solidarity, and not all Western nations grasped the fact that the West must be strong in manpower as well as in technology if it were to contain the Red axis. Moreover, the majority of Americans knew little or nothing about the Muslim world and few were aware of the postwar realignment into Muslim and non-Muslim orbits in Asia.

As we have seen, it was the Truman Doctrine which laid the cornerstone for an American rapprochement with the Muslim world, by extending military and economic aid to save Turkey from Soviet encroachment. Subsequent to 1947 the United States continued its efforts to unite the Muslim peoples of the Arab states against the Communist menace. These efforts did not succeed, in part because of the establishment of the State of Israel in 1948, and also due to bitter rivalries among the Arab states. Had the seven states that comprise the Arab League—Egypt, Lebanon, Syria, Iraq, Jordan, Saudi Arabia, and Yemen—not vacillated too long, with Egypt at the head they might have become the focal point of a Western-sponsored defensive alliance against communism. Egypt, which expected to assume the leadership of the Arab world, temporarily fell prey to internal disunity, and the struggle between General Muhammed Naguib and Lieutenant-Colonel Gamal Abdel Nasser militated against prompt and decisive action. Egyptian nationalists were more intent at that time on the control of the Sudan and the Suez Canal, issues that were of more immediate concern to Egypt than the containment of the Soviet Union.

Turkish-Pakistani Pact. Frustrated in this direction, the United States won a major diplomatic and strategic victory in bringing about the Turkish-Pakistani Mutual Aid Agreement of April 2, 1954. To put more teeth into the pact the United States and Pakistan on May 19 signed an agreement providing American war materiel and technical assistance to Pakistan. The Turkish-Pakistani Pact united the two strongest Muslim states, comprising about one hundred million people, or one-fourth of the Muslim world, located on the southern periphery of the USSR.

Although the Turks had been the most reliable ally of the United States in the Near and Middle East, they were far from enthusiastic about an alliance embracing the Muslim world, especially one that included the Arabs. They were apprehensive that the Arab states might prove to be more intent on the elimination of Israel, with which Turkey carried on a thriving trade, than in concentrating on the Communist menace. The Turks also appeared to prefer a limited alliance, possibly including Iran and Afghanistan to close the gap between Turkey and Pakistan, but they did not seek closer ties with the states of the Arab League. Modern Turkey, where Westernization and secularization have taken deep root, does not look with favor on any resurgence of Islam as practised in the Arab world. Nevertheless, under Western pressure the Turks were persuaded that Pan-Islamism offered better protection against Communist aggression than could be found in a divided Muslim world. Following the unanimous ratification of the Turkish-Pakistani Pact by the Turkish Grand National Assembly on June 11, 1954, Turkey and Pakistan announced that they would henceforth shift from a passive to an active policy in seeking to induce other Muslim countries of the Near and Middle East, especially those in the north, to join forces with them to establish an effective system of collective security.

Had the United States succeeded in implementing an Arab alliance against communism, Soviet leaders would have displayed no great concern, for the Arab states were divided and weak. With Turkey and Pakistan at the helm the situation was different. The Soviet government was fully aware that every effort would be made to create an unbroken chain of alliances from Turkey to Pakistan, which would include Iraq and Iran, if not Afghanistan. If Iraq could be induced to break loose from the Arab League to join Turkey and Pakistan, the other Arab states might eventually conclude, no matter how reluctantly, that it was in their own interest to follow suit. The very existence of the Turkish-Pakistani Pact, sponsored by the United States, weakened the hold that the Soviet government still had on Iran by virtue of the 1921 treaty.

Soviet Domestic Counter-Measures

Because the Soviet people are still impressed by man power, at times even more than by technology, the impact on the USSR of the Turkish-Pakistani agreement was therefore instantaneous. It resulted in large-scale, strategic counter-measures involving the status of the thirty million Muslims inside the borders of the Soviet Union. Central Asia, where the bulk of these Muslims resided, was the bulwark for the defense of the Ural Region, the backbone of Soviet industrial development.

Under the guise of a campaign to increase Soviet food production, the Soviet government in the spring of 1954 instituted a program for the reclamation of virgin and idle lands and the opening up of new agricultural areas in Kazakhstan, West Siberia, the Ural and Volga regions, and the North Caucasus. These are highly strategic areas with reference to the Near and Middle East. One of the principal areas selected for cultivation and reclamation was Soviet Central Asia, known before the Revolution as Russian Turkestan, but which now comprises the Soviet Republics of Kazakhstan, Kirghizia, Tadjikistan, Turkmenistan, and Uzbekistan.

Soviet Muslims in World War II. Until the Second World War the bulk of the population in Soviet Central Asia, in both urban and rural areas, was Muslim. The native peoples, irrespective of current nomenclature, considered themselves of Turkish or Iranian origin. Even under the Soviet regime, in these republics nationalism has been associated with Pan-Islamism, Pan-Turkism, or Pan-Iranism, all of which have been denounced repeatedly by the Communist leadership. Together with the Crimean Tatars, the Central Asian peoples proved highly unreliable in their allegiance to the USSR during the conflict with Nazi Germany. This was proved by the aid they rendered the Nazi armies in labor and ordnance battalions, as well as in combat. One of their leaders, Kayum-Khan, an Uzbek exile, succeeded in organizing in Germany 180,000 men from various parts of Central Asia into a force which became an integral part of the Wehrmacht (German armed forces) or the Waffen-S.S. (force for internal security). Of these, three battalions fought to the last man before Stalingrad. Others were destroyed in fierce fighting in the Caucasus. Six battalions of these Muslim recruits for a time held up the Soviet advance into Berlin in 1945. Altogether, it is estimated that they suffered the loss of fifty thousand men.

Compulsory Resettlement. The first step taken by the Soviet government to offset the Muslim threat in the Soviet Union was, as we have seen, the expulsion of all Tatars from the Crimea, facing Turkey, and the resettlement of the area with Slavs. Thereafter, in order to enlist wholehearted Ukrainian support for the defense of this region, the Crimea was "annexed" to the Ukrainian Republic. A second step, immediately following World War II, was the dispatch of many Slavs and other non-Muslim elements to the cities of the Central Asian republics, to places such as Tashkent, Ashkabad, Almu Ata, etc. By 1952 the Slavic element outnumbered the native Muslim population in these urban centers and key posts in the administration were in their hands.

Sovkhozi. In this program for the development of "virgin and idle lands," the Soviet government stressed the establishment of *sovkhozi,* that is state-owned farms, in place of *kolkhozi,* or collective farms. According to Khrushchev, secretary of the Central Committee of the Communist Party, prior to the Soviet campaign to cultivate "virgin and idle lands" there were approximately 4,700 *sovkhozi* in the USSR, in comparison with 94,000 *kolkhozi.* In January, 1956, the Soviet government revealed that since 1954 an additional 560 *sovkhozi* had been established, most of them in desolate, but highly strategic, eastern areas. Over the *sovkhozi* the government retained more direct and rigid controls. In time of national crisis it could carry out a more effective scorched-earth policy along the periphery. As World War II demonstrated, this was difficult to enforce among the *kolkhozi,* where a modicum of private ownership prevailed.

The new *sovkhozi* were likewise expected to offset in some measure the rise of a new middle class in the USSR, which already constituted a problem for the Soviet regime, especially for the Communist Party. On March 9, 1956, the

Soviet government embarked upon a program aimed at the progressive reduction of private plots and privately owned livestock on collective farms to the point where they will merely "decorate" the life of the collective farmer, rather than constitute a threat to collective ownership. If the international situation had been less threatening, it seems likely that the Soviet government would have taken more drastic action to curb the new middle class than was indicated by the campaign for new state farms. Whereas the growth of new middle and upper classes remained a thorn in the flesh to the Communist Party, the military element was inclined to favor this development, in the belief that those who had something at stake were more likely to fight to defend the system in the event of another conflict.

FOREIGN POLICY

Dissension in Pakistan. In the field of foreign affairs the Soviet Union betrayed manifest concern over the impact of the Istanbul-Karachi agreement on the 350,000,000 Muslims beyond Soviet borders, stretching from Chinese Turkestan and Southeast Asia to Morocco and West Africa. The Soviet government immediately focused its attention upon ways of reducing the effectiveness of the pact by stirring up internal dissension in Pakistan. Taking advantage of the geographical division of Pakistan into two parts separated by approximately one thousand miles, and the hostility of India toward this Muslim state, Soviet propagandists fomented strikes and labor riots in the jute and other industries of thickly populated East Pakistan (East Bengal) and encouraged the movement for political independence there. On May 30, 1954, Premier Muhammed Ali of Pakistan was forced to dismiss Fazlul Huq, chief minister of East Pakistan and his associates for "treasonable activities" and to undertake a drastic reorganization of the government. The Communist Party was banned in East Bengal on July 5 and in West Pakistan on July 24.

Turkey. Even without waiting for the formal conclusion of the Turkish-Pakistani Pact, the Soviet government in an official note of protest to Turkey predicted that this agreement would "aggravate the situation in the Near and Middle East, and also in Southeast Asia, and would have a direct bearing on the security of the Soviet Union." It accused the United States of planning to use "the human resources" of this area to carry out American policy, and of "forging a bloc by installments."

Soviet propaganda guns were trained on Turkey following the negotiation of the pact with Pakistan. The Soviet government took the stand that the pact was aggressive in design, since it came when Turkey's security was no longer threatened by any of her neighbors. No doubt this was an indirect allusion to belated Soviet action (May 30, 1953) in officially abandoning all territorial claims against Turkey. *Izvestia,* the official organ of the Soviet government, on June 15, 1954, in a lengthy analysis of the Turkish position, discussed the dispatch of Turkish troops to Korea: "It is quite obvious," commented *Izvestia,* "that Turkish ruling circles would not have sent soldiers abroad if on the Turkish borders there existed any kind of danger. . . . This consideration once again exposes the aggressive and not the defensive role assigned by Washington to the Turkish military forces." The Soviet press tried to incite Arab opposition to the pact by frequent allegations concerning Turkey's irredentist claims on Syria, the other Arab states, and Iran. "Moreover," continued *Izvestia,* "Turkish ruling circles do not help to mitigate the tension that exists in the areas of the Near and Middle East, as well as in the Balkan Peninsula. In spite of the fact that the Soviet government has taken numerous steps to secure good neighborly relations with Turkey, Turkish official circles are acting in such a manner as to make it appear that Turkey is less interested than the Soviet Union in such relations."

Baghdad Pact. As their next strategic move, the United States and England engineered the extension of the Turkish-Pakistani Alliance through a series of agreements which together comprised the Baghdad Pact of 1955. On February 24 Turkey and Iraq signed an alliance, to which Great Britain adhered on April 24, at which time the British government agreed to transfer to Iraq the British air bases at Habaniya and Shaiba. Pakistan, which agreed on June 30 to join the Turkish Iraqi Pact, formally affixed its signature on September 23. In a last-minute effort to forestall Iranian adherence to this new Middle East defense system, the Soviet Union on June 1 returned to Iran eleven tons of long-promised gold and undertook to provide compensation to the extent of £3,000,000 for Iranian supplies appropriated by the USSR during World War II. The United States entered the picture, however, by signing with Iran a treaty of friendship, economic relations, and consular rights on August 15. Two days later the Export-Import Bank announced loans amounting to $14,000,000 to assist Iran to modernize part of its railroad equipment by shifting to diesel power. The contest for Iran was decided in favor of the United States, when on October 11 Premier Hussein Ala announced Iran's intention of adhering to the Baghdad Pact.

Middle Eastern Treaty Organization. In November, 1955, the premiers of Iraq, Iran, Pakistan, and Turkey met with the British foreign secretary, Harold Macmillan, to establish a permanent political, military, and economic organization—in other words, a permanent secretariat—with headquarters in Baghdad. The United States, which originated the idea of the pact but was not a signatory, was represented by political and military observers. On November 22 the five powers comprising the Middle Eastern Treaty Organization (METO) announced the establishment of the "Council of the Baghdad Pact," the purpose of which was defense against "aggression or subversion." The premier of Iraq, Nuri as-Said, became the first chairman.

Effect of the Baghdad Pact. By the Baghdad Pact the Middle East was linked with the North Atlantic Treaty Organization (NATO) through Turkey and Great Britain, and with the Southeast Asian Treaty Organization

(SEATO) through Pakistan. It marked the conclusion, at least on paper, of a United States-sponsored chain of alliances stretching from Norway to the Philippines, the object of which was to prevent further expansion on the part of the Sino-Soviet axis. In the Middle East, although the Bagdad Pact established a three thousand-mile ideological and military *cordon sanitaire* against further Soviet penetration, it still required implementation if it was to prove effective. The signatories, realizing that the effectiveness of the pact depended upon the United States, looked forward to ultimate American membership and to the inclusion of the other Arab states. The Iraq government hastened to announce, in this connection, that its adherence to the pact in no wise conflicted with its membership in the Arab League. The implication was that the pact might be used to aid any Arab state which might become the object of aggression. Nevertheless, the Baghdad Pact split the Arab world, at least temporarily.

Soviet Interpretation. As interpreted by the Soviet press, the Baghdad Pact was an aggressive military alliance, by means of which the United States and Great Britain hoped to saddle "a new form of colonialism" on the Middle East. Soviet writers acclaimed the Arab states of Syria, Lebanon, Jordan, Saudi Arabia, and Egypt for their successful resistance to Western pressure. They likewise welcomed and no doubt helped to instigate the Jordan riots which broke out in December, 1955, as a result of British pressure on that country to join the Baghdad alliance. An *Izvestia* article interpreted the Jordan riots as representative of the opposition of all the Arab states to further outside interference in Arab affairs. Seeking to widen the breach between Iraq and the states of the Arab League, Soviet propaganda charged that the Western powers were inciting Iraq to absorb Syria, and that Turkey intended to occupy Iranian Azerbaijan and Kurdistan. Soviet leaders were even more bitter over the failure of their efforts to keep Iran "neutral." On November 26, 1955, Soviet Foreign Minister Molotov charged Iran with violation of Article III of the Soviet-Iranian Treaty of October 1, 1927, by which both parties promised to avoid alliances or agreements directed against the other. Although it declared the Soviet frontiers to be in danger, the USSR made no move to invoke the famous Treaty of 1921 by taking steps to occupy Iran. Nevertheless a third protest against Iran's accession to the Baghdad Pact was transmitted to the Iranian foreign minister by Soviet ambassador Lavrentyev on February 4, 1956. The Shah's visit to the USSR in June, 1956, was designed to convince Moscow that the Baghdad Pact was a purely defensive instrument and that its signatories had no intention of using Iran as a base for an atack on the Soviet Union. Khrushchev and his cohorts, who showed no more signs of being reconciled to METO than to NATO, took advantage of the tour to continue their efforts to pry Iran loose from the Baghdad defense system.

Soviet-Afghan Agreement. There was still a gap in the Baghdad Pact due to the abstention of Afghanistan. Spurred into action by the Turkish-Pakistani

Agreement of 1954 and by the United States-Pakistan Arms Pact, the Soviet government at once took steps to strengthen its ties with Afghanistan, regarded as the one truly "neutral" Muslim state lying athwart the USSR and Pakistan. Soviet action took the form of economic aid—the construction of an oil pipeline from Uzbekistan to the Afghan city of Mazar-i-sharif and of two huge wheat silos in Kabul and Pul-i-Khumr—and support of Afghan nationalist demands for a plebiscite among the Pathan tribes of Pakistan's northwest frontier province. In the fall of 1955, a Soviet-Afghan agreement for reciprocal free transit of goods through both countries relieved Afghanistan of dependence on Pakistan.

RENEWED EFFORTS IN THE MIDDLE EAST

It was the Baghdad Alliance of 1955 which precipitated the third Soviet drive for penetration of the Near and Middle East.[2] In the early years of the Soviet regime, the Bolsheviks sought to build a Soviet bulwark against England and the West in Turkey, Iran, and Afghanistan, the three countries which they expected to serve as the vanguard for Soviet absorption of the Muslim East. Confronted instead by the Baghdad Pact, in which Turkey and Iran, as well as Iraq and Pakistan, constituted a bulwark against Soviet expansion and subversion, the post-Stalin regime took prompt measures to outflank the new alliance by strengthening its ties with Afghanistan and by joint action with Red China to draw the Arab states into the Sino-Soviet orbit. The destruction of the Baghdad Alliance became a major objective of Soviet foreign policy.

Strategic Importance of Afghanistan. Changes in the Soviet government in February, 1955, led to the replacement of Malenkov by Marshal Nikolai A. Bulganin as chairman of the Council of Ministers of the USSR. In December, in an unprecedented move, Premier Bulganin and Khrushchev, secretary of the Central Committee of the Communist Party, toured India, Burma, and Afghanistan to win friends and influence people. Although the press focused upon the Indi-Burma stages of this barnstorming trip, in reality it was Afghanistan that proved most significant. With extensive atomic research reported in Soviet Kirghizia, northeast of Afghanistan, the USSR could not afford to let its Afghan neighbors go by default into the American-sponsored Muslim alliance in the Middle East. As the climax to the Bulganin-Khrushchev visit to Kabul, the Soviet government on December 18, 1955, announced a Soviet version of the Truman Doctrine—a loan of $100,000,000 to Afghanistan and a ten-year extension of the 1931 Soviet-Afghan Treaty of Neutrality and Mutual Non-Aggression.

Although Afghanistan remained officially "neutral" between the Soviet and

2. Ivar Spector, "Russia in the Middle East," *Current History,* Vol. 32 (No. 186, February 1957), pp. 83–88.

Western blocs, the Soviet-Afghan *rapprochement* appeared to give the Soviet Union a foothold there, which served a twofold purpose: In the first place, it enabled the USSR to maintain the gap in the METO chain of defense along the southern Soviet frontier, thereby compensating in part for the loss of Iran. In the second place, it afforded an opportunity for the Soviet Union to outflank Pakistan, one of the two major partners of the Baghdad Pact, and also to outflank Iran. It soon became clear why the USSR hastily tried to acquire a foothold in Egypt by providing that country with arms from Czechoslovakia and by seeking a contract for the construction of the Aswan Dam. Once successful in Egypt, the Soviet Union would outflank METO in the West as it did via Afghanistan in the East. It would thus hold the Middle East in a pincer grip that would constitute a direct threat to Western defense of that area.

Cinematic Propaganda. Lenin once predicted that the film would be one of the most effective agencies for the spread of communism in the Orient. With a speed even surpassing the production of *Alexander Nevsky, Pravda* announced on January 24, 1956, the appearance of a documentary color film *In Friendly Afghanistan,* recording with an appropriate background of native music the four-day visit of Bulganin and Khrushchev to various historic Afghan sites, their warm welcome in Kabul, and the signing of the Soviet-Afghan agreements concluded at that time. It was generally conceded in the West that until an agreement could be reached on the disposition of the Pathan tribes in northern Pakistan, there was little possibility of inducing Afghanistan to join the Baghdad Alliance.

Iran. The Soviet Union continued to exert every possible pressure to defeat or to delay the implementation of the American program for an effective alliance of the Muslim states against communism. It tried, in particular, to bring about the defection of Iran by means of intimidation and economic pressure. With this in view, it made good use of the Soviet-Iranian economic agreement of June 17, 1954, which called for a sharp increase in shipments of Soviet industrial equipment and durable goods. An Iranian parliamentary delegation, headed by Muhammed Sayed, toured the Soviet Union, including Central Asia, during the winter of 1955–1956 in the interests of better Soviet-Iranian relations, and Shah Muhammed Reza Pahlevi paid an official visit to Moscow in May, 1956.

Turkey. In February, 1956, the Soviet government intensified its propaganda for the "normalization" of Soviet-Turkish relations, in an effort to weaken Turkish adherence to the Baghdad Pact. As if in reply to a lengthy article on the subject in *Pravda,* a Turkish foreign ministry official on February 9 gave voice to his government's continued suspicion of Soviet motives by declaring as follows: "Turkey feels that this activity on the part of the Soviet Union proves beyond a doubt the value of the Baghdad Pact and that the Pact is doing just what it was supposed to accomplish." In spite of the Turkish rebuff, the Soviet government pursued its efforts for "normalization."

Commemorating the thirty-fifth anniversary of the signing of the Soviet-Turkish Treaty of Friendship and Fraternity of 1921, *Izvestia* called for a return to the good relations that prevailed between the two countries under Kemal Pasha and Ismet Inönü, admitted that the subsequent estrangement was a joint responsibility, and emphasized the importance of a new *rapprochement* for the strengthening of peace in the Near and Middle East.

Pakistan. Pakistan, the other major Muslim member of the Baghdad Alliance, on February 8, 1956, approved a recommendation of the Ministry of Economic Affairs for the initiation of formal negotiations for a trade pact with the Soviet Union. The only other trade contracts between the USSR and Pakistan occurred in 1953, when a barter agreement provided for the exchange of Pakistani cotton for Soviet wheat at a time when famine threatened the new Muslim state. The decision to negotiate a trade pact was interpreted by some Western experts as an entering wedge for Soviet economic aid to Pakistan, in competition with the United States. Speaking for the press on March 24, the day following his assumption of office, Iskander Mirza, first president of the Pakistan Republic, left no room for doubt on this matter by repudiating "neutralism" and reaffirming Pakistan's determination to hold fast to the Baghdad Pact and the Southeast Asia Treaty Organization, which he regarded as "agencies for peace."

British Role in the Baghdad Alliance. Irrespective of the outcome of Soviet efforts to undermine the Baghdad Alliance, it can be said that English membership in METO provided the Soviet government with an effective weapon to achieve such an objective. A Kukryniksy cartoon in *Pravda* in 1955 depicted the four Muslim members of the Baghdad Alliance seeking security in the open jaws of the British lion. English membership thus lent weight to Soviet claims that the pact was a ruse to inflict a new form of colonialism on the countries of the Middle East. No doubt the British government, having recently surrendered its former strategic position at Suez to Egypt, being in the process of transferring important air bases to Iraq and facing a serious challenge to British authority in Cyprus, hoped by membership in METO to compensate for its retreat elsewhere in the Near and Middle East. The fact that it still controlled the British-led and British-subsidized Arab Legion of Jordan appreciably strengthened Middle Eastern defenses. Its subsequent failure to bring Jordan into the Baghdad Alliance, followed on March 2, 1956, by King Hussein's abrupt dismissal of Lieutenant-General John Bagot Glubb ("Glubb Pasha"), British commander of Jordan's Arab Legion, raised some doubt as to whether British membership had become more of a handicap than an asset. In retrospect, the question arises as to whether the Baghdad Alliance should not have remained exclusively a Muslim alliance, relying on the leadership of Turkey and Pakistan, with Great Britain following the American example of lending active support without becoming an active member. Unfortunately for the success of the alliance, in the minds of the Arabs and other peoples of the Muslim East, Great Britain, in spite of her genuine efforts to promote the development and stability of this area, was the country most closely associated with colonialism.

POLICY IN THE NEAR EAST AND AFRICA

Sino-Soviet Collaboration. Early in 1956 it became apparent that Red China and the USSR were taking parallel action in the Near East and Africa, probably as a result of the Asian-African Conference in Bandung. The most conspicuous parallels were to be seen in their diplomatic and trade overtures to Lebanon, Syria, Egypt, the Sudan, and Liberia. The expansion of Chinese-Egyptian trade since the trade pact of August, 1955, and the manifest success of the Red Chinese trade fair in Cairo in April, 1956, all without benefit of diplomatic recognition, appeared to augur bigger and better deals to come. Egypt's recognition of Red China on May 16, 1956, undoubtedly accelerated the pace of Sino-Soviet collaboration. Thus, no sooner had the Western democracies reconciled themselves, albeit reluctantly, to the necessity for recognizing the USSR as a factor in eastern Mediterranean affairs, than they were confronted by the sudden and unwelcome impact of Red China in that area.

Arab States. The Soviet Union and the Arab states, with the exception of Iraq, saw eye to eye in their opposition to English membership in the Baghdad Alliance. Agreement on this issue undoubtedly facilitated a Soviet-Arab, and in particular, a Soviet-Egyptian *rapprochement.* The Soviet Union was quick to recognize the new Sudanese Republic (January, 1956). On March 8, 1956, the USSR followed up its treaty of friendship with Yemen (October 30, 1955) with a trade agreement, providing Soviet industrial equipment, oil products, and food in exchange for Yemenite coffee, hides, dried fruits, etc.

In line with its challenge to the United States, the Soviet government offered to build factories, to provide technical assistance, and possibly arms to this Arab state. The first Arab leader to undertake "a mission to Moscow" was the crown prince of Yemen, Seif al-Islam Muhammed el-Badr, who made a three-week tour of the Soviet Union in June, 1956. In March, Soviet cultural and economic delegations were busy in Damascus, while a Syrian military mission was in Prague to negotiate for the purchase of arms. The Soviet government, in addition to providing a market for Syrian cotton, offered to construct a Syrian government oil refinery to process the oil reaching that country from Iraq.

The USSR was likewise instrumental in accelerating the issuing of a joint communiqué (March 12, 1956) by the leaders of Egypt, Saudi Arabia, and Syria for the mobilization of their defenses against Israel and for the formation of a neutral Arab bloc to counteract Western efforts to strengthen the Baghdad Pact. Scarcely a week passed without the announcement of additional economic ties between the Arab states and the Sino-Soviet Axis.

Soviet prospects for further encroachment in the Near East, especially in the Arab World, were enhanced by the withdrawal, July 19–20, 1956, of Anglo-American offers to help Egypt finance the building of the Aswan High Dam on the Nile. By this action, according to Senator J. William Fulbright (August 14, 1957), "we handed communism a key to the Middle East." President Gamal Abdel Nasser promptly retaliated on July 26 by the nationalization of the Suez Canal Company twelve years prior to the end of its concession, with the avowed object of securing revenue to finance the Aswan Dam.

Suez Crisis. As the opponent of all survivals of colonialism in Asia and Africa, the Soviet government found in the Suez crisis of 1956 plenty of grist for its own mill. Soviet Foreign Minister Shepilov no sooner assumed office than he trekked to Cairo in June to celebrate with the Egyptians the end of three-quarters of a century of British occupation of the Suez Canal Zone. Without full assurance of Soviet support, it is unlikely that Nasser would have recklessly defied the West on July 26, within a month of the Shepilov visit, by the nationalization of the Suez Canal Company, long regarded by Moscow as "an important bulwark of colonialism."

In the years immediately following the Bolshevik Revolution, Soviet Russia appeared to be more intent on transforming Persia into "the Suez Canal of the revolution" than in ousting Britain from Egypt and the Suez. A Moscow University history (1954) on the non-Soviet countries of the East states that the initial program of the Communist Party of Egypt, as formulated in 1923, included a plank in support of the nationalization of the Suez Canal. The edition published in 1934 contained no such explicit demand, except insofar as it called for the abolition of all the privileges of the imperialists, including confiscation and nationalization of all their industrial enterprises.

From the moment Egypt took action to nationalize the Suez Canal Company, Soviet support of that action was unqualified. Since Russia was a signatory of the Constantinople Convention of 1888, the Soviet government clearly indicated its intention to participate in any revision of that settlement and demanded the inclusion of the Arab succession states of the Ottoman Empire.

Although unwilling in 1947 that Turkey should have exclusive control of shipping in the Dardanelles and Bosphorus, the USSR now posed as the principal champion of Egyptian sovereignty over the Canal, rejecting Anglo-French plans for its internationalization. After September 12, Soviet pilots supported Nasser's efforts to keep the canal open. On September 16, in a major pronouncement, the Soviet government warned that "any disturbance of peace in the Middle East cannot but affect the security and interests of the Soviet state," and demanded a peaceful settlement through the UN. The "piratical" Users' Association was rejected by Moscow as an American scheme to get control of the canal.

No sooner had the Israeli invasion of Egypt begun, closely followed by Anglo-French intervention, than Bulganin appealed to India and to Indonesia for a special session of the Asian-African bloc that comprised the Bandung Conference. Voroshilov, on November 3, promised Soviet aid to visiting President Shukri al-Kuwatly of Syria. Two days later the USSR warned Britain, France, and Israel of Soviet readiness to use force "to crush the aggressors." On November 10, the Soviet government officially announced that it would permit "volunteers" to go to Egypt to fight the "aggressors," if Britain, France, and Israel refused to withdraw their forces from Egyptian territory. Red China followed suit with an offer of 250,000 "volunteers." Bulganin's call for joint United States-Soviet action to end the Egyptian War appeared to be paving the way for unilateral Soviet action, when the United States government promptly labelled the proposal "unthinkable."

Sino-Soviet intervention in the Suez crisis undoubtedly strengthened the position of President Nasser and the Arab states. Temporarily, at least, the prospect of Soviet "volunteers" in the Near East gave rise to near panic on the part of Egypt's invaders. Without the threat of imminent Soviet military intervention, it is doubtful that the United Nations emergency Assembly meeting would have ordered and achieved a ceasefire in Egypt so quickly, that it would have proceeded so rapidly to authorize and to move into Egypt the new United Nations police force, and that England, France and Israel would have agreed to withdraw from Egyptian territory in favor of UN occupation forces, once they were in a position to assume effective control.

On the other hand, the second conference of the chiefs of state of the Arab League, meeting in Beirut on November 13, amid rumors of substantial Soviet arms shipments and the dispatch of Soviet technical advisers to Syria, viewed with apprehension the pro-Soviet stand of Syria and Egypt. The seven other states of the Arab League, especially Lebanon, Saudi Arabia and Iraq, opposed the use of Soviet "volunteers."

These Arab leaders appeared to be aware that under Soviet domination there would be no room for independent Arab *or* Israeli states. The fate of the thirty million Muslims and of the much advertised Jewish autonomous region of Birobidjan inside the USSR afforded ample demonstration of that. Although since World War II many independent Muslim states have emerged in the Near and Middle East, the Sino-Soviet orbit, having in all probability more Muslims than there are Arabs in the world, has not created a single independent Muslim state.

It was unfortunate that the invasion of Egypt coincided with the Hungarian revolt against Communist tyranny in Europe. Aggression, whatever its motives and justification, is nevertheless aggression. The resort to force by England, France, and Israel muted the protests against Soviet aggression against Hungary. Under other circumstances, it might have been possible to mobilize world sentiment in the United Nations to bring irresistible pressure to bear against the ruthless suppression of the Hungarian uprising by the Red Army.

Eisenhower Doctrine. To prevent any possible repetition in the future of the use of Soviet "volunteers" in the Arab world, on January 5, 1957, President Eisenhower called upon Congress to authorize the use of United States armed forces against Communist or Communist-dominated aggression in the Middle East. After prolonged debate, the Senate on March 5, by a vote of 72 to 19, approved an amended version of the Eisenhower Doctrine, which limited the discretionary power of the President. On March 9, the President signed the Middle East doctrine as passed by Congress.

Following a series of articles in the Soviet press denouncing the proposed Eisenhower Doctrine, the Soviet and Red Chinese governments on January 18 signed in Moscow a joint declaration condemning the doctrine and announcing their readiness to support the peoples of the Near and Middle East in order to prevent "aggression" and interference in their internal affairs. This "Sino-Soviet Doctrine," as reported in the Soviet press, met with an immediate and favorable response in some parts of the Arab world, especially in Cairo and Damascus.

Since the United States government had vigorously opposed the Anglo-French-Israeli invasion of Egypt, it was perhaps unfortunate that the Eisenhower Doctrine was directed solely against the threat of "armed aggression from any country controlled by international communism." At a time when American prestige had soared to new heights in the Muslim world, and especially among the Arab states, the United States government had an opportunity to propose an ironclad guarantee of protection of the Middle East against aggression from any source, communist or noncommunist. In retrospect, it seems likely that such a guarantee would have been accepted eagerly, not only by the members of the Baghdad Alliance, but likewise by the Arab states outside the Middle East bloc, thereby healing instead of accentuating the breach in the Arab world. By uniting all the Muslims states of the Near and Middle East under United States leadership, it would have erected an effective bulwark for the preservation of world peace.

As it was, the Eisenhower Doctrine offered no protection against a repetition of the Anglo-French-Israeli invasion of Egypt, other than that offered by the temporary presence of the United Nations emergency force in the Middle East. In the minds of Arab leaders, especially those in Cairo and Damascus, the recent invaders of Egypt constituted the real threat to peace and security in the Arab world. They rejected an American guarantee directed against the very Communist "volunteers" who ostensibly had just offered them "protection" against Anglo-French-Israeli invasion. Not only did the Eisenhower Doctrine fail to win the unanimous support of the Muslim world, but temporarily, at least, it split the Arab states, thereby providing the USSR with still another opportunity to use the breach to secure a Soviet foothold there.

On February 11 and again on April 21, 1957, in an effort to offset the impact of the Eisenhower Doctrine, the Soviet government called upon Great Britain, France, and the United States to join with the USSR to renounce force in the solution of the problems of the Middle East. Since the acceptance of the Soviet proposals would have been tantamount to the abandonment of the Eisenhower Doctrine and the dissolution of the Baghdad Alliance, the

United States and her European partners promptly rejected it. Shortly thereafter, the United States at a conference in Karachi pledged $12,570,000 in Eisenhower Doctrine funds for financial aid to the Baghdad Pact countries. To further strengthen the Middle East treaty powers, on June 3 the United States formally joined the Baghdad Pact Military Committee. During the Syrian crisis of September–October, 1957, the Soviet government again sought to place the Western powers at a disadvantage by repeating its propaganda gesture in favor of a Big Four declaration "denouncing force" as a means of solving disputes in the Near and Middle East.

Central Treaty Organization. In the summer of 1958 there was widely divergent reaction in the Middle East to the implementation of the Eisenhower Doctrine. Following disturbances in Lebanon and revolution in Iraq, United States troops landed at Beirut in July at the request of the Lebanese government in order to forestall further internal unrest. Although the Turks regarded United States action as "sublime," Lebanese opinion was sharply divided, and in Cairo the official press and radio voiced unqualified opposition. In Iraq, the revolutionary government of Major General Abdul Karim Kassim, undoubtedly under pressure from the USSR which provided the new regime with substantial military aid, virtually abandoned the Baghdad Alliance months before its formal withdrawal on March 24, 1959. This breach in the Northern Tier, which for a time threatened the very existence of the Baghdad Pact, amounted to a victory for the Soviet Union. To prevent further defection, the United States, which had joined the Pact's Military Committee following the Suez crisis of 1956, now agreed to participate in its antisubversive activities. Instead of becoming a formal member of the alliance, however, the Eisenhower government signed bilateral defense agreements with Turkey, Iran, and Pakistan, providing guarantees against aggression. On August 18, 1959, as a result of Iraq's withdrawal, the name of the Baghdad Pact was changed to the Central Treaty Organization.

Soviet Economic Aid. The third Soviet drive to win the Muslim East raised another new problem for the West. Prior to this time the USSR presented a challenge to the West as an ideological and as a military force. It now emerged, in addition, as an economic competitor. Having observed the effectiveness of the Marshall Plan in Europe, of American aid to Turkey and other developing areas, the Soviet government adopted these tactics as its own, not only in Eastern Europe, but in large parts of Asia and Africa. It made loans to Afghanistan, Egypt, and Indonesia, and in November, 1956, a new $126,000,000 credit to India, primarily for the purchase of heavy machinery. In its bilateral agreements the USSR, in contrast to the United States, preferred long-term, low-interest rate loans and barter deals to outright grants, frequently accepted as payment such raw materials as Egyptian cotton, Burmese rice, or Indian jute when these products were a glut on the market, and supplied limited quantities of machine tools and industrial equipment to accelerate industrialization of Asian countries. Its object was to render recipients of Soviet aid like Egypt, Afghanistan, Yemen, and Syria economically dependent on the Sino-Soviet orbit and to cut their ties with the West. One of the more spectacular examples of Soviet technical assistance, which created an impression in many countries of the Middle East, was the Soviet-Indian agreement of February 2, 1955, by which the Soviet Union undertook to provide India with an integrated iron and steel plant at Bhilai, as well as to furnish Soviet technicians to supervise its construction.

After four years of concerted effort the Soviet bloc's economic offensive was still limited in scope. It had nevertheless made significant gains in the Middle East, so much so, in fact, that the vice-president of the United States in October, 1957, termed it a greater cause for concern than the Soviet launching of the first earth satellite (sputnik). In time of crisis, it presented the countries of the Middle East with alternatives. If the West declined to build hydroelectric plants, dams, steel plants, roads, and oil refineries, etc., the USSR exploited the opportunity to its own advantage.

A careful analysis of Soviet economic aid to eighteen countries from 1954 to 1959, to the tune of approximately $2,384,000,000 (over $1,000,000,000 of which was advanced in 1958), reveals that Soviet funds were allocated to the neutrals primarily for industrial purposes.[3] In addition to the $100,000,-000 advanced for the first section of the Aswan High Dam, which serves a twofold purpose, agrarian and industrial, Soviet aid to the United Arab Republic, especially in 1959, helped Cairo to build ships, mines, airports, electric power plants and a dairy. A Soviet credit of $378,000,000 to support the Third Indian Five-Year Plan was slated to cover nine projects, all of them industrial: the expansion of the Bhilai Steel Works, a heavy machine building plant, mining equipment, fertilizer plants, newsprint, paper and printing machinery, aluminum smelting works, and new thermal plants. After the Iraq Revolution in 1958, the USSR supported Kassim's first industrial development program, which included twenty-five new plants for the manufacture of chemicals, farm machinery and electrical equipment, a steel mill, glass works and a cement plant. A Soviet loan to Ethiopia in 1959 was designed to meet similar industrial requirements.

The Soviet economic aid program to the neutral nations of Asia and Africa appeared to have two objectives—immediate and long range. The immediate objective was to create work for the unemployed and to make the recipients economically independent of the West. The long-range purpose—included as one of the objectives of the Soviet Seven-Year Plan—was the creation of an industrial skilled labor class—an Asian-African proletariat.

The failure of communism to make notable headway among the emerging nations has been attributed to the absence of strong proletariats. A revealing

3. Ivar Spector, "Russia and Afro-Asian Neutralism," *Current History,* Vol. 37 (No. 219, November 1959), pp. 272–277, 283.

article in *Kommunist* in 1962 on "The Rise of the Labor Movement in the Countries of Asia and Africa," prepared by the Institute of the Peoples of Asia of the USSR Academy of Sciences, promised that this situation would soon be changed. Since 1955 the Soviet aid and trade drive in Asia and Africa has been directed toward industrialization, with the object of creating proletariats where none existed and strengthening weak proletariats. In the non-Communist countries of Asia and Africa, according to Soviet estimates, there were by 1963 around 100,000,000 hired laborers, half of them in the three great Asian countries of Indonesia, India, and Japan, 4,000,000 in the Philippines, 2,500,000 in the UAR, 2,000,000 in Turkey, 1,500,000 in Iran, and 1,000,000 in Pakistan. These industrial proletariats, according to Soviet claims, are coming under the leadership of their Communist parties. In 1963, the Soviet press was emphasizing not so much the irrigation potentialities of the Aswan Dam as the creation there, with the help of Soviet technicians, of a new working class, fresh from the desert.

Technical Education. In the developing nations, Soviet training of workers, technicians, engineers, and scientists at educational institutions and directly at construction projects has proceeded apace. With Soviet assistance, institutes to train engineers and technicians were established in India and Burma. In December, 1962, the Bombay Technological Institute graduated its first contingent of engineers. More such institutions were planned for Indonesia, Guinea, Afghanistan, and Cambodia. By 1962 over fifty vocational training centers had been completed or were in the process of construction. In India, Soviet and Rumanian specialists trained more than 5,000 oil workers and at least as many skilled laborers at the Bhilai Steel Works. More than 6,500 Afghan workers were taught special trades by Soviet and Soviet satellite experts. In addition, it was estimated that over 10,000 students and workers from developing countries were being trained at institutes and plants in the Soviet Union and the satellite countries. These are the people that the Soviet government expects to become the leaders of tomorrow in their respective countries.

Barriers to Soviet Influence. The third Soviet drive for Muslim Asia and Africa convinced the Soviet government that three factors obstructed their efforts to bring the neutral nations into the Soviet orbit—local nationalism, Islam, and the prevalence of an illiterate and inarticulate fellahin class, or its equivalent, which comprised the bulk of the population of these countries. The Soviets were able to lend outright support to the nationalist cause. Islam they could not support, nor could they win the fellahin and peasant masses, who represented Islam.

Originally, the Soviet purpose was to make the USSR the Mecca of technology vis-à-vis Asia and to provide Soviet aid abroad for the development of agriculture. Experience taught them that Islam was a barrier to headway along these lines. The poverty-stricken fellahin and peasant masses proved to be averse to change, difficult to uproot and opposed to organization.

Industrial workers, on the other hand, are more amenable to new ideas, can be readily transplanted to jobs in other locations, and succumb more quickly to regimentation.

In Soviet Russia, too, it was the peasant class that stood between the Bolshevik regime and Sovietization. One of the main objectives of the First Five-Year Plan in Russia was to overcome this obstacle, no matter what the cost in human suffering, by transforming peasants into industrial workers and creating a Soviet proletariat.

Industrial Class. After 1955, Soviet aid and cultural propaganda were directed toward making the masses of the neutral countries, first of Asia and now of Africa, technology-minded. In other words, by promoting industrialization on these continents, the Russians hoped to accelerate the transformation of the fellahin class into a class of industrial workers. In proportion as technology and science assert themselves in Muslim countries, they believe that the hold of Islam will be weakened. Already in literature widely disseminated throughout Arabic lands, Soviet writers have utilized the sputnik successes to point out that Soviet experiments revealed the presence of neither God nor angels in outer space. Once the barrier created by Islam is broken, the USSR expects to win over the industrial proletariat with comparative ease, as was the case in the Soviet Union itself. Moreover, the Russians expect the Asian industrial proletariat to prove an asset in the contest with bourgeois regimes. The bourgeoisie, according to Soviet thinking, is more afraid of the proletariat than of domination by serfs.

Concentration on the People. In the third Soviet drive, the Russians concentrated, not on territorial annexations, but on winning over the peoples of the emerging nations, especially their intellectuals. To win the intellectuals, the Soviets opened their doors wide to Asian and African students and professional personnel, and expanded the University of the Friendship of Peoples (Lumumba University) in Moscow as a special training ground for them. By June, 1965, when the first class of 228 students were graduated, the enrolment at this university was 3,800, including 150 candidates for advanced degrees, and the faculty numbered 900. The first graduates comprised 57 from Southeast Asia and the Far East; 38 from Africa; 58 from Latin America; 31 from Arab and Near Eastern countries, and 44 from the Soviet Union. The Soviets also provided access to Soviet periodicals—both scholarly, as, for instance, *Narody Azii i Afriki (The Peoples of Asia and Africa)* and semi-popular, *Aziya i Afrika Segodnya (Asia and Africa Today)*—to provide a forum for their views. On the honorarium for a scholarly article published in a Soviet periodical, an Asian scholar is reported to be able to live comfortably for a year. As one indication of its success, the Indian-Soviet Cultural Society, founded in Bombay in 1952, a decade later had established 132 branches in various states, regions, and cities of India.

New Asian Histories. Taking advantage of the intense nationalism of the new Asian intellectuals, Soviet cultural leaders encouraged them to follow the

Wide World

Founded in 1960 especially for students from Asia, Africa, and South America, Patrice Lumumba University was named for the first prime minster of the Congo. The photograph shows students utilizing a modern method of language study.

Soviet example by rewriting their own past from an Asian rather than a Western standpoint, and reinterpreting the history of the Western world in their own image. Every Soviet periodical devoted to Asia and Africa included lists of new Soviet works on the emerging nations, anti-Western in approach, which reemphasized not only the evil influence of the West in the Orient, but also the intellectual debt of the West to the East. These works helped to set the tone for the new Asian histories.

Use of Nationalism. Although Communist ideology had apparently failed to advance Soviet interests in Asia and Africa, Soviet sponsorship and support of nationalist movements, especially in the neutral Arab world, met with considerable success. In spite of the fact that the USSR has not established a single independent Muslim state within its own borders, its perspicacity in posing as "the sole champion" of independent Muslim national states abroad elicited a warm welcome. In other words, Soviet success among the neutral nations of Asia and Africa since 1955 was due, not to its so-called Communist system, but to its constant attack on colonialism and its unequivocal support of nationalist movements. Bulganin and Khrushchev set the tone in their trek through India, Burma and Afghanistan in 1955, when their theme song was "Down with Colonialism." N. A. Mukhitdinov, chairman of the Supreme Soviet's Council of Nationalities, in his visit to the UAR in September, 1958, and other Soviet delegates to the Asian-African Conferences have received the same warm response when they followed the same line. The "thaw" in the attitude of the neutrals toward the USSR has spread, in one way or another, to most of the Arab world.

Although the Soviet regime preached internationalism to the workers of the world, emphasizing that they had no fatherland but the USSR, in Asia and Africa they discovered that nationalism was a much more potent weapon than any other "ism." They therefore used nationalism to attain a communist goal.

Solidarity Conferences. During the third drive, the Soviet government also sought to achieve its goals through the Afro-Asian People's Solidarity Conferences, the first of which was held in Cairo in December, 1957. Unlike its predecessor, the Bandung Conference of 1955, it was subjected to the direct impact of the USSR, which played an active part in the preparation of the agenda and the drafting of the resolutions. Within a few months it became an established institution with headquarters in Cairo. Its main objectives were the promotion of Arab unity and the "liberation" of the remaining dependencies of Africa and Asia from the control of the Western "colonizers." Since its founding, although Cairo has remained the headquarters, some important Asian-African cultural gatherings have been held in Tashkent, the foremost Soviet Middle Eastern center of Oriental Studies. These have included the Afro-Asian Cinema Festival (August 20–September 2, 1958), where eight Soviet Republics and fourteen Afro-Asian countries, including the Arab states of the UAR, Tunisia, and Morocco, were represented; and in October, 1958, an Afro-Asian Writers' Conference with delegates from about fifty countries of the Afro-Asian bloc, who came to seek common ground, a common hero, and a common genre in the literatures of the Afro-Asian peoples. Somewhat to the discomfiture of the Soviet government, Afro-Asian nationalists soon demonstrated their opposition to Soviet "leadership."

Role of Soviet Muslims. The Soviet Union has still another inducement to play an active role in behalf of Arab unity and Afro-Asian solidarity. It enables the Soviet regime to divert the attention of the USSR's thirty million Muslims from domestic anti-Soviet activities to pro-Soviet missionary work among the millions of Muslims beyond Soviet borders, especially in the Muslim lands of the Middle East and Africa.

The Soviet government has exerted every effort to convince its own Muslims that they are the salt of the Muslim world, that they are the most progressive, the best educated, and that it is their mission to assume leadership of the Afro-Asian Muslims. That the Soviet regime was not entirely satisfied with the results was apparent from Radio Moscow's attack on May 22, 1958, on Islam and the Muslims of the Soviet Middle East as reactionary and fanatical. There is reason to believe, however, that Soviet efforts have not been in vain, and that many Soviet Muslims are ready and willing to substitute for the "White Man's Burden" the "Soviet Burden" in Asia and Africa. One example was provided by the "Appeal of the Muslim Spiritual Leaders of the USSR to the Muslims of the World" against the landing in July, 1958, of American and British troops in Lebanon and Jordan respectively, and the demand for their immediate withdrawal. During the Lebanese crisis, there were hints about using Soviet Muslim "volunteers" against the Anglo-American occupation forces. To represent him on a state visit to the United Arab Republic in September, 1958, Nikita Khrushchev sent to Cairo the prominent Soviet Middle Easterner, Mukhitdinov.

It has become apparent that the USSR is using both its own Muslims and the eager exponents of Arab unity to promote the second major objective, the "liberation" of the entire Middle East and Africa, both Arab and non-Arab, from Western hegemony. To date, Soviet intervention has been indirect, rather than direct. Soviet Muslims prod Arab Muslims, especially those of the UAR, to take their place in the vanguard for the elimination of the vestiges of "colonialism." Even during the Near Eastern crisis of 1958, the USSR confined itself to pressing attacks on Anglo-American intervention, supported the UAR before the United Nations Security Council and Assembly, and carefully avoided the landing of Soviet troops on Arab soil.

A New Middle East. A careful study of Soviet sources, such as *Narody Azii i Afriki, Aziya i Afrika Segodnya,* and *Sovetskaya Kultura,* suggests that the ultimate Soviet objective in the Arab world is the creation of a new Middle East—one in the Soviet image. The prerequisite for this is the United Arab States, entirely divorced from the Western orbit, which will then be linked with the Soviet Middle East under Soviet Muslim leadership, that is, under the USSR. This prospect, which is present in Soviet thinking, but not spelled out for all to grasp, may well be of interest to Arab leaders who are seeking to build Arab unity with Soviet political, economic, and cultural aid.

Soviet policy in the Muslim East during the third drive envisaged the complete withdrawal of the West from Asia, physically, economically, intellectually, and spiritually.[4] According to Soviet interpretation, it was the colonial Orient that gave strength and power to the British, French, Dutch, and Portuguese empires. Without Asia (and presumably Africa), Soviet leaders expected that Europe would vegetate and decay. What the USSR had accom-

4. Ivar Spector, "Soviet Policy in Asia: A Reappraisal," *Current History,* Vol. 43 (No. 255, November 1962), pp. 257–262.

plished in forty years, Asians were assured they could do in less time with Soviet help. By advancing economic, technical, scientific, and military assistance to Asian nations, even at the expense of the vast needs of the Soviet peoples, Khrushchev sought to demonstrate that everything Asians required for liberation and development was readily available to them from the Soviet bloc.

Vostok. One of the most dramatic symbols of the Soviet focus on the Orient was the naming of the first Soviet sputnik to orbit the earth, the *Vostok* (Orient, East). As subsequent experiments in manned space flights occurred, Soviet space ships were listed *Vostok I* to *Vostok IV*. In a revealing cartoon, "Light from the *Vostok*" (East), the Soviet humor magazine, *Krokodil* (April 20, 1961) depicted the shepherds of Palestine watching, not the Star of Bethlehem, but the Soviet spaceship. In other words, the Soviet objective remains the complete de-Westernization of Asia and its reorientation toward the Union of Soviet Socialist Republics.

26

A Half Century of Soviet
Arts and Sciences, 1917-1967

LITERATURE

It is difficult to say definitively where Soviet literature begins and Russian literature ends. The Bolshevik Revolution occasioned a great upheaval in the arts as it did in politics. Many Russian writers, artists, and musicians emigrated to the West. In literature, these included Ivan Bunin, Leonid Andreyev, Dmitri Merezhkovsky, Andrei Bely, K. D. Balmont, Alexander Kuprin, Ilya Ehrenburg, and Alexei N. Tolstoy. Although Maxim Gorky, friend of Lenin, remained in Russia until 1922, he spent the following decade in Italy, still in good repute, however, with the Soviet regime. The Russian artist Ilya Repin, and several leading composers, including Sergei Prokofiev and Sergei Rachmaninov, chose the West in preference to revolutionary Russia. There were others, of course, who elected to remain in Russia to continue their work. These included the symbolist poets Alexander Blok (d. 1921) and Valery Bruisov (d. 1924) and the imagist poet Sergei Esenin (committed suicide 1925). Only a handful, including the peasant writer Demyan Bedny and the futurist Vladimir Mayakovsky, the latter boisterously acclaiming Militant Communism, actually threw in their lot with the Revolution. In the confusion of revolution, civil conflict, and foreign intervention, the new regime had little time for writers and artists, other than those who, like Mayakovsky, became willing propagandists. Lenin, Trotsky, Gorky, and Lunacharsky lent their support to *Proletcult,* an organization founded in 1920 to lay the foundations for a communist (proletarian) culture, not only in Russia, but throughout the world.

NEP Policy. Under the NEP the Soviet government in general pursued a policy of free and easy tolerance of writers and artists. This was a period of great, and often exaggerated experimentation in form and style, and also of infinite variety. Soviet fiction began to replace poetry as the chief form of literary expression. In the theater, Vsevelod Meyerhold and Eugene Vakhtangov (d. 1922), pupils of Stanislavsky, voluntarily backed the "Left Front of Literature" (LEF), and the former attempted to bring the spirit of the October Revolution to the stage. Sergei Eisenstein, known for his creative work in cinematography, attained worldwide fame with his film *Potemkin* (1925), an interpretation of the Revolution of 1905. Even Boris Pasternak continued to produce lyrical poems of real merit. Humor and satire found expression in the works of Valentin Katayev, Mikhail Zoshchenko, and the literary collaborators Ilya Ilf and Eugene Petrov. Lulled by this demonstration of tolerance and stirred by the atmosphere of ferment in the arts, some of the émigrés returned to Soviet Russia, including Ilya Ehrenburg and A. N. Tolstoy in 1923, and the composer Prokofiev temporarily in 1927, when he became a Soviet citizen. Many of these "Fellow Travellers," as Trotsky labelled them, went along with the new regime, without actually subscribing to it by joining the Communist Party. Much of the literature produced was devoted to the Revolution, Civil War, and reconstruction periods.

Five-Year Plan Literature. The Five-Year Plan brought the casual handling of the arts to an abrupt conclusion. Under the leadership of the notorious Leopold Averbakh, the Russian Association of Proletarian Writers (RAPP), from its founding in 1928 to its demise in 1932 maintained a literary dictatorship of the arts, under which shock brigades of writers, dramatists, poets, and artists were expected to mobilize their cohorts to achieve the purposes of the Five-Year Plan. There followed an epidemic of Five-Year Plan novels, such as F. V. Gladkov's *Power,* Valentin Katayev's *Time, Forward!,* and much the best work in this category, Mikhail Sholokhov's *Virgin Soil Upturned.* Although in 1932 the RAPP was superseded by the Union of Soviet Writers, of which Maxim Gorky became president, the control of the arts was not substantially relaxed, only its direction changed. Proletarian writers and Fellow Travellers became "Soviet writers." All the arts were expected to conform to the new doctrine of "socialist realism," the three main tenets of which were socialist content, national form, and realistic presentation. Further experimentation in literary techniques was abjured as "formalism." Literature came to be regarded as a "weapon" to stimulate Soviet patriotism and a reinterpretation of the Russian past. In 1934, two years after his death, the leading Soviet historian, Michael Pokrovsky (1868–1932), was denounced for his undiscriminating attack on the rulers of tsarist Russia. Nor did the arts escape the impact of the purges of 1936–1938. D. S. Mirsky, a princely convert to communism, well known for his *History of Russian Literature,* Isaac Babel, and Boris Pilnyak disappeared in 1937. Even Maxim Gorky died under mysterious circumstances in 1936.

Soviet literature, to an even greater extent than tsarist literature, is closely interwoven with current events. For the most part it has mirrored Soviet policies under Militant Communism, the NEP, and the Five-Year Plans. For the study of Soviet history, therefore, the literature is an indispensable collateral, and in many instances, a primary source.

Vladimir Mayakovsky (1893–1930). The works of the extrovert poet, dramatist, and painter, Vladimir Mayakovsky, constitute one of the best sources on the era of Militant Communism, 1917–1922. Mayakovsky, who had predicted for 1916 the "thorny crown of revolution" (*In a Cloud in Trousers,* 1915), was fully prepared "to rush into the future, undismayed." Like others on the extremist fringe, he was prepared to throw overboard Pushkin, Dostoyevsky, and Tolstoy. Even Lenin, who enjoyed Pushkin and Nekrasov, had difficulty in appreciating the staccato rhythm of Mayakovsky's *Left March* (1918). Mayakovsky's play in verse, *Mystery-Bouffe* (1918), a heroic rhapsody of the Revolution, carried out in drama the Trotskyite concept of permanent revolution, which preached no compromise with the capitalist world. Because the Chinese Communists in the 1960's are approximately where the Russians were in the years immediately following the Bolshevik Revolution, this play contributes to an understanding of the ideological controversy between Red China and the USSR.

For a time Mayakovsky, the iconoclast, who discarded all accepted literary canons, was the uncrowned poet laureate of the Russian Revolution. His popularity was due, in part, to the fact that many Russian writers boycotted the Bolshevik Revolution, or their works were totally divorced from the ideology of the new regime. By 1920–1921, however, Mayakovsky was lamenting that the storms of revolt were as dead as the tsar. As Militant Communism receded, his star declined. This man who, according to Ilya Ehrenberg, was "never in conflict with the Revolution," was unable personally to adjust himself to the compromises of the NEP and the regimentation of the Five-Year Plan. He committed suicide on April 14, 1930. Had he lived longer, it is likely that he would have become a victim of the purges, along with other Trotskyites. Since he died in time, he continued to be extolled as the poet of the Revolution, although little or no reference was made to the play *Mystery-Bouffe.*

Panteleiman Romanov (1884–1936). Soviet life under the NEP, 1922–1928, especially the plight of former intellectuals and the intelligentsia, finds its best portrayal in a novel by Fellow Traveller Panteleiman Romanov, published under the title *Comrade Kisliakov, or Three Pairs of Silk Stockings.* Its two principal characters were Hippolite Kisliakov, an ex-engineer who, after the Revolution, sought to bury his former identity as an employee in a museum (the only cultural work remaining for intellectuals like him), and Tamara, wife of the scientist Arkady Nesnamov, who subordinated everything else in life to her passion to become a great actress. Tamara's fleeting interest in Kisliakov, together with her affections, were soon transferred to a foreign cinema producer named Miller, who cynically remarked that any Russian woman could be bought for three pairs of silk stockings, with the addition, in some cases, of a bottle of perfume.

Romanov's novel revealed the prevailing attitude toward the former intelligentsia, appropriately consigned, like mummies, to the museum, along with other relics of the past. It vividly depicted the moral degeneration of the intelligentsia, which reached its nadir under the NEP. Miller's allegation was to Romanov an indictment, not merely of one group, but of all Russian womanhood. At the same time, this novel implied that irrespective of official contempt for the old intelligentsia, a society must have brains as well as brawn. Either an effort must be made to rehabilitate or win over the old intelligentsia for service to the state, or a new Soviet intelligentsia must be created. "If we cannot," wrote Romanov, "then we shall degenerate, because no social group can exist without a purpose." His novel may be said to have inaugurated an era of "self-criticism," which was indispensable to the building of a new society. In this respect, it marked a striking departure from the literature of Militant Communism.

Among the host of Soviet writers during the period of the pre-war Five-Year Plans, the most outstanding were Valentin Katayev, Boris Pilnyak (Vogau), Nikolai Pogodin, Alexei N. Tolstoy, and Mikhail Sholokhov.

Valentin Katayev (1897–   ). Katayev's works included several novels, among them *The Embezzlers* (1926), a clever satire about a couple of rascally Soviet officials who absconded with some 12,000 rubles of state funds; *Time, Forward!* (1933), a racy and original account of a competition in cement pouring at Magnitogorsk; and *Peace Is Where the Tempests Blow (Lonely White Sail,* 1936), a semi-autobiographical account of the Revolution of 1905 in Odessa. His most significant contribution from the standpoint of this period, however, was his play *Squaring the Circle* (1928).

Squaring the Circle dealt with the life and love problems of three serious-minded members of the Komsomol (Young Communist's League), and one flighty "kittenish" young bride, interested in her appearance and in bourgeois creature comforts. Vasya, a simple, direct, and unassuming young Communist, having married the light-headed Ludmilla, brought her home to the bare and unattractive room he shared with his friend Abram. Shortly thereafter, Abram, who had married the serious and bookish but good-looking young Communist Tonya, in complete ignorance of his roommate's action, brought his wife to share the same room. The play deals with the efforts of the two young couples to adjust themselves to the problems of wedded life in such congested quarters. Ludmilla, the domestic type, soon made of her half of the room a home replete with comfort and a well-stocked larder. Tonya, absorbed in Marxist literature, made no effort to improve her living quarters or to attend to domestic affairs. In the course of the play, the young couples discovered that they were badly mated. Abram and Ludmilla fell in love. Vasya and Tonya, unaware of what had happened to the others, followed suit. Comrade Flavius, an older Bolshevik, who acted as benevolent adviser to his young friends, decided that love and the unscrambling of their too hasty marriages could not hurt the Revolution.

Beginning essentially where Romanov left off, *Squaring the Circle* described conditions on the eve of the First Five-Year Plan. Following Romanov's plea for a new or rehabilitated intelligentsia, Katayev made it clear that the forthcoming Soviet leadership, as represented by the existing Komsomol membership, was neither mature enough nor sufficiently well qualified to handle the tremendous tasks that lay ahead. In other words, a bookish knowledge of ideology was no substitute for technological training. By implication, the works of Karl Marx could not in themselves provide the necessities of life for the Soviet people. Thus *Squaring the Circle* helped to condition Russians, and also the Communist Party, for the employment in key positions under the forthcoming Five-Year Plan of non-Party and even foreign specialists from capitalist countries.

Squaring the Circle for the first time removed the taboo on love, as far as Communists were concerned. Heretofore, Party members were discouraged from "falling in love." Relations between the sexes had been placed on a purely physiological basis. In the process of untangling the relations of the two young couples in this play, Katayev showed how matters were remedied when they loved one another. "Love," according to the benevolent old Bolshevik, Comrade Flavius, "cannot hurt the Revolution." In other words, Katayev's play reflected the fact that love had become respectable in Soviet Russia.

Boris Pilnyak (1894–1937?). Boris Pilnyak, more Populist than revolutionary in outlook, first attracted serious attention with *The Naked Year* (1922), an unusual novel of how Russians had rediscovered themselves through the cruelty, lust, and famine of the revolutionary upheaval. In a subsequent work, *The Volga Falls to the Caspian Sea* (1930), Pilnyak went beyond Katayev to present the Five-Year Plan in full swing. The tempo of Moscow at that time was strikingly revealed in one of the early passages of this novel:

> Beneath the walls of the Kremlin spread the Moscow of the year 1929, with its colossal courage and colossal tension. Moscow, highly strung in every respect, to the verge of convulsions, like all of the USSR, maintained a soldier's pace in the military march to socialism, in order to emerge victorious. History in those years did not proceed at a walking pace; it ran; it did not flow, but was built. Had a uniform been introduced for the guilds of builders, Russia would be like an army in motion. Indeed, that year Russia lived the life of an armed camp, with her grey, heroic, humdrum days, which resembled a soldier's great coat; with her heroic orders establishing martial law, brooking no opposition, lining up for her supplies as in an embattled city, yet in a manner that was not terrifying.

Pilnyak's novel was about a huge construction project near Kolomna, a dam on the Moscow-Volga Canal, the ultimate purpose of which was to create an unbroken shipping route from the Caspian Sea to the Soviet capital. Involved in the project were engineers who supported it, as well as others who, instigated by a foreign power (England), plotted to sabotage it. Although the would-be "wreckers" ultimately failed, the Communist hero drowned in the waters held back by the dam. The engineers Sadykov and Lyubov, the woman he loved, found a new horizon in the prospect of a huge irrigation works on the lower Volga, the purpose of which was to stem the advance of the desert into European Russia.

This novel vividly portrayed the clash between the new Russia, which was bent on constructive work, and the old which resisted and sabotaged the changes being wrought by the Five-Year Plan. Through the Communists, Sadykov and Lyubov, Pilnyak registered Soviet Russia's return to conventional morality, labelled a "new morality," which rejected the loose living generally condoned during the early years of the Soviet regime. *The Volga Falls to the Caspian Sea,* in which the author combined two earlier works, amounted to a sweeping reappraisal on the part of the representatives of different classes of people of all aspects of life in Soviet Russia.

In 1931, Pilnyak visited the United States, the inspiration for his novel *O.K.* (1932), which aroused the ire of Soviet critics because it was too friendly to America. Pilnyak disappeared from sight in 1937, presumably a victim of the Stalin purges.

Nikolai Pogodin (1900–1962). Instead of writing of native engineers, as Pilnyak had done, Nikolai Pogodin in his documentary drama *Tempo* (1929) held up for emulation a super-efficient American engineer named Carter, modelled after a Mr. Kidler who actually supervised the construction of the Stalingrad Tractor Plant. Carter effectively demonstrated that with American methods and American direction even the *muzhiks,* "the human raw material of the Five-Year Plan," could break American records of production. Carter, who had no time for, nor inclination toward, Marxist politics, had come to Russia to do a job and to do it efficiently, even when confronted with the ignorant and uncooperative peasant labor available, still in fear of hospitals and cars. This play made the term "American" synonymous with efficiency. It paved the way for the use of American brains and American knowhow in other construction projects under the Five-Year Plans. Probably Americans have never been so popular in Russia before or since. It is significant that *Tempo* was withdrawn from circulation in the USSR when the Cold War began in 1947.

In a later play, *Aristocrats* (1934), based on the construction of the White Sea-Baltic Sea Canal by means of labor from the concentration camp, Pogodin dealt with the regeneration of prostitutes, common criminals, and even *kulaks* through the cleansing process of constructive labor. The moral transformation of class enemies henceforth became a popular theme in Soviet fiction, although it seems to have reflected the influence of Dostoyevsky rather than of Marx.

Alexei N. Tolstoy (1882–1945). After the death of Maxim Gorky in 1936, Alexei Tolstoy, son of an aristocratic landowner and a relative of Leo Tolstoy, became the dean of Soviet writers. In 1919, after serving in the propaganda section of Denikin's army, Tolstoy was forced to leave Russia via Odessa. As an émigré he lived for a time in Paris, where he began his novel *Khozhdenie po mukam (The Road to Calvary),* a picture of Russian society on the eve of the Revolution and during its opening stages, which was later revised in Soviet Russia to eliminate its anti-communist bias, and which was awarded the Stalin Prize in *belles-lettres* in 1942. From Paris Tolstoy proceeded to Berlin where he wrote *Aelita* (1922), a fantastic account after the manner of H. G. Wells of a Soviet expedition to Mars, which culminated in a Marxian revolution there. This pioneer example of Soviet "science fiction" was revised in Russia, dramatized, and filmed in 1924. In the spring of 1923 Tolstoy returned to Soviet Russia, where he became a living example of the Soviet government's reconciliation with the former intelligentsia. Although his outlook was essentially that of a Russian nationalist, Tolstoy enjoyed a huge success in the USSR, lived the comfortable life to which he was addicted, and produced a formidable number of novels, plays, short stories, film scenarios, pamphlets, and articles.

Alexei Tolstoy's fame rests on his two major historical novels, *Peter I* (1929–1934) and *The Road to Calvary* (1921–1942).

Peter I, regarded by some as Tolstoy's masterpiece, is a novel about Peter the Great (1682–1725), based on authentic historical materials. Although RAPP frowned upon the book when it first appeared, it soon became the official Soviet interpretation of the tsar who attempted to Europeanize Russia in a generation. A dramatic version, based on the novel, appeared in 1930. Finally, when Part I was filmed in 1937 under Eisenstein's direction, A. Tolstoy became the most widely known writer in the USSR, with the possible exception of Mikhail Sholokhov. The final sections of the monumental novel were not published until 1944–1945.

Best known for his historical novels, Alexei Tolstoy was also a dramatist. This scene is from a 1944 production of *Ivan the Terrible*, with People's Artist Konstantin Zubov in the title role.

Perhaps the main reason for the popularity of *Peter I* was the striking parallel it afforded between the Russia of Peter and the Russia of Stalin under the Five-Year Plan. Peter was boldly presented as the monarch whose aim was to revolutionize the traditional mode of Russian life, irrespective of the opposition of privileged landowners, hostile clergy, and an apathetic and indifferent public. In spite of Tolstoy's denial of any didactic motives, the picture inevitably called to mind the efforts of Stalin to bring about the collectivization of agriculture and the industrialization of Soviet Russia by means of the Five-Year Plan, no matter what the cost in human or financial terms. In both instances, there was opposition, even to the point of sabotage, to the tempo with which these changes were carried out.

Peter I set in motion a revaluation and reinterpretation of the Russian past on the part of contemporary Soviet writers. From the Russian standpoint, it was an epoch-making work, since it restored the link between Soviet and tsarist Russia, broken by the Bolshevik Revolution of 1917. With the appearance of this novel, it became increasingly clear that there were far-sighted and capable monarchs, military leaders, statesmen, and writers before the Revolution, and that it was no longer possible to tar them all with the same brush. It was, therefore, no accident that innumerable heroes of the past, like Dmitry Donskoi, Alexander Nevsky, General Suvorov, Field Marshal Kutuzov, and Ivan Grozny, were resurrected and presented from the standpoint of socialist realism. This trend reflected the growth of a national socialism in the USSR, soon to be intensified by World War II.

In his trilogy, *The Road to Calvary,* completed on June 22, 1941, the very day of the Nazi invasion of the Soviet Union, Tolstoy dealt with the impact on members of St. Petersburg society of events on the eve of World War I, during that conflict, and in the early stages of the Soviet regime. The results were most convincing. Tolstoy portrayed the moral and spiritual degeneration of the Russian upper classes and intelligentsia in the capital even prior to the outbreak of the war. From the standpoint of the Soviet regime, the real significance of this work lay in its final chapter, which amounted to a justification of the Bolshevik seizure of power. Tolstoy was perhaps the first outstanding novelist of Russian aristocratic origin to accept the October Revolution. As Roshchin whispered into Katya's ear:

> Can you see now how purposeful all our efforts, all the blood we shed, all our unsung and uncomplaining torments have become? We shall rebuild the world, a better world. All these people here in this hall are willing to give their lives for that. And this is not mere words—they can show you the scars and the blue marks of bullets. And this is happening here, in my country, and this is Russia!

Perhaps as a student of technology in Russia and Germany Tolstoy had a particular flair for construction.

It was undoubtedly his glorification of the Bolshevik Revolution that earned Alexei Tolstoy the Stalin Prize in 1942. Like his great predecessor Leo Tolstoy, he hated war. He claimed that he would like to take the reader who clamored for "heroic feats" to the battlefield to show him "a decayed horse or a Turk whose head was devoured by a jackal, or let loose upon that same reader ten thousand lice." *The Road to Calvary* is sometimes compared to *War and Peace,* although Alexei Tolstoy was an eye-witness to the events he described, whereas Leo Tolstoy based his great classic on historical archives.

Mikhail Sholokhov (1905–   ). The most outstanding writer of the Soviet period under consideration was Mikhail Sholokhov, a Don Cossack. He is best known for his *Tales of the Don* (1924–1926), *Virgin Soil Upturned* (1932), and *The Silent Don* (1926–1940).

The sixteen *Tales of the Don* represented the spadework for Sholokhov's masterpiece, *The Silent Don.* In them he recorded dramatic wayside incidents of the Civil War among the Don Cossacks. Sholokhov wrote them during the NEP. These tales were typical of Sholokhov's work, in that they reflected the colors, sights, sounds, and especially the smells of the Cossack village where, instead of automobiles, there were horses; instead of garages, stables; instead of the odor of gasoline, the smell of "horse's sweat" and steaming cow dung. The entire collection depicted the *Klassenkampf* between Cossack converts to the new Soviet regime and the irreconcilable adherents of the traditional Cossack order, especially the *kulaks.* Many tales described the bitter conflict of father against son, and of brother against brother. The disruption of family ties was summed up by Misha, a diehard White officer: "Mother dear, as an officer and loyal son of the silent Don, I must ignore all family ties. Whether it be father or blood brother—it's all the same. I'll hand them over to be court-martialed" (*The Diehard*). In these tales, the White Cossacks were by and large the villains responsible for a succession of unspeakably cruel and sadistic atrocities. Bolshevik sympathizers emerged as more humane and more altruistic than their White counterparts. This apparent lack of objectivity distinguished these tales from *The Silent Don,* where Sholokhov freely attributed atrocities to both sides—the Reds and the Whites. Even in his later work, however, he seemed to feel more sympathy for Ilya Bunchuk and Mishka Koshevoy than for Eugene Listnitsky, the Cossack officer.

In *Virgin Soil Upturned* (1932–1933), Sholokhov portrayed the vicissitudes of collectivization among the Cossacks of Gremachy Log, a village on the Don. This book, an account of the struggle between Davydov, Communist ex-sailor and metal worker turned farm hand, and the local *kulaks,* remains one of the best descriptions of rural collectivization. The novel was expanded by Sholokhov after World War II. As late as the summer of 1963 a dramatized version was presented to enthusiastic Moscow audiences in the Kremlin Theater.

In his great epic, *The Silent Don,* Sholokhov depicted the life of the Melekhovs, a typical Don Cossack family of the village of Tatarsk on the Don. Beginning with the tsarist regime on the eve of World War I, he followed the checkered course of their lives during the war, the Revolution, and the fratricidal Civil War to the triumph of the Soviet regime. Grigory Melekhov, the principal character of the novel, like many of his countrymen during the struggle between the Reds and the Whites, drifted back and forth from one side to the other, returning home after the Civil War disillusioned with the excesses of both factions. It was Dzherzhinsky, who based an opera on this novel, and not Sholokhov, who made of Grigory a real Soviet hero.

Perhaps because Sholokhov depicted for the first time the class struggle among the Cossacks, enjoyed wide popularity as a proletarian writer, and was actually a member of the Communist Party (beginning 1932), as well as a deputy to the Supreme Soviet, *The Silent Don* became one of the rare examples of freedom of thought and expression in Soviet literature. No doubt Soviet policy of conciliating the minorities, instead of continuing to regard them as a liability, was in Sholokhov's favor. In any event, he wrote as a free Cossack, and Soviet literature is much the richer for his efforts.

Like A. N. Tolstoy's *Road to Calvary* and Leo Tolstoy's *War and Peace,* with which it is often compared, *The Silent Don* is an historical epic. Sholokhov, like Alexei Tolstoy, described the tremendous upheaval of his own era in which he participated, and in this sense his novel may be considered autobiographical. Instead of the broad canvas of Leo Tolstoy, Sholokhov's work was regional in scope, confined to the Cossacks of the Don, with whose everyday lives he was intimately acquainted. Both A. N. Tolstoy and Mikhail Sholokhov carried on the tradition of the classical Russian novel.

Sholokhov's works have created a better appreciation of the Russian Cossacks, who before the Revolution were employed by the tsars to break up strikes, suppress liberal movements, and quell uprisings in brief, to make Russia safe for autocracy and reaction. A Cossack himself, Sholokhov was able to show that not all Cossacks were as black as they were painted. He distinguished between rich and poor, good and evil, educated and illiterate, reactionary and progressive. In other words, he showed the Cossacks to be much like other people. Although Lermontov, Gogol, and Leo Tolstoy also wrote of Cossack life, their works were confined mainly to romantic and dashing episodes, reminiscent of the adventures of American cowboys and Indians in the American wild West. Sholokhov's work was an all-embracing epic of an agricultural people, presented from the standpoint of realism, rather than romanticism.

It is no exaggeration to say that Sholokhov's works were an important factor in winning over the younger generation of Cossacks to the Soviet regime. These Red Cossacks played a significant role in the defense of the USSR in World War II. Nor was it an accident that a new edition of the Sholokhov *Tales* was published in the Soviet Union in 1958. The vicissitudes of the herdsman, watchman, farm laborer, felter, and other destitute or maltreated Cossacks served as a reminder of their plight some forty years ago, as compared with their position today.

CONTROVERSY: THE "POSITIVE" SOVIET MAN

The controversy that raged prior to the death of Stalin (March 5, 1953), over the creation and delineation of positive and negative characters in Soviet literature, was revived on the eve of the convocation of the Second All-Union Congress of Soviet Writers in Moscow in December, 1954. As in the case of the First Congress held twenty years earlier (in August, 1934), this was a time for literary stocktaking, designed to set the pattern for Soviet writers in the years ahead. The doctrine of socialist realism, proclaimed at the First Congress, was interpreted in such a way as to ban the presentation of negative leading characters in Soviet literature. This ban was imposed, not only on the literatures of the Slavic and non-Slavic Soviet minorities inside the USSR, but also on the literary output of the Soviet orbit, from the Slavic satellites of Eastern Europe to Red China.

The dispute over the role of positive and negative types in Soviet literature, which reached its peak in 1952, followed the controversy in the USSR over biological science (1948) and that over linguistics (1950). In all three instances, the Stalin government's propaganda tactics were, by and large, the same. The Soviet press aired the pros and cons, following which the mouthpiece of the government and the Party stepped in, rendered a decision, and mapped out the "correct" line of procedure. Although in the settlement of the controversy over genetics the principle of constant change, as set forth in Marxian dialectics, was adhered to, in the linguistic and literary decisions there appeared to be a marked departure from Marxian principles; dynamism gave way to a recognition of the static element, plus natural growth and transformation.

The champions of the positive Soviet type soon discovered that existing Soviet literature provided them with a foundation on which to build and with examples for them to emulate. They traced the positive type back to Gorky, especially to his novel *Mother;* to A. Serafimovitch's *The Iron Stream;* to D. Furmanov's *Chapayev,* where the power behind Chapayev was Klytchkov, the commissar; to A. Fadeyev's *The Rout (The Nineteen),* which was recommended even more than *The Young Guard;* to Sholokhov's *Virgin Soil Upturned;* to Pyotr Pavlenko's *Happiness;* to S. Babayevsky's *Cavalier of the Gold Star;* and to Mikhail Bubennov's war novel, *The White Birch,* where the commissar, Yakhno, although not the main character, plays the same role as Klytchkov in *Chapayev.*

In the spring of 1953, even Russia's distant past was being combed for positive characters. Alexei Yugov, reviewing *Origins of Russian Literature* (1952) by D. S. Likhachev, unearthed positive types in the Russian literature of the tenth to the thirteenth centuries!

Two novels which, because of their wide popularity, became the focal point of much of the discussion about positive and negative types, were Alexander

Fadeyev's *The Young Guard* (1945) and Boris Polevoy's *Story of a Real Man* (1947).

Alexander Fadeyev (1901–1956). *The Young Guard* stressed the superiority of the existing Soviet system from a military, political, economic, and especially from an educational standpoint. By 1947, however, the author was accused of "deviation," because of his failure to portray the leading Bolshevik characters as positive and active types. In compliance with the new trend, Fadeyev in 1951 brought out a revised version of his novel, in which the leader of the underground youth organization, Lyutikov, and his associates stand out as positive characters, worthy of emulation.

Boris Polevoy (1908–   ). *A Story of a Real Man* (1947), by Polevoy, appeared as if in answer to the prayers of Soviet propagandists for some means of stemming the tide of discontent over domestic conditions in the USSR after the close of World War II. It became virtually an integral part of the Soviet program for the readjustment and rehabilitation of millions of Soviet veterans and displaced persons who had returned to their homes following that cataclysm. Although ostensibly a war novel, the indomitable hero Meresyev served as an example for all maimed or destitute Soviet citizens to emulate. The "real man" was soon identified with the "contemporary man" or the "Soviet man," as distinct from the "historical man" who rose to unprecedented popularity in the war years. The heroes of Russia's past—as represented by men like Alexander Nevsky, Ivan Grozny, Peter the Great, Generals Suvorov and Kutuzov, and even Chapayev—once peace was restored gave way to the Soviet hero, the contemporary Soviet man. He was to be, above all, a positive type, in essence a superior man, in marked contrast to most of the fictional characters depicted in postwar Western literature.

Dissenting Viewpoints. Some Soviet writers and critics, like Vera Panova, best known as the author of *The Train* (*Companions,* 1946), resisted the growing pressure for a ban on negative characters. She argued that if all leading characters were to be positive and unmarred by negative traits they would cease to be typical and Soviet literature could no longer claim to be realistic. For having the temerity, in one of her novels, *A Year's Span*, to imply that the children of Communists sometimes turned out to be scoundrels, as in the case of Dorofeya Kuprianova's son, Vera Panova was severely criticized in the Soviet press in 1954. *Pravda* alleged that the author, on three occasions a Stalin prize winner, was out of step with the times, that in the socialist epoch it was unnecessary to write about "petit bourgeois happiness and troubles." In spite of this barrage of criticism, Vera Panova was elected to the board of directors of the Union of Soviet Writers in December, 1954, and was honored by Leningrad writers on her fiftieth birthday (April 1, 1955) for her literary achievements.

B. Rurikov, deputy editor-in-chief of *Literaturnaya Gazeta,* also lashed out at those writers who insisted that all negative characters were untrue to Soviet life, as if chairmen of works committees with disagreeable personalities did not exist; as if there were no women leading idle and useless lives; no managers who failed to support innovations; no collective farmers who persisted in rejecting new methods of cotton growing, etc. He condemned such writers for producing "model picture-book heroes," and insisted that they were all in a muddle as to what was or was not typical. In fact, he claimed that they were using the label "untypical" to distract attention from negative facts. Incidentally, Rurikov was removed from *Literaturnaya Gazeta*'s editorial board in December, 1952, and was not reinstated until August, 1953.

New Definition of "Typical." This literary debate over the delineation of positive and negative characters continued until G. M. Malenkov, in his report to the Nineteenth Party Congress on October 5, 1952, handed down a new definition of the term "typical," which at once set the tone for Soviet writers throughout the USSR, and shortly thereafter throughout the Soviet orbit:

> In creating artistic images, our artists and writers must always bear in mind that the typical is not only what is most often encountered. The typical is that which most fully and vividly expresses the essence of a given social force. In the Marxist-Leninist concept, the typical does not necessarily mean the specific statistical average. Typicalness corresponds to the essence of a given socio-historical phenomenon and is not simply what is most widespread, most often repeated, most common. A deliberately magnified image, brought out in salient relief, does not exclude typicalness, but more fully reveals and emphasizes it. Typicalness is the main sphere of the manifestation of partisanship in realistic art. The problem of typicalness is always the problem of politicality.

Needless to say, Malenkov's pronouncement evoked a flood of favorable comment in the Soviet press and periodicals at various levels. The many articles and editorials that appeared, whether in *Pravda, Kommunist, Literaturnaya Gazeta, Znamya,* or elsewhere, lined up the Soviet literary world on the side of Malenkov, in what amounted to a ban on negative leading characters in Soviet literature. The numerous articles and reviews that appeared following the Malenkov pronouncement, irrespective of the number or where they were published, were all in the same vein.

Literary Climate. After the death of Stalin, Ilya Ehrenburg, writing in *Znamya,* vigorously protested against existing bureaucratic controls on literature and demanded greater freedom for the author and the artist in the USSR. A new Ehrenburg novel, with the suggestive title *The Thaw* (1954), reemphasized the same goal. The flurry of excitement aroused by his temerity was of short duration. On the eve of the convocation of the Second Congress of Soviet Writers, the literary climate in the Soviet Union indicated that instead of greater freedom, more rigid controls were in store for Soviet authors. Following publication of his lengthy and unorthodox poem *Space Beyond Space* (October, 1954), Alexander Tvardovsky was temporarily dismissed from the editorship of *Novyi Mir*. Nevertheless, the literary climate "thawed" sufficiently to permit the republication in 1955 of the works of Dostoyevsky.

The down-grading of Stalin, with the accompanying barrage against "the cult of personality," which began in 1953 and came to the fore with Khrushchev's now famous speech in February, 1956, appeared to herald a radical change in emphasis on positive and negative characters in Soviet literature. Although some Soviet critics have paid lip service to the evils of overemphasis on Soviet hero worship and now quote Lenin instead of Stalin as their authority on literary problems, as yet there appears to be no basic departure from the earlier ban on negative leading characters. When Pogodin's new play, *We Three Went to the Virgin Lands,* was attacked in *Pravda* for its lack of positive characters and positive action, the author promptly succumbed to pressure and promised to revise it. Although Soviet critics, such as V. Ozerov, have continued to demand the liquidation of the remnants of the cult of personality, at the same time they have advocated the delineation of typical, positive groups of characters, with the collective approach at times superseding the emphasis on the individual Soviet hero. B. Rurikov, writing in *Pravda* in 1956 on "Literature and the Life of the People," continued to encourage the depiction of Soviet society as it ought to be, with stress on the positive types. Even while emphasizing that every artist has the right to create freely in accordance with his ideal, Rurikov took his stand with Lenin in the basic qualification of that freedom: "But, of course, we are Communists. We must not stand idly by and permit chaos to develop at will. We must have a complete plan to direct this process and to determine its results."

In 1955 the official Party organ, *Kommunist,* although it denounced the "scholastic" and dogmatic approach of many contemporary Soviet writers and critics to the problem of typicalness in literature, and reinterpreted Gorky's sanction of the use of exaggeration in order to attain typicality, nevertheless reaffirmed the importance of the creation of positive characters, who synthesize "the best, typical traits of character and spiritual make-up of the Soviet man." The Party's warnings against scholasticism and dogmatism produced only a modification of the general thesis—an admission that typicalness can be achieved by various means, and not through exaggeration alone:

> The artistic principles and methods for creating typical characters used in the novel differ from those used in a lyrical or satirical work. Drama has its own laws and its own poetics for the creation of typical characters. The object of delineation and the artist's very approach to delineation, by which the artist is guided, exercise a decisive influence on the methods of typification during the creative process.
>
> Nothing but harm can result from canonizing some single method of typification and dogmatically asserting its priority over many other methods,

without taking into consideration all the complexities of artistic practice and the development of literature and art. The multiform artistic methods of typification cannot be reduced to exaggeration alone.

If the current trend in Soviet literature should continue without drastic change for the next few years, it may well contribute to an unhealthy climate of opinion in the Soviet Union. The emphasis on the positive Soviet man in literature is almost certain to produce a generation imbued with the idea of a Soviet *Herrenvolk,* or superman. In line with the crusade for the transformation of nature, the Soviet people are also to be remade and imbued with the belief that they are superior to anything that has existed before. In the words of Ilya Matveyevitch Zhurbin, veteran shipyard metalworker in V. Kotchetov's novel *The Zhurbins:* "The *human* ore that has been growing hotter year by year since 1917, has started now to boil and bubble; a metal has been smelting there the like of which the world has never seen." In other words, the new Soviet man is not a man created in the image of God, but a product of the Soviet era. He challenges God and seeks to remake both man and nature.

This indoctrination apparently is designed to render Soviet citizens immune to foreign ideologies, as their contacts with the Western world increase. Thus Soviet literature continues to follow Zhdanov's oft-reiterated injunction to serve the interests of the state. This type of literature will continue to provide a distorted and idealistic rather than realistic portrait of the Soviet man. For the characters will be neither positive nor negative, neither realistic nor typical. They can be typical only of the state apparatus—of the Party. This distortion of realism can only produce "lives of Soviet saints." Barring a world upheaval, this fantastic distortion, under the guise of "a positive Soviet man," will affect the thinking of the hundreds of millions of people within the Soviet orbit in Europe and Asia. Finally, the only redeeming feature in connection with this Soviet hero worship is that it may produce an unlooked for and unwanted revival of individualism, which might eventually prove detrimental to Communism and to statism.

V. Dudintsev (1918–   ). The publication in 1956 of V. Dudintsev's novel *Not By Bread Alone,* which clearly revealed the struggle of the positive individual against collectivism, left those responsible for the molding and shaping of Soviet literature profoundly shaken. Although his hero proved to be right and the collective power wrong, obviously it was not the purpose of Dudintsev to undermine the Soviet system of collectivism. His emphasis on the frustrating experiences of the inventor, Lopatkin, who designed a centrifugal pipe-casting machine of considerable value only to have it rejected by the Soviet bureaucracy, nevertheless produced that result. Because of the disturbance created by this novel, Soviet critics who continued to advocate the delineation of the positive character emphasized early in 1957 that this must not be done at the expense of collectivism and Communist discipline:

"Creative activity in the field of literature and art must be imbued with the spirit of the struggle for Communism, must instill in the heart courage and firmness of conviction, must develop socialist consciousness and comradely discipline."

As was the case with many of his predecessors, Dudintsev succumbed to pressure and "revised" his novel. Its very title nevertheless challenged forty years of Soviet materialistic indoctrination, serving as a reminder to the peoples of the USSR that "man does not live by bread alone . . ."

Boris Pasternak (1890–1960). In 1957 another novel, *Dr. Zhivago,* by one of Russia's foremost poets, Boris Pasternak, evoked even greater controversy, both inside the USSR and abroad. The name *Zhivago* is derived from the Russian verb *zhit,* to live, camouflaged in the novel's title in a Latinized form, which could be translated: "I live," "I am living," or "I do live." After twenty-five years of silence, the poet thus announced to the world that he, representing the conscience of Russia, still lived.

As in the case of some other Soviet literary works, *Zhivago* was rejected for publication in the Soviet Union. The novel appeared first in Italy, after which it was translated into many other languages and enjoyed an almost fabulous success. In October, 1958, Pasternak was awarded the Nobel Prize in Literature, ostensibly for his poetry; due to the official furore over *Zhivago,* however, he refused the honor to avoid becoming the storm center of a cold-war controversy.

Pasternak's historical novel about the Russian Revolution rejected communism, Marxism, and collectivism. In it, he spoke of revolutionaries as men who resembled machines that had gone out of control. He labelled Marxism a self-centered movement far removed from the facts, whose leading exponents by seeking to establish their own infallibility prostituted the truth. Collectivization he denounced as a mistake and a failure which the regime could never afford to admit. The professional revolutionists of 1917 he depicted as fanatics, with one-track minds, who preached but did not practise social betterment. For him the groups and societies that flourished after the Revolution were the refuge of mediocrities. Like Dudintsev, Pasternak championed the cause of the individual, for only individuals seek the truth. The novel itself portrays the struggle of Dr. Zhivago, a physician and poet, to preserve his dignity as an individual in revolutionary Russia, 1903–1929. After many years of silence in Stalin's Russia, Pasternak emerged with a strong faith in the redemptive power of Christ.

In the Soviet Union, Pasternak's novel was condemned for its hatred of socialism and because it cast doubt on the validity of the Revolution. In spite of the official denunciation of his work, more than one thousand friends, neighbors, artists, writers, and actors paid a final tribute to the poet and novelist by attending his funeral on June 2, 1960.

Alexander Solzhenitsyn (1918–   ). Perhaps the strongest indictment of Stalinist tyranny was the novel *One Day in the Life of Ivan Denisovich* by

Sovfoto

Refusing throughout his life to write the propagandist verse the government demanded of its poets, Boris Pasternak was the most consistent non-conformist in Soviet literature. *Dr. Zhivago* was the great poet's only novel.

Alexander Solzhenitsyn, which first appeared in the Soviet periodical *Novyi Mir* in November, 1962. This novel, the publication of which was authorized by Khrushchev in person, was an immediate literary and political sensation. It revealed the predicament of a simple Red Army soldier who escaped from the Germans only to find himself falsely accused of high treason and incarcerated in one of Stalin's notorious slave-labor camps. The novel inevitably invited comparisons with Dostoyevsky's *Notes from a Dead House* (1861), written just one century earlier, and seemed to indicate that in this respect, at least, Stalin's regime was no better than that of the tsars. The Soviet humor magazine, *Krokodil,* provided a new slant on the "martyrs" of the Stalin

regime, by implying that some of the noisiest among them deserved punishment (Solzhenitsyn?):

> He was
>> for cowardice sentenced.
>
> Served his time.
> Returned.
> And now he trumpets
>> disgracefully,
>
> That
>> he was a victim
>> of the cult of personality.

—SERGEI SMIRNOV, *Rabbit Warrior*

Limited Freedom of Expression. During the Khrushchev era there was
some relaxation of the literary dictatorship that circumscribed all Soviet art.
Ilya Ehrenburg's memoirs, *People and Life,* were attacked, but the publication of additional volumes continued. A group of young writers, such
as Alexander Solzhenitsyn, Yuri Kazakov, Andrei Voznesensky, and Yevgeni
Yevtushenko, continued to challenge the pattern of conformity with temerity.
Yevtushenko, whose poem *Babi Yar* commemorated the twentieth anniversary of the German slaughter of some 100,000 Jews in a ravine near Kiev,
and who boldly attacked all manifestations of anti-Semitism, survived the
storm of criticism that followed and continued to write. The same is true of
Solzhenitsyn, whose short story, *Matryona's Yard,* provoked the unanimous
disapproval of Soviet critics. Matryona, a "righteous" woman was declared an
anachronism of the past unrepresentative of the new collective farms, which
depend on "active creators, people capable of tilling the soil and remaking the
world." Two of his novels, *In the First Circle* and *The Cancer Ward,* dealing
with police terror under the Stalin regime, have been rejected for publication
in the Soviet Union.

In spite of the seemingly restless search of Soviet writers for the new and
the different, Soviet literature nevertheless continued to be a weapon in the
ideological struggle and was bound by the Party's dictum. In 1963 Khrushchev admonished writers and artists that "the artist must be able to see the
positive things and to rejoice at them as they comprise the essence of our
reality; he must support these things, but at the same time, of course, not
overlook the negative phenomena and all that interferes with the rise of the
new in life." Speaking before writers and artists, March 8, 1965, Khrushchev
prescribed other limits to the freedom of expression of Soviet writers, artists,
and musicians. Never, he said, could he foresee "absolute freedoom" of the
individual, even under full communism. He scathingly repudiated Ehrenburg's
incautious plea for "peaceful coexistence in the field of ideology" as treason
against Marxism. This, he admitted, would be tantamount to welcoming a

Trojan horse, and it would lead inevitably to ideological disarmament of the USSR, with Soviet writers slipping into positions of anti-communism.

MUSIC

As in the case of literature, it is difficult to say explicitly where Soviet music begins and Russian music ends. During the early years of the Soviet regime, there was in music, as in literature, a great deal of experimentation and a drift toward extreme modernism and so-called proletarian music. In general, however, Soviet music has followed the traditions of the great Russian composers of the nineteenth century, and when these have been abandoned in favor of the satirical, exaggerated effects of Western modernism, the Soviet government has stepped in to demand conformity with socialist realism—that is, music that is "socialist in content but national in form," designed for the masses. In practice, socialist realism in music has usually meant the selection of a Soviet or historic patriotic theme, the use of simple, singing melodies, preferably folk tunes, and avoidance of formalism (dissonance, atonality, polytonality, complex rhythms, and American jazz rhythms). Lenin, Stalin, and Khrushchev proved to be anything but revolutionary in their tastes in music and painting. In justice to the Soviet Union, however, it must be said that the government has encouraged the establishment of orchestras and choruses everywhere—in factories, clubs, on the collective farm, as well as in palaces of culture. Practically every Soviet city has its own orchestra. Soviet composers have found it safer to emphasize vocal music which, of course, has deep roots in the Russian past. Russians have always sung at work and in military service, where singing has been of vital importance to morale. In Soviet Russia, singing has simply been organized, and outstanding teachers have been assigned to train workers, peasants, and soldiers.

Among the more outstanding Soviet composers, whose works have become popular in the United States, are Nicholas Myaskovsky, Sergei S. Prokofiev, Dmitry Shostakovitch, and Aram Khatchaturian.

Nicholas Myaskovsky (1881–1950). Myaskovsky, as professor at the Moscow Conservatory and dean of Soviet composers until 1950, helped to train and influence the younger generation of Soviet composers, including Khatchaturian, Shebalin, Muradeli, and Kabalevsky. His twenty-four symphonies reveal the influence of Mussorgsky and Borodin. Although he was a master of technique, his music lacked individuality, and according to Paul Miliukov, at best represented "a balance between modernism and conservatism." That he adapted himself to the Soviet regime is evident, for his *Twelfth (Kolkhoz) Symphony* was dedicated to the fifteenth anniversary of the October Revolution, his *Sixteenth* to Soviet aviation, the *Eighteenth* to the twentieth anniversary of the Revolution, and the *Nineteenth* to the Red Army.

Sergei S. Prokofiev (*1891–1953*). Prokofiev—ordinarily regarded in the West as the greatest composer of the USSR—was believed to be the hope of Russian music even before the Revolution, when his *Scythian Suite* (1914) and *Classical Symphony* (1917) appeared. Although from 1918 to 1932 he spent most of his time abroad, he settled thereafter in the Soviet Union. A pronounced anti-romantic, adept at satire and realism, Prokofiev has listed the following five characteristics of his music: the classical element; innovation (dissonance in harmony); the toccata or motor element; the lyric element; and the grotesque (comic) element. Some of his earlier works, such as *The Buffoon* (1915–1920), *The Scythian Suite,* and *The Love for Three Oranges* (1921), the last of which was produced in Chicago in 1924, reflected the sarcasm and caricature found in Mussorgsky's musical works and Gogol's literary masterpieces. His Soviet biographer has pointed out that Prokofiev's music was at one time or another rejected as "avant-garde" in tsarist Russia and "decadent" in Soviet Russia. After his return to the USSR, however, Prokofiev reverted increasingly to patriotic themes. His *Alexander Nevsky Cantata* (1939), based upon his music for the Sergei Eisenstein film, was a powerful work on the defense of Novgorod against the Teutonic Knights in 1242. The opera *War and Peace* (1945), his most extensive work along nationalist lines, which was based on Tolstoy's masterpiece, was labelled formalistic, due to the excessive use of recitative at the expense of melody.

Prokofiev was a prodigious worker, who produced not only operas, but ballets, choral works, seven symphonies, piano, violin and cello concertos, and many other orchestral works. He made a significant contribution to piano music with what has been termed his *style mécanique,* although his works have not achieved the popular success accorded Sergei Rachmaninov. Among other well-known works are his *Fifth Symphony,* his notable *Second Violin Concerto in G Minor* (1935), *Peter and the Wolf* (1936), one of his many contributions toward music for children, and the ballets *Cinderella* (1940–1944) and *The Stone Flower* (1948–1950).

Prokofiev died on March 5, 1953, the same day as Stalin, although in the confusion that prevailed at the time his death was unreported for three days. As an indication of his continued popularity in the Soviet Union, two unpublished works criticized during the Stalin regime for a lack of melody—*Cantata for the Twentieth Anniversary of the October Revolution* (1936–1937) to the words of Lenin, Stalin, and Marx, and his wartime *Ballad of an Unknown Boy*—were scheduled for performance in the spring of 1966 as part of an elaborate celebration of the seventy-fifth anniversary of the composer's birth (April 23).

Dmitry Shostakovitch (*1906–   *). Dmitry Shostakovitch, whose outstanding musical works belong exclusively to the Soviet era, achieved worldwide fame during World War II for his *Seventh* or *Leningrad Symphony* (1942), dedicated to the "ordinary Soviet citizens who have become the heroes of the present war." This symphony served as a patriotic call-to-arms and was awarded a Stalin Prize. Shostakovitch has been strongly influenced by Tchaikovsky, whom he regarded as a "cornerstone" of Russian and world music, by Western music, and by the Communist program. His technical mastery is unchallenged. His ballet *The Golden Age* (1929–1930), represented a clash between Soviet and Fascist visitors to a capitalist industrial exhibition. His opera *Lady Macbeth of Mtsensk* (1932), based on Nikolai Leskov's novel *Katherine Ismailova,* vividly portrayed the position of women in prerevolutionary Russia, but it was banned in 1936 for its "jarring, irritating, and affected intonations." It was during the furore over the "decadent bourgeois" attributes of this opera that Stalin was reputed to have made his oft-reiterated pronouncement that "music in Soviet Russia should be national in its form and socialist in content." The composer's brilliant *Fifth Symphony,* performed two years later, resulted in his rehabilitation. Since the death of Prokofiev in 1953, Shostakovitch has remained the unchallenged leader of Soviet composers. His *Lake Quartets* (*Ninth* and *Tenth Quartets*), composed at Lake Sevan in Armenia and Lake Balaton in Hungary, two of his more recent chamber works (performed in 1965), have been well received in the Soviet Union.

   Aram Khatchaturian (*1904–   *). The Soviet Armenian composer, Aram Khatchaturian, a product of the Gnesin School of Music who has called himself "the musical grandson of Rimsky-Korsakov," has attracted increasing attention abroad since 1942. Like so many other Russian composers, tsarist and Soviet, he maintained that "Nationality is a cardinal principal of art," and his music is steeped in the folklore of his native Armenia, the Caucasus, and the Transcaucasus. "My cradle song," he has said, "came from the Orient." His best-known works include a *Concerto for Piano and Orchestra* (1936), a *Concerto for Violin and Orchestra* (1940), which won a Stalin Prize, his Second *Symphony* (1942), and his colorful and rhythmic *Gayne Ballet* (1942), a recording from which became a best-seller in the United States. Of the Gayne *Sabre Dance,* Khatchaturian has said that it would never have seen the light of day had he realized that its popularity would obscure his other works. The reception of the *Sabre Dance* recalls the "incredible renown" of Rachmaninov's *Prelude in C Sharp Minor,* which equally nonplussed its composer. Khatchaturian's ballet *Spartacus,* in which he tried to express in music the spirit and mood of ancient Rome, was well received in Moscow and Leningrad. In addition to his creative work, Khatchaturian has taught composition at the Moscow Conservatory and at the Gnesin School of Music, with time out to direct an amateur music group for a factory club.

   Other Soviet composers whose works have attracted attention include Dmitry Kabalevsky, known also as a music critic, whose third opera, *The Taras Family,* has been recognized as one of the best Soviet works in this genre; Vissarion Shebalin, often regarded as one of the most representative Soviet composers; Ivan Dzerzhinsky, who produced a "model" Soviet opera on Sholokhov's novel *The Silent Don;* and the Georgian-born Ivan Muradeli, whose music reflects the folklore of his native environment.

Zhdanov's Decree on Music. In general, it may be said that Soviet composers enjoyed more freedom than Soviet authors and dramatists until 1948, when Zhdanov's notorious Decree on Music subjected them to regimentation. It is said that Prokofiev, who led the list of musicians attacked by the government at that time, turned his back on Zhdanov during that speech, and Myaskovsky refused even to attend the session. After Stalin's death in 1953, Khatchaturian published an article in *Soviet Music,* in which he called for more creative freedom for composers. Shostakovitch followed suit. Although the tension has somewhat abated, it is safe to say that Soviet control measures have obstructed the development of originality and depth in Soviet music, which, with some exceptions, has not yet measured up to prerevolutionary standards.

On February 22, 1965, the Communist Party proclaimed a relaxed attitude toward the arts, with opportunity for "free expression and clashes of viewpoints." It is to be hoped that this will provide the rising generation of Soviet composers, including Georgy Sviridov, Otar Taktashivili (Georgian), Kara Karaev (Azerbaijanian), and Ter-Tatevosian (Armenian), and others whose works are still unknown in the United States, freedom which was not accorded their predecessors.

ART AND ARCHITECTURE

Academy of Art. With the coming of the Revolution, the Travellers and the World of Art groups were soon outmoded. The slogan of "Art for Art's Sake" was scrapped along with the Imperial Academy and other relics of the past. Some artists continued to work under the Soviet regime, including M. Nesterov, P. Konchalovsky, the Palekh and Mtsery artists, and the talented sculptor Konenkov. Others went or remained abroad. After a brief, individualistic fling, which included experimentation with cubism, futurism, constructivism, etc., Soviet artists were forced to conform to socialist realism. Art, like literature and music, was believed to have an educative mission in the building of the new society and could not be permitted to flourish independent of politics. The Soviet government did seek to "democratize" art by carrying it to the people, by establishing free workshops, holding lectures in factories, taking over private art collections, holding revolutionary art festivals, and undertaking the restoration and preservation of historic monuments and paintings. In 1932 the Academy of Art was restored and headed by Isaac Brodsky, erstwhile member of the World of Art Movement and one of the few academicians to remain in Russia.

Socialist Realism. In the field of art, socialist realism usually meant selection by artists of Soviet or national themes and the avoidance of formalistic and abstract art. Soviet artists were expected to produce cheerful, optimistic paintings, reminiscent of the emphasis on the positive man in literature; the results, with some exceptions, were often monotonous, mediocre, and devoid of originality. Some of the best work has been done by P. Filonov, Kapitsa, and Glazunov (portraits), and Konenkov (sculpture). Among the most representative Soviet artists are Isaac Brodsky (1884–1939), who painted well-known portraits of Lenin and Gorky; A. Gerasimov, whose *Hymn to October* depicted the twenty-fifth anniversary of the October Revolution (1942) at the Bol'shoi Theatre; Georgi Nissky, now a member of the USSR Academy of Fine Arts, and N. D. Kuznetsov, known for their industrial landscapes; and Yu. Pimenov, who painted *Novaya Moskva* (1960). The works of some of Russia's talented artists with leanings toward abstract art, such as those of Kandinsky, M. Chagall, Soutine, and De Stael, have not been exhibited because their formalism violates socialist realism. They are said to be in the basement of the Hermitage.

Classical Architecture. In architecture, after faulty beginnings, a tremendous amount of new building, reconstruction, and restoration has been accomplished. The Soviet regime has been interested, not in palaces for aristocrats, or cathedrals, but palaces of soviets, palaces of culture, libraries, schools, hospitals, hotels, subways, etc., for the use of all the people. Vast new public buildings, some of them skyscrapers, housing projects characterized by "gigantism," and entirely new cities have been constructed. With the end of

Sovfoto

The Lenin Mausoleum on Red Square stands deserted, except for its guards, on a winter evening. A. V. Shchussev was one of a number of prerevolutionary architects who received important commissions from the Soviet government.

experimentation, which encouraged individualism rather than collectivism, the classical style once again came into vogue, even for apartment houses. Academician A. V. Shchussev, architect for the Kazan Railroad Station (1913) in Moscow, designed the Lenin Mausoleum and helped to design the Moscow Hotel (1935). The development of the Moscow METRO (subway), with its forty-two or more stations gleaming like a series of underground palaces, each with distinctive decoration, is an example of the mammoth projects undertaken by the Soviet regime. The new Europa Hotel, it is claimed, is the largest in Europe. Although there has been much criticism and self-criticism of Soviet architecture, there have been signs of late that a more modernistic trend is under way.

SCIENCE

Under the Soviet regime the Academy of Sciences has become a truly gigantic organization, unequalled elsewhere as far as scope, versatility, and the size of its staff are concerned. At its peak, the Tsarist Academy is said to have had 212 scientists, 5 laboratories, 1 institute, and several museums. The USSR Academy of Sciences in 1965 included more than 20,000 scientific workers, as well as 166 institutes and laboratories. It is the official Soviet viewpoint that in the competition between capitalism and communism the victor will be the one that makes the most effective use of science. "Science," according to Khrushchev, "is our compass." The Soviet government has therefore devoted almost unlimited funds to scientific research facilities and has accorded salaries and perquisites to scientists that are not available to scholars in other fields.

Emphasis on Applied Science. In the Soviet Union there is no science for science's sake any more than there is art for art's sake. Especially since 1930, the planning of Soviet scientific research has become progressively more systematic and all-embracing. All scientific projects—those of the academy, as well as those of the universities and institutes—must be closely integrated with the Five- or Seven-Year Plans. In other words, the emphasis has been on applied rather than on theoretical science. In its crusade to develop the natural resources of the country in the shortest possible time, it was natural that the Soviet government should emphasize applied science, even sometimes at the expense of theoretical science, although much outstanding work has been accomplished in both areas. Soviet controls have not operated to the same extent in all the sciences. The physical and mathematical sciences have enjoyed a greater degree of freedom than, for example, the biological and social sciences.

Mitchurin School of Biological Science. One of the bitterest and most prolonged scientific controversies of the Soviet period has been waged since World War II in the field of biological sciences. It has involved, on the one hand, the I. V. Mitchurin School of biological science under the leadership of Academician Trofim D. Lysenko, and on the other, those Soviet scientists who adhered to Western concepts of genetics. Mitchurin (1855–1935), a contemporary of the American horticulturists Luther Burbank and Nils Hansen, was a successful plant breeder who, by skilful crossing, produced new varieties of fruit trees adapted to the severe climate of Central Russia. Like his American counterparts, he evolved spurious scientific theories at variance with modern genetics. In brief, the Mitchurinites contended, in line with the basic tenets of Marxian dialectics, that a change in the environment of an organism leads to changes in its heredity. Most Western biologists maintain that the properties of heredity are determined by genes and chromosomes which are independent of environment, although they may be altered by accidental changes, or mutations. In 1948 Lysenko, with the support of Stalin, emerged triumphant, and disaster overtook Soviet genetics, a field in which he became the virtual dictator. With the ouster of Khrushchev in 1964, the Mitchurin School lost its principal supporter among Soviet leaders. Probably as a result of the disillusionment of Soviet hopes for immense achievements in agriculture and forestry, in February, 1965, M. V. Keldysh, president of the USSR Academy of Sciences, announced the dismissal of Lysenko as director of the academy's Institute of Genetics, a post he had held since 1940. With his downfall, another "personality cult" was overthrown and a disgraceful era in Soviet biology appeared to have ended. The supporters of Lysenko, however, have continued to fight a rear-guard action for the "coexistence" of the Lysenko and classical schools of genetics. The sudden change, which required the retraining of thousands of Soviet biology teachers and the rewriting of textbooks, created a crisis in the Soviet school system, which had not been solved by the opening of the 1965–1966 school year.

Research in Physics. The achievements of the USSR in outer space have testified to the enormous progress of Soviet science in areas such as mechanics, mathematics, electronics, chemistry, space biology, and in general to the high level of Soviet research in pure and applied science. Many Soviet scientists have contributed directly or indirectly to Soviet nuclear development. Pyotr L. Kapitsa (1894–   ), predominant in the field of physics, contributed to the theory of supraconductivity and invented a machine to liquefy air or helium. His chief theoretical works have dealt with the study of low temperatures. The Cavendish Magnetic Research Laboratory at Cambridge, England, which Kapitsa headed, was transferred to Moscow after the scientist was enticed to visit the USSR in 1934 and renamed the Institute of Physical Problems. In 1965 Kapitsa was awarded the Niels Bohr Gold Medal (Denmark) for his contribution to the development of nuclear physics and its practical application for peaceful purposes. Another outstanding physicist, Vladimir Veksler, at the age of twenty-eight caught cosmic rays on Mt. Elbrus in the Caucasus, and according to Soviet claims, discovered the principle of "phase stability" a year before the American scientist Dr. Edwin McMillan.

Igor Kurchatov (1903–1960), a professor at Leningrad University and a recognized genius in the field of nuclear physics, worked on the physics of chain reactions of fissionable nuclei. His main objective was the control of thermonuclear reactions, a cardinal problem of contemporary science and technology, if thermonuclear power is to be placed at the service of industry. A Communist since 1948, Kurchatov for many years directed the academy's Institute of Atomic Energy. In 1964 two outstanding Soviet physicists, Nikolai Basov and Alexander Prokhorov, laboratory heads at the Institute of Physics of the USSR Academy of Sciences, shared with an American, Charles Townes, the Nobel Prize in Physics, awarded for basic research on quantum electronics which resulted in the development of generators and amplifiers in the radio and optical wave bands (masers and lasers). The Soviet government has established at Dubna, about eighty miles north of Moscow, an atomic center where theoretical and experimental physicists of many nationalities, including American, work together in the Joint Nuclear Research Institute, studying the fundamental particles of the atom (the proton is one), for the peaceful uses of atomic energy.

Mathematics. Andrei Kolmogorov (1903–   ), a Soviet mathematician of international repute and professor at Moscow University since 1931, discovered the laws of chance, one of the outstanding achievements in world mathematics. He is a leading authority on the theory of probabilities and mathematical logic. Attracted by recent developments in cybernetics, Kolmogorov is convinced that a thinking cybernetic robot can be invented. The Soviet government has placed great hopes in cybernetics as a solution to overall planning in the USSR.

Outer Space. One of the most outstanding Soviet scientists, Konstantin E. Tsiolkovsky (1857–1935), possessed by the idea of flight in cosmic space, created a scientific theory of the movement of rockets. The foundations he laid for rocketry, including his proposals for the multi-stage rocket, have been developed since 1924 by the government's Central Bureau for Research on Rocket Problems and by the Society for Interplanetary Communications. Without the extensive work done in this field, the first sputnik could not have been launched.

Professor Iosif Shklovsky (1916–   ), a leading specialist in radio astronomy, is another Soviet scientist who regards communication with extraterrestrial civilizations as a real rather than a hypothetical problem. A professor at Moscow University, he is the author of *The Physics of Solar Corona* (1951), *Cosmic Radio Emission* (1956), and more than one hundred other works. He heads the radio astronomy section of the Sternberg Astronomical Institute.

Scientific Horizons. Americans interested in Soviet scientific development will need to follow the activities of the Siberian Branch of the USSR Academy of Sciences, with headquarters in the new Science City, Akademgorodok (Academic Town), seventeen miles east of Novosibirsk, where outstanding scholars have been assembled. By 1963 there were twenty research institutes in the Novosibirsk Science Center Complex. At a Physics and Mathematics Boarding School, directly subject to Novosibirsk University, gifted Soviet teenagers were being taught the functions of chromosomes, cell structure, and other basic principles of modern genetics almost a year before the downfall of Lysenko. Affiliates of the Siberian Branch are engaged in research on volcanology, geocryology, and forest products in Kamchatka, Yakutsk, and Krasnoyarsk respectively. In 1967 the population of Akademgorodok reached 50,000, including forty members of the Soviet Academy of Sciences.

There is no doubt but that Soviet scientists have a horizon. They envisage the creation of an artificial sun which can be moved on selected orbits to bring heat and light to the Arctic. They discuss the possibility of using the huge sources of heat represented by the Pacific Ocean to provide a central heating system for the Far North. At the first solar electric station in the world, located in Armenia's Ararat Valley, they study ways and means of using the sun's enormous potential for heat and power through a system of reflecting mirrors, and they hope eventually to store and accumulate this energy.

Under the Stalin regime, the main challenge to Soviet scientists was the "remaking of nature" on this planet. Now the horizon has been widened appreciably. It is in their purview to transform the entire cosmos, and to create new planets comparable to those now in existence. In other words, they believe that science will control the universe, which is one reason why they want coexistence and peace. Soviet progress in science not only has had, but will continue to have, a political and ideological impact abroad, especially on the developing countries of Asia and Africa. If new planets are created first by Soviet man, this will inflict a crushing blow on the religion of Islam, since religion is the main barrier that stands between Soviet ideology and the poverty-stricken masses of Muslim Asia.

27

The Khrushchev Era, 1956-1964

THE DEATH OF STALIN, following years of adulation that virtually amounted to deification, raised the problem of the Soviet succession—a problem that has plagued many dictatorships in the past. Since none of the eligible successors— Malenkov, Beria, and Molotov—had attained Stalin's stature, there was temporarily, at least, a division of power among them, with Georgi M. Malenkov assuming the premiership but surrendering the strategic post of secretary of the Central Committee of the Communist Party to Nikita S. Khrushchev;[1] Lavrenti P. Beria serving as deputy premier and minister of internal affairs; and Vyatcheslav M. Molotov, likewise a deputy premier, returning to his old post as minister of foreign affairs. The inevitable struggle for supremacy among the Soviet Big Three culminated in the announcement on July 10, 1953, of the overthrow of Beria, the head of the dread Soviet secret police (MVD) (see also page 473).

THE DETHRONEMENT OF STALIN

The triumvirate lost no time in playing down the "cult of personality" that had elevated Stalin to the skies and established his reputation for infallibility. In the months that followed his death Stalin's name was rarely mentioned in the Soviet press and then largely in conjunction with the historical figures of Marx, Engels, and Lenin. It seemed as if the triumvirate thus paved the way for a departure from Stalin's policies.

Indictment Speech. Khrushchev's spectacular rise to power dates from the Twentieth Congress of the Communist Party, February 24–25, 1956. The sensation of this congress was Khrushchev's posthumous indictment[2] of "Stalin the Great"—the first time in a quarter of a century that anyone had dared to make such an open attack. His speech amounted to a confession of the iniquities of a "great inquisitor." He condemned not only the "cult of personality," but Stalin's blunders in the early stages of World War II and the purges of 1936–1938, especially the execution of five thousand Red Army

1. On September 12, 1953, the plenary session of the Central Committee of the Communist Party of the Soviet Union (CPSU) elected Khrushchchev as first secretary of the Central Committee of the CPSU, thus formalizing his position.
2. This speech, although secret, was procured by the U.S. Department of State and published June 4, 1956.

officers, thousands of technical specialists, and numerous other government and Party leaders. Anastas Mikoyan supported the indictment by denouncing Stalin's "falsification" of Soviet history and the social sciences, and by casting doubt on the validity of his *Economic Problems of Socialism in the USSR,* which was intended to serve as the basis of the revised program of the Communist Party.

The dethronement of Stalin, often called his "second death," evoked much speculation as to its cause. Many regarded it as the herald of another purge—this time of Stalin's supporters—which indeed followed, not only inside the USSR, but in the satellite states. Others interpreted it as an effort to wipe the slate clean of past mistakes, thereby contributing to a better atmosphere at home and abroad. Some even hoped that it would inaugurate a new era in the Soviet Union, with more freedom and justice for all. The indictment clearly stemmed from a split among top Party members as to the course to be pursued in Soviet domestic and foreign policy. Such drastic action, however, threatened the very foundations of the Party cult. If Stalin, who had been virtually deified for years, could be summarily toppled from his pedestal, the same fate might befall the other Communist prophets, with the result that the entire Communist edifice might come crashing down. Herein may lie the source of the breach between Krushchev and Mao Tse-tung.

Khrushchev Purge. The response and acclaim that followed Khrushchev's speech suggest that he voiced the long pent-up feelings of his audience, many of whom experienced a sense of guilt for the crimes of the Stalin era. There nevertheless remained a hard core of Stalinists in key positions who were prepared to oppose the Khrushchev program, especially his plans for the decentralization of agriculture and industry. The weeks that followed the indictment were marked by the sweeping removal of Stalin's protégés and the rehabilitation of his victims, including Rykov and Gomulka. Khrushchev's campaign of rehabilitation was still in process in 1963.

The climax of the Khrushchev purge came on July 3, 1957, when Malenkov, Molotov, Kaganovitch, and Shepilov—all on grounds of anti-Party activity—were ousted, not only from the Party Presidium and Central Committee, but from their key government posts. Stalin, under these circumstances, would have liquidated the opposition. Under Khrushchev, however, Malenkov was placed in charge of a hydroelectric station at Ust-Kamenogorsk in eastern Kazakhstan; Molotov was appointed Soviet ambassador to Outer Mongolia; Kaganovitch was made head of a cement plant in the Urals; and Shepilov became a school teacher, first in Central Asia, and later at the Institute of Economics in Moscow. Of Stalin's "heirs," only Khrushchev and Mikoyan remained in the Presidium. As late as 1961 the leading Soviet writer, Mikhail Sholokhov, no doubt voiced the feelings of many Soviet citizens on this purge of the "anti-Party" group, when he asked: "Are we not too tolerant of those who have the deaths of thousands of true sons of our motherland and party on their consciences?" He then assured the watchful

West: "We are not thinking of revenge. Nobody is thirsting for the blood of the factionalists, poisoned by intrigues. But they must answer for their crimes against the Party and the people." In 1961 Stalin's body was moved from the Lenin Mausoleum to an inconspicuous resting place beside the Kremlin wall. There followed a rash of name-changing, in the midst of which the "Hero City" of Stalingrad was renamed Volgograd.

Restriction of Criticism. Khrushchev soon felt impelled, however, to bar unrestricted criticism of the Stalin era. At a 1963 meeting of Party and government leaders with writers and artists, in which he referred to Stalin's abuses of power, Khrushchev called attention to his predecessor's services as a Marxist to the Party and to the Communist movement, and insisted that he be rendered his due. The Soviet leader appeared to be drawing a clear distinction between Stalin's earlier contributions and the closing years of his life when, as a sick man suffering from suspicion and persecution mania, he violated the Leninist principles of Party leadership and abused the power entrusted to him.

Khrushchev's Rise to Power. As Stalin was a disciple of Lenin, Khrushchev was a protégé of Stalin. Like Stalin, he rose to power through the Party bureaucracy until he gained control of the Party Secretariat. The son of a coal miner in Kursk Province, Khrushchev as a youth worked as a sheep herder and as a miner. He received little formal education. In 1918, he joined the Communist Party and thereafter served as a political worker on the southern front during the Civil War. Later he was employed as a machinist in factories and mines in the Donbas. Not until 1925 did he complete his elementary and secondary education at a *rabfak* (factory workers' school). In 1929, when he became a student in the Stalin Industrial Academy in Moscow, Khrushchev's chances for advancement improved. In the years that followed, he served the Party in various capacities in Moscow, supporting Stalin against the Rightist Opposition, and in 1934 became a member of its Central Committee. Not only did he survive the Stalin purges, but he emerged with full membership in the Politburo (1939). He was then sent to Kiev, where for twelve years he headed the Ukrainian Communist Party, gaining valuable experience and considerable authority. Khrushchev's return to Moscow opened up new opportunities in the Party hierarchy, which culminated in 1953 in his selection as first secretary. Like Stalin, Khrushchev shared power temporarily with his rivals, but soon emerged triumphant.

Once he had established his grip on the Communist Party, Khrushchev turned to the army. On October 26, 1957, Marshal Rodion Malinovsky replaced Marshal Zhukov as minister of defense. Accused of promoting his own "cult of personality" and of resisting Party control of the Red Army, the renowned Zhukov, viewed by some as a potential successor to Stalin, was removed from the Party Presidium and Central Committee in November and relegated to obscurity. On March 27, 1958, the Supreme Soviet reelected the aging Voroshilov, one of the last of the old Bolsheviks, as chairman of the

Presidium of the USSR. With his chief rivals disposed of, Khrushchev became chairman of the Council of Ministers, replacing Bulganin. Thus, by the spring of 1958 Khrushchev, like Stalin before him, combined in his person leadership of the Communist Party and of the Soviet government.[3] The Party had successfully reasserted its power over the Red Army.

DOMESTIC POLICIES

Agriculture. The most immediate problem confronting Khrushchev was that of Soviet agriculture, long a primary source of domestic discontent. Although the postwar years had witnessed a great increase in agricultural production, Soviet consumption outran Soviet production. The havoc wrought by World War II in European Russia had set back Soviet agriculture for decades, and the gap had not yet been filled. During the war, millions of Soviet men and women in the armed forces had eaten three square meals a day, often faring better than they had ever done at home. When these veterans were demobilized they sought to preserve the same standards. As the Soviet standard of living continued to rise after the war, the entire population, which was on the increase, bought more food. In the USSR a "revolution" of rising expectations was under way. Amid the constant shifting of segments of the Soviet population, many Russians had abandoned the farm for the factory. In the years from 1953 to 1962, the number of persons engaged in agriculture was said to have decreased by 1,200,000. Others had migrated to Siberia and the "virgin lands" to open up new agricultural areas not yet in full production and often plagued by severe cold or drought. Russians who had travelled abroad and observed at first hand the food supplies in Western lands returned to demand improved conditions at home. In other words, it was not solely due to managerial inefficiency and backward methods that Soviet agricultural production failed to meet Soviet requirements.

Decentralization. Unlike Stalin, Khrushchev mingled with the people in factories and on farms during his frequent tours about the country. With his ear to the ground, he heard complaints about red tape, over-centralization of authority in the MTS and in Moscow, and recommendations for more flexibility, as well as for the abrogation of rules and regulations that hampered Soviet production. He soon put some of these recommendations into practice. In the first place, he introduced a modicum of decentralization of planning and management. On June 28, 1958, compulsory deliveries of agricultural products to the state in return for services furnished by the MTS were discontinued. This action removed a long-standing grievance of *kolkhoz* farmers. To eliminate "two bosses on the land," the MTS were themselves liquidated.

3. On the Khrushchev succession, see Harrison Salisbury in the *New York Times* (March 16, 1956); also, *Report on the Soviet Union in 1956* (Munich: Institute for the Study of the USSR, 1956).

They were converted into service and supply centers, renamed "Repair-Technical Stations" (RTS), and their machinery, for the most part, was sold to the *kolkhozi* on a cash or credit basis. By July, 1959, almost 95 per cent of the collective farms had taken advantage of the opportunity to purchase tractors, grain combines, and other agricultural machinery. The government compensated for this relaxation of MTS control by stronger Party control commissions. Khrushchev's visit to the United States in September, 1959, which included the Middle West corn belt, led to his promotion of large-scale corn production in the USSR, mainly as food for cattle, and even to the introduction of cornflakes.

Seven-Year Plan. The Soviet Seven-Year Plan (1959–1965) provided for an increase in agricultural production 80 per cent above the 1958 level. The continued barrage of self-criticism over agricultural management and production soon indicated that these expectations would not be realized. Unseasonable cold weather led to the wheat crop failure of 1963. Khrushchev was forced to resort to extensive purchases of wheat (10,000,000 tons) abroad to prevent undue privation at home. In response to domestic criticism of these purchases, he pointed out that in 1947 many Soviet citizens died of hunger because Stalin and Molotov continued to export grain in a poor crop year. On December 9, 1963, before the Party's Central Committee, Khrushchev announced a $46 billion, seven-year crash program of expansion of the chemical industry, "the Industry of Abundance," designed to produce enough fertilizer to double farm production by 1970. He ascribed high United States agricultural output, not to "any special American wisdom," but to the fact that the USA used four times as much chemical fertilizer per acre as did the Soviet Union. In his marathon four and one-half hour speech, Khrushchev explained that one fourth of the vast capital investment in the chemical industry was destined for farm chemicals, another fourth for consumer products such as textiles and footwear, and the balance for heavy industry. The Soviet Academy of Sciences promptly called for a national center to coordinate chemical research. Victor V. Grishin, Soviet trade-union leader, demanded higher wages for chemical workers to bring them in line with those of other industries. The new program, dependent on credits from abroad for the purchase of machinery and equipment to insure the rapid development of the chemical industry, appeared to foreshadow renewed efforts toward improved economic relations with the West.

Industry. In Soviet industry Khrushchev also carried out a radical policy of decentralization, 1957–1958. Some of the pressure on Soviet workers was reduced by improved working conditions. In April, 1957, a six-hour day was established for workers in mines and a seven-hour day for those in heavy industry. In 1960 the seven-hour day was extended to all factory and office workers, and wages were increased. The minimum wage of Soviet workers, as announced in December, 1963, was from forty to fifty rubles ($44.90 to $49.95) per month. Although these figures suggest starvation wages, the

Soviet worker pays very low rent ($10 per month on the average), and receives free medical and dental services. Clothing, food, and non-staple commodities, however, remain very expensive. Under the impact of his tour of the United States in 1959, Khrushchev introduced purchases on the installment plan for expensive consumer goods—a strictly capitalistic practice which proved highly popular among Soviet citizens.

Soviet industry was growing temporarily at an annual rate of 9.5 per cent, as compared to 3.6 per cent for the United States. The Seven-Year Plan stepped up the nation's industrial program to complete by 1965 what was to have been accomplished by 1972. Somewhat prematurely, as events were to prove, Khrushchev boasted that its purpose was to enable the USSR to overtake the United States in production by 1970.

When the Soviet goal was to surpass the United States, the USSR of necessity had to adopt American methods. In his Budapest speech of April 1, 1964, Khrushchev inadvertently revealed how far the Soviet Union had progressed from the Militant Communism of 1917 to 1921, when revolution was the Party's primary concern. Indirectly taking issue with the Red Chinese, whose paramount consideration today is revolution, he emphasized the need to strive for "a better life":

> The important thing is that we should have more to eat—good goulash— schools, housing, and ballet. How much more do these things give to the enlargement of man's life? It is worth fighting and working for these things.

The new plan, Khrushchev said, was the government's response to economic decentralization, new mineral resources, new power developments, and the need for plastics and synthetics fibers. When the experiment with decentralization failed to live up to expectations, Khrushchev, who abjured inflexibility and dogmatism, resorted once again to centralized control of industry. At the Party's Central Committee session of November, 1962, a decision was made to set up two independent administrative systems, one for industry and the other for agriculture.

Supreme Council of the National Economy. On March 13, 1963, the Soviet government virtually scrapped the already obsolete Seven-Year Plan in favor of a new two-year program reflecting major changes in economic policy and technology. Embarking on what appeared to be a program of military discipline in industry, it established the Supreme Council of the National Economy to coordinate industrial planning, management, and construction on a nationwide basis. The head of the new industrial super-agency was Dmitry F. Ustinov, former administrator of the Soviet defense industries, who now became a first deputy premier under Khrushchev, a position held only by Anastas Mikoyan and Alexei N. Kosygin. Ustinov's appointment appears to have stemmed from his success in achieving the smooth operation of the nation's vital armament production.

Oil and Gas Pipelines. One of the high priority projects to expand the economic potential of the Soviet bloc in the Khrushchev era was the construction of a system of oil and natural gas pipelines inside the Soviet Union and from the USSR to the satellite states of Eastern Europe. From far-off Bukhara in Central Asia a 1500-mile line was undertaken to furnish gas for heavy industry in the Urals. By the 2500-mile "Friendship" (*Druzhba*) pipeline the Soviet government prepared to link the vast Transvolga oil fields near Kuibyshev with refineries in Czechoslovakia, Hungary, Poland, and East Germany, with the terminus of the last near Berlin. These were but the advance stages of a network to be extended eventually to the Black and Baltic Seas and possibly via Irkutsk to the Sea of Japan. In East Germany, the new pipeline was expected to provide fuel for a huge chemical industry planned at Schwedt, on the Oder River.

Petroleum Production. A phenomenal rise in Soviet petroleum production had occurred since World War II. As compared with 44,000,000 tons in 1950, Soviet production was expected to reach 265,000,000 tons in 1965. Annual exports to the free world, which were limited to 1,000,000 tons in 1950, were scheduled to reach 50,000,000 tons in 1965. West German imports of Soviet oil rose 1600 per cent from 1957 to 1963. By March, 1963, it was estimated that of the NATO members, Italy obtained 23 per cent of its oil from the USSR, West Germany 11 per cent, Greece 38 per cent, and Iceland 98 per cent. In May of the same year the USSR launched the second of a high-priority series of large tankers to provide facilities for the increased export of Soviet oil. In the Western world, it was feared that Soviet oil would be dumped in Western markets at greatly reduced prices.

Western Ban on "Strategic" Goods. The Khrushchev government originally planned to complete both the oil and the gas pipelines in 1963, even at the cost of purchasing large quantities of "big-inch" (forty-inch) pipe from Germany, Japan, and elsewhere, which it did for three years. Increasingly concerned by the strategic aspects of the Soviet oil project and by the prospect of Soviet competition in oil on the world markets, the Kennedy administration then put pressure on its NATO allies to place "big-inch" pipe on the strategic list, thereby cutting off further shipments to the Soviet Union. Although the NATO Council made such a recommendation for an embargo on November 21, 1962, the move proved to be a source of great dissension between the United States on the one hand and West Germany, England, Italy, and Japan on the other. The Adenauer government reluctantly cancelled orders for 163,000 tons of pipe (four hundred miles).

The question that has plagued the countries of the West in their trade relations with the USSR is the interpretation of the term "strategic." A gas pipeline to supply the defense industry of the Urals certainly came into this category. An oil pipeline to East Germany could not fail to be of strategic significance for the supply of the Red Army in that area. The increased dependence of East Germany on the USSR resulting therefrom threatened to obstruct further Western efforts toward German unification. For the United States government, the banning of sales of strategic goods to the Soviet Union and its orbit was an important cold-war weapon. If it accomplished nothing else, it hampered the Soviet construction program and purchased time for the West. America's allies, however, pointed out that this policy was merely promoting Soviet self-sufficiency. Great Britain, in particular, in the interests of her foreign trade, preferred that the term "strategic" be restricted to military supplies and equipment. With his usual "earthy" approach, Khrushchev commented that the American interpretation would make buttons even more strategic than forty-inch pipe, since soldiers with buttonless uniforms would have to abandon their weapons to hold up their trousers!

Although American intervention retarded, it did not halt, the Soviet program. What the USSR was unable to purchase abroad, it was determined to produce at home. In March, 1963, the Chelyabinsk pipe-rolling mill in the Urals, completed ahead of schedule, and the Novomoskovsk plant in the Ukraine, which had begun operations in 1962, concentrated on the production of the much-needed pipe. In May, two more forty-inch pipe-welding mills went into operation, one at Khartsyzsk in the Donetz basin of the Ukraine, and the other at the Zhdanov Steel Plant on the Sea of Azov. By November 7, 1963, in time for the forty-sixth anniversary of the Russian Revolution, Soviet oil had reached Poland, appreciably ahead of schedule. Trial operations were set to begin at Schwedt on April 1, 1964, with full-scale production by July 1 of the same year.

Water Transport. Another project of major consideration for Soviet transportation was the Volga-Baltic Waterway to replace the 150-year-old Mariinsk Canal System with a channel enabling large river barges to traverse European Russia from north to south without reloading into smaller vessels. Planned for 1940, this project was interrupted by World War II. In a country where railroads still carried 80 per cent of the freight traffic, the diversion from rail to water transport was of key significance. The 224-mile Volga-Baltic Waterway was scheduled to open in the spring of 1964, at which time it would provide north Russia with grain, salt, oil, and coal from the south, and southern farm areas with timber, paper, and chemical fertilizer from the north.

Transformation. The rapid industrial development of the USSR has transformed a basically agricultural society into a great industrial power within the span of a single generation. This transformation has undoubtedly had an important impact on the developing countries, especially since the launching of the first sputnik. The question is often asked, therefore, whether the Soviet economic system serves as a model for the emerging nations of Asia and Africa. There seems to be no indication at present that these nations are concerned about the economy that prevails in countries from which they derive economic aid. If they cannot get help from the USA, they will try the USSR. The aid as such is a means to an end—the preservation of the nation—rather than an end in itself. In other words, the USA and the USSR serve as alternatives rather than as models. Nor does it appear to be the Soviet objective to serve as an economic model for the developing countries. Soviet emphasis is on ideology, to which they repeatedly give credit for their new system. As Soviet leaders admit, their economy is not uniform and has not yet crystallized. This is revealed by their fluctuations toward decentralization and back again to centralization. In other words, the Soviet economy is a means to an end—a new society and communism—not an end in itself. Because the means is transient and subject to change (zigzags), it cannot serve as a model to others. It is more likely to be the example of the USSR (its transformation from a backward agrarian to a highly industrialized and creditor nation within a half century) that attracts the new nations.

COMECON. Early in 1963, the Khrushchev regime laid the foundations for a more highly integrated Council for Mutual Economic Assistance (COMECON) (the Soviet bloc's answer to the European Common Market), which comprises the USSR, Czechoslovakia, Poland, Hungary, Rumania, East Germany, and Outer Mongolia. It called for greater study and planning of industry and agriculture in the interests of the bloc as a whole. Preliminary plans implied, not only over-all control of production planning for entire branches of industry, but also the concentration of certain types of industrial development in specific member countries. The program was expected to affect industrial raw materials, fuel power, chemicals, machine construction, and agriculture. Among other things, it envisaged joint hydroelectric and thermonuclear power stations and joint machine-construction enterprises, or at least close cooperation in these areas.

Opposition to the further integration of COMECON soon developed in Rumania, which feared the stifling of its own national program for diversified industrial development. Czechoslovakia showed a like concern that integration might result in the removal of existing industries to other member countries, thereby lowering Czech living standards, the highest in COMECON. Poland and Hungary supported and Rumania opposed a joint capital investment pool to aid the industrial development of the poorer members.

The chief obstacles to COMECON integration, slated for implementation in 1964, appeared to be the conflicting national interests and needs of its members and the diversity of their economic development. East Germany and Czechoslovakia, with more industry and skilled labor, seemed likely to profit more from the proposed division of labor than did Poland, Hungary, and Rumania, still basically producers of raw materials. The weakness of the COMECON members, with the exception of the USSR, is that individually they lack sufficient raw materials and capital reserves to finance their own development and therefore need to pool their resources. In October, 1963, in spite of this apprehension, a COMECON agreement was signed in Moscow to establish a new International Bank for Economic Cooperation to go into operation January 1, 1964. Provision was made also for formal multilateral clearing arrangements through the bank, based on the new "gold-backed" convertible ruble (1 ruble = $1.11). There were indications that transactions in convertible rubles might be extended to non-Communist countries, thereby transforming the ruble into a genuine international currency.

Integration of Minorities. Whereas in the 1960's segregation constituted a problem for the United States, the USSR confronted the problem of integration, not only in COMECON, but among the Soviet minorities. Before World War II the Stalin regime pursued a policy toward its minorities of "divide and rule." In the post-Stalin years the Khrushchev regime moved cautiously in the direction of a policy of "unite and rule." Not that it had any fears of counter-revolution, especially in time of peace. The members of the White Russian armies that fought in the Civil War had grown old or died. After the atrocities of the Nazi "liberators," Soviet minority groups had no expectation of salvation from the outside. In general, the Soviet population was too busy working and exceeding quotas to find time for subversive activities on any substantial scale.

The Khrushchev government was still conscious, nevertheless, of the strategic weakness of a belt of minority republics along the periphery of the USSR, especially in Asia. It would prefer the American pattern where minorities, instead of remaining as geographical entities, are generally scattered throughout the country and readily assimilated. In the USSR assimilation has been promoted with limited results by the Soviet school system and by the shifting of segments of the Soviet population. Athough Soviet leaders are proceeding slowly, their objective, as defined by the Twenty-Second Congress of the Communist Party in 1961, is to develop a unitary nation, with one basic language, Russian; one creed, communism; and one integrated Communist culture. To transpose the American formula, they want to become "One nation under communism, indivisible . . ."

Regional Federations. The next step in this direction was to be the conversion of the existing structure of national republics into a system of regional federations that would downgrade the national particularism of non-Russian ethnic groups. In 1962, in preparation for this development, the four Central Asian republics of Uzbekistan, Turkmenistan, Tajikistan, and Kirghizia were placed under a unified Communist Party command, and a single system of management was established in the areas of industry, construction, and cotton irrigation. This was followed in the Transcaucasian republics of Armenia, Georgia, and Azerbaijan by the adoption of a similar unified Party organization with looser economic coordination. Among the Baltic republics of Esthonia, Latvia, and Lithuania, the movement for integration was confined to joint conferences and cultural exchanges. In November, 1963, a joint conference of sociologists, economists, lawyers, and linguists was held in Frunze, capital of Kirghizia, which recommended the establishment of scholarly study groups in Central Asia, Transcaucasia, and the Baltic States to devise ways and means for the establishment of new federations in those areas. The conferees, according to press reports in *Sovetskaya Kirghizia,* attacked the "pseudo-scientific theory" of linguistic purity, acclaimed the Russian language as an important means of communication among Soviet peoples and ethnic groups, and called for an investigation of nationalist ideology that might be expected to oppose regional entities. The chief barrier to integration, especially in Central Asia and Transcaucasia, is still Islam. The Soviet government therefore intensified the training of atheistic native speakers and exhorted the Communist Party to break through the religious barrier.

Among the factors likely to promote the integration of Soviet minorities, the conference listed economic growth, common social change, greater communication between ethnic groups, and the increasing mobility of the Soviet population. The new Soviet constitution now being drafted to replace the Stalin Constitution of 1936 is expected to make provision for a new regional organization, as the first step toward the achievement of a unitary system of government.

Campaign Against Religion. One result of Soviet efforts to integrate the multi-national state was an intensification of the campaign against all religion —Orthodox, Muslim, Jewish, and other groups—in the USSR. Religion, even when professed by a minority, had proved to be a divisive factor in a country where the first commandment might well be phrased: "Thou shalt have no other god before Communism." The institution which holds the people together and serves as a strongly integrating force is the Communist Party. Communism is preached daily throughout the Soviet communications and educational systems. Anything that detracts from Communism, such as the historic religions, therefore, makes the government and Party leaders sensitive and apprehensive. The chief reason a measure of tolerance continues to prevail appears to be the confidence of Soviet officials that conventional religion is rapidly dying out. All that is required, therefore, is to facilitate the process by persuasion and indoctrination rather than by force.

"Scientific Atheism." The campaign for the dissemination of "scientific atheism," as it is called, is being carried out through two main channels—the churches and the sciences. Tourists, including the rapidly increasing masses of Soviet citizens on holidays, are encouraged to visit historic Russian churches and monasteries, such as those inside the Kremlin walls and in Kiev, the birthplace of Russian Christianity, preferably under efficient and well-trained atheistic guides. These shrines, most of them now museums, are interpreted as we would interpret the pagan temples of Greece and Rome—as something belonging to a bygone age, which Soviet citizens have long since outgrown. The visitors, especially the younger generation, can hardly fail to emerge from these empty religious centers more atheistically inclined than when they entered.

The Russian Orthodox church, the largest, has suffered proportionately more than other faiths. From 1960 to 1963, some 3500 Orthodox churches in the USSR were closed for lack of congregations able to maintain their upkeep. In 1963, only 10,000 churches, 17 monasteries, and five seminaries for the training of Orthodox priests remained.

In the Muslim areas of the USSR, especially in Soviet Central Asia and Transcaucasia, it is science that serves as the Soviet government's handmaiden to break down the religious barrier. Here regular evening sessions have been devoted to "Miracles Without Miracles." Scientific experiments (miracles) are performed, usually by teachers or other members of the "intelligentsia," whose object is to demonstrate that miracles are performed by Soviet man rather than by any deity. Part of the evening is devoted to belittling religious miracles, fasts, holy days, etc. The sputniks have been used to demonstrate man's power over nature. Already some Soviet scientists are advancing the theory that the planets were made by man, not by God, and that in the years to come Soviet scientists will create new planets in the heavens commensurate in size with those now in existence.

Secular Rituals. To insure the effectiveness of its anti-religious program, however, the Khrushchev regime began to devise a series of secular rituals, patterned after those of the major churches. The first strong appeal for "Soviet ritualism" appeared in *Izvestia,* October 4, 1959. Shortly thereafter, to stem the tide in favor of colorful church weddings, the now famous "Palaces of Weddings" in Moscow, Leningrad, and other centers, were set up to provide a secular ceremony that would add glamor to the institution of marriage completely lacking in the registry office. The Soviet marriage ritual proved so popular that nonreligious spring and harvest festivals were promoted on economic and ideological grounds, timed so as not to disrupt the agricultural season. Many religious holidays, such as Easter and Trinity Sunday in the Russian Orthodox church and the Bairam festivals of Muslim Central Asia, interfered with peasant labor in the fields, thereby resulting in substantial losses to the national economy. It is planned eventually to devise special Soviet ceremonies for the celebration of all major events in the lives of Soviet citizens.

Priority of Science. To make the twentieth century the era of Soviet technological development, the Soviet government accorded priority to the sciences over the humanities in education. The decree of the Council of Ministers of the USSR on the occasion of the opening on September 1, 1953, of the new buildings of the Moscow State University named after N. V. Lomonosov specifically directed the university administration to begin instruction and research at once in physics, chemistry, engineering mathematics, geology, and geography. In 1954 there were 54,000 graduates from Soviet engineering schools. By 1956 Soviet institutions of higher learning were said to be graduating almost twice as many scientists and engineers as were the institutions in the United States.

Sputnik. The urgency behind the Soviet priority for science and technology was revealed in memorable fashion in 1957. In August, the Khrushchev government announced its possession of an intercontinental ballistic missile (ICBM), with a range of 5,000 miles at 13,000 miles per hour. This was used in the autumn of the same year to place Sputniks I and II into orbit. On October 4 the free world was shocked to learn that the USSR had successfully

On November 3, 1963, the Soviet Palace of Weddings in Moscow was the scene of a noteworthy wedding. The first woman cosmonaut, Valentina Tereshkova, was married to Major Andryan Nikolayev, who piloted one of the spacecrafts in the world's first twin-orbit flight.

launched a 184-pound earth satellite which, at 18,000 miles per hour reached a maximum altitude of 560 miles. On November 3 a 1,129-pound rocket cone, which carried the dog Laika, began circling the earth at a maximum height of 1,056 miles. The Sputnik Age had dawned.

In space research and experimentation the USSR made significant advances in the Khrushchev era. In 1959 the Soviet Union launched rockets past the moon, onto the moon, and around it—achievements hailed by scientists throughout the world for the new knowledge acquired thereby and for the degree of control achieved by Soviet rocketry. Another achievement was the inauguration of manned space flights on April 12, 1961, with Yuri Gagarin,[4] the world's first cosmonaut, piloting *Vostok I*. He was followed by Herman Titov in *Vostok II*. In August, 1962, came the world's first twin-orbit space flight, with Major Andryan Nikolayev and Lieutenant Colonel Pavel Popovich. This marked the first time that information from a space ship was telecast on a large scale and relayed to numerous countries. The USSR also launched an automatic interplanetary station bound for Mars on November 1, 1962. Still another space precedent was set in June, 1963, when Valentina Tereshkova, the first woman cosmonaut, was launched in *Vostok VI*. Her subsequent marriage to cosmonaut Nikolayev at the Soviet Palace of Weddings in Moscow received sensational coverage in the Soviet press.

Khrushchev Versus Stalin. Although he denounced Stalin, Khrushchev perpetuated many of his predecessor's policies, including priority to heavy industry and the drive to overtake the capitalist countries, especially the United States. Khrushchev, however, was closer to the agriculturist than Stalin. His strongly developed political sense led him to make concessions to the *kolkhoz* farmers, and when harvests failed he imported grain rather than permit the population to starve. Whereas Stalin had purged the Old Bolsheviks, Khrushchev released and rehabilitated many of Stalin's victims. Unlike Stalin, Khrushchev travelled widely throughout the world—to Poland, Hungary, India, Burma, Yugoslavia, the UAR, the United States, and Scandinavia. More knowledgeable about world affairs, he abandoned the Stalin thesis of the inevitability of war under conditions of capitalist encirclement in favor of the policy of peaceful coexistence.

FOREIGN POLICY

Soviet-American Relations. American and Soviet reliance on strategy rather than on diplomacy after World War II resulted in a stalemate, the most graphic illustration of which was the continued partition of disputed areas—Berlin, Germany, Korea, Vietnam, and China—as a substitute for a permanent settlement. By 1957, when it appeared that neither the USA nor the USSR could make a major move on this planet without the danger of involvement in a nuclear holocaust, the first sputnik opened new vistas for competition in outer space. Tensions on earth seemed to relax temporarily. The threat of nuclear annihilation led to renewed efforts on the part of both protagonists

4. Gagarin was killed on March 27, 1968, when his MIG-15 jet fighter crashed on a training mission. He was given a hero's funeral and his ashes were placed in the Kremlin wall.

in the cold war to return to diplomacy. As interpreted by George F. Kennan, the concept of "disengagement"—the withdrawal of NATO forces from West Germany and the neutralization of that country—was viewed as an alternative to rigid "containment" of the USSR by many European liberals, but unqualifiedly rejected by Dean Acheson. In the United States and England, the advocates of negotiation recalled that even during the Stalin regime some agreements had been reached. The treaties with Italy and the Balkan states in 1946 and the peace settlement for Austria on February 10, 1947, although not entirely satisfactory to either side, had contributed to the restoration of stability in Europe. The postponement of major issues, such as the German question, in the name of "a cooling-off period" had resulted in no settlement at all and little or no prospect of one a decade later. The Japanese peace settlement at the San Francisco Conference on September 5, 1951, was achieved by the West without benefit of the USSR, which continued to regard it as a violation of Allied pledges in World War II not to make a separate peace. In retaliation, the Kremlin threatened to make a separate peace with East Germany. Unlike Japan, however, Germany was divided, and any attempt to end the *status quo* involved the risk of an East-West conflict. A German settlement required negotiation.

For the United States and the Soviet Union, the road back to diplomacy was strewn with obstacles. As they reacted to one another's strategic moves in the cold war following World War II, through long disuse the diplomatic gears became rusty. In the absence of regular diplomatic negotiations, American and Soviet diplomats ceased to know and understand one another. The very language of diplomacy appeared to have been shelved as both sides resorted to epithets in the cold war. In other words, being "tough" had taken precedence over being diplomatic. Americans and Russians, it seemed, were prepared to negotiate only on their own terms, but without yielding one iota of their respective demands. Concessions were still regarded as "appeasement," a term that had acquired disagreeable connotations in the days of Munich. On January 27, 1958, a simple beginning was made with the signing of the Soviet-American Cultural Agreement, which provided for the exchange of scientists, artists, teachers, students, athletes, and journalists. In September, 1959, in the interests of better Soviet-American relations, Khrushchev paid his memorable visit to the United States, where he could not help but be profoundly impressed by American living standards. In conference with Eisenhower at Camp David, Khrushchev won the president's consent to a "summit" meeting to reduce international tensions and seek agreement on outstanding issues. The "spirit of Camp David" raised hopes of the end of the cold war.

Paris Summit Conference. Khrushchev's insistence on summitry was a natural outgrowth of the highly centralized Soviet system, where important decisions could be made only by the head of the government. He therefore assumed that a conference of the heads of state could produce a settlement without unnecessary loss of time. He was completely unversed in the more complex machinery of the American system, by which decisions are made at the top only after long and careful preparation at lower levels. To Khrushchev in 1959, rejection of a summit meeting would have been equivalent to a refusal to negotiate. In spite of American qualms about going straight to the summit without adequate preparation, President Eisenhower agreed to make the effort in the interests of peace. The summit conference was scheduled to be held in Paris on May 16, 1960.

Although there were numerous issues that merited consideration in Paris, including Poland, Hungary, Korea, Allied bases encircling the USSR, and disarmament, the Soviet government was interested primarily in Germany, and especially in Berlin, the most dangerous trouble spot in Europe. At the very least, it anticipated that Soviet concessions elsewhere would make possible some modification of the status of Berlin. The USSR had emerged from World War II with a German complex—an abiding fear of another German invasion. This was a natural result of the loss of over twenty million people (soldiers and civilians), not to mention the material destruction incurred during the German occupation of the greater part of European Russia. Fear of Germany was not confined to the Soviet Union. It was shared by the Slavic states of Poland, Czechoslovakia, and even Yugoslavia. The dilemma that confronted the Western world, especially the United States, Great Britain, and France, was that without Germany Western Europe could not be defended against aggression from the Soviet orbit. On the other hand, every measure taken by the West to strengthen Germany bound the Slavic countries, which the West hoped to liberate, closer to the USSR. In the West the threat of the USSR preserved NATO. In the East the threat of Germany insured the unity of the Soviet bloc.

It is understandable, therefore, that the Russians pinned great hopes on Khrushchev's trek to Paris. The Soviet press conditioned them to expect Soviet concessions elsewhere in return for concessions on Germany. Khrushchev himself encouraged Russians to believe that a negotiated settlement was both possible and preferable to one obtained by reliance on military force, a view not concurred in by the Red Army at that time, especially by Marshal Malinovsky. They could not conceive, however, that the Soviet premier would go to Paris without securing concessions on Germany. Like Disraeli, who returned to England from the Berlin Congress of 1878 bearing "peace with Cyprus," Khrushchev was expected to return from Paris with something tangible, such as the end of the Allied occupation of Berlin or recognition of the East German government. Neither the Red Army chiefs nor the civilian population was prepared for him to return empty-handed. Nor is it likely that Khrushchev would have gone to Paris had he not believed that the trip would serve the vital interests of the USSR.

Collapse of the Summit. It was to forestall the possibility of concessions at German expense that Konrad Adenauer conferred in advance of the summit conference with Presidents Eisenhower and DeGaulle. Khrushchev arrived in Paris only to discover that the road was blocked to any concessions on Berlin and Germany. Since it was virtually impossible for him to return to Moscow empty-handed, he was prepared on any pretext to sabotage the conference. It was at this point that strategy entered the picture and once again superseded diplomacy. On May 1 an American U-2 plane on an intelligence flight from Pakistan to Norway was shot down over the city of Sverdlovsk in Siberia. As subsequently revealed, it was not the first such flight, but it provided Khrushchev with a face-saving device by means of which he could abandon a conference that promised no results. To the dismay of the assembled diplomats and a watching world, on May 16, Khrushchev refused outright to participate in the summit conference without a public apology from President Eisenhower for the incident and assurances that there would be no repetition of such flights over Soviet soil and that those responsible for the current flight would be punished. The tone and content of Khrushchev's ultimatum made it impossible for the president to apologize. Under such conditions, the Paris Conference on which by now the hopes of the world were pinned collapsed.

Khrushchev and Kennedy. In spite of the Paris debacle, the American and Soviet governments kept the door ajar for the resumption of summit negotiations under more propitious circumstances in the future. In his inaugural address of January, 1961, President John F. Kennedy held out an olive branch: "Let us never negotiate out of fear," he said, "but let us never fear to negotiate." The impression was given that he was ready to assume the initia-

Sovfoto

Premier Khrushchev and President Kennedy met at the Soviet Embassy in Vienna in June, 1961. Although the encounter was amicable, it produced no positive results.

tive, lest all credit for peace efforts, at least as far as the Afro-Asian world was concerned, should go to the USSR. Early in June President Kennedy and Khrushchev met face-to-face in Vienna—a sobering experience, in which both leaders appeared to learn what was *not* negotiable. There was sharp disagreement between them on Berlin, German unification, and the control of nuclear weapons. President Kennedy was clearly shaken by the discovery that Berlin was of such vital importance to Soviet security. Khrushchev was seriously disturbed by the American determination to preserve, at least for the time being, the *status quo* on Berlin. The outcome was a reversion to cold-war strategy.

Berlin Crisis. On June 15 the Soviet government delivered a virtual ultimatum to the West, by threatening to conclude a separate peace with East Germany—a move that implied the cutting off of Western access to Berlin—unless Soviet terms for a German peace treaty were accepted by the end of the year. In the crisis that followed, the United States government called up military reserves and proceeded to strengthen the defenses of Berlin. In a television address to the nation on July 25, President Kennedy committed the United States to the defense of Germany. "We cannot and will not permit the Communists," he said, "to drive us out of Berlin either gradually or by force." Fulfillment of this pledge he regarded as essential to the morale and security of Western Germany, to the unity of Western Europe, and to the faith of the entire free world.

For Khrushchev, however, Berlin had become a "bone in the throat," which demanded action. He referred to it as "a lit fuse in a powder magazine of a time-bomb which may explode at any moment." This was the third crisis instigated by the Soviets over Berlin, the other two having occurred in 1948 and 1958. Since 1945, four million Germans had escaped from Communist-controlled East Germany to the free world, a large percentage of them skilled technicians and intellectuals. During the critical days of early August (August 1–12), some 22,000 had crossed to freedom. To seal off East Berlin and prevent further loss of skilled manpower, the German Communist regime, backed by Soviet tanks, on the night of August 13 erected the Berlin wall. Since American commitments were to West Berlin only, no action was taken by United States troops. President Adenauer once again stated that there was nothing to negotiate about with the USSR. On August 31 the Soviet government announced the forthcoming renewal of its hydrogen bomb tests, one of which proved to be of fifty-megaton capacity.

United Nations Appearance. In September, 1960, a frustrated and angry Khrushchev appeared before the United Nations in an effort to avoid a major showdown between the East and the West. In a speech memorable for his shoe-banging, Khrushchev reinforced earlier Soviet proposals for general and complete disarmament, including the prohibition of all nuclear weapons and destruction of existing stockpiles of the same. He likewise called for "peaceful coexistence" as "the only sensible path for developing international relations in our time." Having placed the entire blame for failure to secure disarmament and a German peace treaty on the United States and the NATO powers, Khrushchev's behavior before the United Nations was not conducive to better East-West relations. The surprise package in his address—an outgrowth of the Congo crisis—was his proposed reorganization of the United Nations Secretariat, involving the replacement of the secretary-general by a "troika" (three representatives), one each from the Communist, Western, and unaligned blocs. From the Soviet standpoint Dag Hammarskjold, the highly respected UN secretary-general, not being a Communist, was incapable of acting as a neutral administrator. Although until 1960 the USSR had consistently refused to consider amendments of any kind to the UN Charter, the "troika" reflected Soviet demands for "parity" in international negotiations and Soviet efforts to curry favor with the developing nations. With three administrators the chance of securing action to implement UN decisions was about as remote as the efforts of the swan, the pike, and the crayfish in Krylov's fable to draw a cart and freight.

Coexistence. Apparently impressed by the firm stand of the United States on Berlin, Khrushchev went before the Twenty-Second Congress of the Communist Party at the end of October, 1961, to proclaim a policy of peaceful coexistence:

> In adopting our new Program, our great Party solemnly proclaims to all mankind that it considers the principal aim of its foreign policy to be not only the prevention of world war but its elimination forever from the life of society within the lifetime of our generation. . . .

Under the Stalin regime, war was regarded as inevitable in an epoch of imperialism. Only until the USSR achieved nuclear parity with the West was peace secure. By abandoning the Communist thesis of the inevitability of war, Khrushchev completed his official break with Stalinism. Peaceful coexistence was possible, according to the Soviet premier, because imperialism was already on the decline. Socialism was winning by peaceful expansion throughout the world. Under these circumstances, all that was necessary was to concentrate on the growth of the socialist camp into a powerful empire, and to continue economic and ideological competition with the capitalist world. Khrushchev's formal enunciation of a policy of peaceful coexistence and his attack on Albania further alienated the Red Chinese, who were primarily interested in exploiting numerous revolutionary situations in Asia, even at the risk of all-out nuclear war.

It should be understood that the Soviet concept of peaceful coexistence, like that of "democracy," "freedom," and "progress," differed radically from the definition of these terms in the West. It did not involve any abandonment of the Communist goal—the reshaping of the entire world in the communist image. It was not accompanied by any retraction of Khrushchev's threat in

1956 to "bury" the United States. Nor did it eliminate all wars, certainly not local "anti-imperialist" wars of liberation, although it was certainly intended to prevent a world holocaust. A few months later (January 30, 1962), Mikhail Suslov, top Soviet Party theoretician, stated in *Pravda* that "in the realm of ideology" peaceful coexistence with the West was impossible and unthinkable, since it would amount to "ideological disarmament for Communists."

Khrushchev nevertheless demonstrated the positive aspects of coexistence on November 6, 1961, when he abandoned his deadline for a peace treaty with Germany. In December, 1963, President Johnson, obviously unwilling to leave to the Soviets the entire credit for coexistence, announced that "the number one objective" of the United States was to convince the world that "we court no territory, we seek no satellites, that we are trying to live in peace and prosperity." This amounted to an American version of coexistence.

Cuban Crisis. The Cuban crisis of 1962 temporarily threatened the very foundations of the policy of coexistence. Following persistent rumors of a Soviet military build-up in Cuba, President Kennedy in a special broadcast to the nation on October 22 confirmed the "unmistakable evidence" of Soviet construction of a series of offensive long-range missile sites on that island within ninety miles of United States territory. He immediately proclaimed "a strict quarantine on all offensive military equipment under shipment to Cuba," and called upon Khrushchev to "halt and eliminate this clandestine, reckless, and provocative threat to peace." Any missile launched from Cuba against a nation in the western hemisphere, he warned, would be regarded as "an attack by the Soviet Union on the United States, requiring a full retaliatory response upon the Soviet Union." The president offered to provide assurances against an American invasion of Cuba if the USSR would remove its weapons from the island under international inspection. The dispute was carried to the United Nations Security Council by Cuba, the United States, and the Soviet Union. Following a direct appeal by UN Secretary-General U Thant to President Kennedy and Chairman Khrushchev for a voluntary suspension of arms shipments and quarantine measures, the USA and the USSR entered into negotiations for a peaceful settlement of this explosive issue. A Soviet-American agreement was reached on the inspection of Soviet ships and on the removal of missiles and other installations.

Premier Fidel Castro of Cuba proved more difficult to handle. Anastas Mikoyan, first deputy premier of the USSR, spent twenty-four days in Cuba in November without securing an agreement on international inspection of the dismantling of Soviet bases on Cuban soil. Not until November 19 did Castro agree to the withdrawal of Soviet jet bombers. Although he consented to the removal of Soviet property, he contended that no foreign government could legitimately commit the independent state of Cuba to foreign inspection of disarmament, something that the USSR itself had consistently refused to permit. In an effort to prove that Cuba was no Soviet satellite, Castro rejected outside inspection of Cuban sites unless the United States likewise agreed to United Nations inspection of the dismantling of Cuban exile training camps on American soil, from which the "Bay of Pigs" invasion of Cuba allegedly had been launched in 1961. As a result of the failure of the Soviet Union to guarantee international verification of the dismantling and withdrawal of all offensive weapons from Cuba, President Kennedy withheld his no-invasion pledge and the United States continued its aerial surveillance of the island. Nevertheless, by a narrow margin war had been averted.

Throughout the Cuban crisis, the Soviet Union contended that its military bases were for the defense of Cuba, which had been threatened by invasion, and not for offensive purposes. In 1963, however, Premier Castro was said to have stated in an interview with a French correspondent that Soviet bases were established in Cuba, not to insure Cuban defense but for strategic purposes—to strengthen the socialist camp throughout the world. There is reason to believe that at least one of the reasons for the construction of Soviet missile sites on Cuba close to American shores was to demonstrate to the people of the United States what it was like to have American bases along the Soviet periphery. During the crisis, there were reports in the press of "swapping" Turkish bases for Cuban.

The immediate and vigorous reaction of the United States to the Soviet move in Cuba should not have surprised the Soviet government. The United States emerged from World War II with a Pearl Harbor complex, determined to avoid any possibility of a surprise attack on American territory in the future. Hence the American preoccupation with inspection in any disarmament agreement on Cuba or elsewhere. Foreign missiles in Cuba constituted a threat to the vital interests of the United States and to the Organization of American States, which promptly expelled Cuba. Since Cuba was not of primary importance for the defense of the Soviet Union, Khrushchev readily retreated before the threat of nuclear war, which he has consistently sought to avoid. The retreat exposed him to the taunt of cowardice from Red China, but it saved the peace. He continued to reiterate his pledge to support Cuba in the event of that island's invasion.

Sino-Soviet Estrangement. With the denunciation of Stalin at the Twentieth Congress of the Communist Party in 1956, the climate of opinion in Red China toward the USSR began to change. In proportion as Khrushchev turned to the West, especially to the United States to establish a *modus vivendi* and to implement his coexistence policy, Soviet relations with Communist China deteriorated. Stalin's de-Europeanization of the USSR was music to Chinese ears. Moreover, Stalin, who was of Georgian birth, ranked as an Asian. He was a contemporary of Mao Tse-tung, whereas Khrushchev was merely Stalin's assistant and therefore not of equal stature. The real turning point in Sino-Soviet relations appears to have been Khrushchev's visit in 1959 to the United States, Red China's most bitter enemy, the country which blocked the recovery of Formosa and other islands off the Chinese mainland and which prevented Red China's entry into the United Nations. Khrushchev, who denounced the basic tenets of Stalinism and then offered the hand of friendship to the United States, in Chinese eyes was guilty not only of ideological heresy but of violating the spirit of the "unbreakable" alliance of 1950 with Red China. The Sino-Soviet dispute over coexistence seemed to indicate that Red China was still in the stage of Militant Communism abandoned by the Soviet regime in the early 1920's.

There were other reasons for the growing estrangement between the partners of the Sino-Soviet axis. Serious dissatisfaction developed over Red China's interference in Soviet bloc affairs, as in the Polish crisis of 1956, the dispute with Albania, and policy toward Rumania. Khrushchev bluntly voiced his disapproval of Mao Tse-tung's "great leap forward" through the establishment of huge collective communes, scoffed that Russia had tried communes and they did not work. Although Red China received substantial economic and military aid from the USSR after World War II, both indirectly through the allocation of captured Japanese materiel and directly through Soviet economic and technical assistance for Chinese industrialization, this help was never commensurate with Chinese needs. Moreover, it was paid for by exports of food and raw materials to the USSR which the Chinese could ill afford to spare. Mao Tse-tung could not brook the increase of Soviet aid to non-communist countries in Asia and Africa at the expense of Red China, the ally of the Soviet Union. He resented the lack of Soviet cooperation to enable Red China to become a nuclear power. As tension increased, the Soviet government even withdrew several thousand Soviet technical experts from China, many of whom had wounded Chinese pride by their attitudes of superiority. In spite of all the difficulties confronted by the regime of Mao Tse-tung, Red China in the late 1950's not only ceased to be a Soviet satellite, but increasingly became a competitor rather than a partner in Asia, Africa, and more recently in Latin America. Instead of one unchallenged authoritative leadership of the communist world centered in Moscow, as in the Stalin era, there were two, one in Moscow and one in Peking, competing for the allegiance of other so-called communist nations.

With Red China as a rival, the USSR faced competition from two sources in its third drive for the Muslim East and Africa—the Mao Tse-tung regime and the Western democracies. On his extended tour of Africa (the UAR, Algeria, Morocco, Mali, Guinea, Somalia, etc.), in December, 1963–January, 1964, to make contacts with African leaders, Premier Chou En-lai assured President Nasser of the United Arab Republic that there would be no strings attached to Chinese aid to African nations. In his efforts to identify Red China's aspirations with those of the newly emerging African states, the Chinese leader confronted major obstacles. His appeal to the common bond of the ancient cultures of Egypt and China was only of sentimental value to Nasser, who is primarily concerned with the rapid development of the UAR into a modern industrial state toward which Red China has little or nothing to contribute for the present. Nasser's dispatch of Chou En-lai to the Soviet-sponsored Aswan High Dam was a pointed hint of the type of economic and technical assistance he would welcome from Red China. In Algeria, where Chinese aggression against India had created a bad impression, Chou En-lai confronted Arab support for the Khrushchev policy of coexistence.

One of the main sources of dispute between Red China and the USSR has been Chinese pressure for territorial aggrandizement in Asia. The USSR, on the other hand, wished to demonstrate to the West that with the retreat of the colonial powers, Asian problems could be settled peacefully. At the Twenty-Second Congress of the Communist Party Khrushchev stated: "The Soviet Union wishes to live in peace and friendship even with such neighbors as Iran, Pakistan, and Japan," which are tied to Western-sponsored blocs. The Soviet purpose was to transform Asia into a *Zona Mira* (Zone of Peace). Its outstanding pillars, in addition to the USSR, were to be Red China and India, which together would insure the peace of Asia.

In line with this policy, the Red Chinese arranged an amicable and advantageous settlement of their border disputes with Burma and Nepal. Their refusal to recognize the McMahon Line between Tibet and India, however, increasingly threatened Soviet objectives for *Zona Mira*. A situation developed in which the USSR, a socialist state, appeared to be offering India, a capitalist regime, economic and military aid against her communist ally Red China. Likewise, Red China supported the anti-communist state of Pakistan against India in the Kashmir dispute, while the USSR vetoed a Western move in the United Nations Security Council (June 21, 1962) to force India to negotiate this fourteen-year-old territorial issue.

Today, when there is a strong movement in Western Europe to subordinate nationalism to Europeanism and even to promote the interdependence of Europe and America in an Atlantic Union, nationalism in Asia takes precedence over internationalism. In a Moscow speech in 1961 President Sukarno of Indonesia reminded Soviet leaders that what is going on in Asia and Africa is national, not international or world, revolution, and that a recognition of this fact is basic to an understanding of the peoples of these continents. This rising nationalist tide in Asia has made its peoples more territory-conscious than ever before. Protesting Anglo-American opposition to India's stand on Kashmir (June 22, 1962), Prime Minister Nehru made this abundantly clear in his emotionally charged statement: "Kashmir is flesh of our flesh and bone of our bones."

In the summer of 1962 there were signs of a *rapprochement* between the USSR and Red China on Asian policies. On July 23, both signed the Geneva Declaration and Protocol guaranteeing the neutrality and independence of Laos. Two weeks later, on August 6, possibly under Soviet pressure, Mao Tse-tung agreed to India's request for the resumption of negotiations for the peaceful settlement of the Ladakh border dispute in Kashmir on the basis of a 1960 report largely favorable to India. There appeared to be continued collaboration on the Sino-Soviet border in connection with the Amur and Sungari power and transport projects.

The eruption, in October, 1962, of Red China's border dispute with India into extensive armed clashes on several fronts, accompanied by Chinese military penetration of India, was a major blow to the Soviet concepts of the *Zona Mira* and coexistence. Having cultivated Indian friendship for years and advanced substantial economic and some military aid to that country, Chinese aggression placed the Soviet government on the horns of a dilemma. It soon became clear that the USSR would not support the invasion of India by its Chinese ally. To the USSR, the Sino-Indian conflict was no ideological war. It had all the earmarks of old-fashioned imperialistic territorial expansion. Moreover, India was an Asian, not a Western power, and one which had strongly supported the entry of Red China into the United Nations. The fact that Red China was the aggressor relieved the USSR of any obligation under the terms of the Sino-Soviet alliance of 1950. To the outside world, it appeared that Red China was using communist tools to attain a nationalist objective at the same time that the USSR used national tools to serve a communist purpose. Even the staunchly anti-communist regime of Chiang Kai-shek approved Red China's territorial claims on India.

Until 1964 the Soviet government sought to cover up its growing estrangement from Red China and to call off the ideological polemics involved. For the Central Committee's plenary session in February, 1964, however, M. A. Suslov, its secretary, summed up the ideological and political controversy between the two allies. He accused the Mao Tse-tung regime of "rehashing Trotskyism," of promoting subversion inside the Soviet Union, of seeking to disrupt the unity and solidarity of the socialist commonwealth, of belittling the role of world socialism in the national liberation movement in Asia and Africa, of trying to impose on the entire socialist camp its own brand of "sinicized socialism," of pursuing an "adventurist" course in foreign policy, and practicing "the cult of the individual." Although Red China levelled its propaganda guns against the Soviet policy of peaceful coexistence, never before, according to Suslov, had so many businessmen and political leaders from capitalist countries been visiting Peking for the conclusion of agreements on trade, credits, scientific and technological aid, and political issues. The Soviet government pressed for a conference of all the socialist powers to resolve once and for all this troublesome situation, even if it involved the expulsion of Red China from the socialist camp. Apparently on the ground that the USSR still had the power to bring about their exclusion, the Red Chinese promptly rejected such a conference.

From 1960 on, the breach between the Soviets and the Red Chinese was reflected in the curtailment of the Soviet aid program for the Chinese People's Republic. According to Suslov, the USSR had granted Red China 1,816,000,-000 rubles in long-term credits on highly favorable terms. With Soviet assistance the Chinese Communists constructed over two hundred fully equipped major industrial enterprises, shops, and other projects, among them the Changchun Motor Vehicle Plant, the Harbin Electrical Equipment Plant, and the Loyang Tractor Plant. During the decade 1950 to 1960, more than 10,000 Soviet specialists served in China, and from 1951 to 1962 some 10,000 Chinese engineers, technicians, and skilled workers received instruction, scientific training, and practical experience in the USSR, and over 11,000 Chinese students graduated from Soviet higher educational institutions. According to the Soviet version, denied by the Mao Tse-tung regime, in 1960 the Chinese government demanded the complete revision of all existing agreements on economic and scientific-technical cooperation, rejected a substantial part of the scheduled deliveries of Soviet equipment, and proceeded to cut to a minimum the volume of Sino-Soviet trade. In a procedure reminiscent of Soviet action on American Lend-Lease aid, the Red Chinese allegedly removed Soviet trademarks from machine tools and other items and alleged that the USSR had provided China with obsolete equipment. The Mao Tse-tung regime, for its part, claims to have shipped to the USSR large quantities of strategic minerals, including borax, tungsten, mercury, molybdenum, tin, and lithium, and other minerals essential to the development of rocketry and nuclear weapons.

When the Soviet foreign aid drive was first launched, the major Soviet target was the Middle East, especially the Arab world. This area still figures prominently in the Soviet program. After 1960, however, the major emphasis of the aid and trade program shifted to the Far East and South Asia, especially, to Red China's distress, to the heavily-populated non-communist states of Indonesia and India, and more recently, to Japan.

Indonesia. The Republic of Indonesia, for various reasons, became a prime target of the Soviet drive to the East. Indonesia's campaign for the further liquidation of colonialism by annexation of West Irian from the Netherlands received strong moral and material Soviet support. As a major Muslim state (population nearing 100,000,000), Indonesia offset Pakistan, which was tied to the Western-sponsored CENTO and SEATO blocks, and also the Philippines, oriented toward the United States. Although Indonesia was the first Muslim state to meet and win the challenge of communism in Civil War (1958–1961), its Communist Party, over two million strong, was the largest and best disciplined outside the Soviet orbit, and was reputed to be one of the two most important forces backing the Sukarno regime, the other being the officer corps. The objective of the government's Eight-Year-Plan (1961–1969), approved December 3, 1960, was to transform Indonesia from a basically agrarian into an industrial nation. The plan clearly indicated that the Indonesian economy would be based largely on state rather than on private enterprise, a purposeful drift toward socialism or state capitalism welcomed by the USSR.

Soviet credits, it was estimated, covered from 15 per cent to 20 per cent of Indonesian investments in the Eight-Year-Plan. The Soviet-Indonesian Agree-

ment for Economic and Technical Collaboration, February 28, 1960, provided $250,000,000 for economic aid, most of it for industrial enterprises,
including metallurgical plants in Kalimantan (Borneo) and Java, and the
great Asahan industrial complex in Sumatra. The largest stadium in Asia,
built at Sukarno's request to accommodate 100,000 persons and modelled
after the Lenin Stadium in Moscow, was opened in Djakarta, July 21, 1962,
just in time for the Fourth Asian Games in August.

In the area of military aid, in which the United States was handicapped by
friendly relations with the Netherlands, Soviet achievement was even more
spectacular. MIG-15 fighter planes, piloted by Indonesians trained in the
UAR and Czechoslovakia, made their appearance in Indonesia in 1958. It
has been estimated that well over $750,000,000 of Soviet bloc military aid,
fully one-third of that allocated to "neutral" nations, went to Indonesia to
promote the liberation of West Irian. This up-to-date military equipment
included MIG-21 fighter planes armed with missiles, TV-16 medium bombers, amphibious tanks and artillery, as well as submarines and cruisers. Large
numbers of Soviet instructors were assigned to Indonesian ground, air, and
sea forces.

The Dutch-Indonesian agreement for Indonesian occupation of West Irian
by May, 1963, arranged through the good offices of the United States and
signed at the United Nations, August 15, 1962, rendered this military buildup
superfluous. It did not, however, remove the danger of Indonesian military
dependence on the USSR. The Soviet Union reaped much of the credit for the
settlement on the ground that no peaceful solution was possible without
strong Soviet backing and military aid. Sukarno used his military power in
1963 to threaten the new Asian state of Malaysia.

India. Although Nehru's India, which preserved close ties with the West,
especially with the British Commonwealth and the United States, was slow to
respond to Soviet overtures for extended economic and cultural relations, the
success of the Bhilai steel plant, which went into full operation in January,
1961, and the scrupulous behavior of Soviet experts training Indian workers,
encouraged a marked expansion in Soviet-Indian trade. Soviet leaders, impressed by the rapid rise of the Indian proletariat, hoped for a friendly Indian
"socialist" regime in the future. In the elections of February, 1962, Indian
Communists, with 11,473,384 votes, won thirty seats in Parliament. An
informative article by P. Kutsobin in *Pravda* complained, however, that Right-
wing Socialists in both India and Indonesia formed the diehard core of anti-
communism, and that efforts should be made to win them over.

Soviet objectives were advanced by consistent Soviet support of India's
claims to Kashmir and commendation of her contribution to the liquidation of
colonialism through the forcible annexation of Portuguese Goa, Damao, and
Diu, in December, 1961. This was in sharp contrast to British and American
criticism of Indian action in both instances. Fear of Red China, uncertainty
about the amount and continuation of American aid (especially since the

United States Senate's attempted 25 per cent cut in 1962), and about India's relationship to the European Common Market in the event of British membership, no doubt contributed to the Nehru government's interest in closer relations with the USSR. From the Soviet standpoint India served as a counterweight to Communist China, both in the present and for the future.

Soviet loans to India since 1955, amounting to more than $800,000,000, failed to approach the $4,000,000,000 advanced by the United States. Soviet aid, however, was directed toward large state-owned industrial enterprises, such as the Bhilai steel mill, three hydroelectric stations, the heavy-machine building complex at Ranchi (scheduled for completion in 1964), and two oil refineries, all of which demonstrated the progress of Indian industrialization. In June, 1962, the USSR agreed to supply engines for supersonic transport aircraft under construction in India on a British model.

The decision of the Nehru government in July, 1962, to negotiate for the purchase of two squadrons of Soviet MIG-21 jet fighter planes, and for the manufacture of this plane in India, marked a new trend in Soviet military aid to the Nehru regime, which earlier rejected American military assistance and a plane deal with Britain. When these negotiations were announced, the Indian government resented British and American protests as unwarranted interference in India's domestic affairs, especially in view of United States military aid to Pakistan. Heretofore, Soviet military aid had gone mainly to the UAR, Indonesia, and Iraq.

Taking advantage of the favorable climate of official Indian opinion, Anastas I. Mikoyan, Soviet deputy premier, cut short his visit to Indonesia in July, 1962, to enter into broad discussions with Nehru for still greater economic collaboration, which would demonstrate to the world "the peaceful coexistence of two countries with divergent social structures." Mikoyan's plea for time to plan such large-scale aid and the subsequent Soviet announcement of delay in the delivery of electrical generators already pledged for India's Third Five-Year Plan suggested the overextension of Soviet commitments, which even the COMECON could not solve.

Red China's invasion of India resulted in a comparative lull in Soviet-Indian relations. Since that conflict was not formally settled, the USSR, as an ally of Red China, became wary of committing itself to large-scale Indian aid. Soviet caution may have stemmed from Nehru's avowed intention "to recover territory illegally occupied by the Chinese." The Nehru government, aware of the Soviet predicament, refrained from putting undue pressure on the Soviet Union, and turned more and more to the West, especially to Great Britain and the United States, for military aid. At the close of 1963, however, Khrushchev scheduled another tour of India and South Asia for February, 1964.

Japan. The USSR, in search of new sources of industrial equipment to supplement shortages at home, turned to industrialized Japan in the summer of 1962. The first long-term trade agreement between Japan and the Soviet Union was concluded in March, 1960, by the Japanese Sea, a private company representing firms interested in Japan-USSR trade. Within two years the trade volume was said to have reached $225,000,000, exceeding all expectations. Progress with Japan was slow, partly because of official distrust of Soviet motives and apprehension of endangering the Japanese-American Alliance.

When the Japanese had neared the saturation point in Western markets and were jolted by the 1962 slump on the New York Stock Exchange, the Khrushchev government dangled before them the irresistible bait of a vast Siberian market, which might increase the trade turnover to $1,000,000,000 within a few years. With Soviet plans for the industrialization of Siberia and the Soviet Far East lagging behind Soviet goals, Khrushchev and Mikoyan proposed to Agriculture Minister Kono in the early summer of 1962 the possibility of using Japanese production to accelerate development there. As in other Asian countries, one Soviet objective was the reduction of Japanese dependence on the West, in this case on the United States. The Russians took the precaution to emphasize that this was no Far Eastern Rapallo Treaty, by means of which the Japanese would develop munitions factories in Siberia and train Japanese forces there.

Kono recognized the vast ideological gulf that separated Japan from the Communist orbit. Nonetheless, on August 8, 1962, a high-level Japanese trade mission to Moscow was led by Yoshinari Kawai, president of the important machinery producer, the Komatsu Manufacturing Company. Kawai's delegation of about sixty, including bankers and representatives of the machine-construction, shipbuilding, and synthetic fibers industries, was ostensibly a private, not a government, venture. It had the backing of top Japanese business interests, who felt that they must assume the initiative to end economic depression and unemployment, especially in the oil and steel industries, thereby helping to preserve capitalism at home. The recent success of Japanese private industry in establishing trade relations with Red China, which led to government moves to expand that trade, appeared to set a precedent for dealings with the USSR.

For the USSR, an industrialized and populated Siberia provided a "cushion" in the event of conflict either in Europe or Asia. From a long-range viewpoint, the contemplated economic collaboration might be regarded as a Soviet-Japanese insurance policy against Red Chinese expansion. The Soviet drive to double the population of the sparsely settled Soviet Far East within a decade was due not only to the normal expansion of Soviet industrial capacity north and east of Lake Baikal, but to the revival of Red China's long dormant claims to that area. Peking's protests against the "unequal" treaties of Aigun (1858), Peking (1860), and St. Petersburg (1881)—the last two signed under duress—have suggested that the Sino-Soviet border is no more acceptable to the Red Chinese than the Sino-Indian frontier. The area in dispute may involve as much as 500,000 square miles of territory with a population somewhat in excess of 10,000,000.

In spite of the visible estrangement of the Sino-Soviet partners, their alliance has proved to be of mutual benefit in the past and may continue to be useful in the future. Without the backing of the USSR, Red China would have enjoyed no security against a Western-sponsored invasion of the mainland. Since 1950 the alliance has strengthened Soviet power and prestige in Asia, Europe, and the emerging nations. Both Khrushchev and Red China's leaders have recognized these facts and have left the door open to reconciliation. From Cairo in December, 1963, Chou En-lai warned the West that the rift is not permanent: "If anything unusual happens," he prophesied, "the Soviet Union and China will stand shoulder to shoulder and arm to arm." Sino-Soviet estrangement appears to have resulted, in part at least, from the absence of any undue threat from the outside which would require a solid front.

Limited Agreement on Disarmament. One positive step toward the end of the cold war—a limited agreement on disarmament—was achieved in 1963. After protracted negotiations to end the disarmament deadlock, the United States and the USSR initialed in Moscow in August a test-ban treaty to outlaw nuclear tests everywhere except underground. This agreement was formally ratified in October. In the United States it was followed by the announcement of limited withdrawals of American troops from overseas bases and the reduction of military expenses at home. In the Soviet Union Khrushchev also announced an appreciable reduction in the size of the Red Army and proceeded to divert funds earmarked for military purposes to industrial expansion. This accord on disarmament, regarded as one of a series of steps to relieve international tensions, was almost universally acclaimed. The assassination of President Kennedy, November 22, 1963, aroused worldwide apprehension as to the continuation of this effort to promote peace and security. President Lyndon B. Johnson promptly assured Premier Khrushchev by telegram (November 24) of his intention to continue President Kennedy's efforts in "the cause of peace and the peaceful settlement of international problems" and to work for the improvement of "relations between all countries, including the Soviet Union and the United States."

End of the Khrushchev Era. The overthrow of seventy-year-old Nikita Khrushchev came suddenly and without warning. On October 16, 1964, the Central Committee of the Communist Party, in plenary session, announced that "at his own request" Khrushchev had been relieved of his duties for reasons of "age and deteriorating health." His party and government offices were divided between two of his former supporters, with Leonid I. Brezhnev becoming first secretary of the Party's Central Committee and Alexei N. Kosygin assuming the post of premier. *Pravda* subsequently accused Khrushchev of a whole series of sins of commission and omission—"hairbrained schemes, immature conclusions, hasty decisions, bragging and phrasemongering, commandism, unwillingness to take into account the achievements of science and practical experience. . . ." To allay the misgivings of the Western powers that this change in leadership heralded a major shift in Soviet foreign policy, the Kremlin hastened to assure them, including the United States, that the USSR would continue to pursue its policy of peaceful coexistence. Since Khrushchev's personal vendetta with Mao Tse-tung had proved to be a major obstacle to the improvement of Sino-Soviet relations, his removal appeared to provide fresh opportunities to heal the breach between the two allies. These expectations, however, have not yet been realized, no doubt because Khrushchev's successors failed to repudiate the policy of coexistence with the West, especially with the United States.

28

Khrushchev's Successors, 1964-1968

ESCHEWING ANY RESORT to sensationalism or the "cult of personality," Khrushchev's successors, Leonid I. Brezhnev (1906–   ), general secretary of the Central Committee of the Communist Party of the Soviet Union, and Alexei N. Kosygin (1904–   ), premier, with Anastas I. Mikoyan serving as president (chairman of the Presidium), proceeded in businesslike fashion to consolidate their position. Fourteen months later, on December 9, 1965, Nikolai V. Podgorny (1903–   ) replaced the seventy-year-old Mikoyan, almost the last of the Old Bolsheviks, as chairman of the Presidium and nominal chief of state. In spite of rumors that the new regime would prove ephemeral, in the almost fifty years since the Revolution the Soviet government had developed a measure of stability and its peoples were more conditioned to change than during the Stalin era. The stability of the new regime was further emphasized by the Supreme Soviet's prompt reelection of Kosygin as Premier on August 2, 1966, for a term of four years.

For the first time since 1917, the three key positions in the Soviet government were held by graduates of higher schools of learning, all engineers and technologists, who had a better knowledge of the outside world and of the USSR than had most of their predecessors. Brezhnev, a native of the Ukraine, was graduated from the Dneprodzerzhinsk Metallurgical Institute in 1935. During World War II he served in the Red Army as chief of the political administration of the Fourth Ukrainian Front, rising to the rank of lieutenant-general. At the Nineteenth Congress of the Communist Party of the Soviet Union in 1952, he became a member of the Party's Central Committee. From 1960 to 1964 he was president of the Supreme Soviet of the USSR. Kosygin, a native of Leningrad, was graduated from the Leningrad Textile Institute in 1936. At the age of thirty-five he became people's commissar for the textile industry of the USSR and later mayor of Leningrad. From 1948 to 1952 he was a member of the Politburo of the Communist Party. In 1960 he became first deputy chairman of the USSR Council of Ministers. A specialist in external economic relations, Kosygin has been in contact with trade and economic delegations from scores of countries and has travelled extensively in Europe and Asia. A versatile and well-informed person, he is also known for his interest in Soviet sports, the Moscow Theatre, and contemporary literature. Podgorny, another native of the Ukraine, was graduated from the Kiev Technological Institute in 1931 and worked as an engineer until 1939. A

When Khrushchev resigned in October, 1964, Alexei Kosygin (on the left) and Leonid Brezhnev took over his posts. They are shown here during a 1960 appearance at Moscow's Sports Palace.

member of the Communist Party since 1930, he rose to prominence in the Ukrainian Party apparatus, which he headed following Khrushchev's departure for Moscow. He became a full member of the Party Presidium in 1960 and Central Committee secretary in 1963.

Although Khrushchev initiated the Soviet rapprochement with the Western powers, especially with the United States, he was not sufficiently knowledgeable about Europe and his policy often met with frustration. On the other hand, the visits of Kosygin to France (1966) and England (1967) and Podgorny to Austria and Italy (1966–1967) demonstrated that they acted and were received as if they were at home in the European family of nations.

DOMESTIC AFFAIRS

Khrushchev's erratic efforts to improve Soviet economic conditions resulted in extensive disorganization, especially in agriculture. Measured by the gross national product (GNP), the growth rate in the output of all goals and services, which averaged 7.1 per cent from 1950 to 1958, slipped to an average of 5.3 per cent thereafter. Soviet per capita consumption, which had grown at an average rate in excess of 5 per cent per annum, 1950 to 1958, fell to 2.5 per cent in the years that followed.

Economic Reforms. The Brezhnev-Kosygin team realized that drastic measures must be taken to revive the nation's economy and to raise Soviet living standards. As compared with American, European, and Japanese economic booms, Soviet production, subject entirely to government control, was seriously lagging. Increased Soviet travel abroad and the impact at home of greater numbers of foreign tourists with higher living standards contributed to the rising expectations of the Soviet people, who were no longer willing to tolerate austerity, but demanded more and better facilities and food without delay.

As in the Lenin and Stalin eras, the inauguration of any crash program to improve the economy involved a resort to capitalist methods. Almost a year after the fall of Khrushchev, Premier Kosygin (September 27, 1965) announced sweeping reforms designed to put the planning and administration of the Soviet government-run industry on a profit basis. The regional industrial councils and the two high-level economic agencies established by Khrushchev in 1957 and 1962 respectively, were abandoned. They were replaced by central industrial ministries such as existed prior to 1957. In contrast to the rigid Stalinist controls over these ministries, however, the Brezhnev-Kosygin regime permitted greater independence of industrial managers in running the day-to-day operations of their plants.

New Five-Year Plan. On February 20, 1966, the Soviet news agency TASS announced the adoption of a new Five-Year Plan, the eighth since 1929, for the development of the Soviet national economy, 1966–1970. This Plan envisaged a 49 to 52 per cent increase in the output of the means of production and a 43 to 46 per cent increase in the production of consumer goods. It stressed the importance of faster scientific and technical progress and the streamlining of industrial production, with emphasis on speeding up developments in electrical engineering, the chemical industry, and metallurgy. The goal was a 25 per cent increase in the annual volume of farm production (30 per cent for grain) and an increase of approximately 50 per cent in industrial production. Soviet leaders, concerned about the gap in living standards between the urban and rural populations, provided for the doubling of capital investments in agriculture in the five-year period. The collective farmer's income in cash and kind from the collectively-owned husbandry was to be increased from 35 to 40 per cent and he was to receive a monthly guaranteed remuneration corresponding to the level of wages for State Farm (*sovkhoz*) workers. In urban areas provision was made for a minimum increase of 20 per cent for certain low-paid categories of factory and office workers. Reflecting the growing obsession of Soviet citizens for the acquisition of cars and household appliances, the plan called for an approximate quadrupling of the passenger car output, the doubling of television sets, and the production of three times as many refrigerators. Addressing Hungarian workers in Budapest in December, 1966, Brezhnev predicted that the road to communism would be filled with private cars.

Automobile Production. To meet the goal of the Eighth Five-Year Plan for automobile output (800,000 cars a year by 1970), the Soviet Government turned for help to foreign sources. In the spring of 1966 it contracted with Italy's Fiat Automobile Company for the construction in the USSR of a plant to manufacture a modified version of the Fiat 124, adapted to Russian weather conditions. The new Russian "Detroit" is the Volga River city of Togliatti (formerly Stavropol), five hundred miles east of Moscow. The Renault Company of France also contracted to help the USSR increase its automobile output. American automobile firms initially showed little direct interest in the vast expansion of the Soviet auto-building facilities, partly on the ground that the United States government "discourages any such ventures."

Land Reclamation. In line with the greater agricultural development envisaged in the new Five-Year Plan, in May, 1966, the Communist Party's Central Committee outlined a broad program of land improvement and reclamation to provide more stability in the country's harvests. Drought conditions periodically deplete the harvests of the black-soil steppes of the southern Ukraine. The Soviet government therefore turned its attention to the Russian Republic's underdeveloped forest zone to the north. In this area, it planned large-scale drainage of six million acres of swampland, the clearing of thousands of miles of brush, removal of stones, and application of lime to the acid forest soil. By such programs the USSR hoped to avoid a repetition of the grain harvest disaster of 1963. To provide for immediate needs, however, in June, 1966, the Brezhnev-Kosygin regime contracted with Canada for the cash purchase of 336,000,000 bushels of wheat at a cost of $800,000,000, to be delivered over the next three years. It also arranged for the purchase of eight hundred thousand tons of wheat from France. To avoid dipping into its own reserves, the USSR needs a minimum quantity of from sixty-nine to seventy million tons of wheat per annum.

Siberian Oil and Natural Gas. Vast oil and natural gas reserves are being tapped by thousands of Soviet engineers and geologists working in the taiga and tundra of the West Siberian lowlands north of Novosibirsk, Omsk, and Tomsk. According to Soviet specialists (September, 1966), reservoirs of about six trillion cubic meters of natural gas have been discovered beneath the tundra. Plans were made to pipe this gas three thousand miles across the Urals to the large cities of European Russia by 1980. So rich are the oil resources of this area, according to Soviet sources, that the West Siberian lowlands are expected to produce as much oil in one year as the entire USSR produced in 1965.

Diamond Mining. In isolated Yakutia in northeastern Siberia, still another industry made great strides. Diamond mining was greatly expanded and accelerated in 1966, according to *Pravda,* and has become a "gigantic" industry.

Railroads. The new regime promptly stepped up its program to improve railroad communications inside the USSR and abroad. In February, 1965, the opening of the four-hundred-mile Abakan-Taishet line (begun 1958) filled a crucial gap in the Soviet transport system by linking the Trans-Siberian main line with the South Siberian Railroad. The new line opened up the vast mineral resources of the Sayan Mountains and reduced the haul between Siberian steel plants (Magnitogorsk) and their sources of coking coal and iron ore. New Siberian express trains in 1965 covered the distance between Moscow and Vladivostok (5,787 miles) in six days and nineteen hours, cutting the previous schedule by five hours. In the same year, Soviet rail links with Scandinavian countries were completed, with the opening of direct express service from Moscow to Stockholm and Oslo, via Poland, East Germany, and Baltic rail ferry.

To provide access to the rich new mineral areas of eastern Siberia (the "Wild East"), Soviet leaders announced in the spring of 1966 their plans to build a new trans-Siberian railway, about five thousand miles in length, to the Pacific. The new line, scheduled for completion between 1981 and 1986, will run north of the present Trans-Siberian Railroad through remote areas rich in coal, iron, and copper. In addition to its economic advantages, the railroad will be of great strategic importance, running far north of the Soviet Union's long border with China.

Japanese Cooperation in Siberia. To accelerate the development of Siberia, which is to become the scientific and industrial center of the USSR, the Brezhnev-Kosygin regime turned to Japan for help. In January, 1966, a five-year trade and payments agreement was signed to expand Soviet-Japanese trade by ten per cent per annum. By this agreement Japan undertook to export to the Soviet Union ships, industrial plants, machinery, chemical goods, textiles, and steel products, in return for timber, petroleum, pig iron, and coal.[1] A Soviet-Japanese civil aviation agreement for a jointly operated air route between Tokyo and Moscow, negotiated at the same time, was signed in Tokyo, January 20, 1967. It provided for weekly trans-Siberian air service beginning April 17, 1967. In July, 1966, Andrei A. Gromyko paid an official six-day visit to Tokyo, the first Soviet foreign minister to visit Japan. One concrete outcome of this visit was the signing of the first consular treaty between Moscow and Tokyo, providing for a Soviet consulate in Osaka and its Japanese counterpart in the rapidly growing Soviet commercial port of Nakhodka, one hundred miles southeast of Vladivostok, which lies in the path of the Japan Current and is therefore ice-free. The USSR has shown particular interest in securing Japanese cooperation in the construction of an oil pipeline across Siberia to the western coast of the Sea of Japan and in the

1. On August 17, 1968, a still broader agreement was reached for Soviet-Japanese collaboration in the development of Siberia.

exploitation of natural gas resources on the Island of Sakhalin. The two governments agreed to hold periodic conferences for the settlement of troublesome issues, such as the conclusion of a peace treaty (a 1956 agreement ended the state of war), the disposition of two southern Kurile Islands, Kunashiri and Etorofu, which the Soviets have refused to return to Japan, and agreement on the long-standing fisheries dispute in northern waters.

The efforts of the Brezhnev-Kosygin regime "to catch up with America" by accelerating the industrialization of Siberia and by satisfying the Soviet public's craving for consumer goods with the assistance of foreign firms in capitalist countries greatly increased the USSR's vested interest in coexistence. For many years, the United States depended on military strategy and alliances to contain Communism. The impact of American (and Western) living standards, however, proved to be a more positive deterrent to Soviet aggression and Soviet interference abroad, and in the long run, a more effective means for the "containment" of Communism.

Foreign Policy

Attempted Reconciliation with China. One of the many reasons assigned for the fall of Khrushchev was his responsibility for the deterioration of Sino-Soviet relations, especially from 1960 to 1964. The personal vendetta between Khrushchev and Mao Tse-tung, it was believed, made a reversal of this trend virtually impossible. From 1964 to 1966 Khrushchev's successors made serious efforts to improve Soviet relations with China and to rehabilitate the Sino-Soviet Alliance of February 14, 1950. Within a year, *Pravda* admitted that on the part of the Communist Party of China there had been no response whatsoever to Soviet efforts. On February 16, 1966, the sixteenth anniversary of the Sino-Soviet Alliance, *Izvestia* nevertheless undertook to reassure Mao's China that the Soviet government still placed great value on the alliance, continued to carry out its sacred obligations under the treaty, and hoped to make it a real lever in the struggle for peace and friendly Sino-Soviet relations. Once again, on July 1, 1966, the forty-fifth anniversary of the founding of the Chinese Communist Party, *Pravda* issued a strong appeal for unity, which constituted a rebuttal of Chinese complaints about the inadequacy of Soviet aid and the subordination of Chinese interests to those of non-Communist countries. *Pravda* reminded the Chinese that without Soviet help there would be no Chinese People's Republic; that Russia's role in the defeat of Nazi Germany created favorable circumstances for the victory of the Chinese People's Revolution; that the Soviet defeat of the Japanese Kwangtung Army in Manchuria eliminated from the Asian mainland China's foremost enemy, Japan (the United States role in the Pacific was not mentioned); that Soviet transfer to the Chinese Communists of large quantities of captured Japanese arms was instrumental in bringing about the expulsion of Chiang Kai-shek's forces from China proper, thereby eliminating the "threat" of American control over China. In other words, the Soviets insisted that they had eliminated the three major, actual or potential, enemies of the Chinese Communists. The Soviet press also credited the USSR with the founding of the Chinese Communist Party. The Comintern, according to *Izvestia* in 1966, in the spring of 1920 dispatched to China G. N. Voytinsky, who initiated contacts with Chinese Marxists in Shanghai and Peking,[2] with the result that the first Marxist circles were organized there. In 1921 these circles united to form the Communist Party of China.

Chinese Purges. The Chinese purges of 1966–1967, which swept into oblivion the political, military, and intellectual leaders opposed to Mai Tse-tung's policies, including those predisposed toward a reconciliation with the USSR, for the time being appeared to slam the door against any improvement in Sino-Soviet relations. These purges highlighted the fact that Mao's China was characterized not only by Militant Communism, which Soviet leaders understand although they have long since ceased to subscribe to it, but also by a Chinese version of Nazism (National Socialism), with racial and irredentist overtones, which constituted a threat to Soviet territorial integrity. Both Soviet and American leaders were slow to recognize the elements of Chinese Nazism underlying Chinese Militant Communism.

"Paper War." Following the violent anti-foreign Chinese Red Guard demonstrations in August, 1966, the Soviet Communist Party's Central Committee, in its first public anti-Chinese statement (August 31, 1966) since the fall of Khrushchev, placed on Peking the entire blame for the Sino-Soviet rift. Using much the same language as the Chinese had employed against the Russians, it accused the Mao Tse-tung regime of "damaging the cause of unity of the International Communist movement," and of impeding the "struggle for socialism, national liberation, peace, and the security of peoples." Chinese policy, according to the Soviets, rendered outstanding service to imperialism and reaction at the very moment of the escalation of the war in Vietnam.

Ideologically, the erstwhile partners indulged in a "paper war," in which virtually no one was killed, but recrimination ran rampant. From this ideological controversy it became clear that Soviet Marxism was Europe-centered, whereas Chinese Marxism was Asia-centered. This dictum is indispensable to an understanding of the Sino-Soviet rift. Mao Tse-tung developed what he termed "a higher, Asian concept of Marxism." Emphasizing a life of austerity almost monastic in concept, his regime insisted on the subordination of the material welfare of China's teeming millions to "spiritual" ideology. In other words, Mao wanted to do for "materialistic" Europe in ideology what Near Eastern Asia originally did for "spiritually underdeveloped" Europe in theology. Thus the Chinese interpreted the Soviet fetish about raising the living standards of Soviet citizens as a threat to collectivism—the essence of Marxism—which would ultimately blot out the differ-

2. The Peking Marxist circle was headed by Li Ta-chao, a professor of history at Peking University.

ences between the Soviet and capitalist economies. To the Chinese this amounted to "Khrushchevism without Khrushchev." The Soviets contended, on the other hand, that Marxism-Leninism was based on materialism, as all Communist literature for the past forty-five years has represented; and that Communism was international in concept, whereas Sinicized Marxism was imbued with nationalism. According to Soviet theoreticians, there can be no such thing as "national Marxism"—Chinese, Russian, Polish, African, or Latin American. Soviet writers pointed out that Chinese ideology was dominated not by the working class (the proletariat), which both Marx and Lenin envisaged as the vanguard of the revolution, but by peasants and the petty bourgeoisie. Although the followers of Maoism constantly alleged that the Soviets are "revisionists," it seems legitimate to consider Mao Tse-tung himself a "revisionist."

Militant Chinese Communism. Both Khrushchev and his successors warned the Mao Tse-tung regime against spreading Militant Communism in newly established and developing countries where nationalism was especially strong. This advice was founded on Soviet experience in Europe (Italy, Germany, Hungary, etc.) in the 1920's where Militant Communism gave birth to Fascism and Nazism, which very nearly destroyed the USSR in World War II. It also created in England, France, and the United States a hostile attitude toward Soviet Russia. In Asia it made Japan an implacable enemy of the USSR and in China it resulted in the suppression of the Communist Party and the consolidation of Kuomintang power under Chiang Kai-shek. From sad experience Soviet leaders learned that as they receded from the practice of Militant Communism in foreign policy, Soviet relations with the rest of the world proportionally improved. Coexistence, practiced long before it became a Khrushchev slogan, seemed to afford a better opportunity for the establishment of an exemplary "Communist society" at home, served as an antidote to the revival of Fascism and Nazism abroad, and lulled the fears of capitalist countries in regard to the eventual triumph of world Communism.

Chinese failure to heed Soviet warnings led, from 1965 to 1967, to a series of Chinese setbacks in the developing countries. The Sukarno regime in Indonesia, a recognized friend of the Socialist camp, was reduced to impotence by a military coup. The subsequent purge of the Indonesian Communist Party, the largest outside the Communist bloc, in a ruthless blood bath, startled the world and wiped out Soviet achievements of the previous decade in Indonesia. The Chinese met with similar defeat in their efforts to establish a pro-Chinese Communist regime in Zanzibar (the Cuba of Africa). Ben Bella, pro-Chinese head of the Algerian government, was ousted from power in the spring of 1965 on the very eve of the abortive Afro-Asian Summit Conference. A similar fate befell President Nkrumah of Ghana on the day he arrived in Peking for a state visit. Subsequently Odinga Oginga was supplanted in Kenya. Fidel Castro of Cuba, ideologically attuned to the Chinese concept of "permanent revolution," also abandoned the Chinese for the Soviet camp. In spite of these widespread setbacks, the Chinese continued to assert the "infallibility" of Mao Tse-tung.

Irrespective of the outcome of the Sino-Soviet rift from the international standpoint, its positive aspect for Soviet domestic policy was soon apparent. The Soviets observed with growing distaste the excesses of Maoism and the Maoist Red Guards, knowing full well that what they criticized in China was in many respects characteristic of Soviet Russia in the years of Militant Communism and during the purges of the reactionary Stalin regime. Soviet disparagement of Maoist excesses amounted to self-criticism, and hopefully constituted a guarantee that the Soviet regime will not return to similar tactics.

India and Pakistan: Tashkent. Although the Brezhnev-Kosygin regime failed to improve Sino-Soviet relations, it successfully performed the role of "mediator" and "peacemaker" between India and Pakistan in their dispute over Kashmir in 1965. With the United Nations seemingly helpless, the United States preoccupied by the war in Vietnam, and China prepared to fan the flames of conflict, the USSR emerged as the only great power which could bring the two protagonists, already locked in battle, to the peace table. On September 17, 1965, Premier Kosygin offered the combatants the good offices of the Soviet Union for a summit meeting in the city of Tashkent, Soviet Central Asia—a new venture in Soviet diplomacy. The Soviet gesture, widely acclaimed throughout the world, including the United States, culminated in the Tashkent Declaration of January 10, 1966, in which India and Pakistan agreed to cease hostilities and to withdraw their armed forces by February 25, 1966, to lines occupied prior to the conflict. Kosygin's acknowledged diplomatic skill at Tashkent enhanced the prestige of the Soviet Union in Asia and throughout the world.

Reappraisal. The international situation which confronted Brezhnev and Kosygin differed substantially from the bipolar world of the years following World War II, in which the "Free World" under the leadership of the United States faced the "Communist Bloc" led by the Soviet Union. Containment at that time meant primarily containment of the USSR. With the rise of Red China, the establishment of many new Afro-Asian nations, and the political, economic, and military revival of German power (West Germany), both the Western and the Sino-Soviet systems of alliances began to disintegrate and were subjected to "agonizing" reappraisal.

Complication of Diplomacy: The "Enemy." Complicating the conduct of foreign policy, especially for the United States and the Soviet Union, was the fact that each country, including the new nations, had a "public enemy number one" compared to which all other issues, including formal alliances, were subordinated. China's "enemy" was the United States, which had refused her diplomatic recognition, effectively prevented her entry into the United Nations, her recover of Formosa (Taiwan) and the offshore islands, and worked to isolate her from the free world. In seeking a *rapprochement* with the United States, the USSR was immediately suspect and proclaimed by China a traitor to the Sino-Soviet Alliance. The Soviet Union's "enemy" (and the same is true for the other Slavic countries) was a rearmed and unified Germany. Soviet leaders therefore regarded the NATO Alliance, backed by the United States, as a major threat, even after it was substantially weakened by the "defection" of France.

Other countries have displayed similar reactions when confronted by American or Soviet aid to the "enemy." Pakistan's enemy was India. As an ally of the United States, the Karachi government expected American aid not only against Communism but against India. United States aid to India to stem the tide of Chinese aggression so estranged Pakistan that its leaders signed a border agreement with China, took no part in SEATO military exercises in September, 1965, on the pretext of the conflict with India, and refused to participate in SEATO naval exercises in May, 1966, in the South China Sea.[3] The Soviet Ministry for Defense, taking advantage of Pakistan–United States friction, at once invited the Karachi government to send a military delegation to Moscow. The first Pakistani military delegation to the USSR arrived in the Soviet Union on June 25, 1966. In August Pakistan flatly rejected a proposal by Chester Bowles, United States ambassador to India, that the non-Communist Asian states of India, Japan, Indonesia, and Pakistan cooperate to build a "bulwark against Communist China." To allay Pakistani fears, Prime Minister Indira Gandhi proposed (by radio) September 4, 1966, unrestricted travel and economic cooperation between the two countries. Except for the withdrawal of troops and an exchange of ambassadors, however, no further steps were taken to implement the Tashkent Declaration of January, 1966. India's "enemy" was Pakistan, although China now ranks as a close competitor. Small wonder that United States consideration of the resumption of American military aid to Pakistan in the summer of 1966 met with noisy protests in the Indian National Congress. Nor, under these circumstances, did it placate Pakistan or China when the Soviet government (December 10, 1966) agreed to provide India with a new credit of $330,000,000 in support of that country's fourth five-year plan; or when the United States and the USSR (December 22, 1966) allocated large quantities of grain (the United States 900,000 tons of food grains and the USSR 200,000 tons of wheat) to meet India's food shortage emergency.

To most of the Arab world, Israel was the "enemy." Although the United States extended billions of dollars in aid to Arab countries and was greatly instrumental in forcing Anglo-French-Israeli withdrawal from Suez in 1956, American assistance to Israel virtually nullified this effort. On the other hand,

3. On June 6, 1968, Foreign Minister Arshad Husain of Pakistan informed the National Assembly that Pakistan is progressively disengaging itself from both the Southeast Asia Treaty Organization and the Central Treaty Organization defense pacts, its role having been reduced to that of "a virtual observer." In May, 1968, Pakistan notified the United States that it would not renew the ten-year pact on the electronic surveillance station near Peshawar, which expires in 1969.

the Soviet Union, which cast its lot unqualifiedly with the Arab world, was able to claim in 1966 that relations between the United Arab Republic and the Soviet Union had become "the most important political factor in the Near East and in Africa."

Prior to the eruption of Greco-Turkish communal strife in Cyprus in December, 1963, Turkey's "enemy" was the USSR, which was prevented by the Truman Doctrine (March 12, 1947) from expanding to the Straits following World War II. Unable to understand why her American ally failed to rush to her aid when the Turkish minority on Cyprus was threatened by Greece, the Turkish attitude toward the United States cooled appreciably. It appeared that the Cyprus issue had become Turkey's most sensitive spot, superseding even the Soviet threat. In December, 1966, Premier Kosygin paid an official visit to Ankara, becoming the first Soviet premier to visit Turkey, ostensibly to improve Soviet-Turkish economic and cultural relations. The cool reception accorded to him was due in large part to a recent Czechoslovak arms sale to pro-Greek President Archbishop Makarios of Cyprus. When Kosygin publicly expressed regret over the Czech action, and further shipments were cancelled, he created bad feeling between the USSR and Greece.

For many years, the United States "enemy" has been Communism. Formerly this meant Soviet Communism, but in the late 1950's it came to mean primarily Chinese Communism. The United States Congress originally threatened to cut off aid to any ally that succumbed to the temptation to do strategic business with the USSR, as in the case of West Germany's proposed deal for the sale of "big-inch" pipe to the Soviets (1962) for the piping of Soviet oil to Eastern Europe. Similarly the United States government prevented or curtailed trade by America's allies with Communist Cuba and Communist China.

The existence of so many sensitive spots throughout the world greatly complicated the tasks of diplomacy for both the United States and the Soviet Union, and obstructed a return to normalcy, even among allies. No matter how much economic and military aid was advanced to a particular country to expedite its development and to strengthen its security, the reward was cancelled by the extension of similar assistance to its "enemy."

Partial Soviet-American Detente. In spite of the adverse international situation, relations between the United States and the Soviet Union progressed, especially in the area of cultural and scientific exchange. In March, 1966, agreement was reached on a fifth two-year extension of the Soviet-American Cultural Exchange Pact initiated in 1958, which covered exchanges in science, technology, agriculture, public health, medicine, education, the performing arts, publications, culture, the professions, and athletics. Some of the more spectacular cultural and sports interchanges, such as the Soviet and Polish track and field meets scheduled for July, 1966, at Los Angeles and Berkeley, California, were cancelled by the Soviet government as a result of ill feeling bred by the Vietnamese War. The exchange of scholars, however, continued on a cordial basis, with arrangements for the exchange of thirty-two

Soviet and thirty-two American graduate students for one year of study and research and the expansion of the language-teacher exchange program. From 1958 to 1966 approximately six hundred young scholars (about three hundred from each country) participated in the exchange, those from the USSR representing, for the most part, the scientific and technological disciplines and those from the United States pursuing mainly the fields of history, literature, and government. Among the more than thirty thousand American tourists in the Soviet Union in 1966 were twenty-two Jewish rabbis, members of the Conference of American Rabbis, who visited Moscow, Vilna, Leningrad, and Kiev and participated in Jewish services in the USSR. As a gesture toward American Jewry and world public opinion, Premier Kosygin promised, during his visit to Paris (December 3, 1966), that the Soviet government would "open the road" for those Soviet Jews who wished to leave the USSR to be reunited with their families in the West. In an unprecedented gesture toward world Catholicism, Soviet President Nikolai Podgorny (January 29, 1967) was received by Pope Paul VI in the first papal audience ever granted such a high-ranking Communist official.

There were other areas in which contacts were made and agreements reached. In July, 1966, at Geneva, the USA and the USSR, working on the United Nations twenty-eight-nation legal subcommittee drafting a treaty to govern space exploration, reached agreement on a treaty article barring any state from claiming sovereignty over space, including the moon and other planets. The subsequent United Nations peace-in-space treaty was signed in Washington, London, and Moscow, January 27, 1967. In August, 1966, the Soviet government concluded a contract with Capitol Records for the first time conferring on an American company the exclusive right to manufacture, license, and distribute in the United States and the Western hemisphere all recordings by Russian artists. Shortly thereafter (September 1, 1966), the American Broadcasting Company obtained Soviet approval to film in the USSR a documentary dealing with the daily life of a Soviet family. Progress was also made in the exchange of weather data. On August 20, 1966, the Soviets for the first time permitted the broadcast of weather data picked up by Cosmos 122 (launched June 25, 1966) over the regular weather communication link (the "cold" line) with the United States. A few weeks later (September, 1966) the United States and the Soviet Union began the daily exchange of photographs taken by weather satellites. The weather communication link, established in 1964, was one of three direct telecommunication channels between Washington and Moscow, the others being for transmission of diplomatic messages and for direct emergency communication between the heads of the two governments (the "hot" line). Although earlier efforts to establish direct commercial air communications between the United States and the USSR were blocked by the deterioration of Soviet-American relations under the impact of the Vietnamese conflict, on November 4, 1966, representatives of the two countries signed an agreement providing for nonstop, 4,200-mile flights between New York and Moscow via Pan American Airways and the Soviet air line, Aeroflot. Service began July 14, 1968.

Still another indication of efforts to improve Soviet-American relations was the ratification by the United States Senate (March 16, 1967) of the United States-Soviet Consular Treaty signed in June 1964, the first bilateral treaty between the two countries requiring Senate approval. This treaty, which covered the establishment of consulates outside Moscow and Washington, was designed to provide greater protection for United States citizens travelling in the USSR and reciprocal rights for Soviet citizens in the USA. After four years, the Soviet government ratified the Consular Treaty on May 4, 1968.

The Vietnamese War. The escalation of the war in Vietnam, 1965–1967, impeded still further progress in the improvement of Soviet-American relations. The air bombardment of North Vietnam, which American military advisers regarded as strategically necessary, proved to be a deterrent to diplomatic efforts to end the Vietnamese conflict. The resulting hysteria in the Soviet Union, manifested daily in the Soviet press, can be understood only by comparing it to the similar reaction in the United States and Western Europe that accompanied the Soviet-Finnish War, 1939–1940. The average Soviet citizen, especially in rural Russia, with no background on the origins of this conflict and ever conscious that he had been the victim of the German invasion in World War II, was easily aroused by the plight of his Communist brethren in North Vietnam in their stand against the American leviathan. In this instance, Soviet sympathy for "little Vietnam" recalled American feeling for "little Finland" in its unequal struggle with the USSR. Whereas the Vietcong obtained substantial assistance from the Communist bloc, however, Finland received no comparable military aid from the West.

Trade Bridge. The most significant positive response to President Lyndon B. Johnson's efforts to build a trade bridge to the USSR occurred on January 16, 1967, when, in an unprecedented two-page Soviet advertisement in the *New York Times,* American businessmen were invited to advertise American wares in Soviet newspapers, magazines, and on Soviet radio and television, with a view to exploiting a rich Soviet market. In a vein reminiscent of the early *Rūs* appeal to the Norsemen "to come and govern us" because "our land is great and rich, but there is no order in it," the Soviets have eagerly invited Americans "to come and do business with us," because a rich market awaits them and there is no economic order to enable Russians to fulfill the rising expectations of the Soviet peoples for consumer goods.

FIFTY YEARS AFTER THE REVOLUTION

Fifty years of Soviet rule, 1917–1967, have transformed the USSR from a basically agrarian to an urban society, from a relatively "poor" and under-developed to a "rich," industrialized country, from a debtor to a creditor nation, from one defeated and dismembered to a world power, second only to the United States. This transformation, which is still in progress, has been achieved in proportion to the Soviet retreat from Militant Communism. It has changed the outlook and mode of living not only of the Russian people but of the many peoples that comprise the Soviet Union. Today the country is far removed from the goals envisaged by the revolutionary founders of the new society, in which government would "wither away." Although no longer a police state as under Stalin, politically the USSR is still a totalitarian regime, based on one-party rule, that of the Communist Party. Socially, it remains a class, not a classless, society, characterized by "socialist competition," which provides for "each according to his work" rather than for "each according to his need." Economically, the prevailing system is state capitalism, in which the entire economy is based on profit, and profit is the soul of capitalism. Unlike the Chinese Revolution, after fifty years the Revolution in Russia essentially has run its course and a new equilibrium appears to have been established. Although Soviet leaders still profess the ultimate triumph of their version of Communism, today the USSR is regarded more and more as a *status quo* power, with a vested interest in preventing a world holocaust and in preserving world peace.

From the Soviet standpoint, the crowning diplomatic achievement of the USSR is the Soviet "presence" in the eastern Mediterranean and Middle East. As an aftermath of the Six-Day Israeli-Arab War in June, 1967, the USSR in 1968 virtually controlled the armed forces of several Arab states. A formidable Soviet fleet, operating from Arab ports in the eastern Mediterranean, outflanked Europe, North Africa, and Istanbul (Constantinople), coveted by Russians since 1453. From 1967 to 1968 the presence of the United States Sixth Fleet in the Mediterranean in all probability forestalled a complete "take-over" of the Middle East. One of the great tasks of diplomacy promises to be the avoidance of a violent confrontation between the United States and the Soviet Union in the Mediterranean.

On August 20, 1968, Soviet armed forces, supported by East German, Polish, Bulgarian, and Hungarian troops, without warning crossed the borders of Czechoslovakia to suppress an allegedly anti-socialist movement inimical to the security of the Warsaw bloc. The military occupation of Czechoslovakia demonstrated how desperate is the struggle for the survival of the authority of the Communist Parties in the invading socialist countries. This blatant attack on a member of the Warsaw Pact was not perpetrated to save communism (for there exists no such thing as a communist society), but to enforce allegiance to a collective secular deity—the Communist Party. Irrespective of the outcome of this struggle, two conclusions can be reached: 1. The infallibility of the Communist Party has suffered a body blow; and 2. The oft-reiterated claim of the Soviet government that it pursues a policy of non-intervention in the internal affairs of other nations has been seriously undermined.

Appendix I: Chronology

862	Traditional date of summons from Slavonic tribes to Norsemen to come and rule.
882	Oleg takes possession of Kiev.
945	Igor negotiates a commercial treaty with Byzantium.
957	Baptism of Grand Pincess Olga.
966	Svyatoslav seizes the Khazar capital of Sarkil
988	Christianity becomes the official religion of the Kievan state.
1051	Metropolitan Hilarion becomes first Russian head of the Kievan Church.
1056–54	Kievan culture reaches its peak under Yaroslav the Wise.
1056–1114	*Russian Primary Chronicle* written.
1147	First written reference to Moscow.
1223	First Mongol Invasion. Battle at the River Kalka.
1237	Return of the Mongols (Tatars).
1238	Moscow destroyed by the Mongols.
1240	Mongols capture Kiev.
1242	Alexander Nevsky defeats Teutonic Knights at Lake Peipus.
1243	Establishment of the Golden Horde at Sarai on the Volga.
1259	Novgorod submits to the Mongols.
1328	Tatars confer upon Ivan I of Moscow the title of Grand Prince.
1342	Metropolitan Peter makes Moscow his ecclesiastical capital.
1380	Dimitri Donskoi defeats Khan Mamai at Kulikovo Meadow.
1382	Tatars sack Moscow.
1453	Constantinople falls to the Turks.
1472	Ivan III marries Sophia Palaeologa, niece of the last Byzantine Emperor.
1480	Ivan III repudiates overlordship of the Golden Horde.
1497	Restriction of Peasants' freedom of movement to a two weeks' period; *Sudebnik,* first unified code of laws published.
1550	Ivan Grozny organizes the *Streltsy.*
1552	Ivan Grozny seizes Tatar stronghold of Kazan.
1553	Chancellor opens White Sea route to Russia.
1554	Muscovy Company chartered by Queen Mary of England.
1556	Seizure of the Khanate of Astrakhan.
1555–61	Construction of St. Basil's Cathedral.
1565–72	Period of the *oprichnina.*
1566	Summoning of the first *Zemsky Sobor.*
1581	Peasants forbidden to leave the estate in certain years. Yermak invades Siberia.

1584	Siberia annexed.
1589	Creation of the Moscow Patriarchate.
1598	End of the Rurik dynasty.
1607	Right of recovery of fugitive peasants extended from five to fifteen years.
1610	Poles seize Moscow.
1612	Moscow liberated under leadership of Minin and Pozharsky.
1613	*Zemsky Sobor* elects Tsar Michael, first of the Romanovs.
1639	Russians reach the Sea of Okhotsk on the Pacific.
1652	Tsar Alexis founds German Suburb of Moscow; foreigners ordered to live there.
1653–54	Annexation of the Ukraine.
1653	Nikon becomes patriarch. Launches Church reforms, which produce the Schism.
1667	By the peace of Andrusovo Russians secure left bank of Dnieper and Kiev.
1670–71	Revolt of Stenka Razin.
1689	Treaty of Nertchinsk with China.
1697–98	"Grand Embassy" of Peter the Great tours Western Europe.
1700	Peter I adopts the Julian calendar. Suspension of the Russian patriarchate.
1703	Founding of St. Petersburg.
1709	Defeat of the Swedes under Charles XII at the Battle of Poltava.
1711	Peter establishes the Senate.
1721	Peter I becomes "Emperor of All the Russias." Holy Synod replaces the Patriarchate. Sale of individual serfs prohibited.
1722	Table of Ranks published.
1725	Imperial Academy of Sciences founded.
1725–30	First Bering expedition.
1727	Kyakhta Treaty regulates Russian trade with China.
1733–42	Second Bering expedition.
1736	Military service for nobility reduced from life to 25 years.
1747	Elizabeth authorizes landowners to sell serfs.
1755	Moscow University founded.
1758	Academy of Arts established.
1760	Landowners permitted to banish serfs to Siberia. Russians occupy Berlin during Seven Years' War.
1762	Peter III frees nobility from compulsory service to the state.
1773	First partition of Poland.
1773–75	Pugachev Revolt.
1774	Treaty of Kuchuk-Kainardji ends First Turkish War.
1791	Jewish "Pale of Settlement" established.
1793	Second partition of Poland.
1795	Third partition of Poland.
1796	Serfdom extended to "New Lands" of southern Ukraine and Caucasus.
1797	Paul I proclaims the "Law of Succession" to the throne. Labor of serfs for landowners restricted to three days per week.
1804–07	Russia joins Third Coalition against Napoleon.
1807	Treaty of Tilsit between Napoleon and Alexander I.
1808	Public sale of serfs in the market place banned.
1809	Russia acquires Finland.

1812	Napoleon invades Russia.
1814	Russian troops under Alexander I enter Paris.
1814–15	Congress of Vienna.
1815	Holy Alliance and Quadruple Alliance.
1816–19	Baltic serfs emancipated.
1825	Decembrist Revolt.
1826	Third Division (Gendarmerie) established. Serfdom banned in Siberia.
1833	*Digest of the Laws of the Russian Empire* issued. Treaty of Unkiar-Skelessi with Turkey.
1838	First Russian railroad, St. Petersburg to Tsarskoe Selo, completed.
1840	Factory owners permitted to liberate serfs.
1842	Emancipation of serfs by landlords permitted.
1842–50	Railroad constructed from St. Petersburg to Moscow.
1848	Communist Manifesto of Karl Marx.
1849	Intervention by Russian troops in Hungary.
1851	Telegraphic communication established between St. Petersburg and Moscow.
1853–56	Crimean War.
1855	Diplomatic relations established between Russia and Japan.
1858	Treaty of Aigun with China. Annexation of the Amur Territory.
1860	Treaty of Peking with China. Annexation of the Ussury Territory. Founding of Vladivostok.
1861	Abolition of serfdom.
1864	Establishment of zemstvos. Court reforms.
1865	Seizure of Tashkent.
1867	United States purchases Alaska from Russia.
1870	Russia scraps Black Sea clauses of Treaty of Paris (1856).
1874	Universal military service. Military reforms.
1877–78	War with Turkey. Treaty of San Stefano. Congress of Berlin.
1881	Loris Melikov's constitutional proposal shelved.
1885	Special Nobles Bank established.
1891	Franco-Russian Alliance. Construction of Trans-Siberian Railway begins.
1897	Working day limited to 11½ hours.
1898	Russia gets 25-year lease on Port Arthur and Liaotung Peninsula. First Conference of Russian Social-Democratic Party.
1899	Witte's "Five-Year Plan" for industrialization of Russia.
1901	Formation of Social Revolutionary Party.
1902	Anglo-Japanese Alliance against Russia.
1904–05	Russo-Japanese War.
1905	
Jan. 9	Bloody Sunday. Revolution of 1905.
Sept. 5	Peace of Portsmouth ends war with Japan.
Oct. 12–18	Convention of Constitutional Democrats (Kadets).
Oct. 17/30	October Manifesto providing for a Duma.
1906	
April 27	First Duma convenes.
Nov. 9	Stolypin's Land Law proclaimed.
1907	
Feb. 20	Second Duma convenes.
August	Anglo-Russian Entente. Triple Entente.

1908	Universal primary education for children 8 to 12 passed.
1911	Stolypin assassinated.
1912	Fourth Duma elected.
1914	
June 28	Assassination of Archduke Franz Ferdinand of Austria.
Aug. 1	World War I begins with German declaration of war on Russia.
1915	
Mar.–April	Allied Secret Agreement on Constantinople and the Straits.
1916	Sykes-Picot Agreement on dismemberment of Turkey.
July 3	Russo-Japanese Secret Agreement for partition of China.
Dec. 18	Murder of Rasputin.
1917	
Feb. 26	Nicholas II prorogues Fourth Duma.
Feb. 27	Formation of St. Petersburg Soviet of Workers' Deputies. Formation of Provisional Committee of the Duma. Termination of the monarchy.
March 1	Order #1 of the Soviet of Workers' and Soldiers' Deputies.
March 2	Provisional government organized with Prince Lvov as chairman. Abdication of Nicholas II.
March 9	United States recognizes Provisional government.
March 14	Petrograd Soviet calls for "peace without annexations and indemnities."
April 3/16	Lenin returns to Petrograd.
May 5	Formation of Coalition Provisional government.
July 3–4	Petrograd uprising inspired by Bolsheviks.
July 24/ Aug. 7	Second Coalition government, with Kerensky as chairman.
Aug. 25	Kornilov affair.
Sept. 24	Third Coalition government.
Oct. 25/ Nov. 7	Bolshevik Revolution. "October Revolution."
Oct. 26	Bolshevik decree on peace. Decree on land.
Dec. 5	Appeal to the Muslims of Russia and the East.
Dec. 20	CHEKA established by Lenin.
1918–20	Civil War in Russia.
1918	
Jan. 1/14	Introduction of new style (Gregorian) calendar.
Jan. 18	Constituent Assembly convenes; dissolved by Bolsheviks after one session.
Feb. 23	Establishment of the Red Army.
March 3	Treaty of Brest-Litovsk signed.
March 9	English troops land at Murmansk.
March 10–11	National capital transferred from Petrograd to Moscow.
April 5	Japanese forces land at Vladivostok.
June 28	Nationalization of large-scale industry.
July 17	Execution of the royal family.
August	American and Allied troops land at Vladivostok.
Dec.	French naval and military forces land at Odessa.
1919	
Mar. 2–6	Creation of the Third International (Comintern).
Summer	End of Allied Intervention in European Russia.

1920
  April   Last American troops withdraw from Siberia.
  April 6   Far Eastern Republic of Siberia established.
  Sept. 2   Congress at Baku convenes.
1921
  Feb. 26   Soviet-Iranian Treaty of Friendship and Fraternity.
  Feb. 28   Soviet-Afghan Treaty of Friendship and Fraternity.
  March 2   Kronstadt Rebellion begins.
  March 8   Tenth Congress of Communist Party convenes in Moscow. Lenin launches the NEP, by March 21.
  March 18   Soviet Russia signs a peace treaty with Poland.
  March 21   Soviet-Turkish Treaty of Friendship and Fraternity.
1922
  April 16   Rapallo Treaty.
  Oct.   Japanese withdraw from Siberian mainland.
  Nov.   Far Eastern Republic merges with the RSFSR.
  Dec.   Formation of the Union of Soviet Socialist Republics (USSR).
1924
  Jan. 3   First USSR Constitution ratified.
  Jan. 21   Death of Lenin.
                During 1924 Great Britain, Italy, Norway, Austria, Greece, Sweden, China, Denmark, Mexico, France all recognize the USSR.
1925   Japan recognizes the USSR.
  Jan.   Trotsky removed as Commissar of War.
1927
  Dec.   Expulsion of Trotsky from the Communist Party. Stalin emerges victorious over the Trotskyite faction.
1928
  April   Sixteenth Congress of the Communist Party. Adoption of First Five-Year Plan. Plan launched October 1.
1931–32   Famine in Soviet Russia.
1931   Japanese occupation of Manchuria.
                Piece work introduced.
1932   Second Five-Year Plan launched.
1933
  Jan. 30   Accession to power of Adolph Hitler.
  Nov. 16   USA recognizes USSR.
1934   Birobidjan autonomous Jewish state created.
  Sept. 18   USSR enters the League of Nations.
1935
  May 2–16   Franco-Russian-Czech Alliance.
  Aug. 31   Stakhanov movement launched.
1936
  June 12   Draft Constitution published.
  August   Stalin Purges begin. "Trial of the 16."
  Dec. 3   Adoption of USSR Constitution.
1937
  Jan.   "Trial of the 17."
  June   Red Army Purge.
1938
  Jan.   Third Five-Year Plan.
  March   Purge of Right-Wing Communists.
  Sept.   Munich crisis.

1939
May–Dec.	Battle of Nomanhan.
May 3	Litvinov replaced as foreign minister by Molotov.
Aug. 23	German-Soviet Non-Aggression Pact.
Sept. 1	Nazi invasion of Poland.
Sept. 17	Red Army enters Western Ukraine.
Nov. 30	USSR invades Finland.
Dec. 14	USSR expelled from the League of Nations.

1940
June 28	USSR occupies Bessarabia and Northern Bukovina.
Aug. 1–8	USSR annexes the Baltic states.

1941
April 13	Soviet-Japanese Neutrality Pact.
June 22	Germany invades the USSR.
July 12	Anglo-Soviet Mutual Aid Agreement.
Sept. 29	Harriman mission to USSR. Initial Lend-Lease aid arranged.
Dec. 7	Pearl Harbor.

1942
May 26	Anglo-Soviet 20-year alliance.
June 11	Joint Allied Communiqué on the Second Front in 1942.
Aug. 22	Siege of Stalingrad begins.

1943
Jan. 18	Siege of Leningrad lifted.
Feb. 2	Surrender of German Sixth Army at Stalingrad.
May 22	Dissolution of Comintern.
Oct. 25	Soviet recovery of Kiev.
Nov.	Teheran Conference.

1944
June 6	D-Day. Allied second front opened in France.
Aug. 15	Red Army reaches Warsaw.
Feb. 4–11	Yalta Conference.
April 13	Red Army occupies Vienna.
May 2	Berlin falls to the Red Army.
May 7	Unconditional surrender of the Germans.
July 17	Potsdam Conference convenes.
Aug. 6	USA drops atomic bomb on Hiroshima.
Aug. 9	USSR enters the war in the Pacific; invades Manchuria, Korea, and Southern Sakhalin.
Sept. 2	Japanese armistice.

1946
March 5	Churchill's "Iron Curtain" speech at Fulton, Missouri.
March	Fourth Five-Year Plan launched.

1946
	Treaties with Italy and the Balkan states.

1947
Feb. 10	Treaty of Peace with Austria.
March 12	Truman Doctrine.

1948
April 1	Berlin blockade.
	USSR introduces high-pressure campaign for profits.
Aug. 29	Construction of private houses permitted in the USSR.
Sept.	Cominform established.
Sept. 23	USSR discloses its possession of the atomic bomb.

1950	Fifth Five-Year Plan.
Feb. 14	Sino-Soviet Alliance.
1951	
Sept. 5	United States makes peace with Japan.
1952	
July 12	Completion of Volga-Don Navigation Canal
1953	
March 5	Death of Stalin.
Aug. 20	First Soviet hydrogen bomb exploded.
Sept. 13	Khrushchev becomes First Secretary of Party Central Committee.
1955	
Feb. 8	Bulganin succeeds Malenkov as premier.
April	Bandung Conference.
1956	
Feb. 24–25	Twentieth Congress of CPSU. Khrushchev demotes Stalin.
Oct. 23	Hungarian revolt. Suppressed by Red Army Nov. 4.
Dec. 26	State of war between USSR and Japan ended.
1957	
Jan. 5	Eisenhower Doctrine.
Jan. 18	Sino-Soviet "Doctrine."
Oct. 4	First sputnik launched.
Dec.	First Asian-African People's Solidarity Conference in Cairo.
1958	
Jan.	Soviet-American Cultural Agreement.
March 27	Khrushchev replaces Bulganin as premier.
1959	
Sept. 15–27	Khrushchev visits the United States.
Oct. 1	Khrushchev visits China. Sino-Soviet relations deteriorate.
1960	
May 1	U-2 Incident over Sverdlovsk, followed by collapse of Paris Summit Conference.
1961	
April 12	Yuri Gagarin pilots *Vostok I*, first Soviet manned space flight.
Aug. 13	Berlin Wall.
Oct.	Twenty-Second Congress of the CPSU. Khrushchev launches "peaceful coexistence" policy.
1962	
Oct. 22	Cuban Crisis.
1963	Council for Mutual Economic Assistance (COMECON) formed.
June	Valentina Tereshkova becomes first woman cosmonaut in *Vostok VI*.
Aug.	USA-USSR Nuclear Test-Ban Treaty.
Fall	Grain harvest disaster in USSR.
1964	Volga-Baltic Waterway opened.
June	US-Soviet Consular Treaty signed.
Oct.	Fall of Khrushchev. Kosygin becomes premier; Brezhnev becomes Secretary of CC of CPSU.
1965	
Sept. 27	Kosygin puts Soviet industry on a profit basis.
1966	
Jan. 10	Tashkent Declaration ends conflict of India and Pakistan over Kashmir.

Feb. 20	Eighth Five-Year Plan announced.
March	Fifth extension of Soviet-American Cultural Exchange Pact.
Spring	Plans for new Trans-Siberian Railway announced.
1967	
March	US Senate ratifies Consular Treaty with USSR.
1968	USSR ratifies Consular Agreement.
August	USSR and four Warsaw Pact members invade Czechoslovakia.

Appendix II: Russian Rulers

Rurik Dynasty (862–1598)

Rurik	862–879
Oleg	879–912
Igor	913–945
Olga	945–969
Svyatoslav	962–972
Yaropolk	973–980
Vladimir, the Saint	980–1015
Sviatopolk	1015–1019
Yaroslav, the Wise	1036–1054
Vladimir Monomakh	1113–1125

GRAND PRINCES OF MOSCOW

Ivan I, Kalita	1328–1341
Simeon, the Proud	1341–1353
Ivan II, the Red	1353–1359
Dimitry II	1359–1362
Dimitry III, Donskoi	1362–1389
Vasily Dimitrievitch I	1389–1425
Vasily Dimitrievitch II	1425–1462
Ivan III, the Great	1462–1505
Vasily Ivanovitch III	1505–1533

TSARS

Ivan IV, Grozny	1533–1584
Fyodor Ivanovitch	1584–1598

Note: The period from 1598 to 1613 is called the "Time of Trouble." None of the rulers, including Boris Godunov (1508–1605), who reigned during this time of unrest and anarchy, was fully acknowledged.

Romanov Dynasty (1613–1917)

TSARS

Michael Fyodorovitch	1613–1645
Alexei Mikhailovitch	1645–1676
Fyodor Alexeyevitch	1676–1682
Ivan V and Peter I	1682–1689

EMPERORS AND EMPRESSES

Peter I, the Great	1682–1725
Catherine I	1725–1727
Peter II	1727–1730
Anna	1730–1740
Ivan VI	1740–1741
Elizabeth	1741–1762
Peter III	1762
Catherine II, the Great	1762–1796
Paul	1796–1801
Alexander I	1801–1825
Nicholas I	1825–1855
Alexander II	1855–1881
Alexander III	1881–1894
Nicholas II	1894–1917

Appendix III: Population and Natural Resources

POPULATION

The Union of Soviet Socialist Republics (USSR) is a multinational state, comprised of 15 constituent republics, 20 autonomous republics, 8 autonomous regions, and many smaller national subdivisions.[1] Ranking next to those of China and India, its total population in 1968 was approximately 238,000,000. The bulk of the population is concentrated in the three Slavic republics, the Russian Soviet Federative Socialist Republic (RSFSR) having in excess of 128,000,000, the Ukrainian SSR over 46,000,000, and the Byelorussian SSR about 9,000,000. According to the 1959 census, the Slavs comprise 76 percent of the population of the USSR, or approximately 160,000,000. There is a substantial and increasing number of Great Russians and Ukrainians in the other Soviet republics. In 1959, of 114,600,000 Great Russians, 97,800,000 resided in the RSFSR. The same census indicated that 19,700,000 non-Russians live in the RSFSR, as compared to 16,700,000 Russians residing beyond its borders.[2] The Russian Federation, which is said to include more than 60 "nationalities," is composed of 16 autonomous republics, 5 autonomous regions, and 10 national areas. Of the 37,000,000 Ukrainians (1959), 32,000,000 were in the Ukraine and around 5,000,000 in other parts of the Soviet Union. Kazakhstan, in Soviet Asia, has a population of 12,400,000 (1967), slightly more than 50 percent of whom are Russians and Ukrainians and the rest largely of Turkic origin. Of the four Central Asian republics—Uzbekistan, Tajikistan, Kirghizia, and Turkmenistan—the most significant is Uzbekistan, with a population of 10,900,000 (1967). On the eve of World War II, approximately one fifth of the Soviet population, or 34,000,000 people, lived in the Asian parts of the USSR. As of 1964, it was estimated that about 53,000,000 were east of the Urals.

The distribution of the Soviet population is far from static. As a result of World War II, the development of the "virgin lands" (Kazakhstan), increased

1. See the map, "The Constituent Republics," on page 375.
2. The proportion of Russians in the various republics of the USSR, although subject to fluctuation, has been estimated as follows: Kazakhstan, 43.1%; Kirghizia, 30.2%; Latvia, 26.6%; Esthonia, 21.7%; the Ukraine, 17.7%; Turkmenistan, 17.3%; Azerbaijan, 13.9%; Uzbekistan, 13.6%; Tajikistan, 13.3%; Georgia, 10.8%; Moldavia, 10.2%; Byelorussia, 9.1%; Lithuania, 8.5%; and Armenia, 3.2%.

emphasis on industrialization, as well as on the exploitation of the vast mineral, forest, and power resources of Asiatic Russia, and the rise of Red China as an Asian power, the proportionate increase in the population of Soviet Asia has been greater than in other parts of the country. From 1939 to 1961, for instance, the population of Kazakhstan is said to have increased 70 percent, that of the republics of Central Asia about 30 percent, Siberia[3] about 35 percent, and the South Caucasus 25 percent. In Eastern Siberia alone, from 1939 to 1960, the population increase was 2,300,000. During the same period, the increase for the USSR as a whole, partly due to the losses of World War II, amounted to only 9 percent. It has been estimated that the USSR lost approximately 25,000,000 people in World War II, and as a result of territorial annexations in east-central Europe gained around 23,000,000.

In spite of the great "eastward movement" during the Soviet period, Soviet Asia is still sparsely populated. Eighty percent of the population of the USSR is concentrated in about one quarter of the territory. The greatest concentration is in European Russia, south of 60 degrees north latitude and west of the Volga River. As of the 1959 census, the population of Siberia was only 23,600,000, of whom 95 percent were Russians and Ukrainians. Although the Soviet Far East increased 70 percent in population from 1939 to 1959, it still boasted only four persons to the square mile. In the Soviet Far North, there are approximately 2.5 persons per square mile.

During the Soviet period, the process of urbanization has been greatly accelerated. The number of cities and towns has more than doubled. This is the result of a number of factors, especially of industrialization, the mechanization of agriculture, and strategic requirements. The Soviet government learned in World War II that cities were easier to defend than rural areas, and its policy has been to increase the number of cities in highly strategic borderlands, especially in Soviet Asia. In 1913, the urban population of Tsarist Russia was 24,700,000 in a total population of 165,000,000. In the nineteen twenties, the Soviet population was still less than 20 percent urban. According to the 1959 census, however, 99,800,000, or 48 percent, were in urban communities, and 109,000,000, or 52 percent, in rural. By the beginning of 1964, the urban population was estimated to have risen to 117,000,000, living in 1,763 cities, 3,255 towns, and other types of urban settlements. The rural population had reached 108,000,000, residing in some 700,000 rural communities. In other words, the urban population is now slightly more than 50 percent of the total. In Siberia, including the Soviet Far East, at least 54 percent of the population is located in urban centers (1959). In the Soviet Far East itself, 69 percent of the population has been classified as urban.

Among the largest cities of the USSR are Moscow, the capital, with an estimated population of about 7,000,000; Leningrad, with over 3,600,000; and Kiev, capital of the Ukraine, with 1,417,000 (1967). Other cities that have passed the million mark include Baku (Azerbaijan), with 1,088,000 (January 1, 1963),

3. The Asian areas of the RSFSR are usually divided into the following regions: Western Siberia, which denotes the vast lowland from the foot of the Urals to the Yenisei, and north to the Kara Sea; Eastern Siberia, which covers about one third of the USSR (2,800,000 square miles) and extends from the Yenisei beyond the Lena to the Verkhoyansk and other mountain ranges running parallel to the Pacific; and the Soviet Far East (over 1,000,000 square miles), sometimes called the "Maritime Province," which lies between the aforementioned mountains and the Pacific, includes the Kamchatka Peninsula and the Island of Sakhalin, and extends from Korea to the Bering Strait.

Gorky (RSFSR) with 1,042,000; Tashkent (Uzbekistan), with 1,241,000 (1967); and Kharkov (Ukraine), with 1,006,000. Novosibirsk, the "Chicago of Siberia," likewise passed the million mark in 1963, and Sverdlovsk, with over 869,000, was rapidly approaching the same level. Khabarovsk, the chief Soviet city of the Far East, has a population exceeding 330,000, and Vladivostok is not far behind with 285,000.

New towns have continued to spring up in all parts of the USSR, around factories, mines, and hydro-electric plants, faster, in some cases, than cartographers can record them on the map. According to Soviet claims, two thirds of the towns in the Urals, Siberia, and the Soviet Far East, and half of those in Central Asia, have developed in the Soviet period. Typical of this trend are Karaganda (459,000), in the rich coal-mining center of Kazakhstan; Igarka, one of the biggest lumber milling centers of Siberia, at the mouth of the Yenisei; nearby Noril'sk, an Arctic copper-smelting center, which in 1962 had a population of 117,000; and Bratsk, the site of a great new hydro-electric project on the Angara River, already said to have a population of 100,000 workers. Svetly, begun in 1960 in the vicinity of new discoveries of nickel-cobalt deposits on the Orenburg steppe (RSFSR), was built mainly by young people as the site of a new iron and steel mill and by 1964 its population had reached 60,000. Temir-Tau, a satellite of Karaganda, begun in 1957 by 12,000 young people as the center for Kazakhstan's new metallurgical plant, five years later had a population of more than 130,000. Such instances can be multiplied indefinitely.

The frequent change of place names in the USSR, as leaders fall from grace or new territories are annexed, is likely to be confusing to outsiders. Stalingrad, for instance, is now Volgograd, Stalino is Donetsk, Stalinabad has become Dushanbe, and Stalinsk in the Kuznetsk Basin is now called Novokuznetsk. Molotov has reverted to its former name, Perm. The Baltic port of Königsberg, acquired from Germany in 1945, is known as Kaliningrad, and the former Finnish port of Petsamo on the Barents Sea has become Pechenga.

In spite of the strong national sentiment prevailing in the fifteen republics, the process of integration proceeds apace. Of the 108 languages and "other nationalities" listed in the 1959 census, fewer than half (48 percent) were claimed by as many as 100,000. Already a substantial number of Soviet citizens born outside the RSFSR, including representatives of the minorities, have declared Russian to be their mother tongue. Increased industrialization, compulsory education, and the migration of large numbers of the Soviet population undoubtedly contribute to integration, especially among the youth.

The republican boundaries of the USSR, to a limited extent, have ceased to be linguistic boundaries. Beyond the Soviet borders, however, live many national and ethnic groups akin to those inside the country. Since World War II this is no longer true, in any real sense, of the USSR's European borders, with the exception of Finland. It is, however, a matter of increasing concern along the Asian borders of the Soviet Union, where Kurds, Armenians, Azerbaijanians, Tajiks, Kirghiz, Kazakhs, and Uighurs live on both sides of the line, and most of them have a history of migration back and forth by way of mountain passes and navigable rivers, over the medieval silk route, and so on. The most recent adjustment of the Soviet-Asian border occurred in 1944, when the USSR incorporated Tannu Tuva, formerly part of Outer Mongolia, to straighten and improve the boundary. Although such conditions have, at least in the past, provided an incentive for further Soviet expansion (for instance, in Iran and Sinkiang), with the rise of Red China they have emerged as potential sources of trouble. Along the 4,500 miles of Sino-Soviet-Mongolian border from the Pamirs to the Pacific there remain sections that the Chinese still regard as undetermined.

Natural Resources

The USSR covers a vast area of 8,650,000 square miles, about one sixth (17 percent) of the land surface of the globe and more than two fifths of the Eurasian continent. From the westernmost to the easternmost point, its territory extends 6,215 miles, spanning eleven time zones; from north to south, as much as 3,110 miles. The RSFSR alone, stretching from the Baltic to the Pacific, covers almost three quarters of the area of the Soviet Union and includes more than half its population. In a country of such size, there is great diversity of climatic conditions, vegetation, soil, altitude, and natural resources. Its chief physical handicaps are its northerly location, climatic extremes, inadequate rainfall, and shortage of arable land.

Ninety percent of the Soviet Union lies closer to the North Pole than to the Equator. Few persons realize that Moscow is farther north than Edmonton, Canada, and Leningrad than Anchorage, Alaska. More than 40 percent of the country (3,500,000 square miles) lies in the permafrost zone (frozen subsoil)—a serious disadvantage from the standpoint of agriculture, transportation, and mining. The Soviet Arctic, or cold desert, the land of the tundra, covers about one tenth of the country. The hot desert, most of which is to be found east, north, and west of the Caspian Sea, covers nine percent of the land, or 760,000 square miles. Only a small fraction of the USSR—the South Crimea and the Transcaucasian republics—enjoys a subtropical or Mediterranean climate. The vast mountain ranges in the Caucasus and those of Central Asia—the Kopet Dagh range, the Pamirs, and the Tien Shan, whose peaks, the highest in the USSR, rise to 25,000 feet—cut off the warm air from the south. In the north, there exists no barrier to the sweep of the cold Arctic winds. The Ural Mountains, 1,500 miles in length, the traditional boundary between European and Asiatic Russia, with an average elevation of but 1,600 feet and a maximum of 6,000 feet, constitute no real barrier to east-west communications. The Great Russian lowland west of the Urals, lying mainly from 600 to 1,000 feet above sea level, remains the most populous region in the USSR.

Although the USSR has 30,000 miles of coastline, most of it lies in the Arctic, and is open to commercial traffic for only two or three months per year. Murmansk (300,000) on the Barents Sea is the only "open" port in the far north, although Archangel (276,000) can be used throughout the year by means of icebreakers. Even the Baltic Sea is subject to winter freeze. On the Pacific, the port of Vladivostok is kept open with the help of icebreakers. Although the Azov and Black Seas remain open to navigation throughout the year (the port of Odessa sometimes requires icebreakers), the outlet to the Mediterranean via the Dardanelles and the Bosphorus is not under Soviet control. Three of the great river systems of Siberia—the Ob-Irtysh, the Yenisei (2,700 miles), and the Lena (2,800 miles, with 270 tributaries)—as well as the Dvina in European Russia, flow into the Arctic. The Volga flows to the enclosed Caspian Sea, and the Don and Dnieper to the Black Sea.

According to Soviet estimates, the USSR has 534,000,000 acres of arable land, of which 320,000,000 are in the RSFSR. The Ukraine, however, with its rich black soil, has a higher proportion of sown area, mainly in cereals, than any other region. Actually, only 10 percent of Soviet land is under cultivation, as compared to 7 percent in 1913. By the eve of World War II, almost all of Soviet Russia's farmlands, within the pre-1939 borders, were already being cultivated by *kolkhozy* (collective farms) or *sovkhozy* (state farms). With approximately nine tenths of the country unsuited to commercial agriculture, due to tundra, desert, marshes, mountains, and permafrost, some geographers question whether cultivation can be substantially increased, except where irrigation is made available. Since the Revolution there has, nevertheless, been a great increase in crop production. The corresponding increase in the Soviet population, however, has led to recurring food shortages in years of adverse climatic conditions, as in 1963. In October of that year, Khrushchev announced that the Republic of Uzbekistan, which has produced four fifths of the cotton of Central Asia, would also become a granary, with an increasing part of its productive land being devoted to corn and wheat. The Khrushchev regime hoped to ameliorate this problem of agricultural shortages by its crash program for the development of chemical fertilizers. Some Western geographers are inclined to believe that fertilizers and greater efficiency will not be enough—that the only satisfactory solution is the continued importation of grain in exchange for Soviet minerals, machines, and manufactured goods.

The Soviet regime envisaged its serious geographical handicaps as a challenge. Determined to convert these liabilities into assets, it has developed a grandiose, but imaginative, program "to transform nature" by the establishment of forest shelter belts on the semi-arid steppes of European Russia to hold back the dry winds from Central Asia, by diverting the waters of its great river systems and some lesser waterways for purposes of irrigation and hydroelectric power, by overcoming distance through greatly improved networks of land, water, air, and pipeline communications, and by opening up new "virgin lands" in Kazakhstan, Siberia, and the Urals, for increased food production. Instead of permitting nature to dominate man, it is the Soviet objective that man should change nature. These programs have met with varying degrees of success, but they still challenge the Soviet population, especially its youth, in the interests of progress.

Through the complex Volga-Don Canal system, Moscow, an inland city, has been transformed into a port of five seas: the Black, Azov, Caspian, Baltic, and White seas. By the North Crimean Irrigation Canal, the first stage (125 kilometers) of which was completed in October, 1963, the waters of the Dnieper River are being brought to the Crimea to open up new areas for the production of grain, vegetables, and fruit. This is but the beginning of a project eventually expected to provide a new inland waterway from the Sea of Azov via the Dnieper to the Baltic. In Uzbekistan, since the nineteen thirties, the Great Fergana Canal, using the waters of the Syr Darya (Jaxartes) and its tributary, the Narym, has opened the Fergana Valley to lucrative cotton production. The Kara-Kum Canal in Turkmenistan, the third section of which was completed in May, 1962, has provided a five-hundred mile irrigation and small craft waterway from the Amu-Darya (Oxus) to Dushanbe (Stalinabad), the capital. The ploughing of the "virgin lands" of Kazakhstan, which brought such an influx of Russians and Ukrainians to that republic, has provided, so far with limited success, an important new wheat-growing area in the Soviet East. Established in December, 1960, as a distinct administrative area, the Virgin Lands *Krai* (territory) comprises 600,000 square kilometers, with a population of around 3,000,000. In its efforts to utilize the dry lands of Central Asia, the government has envisaged the diversion of the waters of the Yenisei to the Aral Sea by means of atomic energy.

The Soviet government likewise displayed unusual energy and initiative in the discovery and exploitation of its vast and diversified mineral resources. Before the October Revolution of 1917, most Russian mines were operated by foreign capital. So limited were Russian efforts to discover and exploit Russian resources that the country was importing even common minerals, such as chalk, gypsum, and building stone. There was no mining of nickel, aluminum, and magnesium, and no prospecting for new sources of potassium salts and other much-needed mineral fertilizers. Immediately following the Revolution, the Soviet government made provision for planned geological surveys. New sources of coal were located near Moscow, new iron ore deposits near Kursk, and bauxites, which formed the basis of the new aluminum industry, on the Kola Peninsula. Initial successes whetted the Soviet appetite for further discoveries, even in the remote areas of Soviet Siberia, which had hitherto been neglected. By 1956, the USSR claimed to have 41 percent of the prospected world reserves of iron ore, 88 percent of the manganese ores, 54 percent of the potassium salts, over 30 percent of the phosphates, 60 percent of the peat, 57 percent of the coal, and huge oil reserves. It likewise claimed to rank first in the world in prospected reserves of iron and manganese ores, copper, lead, zinc, nickel, bauxites, tungsten, mercury, sulphur, potassium salts, phosphates, peat, and timber. Although Western mining experts believe some of these claims to be exaggerated, known Soviet mineral reserves are nonetheless impressive. In recent years, diamonds suitable for industrial purposes were discovered in far-off Yakutia. In 1964, as the search proceeded, 15,000 Soviet geologists were prospecting for minerals in the Irkutsk region of Siberia alone, with the help of the local population, old and young.

To accelerate the process of industrialization, the Soviet government has greatly increased its resources of energy. Since 1948, when the first natural gas line was completed from Dashava to Kiev (over 300 miles), a pipeline network has reached Moscow, Leningrad, the Ukraine, the Caucasus, the Urals, and Central Asia. Recent important discoveries in the vicinity of Bukhara and Khiva in Central Asia have led to the construction of another pipeline from Bukhara to the Urals (over 1,200 miles). According to Soviet experts, by 1965 natural gas provided one quarter of the total energy of the USSR.

The oil industry developed in Russia long before the Revolution. At the beginning of the twentieth century, tsarist Russia was producing half the world's total oil supply. An oil pipeline, one of the first in Europe, was completed from Baku to Batumi on the Black Sea shortly thereafter. By World War II, the Azerbaijan-Baku fields on the Caspian accounted for 71.5 percent of the Soviet Union's oil supply. Since the war, many new sources have been developed, the most important of which are those in the Ural-Volga area, in the Bashkir and Tatar republics, known as the "Second Baku," which now provide 70 percent of the oil extracted in the USSR and have superseded Baku and the North Caucasus. The Soviet Union claims to have 54.8 percent of the world's oil reserves, although these claims are generally challenged by Western experts, who estimate the supply closer to 26 percent. Less spectacular, but commercially valuable sources of oil have been exploited around Pechora in the north, in Central Asia, and on the Island of Sakhalin, which supplies the Soviet Far East. In the years since World War II, oil transportation has been transformed by the development of an extensive pipeline network from the Urals to Irkutsk (Siberia) and Atbazar (Kazakhstan), and from the Tatar Republic to Moscow. These pipelines help to relieve the heavy pressure on the country's railroads. The Druzhba (Friendship) International Pipeline (3,100 miles) from the Urals to Poland, East Germany, Hungary, and Czechoslovakia, part of which is in operation, opens up the possibility of future oil deliveries even to Western Europe. The Soviet oil output, which quadrupled in the decade 1954–1964, already furnishes the country's leading export. The discovery in 1961 and development thereafter of "tremendous" oil and gas resources around Ust-Belyk in the Tyumen *Oblast* in Siberia (a center not recorded on Soviet maps by 1964) suggests that an "oil rush" in some respects reminiscent of the California and Alaska gold rushes has occurred there (*Izvestia,* July 12, 1964). The Ust-Belyk oil deposits were reported to be greater than those of Bashkiria, Tatariya, and Udmurtiya, the Saratov, Orenburg and Volgograd regions combined. Estimates of the gas reserves in this area exceed five trillion cubic meters. And the end is not yet in sight. Some two hundred kilometers from Ust-Belyk new oil deposits have been located, allegedly exceeding all previous findings. As a result, Ust-Belyk is expected to become a new center for the chemical industry.

In spite of the growing importance of natural gas and oil, coal remains the most important energy source in the Soviet Union. Although coal deposits are widely dispersed throughout the USSR and important new discoveries have been made, the principal coal basins are the Donbas (Ukraine), the Kuzbas or Kuznetsk Basin (Siberia), the Karaganda (Kazakhstan), and the Pechora (RSFSR). From 1855 to 1938, approximately two thirds of Russia's coal was produced in the Donets Basin. The exploitation of new sources in Siberia and Kazakhstan, where mining is cheaper, have reduced this proportion to one third. A large proportion of the USSR's rich coal reserves, such as those on the Lena and Tunguska rivers, is in remote areas of the Arctic and subarctic, where distance and transportation still present serious handicaps to exploitation.

Tsarist Russia was more backward, proportionately, than any of the other great powers in the production of electric energy. Since the Revolution, spurred on by Lenin's program for the electrification of the country, the Soviet government has undertaken many great hydroelectric projects. Prior to World War II, the greatest of these was the Dneproges hydroelectric installation at Zaporozhye on the Dnieper, which began operation in 1932. Until the construction of the Grand Coulee Dam in the United States, it was the biggest in the world. The Volga hydroelectric projects, begun before the war at Uglich and Shcherbakov (now Rybinsk) as part of the Volga-Don waterway and irrigation program, have been further increased since 1945, with the completion of a great plant on the Don at Tsimlyansk, and the construction of others at Kuibyshev and Volgograd (Stalingrad). Some of the more spectacular developments in Eastern Siberia since World War II are the mammoth hydroelectric plants at Bratsk (population 100,000) on the Angara River, and at Krasnoyarsk (465,000) on the Yenisei. Plans are under way to weld the various electric power projects west of the Yenisei into an all-Union power grid, which will make possible the adjustment of power supply to industrial needs and to the seasons. Although the Soviet government has never failed to publicize its hydroelectric projects, some Western experts are inclined to discount their significance in the production of Soviet energy. Most of the electricity generated in the Soviet Union still comes from thermal electric stations, which utilize cheap coal, gas, and oil, and these are being given priority. In the USSR, the need for electric energy still greatly exceeds the supply.

The development of Soviet resources, especially those of Siberia and the East, depends on improved transportation facilities. By 1913 tsarist Russia had 43,000 miles of railroads. Under the Soviet regime, this mileage has been doubled (82,000 miles of track as of 1968), with special emphasis on Siberia, Kazakhstan, and Central Asia. The Turksib (Turkestan-Siberian) Railway, linking Tashkent (Uzbekistan) with Alma-Ata and Semipalatinsk (Kazakhstan), was completed in 1930. The double-tracking of the Trans-Siberian Railway was finished prior to World War II. The South Siberian Railway, connecting the metallurgical center of Magnitogorsk in the Urals with Akhmolinsk, Barnaul, and Novokuznetsk (Stalinsk) in the Kuzbas, is one of many significant railroad projects in Asiatic Russia. Since World War II, the conversion of Soviet railways from steam to diesel and electric power (15,500 miles electrified by 1968) has been carried out over wide areas. The Moscow-Leningrad, the Moscow-Donbas-Caucasus, and the Trans-Siberian as far east as Irkutsk have been electrified, and the process continues.

The Soviet Union's vast system of inland waterways, which has been of vital importance throughout the country's history, continues to supplement the railroads for at least part of the year. The Baltic-White Sea and Volga-Don Canal systems are used extensively for inland shipping of lumber, petroleum, building materials, coal, grain, fish, salt, etc. The Siberian rivers, where no railroads are available, are employed for the shipment of freight during the summer season. The busy port of Igarka at the mouth of the Yenisei has already outgrown its facilities and new ones are planned. When the great projects on the Angara and Yenisei are completed, the USSR expects freighters to travel from London to Lake Baikal (area, 11,580 square miles) in the heart of Siberia. The USSR claimed to have 85,000 miles of inland waterways in 1960, as compared to 40,000 in 1913.

The Northern Sea Route, 7,000 statute miles by way of the Arctic from Archangel to Vladivostok, was put into operation by the Soviet regime in 1932, although it can be used for only two or three months per year. The Soviet merchant fleet is small, but increasing. By the early nineteen sixties, the USSR accounted for little more than 3 percent of the world's trade, mainly in oil, timber, ores, and coal.

The Soviet air routes, which have developed since 1923, have greatly improved communications, especially in the more remote areas of the USSR where neither roads nor railroads are available. Regular air service connects the principal cities in the Union, and an increasing number of European and Asian capitals. From Moscow to Irkutsk takes six hours, to Tbilisi (Georgia), two and one-half hours, and to Tashkent, four hours. By Soviet jet aircraft (TU-114), the trip from Moscow to Peking (6,000 miles) can be made in eight and one-half hours. In 1968 direct air communications were opened between Moscow and New York.

In spite of the extensive development of natural resources and industries in all the republics of the Soviet Union, the vast Russian Federation continues to be the country's principal industrial base. In the Urals and Siberia, it has the second biggest coal and metal base in the USSR, as well as the great machine-building centers of Novosibirsk, Omsk, and Krasnoyarsk. It produces over half the output of pig iron, 60 percent of the steel and coal, nearly three quarters of the oil, and four fifths of the machines in the Soviet Union. According to Soviet claims, it has 60 percent of the country's arable land.

Although they cannot compete with the RSFSR in overall natural resources and industrial power, the republics of Central Asia and Kazakhstan, which cover 7.8 percent of the area and include 11 percent of the population of the USSR, do furnish variety and contribute substantially to the self-sufficiency of the Union. They continue to develop their own industrial plants and practice irrigated agriculture on an expanding scale. The Uzbek Republic, in the heart of the Central Asian plateau, boast two thirds of the population, four fifths of the gross industrial output, and four fifths of the cotton production of Central Asia. It has its own steel and rolled iron industries, and its own chemical, machine-building, and food processing plants. Its new industrial centers include Chirchik (chemical, power, and machine-building plants), Yangi-Yul (food processing and light industry), Angren (the Uzbek "coal pit" near Tashkent), and Kuvasai (building materials). The Kirghiz Republic, whose population was nomadic a half-century ago, now has non-ferrous metallurgical plants, as well as oil, silk, building materials, canned foods, and meat-packing industries. Its rich mineral resources include coal, mercury, wolfram, lead, and antimony. The Tajik Republic, the most mountainous region of the Soviet Union and its "gateway to India," which was one of the most backward areas prior to the Revolution, ranks second to Uzbekistan in cotton and has developed its own oil resources, bismuth and tungsten mines, as well as its silk, textile, canned foods, and leather industries. In the Turkmen Republic, 80 percent of which is covered by the Kara Kum

(Black Sands) Desert, industry has superseded agriculture, with new cotton and silk mills, shoe factories, and meat processing plants. The Republic is developing its natural gas resources and has founded a chemical industry. Irrigated agriculture is practiced in its oases.

Kazakhstan, second in size to the RSFSR, is said to have over one half the copper ore reserves of the USSR, three quarters of the lead, one half of the zinc, and two thirds of the silver, not to mention again its oil and its rich reserves of coal and iron ore. Kazakhstan now ranks first in the USSR for non-ferrous metallurgy. Long important for stock raising, it is developing its agricultural areas against heavy climatic disadvantages. Its chief industrial centers include Karaganda, Balkhash, Leninogorsk, and Ust-Kamenogorsk. Alma-Ata, its picturesque mountain capital, has become the Soviet Hollywood.

In Transcaucasia, the Republic of Georgia is famous for its vineyards and its substropical crops of tea, lemons, and other citrus fruits. Its great manganese mines at Chiatura were once headed by W. Averill Harriman. Today, it has its own machine-building plants, textile mills, and boot and shoe works. Its Black Sea coast has become a Soviet Riviera. The Armenian Republic, in the shadow of Mount Ararat, is producing cotton, grapes, fruit, tobacco, and silk by means of irrigation. It is gradually exploiting its extensive reserves of copper, molybdenum, iron ore, chromite, and building materials, and expanding its cotton and wine industries.

In all Soviet Asia, the USSR is perpetually seeking to demonstrate to Asians beyond its borders the material and cultural progress that has occurred in little more than half a century. Many parts of the USSR are still backward and underdeveloped by American standards, but the population is conscious of the progress that has been achieved, often in the face of adverse climatic and geographical conditions.

The sheer preponderance of the RSFSR and the fact that the political boundaries of the Soviet republics no longer coincide with economic reality have resulted in preliminary steps toward regional organization. Already in 1962, the four republics of Central Asia, in accordance with policies outlined by the Twenty-Second Congress of the Communist Party, were placed under a unified Party command, with unified management of industry, construction, and cotton irrigation. Similar steps were taken in the Transcaucasian republics of Armenia, Georgia, and Azerbaijan, but with looser economic coordination. It is to be assumed that the Baltic states of Latvia, Estonia, and Lithuania will follow the same pattern. Whether the increasingly close economic interests of the Urals and West Siberia with Kazakhstan will lead to further regional reorganization has not yet been indicated.

Geographic conditions in the Soviet Union are dynamic rather than static. Where a government has absolute power to determine which resources will be developed and to distribute labor forces and specialists wherever necessary to accomplish this purpose, much can be done, albeit at great cost in terms of human values and efficiency, to change the face of nature. Americans who are impressed by the wealth and diversity of natural resources in the Soviet Union and by the nature of its dynamism should bear in mind that in spite of the herculean efforts of the Soviet government the USSR is still far behind the United States in the exploitation of these resources, in the development of transportation and industry, and in the standard of living it is able to provide for the average citizen.

Bibliography

Because a veritable avalanche of books on Russia and the Soviet Union have appeared in the nineteen sixties, this bibliography is a selected list, suggesting the wealth of material available for basic and collateral reading.

GEOGRAPHY AND POPULATION

Adams, Arthur E., Ian M. Matley, and W. O. McCagg, *An Atlas of Russian and East European History*, Frederick A. Praeger, 1966.
Chew, Allen F., *An Atlas of Russian History. Eleven Centuries of Changing Borders*, Yale University Press, 1967.
Cole, J. P., and F. C. German, *A Geography of the USSR: The Background to a Planned Economy*, Butterworths (London), 1961.
Cressey, George B., *Soviet Potentials: A Geographic Appraisal*, Syracuse University Press, 1962.
East, W. Gordon, *The Soviet Union*, D. Van Nostrand Company, Inc., 1963.
Fullard, Harold, ed., *Soviet Union in Maps. Its Origin and Development*, Denoyer-Geppert, 1961.
Hodgkins, J. A., *Soviet Power: Energy, Resources, Production and Potentials*, Prentice-Hall, Inc., 1961.
Hooson, David, *A New Soviet Heartland?* A Searchlight Original, D. Van Nostrand Company, Inc., 1964.
Jackson, W. A. Douglas, *Russo-Chinese Borderlands. Zone of Peaceful Contact or Potential Conflict?* A Searchlight Original, D. Van Nostrand Company, Inc., 1962.
Jorré, Georges, *The Soviet Union: The Land and Its People*, 2nd ed., Longmans, Greene & Co. (London), 1961.
Miller, Wright W., *Russians as People*, E. P. Dutton & Co., 1961.
Suslov, S. P., *Physical Geography of Asiatic Russia*, W. H. Freeman, 1961.
Taaffe, Robert N., *An Atlas of Soviet Affairs*. Maps by Robert C. Kingsbury, Frederick A. Praeger, 1965.

PREREVOLUTIONARY RUSSIA

Adams, Arthur E., ed., *Imperial Russia After 1861. Modernization or Revolution?*, D. C. Heath, 1965.
Almedingen, Martha E., *The Romanovs. Three Centuries of an Ill-Fated Dynasty*,

Bodley Head (London), 1966; *The Emperor Alexander I*, Vanguard Press, 1966. *The Emperor Alexander II: A Study*, Bodley Head (London), 1962.

Avrich, Paul, *The Russian Anarchists*, Princeton University Press, 1967.

Barbour, Philip L., *Dimitry Called the Pretender. Tsar and Great Prince of All Russia, 1605–1606*, Houghton Mifflin, 1966.

Baron, Samuel H., *Plekhanov: the Father of Russian Marxism*, Stanford University Press, 1963.

Bell, John, *A Journey from St. Petersburg to Pekin, 1719–22*, edited by J. L. Stevenson, Edinburgh University Press, 1965.

Billington, James H., *Mikhailovsky and Russian Populism*, Clarendon Press (Oxford), 1958; *The Icon and the Axe. An Interpretive History of Russian Culture*, Alfred A. Knopf, 1966.

Black, Cyril E., ed., *The Transformation of Russian Society. Aspects of Social Change Since 1861*, Harvard University Press, 1960.

Blum, Jerome, *Lord and Peasant in Russia from the Ninth to the Nineteenth Century*, Princeton University Press, 1961.

Cherniavsky, Michael, *Tsar and People. Studies in Russian Myths*, Yale University Press, 1961; *Prologue to Revolution: Notes on the Secret Meetings of the Council of Ministers, 1915*, Prentice-Hall, Inc., 1967.

Cross, Samuel H., tr., *The Russian Primary Chronicle*, Harvard University Press, 1930; *Slavic Civilization Through the Ages*, Harvard University Press, 1948.

Curtiss, John Shelton, ed., *Essays in Russian and Soviet History*, E. J. Brill (Leiden), 1963; *The Russian Army Under Nicholas I, 1825–1855*, Duke University Press, 1965.

Fennell, J. L. I., *Ivan the Great of Moscow*, St. Martin's Press, 1961; ed. and tr., *Prince A. M. Kurbsky's History of Ivan IV*, Cambridge University Press, 1965.

Fischer, George, *Russian Liberalism from Gentry to Intelligentsia*, Harvard University Press, 1958.

Fitzlyon, Kyril, tr. and ed., *The Memoirs of Princess Dashkov*, John Calder (London), 1958.

Florinsky, Michael T., *The End of the Russian Empire*, Collier, 1961.

Grekov, B. D., *The Culture of Kiev Rus*, Foreign Languages Press (Moscow), 1947.

Grey, Ian, *Peter the Great. Emperor of All Russia*, J. B. Lippincott Co., 1960; *Catherine the Great. Autocrat and Empress of All Russia*, J. B. Lippincott Co., 1962.

Grunwald, Constantin de, *Tsar Nicholas I*, Macmillan Company, 1955.

Haimson, Leopold H., ed., *The History of Menshevism*, University of Chicago Press, 1966.

Harcave, Sidney, *First Blood—The Russian Revolution of 1905*, Macmillan Company, 1964.

Hare, Richard, *Pioneers of Russian Social Thought: Studies of Non-Marxian Formation in 19th Century Russia and Its Partial Revival in the Soviet Union*, Oxford University Press, 1951.

Karpovich, M., *Imperial Russia, 1801–1917* (Berkshire Studies), Henry Holt and Co., 1932.

Kennan, George, *Siberia and the Exile System* (2 Vols.), Century Co., 1891.

Kliuchevsky, V. O., *A History of Russia* (5 Vols.), E. P. Dutton & Co., Inc., 1911–1931; *Peter the Great*, tr. by Liliana Archibald, Vintage Books, 1961.

Kohler, Phyllis P., ed. & tr., *Journey for Our Time: The Journals of the Marquis de Custine*, Pellegrini & Cudahy, 1951.

Kohn, Hans, *Pan-Slavism: Its History and Ideology*, University of Notre Dame Press, 1953.

Kornilov, Alexander, *Modern Russian History*, Alfred A. Knopf, 1952.

Laserson, M. M., *The American Impact on Russia: Diplomatic and Ideological, 1784–1917*, Macmillan Company, 1950.

Lensen, George Alexander, ed., *Russia's Eastward Expansion*, Prentice-Hall, Inc., 1964.

Leroy-Beaulieu, A., *The Empire of the Tsars and the Russians* (3 Vols.), G. Putnam's Sons, 1896.

Longworth, Philip, *The Art of Victory: The Life and Achievements of Field-Marshal Suvorov, 1729–1800*, Holt, Rinehart and Winston, 1966.

Lyashchenko, P. I., *History of the National Economy of Russia to the 1917 Revolution*, Macmillan Company, 1949. A Soviet interpretation.

Maroger, Dominique, ed., *The Memoirs of Catherine the Great*, Hamish Hamilton (London), 1955.

Masaryk, Thomas G., *The Spirit of Russia*, Macmillan Company, 1955.

Mazour, Anatole G., *The First Russian Revolution, 1825*, University of California Press, 1937; *The Rise and Fall of the Romanovs* (Anvil Books), D. Van Nostrand Company, Inc., 1960.

Michell, R., and R. Forbes, eds. & trs., *Chronicle of Novgorod, 1016–1471*, Camden Society (London), 1914.

Mosse, W. E., *Alexander II and the Modernization of Russia*, The English Universities Press, 1958.

Olivier, Daria, *The Burning of Moscow 1812*, Allen & Unwin (London), 1966.

Page, Stanley W., ed., *Russia in Revolution: Selected Readings in Russian Domestic History Since 1855*, D. Van Nostrand Company, Inc., 1965.

Paléologue, G. M., *The Enigmatic Czar: The Life of Alexander I of Russia*, Hamish Hamilton (London), 1938; *An Ambassador's Memoirs*, tr. by F. A. Holt (3 Vols.), Hutchinson & Co., Ltd. (London), 1923–25.

Pares, Bernard, *A History of Russia*, Alfred A. Knopf, 1947; *The Fall of the Russian Monarchy*, Alfred A. Knopf, 1939.

Pipes, Richard, tr. & ed., *Karamzin's Memoir on Ancient and Modern Russia*, Harvard University Press, 1959; *Social Democracy and the St. Petersburg Labor Movement*, Harvard University Press, 1963; *The Russian Intelligentsia*, Columbia University Press, 1961.

Platonov, S. F., *A History of Russia*, Macmillan Company, 1925.

Pobedonostsev, C., *Reflections of a Russian Statesman*, University of Michigan Press, 1965.

Putnam, Peter, ed., *Seven Britons in Imperial Russia, 1698–1812*, Princeton University Press, 1952.

Radishchev, Alexander N., *A Journey from St. Petersburg to Moscow*, tr. by Lev Wiener and ed. by Roderick P. Thaler, Harvard University Press, 1958.

Raeff, Marc, *The Decembrist Movement*, Prentice-Hall, 1966; *Plans for Political Reform in Imperial Russia, 1730–1905*, Prentice-Hall, Inc., 1966; *Russian Intellectual History. An Anthology*, Harcourt, Brace & World, 1966.

Rambaud, Alfred, *The History of Russia*, J. Balden, 1886.

Reddaway, W. F., ed., *Documents of Catherine II*, Macmillan Company, 1931.

Riasanovsky, Nicholas, *Russia and the West in the Teaching of the Slavophiles*, Harvard University Press, 1952; *Nicholas I and Official Nationality in Russia, 1825–1855*, University of California Press, 1959.

Robinson, Geroid T., *Rural Russia Under the Old Regime*, 6th Printing, Macmillan Company 1967.

Rogger, Hans, *National Consciousness in Eighteenth Century Russia*, Harvard University Press, 1960.

Schwarz, Solomon M., *The Russian Revolution of 1905. The Workers' Movement and the Formation of Bolshevism and Menshevism,* University of Chicago Press, 1967.

Seton-Watson, Hugh, *The Decline of Imperial Russia, 1855–1914,* Frederick A. Praeger, 1956.

Shoemaker, M. M., *The Great Siberian Railway from St. Petersburg to Peking,* G. Putnam's Sons, 1903.

Spector, Ivar and Marion, eds., *Readings in Russian History and Culture,* Allyn and Bacon, Inc., 1965.

Strakhovsky, L. I., *Alexander I of Russia,* W. W. Norton & Co., 1947.

Sumner, B. H., *A Short History of Russia,* Harcourt, Brace and Co., 1949; *Peter the Great and the Emergence of Russia,* Macmillan Company, 1951.

Tarle, Eugene, *Napoleon's Invasion of Russia—1812,* Oxford University Press, 1942.

The Life of the Archpriest Avvakum by Himself, tr. by Jane Harrison and Hope Mirrlees, Archon Books, 1963.

Thomsen, Vilhelm Ludwig Peter, *The Relations Between Ancient Russia and Scandinavia, and the Origin of the Russian State,* Burt Franklin (1887), 1964.

Thomson, G. S., *Catherine the Great and the Expansion of Russia,* Macmillan Company, 1950.

Tikhomirov, M., *The Towns of Ancient Rus,* Foreign Languages Publishing House (Moscow), 1959. A Soviet interpretation.

Troyat, Henri, *Daily Life in Russia Under the Last Tsar,* Macmillan Company, 1962.

Utechin, S. V., *Russian Political Thought: A Concise History,* Frederick A. Praeger, 1964.

Venturi, Franco, *Roots of Revolution: History of the Populist and Socialist Movements in 19th Century Russia,* Alfred A. Knopf, 1960.

Vernadsky, George, *Ancient Russia,* Yale University Press, 1943; *A History of Russia,* Yale University Press, 1961; *Medieval Russian Laws,* Columbia University Press, 1947; *Kievan Russia,* Yale University Press, 1948; *The Mongols and Russia,* Yale University Press, 1953.

Von Laue, Theodore H., *Sergei Witte and the Industrialization of Russia,* Columbia University Press, 1963.

Wallace, Sir Donald Mackenzie, *Russia on the Eve of War and Revolution,* edited and introduced by Cyril E. Black, Vintage Books, 1961.

Walsh, Warren B., *Readings in Russian History* (3 Vols.), Syracuse University Press, 1963.

Wipper, R., *Ivan Grozny,* Foreign Languages Publishing House (Moscow), 1947. A Soviet interpretation.

Yarmolinsky, Avrahm, *Road to Revolution,* Macmillan Company, 1959; ed. & tr., *Memoirs of Count Witte,* Doubleday, Page & Co., 1921.

Zeman, Z. A. B., and W. B. Scharlau, *The Merchant of Revolution—The Life of Alexander Israel Helphand (Parvus), 1867–1924,* Oxford University Press, 1965.

Soviet Russia

Bauer, Raymond A., and Edward Wasiolek, *Nine Soviet Portraits,* The M. I. T. Press, 1965.

Baykov, Alexander, *The Development of the Soviet Economic System,* Macmillan Company, 1948.

Beck, F., and W. Goden, *Russian Purge and the Extraction of Confessions,* Viking Press, 1951.

Belov, Fedor, *A History of a Soviet Collective Farm,* Frederick A. Praeger, 1955.
Benton, William, *The Teacher and the Taught in the USSR,* Atheneum, 1966.
Berdyaev, Nicholas, *The Origins of Russian Communism,* University of Michigan Press, 1960.
Bergson, Abram, *Economic Trends in the Soviet Union,* Harvard University Press, 1963.
Berman, Harold, *Soviet Criminal Law and Procedure: The RSFSR Codes,* Harvard University Press, 1966.
Black, Cyril E., ed., *Rewriting Russian History,* 2nd ed., Vintage Books, 1962.
Browder, Robert Paul and Alexander F. Kerensky, eds., *The Russian Provisional Government 1917. Documents* (3 Vols.), Stanford University Press, 1961.
Brumberg, Abraham, ed., *Russia Under Khrushchev. An Anthology,* Frederick A. Praeger, 1962.
Brzezinski, Zbigniew, *The Permanent Purge,* Harvard University Press, 1956.
Carr, Edward H., *A History of Soviet Russia, 1917–1926* (6 Vols.), Macmillan Company, 1951–60.
Chamberlin, William H., *Russia's Iron Age,* Little, Brown and Co., 1934; *The Russian Revolution, 1917–1921* (2 Vols.), Macmillan Company, 1952.
Chernov, Victor, *The Great Russian Revolution,* Yale University Press, 1936.
Chuikov, Vasili I., *The Battle for Stalingrad,* Holt, Rinehart and Winston, 1964.
Conquest, Robert, *Russia After Khrushchev,* Frederick A. Praeger, 1965.
Crankshaw, Edward, *Khrushchev's Russia,* Penguin Books, Inc., 1959; *Khrushchev: A Career,* Viking Press, 1966.
Curtiss, John Shelton, *The Russian Revolutions of 1917,* D. Van Nostrand Company, Inc., 1957.
Dallin, Alexander, *German Rule in Russia, 1941–1945,* Macmillan and Co., Ltd. (London), 1957.
Dallin, D. J., and B. S. Nicolaevsky, *Forced Labor in Soviet Russia,* Yale University Press, 1947.
De George, Richard T., *Patterns of Soviet Thought. The Origins and Development of Dialectical and Historical Materialism,* University of Michigan Press, 1966.
Degras, Jane T., ed., *The Communist International, 1919–1943,* Oxford University Press, 1956.
Deutscher, Isaac, *The Unfinished Revolution—Russia 1917–1967,* Oxford University Press, 1967; *Stalin. A Political Biography,* Oxford University Press, 1949.
Djilas, Milovan, *Conversations with Stalin,* Harcourt, Brace and World, 1962.
Dobb, Maurice Herbert, *Soviet Economic Development Since 1917,* Routledge and Kegan Paul, Ltd. (London), 1958.
Education in the USSR, International Arts and Sciences Press, 1963.
Ehrenburg, Ilya, *Memoirs, 1921–1941,* World Publishing Co., 1964; *The War, 1941–1945,* World Publishing Co., 1966; *The Thaw,* MacGibbon and Kee (London), 1961.
Fainsod, Merle, *How Russia Is Ruled,* 2nd ed., Harvard University Press, 1963.
Feifer, George, *Justice in Moscow,* Simon and Schuster, 1964.
Fischer, Louis, *The Life of Lenin,* Harper and Row, 1964.
Fitzsimmons, Thomas, *et al., USSR: Its People, Its Society, Its Culture,* Human Relations Area Files Press, 1960.
Footman, David, *Civil War in Russia,* Frederick A. Praeger, 1961.
Francis, David R., *Russia from the American Embassy,* Scribner, 1921.
Gallagher, Matthew P., *The Soviet History of World War II. Myths, Memories, and Realities,* Frederick A. Praeger, 1963.
Gankin, O. H., and H. H. Fisher, *The Bolsheviks and the World War: The Origins of the Third International,* Stanford University Press, 1940.

Gorbatov, A. V., *Years of My Life. A Red Army General's Experiences of the Soviet Purges,* W. W. Norton & Co., Inc., 1965.

Graves, William S., *America's Siberian Adventure, 1918–1920,* J. Cape and H. Smith, 1931.

Hazard, John, *The Soviet System of Government,* University of Chicago Press, 1957.

Hendel, Samuel, ed., *The Soviet Crucible,* 3rd ed., D. Van Nostrand Company, Inc., 1967.

Herz, Martin, *Beginnings of the Cold War,* Indiana University Press, 1966.

Hindus, Maurice, *House Without a Roof. Russia After Forty-Three Years of Revolution,* Doubleday and Co., 1961.

Hulicka, Karel and Irene, *Soviet Institutions, the Individual and Society,* Christopher Publishing House, 1967.

Inkeles, A., *Public Opinion in Soviet Russia,* Harvard University Press, 1950.

Jasny, Naum, *The Socialized Agriculture of the U.S.S.R.,* Stanford University Press, 1949; *Soviet Industrialization, 1928–1952,* University of Chicago Press, 1961; *Essays on the Soviet Economy,* Frederick A. Praeger, 1962.

Kassof, Allen, *The Soviet Youth Program,* Harvard University Press, 1965.

Katkoff, Vladimir, *Soviet Economy, 1940–1965,* Dangary Publishing Co., 1961.

Kathov, George, *Russia 1917. The February Revolution,* Harper & Row, 1967.

Keep, John, ed., with the assistance of Liliana Busby, *Contemporary History in the Soviet Union,* Frederick A. Praeger, 1964.

Kerensky, Alexander F., *The Catastrophe: Kerensky's Own Story of the Russian Revolution,* Appleton-Century-Crofts, Inc., 1927; *Russia and History's Turning Point,* Duell, Sloan and Pearce, 1965.

Koestler, Arthur, *Darkness at Noon,* Macmillan Company, 1941.

Kruglak, Theodore Edward, *The Two Faces of TASS,* University of Minnesota Press, 1962.

Leonhard, Wolfgang, *The Kremlin Since Stalin,* Frederick A. Praeger, 1962.

Liberman, Simon, *Building Lenin's Russia,* University of Chicago Press, 1945.

Linden, Carl A., *Khrushchev and the Soviet Leadership, 1957–1964,* The Johns Hopkins Press, 1966.

Lyons, Eugene, *Assignment in Utopia,* Harcourt, Brace, 1937; *The Red Decade,* The Bobbs Merrill Co., 1941.

McNeal, Robert H., ed., *Lenin, Stalin, and Khrushchev: Voices of Bolshevism,* Prentice-Hall, Inc., 1963.

Mazour, Anatole G., *Soviet Economic Development: Operation Outstrip, 1921–1965,* D. Van Nostrand Company, Inc., 1967.

Mehnert, Klaus, *Soviet Man and His World,* Frederick A. Praeger, 1962.

Meyer, Alfred G., *Communism,* Random House, 1960; *The Soviet Political System: An Interpretation,* Random House, 1965.

Milenkovitch, Michael, M., *The View from Red Square: A Critique of Cartoons from* PRAVDA *and* IZVESTIA, *1947–1964,* Hobbs, Dorman, 1966.

Moorehead, Alan, *The Russian Revolution,* Harper & Row, 1958.

Nicolaevsky, Boris I., *Power and the Soviet Elite,* ed. by Janet Zagoria, Stanford University Press, 1965.

Nove, Alec, *The Soviet Economy,* Frederick A. Praeger, 1966.

Nove, Alec, and J. A. Newth, *The Soviet Middle East. A Communist Model for Development,* Frederick A. Praeger, 1967.

Pavlov, D. V., *Leningrad 1941: The Blockade,* University of Chicago Press, 1965.

Pipes, Richard, *The Formation of the Soviet Union: Communism and Nationalism, 1917–1923,* Harvard University Press, 1954.

Pope, Arthur Upham, *Maxim Litvinoff,* L. B. Fischer, 1943.

Radkey, Oliver H., *Agrarian Foes of Bolshevism; Promise and Default of the Russian Social Revolutionaries,* Columbia University Press, 1958.
Randall, Francis B., *Stalin's Russia—An Historical Reconsideration,* Free Press, 1965.
Reed, John, *Ten Days That Shook the World,* Modern Library, 1935.
Reshetar, John S., *A Concise History of the Communist Party of the Soviet Union,* Frederick A. Praeger, 1960.
Rigby, T. H., ed., *Stalin. Great Lives Observed.* Prentice-Hall, 1967.
Rush, Myron, *Political Succession in the U. S. S. R.,* Columbia University Press, 1965; *The Rise of Khrushchev,* Public Affairs Press, 1958.
Schapiro, Leonard B., *The Communist Party of the Soviet Union,* Random House, 1960.
Schueller, George K., *The Politburo,* Stanford University Press, 1951.
Schuman, Frederick L. *Russia Since 1917; Four Decades of Soviet Politics,* Alfred A. Knopf, 1957; *Government in the Soviet Union,* Thomas Y. Crowell Co., 1961.
Schwartz, Harry, *The Red Phoenix. Russia Since World War II,* Frederick A. Praeger, 1961.
Shaffer, Harry G., ed., *The Soviet Economy: A Collection of Western and Soviet Views,* Appleton-Century-Crofts, 1963.
Scott, John, *Behind the Urals,* Houghton Mifflin Company, 1942.
Shteppa, Konstantin F., *Russian Historians and the Soviet State,* Rutgers University Press, 1962.
Shub, David, *Lenin: A Biography,* Doubleday, 1948.
Sukhanov, N. M., *The Russian Revolution 1917,* Oxford University Press, 1955.
Timasheff, Nicholas S., *The Great Retreat,* E. P. Dutton & Co., Inc., 1946.
Thompson, John M., *Russia, Bolshevism, and the Versailles Peace,* Princeton University Press, 1966.
Tolstoy, A., *I Worked for the Soviets,* Yale University Press, 1935.
Treadgold, Donald, *Twentieth Century Russia,* 2nd ed., Rand, McNally and Co., 1964; ed., *Soviet and Chinese Communism. Similarities and Differences,* University of Washington Press, 1967.
Trotsky, L., *The History of the Russian Revolution,* University of Michigan Press, 1957.
Ulam, Adam B., *The Bolsheviks. The Intellectual, Personal and Political History of the Origins of Russian Communism,* Macmillan Company, 1965.
Von Laue, T. H., *Why Lenin? Why Stalin? A Reappraisal of the Russian Revolution, 1900–1930,* J. B. Lippincott Co., 1964.
Voznesensky, N. A., *The Economy of the U. S. S. R. During World War II,* Public Affairs Press, 1948.
Vyshinsky, Andrei, *The Law of the Soviet State,* tr. by Hugh W. Babb, Macmillan Company, 1948.
Walsh, E. A., *The Fall of the Russian Empire,* Little, Brown and Co., 1928.
Webb, Sidney and Beatrice, *Soviet Communism: A New Civilization?,* Charles Scribner's Sons, 1936.
Werth, Alexander, *Russia at War, 1941–1945,* Avon Books, 1965.
Westwood, J. N., *Russia, 1917–1964,* Harper & Row, 1966.
Whiting, Kenneth R., *The Soviet Union Today.* A Concise Handbook, Frederick A. Praeger, 1966.
Wolfe, Bertram, *Three Who Made a Revolution,* Dial Press, Inc., 1948.
Wolin, Simon and Robert M. Slusser, eds., *The Soviet Secret Police,* Frederick A. Praeger, 1957.
Woytinsky, W. A., *Stormy Passage. A Personal History Through Two Russian*

Revolutions to Democracy and Freedom: 1905–1960, The Vanguard Press, Inc., 1961.

FOREIGN POLICY

Adams, Arthur E., *Readings in Soviet Foreign Policy. Theory and Practice,* D. C. Heath and Co., 1961.

Bailey, T. A., *America Faces Russia: Russian-American Relations from Early Times to Our Day,* Cornell University Press, 1950.

Beloff, Max, *The Foreign Policy of Soviet Russia,* 2 Vols., Oxford University Press, 1947–49; *Soviet Policy in the Far East, 1944–1951,* Oxford University Press, 1953.

Berliner, Joseph S., *Soviet Economic Aid to Underdeveloped Countries,* Frederick A. Praeger, 1958.

Boorman, Howard L., et al., *Moscow-Peking Axis: Strengths and Strains,* published for the Council on Foreign Relations by Harper, 1957.

Brinkley, George A., *The Volunteer Army and Allied Intervention in South Russia, 1917–1921,* University of Notre Dame Press, 1966.

Browder, Robert P., *The Origins of Soviet-American Diplomacy,* Princeton University Press, 1953.

Brzezinski, Zbigniew, *The Soviet Bloc, Unity and Conflict,* rev., Frederick A. Praeger, 1961.

Byrnes, James F., *Speaking Frankly,* Harper and Brothers, 1947.

Cahen, Gaston, *Histoire des Relations de la Russie avec la Chine, sous Pierre Le Grand* (1689–1730), F. Alcan (Paris), 1912.

Carr, Edward H., *German-Soviet Relations between the Two World Wars, 1919–1939,* Harper & Row, 1966.

Crankshaw, Edward, *The New Cold War: Moscow vs. Peking,* Penguin Books, Inc., 1963.

Curzon, George N., *Russia in Central Asia in 1889 and the Anglo-Russian Question,* Reprint of 1889 ed., Barnes & Noble, Inc., 1966.

Dallin, Alexander, *The Soviet Union at the United Nations,* Frederick A. Praeger, 1962.

Dallin, David J., *Soviet Russia's Foreign Policy, 1939–42,* Yale University Press, 1942; *The Rise of Russia in Asia,* Yale University Press, 1949; *Soviet Russia and the Far East,* Yale University Press, 1948.

Davies, Joseph, *Mission to Moscow,* Simon and Schuster, 1941.

Deane, John R., *The Strange Alliance,* Viking Press, 1947.

Degras, J., ed., *Soviet Documents on Foreign Policy* (3 Vols.), Oxford University Press, 1951–1953.

Dennett, Tyler, *Roosevelt and the Russo-Japanese War,* Doubleday, Page & Co., 1925.

Dyke, Harvey L., *Weimar Germany and Soviet Russia, 1926–1933. A Study in Instability,* Columbia University Press, 1966.

Eudin, Xenia Joukoff, and R. C. North, *Soviet Russia and the East, 1920–1927: A Documentary Survey,* Stanford University Press, 1957.

Eudin, Xenia Joukoff, and Robert M. Slusser, *Soviet Foreign Policy, 1928–1934. Documents and Materials,* Vol. I, Pennsylvania State University Press, 1966.

Filene, Peter G., *Americans and the Soviet Experiment, 1917–1933,* Harvard University Press, 1967.

Fischer, Louis, *The Soviets in World Affairs, 1917–1929,* 2nd ed. (2 Vols.), Princeton University Press, 1960.

Fisher, H. H., *The Famine in Soviet Russia, 1919–1923: The Operations of the American Relief Administration*, Macmillan Company, 1927.

Floyd, David, *Mao Against Khrushchev—A Short History of the Sino-Soviet Conflict*, Frederick A. Praeger, 1963.

Garthoff, Raymond L., *Soviet Strategy in the Nuclear Age*, Frederick A. Praeger, 1958.

Graebner, Norman A., *Cold War Diplomacy, 1945–1960*, D. Van Nostrand Company, Inc., 1962.

Griffith, William E., *The Sino-Soviet Rift*, The M. I. T. Press, 1964.

Hilger, G. and A. G. Meyer, *The Incompatible Allies: A Memoir-History of German-Soviet Relations, 1918–1941*, Macmillan Company, 1953.

Horelick, Arnold L., and Myron Rush, *Strategic Power and Soviet Foreign Policy*, University of Chicago Press, 1966 (The Rand Corporation).

Jelavich, Barbara, *A Century of Russian Foreign Policy, 1814–1914*, J. B. Lippincott Co., 1964.

Jelavich, Charles, *Tsarist Russia and Balkan Nationalism*, University of California Press, 1958.

Jelavich, Charles and Barbara, eds., *The Education of a Russian Statesman: The Memoirs of Nicholas Karlovich Giers*, University of California Press, 1962.

Kennan, George, *Russian-American Relations, 1917–1920*, Vol. I, *Russia Leaves the War*, Princeton University Press, 1956; *Soviet Foreign Policy, 1917–1941*, D. Van Nostrand Company, Inc., 1960; *Russia and the West Under Lenin and Stalin*, The New American Library, 1962.

Konovalov, S., ed., *Russo-Polish Relations: An Historical Survey*, Princeton University Press, 1945.

Korff, S. A., *Russian Foreign Relations During the Last Half Century*, Macmillan Company, 1922.

Laqueur, Walter Z., ed., *The Middle East in Transition*, Frederick A. Praeger, 1958; *The Soviet Union and the Middle East*, Frederick A. Praeger, 1959.

Lederer, Ivo J., ed., *Russian Foreign Policy. Essays in Historical Perspective*, Yale University Press, 1962.

McKenzie, Kermit E., *Comintern and World Revolution, 1928–1943*, Columbia University Press, 1963.

McLane, Charles B., *Soviet Strategies in Southeast Asia. An Exploration of Eastern Policy*, Princeton University Press, 1966.

Mackintosh, J. M., *Strategy and Tactics of Soviet Foreign Policy*, Oxford University Press, 1963.

Malozemoff, Andrew, *Russian Far Eastern Policy, 1881–1904. With Special Emphasis on the Causes of the Russo-Japanese War*, University of California Press, 1958.

Mehnert, Klaus, *Peking and Moscow*, G. P. Putnam's Sons, 1963.

Mosely, Philip E., *Russian Diplomacy and the Opening of the Eastern Question in 1838 and 1839*, Harvard University Press, 1934; *The Kremlin and World Politics*, Vintage Books, 1960; *The Soviet Union, 1922–1962. A Foreign Affairs Reader*, published for the Council on Foreign Affairs by Frederick A. Praeger.

Mosse, W. E., *The Rise and Fall of the Crimean System*, St Martin's Press, 1963.

North, Robert C., *Moscow and the Chinese Communists*, 2nd ed., Stanford University Press, 1962.

Price, E. B., *The Russo-Japanese Treaties of 1907–1916 Concerning Manchuria and Mongolia*, Johns Hopkins University Press, 1933.

Rubinstein, Alvin Z., *The Foreign Policy of the Soviet Union*, 2nd ed., Random House, 1966.

Schuman, Frederick L., *The Cold War: Retrospect and Prospect,* Louisiana State
    University Press, 1962.
Senn, Alfred E., *Readings in Russian Political and Diplomatic History* (2 Vols.),
    Dorsey Press, 1966.
Seton-Watson, Hugh, *From Lenin to Khrushchev. The History of World Com-
    munism,* Frederick A. Praeger, 1962.
Shulman, Marshall D., *Stalin's Foreign Policy Reappraised,* Harvard University
    Press, 1963.
Smith, Walter Bedell, *My Three Years in Moscow,* J. B. Lippincott, 1950.
Sontag, R. J., and J. S. Beddie, eds., *Nazi-Soviet Relations, 1938–1941,* Didier
    Press (Washington, Department of State), 1948.
Spector, Ivar, *The First Russian Revolution (1905): Its Impact on Asia,* Prentice-
    Hall, Inc., 1962.
Stettinius, Edward R., Jr., *Roosevelt and the Russians,* Doubleday & Co., 1949.
Sumner, B. H., *Russia and the Balkans,* Oxford University Press, 1937; *Peter the
    Great and the Ottoman Empire,* William Salloch, 1950.
Thaden, Edward C., *Russia and the Balkan Alliance of 1912,* Pennsylvania State
    University Press, 1967.
Thompson, John M., *Russia, Bolshevism and the Versailles Peace,* Princeton Uni-
    versity Press, 1966.
Ullman, Richard H., *Intervention and the War: Anglo-Soviet Relations, 1917–
    1921,* Princeton University Press, 1966.
Unterberger, Betty Miller, *America's Siberian Expedition, 1918–1920: A Study of
    National Policy,* Duke University Press, 1956.
Vernadsky, George, *Political and Diplomatic History of Russia,* Little, Brown &
    Company, 1936.
Wheeler-Bennett, John W., *The Forgotten Peace, Brest-Litovsk, March, 1918,*
    Macmillan Company, 1939; *Munich: Prologue to Tragedy,* Duell, Sloan and
    Pearce, Inc., 1948.
White, J. A., *The Siberian Intervention,* Princeton University Press, 1950.
Whiting, Allen S., *Soviet Policies in China, 1917–1924,* Columbia University
    Press, 1954.
Williams, William A., *American-Russian Relations: 1781–1947,* Rinehart, 1952.
Wuorinen, John H., *Finland and World War II, 1939–1944,* Ronald Press Co.,
    1948.
Zabriskie, Edward H., *American-Russian Rivalry in the Far East: A Study in
    Diplomacy and Power Politics, 1895–1914,* University of Pennsylvania Press,
    1946.
Zagoria, Donald S., *The Sino-Soviet Conflict, 1956–1961,* Princeton University
    Press, 1962.
Zenkovsky, Serge A., *Pan-Turkism and Islam in Russia,* Harvard University
    Press, 1960.

RUSSIAN CULTURE

General

Billington, James H., *The Icon and the Axe. An Interpretive History of Russian
    Culture,* Alfred A. Knopf, 1966.
London, Kurt, *The Seven Soviet Arts,* Yale University Press, 1938.
Masaryk, Thomas G., *The Spirit of Russia: Studies in History, Literature and
    Philosophy* (2 Vols.), 2nd ed., New York, Macmillan Company, 1955.

Raeff, Marc, *Russian Intellectual History. An Anthology. Documents of the 18th and 19th Century Russian Intelligentsia,* Harcourt, Brace, and World, 1966.
Spector, Ivar and Marion, eds., *Readings in Russian History and Culture,* Allyn and Bacon, Inc., 1965.

Art and Architecture

Alpatov, Mikhail, *Russian Impact on Art,* ed. by Martin L. Wolf and tr. by Ivy Litvinov, Philosophical Library, 1950.
Benois, Alexandre, *The Russian School of Painting,* Alexander A. Knopf, 1916.
Buxton, David R., *Russian Mediaeval Architecture,* Cambridge University Press, 1934.
Bunt, Cyril G. E., *A History of Russian Art,* Studio-Crowell, 1946.
Cross, Samuel H., *Mediaeval Russian Churches,* The Mediaeval Academy of America, 1949.
Duncan, David Douglas, *The Kremlin,* New York Graphic Society, 1960.
Gray, Camilla, *The Great Experiment: Russian Art, 1869–1922,* Abrams (London), 1962.
Kondakov, N., *The Russian Icon,* tr. by H. Minns, Clarendon Press (Oxford), 1927.
"The Hermitage," *Life Magazine,* Part I, March 26, 1965; Part II, April 2, 1965; Part III, April 9, 1965.
Miliukov, Paul, *Outlines of Russian Culture,* Part III, *Architecture, Painting and Music,* A. S. Barnes and Company, Inc., 1960.
Rice, Tamara Talbot, *A Concise History of Russian Art,* Frederick A. Praeger, 1963.
Rubissow, Helen, ed., *The Art of Russia,* Philosophical Library, 1946.
Spector, Ivar and Marion, eds., *Readings in Russian History and Culture,* Allyn and Bacon, Inc., 1965. *See* "Andrei Rublev: Icon Painter, 1360(?)–1430(?)," by Lazarev; and "P. M. Tretyakov and His Art Gallery," by Mudrogel.
Voyce, Arthur, *Russian Architecture: Trends in Nationalism and Modernism,* Philosophical Library, 1948.

Literature

Blake, Patricia and Max Hayward, eds., *Half-Way to the Moon: New Writing from Russia,* Holt, Rinehart and Winston, 1964; *Dissonant Voices in Soviet Literature,* Harper Colophon Books, 1964.
Borland, H., *Soviet Literary Theory and Practice During the First Five-Year Plan, 1928–1932,* King's Crown Press, 1950.
Deutsch, Babette, and A. Yarmolinsky, trs. & eds., *Russian Poetry: An Anthology,* International Publishers, 1927.
Gibian, George, *Internal of Freedom—Soviet Literature During the Thaw,* University of Minnesota Press, 1960.
Gregoire, Henri, *et al.,* eds. & trs., *La Geste du Prince Igor,* Rausen Brothers, Printers, 1948.
Gudzy, N. K., *History of Early Russian Literature,* tr. by Susan W. Jones, Macmillan Company, 1949.
Guerney, Bernard G., ed., *Treasury of Russian Literature,* Vanguard Press, Inc., 1943.
Guterman, Norbert, tr., *Russian Fairy Tales,* Pantheon Books, 1945.
Hayward, Max, and Leopold Labedz, eds., *Literature and Revolution in Soviet Russia, 1917–1962,* Oxford University Press, 1963.

Hayward, Max, and Edward L. Crawley, eds., *Soviet Literature in the Sixties,* Frederick A. Praeger, 1964.

Jarintzov, N., *Russian Poets and Poems,* B. H. Blackwell (Oxford), 1917.

Jelagin, Juri, *Taming of the Arts,* E. P. Dutton & Company, Inc., 1951 (Theater and Music).

Maslenikov, Oleg, *The Frenzied Poets: Andrey Biely and the Russian Symbolists,* University of California Press, 1952.

Mirsky, D. S., *A History of Russian Literature,* Alfred A. Knopf, 1949.

Muchnic, Helen, *From Gorky to Pasternak. Six Writers in Soviet Russia,* Random House, 1961.

Munk, Erika, ed., *Stanislavski and America: An Anthology,* Hill and Wang, 1966.

Nabokov, Vladimir, tr., *The Song of Igor's Campaign: An Epic of the Twelfth Century,* Vintage Books, 1960.

Noyes, Rapall, ed., *Masterpieces of the Russian Drama,* D. Appleton and Company, 1933.

Poggioli, Renato, *The Poets of Russia, 1890–1930,* Harvard University Press, 1960.

Reavey, George, ed. & tr., *The Poetry of Yevgeny Yevtushenko—1953–1965,* October House, 1965; *The New Russian Poets: 1953–1966. An Anthology,* October House, 1966.

Simmons, Ernest J., *Through the Glass of Soviet Literature,* Columbia University Press, 1953.

Slonim, Marc, *The Epic of Russian Literature: From Its Origins Through Tolstoy,* Oxford University Press, 1950; *Modern Russian Literature: From Chekhov to the Present,* Oxford University Press, 1953.

Sokolov, Academician Y. M., *Russian Folklore,* Macmillan Company, 1950.

Spector, Ivar, *The Golden Age of Russian Literature,* 5th ed., The Caxton Printers, 1952.

Struve, Gleb, *Soviet Russian Literature, 1917–1950,* University of Oklahoma Press, 1951.

Swayze, Harold, *Political Control of Literature in the USSR, 1946–1959,* Harvard University Press, 1962.

Tertz, Abram (Andrei Donatevich Siniavskii), *On Socialist Realism.* Introduction by Czeslaw Milosz, Pantheon Books, 1960. *See also,* Hayward, Max, ed. & tr., *On Trial: The Soviet State Versus "Abram Tertz" and "Nikolai Arzhak,"* Harper and Row, 1966.

Varnecke, B. V., *History of the Russian Theatre,* Macmillan Company, 1951.

Vickery, Walter N., *The Cult of Optimism: Political and Ideological Problems of Recent Soviet Literature,* Indiana University Press, 1963.

Whitney, Thomas P., ed., *The New Writing in Russia,* University of Michigan Press, 1964.

Yarmolinsky, Avrahm, ed., *Treasury of Great Russian Short Stories,* Macmillan Company, 1944; *Russians Then and Now. Selected Russian Writings from Early Times to the Present,* Macmillan Company, 1963.

Zenkovsky, Serge A., ed., *Medieval Russia's Epics, Chronicles, and Tales,* E. P. Dutton & Co., Inc., 1963.

Music

Abraham, Gerald, *Eight Soviet Composers,* Oxford University Press, 1943.

Bakst, James, *A History of Russian-Soviet Music,* Dodd, Mead, 1966.

Calvocoressi, M. D., *A Survey of Russian Music,* Penguin Books, 1944.

Calvocoressi, M. D., and Gerald Abraham, *Masters of Russian Music,* Tudor Publishing Company, 1944.
Hanson, Lawrence and Elizabeth, *Tchaikovsky—The Man Behind the Music,* Dodd, Mead, 1966.
Leonard, Richard A., *A History of Russian Music,* Macmillan Company, 1956.
Nestyev, Israel, *Sergei Prokofiev. His Musical Life,* Alfred A. Knopf, 1946.
Roslavleva, Natalia, *Era of the Russian Ballet,* E. P. Dutton, 1966.
Seroff, Victor I., *Dmitri Shostakovich. The Life and Background of a Soviet Composer,* Alfred A. Knopf, 1943; *The Mighty Five. The Cradle of Russian Music,* Allen, Towne & Heath, Inc., 1948.
Shneerson, Grigory, *Aram Khachaturyan,* Foreign Languages Publishing House (Moscow), 1959.
Spector, Ivar and Marion, eds., *Readings in Russian History and Culture,* Allyn and Bacon, Inc., 1965. *See* "The Basic Principles of the New Russian Musical School," by V. Stasov.
Zetlin, Mikhail, *The Five. The Evolution of the Russian School of Music,* International Universities Press, 1959.

Philosophy and Religion

Anderson, Paul B., *People, Church and State in Modern Russia,* Macmillan Company, 1944.
Berdyaev, Nicolas, *The Russian Idea,* The Centenary Press (London), 1948.
Bolshakoff, Serge, *Russian Nonconformity,* Westminster Press, 1950.
Bulgakov, Scrgius, *The Orthodox Church,* The Centenary Press (London), 1935.
Curtiss, J. S., *The Russian Church and the Soviet State, 1917–1950,* Little, Brown and Company, 1953; *Church and State in Russia; the Last Years of the Empire,* Octagon Books, 1965.
Edie, James M., ed., *et al., Russian Philosophy* (3 Vols.), Quadrangle Books, 1965.
Fedotov, G. R., *The Russian Religious Mind· Kievan Christianity,* Harvard University Press, 1946; *A Treasury of Russian Spirituality,* Sheed & Ward, 1948.
French, R. M., *The Eastern Orthodox Church,* Hutchinson's University Library (London), 1951.
MacMaster, Robert E., *Danilevsky—A Russian Totalitarian Philosopher,* Harvard University Press, 1967.
Meyendorff, John, ed., *Kievan Christianity,* Vol. I, The 10th to the 13th Centuries; Vol. II, *The Middle Ages: the 13th to the 15th Centuries,* Harvard University Press, 1966.
Somerville, John, *Soviet Philosophy,* Philosophical Library, 1946.
Spinka, Matthew, *The Church in Soviet Russia,* Oxford University Press, 1956.
Timasheff, Nicholas S., *Religion in Soviet Russia, 1917–1942,* Sheed and Ward, Inc., 1942.
Ware, Timothy, *The Orthodox Church,* Penguin Books, 1964.
Zenkovsky, V. V., *A History of Russian Philosophy* (2 Vols.), Columbia University Press, 1953.
Zernov, Nicolas, *Moscow the Third Rome,* Macmillan Company, 1937.

Science

Ashby, Eric, *Scientist in Russia,* Penguin Books, 1947.
Field, Mark G., *Doctor and Patient in Soviet Russia,* Harvard University Press, 1957.

Joransky, David, *Soviet Marxism and Natural Science, 1917–1932,* Columbia University Press, 1961.

Korol, Alexander G., *Soviet Education for Science and Technology,* Technology Press of M. I. T., 1957.

Lipski, Alexander, "The Foundations of the Russian Academy of Sciences," *Isis,* Vol. 44, Part 4, No. 138 (1953), pp. 349–54.

Menshutkin, B. N., *Russia's Lomonosov, Chemist, Courtier, Physicist, Poet,* Princeton University Press, 1952.

Schwartz Harry, *The Red Phoenix. Russia Since World War II,* Frederick A. Praeger, 1961, Chapter 5, pp. 191–227.

Turkevich, John, "Soviet Science in the Post-Stalin Era," *Annals of the American Academy of Political and Social Science,* CCCIII (January, 1956), 139–151.

Vucinich, Alexander, *The Soviet Academy of Sciences,* Stanford University Press, 1956; *Science in Russian Culture. A History to 1860,* Stanford University Press, 1963.

Zirkle, Conway, ed., *Death of Science in Russia,* University of Pennsylvania Press, 1949.

MINORITIES

Allen, W. E. D., *The Ukraine: A History,* Cambridge University Press, 1941.

Armstrong, John A., *Ukrainian Nationalism, 1939–1945,* Columbia University Press, 1956.

Bacon, Elizabeth E., *Central Asians Under Russian Rule,* Cornell University Press, 1966.

Bilmanis, Alfred, *A History of Latvia,* Princeton University Press, 1951.

Caroe, Sir Olaf, *Soviet Empire: The Turks of Central Asia and Stalinism,* 2nd ed., St Martin's Press, 1967.

Goldberg, Ben Zion, *The Jewish Problem in the Soviet Union. Analysis and Solution,* Crown Publishers, Inc., 1961.

Greenberg, Louis, *The Jews in Russia* (2 Vols. in 1), Yale University Press, 1967.

Halecki, Oskar, *A History of Poland,* Roy Publishers, 1956.

Konovalov, S., ed., *Russo-Polish Relations,* Princeton University Press, 1945.

Kuznetsov, Anatoly, *Babi Yar: A Documentary Novel,* tr. from the Russian by Jacob Guralsky, Dial Press, 1967.

Park, Alexander G., *Bolshevism in Turkestan, 1917–1927,* Columbia University Press, 1957.

Pierce, Richard, *Russian Central Asia: 1867–1914. A Study in Colonial Rule,* University of California Press, 1960.

Reshetar, J., *The Ukrainian Revolution, 1917–1920,* Princeton University Press, 1952.

Samuel, Maurice, *Blood Accusation. The Strange History of the Beiliss Case,* Alfred A. Knopf, 1966.

Schwarz, Solomon M., *The Jews in the Soviet Union,* Syracuse University Press, 1951.

Vakar, Nicholas P., *Belorussia: The Making of a Nation,* Harvard University Press, 1956.

Wheeler, Geoffrey, *The Peoples of Soviet Central Asia,* Dufour Editions (Chester Springs, Pa.), 1966.

Index